Time Out

New York

timeoutnewyork.com

Time Out Guides Ltd
Universal House
251 Tottenham Court Road
London W1T 7AB
United Kingdom
Tel: +44 (0)20 7813 3000
Fax: +44 (0)20 7813 6001
Email: guides@timeout.com
www.timeout.com

Published by Time Out Guides Ltd, a wholly owned subsidiary of Time Out Group Ltd.
Time Out and the Time Out logo are trademarks of Time Out Group Ltd.

Previous editions 1990, 1992, 1994, 1996, 1997, 1998, 1999, 2000, 2001, 2002, 2003, 2004, 2005, 2006, 2007, 2008, 2009, 2010.

10 9 8 7 6 5 4 3 2 1

This edition first published in Great Britain in 2011 by Ebury Publishing.
A Random House Group Company
20 Vauxhall Bridge Road, London SW1V 2SA

Random House Australia Pty Ltd 20 Alfred Street, Milsons Point, Sydney, New South Wales 2061, Australia

Random House New Zealand Ltd 18 Poland Road, Glenfield, Auckland 10, New Zealand

Random House South Africa (Pty) Ltd Isle of Houghton, Corner Boundary Road & Carse O'Gowrie, Houghton 2198, South Africa

Random House UK Limited Reg. No. 954009

Distributed in the US and Latin America by Publishers Group West (1-510-809-3700)
Distributed in Canada by Publishers Group Canada (1-800-747-8147)

For further distribution details, see www.timeout.com.

ISBN: 978-1-84670-210-5

A CIP catalogue record for this book is available from the British Library.

Printed and bound by Firmengruppe APPL, aprinta druck, Wemding, Germany.

The Random House Group Limited supports The Forest Stewardship Council (FSC), the leading international forest certification organisation. All our titles that are printed on Greenpeace approved FSC certified paper carry the FSC logo. Our paper procurement policy can be found at http://www.randomhouse.co.uk/environment.

Time Out carbon-offsets its flights with Trees for Cities (www.treesforcities.org).

Contents

Introduction

'New York will be a great place if they ever finish it,' observed the American short-story writer O Henry a century ago, and his wry sentiments have been echoed by New Yorkers down the years. This sense of the city in perpetual construction, inching towards an ever-changing vision of a future it can never quite reach, has gained special currency since the attacks on the World Trade Center a decade ago; the construction site as tourist sight has taken on a powerful, if haunting, resonance.

New York City's constant physical evolution is perhaps felt most keenly in its neighborhoods. The Lower East Side has become an increasingly crucial player in the art world in the past few years; Chinatown's continued and inexorable expansion – albeit at the expense of Little Italy – has given birth to several palpable sub-Chinatowns; and Harlem's gentrification has witnessed its first real influx since its famous 1920s renaissance, helping it to become a vibrant nightlife destination once again. And while Manhattan may still be the core of the Big Apple, high rents and limited space have obliged many creatives to put down roots in the Outer Boroughs. A dozen years ago, few Gothamites – let alone visitors – would have sought out Brooklyn's Bushwick and Red Hook, or Queens' Long Island City for trendsetting cocktail bars or innovative dining hot spots. Today, any nightlife maven worth his or her *Time Out New York* subscription would find it unthinkable to ignore them.

Despite the eternal quest for the hot and new, the city is ultimately sustained by what endures. The iconic skyline – irrevocably scarred by 9/11 – still boasts some of the world's most distinctive skyscrapers, including the Chrysler, Woolworth and Empire State buildings. Strolling over the Brooklyn Bridge at sunset or catching the Staten Island Ferry at sunrise are still magical, revelatory experiences. The world-class museums of the Upper East Side and the stages of Broadway are as vital as ever, and Central Park remains the city's garden, meat market, playpen and stomping ground of the great human parade.

It's an old cliché that you'll always need more than one visit to take it all in, but we've tried to offer enough guidance to find whatever you seek – and then some. 'Something's always happening here,' remarked silver-screen siren Myrna Loy. 'If you're bored in New York, it's your own fault.'

Richard Koss, Author

New York in Brief

IN CONTEXT

To open the book, this series of features tells the city's fascinating back story, covering everything from the immigrant influx that helped to define its modern identity to the evolution of its iconic skyscrapers. We also look at the impact of Mayor Michael Bloomberg on the post-9/11 city, before exploring the city's musical legacy.

▶ *For more, see pp17-54.*

SIGHTS

As well as in-depth insights into the city's best-known attractions – the Statue of Liberty and the Metropolitan Museum of Art, to name a couple – the Sights section illuminates the shifting character of New York's local neighbourhoods. Here's where you'll find pointers about the latest art districts and fashionable areas, underrated small museums and less- celebrated architectural highlights.

▶ *For more, see pp55-151.*

CONSUME

One of the most exciting eating and drinking playgrounds is also among the most changeable, but that doesn't mean you should neglect old favourites. We've combined the best of the recent openings with trusty classics and wallet-friendly pit stops, all reviewed by critics from *Time Out New York* magazine. Insider guides to shops and hotels round out this section.

▶ *For more, see pp153-260.*

ARTS & ENTERTAINMENT

Beyond the razzle-dazzle of Broadway, this cultural capital is also home to top-notch repertory theatre and intrepid fringe companies. The underground club scene may have shrunk, but live music still thrives and the city holds a prominent place in rock and jazz history. Also in this section, you'll find details of everything from literary salons to gay nightclubs, children's museums to sports stadiums.

▶ *For more, see pp261-360.*

ESCAPES & EXCURSIONS

If you need respite from the non-stop activity that defines New York City, or if you simply want to explore further afield, you're in luck. Whether you crave culture in a country setting, bracing wilderness walks, a beach day, or the retro glamour and gaming tables of Atlantic City, there are many worthwhile destinations within easy reach of the city.

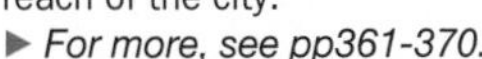

▶ *For more, see pp361-370.*

New York in 48 hours

Day 1 Downtown History & Hot Spots

8AM Start your New York odyssey Downtown, where Manhattan began and where millions of immigrants embarked on a new life. Get an organic caffeine jolt at **Jack's Stir Brew Coffee** (*see p183*), then stroll down to **Pier 17** for great views of the East River and the Brooklyn Bridge. Head further south if you want to hop on the free **Staten Island Ferry** (*see p59*) for classic panoramas of New York Harbor and the Statue of Liberty.

11AM To get a sense of how the ancestors of many New Yorkers lived, take the subway to Delancey Street for a tour of one of the reconstructed immigrants' apartments at the **Lower East Side Tenement Museum** (*see p80*). For a more literal taste of the old neighbourhood, order a pastrami on rye at the classic **Katz's Delicatessen** (*see p191*), or take a detour into Chinatown for superior fare at **Ping's** (*see p189*).

3PM The Lower East Side has changed considerably since its turn-of-the nineteenth-century squalor. Not only is it bursting at the seams with idiosyncratic shops – boutique-cum-bar the **Dressing Room** (*see p243*), gothic-tinged clothier **Thecast** (*see p239*) or new-wave hatters **Victor Osborne** (*see p247*) and **Still Life** (*see p247*) – but it's also now a booming art district. Once you've checked out the **New Museum of Contemporary Art** (*see p81*), gallery-hop the art spaces in the vicinity, especially on Chrystie, Orchard and Rivington Streets (for highlights, *see p293*). When you've worked up an early-evening thirst, suss out one of the many happening bars in the area: try **Mayahuel** (*see p221*), **Bourgeois Pig** (*see p219*) or **PDT** (*see p221*).

8PM At this point, you can either stay on the island or exit to Brooklyn. You'll take Manhattan? If you've managed to secure a table, head west for Keith McNally's hotspot, the **Minetta Tavern** (*see p197*), and a musical pot-pourri at eclectic **(Le) Poisson Rouge** (*see p324*). Alternatively, cross the East River for what many consider to be New York's best steakhouse, Williamsburg's **Peter Luger** (*see p215*), before a bar-crawl that might take in brewpub **Spuyten Duyvil** (*see p229*) or overlooked indie-music gem **Pete's Candy Store** (*see p327*).

NAVIGATING THE CITY

Thanks to the famous grid system of conveniently interconnecting streets, much of Manhattan is relatively easy to navigate. However, the older, more complex layout in Lower Manhattan and the less orderly arrangements in the outer boroughs are more of a challenge. When heading to a particular address, find out its cross-street: it may be more useful than the street number. We've included cross-streets in all our listings.

The subway is the simplest way to get around town, while the bus system is reliable. Be sure to pound the sidewalk: New York is best experienced from street level. And then there's the water: boats run all day around Manhattan. For more on transport and guided tours, *see p372*.

SEEING THE SIGHTS

Your first problem when sightseeing in New York will be deciding which sights to see: the choice is immense. Don't try to

Day 2 Uptown-Midtown Culture Crawl

9AM A short break in the Big Apple involves some tough choices: the Upper East Side alone is home to a dozen world-class institutions. Fortify yourself with sumptuous pastries and exquisite coffee at **Café Sabarsky** (*see p207*), on the Museum Mile, as you mull over your itinerary.

If you opt for the **Metropolitan Museum of Art** (*see p114*), you can either take a brisk two-hour essentials tour or forget the rest of the itinerary entirely – it's a vast place. In the warm-weather months, don't miss the view over Central Park from the Iris & B Gerald Cantor Roof Garden. But if the Met seems too overwhelming, opt instead for the easily manageable **Frick Collection** (*see p111*), a hand-picked cache of masterpieces in an exquisite early-20th-century mansion.

NOON If you decided on working through some of the art at the Metropolitan Museum of Art, slip a few blocks north to admire the gleaming façade of the **Guggenheim Museum** (*see p114*). Then stroll south through Central Park; if you pause for a drink at the **Boathouse Restaurant**'s bar (*see p107*), you can gaze at the strange sight of gondolas on the lake. Exit at the south-east corner of the park and window-shop your way down Fifth Avenue to **MoMA** (*see p102*) – but before you start taking in more art, lunch at the more affordable of its two exemplary eateries: the **Bar Room at the Modern** (*see p205*).

5PM Once you've had your fill of Alsatian-inspired fare and modern masterworks, it's time to get high. Rockefeller Center's **Top of the Rock** (*see p102*) is a less-mobbed alternative to the Empire State Building – and affords a good view of the latter iconic structure.

8PM Evening, though, brings more dilemmas. Should you head back uptown for soul food (**Amy Ruth's**; *see p212*) and jazz (**Lenox Lounge** or **St Nick's Pub**; *see pp330-332*) in Harlem? Or maybe it would be better to stick to Midtown for a dozen Long Island oysters at the **Grand Central Oyster Bar & Restaurant** (*see p207*), followed by a Broadway or Off-Broadway show (*see p347*) and a nightcap at any number of Midtown bars (*see pp223-225*)? It's simply a matter of taste.

do too much. Your second problem will be finding the money. As most of the city's museums are privately funded, admission prices can be steep. However, a number of them either waive admission fees or make them voluntary once a week. Check the listings for details.

PACKAGE DEALS

If you're planning to visit a number of attractions, it's worth considering a pair of cards that offer free entry to a number of attractions. The **New York CityPass** (www.citypass.com) gives pre-paid, queue-jumping access to six big-ticket attractions, among them the Empire State Building and the Met; it lasts nine days and costs $79 (or $59 for six- to 17-year-olds). Meanwhile, the **New York Pass** (www.newyorkpass.com) grants admission to over 50 museums, sights and tours. The card is time-tied: it costs from $75 for a one-day pass up to $190 for seven days ($55-$150 for under-13s).

ART DECO LANES

THE CONEY ISLAND ROOM

THE STADIUM GRILL

FOOD BY DAVID BURKE

CHINATOWN LANES

New York in Profile

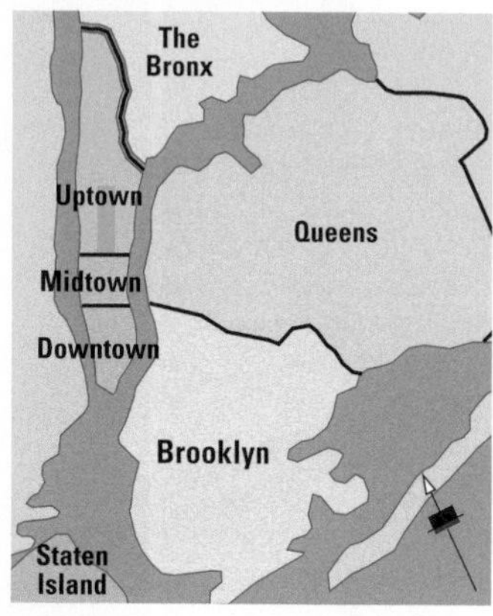

DOWNTOWN

The oldest part of Manhattan also boasts its most happening nightlife. The tip of the island is the seat of local government and the epicentre of capitalism, but to the north-east, trendy bars, boutiques and galleries have moved into the tenement buildings of erstwhile immigrant stronghold the **Lower East Side**. Former bohemian stomping ground **Greenwich Village** still resounds with cultural associations; to the west, leafy, winding streets give way to the **Meatpacking District**'s warehouses, now largely colonised by designer stores, while the once-radical **East Village** brims with bars and cheap eateries. Former art enclave **Soho** is now a prime shopping and dining destination, along with well-heeled neighbour **Tribeca**. Meanwhile, **Little Italy** is being squeezed out by ever-expanding **Chinatown** and, to the north, the fashion-conscious **Nolita**.

► *For more, see pp62-87.*

MIDTOWN

Now New York's main gallery district, **Chelsea** is also the city's most prominent gay enclave. Along with **Union Square**, which hosts the city's best-known farmers' market, the nearby **Flatiron District** has now become a fine-dining destination. Among the skyscrapers of Midtown's prime commercial stretch are some of NYC's most iconic attractions, such as the Empire State Building. Here, **Fifth Avenue** is home to some of the city's poshest retail, while **Broadway** is the world's most famous theatreland. Garish **Times Square** is a must-see spectacle at night.

► *For more, see pp88-105.*

UPTOWN

Bucolic **Central Park**, with its picturesque lakes, expansive lawns and famous zoo, is the green divider between the patrician **Upper East Side** and the more liberal but equally well-heeled **Upper West Side**. Between them, these wealthy districts contain the lion's share of the city's cultural institutions: the majority of museums are on the Upper East Side – the mammoth Metropolitan Museum

of Art, plus others on Fifth Avenue's **Museum Mile**, housed in the stately former mansions of the 20th-century elite – but the Upper West Side has the world-class Metropolitan Opera, the New York Philharmonic and the New York City Ballet at Lincoln Center. Famed designer strip **Madison Avenue** offers more materialistic thrills. Further uptown, regenerated **Harlem** offers vibrant nightlife, soul food and plenty of history.
▶ *For more, see pp106-125.*

BROOKLYN

Giving Manhattan a run for its money as the hippest part of town, the second borough contains some of New York's best nightlife, dining and shopping. **Williamsburg** and neighbouring **Bushwick** are the uncontested hipster hubs, brimming with music spots, galleries, retro eateries and interesting shops, but it's also worth exploring historic **Fort Greene**, rejuvenated **Coney Island** and up-and-coming **Red Hook**. Historic **Brooklyn Heights** and former industrial district **Dumbo** afford great views of Manhattan, while **Park Slope**, where leafy streets are lined with classic brownstones, is home to a celebrated museum, a botanical garden and the borough's intelligentsia. **Prospect Park** is the borough's answer to Central Park, and the amazing Green-Wood Cemetery is the final resting place of the great, the good and the notorious.
▶ *For more, see pp126-136.*

QUEENS

The melting pot personified, this diverse borough serves up a slew of ethnic dining opportunities. Try **Astoria** for Greek, **Jackson Heights** for Indian and South American, or **Flushing** for Korean and Chinese. **Long Island City** is also a burgeoning art district, with the MoMA P.S.1 Contemporary Art Center and one of the more engaging displays of graffiti you've ever seen.
▶ *For more, see pp137-142.*

THE BRONX

One of the country's poorest urban districts, the Bronx is slowly improving through government initiatives, and provides studio space for the latest wave of priced-out artists. The inner-cityscape has some standout features: the art deco architecture of the **Grand Concourse**, the sprawling Bronx Zoo, the lush greenery of the New York Botanical Garden and the gleaming new Yankee Stadium.
▶ *For more, see pp143-148.*

STATEN ISLAND

Best known for the free ferry that serves it, which offers stunning harbour views to an unusual mix of tourists and commuters, Staten Island has a small-town vibe and a handful of historic sites (the city's oldest concert venue, centuries-old fortifications). With an abundance of parkland, it also offers a tranquil urban escape.
▶ *For more, see pp149-151.*

Time Out New York

Editorial
Author Richard Koss
Deputy Editor Edoardo Albert
Proofreader Marion Moisy
Indexer Alice Harman

Managing Director Peter Fiennes
Editorial Director Ruth Jarvis
Business Manager Dan Allen
Editorial Manager Holly Pick
Assistant Management Accountant Ija Krasnikova

Design
Art Director Scott Moore
Art Editor Pinelope Kourmouzoglou
Senior Designer Kei Ishimaru
Group Commercial Designer Jodi Sher

Picture Desk
Picture Editor Jael Marschner
Acting Deputy Picture Editor Liz Leahy
Picture Desk Assistant/Researcher Ben Rowe

Advertising
New Business & Commercial Director Mark Phillips
International Advertising Manager Kasimir Berger
International Sales Executive Charlie Sokol
Advertising Sales Julia Keefe-Chamberlain (Time Out New York)

Marketing
Sales & Marketing Director, North America & Latin America Lisa Levinson
Senior Publishing Brand Manager Luthfa Begum
Group Commercial Art Director Anthony Huggins
Marketing Co-ordinator Alana Benton

Production
Group Production Manager Brendan McKeown
Production Controller Katie Mulhern

Time Out Group
Chairman & Founder Tony Elliott
Chief Executive Officer David King
Group Financial Director Paul Rakkar
Group General Manager/Director Nichola Coulthard
Time Out Communications Ltd MD David Pepper
Time Out International Ltd MD Cathy Runciman
Time Out Magazine Ltd Publisher/MD Mark Elliott
Group Commercial Director Graeme Tottle
Group IT Director Simon Chappell

Contributors
Introduction Richard Koss. **History** Kathleen Squires and Richard Koss (*Profile: Alexander Hamilton, What's in a Naam, Sweatshop Inferno* Richard Koss). **New York Today** Howard Halle and Richard Koss. **Architecture** Eric P Nash (*Rebuilding Ground Zero* Lisa Ritchie, Richard Koss). **A Walk on the Wild Side** Richard Koss. **Tour New York** Erin Clements, Lee Magill. **Downtown** Richard Koss (*Walk Drew Toal; Profile: Statue of Liberty, Urban Myth* Richard Koss). **Midtown** Richard Koss (*Walk Carl Williott; Profile: New York Public Library, Urban Myth* Richard Koss). **Uptown** Richard Koss (*Profile: Metropolitan Museum of Art, Profile: Museum for African Art, Walk* Richard Koss). **Brooklyn** Richard Koss (*Walk* Mike Olsen; *New Life at the Old Fairground* Richard Koss). **Queens** Richard Koss (*Profile: Museum of the Moving Image* Richard Koss). **The Bronx** Richard Koss. **Staten Island** Richard Koss. **Hotels** Lisa Ritchie, Richard Koss. **Restaurants and Cafés** contributors to *Time Out New York* magazine. **Bars** contributors to *Time Out New York* magazine. **Shops & Services** contributors to *Time Out New York* magazine. **Calendar** Richard Koss. **Books & Poetry** Michael Miller. **Children** Julia Israel. **Comedy** Matthew Love. **Dance** Gia Kourlas. **Film & TV** Joshua Rothkopf. **Galleries** Howard Halle. **Gay & Lesbian** Les Simpson. **Music** Adam Feldman, Olivia Giovetti, Jay Ruttenburg, Richard Koss. **Nightlife** Bruce Tantum. **Sports & Fitness** Drew Toal, Richard Koss. **Theater** Adam Feldman. **Escapes & Excursions** adapted from *Time Out New York* magazine. **Directory** Richard Koss.

Maps john@jsgraphics.co.uk, except: pages 413-416, used by kind permission of the Metropolitan Transport Authority.

Photography Michael Kirby, except pages 3, 13 (bottom), 17, 83, 96, 112, 164, 166, 184 (bottom), 238, 246, 251, 273, 281, 295, 320, 333, 345 Wendy Connett; pages 7, 56, 59, 66, 67, 77, 103, 117, 146, 151, 274 (right), 275 (left), 279, 289, 311, 319, 322, 367 Ben Rosenzweig; pages 7 (top), 12 (center and bottom), 13 (top left), 41, 55, 92, 262 Shutterstock; pages 7 (bottom left), 31, 272, 326 Jonathan Perugia; pages 38, 71, 107 Jael Marschner; pages 18, 28 Bettman/Corbis; page 20 Blue Lantern Studio/Corbis; page 25 Historical Picture Archive/Corbis; pages 27, 37, 48, 51, 52 Getty Images; page 30 akg-images/North Wind Picture Archives; pages 101, 220 Time Out NY; pages 133, 269, 274 (left), 275 (right), 299, 335, 368 (bottom) Alys Tomlinson; page 154 The Chatwal; page 184 (top) James Hamilton; pages 196, 211 (top), 221, 228 Roxana Marroquin; pages 200, 206, 207, 241, 254, 255 Jeff Gurwin; page 203 Andrew Fladeboe; page 204 Marianne Rafter; page 208 (top) Clotilde Testa; page 208 (bottom) Noah Fecks; page 211 (bottom) Jolie Ruben; pages 214, 215 David Rosenzweig; pages 217, 222, 342 Lizz Kuehl; page 227 Keith Morrison; page 230 Fumie Suzuki; page 244 Heami Lee; page 266 Paul J Sutton/PCN; page 276 Life Underground (2001) © Tom Otterness, MTA New York City Transit. Commissioned and owned by Metropolitan Transportation Authority Arts for Transit. Photo: Rob Wilson; page 282 Stephanie Berger; page 285 (top) Laurent Philippe/ fedephoto; (bottom) Susana Millman; page 287 New Line Cinema; page 288 United Artists/Photofest; page 302 Michael Alexander; pages 347, 353 Joan Marcus; page 351 Paul Kolnik.

The following pages we supplied by the featured establishments/artists: pages 44, 45, 98, 109, 136, 140, 155, 158, 163, 171, 176, 210, 264, 267, 293, 338, 339, 340, 343, 353 (center), 356, 358.

Front Cover Photography Corbis
Back Cover Photography Jeff Gurwin and Ben Rosenzweig

About the Guide

GETTING AROUND

The back of the book contains street maps of New York City, as well as overview maps of the city and its surroundings. The maps start on page 397; on them are marked the locations of hotels (❶), restaurants and cafés (❶), and pubs and bars (❶). The majority of businesses listed in this guide are located in the areas we've mapped; the grid-square references in the listings refer to these maps.

THE ESSENTIALS

For practical information, including visas, disabled access, emergency numbers, lost property, useful websites and local transport, please see the Directory. It begins on page 371.

THE LISTINGS

Addresses, phone numbers, websites, transport information, hours and prices are all included in our listings, as are selected other facilities. All were checked and correct at press time. However, business owners can alter their arrangements at any time, and fluctuating economic conditions can cause prices to change rapidly.

The very best venues in the city, the must-sees and must-dos in every category, have been marked with a red star (★). In the Sights chapters, we've also marked venues with free admission with a FREE symbol.

PHONE NUMBERS

New York has a number of different area codes. Manhattan is covered by 212 and 646, while Brooklyn, Queens, the Bronx and Staten Island are served by 718 and 347. Even if you're dialling from within the area you're calling, you'll need to use the area code, always preceded by 1.

From outside the US, dial your country's international access code (00 from the UK) or a plus symbol, followed by the number as listed in the guide; here, the initial '1' serves as the US country code. So, to reach the Metropolitan Museum of Art, dial +1-212 535 7710. For more on phones, *see p382*.

FEEDBACK

We welcome feedback on this guide, both on the venues we've included and on any other locations that you'd like to see featured in future editions. Please email us at guides@timeout.com.

Time Out Guides

Founded in 1968, Time Out has grown from humble beginnings into the leading resource for anyone wanting to know what's happening in the world's greatest cities. Alongside our influential weeklies in London, New York and Chicago, we publish more than 20 magazines in cities as varied as Beijing and Beirut; a range of travel books, with the City Guides now joined by the newer Shortlist series; and an information-packed website. The company remains proudly independent, still owned by Tony Elliott four decades after he launched *Time Out London*.

Written by local experts and illustrated with original photography, our books also retain their independence. No business has been featured because it has advertised, and all restaurants and bars are visited and reviewed anonymously.

ABOUT THE AUTHOR

Native New Yorker **Richard Koss** is a travel writer based in Manhattan, who has also lived in Brooklyn and Queens. This is the ninth New York-related guide he has worked on for Time Out.

A full list of the book's contributors can be found opposite. However, we've also included details of our writers in selected chapters through the guide.

In Context

Times Square. *See p94.*

History

The seeds of the Big Apple.

TEXT: KATHLEEN SQUIRES & RICHARD KOSS

More than 400 years ago, Henry Hudson, an English explorer in the service of the Dutch East India Company, sailed into New York Harbor, triggering events that would lead to the creation of the most dynamic and ethnically diverse city in the world. A steady flow of settlers, immigrants and fortune-seekers has seen New York evolve with the energy and aspirations of each successive wave of new arrivals. Intertwining cultural legacies have produced the densely layered character of the metropolis, from the wealthy and powerful Anglos who helped build the city's riches to the fabled tired, poor huddled masses who arrived from far-off lands and faced a tougher struggle. From its beginnings, this forward-looking town has been shaped by a cast of hard-working, ambitious characters, and continues to be so today.

NATIVE NEW YORKERS

The area's first residents were the indigenous Lenape tribe. They lived among the forests, meadows and farms of the land they called Lenapehoking, pretty much undisturbed by outsiders for thousands of years – until the 16th century, when their idyll was interrupted by European visitors. The first to cast his eyes upon this land was Giovanni da Verrazano in 1524. An Italian explorer commissioned by the French to find a shortcut to the Orient, he found Staten Island instead. Recognising that he was on the wrong track, Verrazano hauled anchor nearly as quickly as he had dropped it, never actually setting foot on dry land.

Eighty-five years later, Henry Hudson happened on New York Harbor in the same way. After trading with the Lenape, he ventured up the river that now bears his name, thinking it offered a north-west passage to Asia, but halted just south of present-day Albany when the river's shallowness convinced him it didn't lead to the Pacific. Hudson turned back, and his tales of the lush, river-crossed countryside captured the Dutch imagination. In 1624, the Dutch West India Company sent 110 settlers to establish a trading post here, planting themselves at the southern tip of the island called Mannahata and christening the colony Nieuw Amsterdam (New Amsterdam). In many bloody battles against the local Lenape, they did their best to drive the natives away from the little company town. But the tribe were immovable.

In 1626, Peter Minuit, New Amsterdam's first governor, thought he had solved the Lenape problem by pulling off the city's very first real-estate rip-off. He made them an offer they couldn't refuse: he 'bought' the island of Manhattan – all 14,000 acres (56 square kilometres) of it – from the Lenape for 60 guilders' worth of goods. Legend famously values the purchase price at $24, but modern historians set the amount closer to $500. (These days, that would only cover a fraction of a month's rent for a closet-size studio apartment in Manhattan.) It was a slick trick, and set a precedent for countless future self-serving business transactions.

The Dutch quickly made the port of New Amsterdam a centre for fur trading. The population didn't grow as fast as the business, however, and the Dutch West India Company had a hard time finding recruits to move to this unknown island an ocean away. The company instead gathered servants, orphans and slaves, and other more unsavoury outcasts such as thieves, drunkards and prostitutes. The population grew to 400 within ten years, but drunkenness, crime and squalor prevailed. If the colony was to thrive, it needed a strong leader. Enter Dutch West India Company director Peter Stuyvesant.

PEG-LEG PETE

A one-legged, puritanical bully with a quick temper, Stuyvesant – or Peg-leg Pete, as he was known – may have been less than popular but he was the colony's first effective governor. He made peace with the Lenape, formed the first policing force (consisting of nine men), cracked down on debauchery by shutting taverns and outlawing drinking on Sunday, and established the first school, post office, hospital, prison and poorhouse. Within a decade, the population had quadrupled, and the settlement had become an important trading port.

Lined with canals and windmills, and dotted with gabled farmhouses, New Amsterdam slowly began to resemble its namesake. Newcomers arrived to work in the fur and slave trades, or to farm. Soon, a dozen and a half languages could be heard in the streets – a fact that made Stuyvesant nervous. In 1654, he attempted to quash immigration by turning away Sephardic Jews who were fleeing the Spanish Inquisition. But, surprisingly for the time, the corporate honchos at the Dutch West India Company reprimanded him for his intolerance and overturned his decision, leading to the establishment of the earliest Jewish community in the New World. It was the first time that the inflexible Stuyvesant was forced to mend his ways. The second time put an end to the 40-year Dutch rule for good.

By Any Other Naam

How the Dutch left their mark.

Traces of the former Nieuw Amsterdam colony are visible in the anglicized Dutch names that still dot New York, many bestowed to commemorate places from the settlers' native Holland. Brooklyn, most famously, has evolved from Breukelen, while Harlem is derived from Haarlem; Staten Island was known as Staaten Eylandt in honour of the Staaten-Generaal, Holland's parliament. Most names paid reassuring homage to the Old World, yet some attest to the harshness of the New: sailors encountering deadly currents in the reek between the Hudson and Harlem rivers christened it Spuyten Duyvil, or devil's spout, the name that has stuck to the portion of the Bronx that overlooks that narrow waterway.

While evoking memories of the old Amsterdam that they had left behind, many Dutch names reflect the pastoral nature of the land that they had settled. Greenwich Village comes from *groenwijck*, meaning green or pine district (and not, as many believe, a nod to the London suburb). The Bowery is derived from the archaic Dutch word *bouwerij*, or farm – hardly the image a stroll down that lower Manhattan street suggests today. Even more unlikely is the derivation of Coney Island. Dutch settlers who first ventured to that extremity of Brooklyn found it overrun with rabbits, or *konijnen*, and called it Konijnen Eiland. Evidently, the rabbits moved out long before the fairgrounds moved in.

'Brutal gangs with colourful names such as the Forty Thieves, Plug Uglies and Dead Rabbits often met in bloody clashes in the streets.'

BRITISH INVASION

In late August 1664, English warships sailed into the harbour, set on taking over the now prosperous colony. To avoid bloodshed and destruction, Stuyvesant surrendered quickly. Soon after, New Amsterdam was renamed New York (after the Duke of York, brother of King Charles II) and Stuyvesant quietly retired to his farm. Unlike Stuyvesant, the English battled with the Lenape; by 1695, those members of the tribe who hadn't been killed off were sent packing upstate, and New York's European population shot up to 3,000. Over the next 35 years, Dutch-style farmhouses and windmills gave way to stately townhouses and monuments to English royals. By 1740, the slave trade had made New York the third-busiest port in the British Empire. The city, now home to more than 11,000 residents, continued to prosper for a quarter-century. But resentment was beginning to build in the colony, fuelled by the ever-heavier burden of British taxation.

One very angry young man was Alexander Hamilton, the illegitimate son of a Scottish nobleman born in the West Indies. A fierce intellectual, Hamilton enrolled in King's College (now Columbia University) in 1773 and became politically active writing anti-British pamphlets.

Fearing revolution, New York's citizenry fled the city in droves in 1775, causing the population to plummet from 25,000 to just 5,000. The following year, 100 British warships sailed into the harbour of this virtual ghost town, carrying with them an intimidating army of 32,000 men – nearly four times the size of Washington's militia. Despite the British presence, Washington organised a reading of the Declaration of Independence, and American patriots tore the statue of King George III from its pedestal. Revolution was inevitable.

The battle for New York officially began on 26 August 1776, and Washington's army sustained heavy losses; nearly a quarter of his men were slaughtered in a two-day period. As Washington retreated, a fire – thought to have been lit by patriots – destroyed 493 buildings, including Trinity Church, the tallest structure on the island. The British found a scorched city, and a populace living in tents.

The city continued to suffer for seven long years. Eventually, of course, Washington's luck turned. As the British forces left, he and his troops marched triumphantly down Broadway to reclaim the city as a part of the newly established United States of America. A week and a half later, on 4 December 1783, the general bade farewell to his dispersing troops at Fraunces Tavern, which still stands on Pearl Street.

For his part, Hamilton got busy in the rebuilding effort, laying the groundwork for New York City institutions that remain vital to this day. He started by establishing the Bank of New York, the city's first bank, in 1784. When Washington was inaugurated as the nation's first president in 1789, at Federal Hall on Wall Street, he brought Hamilton on board as the first secretary of the treasury (*see p30* **Profile**). Thanks to Hamilton's business savvy, trade in stocks and bonds flourished, leading to the establishment in 1792 of what would eventually be known as the New York Stock Exchange.

THE CITY TAKES SHAPE...

New York continued to grow and prosper for the next three decades. Maritime commerce soared, and Robert Fulton's innovative steamboat made its maiden voyage

on the Hudson River in 1807. Eleven years later, a group of merchants introduced regularly scheduled shipping (a novel concept at the time) between New York and Liverpool on the Black Ball Line. A boom in the maritime trades lured hundreds of European labourers, and the city, which was still entirely crammed in below Houston Street, grew more and more congested. Where Dutch farms and English estates once stood, taller, far more efficient structures took hold. Manhattan real estate became the most expensive in the world.

The first man to tackle the city's congestion problem was Mayor DeWitt Clinton, a brilliant politician and a protégé of Hamilton. Clinton's dream was to organise the entire island of Manhattan in such a way that it could cope with the eventual population creep northwards. In 1807, he created a commission to map out the foreseeable sprawl. It presented its work four years later, and the destiny of this new city was made manifest: it would be a regular grid of crossing thoroughfares, 12 avenues wide and 155 streets long.

Then Clinton simply overstepped the city's boundaries. In 1811, he presented a plan to build a 363-mile canal linking the Hudson River with Lake Erie. Many of his contemporaries thought it was simply an impossible task: at the time, the longest canal in the world ran a mere 27 miles. But the silver-tongued politician pressed on and raised a truly staggering $6 million for the project.

Work on the Erie Canal began in 1817 and was completed in 1825 – three years ahead of schedule. It shortened the journey between New York City and Buffalo from three weeks to one, and cut the shipping cost per ton from about $100 to $4. Goods, people and money poured into New York, fostering a merchant elite that moved northwards in Manhattan to escape the urban crush. Estates multiplied above Houston Street – all grander and more imposing than their modest colonial forerunners. Once slavery was abolished in New York in 1827, free blacks became an essential part of the workforce. In 1831, the first public transport system began operating, pulling passengers in horse-drawn omnibuses to the city's far reaches. With the inrush of people and money, there was only one thing New York could do: grow.

... AND SO DO THE SLUMS

As the population grew (swelling to 240,000 by 1830 and 700,000 by 1850), so did the city's problems. Tensions bubbled between immigrant newcomers and those who could trace their American lineage back a generation or two. Crime rose and lurid tales filled the 'penny press', the city's proto-tabloids. While wealthy New Yorkers were moving as far 'uptown' as Greenwich Village, the infamous Five Points neighbourhood – the city's first slum – festered in the area now occupied by City Hall, the courthouses and Chinatown. Built on a fetid drained pond, Five Points became the ramshackle home of poor immigrants and blacks. Brutal gangs with colourful names such as the Forty Thieves, Plug Uglies and Dead Rabbits often met in bloody clashes in the streets, but what finally sent a mass of 100,000 people scurrying from Downtown was an outbreak of cholera in 1832. In just six weeks, 3,513 New Yorkers died.

In 1837, a financial panic left hundreds of Wall Street businesses crumbling. Commerce stagnated at the docks, the real-estate market collapsed, and all but three city banks closed down. Some 50,000 New Yorkers lost their jobs, while 200,000 teetered on the edge of poverty. The panic sparked an era of civil unrest and violence. In 1849, a xenophobic mob of 8,000 protesting the performance of an English actor at the Astor Place Opera House was met by a militia that opened fire, killing 22 people. But the Draft Riots of 1863, known as 'the bloodiest riots in American history', were much worse. After a law was passed exempting men from the draft for a $300 fee, the (mostly Irish) poor rose up, forming a 15,000-strong force that rampaged through the city. Fuelled by anger about the Civil War (for which they blamed blacks), the rioting gangs set fire to the Colored Orphan Asylum and vandalised black homes. Blacks were beaten in the streets, and some were lynched. A federal force of 6,000 men was sent to subdue the violence. After four days and at least a hundred deaths, peace was finally restored.

ON THE MOVE

Amid the chaos of the mid 19th century, the pace of progress continued unabated. Compared to the major Southern cities, New York emerged nearly unscathed from the Civil War. The population ballooned to two million in the 1880s, and new technologies revolutionised daily life. The elevated railway helped New Yorkers to move into what are now the Upper East and Upper West Sides, while other trains connected the city with upstate New York, New England and the Midwest. By 1871, regional train traffic had grown so much that rail tycoon Cornelius Vanderbilt built the original Grand Central Depot, which could accommodate no fewer than 15,000 passengers at a time. (It was replaced in 1913 by the current Grand Central Terminal.)

One ambitious project was inspired by the harsh winter of 1867. The East River froze over, halting ferry traffic between Brooklyn and Manhattan for weeks. Brooklyn, by then, had become the nation's third most populous city, and its politicians, businessmen and community leaders realised that the boroughs had to be linked.

The New York Bridge Company's goal was to build the world's longest bridge, spanning the East River between downtown Manhattan and south-western Brooklyn. Over 16 years (four times longer than projected), 14,000 miles of steel cable were stretched across the 1,595-foot (486-metre) span, while the towers rose a staggering 276 feet (84 metres) above the river. Worker deaths and corruption dogged the project, but the Brooklyn Bridge opened in triumph on 24 May 1883.

THE GREED OF TWEED

As New York recovered from the turmoil of the mid 1800s, William M 'Boss' Tweed began pulling the strings. Using his ample charm, the six-foot-tall, 300-pound bookkeeper, chair-maker and volunteer firefighter became one of the city's most powerful politicians. He had been an alderman and district leader; he had served in the US House of Representatives and as a state senator; and he was a chairman of the Democratic General Committee and leader of Tammany Hall, a political organisation formed by local craftsmen ostensibly to keep the wealthy classes' political clout in check. But even though Tweed opened orphanages, poorhouses and hospitals, his good deeds were overshadowed by his and his cohorts' gross embezzlement of city funds. By 1870, members of the 'Tweed Ring' had created a new city charter, granting themselves control of the City Treasury. Using fake leases and wildly inflated bills for city supplies and services, Tweed and his cronies may ultimately have pocketed as much as $200 million.

Tweed was eventually sued by the city for $6 million, and charged with forgery and larceny. He escaped from debtor's prison in 1875, but was captured in Spain a year later and died in 1878. But Tweed's greed hurt many. As he was emptying the city's coffers, poverty spread. Then the stock market took a nosedive, factories closed and railroads went bankrupt. By 1874, New York estimated its homeless population at 90,000. That winter, *Harper's Weekly* reported, 900 New Yorkers starved to death.

IMMIGRANT DREAMS

In September 1882, a new era dawned brightly when Thomas Alva Edison lit up half a square mile of lower Manhattan with 3,000 electric lamps. One of the newly illuminated offices belonged to financier JP Morgan, who played an essential part in bringing New York's, and America's, economy back to life. By bailing out a number of failing railroads, then merging and restructuring them, Morgan jump-started commerce in New York once again. Goods, jobs and businesses returned to the city, and very soon such aggressive businessmen as John D Rockefeller, Andrew Carnegie and

'New York City was the site of the largest women's suffrage rallies in the United States.'

Henry Frick wanted a piece of the action. They made New York the HQ of Standard Oil and US Steel, corporations that went on to shape America's economic future.

A shining symbol for less fortunate immigrants also made New York its home around that time. To commemorate the centennial of the Declaration of Independence, the French gave the United States the Statue of Liberty, which was dedicated in 1886. Between 1892 and 1954, the statue ushered more than 12 million immigrants into New York Harbor, and Ellis Island processed many of them. The island had opened as an immigration centre in 1892 with expectations of accommodating 500,000 people annually, but it welcomed twice that number in its first year. In the 34-building complex, crowds of would-be Americans were herded through examinations, inspections and interrogations. Four million got through, turning New York into what British playwright Israel Zangwill optimistically called 'the great melting pot where all the races of Europe are melting and reforming'.

Many of these new immigrants crowded into dark, squalid tenements on the Lower East Side, while millionaires such as Vanderbilt and Frick constructed huge French-style mansions along Fifth Avenue. Jacob A Riis, a Danish immigrant and police reporter for the *New York Tribune*, made it his business to expose this dichotomy, scouring filthy alleys and overcrowded tenements to research and photograph his 1890 book, *How the Other Half Lives*. Largely as a result of Riis's work, the state passed the Tenement House Act of 1901, which called for drastic housing reforms.

Building **Brooklyn Bridge**.

'Prohibition turned the city into the epicentre of bootlegging, speakeasies and organised crime.'

SOARING ASPIRATIONS

By the close of the 19th century, 40 fragmented governments had been formed in and around Manhattan, creating a state of wholesale political confusion. So, on 1 January 1898, the boroughs of Manhattan, Brooklyn, Queens, Staten Island and the Bronx consolidated to form New York City, the largest metropolis in America with over three million residents. More and more companies started to move their headquarters to this new city, increasing the demand for office space. With little land left to develop in lower Manhattan, New York embraced the steel revolution and grew steadily skywards (*see p40* **Race to the Top**).

By 1920, New York boasted over 60 skyscrapers, including the 20-storey Fuller Building (now known as the Flatiron Building; *photo p31*) at Fifth Avenue and 23rd Street, and the 25-storey New York Times Tower in Longacre (now Times) Square. Within four years, these two buildings would be completely dwarfed by the 47-storey Singer Building on lower Broadway, which enjoyed the status of tallest building in the world – but only for 18 months. The 700-foot (213-metre) Metropolitan Life Tower in Madison Square claimed the title from the Singer Building in 1909, but the 793.5-foot (241-metre) Woolworth Building on Broadway and Park Place topped it in 1913 – and, amazingly, held the distinction for nearly two decades.

If that weren't enough to demonstrate New Yorkers' unending ambition, the city burrowed below the streets at the same time, starting work on its underground transit system in 1900. The $35-million project took nearly four and a half years to complete. Less than a decade after opening, it was the most heavily travelled subway system in the world, carrying almost a billion passengers on its trains every year.

CHANGING TIMES

By 1909, 30,000 factories were operating in the city, churning out everything from heavy machinery to artificial flowers. Mistrusted, abused and underpaid, factory workers faced impossible quotas, had their pay docked for minor mistakes and were often locked in during working hours. In the end, it took the inevitable tragedy, in the form of the Triangle Shirtwaist Company fire (*see right* **Sweatshop Inferno**), to bring about real changes in employment laws.

Another sort of rights movement was taking hold during this time. Between 1910 and 1913, New York City was the site of the largest women's suffrage rallies in the United States. Harriet Stanton Blatch (the daughter of famed suffragette Elizabeth Cady Stanton, and founder of the Equality League of Self-Supporting Women) and Carrie Chapman Catt (the organiser of the New York City Women's Suffrage party) arranged attention-grabbing demonstrations intended to pressure the state into authorising a referendum on a woman's right to vote. The measure's defeat in 1915 only steeled the suffragettes' resolve. Finally, with the support of Tammany Hall, the law was passed in 1919, challenging the male stranglehold on voting throughout the country. With New York leading the nation, the 19th Amendment was ratified in 1920.

In 1919, as New York welcomed troops home from World War I with a parade, the city also celebrated its emergence on the global stage. It had supplanted London as the investment capital of the world, and had become the centre of publishing, thanks to two men: Joseph Pulitzer and William Randolph Hearst. The *New York Times* had become the country's most respected newspaper; Broadway was the focal point of

American theatre; and Greenwich Village had become an international bohemian nexus, where flamboyant artists, writers and political revolutionaries gathered in galleries and coffeehouses.

The more personal side of the women's movement also found a home in New York City. A nurse and midwife who grew up in a family of 11 children, Margaret Sanger was a fierce advocate of birth control and family planning. She opened the first ever birth-control clinic in Brooklyn on 16 October 1916. Finding this unseemly, the police closed the clinic soon after and imprisoned Sanger for 30 days. She was not deterred, however, and, in 1921, formed the American Birth Control League – the forerunner of the organisation Planned Parenthood – which researched birth control methods and provided gynaecological services.

Sweatshop Inferno

A reform movement rises from the Ashes tragedy.

As 25 March 1911 fell on a Saturday, the roughly 500 garment workers – many of them teenage girls – at the Triangle Shirtwaist Company were only putting in a seven-hour shift, as opposed to the nine demanded of them on weekdays. At 4.45pm, they were only fifteen minutes from their brief weekends, when fire broke out on the eighth floor of the ten-storey building on the corner of Greene Street and Washington Place in Greenwich Village, where Triangle owned the top three floors. Fed by the fabrics, the flames spread rapidly up the building, engulfing the sewing room on the ninth floor. As workers rushed to escape, they found many of the exits locked, and the single flimsy fire escape melted in the heat and fell uselessly away from the building. Roughly 350 made it out on to the adjoining rooftops before the inferno closed off all the exits. New Yorkers spending a leisurely Saturday in Washington Square Park a block away, rushed to the scene only to watch in horror as 54 workers jumped or fell to their deaths from the windows. One hundred and forty-six perished in all. Two of the victims were 14 years old.

The Triangle Shirtwaist Fire was the most traumatic disaster in New York City until 9/11. Over 100,000 people attended the funeral procession. The two factory owners who were tried for manslaughter were acquitted, but the fire did at least spur labour and union organisations, which won major reforms. The Factory Commission of 1911 was established by the State Legislature, headed by Senator Robert F Wagner, Alfred E Smith and Samuel Gompers, president of the American Federation of Labour. It spawned the Fire Prevention division of the Fire Department, which enforced the creation and maintenance of fire escape routes in the workplace. The fire also garnered much-needed support for the Ladies Garment Workers Union, which became a major force in the 1920s and 1930s.

ALL THAT JAZZ

Forward-thinking women such as Sanger set the tone for an era when women, now a voting political force, were moving beyond the moral conventions of the 19th century. The country ushered in the Jazz Age in 1919 by ratifying the 18th Amendment, which outlawed the distribution and sale of alcoholic beverages. Prohibition turned the city into the epicentre of bootlegging, speakeasies and organised crime. By the early 1920s, New York boasted 32,000 illegal watering holes – twice the number of legal bars before Prohibition.

In 1925, New Yorkers elected the magnetic James J Walker as mayor. A charming ex-songwriter (as well as a speakeasy patron and skirt-chaser), Walker was the perfect match for his city's flashy style, hunger for publicity and consequences-be-damned attitude. Fame flowed in the city's veins: home-run hero Babe Ruth drew a million fans each season to baseball games at the newly built Yankee Stadium, and sharp-tongued Walter Winchell filled his newspaper columns with celebrity titbits and scandals. Alexander Woollcott, Dorothy Parker, Robert Benchley and other writers met up daily to trade witticisms around a table at the Algonquin Hotel; the result, in February 1925, was *The New Yorker*.

The Harlem Renaissance blossomed at the same time. Writers Langston Hughes, Zora Neale Hurston and James Weldon Johnson transformed the African-American experience into lyrical literary works, and white society flocked to the Cotton Club to see genre-defining musicians such as Bessie Smith, Cab Calloway, Louis Armstrong and Duke Ellington. (Blacks were only allowed into the club if they were performing on the stage, they could not be part of the audience.)

Downtown, Broadway houses were packed out with fans of George and Ira Gershwin, Irving Berlin, Cole Porter, Lorenz Hart, Richard Rodgers and Oscar Hammerstein II. Towards the end of the 1920s, New York-born Al Jolson wowed audiences in *The Jazz Singer*, the first talking picture.

See pp48-54 **A Walk on the Wild Side** for more on NYC's musical history.

Robert Moses.

AFTER THE CRASH

The dizzying excitement ended on Tuesday, 29 October 1929, when the stock market crashed. Corruption eroded Mayor Walker's hold on the city: despite a tenure that saw the opening of the Holland Tunnel, the completion of the George Washington Bridge and the construction of the Chrysler and Empire State Buildings, Walker's lustre faded in the growing shadow of graft accusations. He resigned in 1932, as New York, caught in the depths of the Great Depression, had a staggering one million unemployed inhabitants.

In 1934, an unstoppable force named Fiorello La Guardia took office as mayor, rolling up his sleeves to crack down on mobsters, gambling, smut and government corruption. The son of an Italian father and a Jewish mother, La Guardia was a tough-talking politician who was known for nearly coming to blows with other city officials; he described himself as 'inconsiderate, arbitrary, authoritative, difficult, complicated, intolerant and somewhat theatrical'. La Guardia's act played well: he ushered New York into an era of unparalleled prosperity over the course of his three terms. The 'Little Flower', as La Guardia was known, streamlined city government, paid down the debt and updated the transportation, hospital, reservoir and sewer systems. New highways made the city more accessible, and North Beach (now La Guardia) Airport became the city's first commercial landing field.

Helping La Guardia to modernise the city was Robert Moses, a hard-nosed visionary who would do much to shape – and in some cases, destroy – New York's landscape. Moses spent 44 years stepping on toes to build expressways, parks, beaches, public housing, bridges and tunnels, creating such landmarks as Shea Stadium, Lincoln Center, the United Nations complex and the Verrazano-Narrows Bridge, which connected Staten Island to Brooklyn in 1964.

MOSES IMPOSES

Despite La Guardia's belt-tightening and Moses's renovations, New York began to fall apart financially. When World War II ended, 800,000 industrial jobs disappeared from the city. Factories in need of more space moved to the suburbs, along with nearly five million residents. But more crowding occurred as rural African-Americans and Latinos (primarily Puerto Ricans) flocked to the metropolis in the 1950s and '60s, only to meet with ruthless discrimination and a dearth of jobs. Moses's Slum Clearance Committee reduced many neighbourhoods to rubble, forcing out residents in order to build huge, isolating housing projects that became magnets for crime. In 1963, the city also lost Pennsylvania Station, when the Pennsylvania Railroad Company demolished the site over the protests of picketers in order to make way for a modern station and the new Madison Square Garden, home to basketball's Knicks, hockey's Rangers and blockbuster concerts. It was a wake-up call for New York: architectural changes were hurtling out of control.

But Moses and his wrecking ball couldn't knock over one steadfast West Village woman. Architectural writer and urban-planning critic Jane Jacobs organised local residents when the city unveiled its plan to clear a 14-block tract of her neighbourhood to make space for yet more public housing. Her obstinacy was applauded by many, including an influential councilman named Ed Koch (who would become mayor in 1978). The group fought the plan and won, causing Mayor Robert F Wagner to back down. As a result of Jacobs's efforts in the wake of Pennsylvania Station's demolition, the Landmarks Preservation Commission – the first such group in the US – was established in 1965.

At the dawning of the Age of Aquarius, the city harboured its share of innovative creators. Allen Ginsberg, Jack Kerouac and others gathered in Village coffeehouses to create a new voice for poetry. A folk music scene brewed in tiny clubs around Bleecker Street, showcasing musicians such as Bob Dylan. A former advertising illustrator named Andy Warhol turned images of mass consumerism into deadpan,

Profile Alexander Hamilton

The Founding Father had a full life – and a violent death.

The ultimate self-made man, Alexander Hamilton was born on the Caribbean island of Nevis in 1755, the illegitimate son of a Scottish nobleman. Left to fend for himself at the death of his mother, he became an apprentice to a counting house before he'd entered his teens. In 1773, he moved to New York to attend King's College, now Columbia University. His studies were interrupted by the Revolutionary War, for which he volunteered a year later, rising through the ranks of the American army to be promoted to lieutenant colonel at the age of 21 by George Washington.

After the war, Hamilton represented New York at the Continental Congress in Philadelphia, but soon returned to the city to found the Bank of New York. He attended the Constitutional Convention in Philadelphia in 1787 as one of New York's delegates, was the only person from the state to sign the Constitution, and served as America's first Secretary of the Treasury from 1789 to 1795. A federalist who believed in strong central government, Hamilton was instrumental in founding the US Mint and the First National Bank.

After an attempted blackmail over an adulterous affair led to his resignation, Hamilton returned to New York and, in 1801, established the *Evening Post*, which is still in circulation today as the *New York Post*. What Hamilton would have made of its populist take on journalism is destined to remain a mystery. He continued to be involved in national politics, working to defeat John Adams in the presidential election of 1800, but he is best remembered today for the tragic outcome of his longstanding feud with Vice President Aaron Burr.

Ostensibly political (Hamilton had backed Thomas Jefferson in the 1800 fight for the presidency), their rivalry grew personal, resulting in a duel that was held on 11 July 1804, in Weehawken, New Jersey. Burr shot Hamilton – Hamilton missed – and Hamilton died next day. Hamilton is buried in the graveyard of Trinity Church (*see p72*), not far from the centres of the financial world he helped to create. His 1802 estate, Hamilton Grange, is expected to reopen to the public after a lengthy renovation in the summer of 2011.

IN CONTEXT

ironic art statements. And in 1969, the city's long-closeted gay communities came out into the streets, as patrons at the Stonewall Inn on Christopher Street demonstrated against a police raid. The protests, known as the Stonewall riots, gave birth to the modern gay rights movement.

MEAN STREETS

By the early 1970s, deficits had forced heavy cutbacks in city services. The streets were dirty, and subway cars and buildings were scrawled with graffiti; crime skyrocketed as the city's debt deepened to $6 billion. Despite the huge downturn, construction commenced on the World Trade Center; when completed, in 1973, its twin 110-storey towers were the world's tallest buildings. Even as the WTC rose, the city became so desperately overdrawn that Mayor Abraham Beame appealed to the federal government for financial assistance in 1975. Yet President Gerald Ford refused to bail out the city, a decision summed up by the immortal Daily News headline: 'Ford to City: Drop Dead'.

Times Square had degenerated into a morass of sex shops and porn theatres, drug use rose and subway use hit an all-time low. In 1977, serial killer Son of Sam terrorised the city with six killings, and a blackout one hot August night that same year led to widespread looting and arson. The angst of the time fuelled the punk culture that rose in downtown clubs such as CBGB. At the same time, celebrities, designers and models converged on Midtown to disco their nights away at Studio 54.

The Wall Street boom of the 1980s and fiscal petitioning by Mayor Ed Koch brought money flooding back into New York. Gentrification glamorised neighbourhoods such as Soho, Tribeca and the East Village, but deeper societal ills lurked. In 1988, a protest against the city's efforts to impose a strict curfew and displace the homeless away from Tompkins Square Park erupted into a violent clash with the police. Crack use became endemic in the ghettos, homelessness rose and AIDS emerged into a new scourge.

By 1989, citizens were restless for change. They turned to David N Dinkins, electing him the city's first African-American mayor. A distinguished, softly spoken man, Dinkins held office for only a single term, marked by a record murder rate, flaring racial tensions in Manhattan's Washington Heights and Brooklyn's Crown Heights and Flatbush neighbourhoods, and the explosion of a bomb in the basement parking garage of the World Trade Center in 1993 that killed six, injured 1,000 and foreshadowed the attacks of 2001.

Flatiron Building. *See p26.*

Deeming the polite Dinkins ineffective, New Yorkers voted in former federal prosecutor Rudolph Giuliani. Like his predecessors Peter Stuyvesant and Fiorello La Guardia, Giuliani was an abrasive leader who used bullying tactics to get things done, as his 'quality of life' campaign cracked down on everything from drug dealing and pornography to unsolicited windshield washing and drinking in public. As cases of severe police brutality grabbed the headlines and racial polarisation was palpable, crime plummeted, tourism soared and New York became cleaner and safer than it had been in decades. Times Square was transformed into a family-friendly tourist destination, and the dot-com explosion brought young wannabes to the Flatiron District's Silicon Alley. Giuliani's second term as mayor would close, however, on a devastating tragedy.

9/11 AND BEYOND

On 11 September 2001, terrorists flew two hijacked passenger jets into the Twin Towers of the World Trade Center, collapsing the entire complex and killing nearly 3,000 people. Amid the trauma, the attack triggered a citywide sense of unity, as New Yorkers did what they could to help their fellow citizens – from feeding emergency crews around the clock to cheering on rescue workers en route to Ground Zero.

Two months later, billionaire Michael Bloomberg was elected mayor and took on the daunting task of repairing not only the city's skyline but also its battered economy and shattered psyche. He proved adept at steering New York back on the road to health as the stock market revived, downtown businesses re-emerged and plans for rebuilding the World Trade Center were drawn. True to form, however, New Yorkers debated the future of the site for more than a year until architect Daniel Libeskind was awarded the redevelopment job in 2003; since then progress has been slow. David Childs's central skyscraper, 1 World Trade Center (formerly known as the Freedom Tower), rose by 15 feet in spring 2008, but just weeks later, Chris Ward, executive director of the Port Authority of New York (which owns the site), reported that 'schedule and cost estimates of the rebuilding effort that have been communicated to the public are not realistic.' Now visible above the hoardings, the 1,776-foot (541-metre) tower is expected to be completed by 2013, although the 9/11 Memorial Plaza is still on schedule for the 2011 target date (*see p44* **Rebuilding Ground Zero**).

Yet despite Bloomberg's many efforts to make New York a more considerate and civil place – imposing a citywide smoking ban in bars and restaurants and a strict noise ordinance that would silence even the jingling of ice-cream vans – New Yorkers continue to uphold their hard-edged image. The 2004 Republican National Convention brought out hundreds of thousands of peace marchers who had no trouble expressing how they felt about the war in Iraq. Local activism helped to kill a plan to build a 75,000-seat stadium on Manhattan's West Side, squashing Bloomberg and Co's dream to bring the 2012 Olympic Games to the Big Apple. In 2007, Bloomberg jumped on the eco bandwagon and announced plans to 'green up' NYC, aiming to reduce carbon emissions by 30 per cent and to fight traffic jams by making motorists pay driving fees in parts of Manhattan. His congestion pricing plan was so opposed it didn't even make it to the State assembly.

As Bloomberg's second term neared its end, he became increasingly frustrated that some of his pet proposals hadn't been realised. In the midst of 2008's deepening financial crisis, he proposed a controversial bill to extend the tenure of elected officials from two four-year terms to three. Although it was narrowly passed by the New York City Council in October 2008, many politicos (and citizens) opposed the law change. The encumbent poured a record sum of money into his campaign the following year, beating Comptroller William Thompson Jr with just 51 per cent of the vote to become the fourth mayor in New York's history to serve a third term. In October 2010, in a remarkable display of *chutzpah*, Bloomberg reversed himself and voted to restore the two-term limitation. The crisis alone had justified the extension, he reasoned – implying that exceptional times demanded an exceptional man.

Key Events

New York in brief.

1524 Giovanni da Verrazano sails into New York Harbor.
1624 First Dutch settlers establish Nieuw Amsterdam at foot of Manhattan Island.
1626 Peter Minuit purchases Manhattan for goods worth 60 guilders.
1639 The Broncks settle north of Manhattan.
1646 Village of Breuckelen founded.
1664 Dutch rule ends; Nieuw Amsterdam renamed New York.
1754 King's College (now Columbia University) founded.
1776 Battle for New York begins; fire ravages city.
1783 George Washington's troops march triumphantly down Broadway.
1784 Alexander Hamilton founds the Bank of New York.
1785 City becomes nation's capital.
1789 President Washington inaugurated at Federal Hall on Wall Street.
1792 New York Stock Exchange opens.
1804 New York becomes country's most populous city, with 80,000 inhabitants.
1811 Mayor DeWitt Clinton's grid plan for Manhattan introduced.
1827 Slavery officially abolished in New York State.
1851 The *New York Daily Times* (now the *New York Times*) launched.
1880 Metropolitan Museum of Art opens to the public.
1883 Brooklyn Bridge opens.
1886 Statue of Liberty unveiled.
1891 Carnegie Hall opens.
1892 Ellis Island opens.
1898 The five boroughs are consolidated into the city of New York.
1900 Electric lights replace gas along lower Broadway.
1902 The Fuller (Flatiron) Building becomes the world's first skyscraper.
1904 New York's first subway line opens.
1908 First ball dropped to celebrate the new year in Times Square.
1911 Fire in the Triangle Shirtwaist Company kills 146.
1913 Woolworth Building completed; Grand Central Terminal opens.
1923 The first Yankee Stadium opens.
1929 Stock market crashes; Museum of Modern Art opens.
1931 George Washington Bridge completed; Empire State Building completed; Whitney Museum opens.
1934 Fiorello La Guardia elected mayor.
1939 New York hosts the World's Fair.
1950 United Nations complex finished.
1953 Robert Moses spearheads building of the Cross Bronx Expressway.
1957 Brooklyn Dodgers baseball team move to Los Angeles; New York Giants moves to San Francisco.
1962 New York Mets debut at the Polo Grounds; Philharmonic Hall (later Avery Fisher Hall), first building in Lincoln Center, opens.
1964 Verrazano-Narrows Bridge completed; World's Fair held in Flushing Meadows-Corona Park in Queens.
1970 First New York City Marathon held.
1973 World Trade Center completed.
1975 On verge of bankruptcy, city is snubbed by federal government.
1977 Woody Allen's *Annie Hall* comes out; Studio 54 opens; 4,000 arrested during citywide blackout.
1989 David N Dinkins elected city's first black mayor.
1993 Bomb explodes in World Trade Center, killing six and injuring 1,000.
2001 Hijackers fly two jets into World Trade Center, killing nearly 3,000.
2004 Statue of Liberty reopens for first time since 9/11.
2007 Mayor Bloomberg unveils long-term vision for more eco-friendly city.
2007 Murder rate is lowest in 40 years.
2009 Yankees and Mets move into new state-of-the-art stadiums.
2010 Mayor Bloomberg is inaugurated as the fourth mayor in New York's history to serve a third term.

New York Today

Bloomberg's final term (no, really); building up and out.

TEXT: RICHARD KOSS AND HOWARD HALLE

As New York approaches the tenth anniversary of the attacks of 9/11, Gotham finds itself – much like the rest of the world – grappling with the Great Recession. Although the ranks of the jobless have grown and budget cuts have had palpable affects on such municipal sectors as public transport and the police department, the city's overall mood is not despondent. Part of this stoicism is because most New Yorkers can recall the apocalyptic visions of urban chaos – the graffiti-encrusted subway cars, burning tenement buildings, rampant crime, chronic drug use – that marked the city during the 1970s and '80s, when things were decidedly worse. Another cause for optimism (or, at least, for fending off pessimism) is the knowledge that the city's economic struggle is in fact a global one, that things are tough all over, and, as a result, New York has managed to remain one of the world's brightest cultural, architectural, culinary and financial lights. Throughout the economic storm, the world continues to look to Wall Street, where the fact that the stock market has made a slow but steady recovery from its near collapse in autumn 2008 is cause for some cheer.

ON THE STREETS AND IN THE SKY

Sadly, that cheer has yet to trickle down into the streets, and as 2010 drew to a close, the homeless presence in the city was increasingly evident. It is estimated that as many as 37,000 people live in the city's homeless shelters, including almost 15,000 children. While the breadlines and 'Hooverville' homeless communities of Depression-era Gotham have not sprung up, the sight of beggars on street corners is a hard reminder that, for many, the good times have clearly passed.

High above those streets, additions to the skyline continue to rise, most notably Frank Gehry's twisty, silvery, 76-storey 8 Spruce Street, formerly known as the Beekman Tower, within hailing distance of the gothic elegance that is the Woolworth Building. In November 2009, at the building's 'topping-out' ceremony (when the last bone of a building's skeleton is put into place), Gehry was reported to have pointed to its summit and proclaimed, 'No Viagra' of the successful erection. Whether the tower, like scores of similarly grandiose residential projects sitting empty across town, is able to find occupants is another matter, but it wasn't an auspicious omen when a wind storm in January 2010 sent debris from its upper storeys tumbling into the streets. Another celebrated would-be giant, Jean Nouvel's Tower Verre, was held up when its proposed 1,250 feet (the same height as the Empire State Building) were deemed too tall for midtown by the Planning Commission in 2009, so 200 critical feet were lopped off the plans. It should be ready by 2013.

MAYORAL CHUTZPAH

The Great Recession might scale back building blueprints but it couldn't blunt New Yorkers' propensity for chutzpah – a quality that can be found in rich abundance at the office of Mayor Michael Bloomberg. After serving the maximum limit of two consecutive terms called for by the city's charter, in October 2008 Bloomberg had his allies in the City Council amend the document to allow third terms for all elected officials. At the time the mayor started manoeuvring to change term limits, Wall Street was in full financial meltdown, engendering a surprisingly popular belief that only a billionaire like Bloomberg could steer New York through the tempest without heaving it on to the rocks. And so the change was passed.

Unsurprisingly, Bloomberg did little to dispel the impression of his indispensability, spending a record $102 million to $108 million on his 2009 re-election campaign (accounts of the sum vary). Democrats helped Bloomberg (running as both a Republican and an Independent) by putting up a lacklustre candidate as his opponent: former comptroller Bill Thompson, a bland party hack who seemed to think he was running in the city of 30 years ago. Yet the incumbent won by the barest majority – 51 per cent – reflecting voters' anger that he had overturned term limits to suit his cause and also a backlash against wealthy candidates that was sweeping the nation.

Bloomberg looked abashed on the day of his swearing in. In his speech, he assured New Yorkers that he'd 'heard them'. But his performance since then suggests that humility does not come easily for him. When, for instance, it was announced at the beginning of 2010 that the state government in Albany was proposing to slash money for the city government by $1.3 billion, Bloomberg countered by saying that the budget 'utterly fails the test of fairness.' Then he threatened to lay off 19,000 city workers, including 8,500 teachers, 3,150 cops and 1,050 firemen. This could be seen as a form of political blackmail: those 19,000 jobs, plus the families and other businesses that they support, represent a significant block of voters who might go against the already unpopular Governor David Paterson.

In October 2010, the mayor stunned most observers by coming out in favour of a bill to restore the two-term limits for elected officials – the same bill he'd overridden to achieve his third term. His reasoning was that special circumstances called for special leaders. Whether such chutzpah might translate on to the national level has been a perennial topic, but at the time of writing, such speculation seems on the wane.

'In October 2010, the mayor stunned observers by coming out in favour of a bill to restore the two-term limits for elected officials – the same bill he'd overridden to achieve his third term.'

MANHATTAN MAKEOVER

Meanwhile, little has dampened Bloomberg's enthusiasm for altering the city's appearance and reforming the behaviour of its citizens. In spring 2009, he ordered the closing of seven blocks along Broadway in Times Square, between 42nd and 47th Streets (the area's famed 'bow tie'), to vehicular traffic. He did the same further south around Herald Square – home to Macy's – but on a somewhat more modest scale: just the two blocks along Broadway between 33rd and 35th Streets. While tourists and perambulating New Yorkers have hailed these pedestrian malls, they've caused consternation for cabbies, bus drivers and other motorists.

Also, in April 2009, the mayor, along with City Council speaker Christine Quinn, announced a major package of legislation to significantly reduce greenhouse emissions from government, commercial and residential buildings in New York City. The six-point plan, called PlaNYC: A Greener, Greater New York, is intended to reduce the city's energy usage, saving consumers money while creating thousands of new jobs, and is part of an ongoing initiative first announced in 2007 to make Gotham totally green by 2030. It is widely admired among American urban planners.

Bloomberg's most famous curtailment of emissions, however, was the smoking ban he enacted in 2003: first for bars and restaurants; then in public buildings, offices and businesses. Now, some landlords are taking it upon themselves to extend the ban into apartments. Occasionally, the prohibition seems to be cracking. In autumn 2009, the foodie blog Eater reported that the owners of clubs and lounges are increasingly turning a blind eye to patrons who light up, knowing that the chances of being caught by the city are practically nil.

ADOPT, ADAPT AND IMPROVE

It's no wonder, then, that Bloomberg has kept resorting to micro-managing; in a poor economy, it's so much simpler than enacting grander plans. Indeed, compounded by the collapse of the New York housing market in 2009, a number of large-scale projects on which the mayor staked his administration have either been drastically cut back, or put on permanent hold. Chief among these are the redevelopment of the Atlantic Yards in Brooklyn, and the Hudson Yards on Manhattan's far West Side.

The $4.9 billion Atlantic Yards, brainchild of Cleveland, Ohio-based developer Bruce C Ratner, has been bedevilled by objecting neighbours and a flurry of lawsuits almost since its inception in 2003. In November 2009, New York's State Supreme Court dismissed the final major legal challenge, brought by local opponents of the project who claimed that the state could not use the laws of eminent domain to seize private property on the 22-acre parcel stretching from downtown Brooklyn to the borough's Prospect Heights neighbourhood. The justices found that the state could, in fact, do just that, ruling in Ratner's favour. However, once again, the economy intervened, forcing the developer to dramatically downsize his original plans.

Now just the sports complex, future home for the current New Jersey Nets basketball team, will be built in the foreseeable future. But even there, Ratner was forced to cut costs, firing his original architect, Frank Gehry, and going with a cheaper iteration by the firm SHoP. Likened to a futurist bicycle helmet, the edifice, to be named the

Barclays Center after its British-bank sponsor, is expected to be finished in 2012. When completed, the arena will be Brooklyn's first major sports facility – and home to its first major-league team – since the Brooklyn Dodgers played their last game at Ebbets Field (since torn down) in 1957 and moved to Los Angeles. It will join the new Yankee Stadium in the Bronx and the Mets' Citi Field in Queens.

Hudson Yards, however, is another story. Bounded by Tenth and Twelfth Avenues, between 30th and 33rd Streets, this huge site, currently a Metropolitan Transit Authority rail yard, has also had a chequered past. Originally, Bloomberg had proposed putting a new stadium there for the New York Jets football team as well as the 2012 Olympics, which New York had been hoping to host at the time. But the owners of nearby Madison Square Garden, sensing competition, and neighbourhood activists, fearing the mother of all traffic gridlocks in downtown, led a successful effort to sink the project. After several failed bids from various developers, the MTA struck a deal in May 2010 with two development companies to whom it will lease the site for 99 years, providing $1 billion in much-needed funds for the transit authority.

THE 'MOSQUE' THAT ROARED

In August and September 2010, New York found itself the centre of a political maelstrom that swept the country. The cause was the proposed construction of Park51, an Islamic community centre just two blocks from the site of the World Trade Center. Despite the centre's planned public auditorium, swimming pool, bookstore, memorial to the victims of 9/11 and its promoters' avowals that it would serve as an interfaith centre, Park51's plans to include a prayer space for Muslims struck a raw nerve among right-wing politicians, who protested the 'Ground Zero Mosque'. Republican bigwig Newt Gingrich suggested it 'would be like putting a Nazi sign next to the Holocaust Museum', former mayor Rudy Giuliani called it a 'desecration' and Sarah Palin called upon moderate Muslims to 'refudiate'[sic] the centre. The fact that a mosque even closer to Ground Zero already exists was ignored by opponents of the 'mosque', who used it as political fodder in the November 2010 elections.

Mayor Bloomberg and city officials were near unanimous in their support of the centre as well as the freedom of religious expression ensured by the First Amendment of the Constitution. Demonstrations outside the site were occasionally heated, however. At the time of writing, Park51 has been given the green light to proceed from the city but the project has stalled as its backers lack funds to finance the $150 million building. The controversy has not faded and is certain to flare up again as the tenth anniversary of 9/11 nears and New York continues to grapple with the legacy of that tragedy.

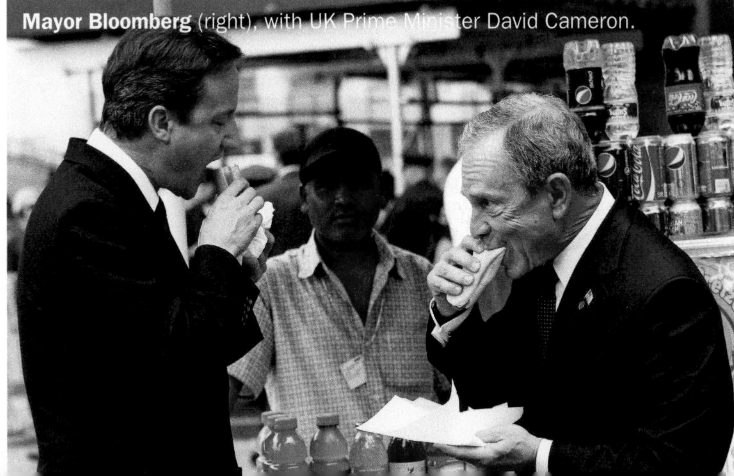

Mayor Bloomberg (right), with UK Prime Minister David Cameron.

Architecture

The ups and downs of the world's most famous skyline.

TEXT: ERIC P NASH

Manhattan, of course, is synonymous with skyscrapers. Following advances in iron and steel technology in the middle of the 19th century, and the pressing need for space on an already overcrowded island, New York's architects realised that the only way was up. The race to reach the heavens in the early 20th century was supplanted by the minimalist post-war International Style, which saw a rash of towering glass boxes spread across Midtown. Even now, despite less than favourable economic conditions, a surprising number of new high-rises are soaring skyward.

However, those with an architectural interest and an observant eye will be rewarded by the fascinating mix of architectural styles and surprising details closer to the ground in virtually every corner of the metropolis, from gargoyles crouching on the façade of an early 20th-century apartment building to extravagant cast-iron decoration adorning a humble warehouse. And it's worth remembering that under New York's gleaming exoskeleton of steel and glass lies the heart of a 17th-century Dutch city.

LOWLAND LEGACY

The Dutch influence is still traceable in the Downtown web of narrow, winding lanes, reminiscent of the streets of medieval European cities. Because the Cartesian grid that rules the city was laid out by the Commissioners' Plan in 1811, only a few samples of Dutch architecture remain, mostly off the beaten path. One is the 1785 **Dyckman Farmhouse Museum** (4881 Broadway, at 204th Street, www.dyckmanfarmhouse.org, 11am-4pm Wed-Sat; noon-4pm Sun) in Inwood, Manhattan's northernmost neighbourhood. Its decorative brickwork and gambrel roof reflect the architectural fashion of the late 18th century. The single oldest house still standing today in the five boroughs, however, is the **Pieter Claesen Wyckoff House Museum** (5816 Clarendon Road, at Ralph Avenue, Flatbush, Brooklyn, www.wyckoffassociation.org, 10am-4pm Tue-Sat). First erected around 1652, it's a typical Dutch farmhouse with deep eaves and roughly shingled walls.

In Manhattan, the only building left from pre-Revolutionary times is the stately columned and quoined **St Paul's Chapel** (*see p70*), completed in 1766 (a spire was added in 1796). George Washington, a parishioner here, was officially received in the chapel after his 1789 presidential inauguration. The Enlightenment ideals upon which the nation was founded influenced the church's highly democratic, non-hierarchical layout. **Trinity Church** (*see p70*) of 1846, one of the first and finest Gothic Revival churches in the country, was designed by Richard Upjohn. It's difficult to imagine now that Trinity's crocketed, finialed 281-foot (86-metre) spire held sway for decades as the tallest structure in Manhattan.

Holdouts remain from each epoch of the city's architectural history. An outstanding example of Greek Revival from the first half of the 19th century is the 1842 **Federal Hall National Memorial** (*see p70*), the mighty marble colonnade built to mark the site where George Washington took his oath of office. A larger-than-life statue of Washington by the sculptor John Quincy Adams Ward stands in front.

The city's most celebrated blocks of Greek Revival townhouses, built in the 1830s, are known simply as the **Row** (1-13 Washington Square North, between Fifth Avenue & Washington Square West); they're exemplars of the more genteel metropolis of Henry James and Edith Wharton.

Greek Revival gave way to Renaissance-inspired Beaux Arts architecture, which itself reflected the imperial ambitions of a wealthy young nation during the Gilded Age of the late 19th century. Like Emperor Augustus, who boasted that he had found Rome a city of brick and left it a city of marble, the firm of McKim, Mead & White built noble civic monuments and palazzi for the rich. The best-known buildings of the classicist Charles Follen McKim include the main campus of **Columbia University** (*see p119*), begun in the 1890s, and the austere 1906 **Morgan Library** (*see p93*), whose interior renovation was completed this past year. His partner, socialite and bon vivant Stanford White (scandalously murdered by his mistress's husband in 1906 on the roof of the original Madison Square Garden, which he himself designed), designed more festive spaces, such as the **Metropolitan Club** (1 E 60th Street, at Fifth Avenue) and the luxe Villard Houses of 1882, now part of the 100-year-old **New York Palace Hotel** (*see p177*).

Downtown, the old **Alexander Hamilton US Custom House**, which now houses the National Museum of the American Indian (*see p63*), was built by Cass Gilbert in 1907 and is a symbol of New York Harbor's significance in Manhattan's growth (before 1913, the city's chief source of revenue was customs duties). Gilbert's domed marble edifice is suitably monumental – its carved figures of the Four Continents are by Daniel Chester French, the sculptor of the Lincoln Memorial in Washington, DC. Another Beaux Arts treasure from the city's grand metropolitan era is Carrère & Hastings' sumptuous white marble **New York Public Library** of 1911 (*see p99*), built on the site of a former Revolutionary War battleground. The 1913 travertine-lined **Grand Central Terminal** (*see p104*) remains the most elegant foyer, thanks to preservationists (including Jacqueline Kennedy Onassis) who saved it from the wrecking ball.

VERTICAL REALITY

Cast-iron architecture peaked in the latter half of the 19th century, coinciding with the Civil War. Iron and steel components freed architects from the bulk, weight and cost of stone, and allowed them to build taller structures. Cast-iron columns – cheap to mass-produce – could support a tremendous amount of weight. The façades of many Soho buildings, with their intricate details of Italianate columns, were manufactured on assembly lines and could be ordered in pieces from catalogues. This led to an aesthetic of uniform building façades, which had a direct impact on later steel skyscrapers and continues to inform New York's skyline today. To enjoy one of the most telling vistas of skyscraper history, gaze north from the 1859 **Cooper Union** building (*see p82*) in the East Village, the oldest existing steel-beam-framed building in America.

Race to the Top

How NYC's architects egged each other onwards and upwards.

Woolworth Building.

For nearly half a century after its 1846 completion, the 281-foot (86-metre) steeple of Richard Upjohn's Gothic Revival **Trinity Church** (*see p70*) reigned in lonely serenity at the foot of Wall Street as the tallest structure in Manhattan. The church was finally topped in 1890 by the since-demolished, 348-foot (106-metre) **New York World Building**. But it wasn't until the turn of the century that New York's architects started to reach for the skies. And so began a mad rush to the top, with building after building capturing the title of the world's tallest.

When it was completed in 1899, the 30-storey, 391-foot (120-metre) **Park Row Building** (15 Park Row, between Ann & Beekman Streets) became the tallest building in the world. However, its record was shattered by the 612-foot (187-metre) **Singer Building** in 1908 (which, in 1968, became the tallest building ever to be demolished); the 52-storey, 700-foot (213-metre) **Metropolitan Life Tower** (*see p91*) of 1909; and the 793-foot (242-metre) **Woolworth Building** (*see p73*), Cass Gilbert's Gothic 1913 masterpiece.

The Woolworth stood in solitary splendour until skyscraper construction reached a crescendo in the late 1920s, with a famed three-way race. The now largely forgotten **Bank of Manhattan Building** (now known as the Trump Building) at 40 Wall Street was briefly the record-holder, at 71 storeys and 927 feet (283 metres) in 1930. Soon after, William Van Alen, the architect of the **Chrysler Building** (*see p105*), unveiled his secret weapon: a 'vertex', a spire of chrome nickel steel put together inside the dome and raised from within, which brought the building's height to 1,046 feet (319 metres). But then, 13 months later, Van Alen's homage to the Automobile Age was itself outstripped by Shreve, Lamb & Harmon's 1,250-foot

The most visible effect of the move towards cast-iron construction was the way it opened up solid-stone façades to expanses of glass. In fact, window-shopping came into vogue in the 1860s. Mrs Lincoln bought the White House china at the **Haughwout Store** (488-492 Broadway, at Broome Street). The 1857 building's Palladian-style façade recalls Renaissance Venice, but its regular, open fenestration was also a portent of the future. (Look carefully: the cast-iron elevator sign is a relic of the world's first working safety passenger elevator, designed by Elisha Graves Otis in 1852.)

Once engineers perfected steel, which is stronger and lighter than iron, and created the interlocking steel-cage construction that distributed the weight of a building over its entire frame, the sky was the limit. New York has one structure by the great Chicago-based innovator Louis Sullivan: the 1898 **Bayard-Condict Building** (65-69 Bleecker

Chrysler Building.

Empire State Building.

(381-metre) **Empire State Building** (*see p99*). With its broad base, narrow shaft and needled crown, it remains the quintessential skyscraper, and one of the most famous buildings in the world.

Incredibly, there were no challengers for the title of New York's – and the world's – tallest building for more than 40 years, until the 110-storey, 1,362- and 1,368-foot (415- and 417-metre) **Twin Towers** of Minoru Yamasaki's World Trade Center were completed in 1973. They were trumped by Chicago's Sears Tower a year later but reigned as the city's tallest buildings until 11 September 2001, when the New York crown reverted to the Empire State Building. **One World Trade Center** (formerly known as the Freedom Tower), designed by David Childs of Skidmore, Owings & Merrill to replace the Twin Towers, has been bogged down by problems, but it's eventually expected to surpass the originals with a completed height of 1,776 feet (541 metres). Don't look down...

'With its heady combination of grandeur and attention to detail, the Seagram Building is the Rolls-Royce of skyscrapers.'

Street, between Broadway & Lafayette Street). Though only 13 storeys tall, Sullivan's building, covered with richly decorative terracotta, was one of the earliest to have a purely vertical design rather than one that imitated the horizontal styles of the past. Sullivan wrote that a skyscraper 'must be tall, every inch of it tall... From bottom to top, it is a unit without a single dissenting line.'

The 21-storey **Flatiron Building** (*see p91*), designed by fellow Chicagoan Daniel H Burnham and completed in 1902, is another standout of the era. Its height and modern design combined with traditional masonry decoration, breathtaking even today, was made possible only by its steel-cage construction.

The new century saw a frenzy of skyward manufacture, resulting in buildings of record-breaking height. When it was built in 1899, the 30-storey, 391-foot (120-metre) **Park Row Building** (15 Park Row, between Ann & Beekman Streets) was the tallest building in the world; by 1931, though, Shreve, Lamb & Harmon's 1,250-foot (381-metre) **Empire State Building** (*see p99*) had more than tripled its record. (For more on the battle for the city's tallest building, *see p40* **Race to the Top**.)

Although they were retroactively labelled art deco (such buildings were then simply called 'modern'), the Empire State's setbacks were actually a response to the zoning code of 1916, which required a building's upper storeys to be tapered in order not to block out sunlight and air circulation to the streets. The code engendered some of the city's most fanciful architectural designs, such as the ziggurat-crowned 1926 **Paramount Building** (1501 Broadway, between 43rd & 44th Streets) and the romantically slender spire of the former **Cities Service Building** (70 Pine Street, at Pearl Street), illuminated from within like an enormous rare gem.

OUTSIDE THE BOX

The post-World War II period saw the rise of the International Style, pioneered by such giants as Le Corbusier and Ludwig Mies van der Rohe. The International Style relied on a new set of aesthetics: minimal decoration, clear expression of construction, an honest use of materials and a near-Platonic harmony of proportions. The style's most visible symbol was the all-glass façade, similar to that found on the sleek slab of the **United Nations Headquarters** (*see p105*).

Designed by Gordon Bunshaft of Skidmore, Owings & Merrill, **Lever House** (390 Park Avenue, between 53rd & 54th Streets) became the city's first all-steel-and-glass structure when it was built in 1952. It's almost impossible to imagine the radical vision this glass construction represented on the all-masonry corridor of Park Avenue, because nearly every building since has followed suit. Mies van der Rohe's celebrated bronze-skinned **Seagram Building** (375 Park Avenue, between 52nd & 53rd Streets), which reigns in imperious isolation in its own plaza, is the epitome of the architect's cryptic dicta that 'Less is more' and 'God is in the details'. The detailing on the building is exquisite – the custom-made bolts securing the miniature bronze piers that run the length of the façade must be polished by hand every year to keep them from oxidising and turning green. With this heady combination of grandeur and attention to detail, it's the Rolls-Royce of skyscrapers.

High modernism began to show cracks in its façade during the mid 1960s. By then, New York had built too many such structures in Midtown and below. The public had never fully warmed to the undecorated style, and the International Style's sheer arrogance in trying to supplant the traditional city structure didn't endear the movement to anyone. The **MetLife Building** (200 Park Avenue, at 45th Street), originally the Pan Am Building of 1963, was the prime culprit, not so much because of its design (by Walter Gropius of the Bauhaus) but because of its presumptuous location, straddling Park Avenue and looming over Grand Central. There was even a plan to raze Grand Central and construct a twin Pan Am in its place. The International Style had obviously reached its end when Philip Johnson, instrumental in defining the movement with his book *The International Style* (co-written with Henry-Russell Hitchcock), began disparaging the aesthetic as 'glass-boxitis'.

Plainly, new blood was needed. A glimmer on the horizon was provided by Boston architect Hugh Stubbins' silvery, triangle-topped **Citicorp Center** (Lexington Avenue, between 53rd & 54th Streets), which utilised contemporary engineering (the building cantilevers almost magically on high stilts above street level) while harking back to the decorative tops of yesteryear. Sly old Johnson turned the tables on everyone with the heretical Chippendale crown on his **Sony Building**, originally the AT&T Building (350 Madison Avenue, between 55th & 56th Streets), a bold throwback to decoration for its own sake.

Postmodernism provided a theoretical basis for a new wave of buildings that mixed past and present, often taking cues from the environs. Some notable examples include Helmut Jahn's **425 Lexington Avenue** (between 43rd & 44th Streets) of 1988; David Childs's retro diamond-tipped **Worldwide Plaza** (825 Eighth Avenue, between 49th & 50th Streets) of 1989; and the honky-tonk agglomeration of Skidmore, Owings & Merrill's **Bertelsmann Building** (1540 Broadway, between 45th & 46th Streets) of 1990. But even postmodernism became old hat after a while: too many architects relied on fussy fenestration and passive commentary on other styles, and too few began to create vital new building façades.

The electronic spectacle of **Times Square** (*see p94*) provided, and continues to provide, one possible direction for architects. Upon seeing the myriad electric lights of Times Square in 1922, British wit GK Chesterton remarked: 'What a glorious garden of wonder this would be, to anyone who was lucky enough to be unable to read.' This particular crossroads of the world continues to be at the cybernetic cutting edge, with the 120-foot-tall (37-metre), quarter-acre-in-area NASDAQ sign; the real-time stock

Bronx Museum of the Arts. *See p46.*

tickers and jumbo TV screens; and the news ticker on the original **New York Times Tower** (1 Times Square, between Broadway & Seventh Avenue). The public's appetite for new images seems so insatiable that a building's fixed profile no longer suffices here – only an ever-shifting electronic skin will do. The iconoclastic critic Robert Venturi calls this trend 'iconography and electronics upon a generic architecture.'

RADICAL RETHINKS

Early 21st-century architecture is moving beyond applied symbolism to radical new forms, facilitated by computer-based design methods. A stellar example is Kohn Pedersen Fox's stainless-steel and glass 'vertical campus', the **Baruch College Academic Complex** (55 Lexington Avenue, between 24th & 25th Streets). The resulting phantasmagoric designs that curve and dart in sculptural space are so beyond the timid window-dressing of postmodernism that they deserve a new label.

Frank Gehry's ten-storey, white-glass mirage of a building on the Lower West Side,

Rebuilding Ground Zero

A new centre offers a preview of the plans.

For nearly a decade, visitors to New York have made the pilgrimage to the site of the defining disaster of recent times. But a stop at Ground Zero has largely been an exercise in empathetic imagination. The gaping hole in the middle of lower Manhattan has been fenced off since the tragedy, and although plans for its redevelopment were announced in 2003, there hasn't been much evidence until the past two years. At the **9/11 Memorial Preview Site**, which opened in 2009, visitors can see an architectural model of the plans, and live webcam images of construction displayed on interactive kiosks. Almost ten years on, the World Trade Center site is still a draw, and the Preview Site received its millionth visitor within a year of opening.

The **National September 11 Memorial & Museum** will occupy half of the WTC site's 16 acres. The memorial itself, *Reflecting Absence*, designed by architects Michael Arad and Peter Walker, comprises two one-acre 'footprints' of the destroyed towers, with 30-foot man-made waterfalls – the country's largest – cascading down their sides. Bronze parapets around the edges will be inscribed with the names of those who died. As the title makes

completed in 2007, is emblematic of the radical reworking of the New York cityscape. Gehry's first glass building, and his first office building in New York, the headquarters for Barry Diller's **InterActiveCorp** (555 W 18th Street, at West Side Highway) comprises tilting glass volumes that resemble a fully rigged tall ship. Change is quite literally in the air in this area. Once an ugly-duckling neighbourhood of warehouses and industrial buildings, it is being transformed by the **High Line**, a former elevated railroad viaduct that has been reconceived as a cutting-edge urban park (*see p96* **Profile**). Down south, the **Urban Glass House** (330 Spring Street, at Washington Street), one of the late Philip Johnson's last designs, sprang up in 2006 amid Tribeca's hulking industrial edifices. The mini-skyscraper is a multiplication of his iconic Glass House in New Canaan, Connecticut. Nearby, Mexican architect Enrique Norten's crisply planed 14-storey glass tower rises from an antebellum warehouse at **One York Street** (at Sixth Avenue & Laight Street).

Midtown West has recently become an unlikely hotbed of new construction, with its

clear, it will convey a powerful sense of loss. 'When people approach these pools and see the names of the 2,982 victims arrayed around them they're going to get a sense of what was here and what is no longer with us – that they're standing at a spot where ten years ago these buildings stood and now there is only a void and sky,' says Joe Daniels, president and CEO of the National September 11 Memorial & Museum.

The surrounding plaza will be planted with around 400 swamp white oak and sweetgum trees that will be a dazzling spectacle of red, gold, pink and purple foliage in the autumn. The pavilion of the museum, designed by Snøhetta – the Oslo-based firm behind its home city's New Norwegian National Opera & Ballet building (2008) – will rise between the waterfalls. Its web-like glass atrium will house two steel trident-shaped columns salvaged from the base of the Twin Towers. Inside, visitors will descend to the vast spaces of the original foundations alongside a remnant of the Vesey Street staircase known as the 'Survivors' Stairs', as it was used by hundreds escaping the carnage.

'We're basically building an eight-acre green roof that will introduce this

area of lower Manhattan back into lower Manhattan,' explains Daniels. 'Beneath it will be the heart of the Memorial Museum. When you go down to bedrock, you'll be able to walk on the very space where the Twin Towers stood and view the actual slurry wall that held back the Hudson. We didn't want to change these spaces; we wanted to have the roof and the pools define the spaces beneath, then fit the exhibition into those defined spaces.

architectural attractions boosted in 2006 by Norman Foster's elegant, 46-storey, 597-foot (182-metre) crystalline addition to the art deco base of the **Hearst Magazine Building** (300 W 57th Street, at Eighth Avenue). The structure is a breathtaking combination of old and new, with the massive triangular struts of the tower penetrating the façade of the base and opening up great airy spaces within.

Further north, and among the more controversial facelifts of recent years, is Brad Cloepfil's renovation of Edward Durell Stone's 1964 modernism meets Venetian palazzo, **2 Columbus Circle**, originally the home of A & P heir Huntington Hartford's Gallery of Modern Art. In the same way that the gallery's collection of mostly figurative painting was seen as reactionary in the face of the abstract art movement, Stone's quotation of a historicist style was laughed into apostasy. However, Stone's work is being re-evaluated as a precursor to postmodernism, and many 20th-century architecture enthusiasts lamented the loss of the original façade after a lengthy, unsuccessful battle by the Landmarks Preservation Commission. The building is the new home of the Museum of Arts & Design (*see p116*).

The activity hasn't been confined to Manhattan. In Brooklyn, Richard Meier has added a glass box condo **On Prospect Park** (1 Grand Army Plaza), upsetting some of the long-standing residents in the process: most preferred the unbroken vista of classic apartment buildings. At $1,200 per square foot for some units, Meier's building set a new real-estate record for Brooklyn; still, it's not as inspired as his more elegantly thought-out apartment buildings at **173** and **176 Perry Street**, which overlook the Hudson. The Bronx got a boost with Arquitectonica's sleek aluminium and glass addition to the **Bronx Museum of the Arts** (*photo p43*), which opens up to narrow strips of windows like accordion pleats.

BEST-LAID PLANS

Some of New York's more ambitious architectural projects have been significantly scaled back in the face of new economic realities. The World Trade Center site, conceived by Daniel Libeskind, has seen frustratingly little progress in the years since the tragedy of 9/11. The 16-acre site's overseers, the Port Authority of New York and New Jersey, reported in 2008 that construction of the 26 interrelated projects was years behind schedule and billions of dollars over its $16 billion budget. However, there is now visible evidence of progress: the steel structure of David Childs's centrepiece 1,776-foot (541-metre) tower, **One World Trade Center** (formerly known as the Freedom Tower), with a revised completion date of 2013, reached 48 storeys by November 2010, and the **9/11 Memorial Plaza** is expected to be ready by the tenth anniversary of the Twin Towers' fall. Santiago Calatrava's spectacular plans for a shimmering, subterranean World Trade Center Transportation Hub, linking the suburban PATH trains to the subway, no longer features retractable roof wings, but the ribbed ceiling will still let in the sun with a skylight. The station is expected to be completed in late 2013.

Scaling back seems to be a key phrase as the city enters the second decade of the 21st century, and grandiose schemes are now settling earthward. The transformation of Brooklyn's **Atlantic Yards** (*see p126*) into a mega-development started boldly as an architectural site for Frank Gehry and Enrique Norten, but Gehry's design for the Nets' arena was rejected as too expensive. The proposed $1.5 billion renovation of **Lincoln Center** was also kept in check, leaving a team of top-notch architects to work with what was already there. Diller Scofidio + Renfro, one of the most creative teams on the scene, turned the travertine marble façade of Alice Tully Hall into a show window, integrating inside and out with glass walls; elsewhere, Billie Tsien and Tod Williams transformed a public atrium across from Lincoln Center, between Broadway and Columbus, and 62nd and 63rd Streets, into a sky-lit 'theatrical garden' lined with ferns, moss and flowering vines for buying tickets and sipping refreshments (*see p98* **Not Just the Ticket**).

'As the age of superblock modernism seems to be coming to a close, a new era of green, eco-conscious architecture is emerging.'

Even as the age of superblock modernism seems to be coming to a close, a new era of green, eco-conscious architecture is emerging. Cook + Fox's **Bank of America Tower** at 1 Bryant Park (Sixth Avenue, between 42nd & 43rd Streets) bills itself as the greenest skyscraper in the city, with torqued, glass facets reaching 54 storeys. The structure has a thermal storage system, daylight dimmers, green roofs and double-wall construction to reduce heat build-up, and the company is even looking into an anaerobic digester that will turn leftover food into electricity. Renzo Piano's sparkling 2007 tower for the *New York Times* at **620 Eighth Avenue** (between 40th & 41st Streets) also offers such green amenities as automatic shades that respond to the heat of the sun and recycled air. The glass-walled design is a literal representation of the newspaper's desire for transparency in reporting; the lobby moss garden with birch trees is also an interesting metaphor for an old-fashioned, paper-based industry in the computer age.

Unfortunately, the pace of construction lags considerably behind fashion trends and volatile economic markets; some buildings, such as the boxy **11 Times Square**, look old as soon as they are finished. Seeing no end in sight to growth and profits, developers tend to overbuild commercial space until there's a bust – plans for the World Trade Center site alone call for new office space that equates to five times the amount in downtown Atlanta, but there have been difficulties attracting tenants.

Setbacks have also met Pritzker Prize-winner Jean Nouvel's exciting plan for the sloped, crystalline Tower Verre, with an exoskeleton of irregularly crossing beams, that is planned to rise next door to the Museum of Modern Art. Initially proposed to reach 1,250 feet (the same height as the Empire State Building), the tower was opposed by activists who feared its shadow would loom over Central Park and it was rejected by the city's Planning Commission. After 200 feet were snipped off the top, the plan received the green light and should be a glamorous presence on the city skyline. And in a reversal of the city's historical pattern of development, most of the money is migrating downtown. The **Blue Building**, Bernard Tschumi's multifaceted, blue-glass-walled condominium, is a startling breakaway from the low-rise brick buildings that make up the Lower East Side.

Also noteworthy is the Japanese firm SANAA's **New Museum of Contemporary Art** (*see p80*); its asymmetrically staggered boxy volumes covered in aluminum mesh shake up the traditional street front of the Bowery. A block north, at **257 Bowery** (between Stanton & Houston Streets), Norman Foster's slender gallery building for Sperone Westwater art dealers – complete with a 12 by 20 foot lift that doubles as a moving exhibition space – has taken shape in a narrow gap. Meanwhile, the curled and warped façade of Frank Gehry's 76-storey **8 Spruce Street** (formerly known as the Beekman Tower) just south of City Hall will revitalise downtown when it's completed in 2011. Other projects exist tantalisingly on the drafting board, but groundbreaking for Renzo Piano's downtown satellite of the Whitney Museum at the southern end of the High Line will take place in May 2011. The museum, which will have double the floor space of the existing museum uptown, is expected to be finished in 2015.

To keep up with what's going up in New York, visit the **AIA Center for Architecture** (*see p86*), the **Skyscraper Museum** (*see p69*) and the **Storefront for Art & Architecture** (97 Kenmare Street, between Mulberry Street & Cleveland Place, 1-212 431 5795, www.storefrontnews.org, closed Mon & Sun), a non-profit organisation that hosts a programme of exhibitions, talks, screenings and more.

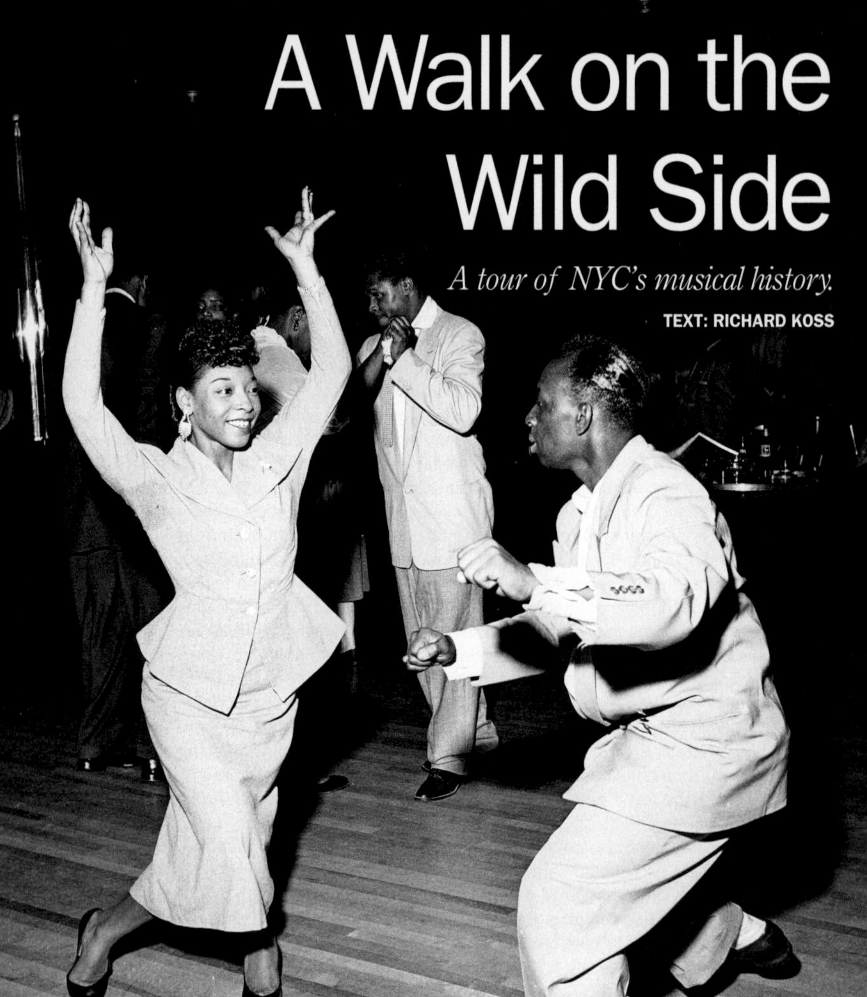

A Walk on the Wild Side

A tour of NYC's musical history.

TEXT: RICHARD KOSS

There are cities around the world that can lay claim to a music scene or genre, from Vienna's waltz through to Liverpool's Merseybeat and Seattle's grunge. But New York was the birthplace of a veritable orchestra of musical styles. In fact, no other city contributed so heavily to the soundtrack of the 20th century as did NYC. From the stages of Broadway and the speakeasies of Harlem to the downtown clubs and the block parties of the Bronx, the city gave birth to melodies, rhythms, lyrics, looks and attitudes that were embraced and adopted the world over. We've surveyed five musical genres – the Broadway musical, jazz, salsa, punk rock and hip-hop – on which the city left its indelible mark, and vice versa.

'Segregation confined black musicians uptown, but they managed to thrive there during the Harlem Renaissance.'

THE GREAT WHITE WAY

Like the frenetic boulevard to which it owes its name, the **Broadway musical** feeds off numerous arteries, including vaudeville comedy, drama, opera, ballet and the burlesque. Each made its own separate mark on 19th-century New York, but it wasn't until the city began to evolve into a world metropolis that the musical emerged as an art form in and of itself.

Although there's some debate as to exactly when musicals began, most recognise the 1866 production of *The Black Crook* as the first authentic musical. Weeks before the curtain was to go up on this uninspiring melodrama, a fire burned down another theatre, where a Parisian dance troupe was scheduled to perform. William Wheatley, the impresario behind *The Black Crook*, had the bright idea of combining both companies to produce a musical-theatre extravaganza – a drama with an orchestra, dancing and acting. Despite its four-and-a-half hour length, the show was popular enough to run for 16 months.

Around then, Union Square was the heart of New York's theatre district, but it soon began to migrate uptown along Broadway, gravitating toward Madison Square around the end of the century and settling around Times Square about a decade later. This progression coincided with the introduction of electric signs (using white bulbs, which lasted longer than coloured) outside the theatres, and their glow soon gave the boulevard its nickname, '**the great white way**'. During the 1900-1901 theatre season, over 70 musicals or plays were produced along Broadway.

The early 20th-century Broadway musical was largely propelled by the compositional abilities of the songwriters of **Tin Pan Alley**, a single, cacophonous block along 28th Street, where composers and their publishers (essentially, the music industry in those pre-radio days) worked. Many of their songs were novelties, but the best of them – by the likes of George M Cohan, Irving Berlin and George Gershwin – essentially wrote America's subconscious score. Cohan's *Little Johnny Jones* (1904) featured the anthems 'Give My Regards to Broadway' and '(I'm a) Yankee Doodle Dandy'. Brooklynite Gershwin, often in collaboration with his lyricist brother Ira, scored *Strike up the Band* (1927), *Girl Crazy* (1930), featuring the standard 'I Got Rhythm', and *Of Thee I Sing* (1931), which won a Pulitzer Prize. Russian-born Berlin, who grew up on the Lower East Side, composed the scores of some 19 musicals, highlighted by *This Is the Army* (1942) and *Annie Get Your Gun* (1946), with the iconic 'There's No Business Like Show Business'.

Surprisingly, the rise of Hollywood did not spell doom for Broadway, and the 1940s and '50s are actually regarded as the golden age of the musical. Richard Rodgers and Oscar Hammerstein II's *Oklahoma!* (1943) ran for 2,212 performances on Broadway, and their collaborations *South Pacific* (1949), *The King and I* (1951) and *The Sound of Music* (1959) are still part of the Broadway canon. A focus on social issues marked Leonard Bernstein and Stephen Sondheim's *West Side Story* (1957), which transposed *Romeo and Juliet* on to the ethnic battlegrounds of New York's Upper West Side. Sondheim would go on to become one of Broadway's most respected composer-lyricists with challenging (and occasionally dark) works, such as *Sweeney Todd* (1979) and *Sunday in the Park with George* (1984).

Today, Broadway boasts 39 official theatres and sells over $1 billion of tickets annually. For more on what's playing, *see p347*.

'Puente declared, "The only salsa I know comes in a bottle."'

THE BIRTH OF COOL

Jazz, of course, was born in New Orleans and made its syncopated way north during the great African-American migration of 1910-1930. Chicago was the first nerve center of the **big band** format, but New York gradually overtook the second city, thanks to its status as a recording, radio and music publishing capital, as well as the ease with which its speakeasy clubs circumvented Prohibition. A gig in New York meant having made it. Legend has it that travelling musicians would salute each other on the road with the hopeful 'see you at the Big Apple', referring to a Harlem nightclub of that name; soon the city appropriated the moniker.

Segregation confined black musicians uptown, but they managed to thrive there during the Harlem Renaissance of the 1920s and '30s. At the famous Cotton Club, where black musicians played for white audiences who ventured uptown, Fletcher Henderson put together a seminal band in 1923 featuring Coleman Hawkins and Donald Redmond; it was later joined by Louis Armstrong. In 1927, the Duke Ellington Orchestra began its residency there, followed in 1931 by Cab Calloway and the Missourians. At the 'home of the happy feet', the racially integrated Savoy Ballroom, Chick Webb's house band galvanised the new **swing** movement. A 'battle of the bands' regularly pitted Webb and his musical troops against the bands of such visiting heavyweights as Henderson, Ellington (who declared 'it don't mean a thing if it ain't got that swing'), Armstrong, Count Basie and Benny Goodman, a white clarinettist who led an integrated band. The Savoy gave birth to the Lindy Hop dance craze, named in honour of Charles Lindbergh's historic 1927 transatlantic crossing.

As the repeal of Prohibition in 1933 released jazz from the illicit world of the speakeasy, it began to shift operations downtown. An array of 'legit' clubs sprung up along 'The Street', a two-block stretch of **52nd Street** from Fifth to Seventh Avenues in the 1930s and '40s, showcasing the talents of Dizzy Gillespie, Billie Holliday, Ella Fitzgerald, Charlie Parker, Thelonious Monk, Art Tatum, Miles Davis and countless others for a mixed-raced crowd of jazz enthusiasts. The Street, which also housed the influential CBS recording studio, became the epicentre of jazz, the first stop for musicians arriving in New York. Jazz slipped further into the mainstream when Benny Goodman and his band gave a watershed concert at venerable Carnegie Hall in January 1938, thus signifying its arrival as 'respectable music'.

Nevertheless, Harlem remained the keeper of jazz's soul, the neighbourhood where most musicians and singers continued to live, and Ellington's famous 1941 'Take the A Train' uptown was no idle invitation. During the 1940s, when Monk was resident pianist there, Minton's Playhouse, a small club in Harlem that Davis called 'the black jazz capital of the world', held late-night jams that lured such luminaries as Gillespie and Parker, giving birth to the freestyle virtuoso jazz form of **bebop**, which rejuvenated jazz is the wake of the swing era.

By the early 1950s, the clubs on 52nd Street were losing their luster and the ones in Harlem were largely shuttered. But while the heyday of the New York jazz scene has passed, innovative jazzmen still journeyed to the Big Apple to make it their own in the 1950s and '60s. Maverick alto saxophonist Ornette Coleman introduced the concept of formless **free jazz** during a lengthy run at Manhattan's Five Spot in 1959, discarding preset tempos and fixed chord changes; trumpeter Miles Davis experimented with a variety of styles from **hard bop**, with its slow tempos and hard beats, to funk in the 1960s and '70s; and revolutionary saxophonist John Coltrane's *A Love Supreme* (1965) remains a New York classic.

Dizzy Gillespie.

Ella Fitzgerald.

Bob Dylan.

Ramones.

OYE COMO VA

Like jazz, **salsa** did not originate in New York, but the city became its throbbing heart during the 1950s and '60s, and played a critical role in the music's evolution. Today, the various strains of salsa are as much a part of the *nuyorican* soundscape as Spanish, which is spoken by almost 20 per cent of the city's residents.

The roots of salsa as we know it can be traced to the islands of the Spanish-speaking Caribbean, where African and Spanish musical traditions began to mix at the end of the 19th century following the abolition of slavery and galvanised by independence from Spain and increased urbanisation. The sound varied across the Caribbean, but the foundation for salsa is widely regarded as the **son Cubano,** a form that originated in Cuba in the 1930s and is distinguished by its use of the *trés* (derived from the Spanish guitar), the double bass, the trumpet and numerous African-inspired percussion instruments (including the bongos, *güiros*, claves and maracas). Among other Caribbean variations of the *son Cubano* that were to influence salsa were the Puerto Rican **bomba** and **plena** forms as well as the Dominican **merengue** and **carabiné.**

Contact with the American mainland – particularly New York, which has had a sizeable Latino population ever since the 1917 Jones Act conferred American citizenship on Puerto Ricans – introduced Latin music to jazz, and vice versa. Afro-Cuban musicians, notably Alberto Socarras and Mario Bauza, saw no barriers to them playing in jazz outfits; Bauza, who played with Dizzy Gillespie in Cab Calloway's band at one point, helped form Machito and His Afro-Cubans in 1940 with the bandleader Machito, who incorporated jazz harmonies and ideas into Latin music. Increasingly, Caribbean musicians began to expand their bands to include pianos and larger horn sections.

One of the results of this blend of Latin music and jazz was **mambo**, which sparked an international dance craze in 1950, as did the **chachachá** four years later. From its opening in 1948, thousands descended on the **Palladium Ballroom** on 53rd Street and

'When Run DMC stamped their Adidas on the scene in the early 1980s, hip-hop was here to stay.'

Broadway, *the* hotspot of Latin dance until it closed in 1966. In 1950, the Palladium became home to the 'big three' – Tito Puente, Machito and Tito Rodríguez – a trio of bandleaders who would take turns on stage night after night without letting the music pause. Spanish-Harlem-born Puente's career spanned six decades, earned him the title of 'Mambo King' and made him one of New York's most beloved sons; today, Tito Puente Way runs along 110th Street from Fifth to First Avenues in Spanish Harlem.

Although the suspension of ties between the United States and Cuba in 1961 cut musicians from the island from the New York scene, the subsequent relaxation of immigration restrictions on other Latin American countries brought new musical influences, such as cumbia from Colombia. Unsurprisingly, given their numbers, Puerto Ricans began to dominate. **Bugalú**, a Puerto Rican-inspired fusion of Latin music and rhythm and blues, became very popular, thanks to such musicians as Joe Cuba, percussionist Ray Baretto (who played with Charlie Parker), the Lebrón Brothers and the great trombonist Willie Colón.

But it was not until the late 1960s that the term 'salsa' was used to describe the various strands of Latin dance music that thrived in New York City. The word itself means 'sauce', and radio DJs began to use it to suggest the spiciness or hotness of the songs they touted. Most purists disdain it however (Puente himself declared 'the only salsa I know comes in a bottle'), and it's largely an Anglo label for a variety of Latino musical styles. Whatever you call it, you'll know it when you hear it, for it has a language all its own.

BURNING DOWN THE HOUSE

New York was firmly on the rock 'n' roll map by the time the 1970s came crashing around. Much as the jazzmen flocked to Harlem in the 1920s and '30s, rock musicians began to make their way to New York in the 1960s, settling downtown where Bohemia reigned and the rents were cheap. Like innumerable writers, artists and actors, musicians such as Bob Dylan and Jimi Hendrix made the pilgrimage to New York; of course, they could have made it anywhere – but they made it here.

And many found their way to **Max's Kansas City**, a nightclub on Park Avenue South and 17th Street that opened in 1965 and became something of a salon for artists and performers. Andy Warhol and his entourage commandeered a round table in the (in)famous back room almost every night; Willem de Kooning and William S Burroughs were regulars; Bob Marley opened for Bruce Springsteen in 1973; and a young Debbie Harry waited tables. Max's was also the epicenter of New York's burgeoning **glam-rock** scene, luring David Bowie, Iggy Pop and the cross-dressing, needle-kissing New York Dolls, who made their own bones at the Mercer Arts Center in Greenwich Village (and befriended Malcolm McLaren, who would later become the Sex Pistols' impresario). A Warhol collaboration, the Velvet Underground, love children of '60s rock and the avant garde, had a celebrated residency in the summer of 1970, after which Lou Reed quit the band, which was captured on their 1972 release *Live at Max's Kansas City*.

From these hazy beginnings, the New York **punk** movement burst into haphazard shape. In 1973, **CBGB** club opened on the Bowery, attracting a variety of bands joined by their energy, chutzpah, and do-it-yourself ethic. Among its regulars – many of whom also played Max's – were the Patti Smith Group, fronted by the Chicago-born poet, feminist and 'godmother of punk'; artsy garage band Television; leather-clad, four-chord warriors the Ramones, who hailed from Queens; Blondie, fronted by sexy, tough and aloof Debbie Harry, which later experimented with disco and even hip-hop; and Richard

Hell and the Voidoids, who served up the punk anthem 'Generation Damned' and whose lead singer pioneered the classic punk look of studs, spiked hair, and ripped clothing and safety pins. Punk songs tended to be stripped down, short and lyrically acerbic, a reaction against the bloated excess of mainstream rock of the time. However, the New York punks were also capable of fine musicianship (the dexterous guitar interplay of Television) and even romanticism (the lyrics of Patti Smith).

Punk found a second home in London, where it had far more commercial success under the wings of such bands as the Sex Pistols and the Clash. Remarkably, given their widespread use of heroin, many of the New York punks survived their raucous heyday and are still performing in various guises. Max's and CBGB did not survive, however, closing in 1981 and 2006 respectively, long after punk had flamed out.

BLOCK-ROCKIN' BEATS

No musical form is as fiercely tied to its New York roots as **hip-hop**, and it's hard to conceive of an artistic birthplace more desolate and economically blighted than the slums of the South Bronx in the mid 1970s. Instead of fiddling as the tenements burned, locals met up at block parties, where funk, soul music, Latin percussion and the disco so popular at the time in the city were played on turntables by neighbourhood DJs. One, Kool Herc, a young Jamaican immigrant named Clive Campbell, inaugurated the practice of using two turntables simultaneously to isolate, repeat and prolong a percussive '**breakbeat**', which became the basis of hip-hop music. Other neighbourhood DJs took note: Afrika Bambaataa expanded the vinyl repertoire to include cartoon music, salsa, calypso and other styles; Grandmaster Flash deployed a 'backpsin' technique to extend drum breaks by repeating them on both turntables; and Grand Wizard Theodore is generally credited with inventing the technique of '**scratching**' records.

So far so fresh, but it wasn't until the DJs began to use MCs to **rap** over the music that hip-hop's popularity began to take off. Initially enlisted to exhort partiers to dance, the rappers began to expand their role, making hip-hop more accessible to the recording studio and the airwaves. The first real hit was 1979's multi-platinum 'Rappers Delight' by the Sugar Hill Gang, three MCs from New Jersey who rapped over the Chic disco track 'Good Times'. Hip-hop staked a claim to be pop music's social conscience with 1982's seminal 'The Message' by Grandmaster Flash and the Furious Five, an unflinching take on the many hardships of ghetto life. Yet despite these forays into the mainstream, many critics regarded hip-hop music as a fad, dismissing it much as they did its urban cousins **breakdancing** and graffiti art.

When Run DMC stamped their Adidas on the scene in the early 1980s, hip-hop was here to stay. The popularity of the Queens trio's *Kings of Rock* (1985) earned them a spot on Live Aid, while *Raising Hell* (1986) – featuring a collaboration with hard rockers Aerosmith, the most audacious crossover of its time – went triple platinum. Several other NYC rap groups soon found international fame in the wake of Run DMC's popularity, most notably suave ladies' man LL Cool J, Caucasian clown princes the Beastie Boys, hardcore political agitpopsters Public Enemy and witty rhyme innovators De La Soul.

As hip-hop's audiences expanded beyond New York in the 1990s, so did its horizons. Gangsta rap put LA on the map, while numerous outfits from Atlanta, New Orleans and the rest of the 'Dirty South' have achieved enormous commercial success over the years. New York has always remained critical, however, periodically reinvigorating the genre with such acts as the ball of organised confusion that is the Wu-Tang Clan, the effortless lyricism of the late gangsta/trickster Notorious B.I.G and the commercial savvy of Jay-Z. Today, as hip-hop has been co-opted by advertising and found new scenes as far afield as Johannesburg, Rio de Janeiro and Tokyo, it still occasionally manages to offer up echoes (however distant) of those original South Bronx block parties.

Sights

Central Park. *See p106*.

Tour New York

See the city from the water, the sky or the street.

Navigating New York may at first appear to be a daunting task: it's big, it's busy and it doesn't have any interest in waiting for you while you rustle around in the bottom of your bag for your pocket map. Fortunately, there are countless options for exploring the city's attractions, whether your pleasure is cycling, sailing, bonding with fellow sightseers on a crowded tour bus, or simply hoofing it – with or without a chaperone. For additional inspiration, refer to the Own This City section of *Time Out New York* magazine (or the website www.timeoutnewyork.com), which offers weekly listings for urban outings.

BY BICYCLE

For more on cycling, *see p344 and p374.*

★ Bike the Big Apple

1-877 865 0078, www.bikethebigapple.com.
Tours vary. **Tickets** (incl bicycle & helmet rental) $80-$90. **Credit** AmEx, DC, Disc, MC, V.

You don't have to be Lance Armstrong to join these gently paced five- to seven-hour rides. Licensed guides lead cyclists through historic and newly hip neighbourhoods: popular tours include Harlem (the 'Sensational Park and Soul' tour), Chinatown ('From High Finance to Hidden Chinatown'), Williamsburg and a twilight ride across the Brooklyn Bridge.

Central Park Bike Tours

1-212 541 8759, www.centralparkbiketour.com.
Tours *Apr-Nov* 10am, 1pm, 4pm daily. *Dec-Mar* 10am, 1pm daily. **Tickets** (incl bicycle rental) $49; $40 reductions. **Credit** AmEx, DC, Disc, MC, V.

Central Park Bike Tours focuses its attentions on – yes! – Central Park. The main two-hour tour visits the John Lennon memorial at Strawberry Fields, Belvedere Castle and the Shakespeare Garden. Film buffs will especially enjoy the 'Central Park Movie Scenes Bike Tour', which passes locations from *When Harry Met Sally…* and *Wall Street*. You can also book your own tailor-made private tour.

BY BOAT

★ Circle Line Cruises

Pier 83, 42nd Street, at the Hudson River, Midtown (1-212 563 3200, www.circleline42.com). Subway A, C, E to 42nd Street-Port Authority.
Tours vary. **Tickets** $35; $22-$30 reductions. **Credit** AmEx, DC, Disc, MC, V. **Map** p404 B24.

The Circle Line's famed three-hour guided circumnavigation of Manhattan Island is a fantastic way to get your bearings and see many of the city's sights as you pass under its iconic bridges. Themed tours include a New Year's Eve cruise, a Fourth of July celebration, an evening 'Harbor Lights' sailing and an autumn foliage ride to Bear Mountain in the Hudson Valley. If you don't have time for the full round trip, there's a two-hour 'Liberty' tour that takes you around Downtown to the Brooklyn Bridge and back.

The separately run Circle Line Downtown (1-212 630 8888, www.circlelinedowntown.com) has a more intimate vessel, the *Zephyr*, for tours of lower Manhattan (Apr-Dec, $27), including summertime Happy Hour cruises from Thursday to Sunday ($25); these depart from Pier 16 at the South Street Seaport. From April to October, the two companies' rival speedboats – the *Beast* and the *Shark* – offer fun, adrenalin-inducing and splashy 30-minute rides ($24). *Photo p59.*

Manhattan by Sail

North Cove, Hudson River, between Liberty & Vesey Streets, Financial District (1-212 619 0885, 1-800 544 1224, www.manhattanbysail.com). Subway R to City Hall; A, C, 2, 3, 4, 5 to Fulton Street/Broadway-Nassau Street. **Tours** *mid Apr-Oct* 5 daily; times vary. **Tickets** *Shearwater* $45-$50, $25-$38 reductions. *Clipper City* $39, $17-$35 reductions. **Credit** AmEx, DC, Disc, MC, V. **Map** p402 D32.

Running Commentary

Your cultural and physical kicks rolled into one.

Whether you're a seasoned marathoner or just a jogging junkie, getting your daily endorphin fix can be a must – even while on holiday. You may be reluctant, however, to waste valuable sightseeing time within the confines of a hotel gym or aimlessly hitting the streets. Fortunately, you don't have to.

Michael Gazaleh, founder and president of of **City Running Tours** (*see p61*), offers a dozen different routes for fleet-footed visitors to explore New York at their preferred running pace. Groups are kept small – just two or three people, on average – so Gazaleh and the 18 guides he employs are able to customise each tour to fit the participants' athletic abilities and cultural interests, even lengthening or shortening a given itinerary. Worry not: if you want to slow down for a photograph or a closer look at a landmark, Gazaleh is happy to wait.

Gazaleh, a licensed chiropractor and lifelong exercise enthusiast, says his most popular excursion is the New York run, which starts in Brooklyn Heights, traverses the Brooklyn Bridge, then proceeds through the Financial District, Tribeca, Chinatown, Soho, the Village, Gramercy and Times Square before ending at Central Park.

His personal favourites are the eight-mile Harlem run, which takes in sites in northern Manhattan and the Bronx such as Columbia University and Yankee Stadium, and the ten-mile Brooklyn run, which traverses Green-Wood Cemetery, Prospect Park and the Brooklyn Heights Promenade.

There's also a jaunt through Central Park and a trip through the ethnically rich Lower East Side (where Gazaleh lives). The $60-and-up cost includes a T-shirt, a souvenir photo, product samples and discount coupons for local athletics shops.

One obvious advantage to Gazaleh's service is the vast amount of territory he covers in a mere one to two hours. 'We can go as far as a bus tour, and we take people on a lot of streets that buses can't,' he notes. He also points out that guides are able to connect with participants on a personal level. 'We're runners, so we have that common interest. And we know that if they go too long without a run, they just don't feel like themselves, so we're able to give them that sense of accomplishment.'

City Running Tours.

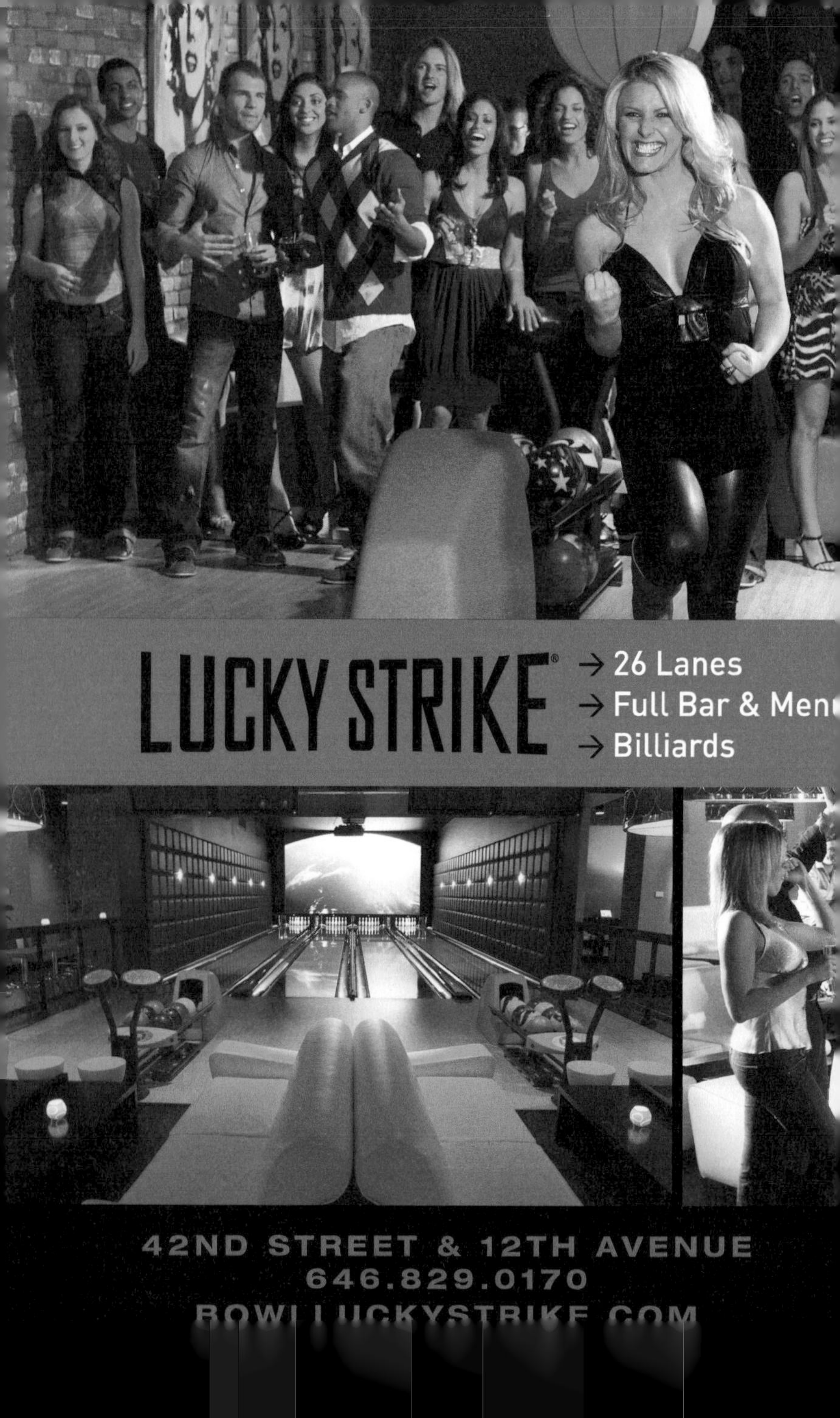
LUCKY STRIKE®
→ 26 Lanes
→ Full Bar & Men
→ Billiards
42ND STREET & 12TH AVENUE
646.829.0170
BOWLLUCKYSTRIKE.COM

Set sail on the *Shearwater*, an 82ft (25m) luxury yacht built in 1929. The champagne brunch ($79) or full-moon ($45) sail options are lovely ways to take in the skyline. The eight-sail tall ship, *Clipper City,* embarks from Pier 17 at the South Street Seaport.

New York Water Taxi

1-212 742 1969, www.nywatertaxi.com.
Like their earth-bound counterparts, New York water taxis are bright yellow, speedy and a great way to get around town. Unlike street taxis, however, they run on a set schedule, and at weekends you can hop on and off any one of them with a day pass, enjoying neighbourhood attractions along the way. The company also runs daily Statue of Liberty Express tours ($25; $15-$20 reductions) year-round and daily sunset cruises ($25) in the summer, including the 'Audubon Eco-Cruise' ($35) on summer Sunday evenings.

NY Waterway

Pier 78, 38th Street, at Hudson River, Midtown (1-800 533 3779, www.nywaterway.com). Subway A, C, E to 42nd Street-Port Authority. **Tours** vary. **Tickets** $26; $15-$21 reductions. **Credit** AmEx, DC, MC, V. **Map** p404 B24.
NY Waterway's scenic 90-minute harbour tour takes you on a complete circuit around Manhattan's landmarks. Choose from the 'City Lights' evening excursion, or a daytime cruise that focuses on the skyline of lower Manhattan. A variety of more specialist tours are also available, including the 'New York Historical Society History Cruise'.
Other locations World Financial Center Pier, Pier 11, Wall Street, Financial District (1-800 533 3779).

Pioneer

South Street Seaport Museum, 12 Fulton Street, between Water & South Streets, Financial District (1-212 748 8786, www.southstreetseaportmuseum.org). Subway A, C to Broadway-Nassau Street; J, M, Z, 2, 3, 4, 5 to Fulton Street. **Tours** *May-Oct* times vary. **Tickets** $25-$30; $15-$25 reductions. **Credit** AmEx, DC, MC, V. **Map** p402 F32.
Built in 1885, the 102ft (31m) *Pioneer* is the only iron-hulled merchant sailing ship still in existence. Rebuilt with steel plating in the 1960s, and with a restored rig, now her sails billow as you cruise the East River and New York Harbor. A range of highly educational on-board adult and children's programmes is also offered.

★ FREE Staten Island Ferry

Battery Park, South Street, at Whitehall Street, Financial District (1-718 727 2508, www.siferry.com). Subway 1 to South Ferry; 4, 5 to Bowling Green. **Tickets** free. **Map** p402 E34.
During this commuter barge's 25-minute crossing, you get superb panoramas of lower Manhattan and the Statue of Liberty. Boats leave South Ferry at

Circle Line Cruises. *See p56.*

BY BUS

Gray Line

777 Eighth Avenue, at 48th Street, Theater District (1-212 445 0848, www.newyorksightseeing.com). Subway A, C, E to 42nd Street-Port Authority. **Tours** vary. **Tickets** $39-$104; $29-$94 reductions. **Credit** AmEx, DC, Disc, MC, V. **Map** p404 D23.
Gray Line offers more than 20 bus tours, from a basic two-hour ride (with 40-plus hop-on, hop-off stops) to the guided 'Manhattan Comprehensive' tour, which includes lunch, admission to Top of the Rock or the Empire State Building, and a boat ride to Ellis Island and the Statue of Liberty.

On-Location Tours

1-212 683 2027, www.screentours.com. **Tours** vary. **Tickets** $20-$52. **Credit** AmEx, DC, MC, V.
Whether you'd prefer to sip cosmos à la Carrie Bradshaw or visit the Bada Bing, On-Location's well-organised bus trips allow HBO enthusiasts to simulate the experiences of their favourite characters from *Sex and the City* and *The Sopranos.* Or hop aboard the 'New York TV and Movie Sites' tour and visit more than 40 sites from big- and small-screen productions such as *The Godfather* and *Seinfeld.*

BY HELICOPTER

Liberty Helicopter Tours

Downtown Manhattan Heliport, Pier 6, East River, between Broad Street & Old Slip, Financial

www.libertyhelicopter.com). Subway R to Whitehall Street; 1 to South Ferry. **Tours** 9am-6pm daily. **Tickets** $150-$225. **Credit** AmEx, DC, MC, V. **Map** p402 E34.

There'll be no daredevil swooping around the city (Liberty's helicopters provide a fairly smooth flight), but the views are thrilling. Even a seven-minute ride (durations vary) is long enough to get an adrenalin-pumping look at the Empire State Building.

Other locations VIP Heliport, Twelfth Avenue, at 30th Street, Midtown (1-800 542 9933).

ON FOOT

Adventure on a Shoestring

1-212 265 2663. **Tours** daily; times vary. **Tickets** $10. **No credit cards.**

The motto of this organisation, now in its 46th year, is 'Exploring the world within our reach... within our means', and founder Howard Goldberg is dedicated to revealing the 'real' New York. Walks take you from one charming neighbourhood to another, and topics can include 'Millionaire's Row' and 'Greenwich Village Ghosts Galore'. Special celebrity theme tours, including tributes to Jackie O, Katharine Hepburn and Marilyn Monroe, are also available.

FREE Big Apple Greeter

1-212 669 8159, www.bigapplegreeter.org. **Tours** by arrangement. **Tickets** free.

Set up in 1992, this independent non-profit scheme offers visitors an alternative to the organised tour format. Sign up through the website at least four to six weeks ahead and you'll be paired with a volunteer 'greeter', who'll give you an informal, personal two- to four-hour tour of one of the city's neighbourhoods (your choice or theirs). All tours are free.

★ Big Onion Walking Tours

1-212 439 1090, www.bigonion.com. **Tours** daily; times vary. **Tickets** $15; $12 reductions. **No credit cards.**

New York was known as the Big Onion before it became the Big Apple. The tour guides will explain why, and they should know – all guides hold advanced degrees in history (or a related field). Among the walks is one devoted to the 'Official Gangs of New York'. Private tours are also available.

★ City Running Tours

1-877 415 0058, www.cityrunningtours.com. **Tours** vary. **Tickets** $20-$60. **Credit** AmEx, DC, Disc, MC, V.

See p57 **Running Commentary**.

Harlem Heritage Tours

1-212 280 7888, www.harlemheritage.com. **Tours** vary. **Tickets** $25-$55. **Credit** DC, MC, V.

Now operating more than ten bus and walking tours, Harlem Heritage aims to show visitors the soul of the borough. The 'Harlem Civil Rights Multimedia' tour takes tourists to landmarks associated with Malcolm X, James Baldwin and Martin Luther King. The 'Harlem Renaissance' tour walks you to the sites of Prohibition-era speakeasies, clubs and one-time residences of artists, writers and musicians.

★ Justin Ferate

1-212 223 2777, www.justinsnewyork.com. **Tours** vary. **Tickets** $20. **No credit cards.**

This venerated historian wrote the book on Gotham walking tours. No, really – the city commissioned him to write the NYC tour-guide licensing exam, which he designed to educate and assess would-be guides. In addition to a regular roster of tours covering everything from Midtown murals to the quaint attractions of the Bronx's City Island, Ferate leads speciality tours – such as one exploring the artwork of historic subway stations around the city – and offers a free 90-minute trek through Grand Central Terminal and its environs every Friday at 12.30pm.

Municipal Art Society Tours

1-212 935 3960, 1-212 439 1049 recorded information, mas.org/tours. **Tours** vary. **Tickets** $15. **No credit cards.**

The Municipal Art Society (MAS) organises bus and walking tours in New York and further afield. Many – such as '42nd Street Deco' – are led by architects, designers and writers, and reflect the society's focus on contemporary architecture, urban planning and historic preservation. There's also a guided walk through Grand Central Terminal on Wednesdays at 12.30pm (suggested donation $10). Private tours are available by appointment.

NoshWalks

1-212 222 2243, www.noshwalks.com. **Tours** vary. **Tickets** $45-$48; $26 reductions.

Each culinary outing is led by company founder Myra Alperson, who's been writing about New York's food scene for more than ten years. Taking you to corners of the city you'd never visit on your own, Alperson fills you in on the neighbourhood's culinary and cultural history, introducing you to chefs and shopkeepers, street food and snacks along the way. Trips have included South Asian cuisine in Jackson Heights, Queens, and the kosher-Caribbean combo tour in Crown Heights, Brooklyn.

INSIDE TRACK GO WILD IN NYC

The **Audubon Eco-Cruise** up the East River (June-mid Aug), run by New York Water Taxi (*see p59*), gives you an entirely new perspective on the city's importance – to birds, that is. You'll ride to uninhabited South Brother Island, a habitat and breeding ground for migratory species such as the great egret.

Downtown

Where it's at.

The southern tip of Manhattan has always been the city's financial, legal and political powerhouse. It's where New York began as a Dutch colony in the 17th century, and where the 19th-century influx of immigrants injected the city with new energy. Yet with much of it off the Big Apple's orderly grid, Downtown doesn't conform to standard.

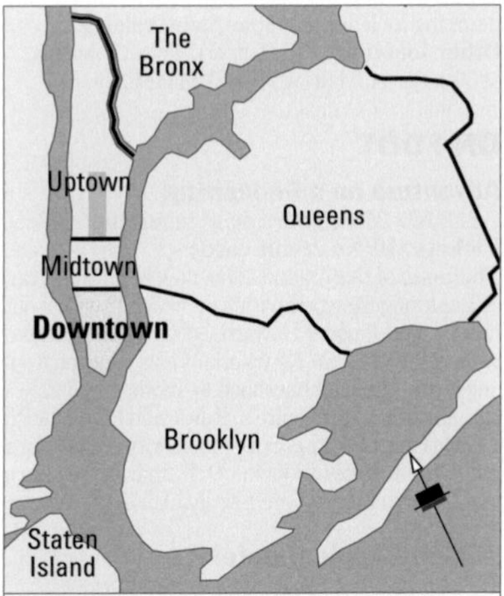

Here, the landscape shifts from block to block. In the **Financial District**, gleaming towers rub shoulders with 18th-century landmarks; **Tribeca**'s haute dining spots are only a short hop from **Chinatown**'s frenetic food markets; and around the corner from the clubs of the **Meatpacking District**, the impeccably dressed bourgeoisie tends to its stately **West Village** brownstones.

The character of these diverse neighbourhoods is constantly changing, but while the counterculture that erupted in **Greenwich Village** and the **Lower East Side** may have been tamed by relentless gentrification and commercial development, iconoclastic art, vibrant nightlife and retail still thrive.

Map pp402-403
Hotels p155
Restaurants & cafés p183
Bars p217

THE FINANCIAL DISTRICT

Battery Park

Subway J, M, Z to Broad Street; N, R to Whitehall Street; 1 to South Ferry; 4, 5 to Bowling Green.

It's easy to forget that Manhattan is an island – what with all those gargantuan skyscrapers obscuring your view of the water. Until, that is, you reach the southern tip, where salty ocean breezes are reminders of the millions of immigrants who travelled on steamers in search of prosperity, liberty and a new home. This is where they landed, after passing through Ellis Island's immigration and quarantine centres.

On the edge of Battery Park, **Castle Clinton** was one of several forts built to defend New York Harbor against attacks by the British in the War of 1812 (others included Castle Williams on Governors Island, Fort Gibson on Ellis Island and Fort Wood, now the base of the Statue of Liberty). After serving as an aquarium, immigration centre and opera house, the sandstone fort is now a visitors' centre and ticket booth for **Statue of Liberty** and **Ellis Island** tours (although it's preferable to book online; *see p65*), as well as an intimate, open-air setting for concerts. The park is a key venue of the annual **River to River Festival** (*see p262*) – a summertime celebration of Downtown culture and the city's largest free arts festival.

Joining the throngs making their way to Lady Liberty, you'll head south-east along the shore, where several ferry terminals jut into the harbour. Among them is the **Whitehall Ferry Terminal**, the boarding place for the famous **Staten Island Ferry** (*see p59*). Constructed in 1907, the terminal was severely damaged by fire in 1991, but was completely rebuilt in 2005. More than 75,000 passengers take the free, 25-minute journey to the Staten Island shore each day; most are commuters but many are tourists, taking advantage of the unparalleled views of the Manhattan skyline and the Statue of Liberty. Before the Brooklyn Bridge was completed in 1883, the **Battery Maritime Building** (11 South Street, between Broad & Whitehall Streets) served as a terminal for the ferry services between Manhattan and Brooklyn. Now, it's the launch point for a free ferry to tranquil **Governors Island** on summer weekends (*see p64* **Profile**).

Just north of Battery Park you'll find the triangular **Bowling Green**, the city's oldest park and a popular lunchtime spot for Financial District workers; it's also the front lawn of the **Alexander Hamilton US Custom House**, now home to the **National Museum of the American Indian** (*see p65*). On its northern side stands a three-and-a-half-tonne bronze sculpture of a bull (symbolizing the bull, or rising, share market). The statue was deposited without permission outside the Stock Exchange by guerilla artist Arturo di Modica in 1989 and has since been moved by the city to its current location on the Green. The bull's enormous balls are often rubbed for good luck by tourists (and perhaps the occasional broker).

Dwarfed by the surrounding architecture, the **Stone Street Historic District** is a small pocket of restored 1830s buildings on the eponymous winding cobblestoned lane, also encompassing South William and Pearl Streets and Coenties Alley. Office workers and tourists frequent its restaurants and bars, including the boisterous **Ulysses** (95 Pearl Street, at Stone Street, 1-212 482 0400) and **Stone Street Tavern** (52 Stone Street, near Broad Street, 1-212 785 5658).

Vestiges of the city's past lurk amid the skyscrapers: the rectory of the **Shrine of St Elizabeth Ann Seton** (7 State Street, between Pearl & Whitehall Streets, 1-212 269 6865, www.setonshrine.com), a 1792 Federal building dedicated to the first American-born saint; and the **Fraunces Tavern Museum** (*see p65*), the restored alehouse where George Washington toasted victory over the British. Marking more recent events, the **New York Vietnam Veterans Memorial** (55 Water Street, between Coenties Slip & Hanover Square) stands one block to the east. Erected in 1985 and recently refreshed with a new plaza, it features the Walk of Honor – a pathway inscribed with the names of the 1,741 New

INSIDE TRACK
THE GHOST SUBWAY STATION

If you take the 6 train to its last downtown stop, Brooklyn Bridge-City Hall, ignore the recorded entreaty to get off. Stay aboard while the train makes its U-turn loop before heading uptown and you'll get a glimpse of the original 1904 City Hall Station (out of use since 1945) and its brass chandeliers, vaulted ceilings, tile mosaics and skylights.

Brooklyn Bridge.

Profile Governors Island

The former military HQ is now an arty seasonal sanctuary.

A 172-acre chunk of prime waterside real estate that can never be developed into luxury condos, **Governors Island** (*see p65*) is a secluded anomaly a scant 800 yards from lower Manhattan. The verdant commons and stately red-brick buildings evoke an Ivy League campus by way of a colonial New England village – oddly emptied of its inhabitants.

The peaceful backwater has had a tumultuous history. Initially a seasonal fishing and gathering ground for the Lenape Indians, it was particularly plentiful in nut trees, earning it the name 'Noten Eylant' when the Dutch arrived in the 1620s. In 1674, the British secured it for 'the benefit and accommodation of His Majesty's Governors'. Perhaps the most colourful of these was Edward Hyde, Viscount Cornbury, Governor of New York and New Jersey from 1702 to 1708. A cousin of Queen Anne, he was alleged to be a cross-dresser (check out the portrait, said to be of Lord Cornbury in drag, at the New-York Historical Society; *see p118*).

The island's strategic position cemented its future as a military outpost (by the late 19th century it was the army's headquarters for the entire eastern US), and it still retains a significant chunk of its military-era construction, including **Fort Jay**, started in 1776, and **Castle Williams**, completed in 1812. When the army began to outgrow the space, excavated soil from the Lexington Avenue subway line was used to enlarge the island by 103 acres.

The modest patch has been the backdrop for some huge events. In 1909, it launched the first overwater flight, when Wilbur Wright circled the Statue of Liberty before flying back. Such legendary figures as Generals Ulysses S Grant and Douglas MacArthur had stints on the island.

Since the island opened to visitors in 2006, the programme of events has increased dramatically. The first phase of the strategy to revitalise the island has been to draw visitors, explains Governors Island Preservation and Education Corporation (GIPEC) president Leslie Koch. The second is the continued investment in the infrastructure and preservation of its 52 historic landmarks.

The third phase is to create 'a world-class set of public spaces and parks.' In 2007, a team of internationally known design firms, led by Rotterdam's West 8, was chosen to develop the plans. Although the details haven't yet been announced, one of the signature features will be new hills constructed from the debris of (non-historic) buildings as they are demolished, providing even more spectacular viewpoints for harbour panoramas.

SIGHTS

Yorkers who lost their lives fighting in the conflict – and a monument etched with excerpts from letters, diary entries and poems written during the war. Nearby, in Hanover Square (William Street at Pearl Street), is the **British Memorial Garden**. Completed in 2007, it commemorates the 67 Britons who died in New York on 9/11, and features hand-carved stone from Scotland, plants from Prince Charles's estate and iron bollards from London.

FREE Alexander Hamilton US Custom House/National Museum of the American Indian

1 Bowling Green, between State & Whitehall Streets (1-212 514 3700, www.nmai.si.edu). Subway N, R to Whitehall Street; 1 to South Ferry; 4, 5 to Bowling Green. **Open** 10am-5pm Mon-Wed, Fri-Sun; 10am-8pm Thur. **Admission** free. **Map** p402 E33.

Cass Gilbert's magnificent Beaux Arts Custom House, completed in 1907, housed the Customs Service until 1973, when the federal government moved it to the newly built World Trade Center complex. Four monumental figures by Lincoln Memorial sculptor Daniel Chester French – representing America, Asia, Europe and Africa – flank the impressive entrance. The panels surrounding the elliptical rotunda dome were designed to feature murals, but this wasn't realised until the 1930s when local artist Reginald Marsh was commissioned to decorate them under the New Deal's Works Progress Administration; the paintings show a ship's progress through New York Harbor.

In 1994, the National Museum of the American Indian's George Gustav Heye Center, a branch of the Smithsonian, moved into the first two floors of the building. On the second level, the life and culture of Native Americans is presented in illuminating rotating exhibitions – from intricately woven fibre Pomo baskets to ceremonial costumes – in galleries radiating out from the rotunda. Craft demonstrations, native dances, films and other events take place in the Diker Pavilion for Native Arts & Culture on the ground floor.

The temporary show, 'A Song for the Horse Nation', exploring the impact of that quadruped on the indigenous populations since its introduction to the New World, is on display until July 7, 2011.

Fraunces Tavern Museum

2nd & 3rd Floors, 54 Pearl Street, at Broad Street (1-212 425 1778, www.fraucestavern museum.org). Subway J, M, Z to Broad Street; 4, 5 to Bowling Green. **Open** noon-5pm Mon-Sat. **Admission** $10; $5 reductions; free under-6s. **Credit** AmEx, Disc, MC, V. **Map** p402 E33.

This 18th-century tavern was favoured by General George Washington, and was the site of his famous farewell to the troops at the Revolution's close. During the mid to late 1780s, the building housed the fledgling nation's departments of war, foreign affairs and treasury. In 1904, it became a repository for artefacts collected by the Sons of the Revolution in the State of New York.

Highlights include a portrait gallery devoted to Washington, and the Long Room, the public dining room where the future president made his emotional leave-taking; relics include one of Washington's false teeth. There are also various temporary exhibitions, though, at the time of writing, the tavern itself has been closed for renovation.

★ FREE Governors Island

1-212 440 2202, www.govisland.com. Subway N, R to Whitehall Street; 1 to South Ferry; 4, 5 to Bowling Green. Then take ferry from Battery Maritime Building at Slip no.7. **Open** *5 June-11 Oct* 10am-5pm Fri; 10am-7pm Sat, Sun.
See p64 **Profile**.

★ Statue of Liberty & Ellis Island Immigration Museum

Liberty Island & Ellis Island (1-212 363 3200, www.nps.gov/stli, www.ellisisland.org). Subway N, R to Whitehall Street; 1 to South Ferry; 4, 5 to Bowling Green. Then take Statue of Liberty ferry (1-877 523 9849, www.statuecruises.com), departing every 30mins from gangway 4 or 5 in southernmost Battery Park. **Open** (ferry runs) 8.30am-4.30pm daily. **Admission** $12; $5-$10 reductions; free under-4s. *Crown access* (reserved in advance) $3. **Credit** AmEx, DC, MC, V.
For the Statue of Liberty, *see p67* **Profile**.

A half-mile across the harbour from Liberty Island is the 32-acre Ellis Island, gateway for over 12 million people who entered the country between 1892 and 1954. In the Immigration Museum (a former check-in depot), three floors of photos, interviews, interactive displays and exhibits pay tribute to the hopeful souls who made the voyage, and the nation they helped to transform. Visitors can also search the museum's registry database and print copies of an ancestor's records. Tickets can be purchased online, by phone or at Castle Clinton in Battery Park. *Photo p66.*

World Trade Center site & Battery Park City

Subway A, C to Broadway-Nassau Street; E to World Trade Center; J, M, Z, 2, 3, 4, 5 to Fulton Street; N, R, 1 to Rector Street; 4, 5 to Bowling Green.

The streets around the site of the former World Trade Center have been drawing the bereaved and the curious since that traumatic day in September 2001. The worst attack on US soil took nearly 3,000 lives and left a gaping hole where the Twin Towers had once helped to define the New York skyline. Since the site was fenced off, there hasn't been much to see, but

SIGHTS

Ellis Island Immigration Museum. *See p65.*

Profile Statue of Liberty

The long history of New York's first lady.

Although she no longer greets new arrivals, the **Statue of Liberty** (*see p65*) is still New York's, if not America's, most iconic sight. The sole occupant of Liberty Island, she stands 305 feet (92 metres) from the bottom of her base to the tip of her gold-leaf torch. Up close, you can really appreciate how huge she truly is: her nose is four and a half feet long.

Lady Liberty was intended as a gift from France on America's 100th birthday. Frédéric Auguste Bartholdi, the statue's designer, was inspired by the ancient Colossus at Rhodes, although it was said that the face was modelled on that of his mother – and the body on that of his mistress. Bartholdi had initially planned a giant lighthouse-statue to stand sentry at the mouth of the Suez Canal, then under construction. But when the Egyptians were unreceptive, Bartholdi turned to New York Harbor. And so the proposed Egypt Bringing Light to Asia was reborn as *Liberty Enlightening the World*, the current statue's official title, as the French raised millions of francs to fund this expression of friendship for their ally from the Revolutionary War.

Construction began in Paris in 1874, with Gustave Eiffel (of Tower fame) crafting the skeletal iron framework. However, the French desire that she should be completed in time for America's centennial proved ill-fated: only the arm and torch were completed in time. The celebrated limb was exhibited at the Centennial Exhibition in Philadelphia and then spent six years on show in Madison Square Park; the head, meanwhile, was first displayed at the 1878 Paris Exposition.

In 1884, the statue was finally completed – only to be taken apart into hundreds of pieces to be shipped to New York, where it was placed on its pedestal and unveiled by President Grover Cleveland in 1886. It served as a lighthouse until 1902 and as the welcoming sign for millions of immigrants. These 'tired... poor... huddled masses' were evoked in Emma Lazarus's poem 'The New Colossus', written in 1883 to raise funds for the pedestal and engraved inside the statue in 1903.

With a Monument Pass, which is free but only available with ferry tickets reserved in advance through Statue Cruises, you can enter the pedestal and view the statue's interior through a glass ceiling. The crown opened to the public for the first time since 9/11 in 2009; tickets cost an extra $3 and must be reserved in advance.

VITAL STATS

There are 345 steps from her base to her top; she weighs 204 tons and has a 35-foot (11-metre) waist.

visitors can learn about the tragedy and find an outlet for their emotions at the **Tribute WTC Visitor Center** (*see p70*), which was opened in 2006 by a not-for-profit organisation formed by families of the victims.

Construction on the new World Trade Center complex – due to include five office buildings, a park, a performing arts centre and a transit hub designed by Santiago Calatrava – has been plagued by infighting, missed deadlines and budget overruns. Although **One World Trade Center** (the renamed Freedom Tower) – the development's 1,776-foot (541-metre) centrepiece – and the proposed **National September 11 Museum** won't be completed by the original 2011 target date, the **Memorial Plaza** is on track to open for the tenth anniversary of the attack. Calatrava's ambitious designs for the PATH train station have been scaled back owing to budget constraints. But visible signs of progress are beginning to rise above the hoardings. In the meantime, stop by the **9/11 Memorial Preview Site** (*see right & p44* **Rebuilding Ground Zero**) to get a sense of how it will look.

Just east of the World Trade Center site, bargain hunters can sift through a seemingly endless stock of designer duds at discount department store **Century 21** (*see p239*). And west of it, the glass and granite office towers of the **World Financial Center** (from Liberty to Vesey Streets, between the Hudson River & West Street, 1-212 417 7000, www.worldfinancialcenter.com) overlook a marina; the complex's Winter Garden hosts numerous arts events, including the annual contemporary-classical music festival Bang on a Can Marathon (www.bangonacan.org) in early June.

The World Financial Center abuts **Battery Park City**, a 92-acre planned community devised in the 1950s to replace decaying shipping piers with new apartments, green spaces and schools. It's a man-made addition to the island, built on soil and rocks excavated from the original World Trade Center construction site and sediment dredged from New York Harbor. Home to roughly 10,000 people, the neighbourhood was devastated after the 9/11 attacks, and nearly half of its residents moved away, although the area has been improved with new commercial development drawn by economic incentives. Visitors can enjoy its esplanade, a favoured route for bikers, skaters and joggers, and a string of parks that run north along the Hudson River from Battery Park.

Providing expansive views of the Statue of Liberty and Ellis Island at its southernmost reaches, the stretch is dotted with monuments and sculptures. Close by the marina is the 1997 **Police Memorial** (Liberty Street, at South End Avenue), a granite pool and fountain that symbolically trace the life span of a police officer through the use of moving water, with names of the fallen etched into the wall. The **Irish Hunger Memorial** (Vesey Street, at North End Avenue) is here too, paying tribute to those who suffered during the famine from 1845 to 1852. Designed by artist Brian Tolle and landscape architect Gail Wittwer-Laird, the quarter-acre memorial incorporates vegetation, soil and stones from Ireland's various counties, and is also home to a reproduction of a 19th-century Irish cottage.

To the north, **Nelson A Rockefeller Park** attracts sun worshippers, kite flyers and soccer players in the warm-weather months. Look out for Tom Otterness's whimsical sculpture installation, the *Real World*.

Just east is **Teardrop Park**, a two-acre space designed to evoke the bucolic Hudson River Valley, and to the south are the inventively designed **South Cove**, with its quays and island, and **Robert F Wagner Jr Park**, where an observation deck offers fabulous views of both the harbour and the Verrazano-Narrows Bridge; below it, Louise Bourgeois's *Eyes* gaze over the Hudson from the lawn. The **Museum of Jewish Heritage** (*see below*), Gotham's memorial to the Holocaust, is on the edge of the green. Across the street at the **Skyscraper Museum** (*see p70*), you can learn about the buildings that have created the city's iconic skyline.

9/11 Memorial Preview Site

20 Vesey Street, at Church Street, Financial District (1-212 267 2047, www.national911memorial.org). Subway A, C to Broadway-Nassau Street; E to World Trade Center; J, M, Z, 2, 3, 4, 5 to Fulton Street. **Open** 10am-7pm Mon-Sat; 10am-6pm Sun. **Admission** free. **Map** p402 E32.
See p44 **Rebuilding Ground Zero**.

Museum of Jewish Heritage: A Living Memorial to the Holocaust

Robert F Wagner Jr Park, 36 Battery Place, at First Place (1-646 437 4200, www.mjhnyc.org). Subway N, R to Whitehall Street; 1 to South Ferry; 4, 5 to Bowling Green. **Open** 10am-5.45pm Mon, Tue, Thur, Sun; 10am-8pm Wed; 10am-5pm Fri, eve of Jewish hols (until 3pm Nov-mid Mar). **Admission** $12; $7-10 reductions; free under-13s. Free to all 4-8pm Wed. **Credit** AmEx, DC, MC, V. **Map** p402 E34.

This museum explores Jewish life before, during and after the Nazi genocide. The permanent collection includes documentary films, thousands of photos and 800 artefacts, many donated by Holocaust survivors and their families. The Memorial Garden features English artist Andy Goldsworthy's *Garden of*

Stones, 18 fire-hollowed boulders embedded with dwarf oak saplings. Special exhibitions tackle historical events or themes, such as 'Fire in My Heart: The Story of Hannah Senesh', which recounts the life of the Jewish resistance fighter, on view until August 7, 2011.

The Keeping History Center brings the core collection to life with interactive displays, including 'Voices of Liberty', a soundscape of émigrés' and refugees' reactions to arrival in the US – made all the more poignant juxtaposed with the museum's panoramic views of Ellis Island and the Statue of Liberty. The second phase of the project, in late 2011, will add more digital exhibits to further illuminate the museum's collection and will allow visitors to contribute to the database.

Skyscraper Museum

39 Battery Place, between Little West Street & 1st Place (1-212 968 1961, www.skyscraper.org). Subway 4, 5 to Bowling Green. **Open** noon-6pm Wed-Sun. **Admission** $5; $2.50 reductions. **Credit** AmEx, DC, Disc, MC, V. **Map** p402 E34.

The only institution of its kind in the world, this modest space explores high-rise buildings as objects of design, products of technology, real-estate investments and places of work and residence. A large part of the single gallery (a mirrored ceiling gives the illusion of height) is devoted to temporary exhibitions (for example, the recent 'The Rise of Wall Street', which detailed the architectural evolution of the street, through photography and architectural drawings).

As you might expect, a substantial chunk of the permanent collection relates to the Word Trade Center, including original models of the Twin Towers and the 1,776ft (541m) One World Trade Center, currently under construction on the site. Other highlights of the display are large-scale photographs of lower Manhattan's skyscrapers from 1956, 1974 and 2004, and a 1931 silent film documenting the Empire State Building's construction.

▶ *For more on the history of New York's skyscrapers, see p40* **Race to the Top**.

Tribute WTC Visitor Center

120 Liberty Street, between Church & Greenwich Streets (1-866 737 1184, www.tributewtc.org). Subway A, C to Broadway-Nassau Street; E to World Trade Center; J, M, Z, 2, 3, 4, 5 to Fulton Street; N, R, 1 to Rector Street. **Open** 10am-6pm Mon, Wed-Sat; noon-6pm Tue; noon-5pm Sun. **Admission** $10; free under-12s. **Credit** MC, V. **Map** p402 E32.

Created by a not-for-profit organisation started by families of 9/11 victims, this centre serves several functions: a collective memorial; a historical testament of the events and aftermath; and a repository of morbidly fascinating artefacts from that unthinkable day. Ground-floor galleries contain a timeline of the tragedy on panels the same width as the Twin Towers' windows, along with recovered objects; a strangely unharmed paper menu from the 106th-floor Windows on the World restaurant contrasts sharply with a twisted steel beam from the wreckage. The final gallery contains photographs and names of the dead; tissues are provided. Downstairs, visitors are invited to write down their own memories or feelings, a selection of which are posted.

Wall Street

Subway J, M, Z to Broad Street; N, R, 1 to Rector Street; 2, 3, 4, 5 to Wall Street.

Since the city's earliest days as a fur-trading post, wheeling and dealing has been New York's main activity, and commerce the backbone of its prosperity. The southern point of Manhattan quickly evolved into the Financial District because, in the days before telecommunications, banks established their headquarters near the city's active port. Although the neighbourhood is bisected vertically by the ever-bustling Broadway, it's the east–west **Wall Street** (or 'the Street' in trader lingo) that's synonymous with the world's greatest den of capitalism.

Wall Street, which took its name from a defensive wooden wall built in 1653 to mark the northern limit of New Amsterdam, is big on aura despite being less than a mile long – blunted by Broadway on its western end, it spans only about half the width of Manhattan. It's at this western intersection that you'll find the Gothic Revival spire of **Trinity Church** (*see p72*). The original church burned down in 1776, and a second was demolished in 1839; the current version became the island's tallest structure when it was completed in 1846. **St Paul's Chapel** (*see p72*), the church's older satellite, is one of the finest Georgian structures in the US.

A block to the east of Trinity Church, at 26 Wall Street, is the **Federal Hall National Memorial**, a rather august Greek Revival building and – in a previous incarnation – the site of George Washington's first inauguration. It was along this stretch that corporate America made its first audacious architectural statements; a walk eastwards offers much evidence of what money can buy. Structures include the Bankers Trust Building at 14 Wall Street (at Broad Street), completed in 1912 and crowned by a seven-storey pyramid modelled on the Mausoleum of Halicarnassus; **40 Wall Street** (between Nassau & William Streets), which battled the Chrysler Building in 1929 for the title of world's tallest building (the Empire State trounced them both in 1931); and the former **Merchants' Exchange** at 55 Wall Street (between Hanover & William Streets), with its stacked rows of Ionic and Corinthian

Wall Street.

columns, giant doors and a remarkable ballroom. Back around the corner is the **Equitable Building** (120 Broadway, between Cedar & Pine Streets), whose greedy use of vertical space helped to instigate the zoning laws that now govern skyscrapers; stand across the street from the building to get the best view. Nearby is the **Federal Reserve Bank** (*see below*), with its huge gold vault.

The nerve centre of the US economy is the **New York Stock Exchange** (11 Wall Street, between Broad & New Streets). For security reasons, the Exchange is no longer open to the public, but the street outside offers an endless pageant of brokers, traders and their minions. For a lesson on Wall Street's influence over the years, and the recent credit crisis, visit the **Museum of American Finance** (*see below*). A few blocks from the East River end of Wall Street, on Old Slip, is the **New York City Police Museum** (*see below*).

FREE Federal Reserve Bank

33 Liberty Street, between Nassau & William Streets (1-212 720 6130, www.ny.frb.org/about thefed/visiting). Subway 2, 3, 4, 5 to Wall Street. **Open** 9am-5pm Mon-Fri. **Tours** (reservations required) every hour on the half-hour (last tour 3.30pm). **Admission** free. **Map** p402 E33.

For security reasons, tours of this important financial institution must be booked in advance by phone or email – the easiest way to do this is online, as a calendar feature shows availability – and a photo ID must be presented upon admission. The Fed recommends reserving at least a month ahead. Descend 50ft (15m) below street level and you'll find roughly a quarter of the world's gold (more than $100 billion dollars' worth), stored in a gigantic vault that rests on the solid bedrock of Manhattan Island. Visitors learn about the precious metal's history and the role of the New York Fed in its safeguarding.

Museum of American Finance

48 Wall Street, at William Street (1-212 908 4110, www.moaf.org). Subway 2, 3, 4, 5 to Wall Street; N, R, 1 to Rector Street. **Open** 10am-4pm Tue-Sat. **Admission** $8; $5 reductions; free under-7s. **Credit** AmEx, MC, V. **Map** p402 E33.

Situated in the old headquarters of the Bank of New York, the permanent collection traces the history of Wall Street and America's financial markets. Displays in the stately banking hall include a bearer bond made out to President George Washington and ticker tape from the morning of the stock-market crash of 1929. A timeline, 'Tracking the Credit Crisis' helps to clarify the current global predicament.

New York City Police Museum

100 Old Slip, between South & Water Streets (1-212 480 3100, www.nycpolicemuseum.org). Subway J, M, Z to Broad Street; 2, 3, 4, 5 to Wall Street. **Open** 10am-5pm Mon-Sat; noon-5pm Sun. **Admission** $8; $5 reductions. **Credit** AmEx, DC, Disc, MC, V. **Map** p402 F33.

Tracking more than 300 years of New York City policing, this museum features exhibits on history and the tools of the trade, including vintage uniforms, squad cars and firearms. More notorious artefacts are also on view, including a gun used by one of Al Capone's minions in the 1928 murder of Frankie Yale. Critics have accused the institution of whitewashing police brutality and other scandals, although visitors can participate in a simulated police gunfight and determine if the shooting was warranted. The museum's ongoing exhibit, 'Policing a Changed City', looks at the force's evolving role in a post-9/11 New York.

FREE Trinity Church & St Paul's Chapel

Trinity Church *89 Broadway, at Wall Street (1-212 602 0800, www.trinitywallstreet.org). Subway N, R, 1 to Rector Street; 2, 3, 4, 5 to Wall Street.* **Open** 7am-6pm Mon-Fri; 8am-4pm Sat; 7am-4pm Sun. **Admission** free. **Map** p402 E33.

St Paul's Chapel *209 Broadway, between Fulton & Vesey Streets (1-212 233 4164, www.saintpaulschapel.org). Subway A, C to Broadway-Nassau Street; J, M, Z, 2, 3, 4, 5 to Fulton Street.* **Open** 10am-6pm Mon-Fri; 10am-4pm Sat; 7am-3pm Sun. **Admission** free. **Map** p402 E32.

Trinity Church was the island's tallest structure when it was completed in 1846 (the original burned down in 1776; a second was demolished in 1839). A set of gates north of the church on Broadway allows access to the adjacent cemetery, where cracked and faded tombstones mark the final resting places of dozens of past city dwellers, including such notable New Yorkers as Founding Father Alexander Hamilton (*see p30* **Profile**), business tycoon John Jacob Astor and steamboat inventor Robert Fulton. The church museum displays an assortment of historic diaries, photographs, sermons and burial records.

Six blocks to the north, Trinity's satellite, St Paul's Chapel, is more important architecturally. The oldest building in New York still in continuous use (it dates from 1766), it is one of the nation's most valued Georgian structures.

▶ *For Trinity's dirt-cheap Concerts at One series, see p315* **Inside Track**.

South Street Seaport

Subway A, C to Broadway-Nassau Street; J, M, Z, 2, 3, 4, 5 to Fulton Street.

New York's fortunes originally rolled in on the swells that crashed into its deep-water harbour. The city was perfectly situated for trade with Europe and, after 1825, goods from the Western Territories arrived via the Erie Canal and the Hudson River. By 1892, New York was also the point of entry for millions of immigrants, so its character was shaped not only by commodities but also by the waves of new workers that arrived at its docks. The **South Street Seaport** is the best place to appreciate this port heritage.

If you enter the Seaport area from Water Street, the first thing you're likely to spot is the whitewashed **Titanic Memorial Lighthouse**. It was originally erected on top of the Seaman's Church Institute (Coenties Slip & South Street) in 1913, the year after the great ship sank, but was moved to its current location at the intersection of Pearl and Fulton Streets in 1976. Check out the magnificent views of the Brooklyn Bridge from this bit of the district.

When New York's role as a vital shipping hub diminished during the 20th century, the South Street Seaport area fell into disuse, but a massive redevelopment project in the mid 1980s saw old buildings converted into restaurants, bars, chain stores and the **South Street Seaport Museum** (*see below*). The public spaces, including pedestrianised sections of both Fulton and Front Streets, are a favourite with sightseers and street performers, but it's only recently that New Yorkers have begun to rediscover the area, attracted by the arrival of cool cafés and bars such as **Jack's Stir Brew Coffee** (222 Front Street, between Beekman Street & Peck Slip, 1-212 227 7631) and sleek wine bar **Bin No. 220** (220 Front Street, between Beekman Street & Peck Slip, 1-212 374 9463). Free summer concerts, held during the River to River Festival (*see p262*), also appeal.

Pier 17 once supported the famous Fulton Fish Market, a bustling, early-morning trading centre dating back to the mid 1800s. However, in 2006 the market relocated to a larger facility in the Hunts Point area of the Bronx (*see p144*). Interest in Pier 17, now occupied by an unremarkable mall, has dwindled since its redevelopment in the 1980s, although recently, the arrival of a new **Water Taxi Beach** on the pier's north side has boosted its appeal. A proposal to replace the mall with a mixed-use complex, including shops and a hotel, has been stalled by local opposition and the recession, but the city has broken ground on its East River Esplanade and Piers Project, which will landscape this stretch of waterfront and transform **Pier 15** into a bi-level lounging space, comprising a lawned viewing deck above a maritime education centre and café.

South Street Seaport Museum

Visitors' centre, 12 Fulton Street, at South Street (1-212 748 8786, www.seany.org). Subway A, C to Broadway-Nassau Street; J, M, Z, 2, 3, 4, 5 to Fulton Street. **Open** *Apr-Dec* 10am-6pm Tue-Sun. *Jan-Mar* 10am-5pm Thur-Sun. **Admission** $15; $12 reductions; free under-5s. *Ships only* $10. **Credit** AmEx, DC, MC, V. **Map** p402 F32.

Set in 11 blocks along the East River, this museum is an amalgam of 19th-century buildings, galleries, historic ships and a visitors' centre. Wander around the rebuilt streets and pop in to see a historical or maritime-themed exhibition before climbing aboard the four-masted 1911 barque *Peking* or the 1930 tug *WO Decker*. The seaport is generally thick with tourists, but it's a lively place in which to spend an afternoon, especially if you're with children.

► *See also p252 for details of the museum's gift shop, Bowne & Co., a working recreation of an 1870s-style letterpress printers.*

CITY HALL PARK

Subway J, M, Z to Chambers Street; R to City Hall; 2, 3 to Park Place; 4, 5, 6 to Brooklyn Bridge-City Hall.

The business of running New York takes place in the grand buildings in and around **City Hall Park**, an area that formed the budding city's northern boundary in the 1700s. The park itself was renovated just before the millennium, and pretty landscaping and abundant benches make it a popular lunching spot for office workers.

At the park's southern end, a granite 'time wheel' tracks the park's history. At the northern end of the park, **City Hall** (*see p75*) houses the mayor's office and the chambers of the City Council, and is frequently buzzing with VIP comings and goings. When City Hall was completed in 1812, its architects were so confident that the city would grow no further north that they didn't bother to put any marble on its northern side. Nevertheless, the building is a beautiful blend of Federalist form and French Renaissance detail. Overlooking the park from the west is Cass Gilbert's famous **Woolworth Building** (233 Broadway, between Barclay Street & Park Place), the tallest building in the world when it opened in 1913. The neo-Gothic skyscraper's grand spires, gargoyles, vaulted ceilings and church-like interior earned it the moniker 'the Cathedral of Commerce'.

Behind City Hall, on Chambers Street, is the 1872 Old New York County Courthouse; it's popularly known as the **Tweed Courthouse**, a symbol of the runaway corruption of mid 19th-century municipal government. William 'Boss' Tweed (*see p24*), leader of the political machine Tammany Hall, famously pocketed some $10 million of the building's huge $14 million construction budget. What he didn't steal bought a beautiful edifice, with exquisite Italianate detailing. These days, it houses the city's Department of Education, but it's also

NYC
SOHO
LOVES
TO SHOP
NYCvisit.com
KORRES
NO PARKING
café
café
apt
Bo
concept
Soho.

open for tours (1-212 639 9675, www.nyc.gov/designcommission). To the east, other civic offices and services occupy the one million square feet of office space in the 1914 **Manhattan Municipal Building** at 1 Centre Street. This landmark limestone structure, built by McKim Mead & White, also houses New York City's official gift shop (www.nyc.gov/citystore, 9am-4.30pm Mon-Fri).

The houses of crime and punishment are located in the **Civic Center**, near Foley Square, once a pond and later the site of the city's most notorious 19th-century slum (Five Points). These days, you'll find the State Supreme Court in the **New York County Courthouse** (60 Centre Street, at Pearl Street), a hexagonal Roman Revival building; the beautiful rotunda is decorated with a mural entitled *Law Through the Ages*. The **United States Courthouse** (40 Centre Street, between Duane & Pearl Streets) is a Corinthian temple crowned with a golden pyramid.

The **Criminal Courts Building & Manhattan Detention Complex** (100 Centre Street, between Leonard & White Streets) is still known as 'the Tombs', a nod to the original 1838 Egyptian Revival building – or, depending on who you ask, to its current grimness. There's no denying that the hall's great granite slabs and looming towers are downright lugubrious.

Nearby, the **African Burial Ground** (*see below*) was officially designated a National Monument in 2006.

FREE African Burial Ground

Duane Street, between Broadway & Centre Streets, behind 290 Broadway (1-212 637 2019, www.nps.gov/afbg). Subway J, M, Z to Chambers Street; R to City Hall; 4, 5, 6 to Brooklyn Bridge-City Hall. **Open** 9am-5pm daily. *Visitor centre* 9am-5pm Tue-Sat. **Admission** free. **Map** p402 E31.

A major archaeological discovery, the African Burial Ground is a small remnant of a 6.6-acre unmarked gravesite where between 10,000 and 20,000 enslaved Africans – men, women and children – were buried. The burial ground, which closed in 1794, was unearthed during the construction of a federal office building in 1991 and designated a National Monument. In 2007, a stone memorial, designed by architect Rodney Leon, was erected; the tall, curved structure draws heavily on African architecture and contains a spiral path leading to an ancestral chamber. A visitor centre is located in the lobby of 290 Broadway.

FREE City Hall

City Hall Park, from Vesey to Chambers Streets, between Broadway & Park Row (1-212 639 9675). Subway J, M, Z to Chambers Street; R to City Hall; 2, 3 to Park Place; 4, 5, 6 to Brooklyn Bridge-City Hall. **Open** *Tours* (individuals) noon Wed, 10am Thur; (groups) 10am Mon, Tue, Wed, Fri. **Admission** free. **Map** p402 E32.

Designed by French émigré Joseph François Mangin and New Yorker John McComb Jr, the fine, Federal-style City Hall was completed in 1812. Tours take in the rotunda, with its splendid coffered dome; the City Council Chamber; and the Governor's Room, which houses a collection of American 19th-century political portraits as well as historic furnishings (notably including George Washington's desk). Individuals can book (at least two days in advance) for the Thursday morning tour; alternatively, sign up at the Heritage Tourism Center at the southern end of City Hall Park on the east side of Broadway, at Barclay Street, for Wednesday's first-come, first-served tour at noon. Group tours should be booked at least a week in advance.

TRIBECA & SOHO

Subway A, C, E, 1 to Canal Street; C, E to Spring Street; N, R to Prince Street; 1 to Franklin Street or Houston Street.

In the 1960s and '70s, artists colonised the former industrial wasteland that was **Tribeca** (the Triangle Below Canal Street), squatting in its abandoned warehouses. Following the example of fellow creatives in neighbouring Soho, they eventually worked with the city to rezone and restore them. The preponderance of large, hulking former industrial buildings gives Tribeca an imposing profile, but fine small-scale cast-iron architecture still stands along White Street and the parallel thoroughfares.

Now a retail mecca of the highest order, **Soho** (the area South of Houston Street) was once a hardscrabble manufacturing zone with the derisive nickname Hell's Hundred Acres. In the 1960s, it was earmarked for destruction by over-zealous urban planner Robert Moses, but its signature cast-iron warehouses were saved by the artists who inhabited them. The **King & Queen of Greene Street** (respectively, 72-76 Greene Street, between Broome & Spring Streets, and 28-30 Greene Street, between Canal & Grand Streets) are both fine examples of the area's beloved architectural landmarks. The most celebrated of Soho's cast-iron edifices, however, is the five-storey **Haughwout Building**, at 488-492 Broadway, at Broome Street. Designed in 1857, it featured the world's first hydraulic lift (still in working condition).

After landlords sniffed the potential for profits in converting old loft buildings, Soho morphed into a playground for the young, the beautiful and the rich. It can still be a pleasure to stroll around the cobblestoned side streets on weekday mornings, and there are some fabulous shops in the area, but the large chain stores and sidewalk-encroaching street vendors along Broadway create a shopping-mall-at-Christmas crush on weekends. Although many of the galleries that made Soho an art capital in the 1970s and '80s decamped to Chelsea and, more recently, the Lower East Side, some excellent art spaces remain (*see pp291-292*). Also in the neighbourhood are the **Museum of Comic & Cartoon Art** (*see right*) and **New York City Fire Museum** (*see right*).

Seeking luxury (and privacy), many celebrities have settled in the area. Robert de Niro is the neighbourhood's best-known resident, founding the **Tribeca Film Center** (375 Greenwich Street, at Franklin Street), with partner Jane Rosenthal in 1988. A few blocks away, De Niro's **Tribeca Cinemas** (54 Varick Street, at Laight Street, 1-212 966 8163, www.tribecacinemas.com) hosts premieres and glitzy parties, when it isn't serving as a venue for the increasingly large and commercial **Tribeca Film Festival** (*see p290*). In 2008, the actor unveiled the exclusive Greenwich Hotel (*see p157*).

Upscale shops, such as an **Issey Miyake** boutique with a Frank Gehry-designed interior (119 Hudson Street, at North Moore Street, 1-212 226 0100), and haute eateries cater to the well-heeled locals. Top dining options include sushi shrines **Nobu** and **Megu** (for both, *see p185*); **Corton** (*see p183*), showcasing the French-accented gastronomic talents of Paul Liebrandt; and the growing empire of celebrity chef David Bouley, including his flagship **Bouley** (163 Duane Street, at Hudson Street, 1-212 964 2525) and **Bouley Marke**t (120 West Broadway, at Duane Street, 1-212 219 1011), which offers some of the city's finest (and priciest) pastries.

Just west of West Broadway, tenement- and townhouse-lined streets contain remnants of the Italian community that once dominated the area. Elderly men and women stroll along Sullivan Street to **St Anthony of Padua Roman Catholic Church** (no.155, at Houston Street), dedicated in 1888. You'll still find old-school neighbourhood flavour in local businesses such as **Joe's Dairy** (no.156, between Houston & Prince Streets, 1-212 677 8780, closed Sun & Mon), **Pino's Prime Meat Market** (no.149, 1-212 475 8134, closed Sun) and **Vesuvio Bakery** (160 Prince Street, between Thompson Street & West Broadway), whose old-fashioned façade has appeared in dozens of commercials over the years.

INSIDE TRACK CHURCH OF THE DAMNED

Michael Corleone (Al Pacino) became an actual godfather at the christening of his nephew, which was filmed in **St Patrick's Old Cathedral** in Little Italy; the church was used again when he received the Order of St Sebastian in *Godfather III*. St Patrick's courtyard was also the scene of the intense heart-to-heart between small-time wiseguys Johnny Boy (Robert de Niro) and Charlie (Harvey Keitel) in Martin Scorsese's *Mean Streets*.

Museum of Comic & Cartoon Art (MoCCA)

594 Broadway, suite 401, between Houston & Prince Streets (1-212 254 3511, www.moccany.org). Subway B, D, F, M to Broadway-Lafayette Street; N, R to Prince Street; 6 to Bleecker Street. **Open** noon-5pm Tue-Sun. **Admission** *Suggested donation* $5; free under-12s. **Credit** AmEx, MC, V. **Map** p403 E29.

Batman, Wolverine, Watchmen… No longer just for pre-pubescent kids and ageing geeks, comic books have made a major comeback on the cultural scene. But MoCCA doesn't stop there: the institution embraces every genre of comic and cartoon art, and hosts regular lectures and events with creators and experts. Revolving exhibitions in its two galleries feature anime, cartoons, comic strips, political satire and graphic novels, among other strands. Each spring, the museum organises the MoCCA Festival, bringing together established and emerging artists and fans for two days.

New York City Fire Museum

278 Spring Street, between Hudson & Varick Streets (1-212 691 1303, www.nycfiremuseum.org). Subway C, E to Spring Street; 1 to Houston Street. **Open** 10am-5pm Tue-Sat; 10am-4pm Sun. **Admission** *Suggested donation* $7; $5 reductions. **Credit** AmEx, DC, Disc, MC, V. **Map** p403 D30.

An active firehouse from 1904 to 1959, this museum is filled with all manner of life-saving gadgetry, from late 18th-century hand-pumped fire engines to present-day equipment.

LITTLE ITALY & NOLITA

Subway B, D, F, M to Broadway-Lafayette Street; J, M, N, Q, R, Z, 6 to Canal Street; J, M, Z to Bowery; N, R to Prince Street; 6 to Spring Street.

Abandoning the dismal tenements of the Five Points district (in what is now Chinatown), immigrants from Naples and Sicily began moving to **Little Italy** in the 1880s. The area once stretched from Canal to Houston Streets, between Lafayette Street and the Bowery, but these days a strong Italian presence can only truly be observed on the blocks immediately surrounding Mulberry Street. As families

Chinatown.

prospered in the 1950s, they moved to the outer boroughs and suburbs; the area has long been shrinking in the face of Chinatown expanding from the south and migrating boutiques from **Nolita** (North of Little Italy).

Another telling change in the district: **St Patrick's Old Cathedral** (260-264 Mulberry Street, between Houston & Prince Streets) no longer holds services in Italian, but in English and Spanish. Completed in 1809 and restored after a fire in 1868, this was the city's premier Catholic church until it was demoted, upon consecration of the Fifth Avenue cathedral of the same name. But ethnic pride remains: Italian-Americans flood in from across the city during the 11-day **Feast of San Gennaro** (*see p265*).

Touristy cafés and restaurants line Mulberry Street between Broome and Canal Streets, but pockets of the past linger nearby. Long-time residents still buy mouth-wateringly fresh mozzarella from **DiPalo's Fine Foods** (200 Grand Street, at Mott Street, 1-212 226 1033), and sandwiches packed with salami and cheeses at the **Italian Food Center** (186 Grand Street, at Mulberry Street, 1-212 925 2954). Legend has it that the first pizzeria in New York was opened by Gennaro Lombardi on Spring Street in 1905. **Lombardi's** moved down the block in 1994 (32 Spring Street, at Mott Street, 1-212 941 7994), but still serves its signature clam pies. These days, the area's restaurants are largely undistinguished grills and pasta houses, but two reliable choices are **Il Cortile** (125 Mulberry Street, between Canal & Hester Streets, 1-212 226 6060) and **La Mela** (167 Mulberry Street, between Broome & Grand Streets, 1-212 431 9493). Drop in for dessert at **Caffè Roma** (385 Broome Street, at Mulberry Street, 1-212 226 8413), which opened in 1891.

Of course, Little Italy is also the site of several notorious **Mafia landmarks**. The brick-fronted store now occupied by a shoe boutique (247 Mulberry Street, between Prince & Spring Streets) was once the Ravenite Social Club, where Mafia kingpin John Gotti made his deals until his arrest in 1990. Mobster Joey Gallo was shot and killed in 1972 while celebrating his birthday at Umberto's Clam House, which has since moved around the corner to 178 Mulberry Street, at Broome Street (1-212 431 7545).

Nolita became a magnet for pricey boutiques and trendy eateries in the 1990s. Elizabeth, Mott and Mulberry Streets, between Houston and Spring Streets, in particular, are home to hip shops such as vintage clothier **Resurrection** (217 Mott Street, at Spring Street, 1-212 625 1374, www.resurrectionvintage.com), beautifully tailored womenswear line **Lyell** (173 Elizabeth Street, between Kenmare & Spring Streets) and chic shoe label **Sigerson Morrison** (28 Prince Street, at Mott Street; *see p249*).

An international cast of pretty young things still gravitates to eateries such as Japanese-fusion joint **Bond St** (6 Bond Street, between Broadway & Lafayette Street, 1-212 777 2500) and rustic Italian **Peasant** (194 Elizabeth Street, between Prince & Spring Streets, 1-212 965 9511, closed lunch & Mon).

CHINATOWN

Subway J, M, N, Q, R, Z, 6 to Canal Street.

Take a walk in the area south of Broome Street and west of Broadway, and you'll feel as though you've entered not just a different country but a different continent. You won't hear much English spoken along the crowded streets of **Chinatown**. Mott and Grand Streets are lined with fish-, fruit- and vegetable-stocked stands selling some of the best and most affordable seafood and fresh produce in the city – you'll see buckets of live eels and crabs, square watermelons and piles of hairy rambutans. Street vendors sell satisfying snacks such as pork buns and sweet egg pancakes by the bagful. Canal Street glitters with cheap jewellery and gift shops, as well as vendors selling bootleg CDs and DVDs. You may also encounter furtive individuals whispering 'Louis Vuitton' and 'Gucci'; don't be drawn in as these are undoubtedly fakes being sold illegally.

Some of the neighbourhood's residents eventually decamp to one of the two other Chinatowns in the city (in Sunset Park, Brooklyn, and Flushing, Queens). However, a steady flow of new arrivals keeps this hub full to bursting, with thousands of both legal and illegal residents packed into the area surrounding East Canal Street, making this among the largest Chinese communities outside Asia. The busy streets get even wilder during the **Chinese New Year** festivities (*see p268*).

Between Kenmare and Worth Streets, Mott Street is lined with restaurants representing the cuisine of virtually every province of mainland China and Hong Kong; the Bowery, East Broadway and Division Street are just as diverse. Adding to the mix are myriad Indonesian, Malaysian, Thai and Vietnamese restaurants and shops.

Cheap eats abound in the area: sample savoury pork buns at Chatham Square dim-sum institution **Chatham Restaurant** (9 Chatham Square, at Mott Street, 1-212 267 0220), or head for Eldridge Street, where Chinese businesses mingle with old Lower East Side landmarks. At tiny, hole-in-the-wall **Prosperity Dumpling** (46 Eldridge Street, between Canal & Hester Streets, 1-212 343 0683), a plate of pork or veggie versions costs a few bucks, and **Super Taste Restaurant** (46 Eldridge Street, between Canal & Division Streets, 1-212 625 1198) serves hand-pulled *la mian* (a Chinese relative of ramen) at around $5 for a bowl.

Explore the Chinese experience on these shores at the stylish **Museum of Chinese in America** (*see right*), which recently reopened in much larger premises. The **Eastern States Buddhist Temple of America** (64 Mott Street, between Bayard & Canal Streets, 1-212 966 6229), founded in 1962, is one of the country's oldest Chinese Buddhist temples.

For an entirely different perspective on the area's culture, visit **Chinatown Fair Arcade** (8 Mott Street, between Mosco & Worth Streets, 1-212 964 1542), a noisy, old-school game hall, where joystick-lovers huddle around *Ms Pac-Man* and *King of Fighters XII*, and some of the East Coast's best *Dance Dance Revolution* players congregate. Older 'kids' hit the **Happy Ending Lounge** (*see p218*), which occupies a former massage parlour – the name is an unabashed nod to its erotically charged roots.

Museum of Chinese in America

215 Centre Street, between Grand & Howard Streets (1-212 619 4785, www.mocanyc.org). Subway J, M, N, Q, R, Z, 6 to Canal Street. **Open** 11am-5pm Mon, Fri; 11am-9pm Thur; 10am-5pm Sat, Sun. **Admission** $7; $4 reductions; free under-12s; free to all Thur. **Credit** AmEx, Disc, MC, V. **Map** p403 E30.

Designed by prominent Chinese-American architect Maya Lin, MoCA has reopened in an airy former machine shop. Its interior is loosely inspired by a traditional Chinese house, with rooms radiating off a central courtyard and areas defined by screens.

MoCA's core exhibition traces the development of Chinese communities in the US from the 1850s to the present through objects, images and video. Innovative displays (drawers open to reveal artwork and documents, portraits are presented in a ceiling mobile) cover the development of industries such as laundries and restaurants in New York, Chinese stereotypes in pop culture, and the suspicion and humiliation Chinese-Americans endured during World War II and the McCarthy era. A mocked-up Chinese general store evokes the feel of these multipurpose spaces, which served as vital community lifelines for men severed from their families under the 1882 Exclusion Act that restricted immigration. A gallery is devoted to temporary exhibitions, such as the work of contemporary Chinese-American artists, and a roster of events includes craft workshops and gallery talks.

LOWER EAST SIDE

Subway B, D to Grand Street; F to East Broadway; F, J, M, Z to Delancey-Essex Streets; F to Lower East Side-Second Avenue; J, M, Z to Bowery.

The **Lower East Side**, a roughly defined area south of Houston Street and west of the East River, is one of the more recent Manhattan neighbourhoods to be radically altered by the forces of gentrification. In the 19th century, tenement buildings were constructed here to house the growing number of German, Irish, Jewish and Italian immigrants – by 1900 it was the most populous neighbourhood in the US. The appalling conditions of these overcrowded, unsanitary slums were captured by photographer and writer Jacob Riis in *How the Other Half Lives* in 1890; its publication spurred activists and prompted the introduction of more humane building codes. The dwellings have since been converted or demolished, but you can see how newcomers once lived by visiting the recreated apartments of the **Lower East Side Tenement Museum** (*see p80*).

This was once the focal point of Jewish culture in New York. Between 1870 and 1920, hundreds of synagogues and religious schools

Lower East Side.

thrived alongside Yiddish newspapers, social-reform societies and kosher bakeries. Vaudeville and classic Yiddish theatre also prospered here – the Marx Brothers, Eddie Cantor and George Gershwin all once lived in the district. Today, the Yiddish theatres are long gone and most of the synagogues founded by Eastern European immigrants in the 19th century have been repurposed or sit empty. But vestiges of the neighbourhood's Jewish roots can be found amid the Chinese businesses spilling over from sprawling Chinatown and the ever-multiplying fashionable boutiques, restaurants and bars. The **Eldridge Street Synagogue** (*see p81*), which has undergone extensive renovation, still has a small but vital congregation. Heading east down Canal Street rewards with a view of the façade of the **Sender Jarmulowsky Bank** (on the corner of Canal & Orchard Streets), which catered to Jewish immigrants until its collapse in 1914; note the reclining classical figures of the sculpture above the door bookending the clock. Further down Canal, at the corner of Ludlow, you'll find the former home of the **Kletzker Brotherly Aid Association**, a lodge for immigrants from Belarus still marked by the Star of David and the year of its opening, 1892.

On the southern edge of Chinatown, the **First Shearith Israel Graveyard** (55-57 St James Place, between James & Oliver Streets) is the burial ground of the country's first Jewish community; some gravestones date from 1683, including those of Spanish and Portuguese Jews who fled the Inquisition. However, the gate is usually locked. The **Forward Building** (175 E Broadway, at Canal Street) was once the headquarters of the *Jewish Daily Forward*, a Yiddish-language paper that had a peak circulation of 275,000 in the 1920s; it's now home to multimillion-dollar condominiums.

Those looking for a taste of the old Jewish Lower East Side should grab a table at **Katz's Delicatessen** (*see p191*). Opened in 1888, this kosher deli continues to serve some of the best pastrami in New York (and was the site of Meg Ryan's famous 'fauxgasm' scene in *When Harry Met Sally…*). A few blocks west, **Yonah Schimmel Knish Bakery** (137 E Houston Street, between First & Second Avenues, 1-212 477 2858) has been doling out its carb-laden goodies since 1910. Traditional potato, kasha and spinach knishes are the most popular varieties, but sweet potato and blueberry fillings are also available. Lox lovers are devoted to **Russ & Daughters** (*see p250*), serving its famous herring, caviar and smoked salmon since 1914. **Essex Market** (www.essexstreetmarket.com), which opened in 1940 as part of La Guardia's plan to get pushcarts off the streets, contains a mix of high-quality vendors selling cheese, coffee, sweets, produce, fish and meat.

By the 1980s, when young artists and musicians began moving into the area, it was a patchwork of Asian, Latino and Jewish enclaves. Hipster bars and music venues sprang up on and around Ludlow Street, creating an annex to the East Village. That scene still survives, but rents have risen dramatically and some stalwarts have closed their doors. Check who's playing at **Arlene's Grocery** (95 Stanton Street, between Ludlow & Orchard Streets, 1-212 995 1652, www.arlenesgrocery.net), the **Bowery Ballroom** (*see p321*) or **Cake Shop** (*see p321*). The radical-political tradition lives on at **ABC No Rio** (156 Rivington Street, between Clinton & Suffolk Streets, 1-212 254 3697). The activist collective's SOS: Sunday Open Series was first established in 1980, when squatters took over an abandoned ground-floor space; it now houses a gallery, studios and a performance area.

These days, visual art is the Lower East Side's main cultural draw. In 2007, the **New Museum of Contemporary Art** (*see p81*) decamped here from Chelsea, opening a $50 million building on the Bowery. A narrow glass tower designed by Norman Foster, rising a block north at 257 Bowery, opened in September 2010 as the HQ for established art dealers **Sperone Westwater** (www.speronewestwater.com), whose high-profile stable includes Bruce Nauman, Susan Rothenberg and William Wegman. Dozens of storefront galleries have opened in the vicinity over the past few years, including **Miguel Abreu**, **Eleven Rivington** and **Lisa Cooley** (*see pp292-293*). They join the early adopter of the neighbourhood, the non-profit gallery **Participant Inc** (*see p294*), which opened its space for experimental work here nearly a decade ago. Not far away, where the Lower East Side and Chinatown borders blur, is **Canada** (*see p292*), directed by four partners, three of whom are artists. On the last Sunday of the month, from spring through autumn, the Lower East Side Business Improvement District sponsors a free tour of neighbourhood galleries. For further information, contact the **Lower East Side Visitor Center** (261 Broome Street, between Allen & Orchard Streets, 1-212 226 9010, www.lowereastsideny.com).

Although the **Orchard Street** bargain district – a row of shops selling utilitarian goods such as socks, sportswear and luggage, and beloved of hagglers – persists, the strip is at the centre of a proliferation of small indie shops, including boutique **Suite Orchard** (*see p245*), eccentric menswear shop **Thecast** (*see p239*), stylist Nikki Fontanella's cool clothing store-cum-bar the **Dressing Room** (*see p243*), and vintage jewellery trove **Doyle & Doyle** (*see p248*).

More mainstream commercial gloss is encroaching on the area in the form of high-rise hotels and apartment buildings. The National Trust for Historic Preservation designated the Lower East Side one of America's 11 most endangered historic places in 2008, but as the area continues to change, groups such as the Lower East Side Conservancy are working to preserve its unique character.

INSIDE TRACK WEATHERMAN PREDICTING...FIRE

On 6 March 1970, an explosion ripped though the basement of a townhouse at 18 W 11th Street, killing three. The inhabitants were members of the **Weathermen**, a militant anti-Vietnam War group, who were making bombs for a planned attack on Fort Dix, New Jersey, when one of their concoctions went off prematurely. Two members survived, escaping to help form the Weather Underground, which was behind several bombings in the 1970s before petering out and surrendering a decade later.

★ Lower East Side Tenement Museum

Visitors' centre, 108 Orchard Street, at Delancey Street (1-212 982 8420, www.tenement.org). Subway F to Delancey Street; F, J, M, Z to Delancey-Essex Streets. **Open** *Museum shop & ticketing* 10am-6pm daily. **Tours** 10.30am-5pm (every 30mins) Mon-Fri; 10.30am-5pm (every 15mins) Sat, Sun. **Admission** $20; $15 reductions. **Credit** AmEx, DC, Disc, MC, V. **Map** p403 G30.

This fascinating museum – actually a series of restored tenement apartments at 97 Orchard Street – is accessible only by guided tour. Tickets can be purchased at the visitors' centre at 108 Orchard Street and tours often sell out, so it's wise to book ahead.

'Getting By' visits the homes of an Italian and a German-Jewish clan; 'Piecing It Together' explores the apartments of two Eastern European Jewish families as well as a garment shop where many of the locals would have found employment; 'The Moores' unfurls the life of an Irish family coping with the loss of their child; and the 'Confino Family Living History Program' takes in the homes of Sephardic Jewish occupants with the help of an interpreter in period costume. From April to December, the museum also conducts themed daily 90-minute walking tours of the Lower East Side ($21).

★ Museum at Eldridge Street (Eldridge Street Synagogue)

12 Eldridge Street, between Canal & Division Streets (1-212 219 0302, www.eldridgestreet.org). Subway F to East Broadway. **Open** 10am-5pm Mon-Thur, Sun. **Tours** (every 30mins) 10am-4pm. **Admission** $10; $6-$8 reductions; free under-5s. **Credit** AmEx, Disc, MC, V. **Map** p402 F31.

With an impressive façade that combines Moorish, Gothic and Romanesque elements, the first grand synagogue on the Lower East Side is now surrounded by dumpling shops and Chinese herb stores, but rewind about a century and you would find delicatessens and *mikvot* (ritual bathhouses). For its first 50 years, the 1887 synagogue had a congregation of thousands and doubled as a mutual-aid society for new arrivals in need of financial assistance, healthcare and employment. But as Jews left the area and the congregation dwindled, the building fell into disrepair.

A recently completed 20-year, $18.5 million facelift has restored its splendour; the soaring main sanctuary features hand-stencilled walls and a resplendent stained-glass rose window with Star of David motifs. The renovations were completed in October 2010, when the east window was replaced by a new stained-glass affair designed by artist Kiki Smith and architect Deborah Gans. Downstairs, touch-screen displays highlight the synagogue's architecture, aspects of worship and local history, including other (extant or long-vanished) Jewish landmarks.

★ New Museum of Contemporary Art

235 Bowery, between Prince & Stanton Streets (1-212 219 1222, www.newmuseum.org). Subway 6 to Spring Street; N, R to Prince Street. **Open** 11am-6pm Wed, Fri-Sun; 11am-9pm Thur. **Admission** $12; $8-$10 reductions; free under-18s. Free to all 7-9pm Thur. **Credit** DC, MC, V. **Map** p403 F29.

Having occupied various sites for 30 years, New York City's only contemporary art museum finally got its own purpose-built space in late 2007. It has since sparked a gallery boom in the area and is dedicated to emerging media and important but under-recognised artists, including sculptor Lynda Benglis, who will have a retrospective show (closing 13 July 2011). The seven-floor museum is worth a look for the building alone – a striking, off-centre stack of aluminium mesh clad boxes designed by cutting-edge Tokyo architectural firm Sejima + Nishizawa/SANAA. At weekends, don't miss the fabulous views from the minimalist seventh-floor Sky Room.

EAST VILLAGE

Subway B, D, F, M to Broadway-Lafayette Street; L to First Avenue or Third Avenue; 6 to Astor Place or Bleecker Street.

Originally part of the Lower East Side, the **East Village** developed its distinct identity as a countercultural hotbed in the 1960s. The seeds had been planted as early as the turn of the century, however, when anarchists such as Emma Goldman and Johann Most plotted revolution in a 1st Street salon owned by Julius Schwab. By the dawning of the Age of Aquarius, rock clubs thrived on almost every corner; among them were the now-demolished Fillmore East, on Second Avenue, between 6th and 7th Streets, and the **Dom** (23 St Marks Place, between Second & Third Avenues), where the Velvet Underground often headlined (the building is now a condo). In the '70s, the neighbourhood took a dive as drugs and crime prevailed – but that didn't stop the influx of artists and punk rockers. In the early '80s, East Village galleries were among the first to display the work of groundbreaking artists Jean-Michel Basquiat and Keith Haring.

The blocks east of Broadway between Houston and 14th Streets may have lost some of their edge, but remnants of their spirited past endure. Although the former tenements are increasingly occupied by young professionals and trust-fund kids, humanity in all its guises converges in the parks, bargain restaurants, indie record stores and grungy watering holes on First and Second Avenues and St Marks Place. For a quintessential old-school East Village experience, grab a stool at **Mars Bar** (25 E 1st Street, at Second Avenue, 1-212 473 9842). The graffiti-plastered hole-in-the-wall has a jukebox stacked with everything from Lou Rawls to the MC5 and is frequented by a rowdy punk and hardcore crowd, as well as slumming yuppies.

Providing a sharp contrast to the radical associations of its more recent past, the **Merchant's House Museum** (*see p84*), on East 4th Street, is a perfectly preserved specimen of upper-class domestic life in the 1800s. A short walk north brings you to the East Village's unofficial cultural centre: **St Mark's Church in-the-Bowery** (131 E 10th Street, at Second Avenue, 1-212 674 6377). Built in 1799, the Federal-style church sits on the site of Peter Stuyvesant's farm; the old guy himself, one of New York's first governors, is buried in the adjacent cemetery. Regular services are still held, as are exhibitions and performances from arts groups.

From the 1950s to the '70s, **St Marks Place** (E 8th Street, between Lafayette Street &

Avenue A) was a hotbed of artists, writers, radicals and musicians, including WH Auden, Abbie Hoffman, Lenny Bruce, Joni Mitchell and GG Allin; the cover of Led Zeppelin's 1975 album *Physical Graffiti* depicts the apartment buildings at nos.96 and 98. St Marks is still fizzing with energy well into the wee hours, but these days, the grungy strip is packed with cheap eateries, shops selling T-shirts, tourist junk and pot paraphernalia, and tattoo parlours – among them the famous **Fun City** (94 St Marks Place, between First Avenue & Avenue A, 1-212 353 8282), whose awning advertises cappuccino and tattoos.

Cutting between Broadway and Fourth Avenue south of East 8th Street, **Astor Place** still attracts young skateboarders and other modern-day street urchins. It is marked by a steel cube that has sat on a traffic island by the entrance to the 6 train since 1968. With a little elbow grease, the cube, whose proper title is *Alamo*, will spin on its axis. This is also the site of the **Cooper Union**; comprising schools of art, architecture and engineering, it bears the distinction of being the only free private college in the United States. It was here, in February 1860, that Abraham Lincoln gave his celebrated Cooper Union Address, which argued for the regulation (though not abolition) of slavery and helped to propel him into the White House. During the 19th century, Astor Place marked the boundary between the slums to the east and some of the city's most fashionable homes. **Colonnade Row** (428-434 Lafayette Street, between Astor Place & E 4th Street) faces the distinguished Astor Public Library building, which theatre legend Joseph Papp rescued from demolition in the 1960s. Today, the old library houses the **Public Theater** (*see p357*), a platform for first-run American plays, and cabaret venue **Joe's Pub** (*see p323*). The Public Theater also stages summer's Shakespeare in the Park festival (*see p359*), held in Central Park. Below Astor Place, Third Avenue (one block east of Lafayette Street) becomes the **Bowery**. For decades, the street languished as a seedy flophouse strip and the home of missionary organisations catering to the down and out. Although the sharp-eyed can find traces of the old flophouses, and the more obvious Gothic Revival headquarters of **Bowery Mission** at no.227 (between Rivington & Stanton Streets), the thoroughfare has been cleaned up and repopulated by high-rise condo buildings, ritzy restaurants and clubs, and the posh **Bowery Hotel** (*see p161*).

One casualty of this gentrification was the hallowed CBGB, once the unofficial home of US punk, which fostered legends such as the Ramones, Talking Heads and Patti Smith (although, let's face it, the average post-1995 show was pretty lame). The site is now occupied by swanky menswear shop **John Varvatos** (315 Bowery, at Bleecker Street, 1-212 358 0315), while growing music-photography chain **Morrison Hotel Gallery** (no.313, 1-212 677 2253) filled the void left by the CBGB Gallery next door. Both the new venues have kept mementos from the club, while other East Village bars and clubs carry on the cheap-beer-and-loud-music formula. Try the **Mercury Lounge** (*see p327*) or the **Bowery Poetry Club** (*see p271*), which has its roots in the poetry-slam scene but also regularly offers concerts (jazz, folk, hip hop), as well as improv theatre.

Elsewhere in the neighbourhood, East 7th Street is a stronghold of New York's Ukrainian community, of which the focal point is the Byzantine **St George's Ukrainian Catholic Church** at no.30. The **Ukrainian Museum** (222 E 6th Street, between Second & Third Avenues, 1-212 228 0110, www.ukrainianmuseum.org, closed Mon & Tue) houses artwork, artefacts and photos from that country. One block over, there's often a long line of loud fraternity types waiting at weekends to enter **McSorley's Old Ale House** (15 E 7th Street, between Second & Third Avenues, 1-212 473 9148). Festooned with aged photos, yellowed newspaper articles and dusty memorabilia, the 157-year-old Irish tavern is purportedly the oldest continually operating pub in New York and the spot where Lincoln repaired after giving his Cooper Union Address. (It still serves just one kind of beer – its own brew, available in light and dark formulas.) Representing a different corner of the globe, **Curry Row** (East 6th Street, between First & Second Avenues) is lined with Indian restaurants that are popular with budget-minded diners.

Alphabet City (which gets its name from its key avenues: A, B, C and D) stretches towards the East River. Once an edgy Puerto Rican neighbourhood with links to the drug trade, its demographic has dramatically shifted over the past 20 years. Avenue C is also known as Loisaida Avenue, a rough approximation of 'Lower East Side' when pronounced with a Hispanic accent. Two churches on 4th Street are built in the Spanish colonial style: **San Isidro y San Leandro** (345 E 4th Street, between Avenues C & D) and **Iglesia Pentecostal Camino Damasco** (289 E 4th Street, between Avenues B & C). The **Nuyorican Poets Café** (*see p271*), a clubhouse for espresso-drinking wordsmiths since 1974, is known for its poetry slams, in which performers do lyric battle before a score-keeping audience.

Dating from 1837, **Tompkins Square Park** (from 7th to 10th Streets, between Avenues A &

Meatpacking District. *See p86.*

B), honours Daniel D Tompkins, governor of New York from 1807 to 1817, and vice-president during the Monroe administration. Over the years, this 10.5-acre park has been a site for demonstrations and rioting. The last major uprising occurred in 1988, when the city evicted squatters from the park and renovated it to suit the influx of affluent residents. Along with dozens of 150-year-old elm trees (some of the oldest in the city), the landscaped green space has basketball courts, playgrounds and dog runs, and remains a place where bongo beaters, guitarists, multi-pierced teenagers, hipsters, local families and vagrants mingle.

North of Tompkins Square, around First Avenue and 11th Street, are remnants of earlier communities: discount fabric dealers, Italian cheese shops, Polish butchers and two great Italian coffee and cannoli houses: **De Robertis** (176 First Avenue, between 10th & 11th Streets, 1-212 674 7137) and **Veniero's Pasticceria & Caffè** (342 E 11th Street, at First Avenue, 1-212 674 7264).

Merchant's House Museum

29 E 4th Street, between Lafayette Street & Bowery (1-212 777 1089, www.merchants house.org). Subway B, D, F, M to Broadway-

Walk Murder Most Cool

Swap the fashionable scene for crime scenes on Downtown's once mean streets.

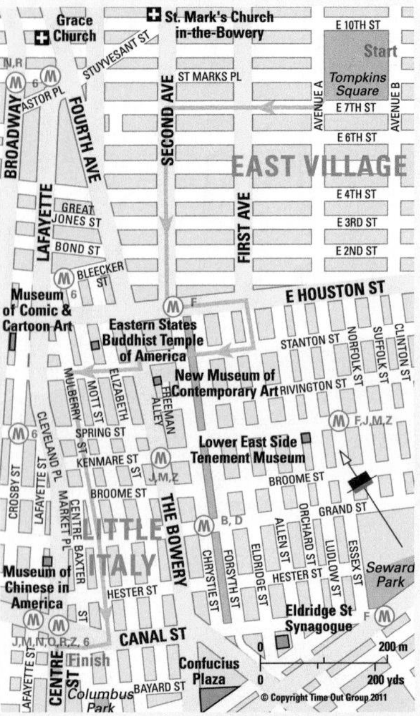

These days, trendy Downtown districts – the East Village, Lower East Side and Nolita/Little Italy – are pretty safe, but they used to be home to a rougher, and in some cases more homicidal, crowd. Start your blood-stained ramble in **Tompkins Square Park** (Avenue A, between 7th & 10th Streets), once the stomping ground of Daniel Rakowitz ('The Butcher of Tompkins Park'). In 1989, the 28-year-old East Village resident, who walked around carrying a live chicken, chopped up his girlfriend Monika Beerle, later serving her in a soup to the Tompkins Square homeless population.

Exit the park on Avenue A and head west on East 7th Street, then take a left on to Second Avenue. As you make your way past what used to be the **Binibon Café** (87 Second Avenue, at 5th Street), now an empty storefront, know that you are in the midst of literary greatness. This is the spot where Norman Mailer's one-time protégé, Jack Henry Abbott, stabbed a waiter to death in the summer of 1981 (after being told that the bathroom was unavailable). Only six weeks earlier, Mailer had helped the author, who had penned the critically acclaimed *In the Belly of the Beast*, earn parole for a murder he had committed while serving a sentence in a Utah prison.

Continue south on Second Avenue until you hit East Houston Street, then turn left. Near the **intersection of East Houston and Allen Streets**, in the early hours of a June day in 1993, serial killer Joel Rifkin picked up his last victim, a prostitute whom he killed in the *New York Post* parking lot at 210 South Street. He kept the body in his car until police pulled him over in Long Island. It turned out that Rifkin had been killing women for years – 17 by his count (though not all were found).

Turn right into Allen Street, then right again at Stanton and make your way to Mulberry Street. Now home to fancy boutiques, this was once a mob-dominated patch, with bodies frequently turning up in dumpsters. Turn left on Mulberry and note first the former **headquarters of John Gotti**

Lafayette Street; 6 to Bleecker Street. **Open** noon-5pm Mon, Thur-Sun. **Admission** $10; $5 reductions; free under-12s. **Credit** ($16 min) AmEx, MC, V. **Map** p403 F29.
Merchant's House Museum, the city's only fully preserved 19th-century family home, is an elegant, late Federal-Greek Revival property kitted out with the same furnishings and decorations as it contained when it was inhabited from 1835 by hardware tycoon Seabury Tredwell and his family. Three years after Tredwell's eighth daughter died in 1933, it opened as a museum. You can peruse the house at your own pace, following along with the museum's printed guide.

Jr (247 Mulberry Street, between Prince & Spring Streets), where the mafia kingpin used to conduct his 'business' affairs, which included racketeering, more than a dozen murders, gambling, extortion and other unsavoury pastimes. When his youngest son, Frank, was accidently struck by a car driven by his neighbour in the Howard Beach section of Queens where the mob boss lived, Gotti allegedly had the neighbour bumped off and his remains dissolved in acid.

As you walk through Little Italy, feast your eyes on what was **Umberto's Clam House** (129 Mulberry, at Hester Street), where 'Crazy' Joey Gallo – a violent gangster who attempted to poison rivals while serving prison time – was shot to death in April 1972 while celebrating his 43rd birthday. Today, it's home to Ristorante Da Gennaro (1-212 431 3934), where you can enjoy a lovely *scaloppini alla caprese* (provided you're not on anyone's hit list).

Turn briefly right on to Walker Street before going south on Centre Street until you get to White Street, where you'll see a series of ominous-looking buildings known as **The Tombs** (125 White Street, between Centre & Lafayette Streets). Police have processed criminals here for almost 170 years. Over time, the buildings may have changed (they have been periodically torn down, rebuilt and renamed), but the clientele has not. Convicts were actually hanged from the gallows here – including members of the Daybreak Boys gang in 1853 – until the electric chair was invented and executions were outsourced.

If it's only your feet that are killing you, count yourself lucky.

GREENWICH VILLAGE

Subway A, B, C, D, E, F, M to W 4th Street; L, N, Q, R, 4, 5, 6 to 14th Street-Union Square; N, R to 8th Street-NYU; 1 to Christopher St-Sheridan Square.

Stretching from Houston Street to 14th Street, between Broadway and Sixth Avenue, **Greenwich Village** has been inspiring bohemians for almost a century. Now that it has become one of the most expensive (and exclusive) neighbourhoods in the city, you need a lot more than a struggling artist's or writer's income to inhabit its leafy streets. However, it's still a fine place for idle wandering, candlelit dining in out-of-the-way restaurants, and hopping between bars and cabaret venues.

Great for people watching, **Washington Square Park** attracts a disparate cast of characters that takes in hippies, students and hip hop kids. Skateboarders clatter near the base of the Washington Arch, a modestly sized replica of Paris's Arc de Triomphe, built in 1895 to honour George Washington. The park hums with musicians and street artists, but the once-ubiquitous pot dealers have largely disappeared thanks to the NYC Police Department's surveillance cameras; today, anyone approaching you offering drugs is probably an undercover cop. However, the 9.75-acre Village landmark has recently been the subject of a different kind of controversy.

In 2007, when the NYC Parks Department embarked on a $16-million redesign of the park, community activists protested strongly, fearing it would ruin the park's bohemian flavour. Yet even vehement detractors have been pleasantly surprised with the results of the first phase, which included new lawns and flower beds in the western section of the park and restoration and a minor relocation of the 19th-century fountain to align it with the arch. The second phase, which turns its attention to the east side, should be completed by the end of 2010.

In the 1830s, the wealthy began building handsome townhouses around the square. A few of those properties are still privately owned and occupied, but many others have become part of the ever-expanding NYU campus. The university also owns the Washington Mews, a row of charming 19th-century former stables that line a tiny cobblestoned alley just to the north of the park between Fifth Avenue and University Place. Several famed literary figures, including Henry James (author of the celebrated novel named after the square), Herman Melville, Edith Wharton, Edgar Allan Poe and Eugene O'Neill, lived on or near the square. In 1871, the local creative community founded the **Salmagundi Club** (47 Fifth Avenue, between

INSIDE TRACK DYLAN'S VILLAGE

Bob Dylan lived at and owned 94 MacDougal Street (on a row of historic brownstones near Bleecker Street) through much of the 1960s, performing in **Washington Square Park** (*see p85*) and at extant clubs such as **Café Wha?** and the **Bitter End** (for both, *see p86*).

11th & 12th Streets, 1-212 255 7740, www.salmagundi.org), America's oldest artists' club. Now situated north of Washington Square on Fifth Avenue, it has galleries open to the public.

Greenwich Village continues to change with the times, for the better and for the worse. In the 1960s, **8th Street** was the closest New York got to San Francisco's hippie Haight Street. Although it's currently a long procession of piercing parlours, punky boutiques and shoe stores, Jimi Hendrix's **Electric Lady Studios** is still at 52 West 8th Street, between Fifth & Sixth Avenues. Once the dingy but colourful stomping ground of Beat poets and folk and jazz musicians, the well-trafficked strip of **Bleecker Street**, between La Guardia Place and Sixth Avenue, is now an overcrowded stretch of poster shops, cheap restaurants and music venues for the college crowd. Renowned hangouts such as Le Figaro Café (184 Bleecker Street, at MacDougal Street), Kerouac's favourite, are no more, but a worthy alternative is **Caffe Reggio** (119 MacDougal Street, at W 3rd Street, 1-212 475 9557). The oldest coffeehouse in the village, it opened in 1927, and appealed to Kerouac, native Villager Gregory Corso and other 1950s poets. Nearby, a former literati hangout (Hemingway and Fitzgerald), **Minetta Tavern** (*see p197*), has been rehabilitated by golden-touch restaurateur Keith McNally.

Although 1960s hotspot **Café Wha?** (115 MacDougal Street, between Bleecker & W 3rd Streets, 1-212 254 3706, www.cafewha.com) is now basically a tourist trap, Brazilian band Brazooka's regular Monday-night party is a genuine happening. Nearby, the **Bitter End** (147 Bleecker Street, between La Guardia Place & Thompson Street, 1-212 673 7030) has proudly championed the singer-songwriter – including a young Bob Dylan – since 1961.

The famed Village Gate jazz club at the corner of Bleecker and Thompson Streets – which welcomed performances by Miles Davis, Nina Simone and John Cage – closed in 1993. However, in 2008, **(Le) Poisson Rouge** (*see p324*) opened on the site with a similar mission to present diverse genres under one roof. Just up the street on La Guardia Place is the **AIA Center for Architecture** (*see below*), which hosts temporary exhibitions on plans and projects in the city.

Not far from here, in the triangle formed by Sixth Avenue, Greenwich Avenue and 10th Street, you'll see the Gothic-style **Jefferson Market Library** (a branch of the New York Public Library). The lovely flower-filled garden facing Greenwich Avenue once held the art deco Women's House of Detention, which was torn down in 1974. Mae West did a little time there in 1926, on obscenity charges stemming from her Broadway show *Sex*.

Just behind the library, off 10th Street, lies **Patchin Place**, which was home to some of the leading luminaries of New York's literary pantheon. This cul-de-sac lined with brick houses built during the mid-19th century is off limits to the public, but through the gate, you can make out no.4, where the poet and staunch foe of capitalisation ee cummings resided from 1923 to 1962; and no.5, where Djuna Barnes, author of *Nightwood*, lived from 1940 to 1982. Indeed, cummings would reportedly check on the reclusive Barnes by calling 'Are you still alive, Djuna?' though his neighbour's window.

FREE AIA Center for Architecture

536 La Guardia Place, between Bleecker & W 3rd Streets (1-212 683 0023, www.aiany.org). Subway A, B, C, D, E, F, M to W 4th Street.
Open 9am-8pm Mon-Fri; 11am-5pm Sat.
Admission free. **Map** p403 E29.

Designed by architect Andrew Berman, this three-storey building is a fitting home for architectural debate: the sweeping, light-filled design is a physical manifestation of AIA's goal of promoting transparency in both its access and programming. Berman cut away large slabs of flooring at the street and basement levels, converting underground spaces into bright, museum-quality galleries.

WEST VILLAGE & MEATPACKING DISTRICT

Subway A, C, E, L to 14th Street; 1 to Christopher St-Sheridan Square; 1, 2, 3 to 14th Street.

In the early 20th century, the **West Village** was largely a working-class Italian neighbourhood. These days, the highly desirable enclave is home to numerous celebrities (including Uma Thurman, Ed Norton, Sarah Jessica Parker and Matthew Broderick), but a low-key, everyone-knows-everyone feel remains. It may not have the buzzy vibe of the East Village, but it has held on to much of its picturesque charm. The area west of Sixth Avenue to the Hudson River, from 14th Street to Houston Street, possesses the quirky geographical features that moulded the Village's character. Only here could West 10th Street cross West 4th Street, and Waverly Place cross… Waverly Place. The West Village's layout doesn't follow the regular grid pattern but rather the settlers' original horse paths.

Locals and visitors crowd bistros along Seventh Avenue and Hudson Street, and patronise the high-rent shops on this stretch of Bleecker Street, including no fewer than three Marc Jacobs boutiques. Venture on to the side streets for interesting discoveries, such as indie boutique **Castor & Pollux** on West 10th Street (*see p240*) and his-and-hers flagships of rustic-chic label **Rag & Bone** (*see p239*) on Christopher Street. The area's bohemian population may have dwindled years ago, but a few old landmarks remain. Solemnly raise a glass in the **White Horse Tavern** (567 Hudson Street, at 11th Street, 1-212 989 3956), a favourite of such literary luminaries as Ezra Pound, James Baldwin, Norman Mailer and Dylan Thomas, who included it on his last drinking binge before his death in 1953. On and just off Seventh Avenue South are jazz and cabaret clubs, including the **Village Vanguard** (*see p332*).

The West Village is also a longstanding gay neighbourhood, although the young gay scene has mostly moved north to Chelsea and Hell's Kitchen. The **Stonewall Inn** (*see p308*), on Christopher Street, is next to the site of the 1969 riots that marked the birth of the modern gay-liberation movement. Inside **Christopher Park**, which faces the Inn, is George Segal's *Gay Pride*, plaster sculptures of two same-sex couples that commemorates the street's role in gay history. Along Christopher Street from Sheridan Square to the Hudson River pier, most of the area's shops, bars and restaurants are out, loud and proud. The Hudson riverfront features grass-covered piers, food vendors and picnic tables.

The north-west corner of the West Village has been known as the **Meatpacking District** since the area was dominated by the wholesale meat industry in the early 20th century. As business waned, gay fetish clubs took root in derelict buildings and, until the 1990s, the area was a haunt for transsexual prostitutes. In recent years, however, following the arrival of pioneering fashion store **Jeffrey New York** (*see p232*), designer flagships started to move in, including Diane von Furstenberg and Stella McCartney. Frequent mentions on *Sex and the City,* along with the arrival of swanky **Hotel Gansevoort** (*see p165*) and self-consciously hip eateries like **Pastis** (9 Ninth Avenue, at Little W 12th Street, 1-212 929 4844) in the noughties, cemented the area's reputation as a consumer playground. Nightclubs such as **Cielo** (*see p336*) draw a young crowd after dark.

The 2009 opening of freight-track-turned-park the **High Line** (*see p96* **Profile**) has brought even bigger crowds to the area. Slick style hotel the **Standard** (*see p165*) straddles the elevated park at West 13th Street, and its beer garden, nestled beneath it, is a great spot for a pint. Ironically, the arrival of the luxury hotel unintentionally restored some of the area's old raunchy reputation when the *New York Post* reported that naked hotel guests were putting on explicit shows in their glass-fronted rooms for the strollers below.

Urban Myths

Dylan Thomas and the fatal glass of scotch. The story behind the legend.

'I've had 18 straight whiskies. I think that's the record,' Welsh poet Dylan Thomas is reputed to have said before dying in November 1953, and the boast has since entered New York bohemian lore. Many believe this heroic feat of alcohol consumption occurred in one sitting at the White Horse Tavern (567 Hudson Street, at 11th Street), where Thomas was a regular and a portrait of him now hangs in the middle room, just above his favourite table in the corner; bar staff have even been known to recount how he expired on the premises following the fatal 18th dram.

In reality, Thomas left his room at the Chelsea Hotel at 2am on 4 November for a bout of drinking at the White Horse, returning after closing time some two hours later to make that highly unlikely claim of 18 scotches to his mistress. He then slept it off before rising mid-morning and heading back with her to the same bar, where he had two glasses of beer. Returning once more to the Chelsea, Thomas – who was also taking medication for depression – suddenly collapsed, and a doctor was summoned. The poet was admitted the following day to St Vincent's Hospital, where he died on 9 November 1953 at the age of 39.

It is alleged that Dylan Thomas's ghost still haunts the White Horse, appearing at the side of his corner table. You would probably have to drink an ungodly amount of whiskey to see it, though – something we can't recommend.

SIGHTS

Midtown

At the heart of things.

The area from 14th to 59th Streets is iconic New York: jutting skyscrapers, crowded pavements and a yellow river of cabs streaming down the congested avenues. The impression is reinforced by the city's most recognisable landmarks being located here, from the iconic spire of the Empire State Building and the stately lions of the New York Public Library to the bright lights of Times Square. But there's a lot more to Midtown than glistening towers and high-octane commerce. It contains the city's most concentrated contemporary gallery district (**Chelsea**), its hottest gay enclaves (Chelsea and **Hell's Kitchen**), some of its swankiest shops (**Fifth Avenue**) and, of course, the majority of its major theatres (along **Broadway**). There are even a few lovely, serene spots where you can retreat from the jostling crowds and traffic. In particular, the city's newest park, the High Line, has boosted the area's green quotient considerably.

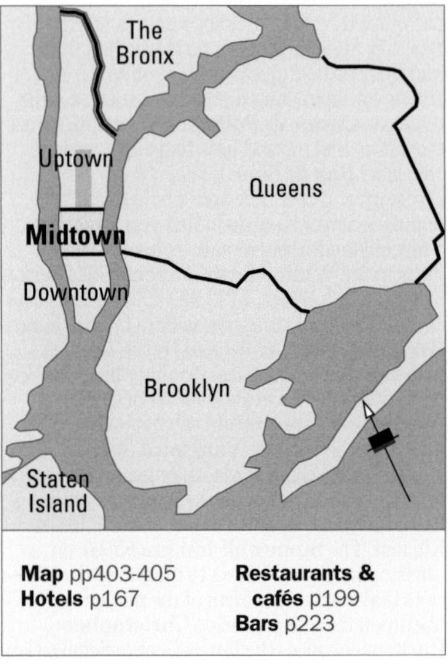

Map pp403-405
Hotels p167
Restaurants & cafés p199
Bars p223

SIGHTS

CHELSEA

Subway A, C, E, 1, 2, 3 to 14th Street; C, E, 1 to 23rd Street; L to Eighth Avenue; 1 to 18th Street or 28th Street.

Formerly a working-class Irish and Hispanic neighbourhood, the corridor between 14th and 29th Streets west of Sixth Avenue emerged as the nexus of New York's queer life in the 1990s. Owing to rising housing costs and the protean nature of the city's cultural landscape, it's being slowly eclipsed by Hell's Kitchen to the north (just as Chelsea once overtook the West Village), but it's undeniably still a homo hotspot with numerous bars, restaurants, clothing stores and sex shops catering to the once-ubiquitous 'Chelsea boys'.

The formerly desolate western edge of the neighbourhood has been the focus of the most eagerly anticipated project in the city's recent history: the transformation of a disused elevated freight train track into a lush, landscaped public park, the **High Line** (*see p96* **Profile**).

In the 1980s, many of New York's galleries left Soho for this patch, from West 20th Street to West 29th Street, between Tenth and Eleventh Avenues (*see pp294-298*). Today, internationally recognised spaces such as **Mary Boone Gallery**, **Gagosian Gallery** and **PaceWildenstein**, as well as numerous less exalted names, attract swarms of art aficionados. The High Line has brought even more gallery-hoppers to the area as it provides a verdant pathway from the boutique- and restaurant-rich Meatpacking District (*see p86*) to the art enclave. Traversing the elevated promenade, you'll pass through the old loading dock of the former Nabisco factory, where the first Oreo cookie was made in 1912. This conglomeration of 18 structures, built between the 1890s and the 1930s, now houses **Chelsea Market** (75 Ninth Avenue, between 15th &

16th Streets, www.chelseamarket.com). The ground-floor food arcade offers artisanal bread, wine, imported Italian foods and freshly made ice-cream, among other treats.

Also among the area's notable industrial architecture is the **Starrett-Lehigh Building** (601 W 26th Street, at Eleventh Avenue). The stunning 1929 structure was left in disrepair until the dot-com boom of the late 1990s, when media companies, photographers and designers snatched up its loft-like spaces. Many of the Hudson River piers, which were once terminals for the world's grand ocean liners, remain in a state of ruin, but the four between 17th and 23rd Streets have been transformed into mega sports centre **Chelsea Piers** (*see p343*).

To get a glimpse of how Chelsea looked back when it was first developed in the 1880s, stroll along **Cushman Row** (406-418 W 20th Street, between Ninth & Tenth Avenues) in the Chelsea Historic District. Just to the north is the block-long **General Theological Seminary of the Episcopal Church** (440 W 21st Street, between Ninth & Tenth Avenues, 1-212 243 5150, www.gts.edu), where the verdant garden courtyard (closed after 3pm & Sun) is a hidden oasis of tranquillity. The seminary's land was part of the estate known as Chelsea, owned by poet Clement Clarke Moore, author of *A Visit from St Nicholas* (more commonly known as *'Twas the Night Before Christmas*).

The nearby **Chelsea Hotel** (*see p167*), on West 23rd Street, has been a magnet for creative types since it first opened in 1884; Mark Twain was an early guest. The list of former residents reads like an international *Who's Who* of the artistic elite: Sarah Bernhardt (who slept in a coffin), William Burroughs (who wrote *Naked Lunch* here), Dylan Thomas, Arthur Miller, Quentin Crisp, Leonard Cohen, Bob Dylan, Janis Joplin and Jimi Hendrix, to name a few. In the 1960s, it was the stomping ground of Andy Warhol's coterie of Superstars, and the location of his 1966 film *The Chelsea Girls*. The Chelsea gained punk-rock notoriety on 12 October 1978, when Sex Pistol Sid Vicious stabbed girlfriend Nancy Spungen to death in Room 100. There are about 95 permanent residents, working artists among them, but 116 traditional (if modest) hotel rooms are available. Under new corporate management, the hotel has lost a measure of its boho glamour, but a tour is offered at least monthly, which visits some of the artists' studios ($40, see www.hotelchelsea.com for dates and details). Occupying a full city block, **London Terrace** (23rd Street, between Ninth & Tenth Avenues) is a distinctive 1920s Tudor-style apartment complex that's home to some rather famous names, including Debbie Harry and *Vanity Fair* photographer Annie Leibovitz.

Chelsea provides a variety of impressive cultural offerings. The **Joyce Theater** (*see p283*) is a renovated art deco cinema that presents better-known contemporary dance troupes, while **New York Live Arts** (*see p283*) performs at the Bessie Schönberg Theater. A dazzling array of Himalayan art and artefacts is on display at the **Rubin Museum of Art** (*see p91*), but if your tastes are more modern, check out pioneering arts centre the **Kitchen** (*see p283*).

The weekend flea markets tucked between buildings along 25th Street, between Seventh Avenue and Broadway, have shrunk in recent years (casualties of development), but you'll still find a heady assortment of clothes, furnishings, cameras and knick-knacks at the rummage-worthy **Antiques Garage** (*see p257*) and the more upmarket **Showplace Antique and Design Center** (*see p257*).

Not far from here, the Fashion Institute of Technology, on 27th Street, between Seventh and Eighth Avenues, counts Calvin Klein, Nanette Lepore and Michael Kors among its alumni. The school's **Museum at FIT** (*see below*) mounts free exhibitions.

FREE Museum at FIT

Building E, Seventh Avenue, at 27th Street (1-212 217 4558, www.fitnyc.edu/museum). Subway 1 to 28th Street. **Open** noon-8pm Tue-Fri; 10am-5pm Sat. **Admission** free. **Map** p404 D26.

The Fashion Institute of Technology owns one of the largest and most impressive collections of clothing, textiles and accessories in the world, including some 50,000 costumes and fabrics dating from the fifth century to the present. The collection is overseen by fashion historian Valerie Steele, and the museum showcases a rotating selection from the permanent collection, as well as temporary exhibitions focusing on individual designers or the role that fashion plays in society.

INSIDE TRACK MYSTERIES OF THE METRONOME

It's not uncommon to see passers-by perplexed by the **Metronome**, a massive sculptural installation attached to 1 Union Square South that bellows steam and generates a barrage of numbers on a digital read-out. Although they appear strange, they're not random numbers – the 15-digit display is actually a clock indicating the time relative to midnight. There's a detailed explanation at the website of Kristin Jones and Andrew Ginzel, the artists responsible; see www.jonesginzel.com.

WORLD YACHT
DUCHESS
Have A Night Out
On The World
WORLD YACHT
AT PIER 81 NYC
Pier 81 at 41st Street • 212.630.8100
contact@worldyacht.com
www.worldyacht.com
Use code: TIMEOUT when booking for free
cocktail onboard. Offer good thru April 2012.

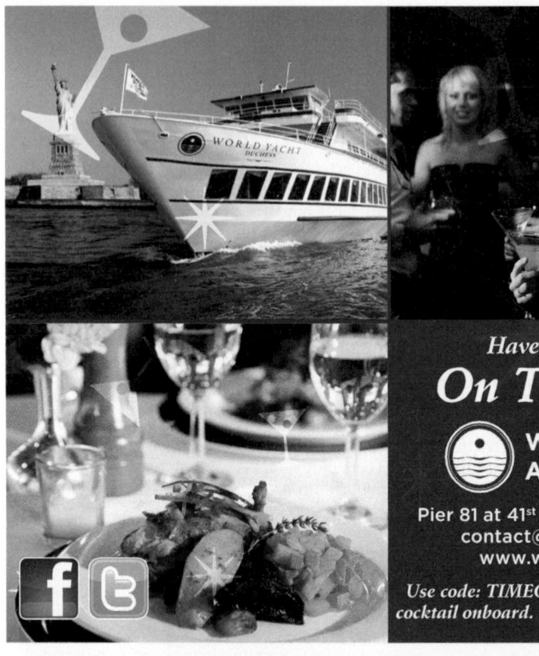

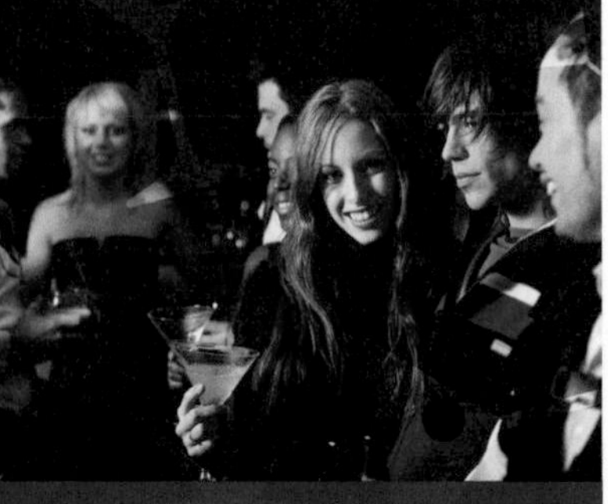

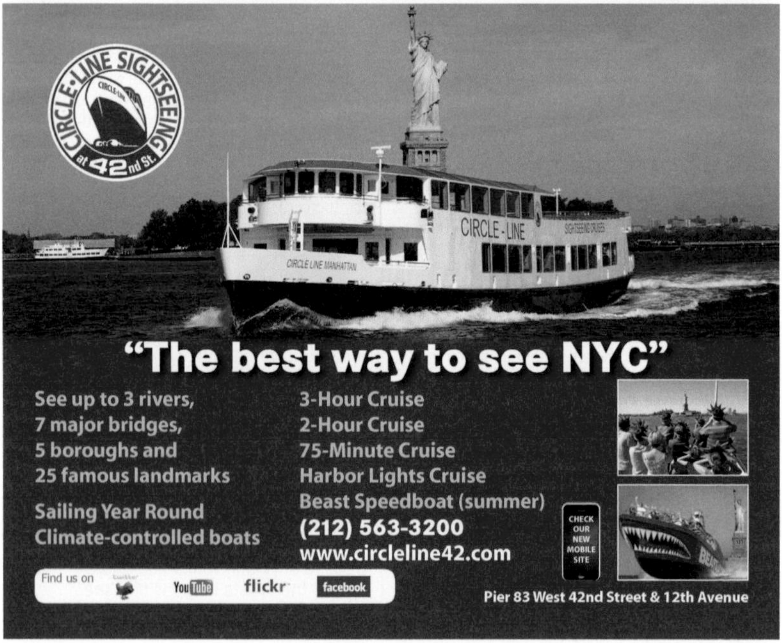
CIRCLE-LINE SIGHTSEEING
at 42nd St.
CIRCLE-LINE
SIGHTSEEING CRUISES
CIRCLE LINE MANHATTAN
"The best way to see NYC"
See up to 3 rivers,
7 major bridges,
5 boroughs and
25 famous landmarks
Sailing Year Round
Climate-controlled boats
3-Hour Cruise
2-Hour Cruise
75-Minute Cruise
Harbor Lights Cruise
Beast Speedboat (summer)
(212) 563-3200
www.circleline42.com
CHECK OUR NEW MOBILE SITE
Find us on
YouTube
flickr
facebook
Pier 83 West 42nd Street & 12th Avenue

Rubin Museum of Art

150 W 17th Street, at Seventh Avenue (1-212 620 5000, www.rmanyc.org). Subway A, C, E to 14th Street; L to Eighth Avenue; 1 to 18th Street. **Open** 11am-5pm Mon, Thur; 11am-7pm Wed; 11am-10pm Fri; 11am-6pm Sat, Sun. **Admission** $10; $5 reductions; free under-12s. Free to all 6-10pm Fri. **Credit** AmEx, DC, Disc, MC, V. **Map** p403 D27.

Dedicated to Himalayan art, the Rubin is a very stylish museum – which falls into place when you learn that the six-storey space was once occupied by famed fashion store Barneys. The ground-floor café, where you can sample inexpensive Himalayan dishes, used to be the accessories department (retail lives on in the colourful gift shop), and a dramatic central spiral staircase ascends to the galleries. Rich-toned walls are classy foils for the serene statuary and intricate, multicoloured painted textiles. The second level is dedicated to 'What Is It? Himalayan Art', an introductory exhibit that displays selections from Donald and Shelley Rubin's collection of more than 2,000 pieces from the second century to the present day. The upper floors are devoted to several temporary themed exhibitions. In 2011, look for 'Pilgrimage and Faith: Buddhism, Christianity and Islam', on view from 1 July to 24 October.

FLATIRON DISTRICT & UNION SQUARE

Subway F, M to 14th Street; L, N, Q, R, 4, 5, 6 to 14th Street-Union Square; L to Sixth Avenue; N, R, 6 to 23rd Street or 28th Street.

Taking its name from the distinctive wedge-shaped Flatiron Building, this district extends from 14th to 29th Streets, between Sixth and Lexington Avenues. Initially, the locale was predominantly commercial, home to numerous toy manufacturers and photography studios. It's still not uncommon to see models and actors strolling to and from their shoots. However, in the 1980s, the district became more residential, as buyers were drawn to its 19th-century brownstones and early 20th-century industrial architecture. Clusters of restaurants and shops soon followed. By the turn of the millennium, many internet start-ups had moved to the area, earning it the nickname 'Silicon Alley'.

The area has two major public spaces: Madison Square Park and Union Square. Opened in 1847, **Madison Square Park** (from 23rd to 26th Streets, between Fifth & Madison Avenues) is the more stately of the two. In the 19th century, the square was a highly desirable address. Winston Churchill's grandfather resided in a magnificent but since-demolished mansion at Madison Avenue and 26th Street; Edith Wharton also made her home in the neighbourhood and set many of her high-society novels here. By the 1990s, the park had become a decaying no-go zone given over to drug dealers and the homeless, but it got a much-needed makeover in 2001 thanks to the efforts of the Madison Square Park Conservancy (www.madisonsquarepark.org), which has created a programme of cultural events, including Mad Sq Art, a year-round 'gallery without walls', featuring sculptural, video and installation exhibitions from big-name artists. A further lure is celebrity chef Danny Meyer's **Shake Shack** (*see p212*), which attracts queues in all weathers for its burgers – considered by many New Yorkers to be top of the heap.

The square is surrounded by illustrious buildings. Completed in 1909, the **Metropolitan Life Tower** (1 Madison Avenue, at 24th Street) was modelled on the Campanile in Venice's Piazza San Marco (an allusion as commercial as it was architectural, for Met Life Insurance wished to remind people that it had raised funds for the Campanile after its fall two years earlier). The **Appellate Division Courthouse** (35 E 25th Street, at Madison Avenue) features one of the most beautiful pediments in the city, while Cass Gilbert's **New York Life Insurance Company Building** (51 Madison Avenue, at 26th Street) is capped by a golden pyramid that's one of the skyline's jewels.

The most famous of all Madison Square's edifices, however, lies at the southern end. The **Flatiron Building** (175 Fifth Avenue, between 22nd & 23rd Streets; *photo p92*) was the world's first steel-frame skyscraper, a 22-storey Beaux Arts edifice clad conspicuously in white limestone and terracotta. But it's the unique triangular shape (like an arrow pointing northward to indicate the city's progression uptown) that has drawn sightseers since it opened in 1902. Legend has it that a popular 1920s catchphrase originated at this corner of 23rd Street – police would give the '23 skidoo' to ne'er-do-wells trying to peek at ladies' petticoats as the unique wind currents that swirled around the building blew up their dresses. Speaking of rampant libidos, the nearby **Museum of Sex** (*see p92*) houses an impressive collection of salacious ephemera.

In the 19th century, the neighbourhood went by the moniker of Ladies' Mile, thanks to the ritzy department stores that lined Broadway and Sixth Avenue. These retail palaces attracted the 'carriage trade', wealthy women who bought the latest imported fashions and household goods. By 1914, most of the department stores had moved north, leaving their proud cast-iron buildings behind. Today, the area is peppered with chain clothing stores, bookshops and tasteful home-furnishing shops such as **ABC Carpet & Home** (*see p258*).

Flatiron Building. *See p91.*

The Flatiron District's other major public space, **Union Square** (from 14th to 17th Streets, between Union Square East & Union Square West) is named after neither the Union of the Civil War nor the labour rallies that once took place here, but simply for the union of Broadway and Bowery Lane (now Fourth Avenue). Even so, it does have its radical roots: from the 1920s until the early '60s, it was a favourite spot for tub-thumping political oratory. Following 9/11, the park was home to candlelit vigils and became a focal point for the city's grief. Formerly grungy, the park is fresh from a rolling renovation project started in the 1980s. It's best known as the home of the **Union Square Greenmarket** (*see right*). The square is flanked by a variety of large businesses, including a **Barnes & Noble** bookstore that hosts an excellent programme of author events (*see p269*).

Museum of Sex

233 Fifth Avenue, at 27th Street (1-212 689 6337, www.museumofsex.com). Subway N, R, 6 to 28th Street. **Open** 10am-8pm Mon-Thur, Sun; 10am-9pm Fri, Sat. **Admission** $16.75; $15.25 reductions. Under-18s not admitted, except 17-year-olds with written parental/guardian consent. **Credit** AmEx, DC, MC, V. **Map** p404 E26.

MoSex explores the subject within a cultural context – but that doesn't mean some content won't shock the more buttoned-up visitor. On the ground floor, 'Action!', which screens around 220 clips from more than 150 years of sex on film, includes explicit scenes from such (literally) seminal porn flicks as *Deep Throat*. Highlights of the permanent collection range from the tastefully erotic to the outlandish. Also of note are the Depression-era Tijuana Bibles and sex machines created by DIYers, such as the 'Monkey Rocker', constructed from a dildo and exercise equipment. The gift shop has books and arty sex toys.

Union Square Greenmarket

From 16th to 17th Streets, between Union Square East & Union Square West (1-212 788 7476, www.greennyc.org/unionsquaregreenmarket). Subway L, N, Q, R, 4, 5, 6 to 14th Street-Union Square. **Open** 8am-6pm Mon, Wed, Fri, Sat. **Map** p403 E27.

Shop elbow-to-elbow with top chefs for all manner of locally grown produce, handmade breads, preserves and desserts at the city's flagship farmers' market around the periphery of Union Square Park. Between Thanksgiving and Christmas, the park is even busier when a holiday market sets up shop. *Photo p95.*

GRAMERCY PARK & MURRAY HILL

Subway L, N, Q, R, 4, 5, 6 to 14th Street-Union Square; L to Sixth Avenue; N, R, 6 to 23rd Street or 28th Street; S, 4, 5, 6, 7 to 42nd Street-Grand Central; 6 to 33rd Street.

A key to **Gramercy Park**, the tranquil, gated square lurking between Union and Madison Squares at the bottom of Lexington Avenue (between 20th & 21st Streets), is one of the most sought-after treasures in all the five boroughs. For the most part, only residents of the beautiful surrounding townhouses and apartment buildings have access to the park, which was developed in the 1830s to resemble a London square. The park is flanked by two private clubs; members of both also also have access to the square. One is the **Players Club** (16 Gramercy Park South, between Park Avenue South & Irving Place, 1-212 475 6116, www.theplayersnyc.org), inspired by London's Garrick Club and housed in an 1845 brownstone formerly owned by Edwin Booth, the celebrated 19th-century actor and brother of John Wilkes Booth, Abraham Lincoln's assassin. Next door at no.15 is the Gothic Revival Samuel Tilden House, which houses the **National Arts Club** (1-212 475 3424, www.nationalartsclub.org, closed Sat, Sun & July, Aug). The busts of famous writers (Shakespeare, Dante) along the façade were chosen to reflect Tilden's library, which, along with his fortune, helped to create the New York Public Library. The galleries are open to non-members, but call before visiting as they may close for private events or between shows.

Leading south from the park to 14th Street, Irving Place is named after author Washington Irving (although he never actually lived here). Near the corner of 15th Street sits the **Fillmore New York at Irving Plaza** (*see p322*), a music venue. At the corner of Park Avenue South and 17th Street is the final base of the once-omnipotent Tammany Hall political machine (*see p24*). Built in 1929, it now houses the New York Film Academy. Popular neighbourhood hangout **75 Irving Place Coffee & Tea Bar** (*see p203*) is a good place to revive with a cup of New York State-roasted java. A few blocks away from here is the **Theodore Roosevelt Birthplace** (*see p94*), a national historic site.

The largely residential area bordered by 23rd and 30th Streets, Park Avenue and the East River is known as **Kips Bay** after Jacobus Henderson Kip, whose farm covered the area in the 17th century. Third Avenue is the district's main thoroughfare, and a locus of restaurants representing a variety of eastern cuisines, including Afghan, Tibetan and Turkish.

Murray Hill itself spans 30th to 40th Streets, between Third and Fifth Avenues. Townhouses of the rich and powerful were once clustered around Madison and Park Avenues. It's now populated mostly by upwardly-mobiles fresh out of university and only a few streets retain their former elegance. One is **Sniffen Court** (150-158 E 36th Street, between Lexington & Third Avenues), an unspoiled row of 1864 carriage houses located within earshot of the Queens Midtown Tunnel's ceaseless traffic. The **Morgan Library & Museum** (*see below*), also on 36th Street, houses some 350,000 rare books, manuscripts, prints, and objects. If you're more interested in contemporary European culture, visit the nearby **Scandinavia House – The Nordic Center in America** (*see below*).

Morgan Library & Museum

225 Madison Avenue, at 36th Street (1-212 685 0008, www.themorgan.org). Subway 6 to 33rd Street. **Open** 10.30am-5pm Tue-Thur; 10.30am-9pm Fri; 10am-6pm Sat; 11am-6pm Sun. **Admission** $12; $8 reductions; free under-12s. **Credit** AmEx, DC, MC, V. **Map** p404 E25.

This Madison Avenue institution began as the private library of financier J Pierpont Morgan, and is his artistic gift to the city. Building on the collection Morgan amassed in his lifetime, the museum houses first-rate works on paper, including drawings by Michelangelo, Rembrandt and Picasso; three Gutenberg Bibles; a copy of *Frankenstein* annotated by Mary Shelley; manuscripts by Dickens, Poe, Twain, Steinbeck and Wilde; sheet music handwritten by Beethoven and Mozart; and an original edition of Dickens's *A Christmas Carol* that's displayed every Yuletide. A massive renovation and expansion orchestrated by Renzo Piano has brought more natural light into the building, doubled the available exhibition space and restored the McKim building, which reopened in October 2010. As a result, visitors can now see Morgan's spectacular library (the East Room), with its 30-ft-high book-lined walls and murals designed by Henry Siddons Mowbray (who also painted the ceiling of the newly restored Rotunda). The 2011 roster of shows includes 'Illuminating Fashion: Dress in the Art of Medieval France and the Netherlands' (until 4 Sept 2011).

FREE Scandinavia House – The Nordic Center in America

58 Park Avenue, at 38th Streets (1-212 879 9779, www.scandinaviahouse.org). Subway S, 4, 5, 6, 7

to 42nd Street-Grand Central. **Open** Hours vary. *Gallery* noon-6pm Tue-Sat. **Admission** free. **Map** p404 E24.
One of city's top cultural centres, Scandinavia House serves as a lifeline between the US and the five Scandinavian nations, and offers a full schedule of film screenings, lectures and art exhibitions. The café, an outpost of small chain Smörgas Chef (open 11am-10pm Mon-Sat, 11am-5pm Sun), serves up tasty Swedish meatballs, and the shop is a showcase for chic Scandinavian design.

FREE Theodore Roosevelt Birthplace

28 E 20th Street, between Broadway & Park Avenue South (1-212 260 1616, www.nps.gov/thrb). Subway 6 to 23rd Street. **Open** 9am-5pm Tue-Sat. **Tours** hourly 10am-4pm, except noon. **Admission** free. **Map** p403 E27.
The brownstone where the 26th President of the United States was born, and where he lived until he was 14 years old, was demolished in 1916. But it was recreated after his death in 1919, complete with authentic period furniture (some collected and restored from the original house), personal effects and a trophy room. The house can only be explored by guided tour, but there's a gallery of artefacts that can be perused independently.

SIGHTS

HERALD SQUARE & THE GARMENT DISTRICT

Subway A, C, E, 1, 2, 3 to 34th Street-Penn Station; B, D, F, M, N, Q, R to 34th Street-Herald Square.

Seventh Avenue, aka Fashion Avenue, is the main drag of the **Garment District** (roughly from 34th to 40th Streets, between Broadway & Eighth Avenue) and where designers – along with their seamstresses, fitters and assistants – feed America's multi-billion-dollar clothing industry. Delivery trucks and workers pushing racks of clothes clog streets lined with wholesale trimming, button and fabric shops. The scene is particularly busy on 38th and 39th Streets.

Taking up an entire city block, from 34th Street to 35th Street, between Broadway and Seventh Avenue, is the legendary **Macy's** (*see p233*). With one million square feet of selling space spread across nine floors, it's the biggest and busiest department store in the world. Facing Macy's, at the intersection of Broadway, 34th Street and Sixth Avenue, is **Herald Square**, named after a long-gone newspaper, the *New York Herald*. The lower section is known as **Greeley Square** after editor and reformer Horace Greeley, owner of the *Herald*'s rival, the *New York Tribune* (the two papers merged in 1924). Once grungy, the square now offers bistro chairs and tables that get crowded with shoppers and office lunchers in the warmer months. To the east, the many spas, restaurants and karaoke bars enlivening **Koreatown** line 32nd Street, between Broadway and Fifth Avenue.

Located not in Madison Square but on Seventh Avenue, between 31st and 33rd Streets, **Madison Square Garden** (*see p338*) is home for the Knicks, the Liberty and Rangers, and has welcomed rock icons from Elvis to Madonna as well as the Barnum & Bailey Circus and other big events. The massive arena is actually the fourth building to bear that name (the first two were appropriately located in the square after which they're named) and opened on Valentine's Day 1968, replacing the grand old Pennsylvania Station razed four years earlier. This brutal act of architectural vandalism spurred the creation of the city's Landmarks Preservation Commission, which has saved countless other edifices from a similar fate.

Beneath Madison Square Garden stands **Penn Station**, a claustrophobic catacomb serving 600,000 Amtrak, Long Island Railroad and New Jersey Transit passengers daily and the busiest train station in America.

A proposal to relocate the entrance of the station across the street to the 24-hour **General Post Office** (formally known as the James A Farley Post Office Building, 421 Eighth Avenue, between 31st & 33rd Streets), was championed by the late Senator Patrick Moynihan in the early 1990s. The project, which has stalled over the years, finally got the necessary funding and government approval, and ground was broken in October 2010. Moynihan Station is expected to be completed in 2016.

THE THEATER DISTRICT & HELL'S KITCHEN

Subway A, C, E to 42nd Street-Port Authority; N, Q, R, S, 1, 2, 3, 7 to 42nd Street-Times Square.

Times Square's evolution from a traffic-choked fleshpot to a tourist-friendly theme park has accelerated in the past few years. Not only has 'the crossroads of the world' gained an elevated viewing platform atop the new TKTS discount booth, from which visitors can admire the surrounding light show (*see p98* **Not Just the Ticket**), in summer 2009 Mayor Bloomberg designated stretches of Broadway pedestrian zones, complete with seating, in an effort to streamline Midtown traffic and create a more pleasant environment for both residents and visitors. In 2009, the mayor decided that these popular plazas, from 47th to 42nd Streets and from 35th to 33rd Streets, would be permanent.

Originally Longacre Square, the junction of Broadway and Seventh Avenue stretching from

Union Square Greenmarket. See p92.

42nd to 47th Streets, was renamed after the *New York Times* moved here in the early 1900s. The first electrified billboard graced the district in 1904, on the side of a bank at 46th and Broadway. The same year, the inaugural New Year's Eve party in Times Square doubled as the *Times*'s housewarming party in its new HQ. More than 300,000 still gather here to watch a glittery mirrorball descend every 31 December.

The paper left the building only a decade after it had arrived (it now occupies an $84-million tower on Eighth Avenue, between 40th and 41st Streets). However, it retained ownership of its old headquarters until the 1960s, and erected the world's first scrolling electric news 'zipper' in 1928. The readout, now sponsored by Dow Jones, has trumpeted breaking stories from the stock-market crash of 1929 to the election of the country's first black president in 2008.

Times Square is also the gateway to the **Theater District**, the zone between 41st Street and 53rd Street, from Sixth Avenue to Ninth Avenue, where extravagant dramatic shows are put on six days a week (Monday is the traditional night off). While numerous off-Broadway theatres stage first-rate productions in the area, only 39 showhouses are officially Broadway theatres. The distinction is based on size rather than location or quality – Broadway theatres must have more than 500 seats.

The Theater District's transformation from the cradle of New York's sex industry began in 1984, when the city condemned properties along 42nd Street ('Forty Deuce', or 'the Deuce' for short), between Seventh and Eighth Avenues. A change in zoning laws meant adult-oriented venues must now subsist on X-rated videos rather than live 'dance' shows; the square's sex trade is now relegated to short stretches of Seventh and Eighth Avenues, just north and south of 42nd Street.

The streets to the west of Eighth Avenue are filled with eateries catering to theatregoers, especially the predominantly overpriced places along **Restaurant Row** (46th Street, between Eighth & Ninth Avenues). Locals tend to walk west to Ninth Avenue – in the 40s and 50s, the Hell's Kitchen strip is tightly packed with inexpensive restaurants serving a variety of ethnic cuisines.

Recording studios, record labels, theatrical agencies and other entertainment and media companies reside in the area's office buildings. The **Brill Building** (1619 Broadway, at 49th Street) has long been the home of music publishers and producers; such luminaries as Jerry Lieber, Mike Stoller and Carole King wrote and auditioned their hits here. **Colony Records** (*see p260*), a fixture of the building for decades, sells sheet music for current Broadway shows and doubles as a museum of pop-culture ephemera, while both visiting rock royalty and aspiring musicians drool over the selection of new and vintage guitars (as well as other instruments) on **Music Row** (48th Street, between Sixth & Seventh Avenues). **ABC Television Studios**, at 7 Times Square, at 44th Street and Broadway, entices early-morning risers hoping to catch a glimpse of the *Good Morning America* crew.

Flashy attractions strive to outdo one another in hopes of snaring the tourist throngs and their wide-eyed progeny. **Madame Tussauds New York** (*see p98*), a Gothamised version of the London-born wax

Profile The High Line

All aboard New York's popular new park.

Back in the early days of the 20th century, the West Side was likened to the Wild West. When freight-bearing trains competed with horses, carts and pedestrians on Tenth Avenue, the thoroughfare was so treacherous it earned the moniker 'Death Avenue'. In an attempt to counteract the carnage, mounted men known as 'West Side Cowboys' would ride in front of the train, waving red flags to warn of its imminent approach. These urban cowboys lost their jobs when the West Side Improvement Project finally raised the railway off street level and put it up on to an overhead trestle – the High Line – in 1934. Originally stretching from 34th Street to Spring Street, the line fell into disuse after World War II as trucks replaced trains. A southern chunk was torn down beginning in the 1960s, and, after the last train ground to a halt in 1980, local property owners lobbied for its destruction.

However, thanks to the efforts of railroad enthusiast Peter Obletz and, later, the Friends of the High Line, which was founded by local residents Joshua David and Robert Hammond, the industrial relic was saved. A decade after the group began advocating for its

museum chain, sits next to **Ripley's Believe It Or Not! Odditorium** (*see p99*), which returned to the locale in 2007 after a 35-year absence. On Broadway, the **ESPN Zone**, so long a noisy multi-screen venue for sports-lovers, has now closed down; the vast **Toys 'R' Us** (1514 Broadway, at 44th Street, 1-800 869 7787) boasts a 60-foot indoor Ferris wheel and a two-floor Barbie emporium.

For more refined entertainments, head further uptown. Open since 1891, **Carnegie Hall** (*see p312*) has staged legendary shows by the likes of Judy Garland, Miles Davis and Yo-Yo Ma. Nearby is the famous **Carnegie Deli** (854 Seventh Avenue, at 55th Street; *see p206*), home to five-inch-tall pastrami and corned beef sandwiches.

West of the Theater District lies **Hell's Kitchen**. The precise origins of the name are unclear, but no doubt arose from its emergence as an Irish-mob-dominated neighbourhood in the 19th-century – the *New York Times* claims that the first known documented reference was in that very paper in 1881, to describe an unsavoury tenement in the locale. In the 1950s, clashes between Irish and recently arrived Puerto Rican factions were dramatised in the musical *West Side Story*. It was a particularly violent incident in 1959, in which two teenagers

reuse as a public space, the first phase of New York's first elevated public park finally opened in summer 2009 (www.thehighline.org).

Running from Gansevoort Street in the Meatpacking District (where groundbreaking for the downtown branch of the Whitney is scheduled for May 2011, with the museum's completion expected in 2015) to 20th Street, the gateway to Chelsea's gallery district, the slender, sinuous green strip has been designed by landscape architects James Corner Field Operations and architects Diller Scofidio + Renfro. As well as lawns, trees and plantings, it has several interesting features along the way. The next phase, from 20th to 30th Streets, is expected to be completed in summer 2011.

Commanding an expansive river view, the 'sun deck' between 14th and 15th Streets features wooden deck chairs that can be rolled along the original tracks, plus a water feature with benches for cooling your feet. The old Nabisco factory that houses Chelsea Market (*see p88*) received deliveries via the line; now the section cutting through the building is devoted to long-term, site-specific art.

Until June 2011, you'll be able to hear Stephen Vitello's *A Bell for Every Minute*, a sonic display that incorporates the recorded ringing of various New York church bells, the United Nations' Peace Bell and the New York Stock Exchange Bell among others; it can be heard between 13th and 14th Streets. Also during the year, sculptor Kim Beck will be installing three skeletal frames resembling the backs of billboards on roofs aligning the High Line in her exhibit *Space Available*. Bereft of actual advertisements, the structures are a poignant allusion to the economic recession.

At 17th Street, steps descend into a sunken amphitheatre with a glassed-over 'window' in the steel structure overlooking the avenue. Further along, look out for the Empire State Building rising above the skyline to the east.

But not all the views from the High Line have been welcome. Soon after the park opened, there were reports in the press of naked antics in the glass-fronted rooms of luxury hotel the Standard, which squats over the park at West 13th Street – in full view of the strollers below.

The High Line is open from to 7am to 10pm daily; the last entrance is 15 minutes before closing time.

FEEDING STATIONS

Places to stop for a bite en route.

Standard Grill. *See p199.*

Chelsea Market. *See p88.*

Cookshop. *See p199.*

SIGHTS

died, that led to an attempt by local businesses to erase the stigma associated with the area by renaming it Clinton (taken from a park named after one-time mayor DeWitt Clinton). The new name never really took, and gang culture survived until the 1980s.

Today, the area is emerging as the city's new queer neighbourhood. A mainly gay crowd frequents nightspots such as **Therapy** (*see p309*) and **Bartini** (*see p308*); theatregoers and locals of every persuasion sup at the profusion of eateries, including celebuchef Mario Batali's **Esca** (402 W 43rd Street, at Ninth Avenue, 1-212 564 7272, closed lunch Sun) and **5 Napkin Burger** (630 Ninth Avenue, at 45th Street).

As gentrification takes hold, new apartment blocks are springing up in the far western wasteland (when they will be occupied, given the current economic climate, remains to be seen). This area is dominated by the massive, black-glass **Jacob K Javits Convention Center** (Eleventh Avenue, between 34th & 39th Streets), host of a never-ending schedule of large-scale trade shows. A couple of major draws are also here: the **Circle Line Terminal**, at Pier 83, the departure point for the cruise company's three-hour circumnavigation of Manhattan Island (*see p56*), and the **Intrepid** (*see p98*), a retired aircraft carrier-cum-naval museum.

★ Intrepid Sea, Air & Space Museum

USS Intrepid, Pier 86, Twelfth Avenue & 46th Street (1-877 957 7447, www.intrepidmuseum.org). Subway A, C, E to 42nd Street-Port Authority, then M42 bus to Twelfth Avenue or 15min walk. **Open** *Apr-Sept* 10am-5pm Mon-Fri; 10am-6pm Sat, Sun. *Oct-Mar* 10am-5pm Tue-Sun. **Admission** $22; $17-$18 reductions; free under-3s, active military & retired US military. **Credit** AmEx, DC, Disc, MC, V. **Map** p404 B23.

Commissioned in 1943, this 27,000-ton, 898ft aircraft carrier survived torpedoes and kamikaze attacks in World War II, served during Vietnam and the Cuban Missile Crisis, and recovered two space capsules for NASA. The 'Fighting I' was finally decommissioned in 1974, but real-estate mogul Zachary Fisher saved it from the scrap yard by resurrecting it as an educational institution. On its flight deck and portside aircraft elevator are stationed top-notch examples of American military might, including the US Navy F-14 Tomcat (from *Top Gun*), an A-12 Blackbird spy plane and a fully restored Army AH-1G Cobra gunship helicopter. (Foreign powers are represented by a French Entendard IV-M, a Polish MiG-21, and the British Airways Concorde, among others.) Following a two-year, $8 million makeover, the museum has a new 12,240sq ft Exploreum featuring interactive exhibits, such as a Bell 47 helicopter you can sit in, while a recreated mess room and sleeping quarters evoke the on-board living conditions of the late 1960s.

Madame Tussauds New York

234 W 42nd Street, between Seventh & Eighth Avenues (1-800 246 8872, www.madame

Not Just the Ticket

Snagging cheap seats can be an entertaining experience.

People usually come to the Theater District to see two things: a Broadway show and the dazzling electronic spectacle of Times Square. The new **TKTS** discount-ticket booth (*see p347*), which has returned to Father Duffy Square after two and a half years at a temporary spot outside a nearby hotel, facilitates both. The word 'booth' doesn't do the structure justice: its 12 ticket windows are encased in a dramatic glass structure that was almost a decade in the making. The brainchild of Australians John Choi and Tai Ropiha, who won the globe-spanning competition for a new design in 1999, it was finally unveiled in October 2008.

An expansive red staircase, illuminated from below with LED technology to create a glowing effect, rises to the roof. Not only is the 'stairway to nowhere', as wags in the press dubbed it, a fittingly razzle-dazzle feature, it helps to solve the practical problem of slow-moving gawkers clogging up the streets. Part of a $19 million project in partnership with the Times Square Alliance to rebuild the square (doubling its size), the stairs are classified as city parkland and offer a place to relax and nosh on your own snacks; there are tables and chairs at street level as well as the 27 handy stoops. The 16-foot summit commands an uninterrupted view of the sweep of the illuminated Great White Way.

Uptown, **Lincoln Center** (*see p312*) has acquired a striking visitor space-cum-cut-price-ticket-facility of its own. Designed by Tod Williams Billie Tsien Architects, the

former Harmony Atrium (between W 62nd & W 63rd Streets, Broadway & Columbus Avenue) has been renamed in honour of patron of the arts and Lincoln Center vice chairman David Rubenstein and transformed into a contemporary interior garden with lush, planted walls and a fountain.

As well as free internet access and snacks from Tom Colicchio's 'Wichcraft, the **David Rubenstein Atrium** (open 8am-10pm Mon-Fri; 9am-10pm Sat, Sun) features a centralised box office where, for the first time, audiences can purchase same-day tickets to Lincoln Center performances, discounted by up to 50 per cent.

The space is the site of genre-spanning free concerts on Thursday nights (see www.lincolncenter.org for details). Performances by rising talent (some studying at the prestigious Juilliard School) will mingle on the schedule with high-profile residents such as the New York Philharmonic, New York City Opera and Jazz at Lincoln Center.

tussauds.com/newyork). Subway A, C, E to 42nd Street-Port Authority; N, Q, R, S, 1, 2, 3, 7 to 42nd Street-Times Square. **Open** 10am-8pm Mon-Thur, Sun; 10am-10pm Fri, Sat. **Admission** $35.50; $28.50-$32.50 reductions; free under-3s. **Credit** AmEx, DC, MC, V. **Map** p404 D24.
With roots in 18th-century Paris and founded in London in 1802, the world's most famous wax museum now draws celebrity-hungry crowds to nine locations worldwide. At the New York outpost, you can get a stalker's-eye view of paraffin doppelgangers of political, sports, film and pop stars, from Miley Cyrus to Barack Obama. A new crop of freshly waxed victims debuts every few months.

Ripley's Believe It or Not! Odditorium

234 W 42nd Street, between Seventh & Eighth Avenues (1-212 398 3133, www.ripleysnewyork.com). Subway A, C, E to 42nd Street-Port Authority; N, Q, R, S, 1, 2, 3, 7 to 42nd Street-Times Square. **Open** 9am-1am daily (last entry midnight). **Admission** $34.73; $27.11 reductions; free under-4s. **Credit** AmEx, DC, MC, V. **Map** p404 D24.
Times Square might be a little whitewashed these days, but you can get a feel for the old freak show at this repository of the eerie and uncanny. Items on display include a two-headed goat, a 3,000lb meteorite, medieval torture devices and the largest collection of shrunken heads in the developed world.

FIFTH AVENUE & AROUND

Subway B, D, F, M, N, Q, R to 34th Street-Herald Square; B, D, F, M to 47-50th Streets-Rockefeller Center; E, M to Fifth Avenue-53rd Street; 7 to Fifth Avenue.

The stretch of Fifth Avenue between Rockefeller Center and Central Park South showcases retail palaces bearing names that were famous long before the concept of branding was developed. Bracketed by **Saks Fifth Avenue** (49th to 50th Streets; *see p233*) and **Bergdorf Goodman** (at 58th Street; *see p231*), tenants include Chanel, Gucci, Prada and Tiffany & Co. Along with Madison Avenue uptown, this is the centre of high-end shopping in New York, and the window displays – particularly during the frenetic Christmas shopping season – are worth a look even if you don't have the cash to splash.

Fifth Avenue is crowned by Grand Army Plaza at 59th Street, presided over by a gilded statue of General William Tecumseh Sherman. To the west stands the **Plaza** (*see p174*), the famous hotel that was home to fictional moppet Eloise. Just south, above 59th Street (the parkside stretch is called Central Park South), is **Central Park** (*see p106*).

Fifth Avenue is the main route for the city's many public processions: the **St Patrick's Day Parade** (*see p268*), the **LGBT Pride March** (*see p263*) and many others. Even without floats or marching bands, the sidewalks are generally teeming with gawking tourists, fashion victims and society matrons. The most famous skyscraper in the world also has its entrance on Fifth Avenue: the **Empire State Building** (*see p101*), located smack-bang in the centre of Midtown.

INSIDE TRACK THE 21 CLUB

A former speakeasy during the Prohibition Era, the **21 Club** (21 W 52nd Street, between Fifth & Sixth Avenues) has since gone decidedly legit and acquired a much loftier profile. Presidents (Roosevelt, Kennedy, Nixon) and Hollywood aristocracy (Frank Sinatra, Marilyn Monroe, Elizabeth Taylor) have supped here over the years. The club has also been widely featured on the screen, most notably in *All About Eve*, *Sweet Smell of Success*, *Sex and the City*, *Wall Street*, and *Manhattan Murder Mystery*

A pair of impassive stone lions, which were dubbed Patience and Fortitude by Mayor Fiorello La Guardia during the Great Depression, guard the steps of the beautiful Beaux Arts humanities and social sciences branch of the **New York Public Library** (*see p102*) at 42nd Street, now officially named the Stephen A Schwarzman Building. Just behind the library is **Bryant Park**, a well-manicured lawn that hosts a popular outdoor film series in summer (*see p290* **Inside Track**) and an ice-skating rink in winter (*see p345*).

The luxury **Bryant Park Hotel** (*see p175*) occupies the former American Radiator Building on 40th Street. Designed by architect Raymond Hood in the mid 1920s, the structure is faced with near-black brick and trimmed in gold leaf. Alexander Woollcott, Dorothy Parker and her 'vicious circle' held court and traded barbs at the nearby **Algonquin** (*see p174*); the lobby is still a great place to meet for a drink. Just north of the park, on Sixth Avenue, is the always thought-provoking **International Center of Photography** (*see p100*).

Step off Fifth Avenue into **Rockefeller Center** (*see p102*) and you'll find yourself in a 'city within a city', an interlacing complex of 19 buildings housing corporate offices, retail space and the popular Rockefeller Plaza. After plans for an expansion of the Metropolitan Opera on the site fell through in 1929, John D Rockefeller Jr set about creating the complex to house radio and television corporations. Designed by Raymond Hood and many other prominent architects, Rock Center grew over the decades, with each new building conforming to the original master plan and art deco design.

On weekday mornings, a (tourist-dominated) crowd gathers at the NBC network's glass-walled, ground-level studio (where the *Today* show is shot), at the south-west corner of Rockefeller Plaza and 49th Street. The complex is also home to art auction house **Christie's** (20 Rockefeller Plaza, 49th Street, between Fifth & Sixth Avenues, 1-212 636 2000, www.christies.com, usually closed Sat & Sun); pop into the lobby to admire a mural by conceptualist Sol LeWitt.

When it opened on Sixth Avenue (at 50th Street) in 1932, **Radio City Music Hall** (*see p327*) was designed as a showcase for high-end variety acts, but the death of vaudeville led to a quick transition into what was then the world's largest movie house. Today, the art deco jewel hosts concerts and a traditional Christmas Spectacular featuring renowned precision dance troupe the Rockettes. Visitors can get a peek backstage, and meet one of the high-kicking dancers, on the Stage Door tour (every 30mins, 11am-3pm daily; $18, $10-$15 reductions; see www.radiocity.com for details).

Facing Rockefeller Center is the beautiful **St Patrick's Cathedral** (*see p104*). Famous couples from F Scott and Zelda Fitzgerald to Liza Minnelli and David Gest have tied the knot here; funeral services for such notables as Andy Warhol and baseball legend Joe DiMaggio have been held in its confines. A few blocks north is a clutch of museums, including the **Museum of Modern Art** (MoMa; *see p102*), the **American Folk Art Museum** (*see below*) and the **Paley Center for Media** (*see p102*).

American Folk Art Museum

45 W 53rd Street, between Fifth & Sixth Avenues (1-212 265 1040, www.folkartmuseum.org). Subway E, M to Fifth Avenue-53rd Street. **Open** 10.30am-5.30pm Tue-Thur, Sat, Sun; 10.30am-7.30pm Fri. **Admission** $12; $8 reductions; free under-12s. Free to all 5.30-7.30pm Fri. **Credit** AmEx, DC, Disc, MC, V. **Map** p404 E22.

The Museum of Modern Art's next-door neighbour celebrates the work of self-taught artists and traditional crafts such as pottery, quilting, woodwork and jewellery design. Recently, the museum has sought to broaden the public perception of outsider art through its temporary exhibitions, such as 'Quilts: Masterworks from the American Folk Art Museum' (until 16 Oct 2011).

The museum's smaller, original Lincoln Center location now houses a satellite gallery and gift shop. Here, the '9/11 National Tribute Quilt', a gargantuan eight-by-30-ft-long quilt consisting of 3,466 blocks in six panels is on permanent display.

Other locations 2 Lincoln Square, Columbus Avenue, at 66th Street, Upper West Side (1-212 595 9533).

> **INSIDE TRACK**
> **EMPIRE STATE EXPRESS**
>
> If you're visiting the **Empire State Building** *(see right)*, allow at least two hours for queueing and viewing. To save time, bypass one of three lines by buying tickets online (the others, for security and entry, are unavoidable), and visit late at night, when most sightseers have turned in. Alternatively, springing for an express pass ($45) allows you to cut to the front.

★ Empire State Building

350 Fifth Avenue, between 33rd & 34th Streets (1-212 736 3100, www.esbnyc.com). Subway B, D, F, M, N, Q, R to 34th Street-Herald Square. **Open** 8am-2am daily (last lift at 1.15am). **Admission** *86th floor* $20; $14-$18 reductions; free under-6s. *102nd floor* add $15. **Credit** AmEx, DC, Disc, MC, V. **Map** p404 E25.

Financed by General Motors executive John J Raskob at the height of New York's skyscraper race, the Empire State sprang up in a mere 14 months, weeks ahead of schedule and $5 million under budget. Since its opening in 1931, it's been immortalised in countless photos and films, from the original *King Kong* to *Sleepless in Seattle*. Following the destruction of the World Trade Center in 2001, the 1,250ft tower resumed its title as New York's tallest building; the nocturnal colour scheme of the tower lights often honours holidays, charities or special events.

The enclosed observatory on the 102nd floor is the city's highest lookout point, but the panoramic deck on the 86th floor, 1,050ft above the street, is roomier. From here, you can enjoy views of all five boroughs and five neighbouring states (when the skies are clear, of course); at sunset, you can glimpse an elongated urban shadow cast from Manhattan all the way across the river to Queens.

International Center of Photography

1133 Sixth Avenue, at 43rd Street (1-212 857 0000, www.icp.org). Subway B, D, F, M, 7 to 42nd Street-Bryant Park; N, Q, R, S, 1, 2, 3, 7 to 42nd Street-Times Square. **Open** 10am-6pm Tue-Thur, Sat, Sun; 10am-8pm Fri. **Admission** $12; $8 reductions; free under-12s. Pay what you wish 5-8pm Fri. **Credit** AmEx, DC, Disc, MC, V. **Map** p404 D24.

Since 1974, the ICP has served as a pre-eminent library, school and museum devoted to the photographic image. Photojournalism remains a vital facet of the centre's programme, which also includes contemporary photos and video. Exhibits in 2011 include 'Signs of Life: Photographs by Peter Sekaer' and 'Hiroshima' (both on view until August 28).

Walk Mad Men in Midtown

Stroll through the sharp-dressed, hard-drinking world of the retro TV series.

Before you get started, suit up! You can't properly be a Mad Man without a grey flannel suit and a skinny tie, so start at **Bloomingdale's** (1000 Third Avenue, between 59th & 60th Streets; *see p231*). If you suffer from buyer's remorse, the store's return policy is generous – although when smarmy Pete Campbell returned a chip 'n' dip here in season one, it cost him his sense of manhood.

We don't want to encourage you to buy a pack of Lucky Strikes, Don Draper's smoke of choice (emphysema never looked so dapper!), so cross the street to pick up some retro candy cigarettes at sugar superstore **Dylan's Candy Bar** (1011 Third Avenue, at 60th Street, 1-646 735 0078). At less than a buck a box, they're a lot cheaper than the real thing. With the 'smoking' comes the drinking, so take a right on Third and stop by **PJ Clarke's** (915 Third Avenue, between 55th & 56th Streets, 1-212 317 1616), where the younger Sterling Cooperites celebrated Peggy's writing achievement.

The **Museum of Modern Art** (11 W 53rd Street, between Fifth & Sixth Avenues; *see p102*) is just a few blocks away. Browse staples of the early '60s such as photorealism and Andy Warhol's pop art paintings, which more or less prove what you've been saying for years: advertising is an art form.

By now it would be wise to stop by the office before Roger Sterling and Bertram Cooper get suspicious, so retrace your steps east to Madison and head south. Step into the lobby of the fictional Sterling Cooper offices at 405 Madison Avenue (between 47th & 48th Streets) – good thing you wore that suit!

Continue south and hang a left on 42nd Street to grab dinner at the **Grand Central Oyster Bar** (89 E 42nd Street, at Park Avenue; *see p207*), inside the terminal, iconic scenes – Don dupes boss Roger into a clam-eating/vodka-drinking contest before the latter famously vomits in front of clients. The super-fresh bivalves here shouldn't leave you with an upset stomach, but the third round of martinis might.

Exit the terminal on Lexington Avenue and head north, before turning left at 45th Street and back to Madison and the **Roosevelt Hotel** (45 E 45th Street, at Madison Avenue, 1-212 661 9600). This was Don's crash pad after Betty kicked him out. Even if you're not spending the night, hop into the Madison Club Lounge for (you guessed it) more drinks.

★ Museum of Modern Art (MoMA)

11 W 53rd Street, between Fifth & Sixth Avenues (1-212 708 9400, www.moma.org). Subway E, M to Fifth Avenue-53rd Street. **Open** 10.30am-5.30pm Mon, Wed, Thur, Sat, Sun; 10.30am-8pm Fri; 10.30am-8.45pm 1st Thur of each mth & every Thur in July & Aug. **Admission** (incl admission to film programmes) $20; $12-$16 reductions; free under-17s. Free to all 4-8pm Fri. **Credit** AmEx, DC, MC, V. **Map** p404 E23.

After a two-year renovation based on a design by Japanese architect Yoshio Taniguchi, MoMA reopened in 2004 with almost double the space to display some of the most impressive artworks from the 19th, 20th and 21st centuries. The museum's permanent collection now encompasses seven curatorial departments: Architecture and Design, Drawings, Film, Media, Painting and Sculpture, Photography, and Prints and Illustrated Books. Highlights include Picasso's *Les Demoiselles d'Avignon*, Dalí's *The Persistence of Memory* and Van Gogh's *The Starry Night* as well as masterpieces by Giacometti, Hopper, Matisse, Monet, O'Keefe, Pollock, Rothko, Warhol and many others. Outside, the Philip Johnson-designed Abby Aldrich Rockefeller Sculpture Garden contains works by Calder, Rodin and Moore. The destination museum also contains a destination restaurant: the Modern, which overlooks the garden; if the prices are too steep, dine in the bar, which shares the kitchen.

Exhibitions for 2011 include 'German Expressionism: The Graphic Impulse' (until 11 July), 'Impressions from South Africa: Printed Art/1960s to Now' (until Aug 2011), 'Projects 96: Haris Epaminonda' (23 Nov-20 Feb 2012), devoted to the works of the Berlin-based photo-collagist, and Sanja Ivekovic: Sweet Violence (18 Dec-26 Mar 2012), the first American museum exhibit of the Croatian video pioneer.

► *For the affiliated MoMA-P.S.1 Contemporary Art Center in Queens, see p139.*

★ FREE New York Public Library

Fifth Avenue at 42nd Street (1-212 930 0830, www.nypl.org). Subway B, D, F, M to 42nd Street-Bryant Park; 7 to Fifth Avenue. **Open** 10am-6pm Mon, Thur-Sat; 10am-8pm Tue, Wed; 1-5pm Sun (see website for gallery hours). **Admission** free. **Map** p404 E24.

See p103 **Profile**.

► *For readings at the library, see p270.*

INSIDE TRACK GRAND CENTRAL'S WHISPERING ARCH

The archway just outside the **Grand Central Oyster Bar & Restaurant** *(see p207)* in Grand Central Terminal creates an interesting acoustical trick. Stand in one corner and whisper a message to a friend standing diagonally across from you. Because of the unique design of the low ceramic arches, it will sound as if you're next to each other.

Paley Center for Media

25 W 52nd Street, between Fifth & Sixth Avenues (1-212 621 6600, www.paleycenter.org). Subway B, D, F, M to 47-50th Streets-Rockefeller Center; E, M to Fifth Avenue-53rd Street. **Open** noon-6pm Wed, Fri-Sun; noon-8pm Thur. **Admission** $10; $5-$8 reductions. **No credit cards**. **Map** p404 E23.

Nirvana for telly addicts and pop-culture junkies, the Paley Center (formerly the Museum of Television & Radio) houses an immense archive of almost 150,000 radio and TV shows. Head to the fourth-floor library to search the system for your favourite episode of *Star Trek*, *Seinfeld*, or rarer fare, then walk down one flight to your assigned console. (The radio listening room operates in the same fashion.) A theatre on the concourse level is the site of frequent screenings, premières and high-profile panel discussions.

★ Rockefeller Center

From 48th to 51st Streets, between Fifth & Sixth Avenues (NBC Studio Tours 1-212 664 3700/7174, Top of the Rock 1-877 692 7625, www.rockefellercenter.com). Subway B, D, F, M to 47-50th Streets-Rockefeller Center. **Open** 7am-11pm daily. *Tours* hourly (except 2pm) 10am-4pm daily. *Observation deck* 8am-midnight daily (last lift at 11pm). **Admission** *Rockefeller Center tours* $15 (under-6s not admitted). *NBC Studio tours* $19.25; $16.25 reductions (under-6s not admitted). *Observation deck* $21; $14-$19 reductions; free under-6s. **Credit** AmEx, DC, Disc, MC, V. **Map** p404 E23.

Constructed under the aegis of industrialist John D Rockefeller in the 1930s, this art deco city-within-a-city is inhabited by NBC, Simon & Schuster, McGraw-Hill and other media giants, as well as Radio City Music Hall, Christie's auction house, and an underground shopping arcade. Guided tours of the entire complex are available daily, and there's a separate NBC Studio tour (call the number above or see website for details).

The buildings and grounds are embellished with works by several well-known artists; look out for Isamu Noguchi's stainless-steel relief, *News*, above the entrance to 50 Rockefeller Plaza, and José Maria Sert's mural *American Progress* in the lobby of 30 Rockefeller Plaza (also known as the GE Building). But the most breathtaking sights are those seen from the 70th-floor Top of the Rock observation deck (combined tour/observation deck tickets are available). In the cold-weather months, the Plaza's sunken courtyard – eternally guarded by Paul Manship's bronze statue of Prometheus – transforms into a picturesque, if crowded, ice-skating rink (*see p345*).

Profile New York Public Library

Heaven for serious bibliophiles.

Guarded by the marble lions *Patience* and *Fortitude*, the main branch of the New York Public Library presents an imposing Beaux-Arts façade that almost belies its mission as a facilitator of learning and an intellectual stimulus. Designed by Carrère and Hastings (who also saw to the chandeliers, tables, chairs and even the wastebaskets), the library was the largest marble edifice in the United States upon its completion in 1911, following 16 years of construction.

In 2008, it was renamed in honour of philanthropist Stephen A Schwarzman, yet Gothamites still know it as the New York Public Library. (The entire NYPL system has 87 branches, spread out over Manhattan, the Bronx and Staten Island; Brooklyn and Queens have their own library systems.) Free hour-long tours (11am and 2pm Mon-Sat; 2pm Sun) are a terrific means of getting to know this vast library and its collections.

The highlight of the building is the enormous Rose Main Reading Room on the third floor, which was restored in 1998. It's 78 feet wide by 297 feet long and 51 feet high (24 metres by 91 metres by 16 metres); almost as large as a football field and divided into two large halls. Its 42 oak tables can seat as many as 16 readers each, and it is not surprising to see most of them full, particularly at weekends. Some 88 miles of bookshelf space lurk below the reading room in eight levels of stacks; another 40 miles of shelving was recently added under Bryant Park just behind the library. Patrons first visit the Bill Blass Public Catalog to find the call numbers of the books they desire then present call slips to staff in the Reading Room, where the books are then brought.

Among the untold thousands who have used the main branch since it opened are Francis Ford Coppola, Princess Grace, Isaac Bashevis Singer, Marlene Dietrich, John Updike and Somerset Maugham. Leon Trotsky spent much of his three-month stay in New York in 1917 here before hightailing it back to Russia to be in time for the revolution.

The specialist collections at the main branch include the Map Division (Room 117), containing some 431,000 maps and 16,000 atlases; the Rare Books Division (Room 328), boasting Walt Whitman's personal copies of the first (1855) and third (1860) editions of *Leaves of Grass*; and the Children's Center (Room 84), home to the original Winnie-the-Pooh, Eeyore, Piglet and Tigger that Christopher Robin Milne played with.

And when you're done with them, you can always play with *Patience* and *Fortitude* on the steps outside.

★ FREE St Patrick's Cathedral

Fifth Avenue, between 50th & 51st Streets (1-212 753 2261, www.saintpatrickscathedral.org). Subway B, D, F, M to 47-50th Streets-Rockefeller Center; E, M to Fifth Avenue-53rd Street. **Open** 6.30am-8.45pm daily. **Admission** free. **Map** p404 E23.

The largest Catholic church in America, St Patrick's counts presidents, business leaders and movie stars among its past and present parishioners. The Gothic-style façade features intricate white-marble spires, but equally impressive is the interior, including the Louis Tiffany-designed altar, solid bronze baldachin, and the rose window by stained-glass master Charles Connick.

► *Further uptown is another awe-inspiring house of worship, the Cathedral of St John the Divine; see p119.*

MIDTOWN EAST

Subway E, M to Lexington Avenue-53rd Street; S, 4, 5, 6, 7 to 42nd Street-Grand Central; 6 to 51st Street.

Shopping, dining and entertainment options wane east of Fifth Avenue in the 40s and 50s. However, the area is home to many iconic landmarks and world-class architecture.

The 1913 **Grand Central Terminal** (*see p105*) is the city's most spectacular point of arrival, although these days it only welcomes commuter trains from Connecticut and upstate New York. Looming behind the terminal, the **MetLife Building** (formerly the Pan Am Building) was the world's largest office tower when it opened in the 1960s. On Park Avenue is the famed **Waldorf-Astoria** hotel (*see p177*), formerly located on Fifth Avenue but rebuilt here in 1931 after the original was demolished to make way for the Empire State Building. Other must-see buildings in the vicinity include **Lever House** (390 Park Avenue, between 53rd & 54th Streets), the **Seagram Building** (375 Park Avenue, between 52nd & 53rd Streets), the slanted-roofed **Citicorp Center** (from 53rd Street to 54th Street, between Lexington & Third Avenues) and the stunning art deco skyscraper that anchors the corner of Lexington Avenue and 51st Street, formerly the **General Electric Building** (and before that, the RCA Victor Building). A Chippendale crown tops the **Sony Building** (550 Madison Avenue, between 55th & 56th Streets), Philip Johnson's postmodern icon.

East 42nd Street has a wealth of architectural distinction, including the Romanesque Revival hall of the former **Bowery Savings Bank**

Urban Myths
The Mole People of Grand Central Terminal

The story behind the legend.

New York City saw an alarming rise in homelessness in the 1980s and early '90s. With shelters overflowing, thousands sought refuge in the subway system and abandoned railway lines, like the Freedom Tunnel running beneath Riverside Park.

Their plight was recounted in Jennifer Toth's *The Mole People: Life in the Tunnels Beneath New York City* (1993), based on her subterranean explorations and anecdotes from tunnel dwellers she met. What emerged was an almost Dickensian vision of underground communities, some as large as two hundred people. According to Toth, six levels below Grand Central Terminal an ordered community existed in one of the abandoned tunnels, getting hot water from a steam pipe and siphoning off the station's electricity – the enclave even had a laundry and an exercise room. A teacher attended to the community's children, while 'runners' were charged with going above ground to scavenge for food.

Although the book proved popular, it also met with considerable scepticism, largely because so much of Toth's work was based on anecdotal accounts from homeless people that could not be verified. Experts on the train system were most dismissive. They insisted that many of Toth's descriptions of stations and tunnels were inaccurate; the tunnels below Grand Central, for example, are very well documented and only consist of two levels. When pressed, the author referred doubters to a woman who spent time in the tunnels – yet rather than corroborating it, Toth's source actually contested portions of the book.

Whatever the truth of *The Mole People*, the problem of homelessness in New York City remains all too real and many people do indeed end up living underground. But perhaps the true nature of these subterranean communities requires a more thorough excavation.

(no.110) and the art deco details of the **Chanin Building** (no.122). Completed in 1930 by architect William Van Alen, the gleaming **Chrysler Building** (at Lexington Avenue) is a pinnacle of art deco architecture, paying homage to the automobile with vast radiator-cap eagles in lieu of traditional gargoyles and a brickwork relief sculpture of racing cars complete with chrome hubcaps. The **Daily News Building** (no.220), another art deco gem designed by Raymond Hood, was immortalised in the *Superman* films. Although the namesake tabloid no longer has its offices here (it moved to 33rd Street in the 1990s), the lobby still houses its giant globe and weather instruments.

To the east lies the literally elevated **Tudor City** (between First & Second Avenues from E 41st to E 43rd Streets), a pioneering 1925 residential development that resembles high-rise versions of England's Hampton Court Palace. The enclave features a charming park, perfect for a respite from the rush of traffic. At the end of 43rd Street is a terrace overlooking, and stairs leading down to, the **United Nations Headquarters** (*see right*). Not far from here is the **Japan Society** (*see below*).

FREE Grand Central Terminal

From 42nd to 44th Streets, between Vanderbilt & Lexington Avenues (tours 1-212 340 2347, www.grandcentralterminal.com). Subway S, 4, 5, 6, 7 to 42nd Street-Grand Central. **Map** p404 E24.

Each day, the world's most famous terminal sees more than 750,000 people shuffle through its Beaux Arts threshold, but not all of them are commuters. After its 1998 renovation, the terminal metamorphosed from a mere transport hub into a destination in itself, with decent shopping and first-rate drinking and dining options such as the Campbell Apartment lounge (located off the West Balcony, 1-212 953 0409) and the Grand Central Oyster Bar & Restaurant (*see p207*).

Don't forget to look up when you're inside the station's 80,000sq ft main concourse. French painter Paul Helleu's astronomical ceiling painting depicts the Mediterranean sky complete with 2,500 stars (some of which are illuminated). Various tour options are available (see website for details); we recommend veteran guide Justin Ferate's free Friday walking tour of Grand Central and its environs (*see p61*).

▶ *For trains from Grand Central, see p373.*

Japan Society

333 E 47th Street, between First & Second Avenues (1-212 832 1155, www.japansociety.org). Subway E, M to Lexington Avenue-53rd Street; 6 to 51st Street. **Open** hours vary; *gallery* 11am-6pm Tue-Thur; 11am-9pm Fri; 11am-5pm Sat, Sun. **Admission** $12; $10 reductions; free under-16s. Free to all 6-9pm Fri. **Credit** AmEx, DC, Disc, MC, V. **Map** p404 F23.

INSIDE TRACK
CRACK(POT) SHOT

In 1967, Andy Warhol moved his Factory from Midtown to the Decker Building, at 33 Union Square West, ostensibly to be nearer to Max's Kansas City cub. So-called because the process for creating his famous silkscreens suggested an assembly line, the Factory was also the scene of legendary debauched parties and the set of Warhol's experimental films. On 3 June 1968, Valerie Solanas, the disturbed author of the *SCUM Manifesto* (which advocated killing all males) and *Up Your Ass*, a play Warhol had briefly expressed an interest in producing before misplacing the script, shot Andy three times in the lobby of the Factory. Warhol survived, and Solanas spent three years in a psychiatric ward. More than a decade after both had died, *Up Your Ass* made it to the stage for a brief run in 2000.

Founded in 1907, the Japan Society moved into its current home, complete with waterfall and bamboo garden, in 1971. Designed by Junzo Yoshimura, it was the first contemporary Japanese building in New York. The gallery mounts temporary exhibitions on such diverse subjects as the art of anime, manga, video games and textile design. In 2011, look out for 'Bye Bye Kitty!!! Between Heaven and Hell in Contemporary Japanese Art' (until 12 June 2011), exploring the works of a new generation of Japanese artists, and 'Deco Japan: Shaping Modern Culture, 1920-1945' (March 2012-June 2012), the first exhibition in the West dedicated to Japanese art deco.

United Nations Headquarters

Visitors' entrance: First Avenue, at 46th Street (tours 1-212 963 8687, www.un.org/tours). Subway S, 4, 5, 6, 7 to 42nd Street-Grand Central. **Tours** 9.45am-4.45pm Mon-Fri; 10am-4.15pm Sat, Sun (escorted audio tour only). **Admission** $16; $9-$11 reductions (under-5s not admitted). **Credit** AmEx, Disc, MC, V. **Map** p404 G24.

Step inside this 18-acre complex and you'll no longer be in New York City – the UN is technically international territory under the jurisdiction of member countries. The Secretariat building, designed by Le Corbusier, is off limits, and the Security Council Chamber is under renovation until at least 2013, but 45-minute public tours discuss the history of the UN and architecture within the complex, visit the General Assembly Hall, and highlight art and objects given by member nations. Visitors can sup from the buffet in the Delegates Dining Room (fourth floor, 1-212 963 7626), which is open to the public 11.30am-2.30pm Mon-Fri (reservations required).

Uptown

Head north for high culture and Harlem hotspots.

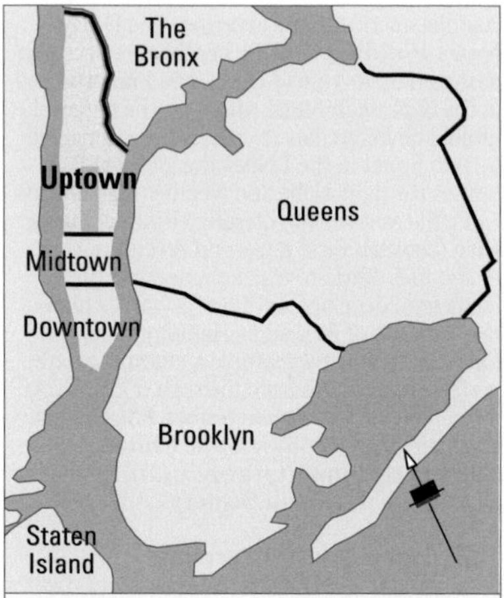

In the early 19th century, the largely rural area above 59th Street was a bucolic getaway for locals living in Manhattan's southern neighbourhoods. Today, much of uptown still feels comparatively serene, thanks largely to **Central Park** and the presence of a number of New York's premier cultural institutions.

Although New York's super-rich have made their gilded nests all over town, the air of old money is most palpable on the **Upper East Side**, where exclusive streets are kept clean by hose-wielding liveried doormen while socialites drift in and out of **Madison Avenue**'s designer flagships. The area also plays host to some of the world's finest museums. Across the park, the **Upper West Side**, hitherto known more for cultural refinement than ostentation, is now home to equally fashionable addresses as well as Lincoln Center. Further north lies **Harlem**, America's most iconic African-American neighbourhood. A dangerous no-go area for visitors in the 1960s and '70s, it has undergone a remarkable renewal over the last decade and features well-preserved architecture and a vibrant nightlife.

The Bronx
Uptown
Queens
Midtown
Downtown
Brooklyn
Staten Island

Map pp405-409
Hotels p178
Restaurants & cafés p207
Bars p225

SIGHTS

CENTRAL PARK

Numerous subway stations on multiple lines.

In 1858, the newly formed Central Park Commission chose landscape designer Frederick Law Olmsted and architect Calvert Vaux to turn a vast tract of rocky swampland into a rambling oasis of lush greenery. Inspired by the great parks of London and Paris, the Commission imagined a place that would provide city dwellers with respite from the crowded streets. It was a noble thought, but one that required the eviction of 1,600 mostly poor or immigrant inhabitants, including residents of Seneca Village, the city's oldest African-American settlement. Still, clear the area they did: when it was completed in 1873, it became the first man-made public park in the US.

Although it suffered from neglect at various points in the 20th century (most recently in the 1970s and '80s, when it gained a reputation as a dangerous spot after dark), the park has been returned to its green glory thanks largely to the Central Park Conservancy. Since this not-for-profit civic group was formed in 1980, it's been instrumental in the park's restoration and maintenance.

The 1872 Gothic Revival **Dairy** (located midpark at 65th Street, 1-212 794 6564, www.centralparknyc.org, open 10am-5pm daily) houses the Central Park Conservancy's information centre and gift shop; there are additional staffed information booths dotted around the park.

The southern section abounds with family-friendly diversions, including the **Central Park Zoo** (*see p108*), between 63rd & 66th

Streets, the **Friedsam Memorial Carousel** (*see p277*) and the **Trump Wollman Rink** (midpark, at 62nd Street; *see p345*), which doubles as a small children's amusement park in the warmer months (*see p277*).

Come summer, kites, Frisbees and soccer balls seem to fly every which way across **Sheep Meadow**, the designated quiet zone that begins at 66th Street. Sheep did indeed graze here until 1934, but they've since been replaced by sunbathers improving their tans and scoping out the throngs. In the former shepherd's residence, the landmark restaurant **Tavern on the Green** (Central Park West, at 67th Street) closed in 2009 after its long-term owners declared bancruptcy. At the time of writing, it has been given over to a visitor centre and gift shop while the park hopes a new restaurant will take over the location. East of Sheep Meadow, between 66th and 72nd Streets, is the **Mall**, an elm-lined promenade that attracts street performers and in-line skaters. And just east of the Mall's Naumburg Bandshell is Rumsey Playfield – site of the annual **Central Park SummerStage** series (*see p262*), an eclectic roster of free and benefit concerts.

One of the most popular meeting places (and loveliest spots) in the park is north of here, overlooking the lake: the grand **Bethesda Fountain & Terrace**, near the midpoint of the 72nd Street Transverse Road. *Angel of the Waters*, the sculpture in the centre of the fountain, was created by Emma Stebbins, the first woman to be granted a major public art commission in New York.

Be sure to admire the Minton-tiled ceiling of the ornate passageway that connects the plaza around the fountain to the Mall – after years of neglect in storage, the tiles, designed by Jacob Wrey Mould, were restored and reinstated in 2007. Mould also designed the intricate carved ornamentation of the stairways leading down to the fountain.

To the west of the fountain, near the West 72nd Street entrance, sits **Strawberry Fields**, which memorialise John Lennon, who lived in, and was shot in front of, the nearby Dakota Building (*see p117*). Also called the International Garden of Peace, it features a mosaic of the word 'imagine' that was donated by the city of Naples. More than 160 species of flowers and plants from all over the world bloom here, strawberries among them. Just north of the fountain is the **Loeb Boathouse** (midpark, at 75th Street). From here, you can take a rowing boat or a gondola out on the lake, which is crossed by the elegant Bow Bridge. The Loeb houses the **Central Park Boathouse Restaurant** (Central Park Lake, park entrance on Fifth Avenue, at 72nd Street,

Central Park.

1-212 517 2233, www.thecentralparkboathouse.com, closed dinner Sat & Sun Nov-Mar), and lake views make it a lovely place for brunch or drinks.

Further north, the popular **Belvedere Castle**, a restored Victorian folly, sits atop the park's second-highest peak. Besides offering excellent views and a terrific setting for a picnic, it also houses the **Henry Luce Nature Observatory** (*see p277*). The nearby Delacorte Theater hosts **Shakespeare in the Park** (*see p359*), a summer run of free open-air performances of plays by the Bard and others. Further north still sits the **Great Lawn** (midpark, between 79th & 85th Streets), a sprawling stretch of grass that doubles as a rallying point for political protests and a concert spot for just about any act that can attract six-figure audiences. At other times, it's put to use by seriously competitive soccer, baseball and softball teams. East of the Great

INSIDE TRACK
EYEING THE NEEDLE

The Central Park **Obelisk** (*see p108*), the only one in the entire Western Hemisphere, is best viewed from the Petrie European Sculpture Court in the Metropolitan Museum.

Lawn, behind the **Metropolitan Museum of Art** (*see p114*), is the **Obelisk**, a 69-foot (21-metre) granite hieroglyphics-covered monument dating from around 1500 BC, which was given to the US by the Khedive of Egypt in 1881.

In the mid 1990s, the **Reservoir** (midpark, between 85th & 96th Streets) was renamed in honour of the late Jacqueline Kennedy Onassis, who used to jog around it. Whether you prefer a running or walking pace, a turn here commands great views of the East and West Sides as well as midtown; in spring the cherry trees that ring the reservoir path and the bridle path below it make it particularly beautiful.

In the northern section, the exquisite **Conservatory Garden** (entrance on Fifth Avenue, at 105th Street) comprises formal gardens inspired by English, French and Italian styles. At the top of the park, next to the Harlem Meer, the **Charles A Dana Discovery Center** (entrance at Malcolm X Boulevard/Lenox Avenue, at 110th Street, 1-212 860 1370, www.centralparknyc.org, closed Mon Apr-Oct, Mon & Tue Nov-Mar) operates a roster of activities and events and lends out fishing rods and bait (for 'catch and release fishing') from April to October. Prospective fishermen need to take photo ID.

Central Park Zoo

830 Fifth Avenue, between 63rd & 66th Streets (1-212 439 6500, www.centralparkzoo.org). Subway N, R to Fifth Avenue-59th Street. **Open** *Apr-Oct* 10am-5pm Mon-Fri; 10am-5.30pm Sat, Sun. *Nov-Mar* 10am-4.30pm daily. **Admission** $12; $7-$9 reductions; free under-3s (under-16s must be accompanied by an adult). **Credit** AmEx, DC, Disc, MC, V. **Map** p405 E21.

A collection of animals has been kept in Central Park since the 1860s. But in its current form, Central Park Zoo dates only from 1988. Around 130 species inhabit its 6.5-acre corner of the park, polar bears and penguins among them. A new habitat dedicated to the endangered snow leopard opened in 2009. The Tisch Children's Zoo houses more than 30 species that enjoy being petted, and the roving characters on the George Delacorte Musical Clock – perched atop a brick arcade between both zoos – delight hordes of children every half-hour.

UPPER EAST SIDE

Subway F to Lexington Avenue-63rd Street; 4, 5, 6 to 86th Street; 6 to 68th Street-Hunter College, 77th Street, 96th Street or 103rd Street.

Gorgeous pre-war apartments owned by blue-blooded socialites, soigné restaurants filled with Botoxed-ladies-who-lunch, the deluxe boutiques of international designers… this is the clichéd image of the **Upper East Side**, and you'll see a lot of supporting evidence on Fifth, Madison and Park Avenues.

Encouraged by the opening of Central Park in the late 19th century, the city's more affluent residents began building mansions along Fifth Avenue. By the start of the 20th century, even the superwealthy had warmed to the idea of giving up their large homes for smaller quarters provided they were near the park, which resulted in the construction of many new apartment blocks and hotels. Working-class folk later settled around Second and Third Avenues, following construction of an elevated East Side train line (now defunct), but affluence remained the neighbourhood's dominant characteristic.

Along Fifth, Madison and Park Avenues, from 59th to 90th Streets, you'll see great old mansions, many of which are now foreign consulates, and stretches of restored carriage houses on the side streets. The 1916 limestone structure at 820 Fifth Avenue (at 63rd Street) was one of the earliest luxury apartment buildings on the avenue, and still has just one residence per floor. Wrapping around the corner of Madison Avenue at 45 East 66th Street, another flamboyant survivor (1906-08) features terracotta ornamentation that would befit a Gothic cathedral. (Andy Warhol lived a few doors up at no.57 from 1974 to 1987.) And further north, Stanford White designed 998 Fifth Avenue (at 81st Street) in the image of an Italian Renaissance palazzo.

Philanthropic gestures made by the moneyed classes over the past 130-odd years have helped to create an impressive cluster of art collections, museums and cultural institutions. Indeed, Fifth Avenue from 82nd to 104th Streets is known as **Museum Mile**, and for good reason: it's lined by the **Metropolitan Museum of Art** (*see p112* **Profile**); the Frank Lloyd Wright-designed **Solomon R Guggenheim Museum** (*see p114*); the **Cooper-Hewitt, National Design Museum** (*see p111*), housed in Andrew Carnegie's former mansion; the **Frick Collection** (*see p111*), lodged in the former mansion of Henry Clay Frick; the **Jewish Museum** (*see p111*); the **Museum of the City of New York** (*see p114*); and the **National Academy Museum** (1083 Fifth Avenue, at 89th Street, 1-212 369 4880, www.nationalacademy.org, closed for renovatons until September 2011), whose collection includes works by Louise Bourgeois, Jasper Johns and Robert Rauschenberg. Museum Mile is lengthening: although technically in Spanish Harlem, **El Museo del Barrio** (*see p111*) recently had a world-class makeover for its 40th birthday. Further north still, the new **Museum for African Art**, rising at the corner of 110th Street (1280 Fifth

Profile Museum of African Art

Africa finds a home on the Museum Mile.

The Museum for African Art has certainly led a nomadic existence since its inception in 1984. It began life in an Upper East Side townhouse, moved in 1992 to a small space in Soho and decamped to Long Island City in 2002. After closing its doors in 2005, it began casting about for a larger, more permanent home, breaking ground in 2007 on a new $95 million museum on Fifth Avenue, right on the cusp of Harlem.

In Sept/Oct 2011, the Museum for African Art will open its doors and become the first addition to Museum Mile since the Guggenheim was completed in 1959. The new space, designed by Robert A.M. Stern Architects, will give the MfAA 75,000 square feet and four floors (one below ground) of a 19-storey residential tower.

A glass atrium guides visitors into a soaring lobby with 45-foot (14-metre) high walls, one of which is formed by an arc of African etimoe wood. In addition to a smaller exhibition space, the lobby contains a shop, a restaurant, a 245-seat theatre and a multimedia education centre.

Upstairs, the first floor is given over to three rotating exhibition galleries making use of 15,000 square feet of space. The MfAA's inaugural shows are 'El Anatsui: When Last I Wrote to You About Africa', a retrospective of some 60 works by the Ghanian-born artist who uses found materials to create large wall sculptures; 'Grass Roots: African Origins of an American Art', which traces the influence of West African basket-making on the American South's adoption of that art form with over 200 coiled baskets; and 'New Premises: Three Decades at the Museum for African Art', a two-part show that will explore the evolution of the Museum for African Art using works from the permanent collection as well as highlights from its 60-plus shows from its previous locales.

The second floor houses the museum's library, offices and a roof terrace overlooking Central Park. Plans are also underfoot on this floor for the MfAA's Mandela Center for Memory and Dialogue, dedicated to programmes examining humanitarian issues and social justice.

In addition to stretching Museum Mile northward, the new MfAA has also broadened its artistic and cultural scope.

Avenue, 1-718 784 7700, www.africanart.org), is slated to open in autumn 2011 (*see p109* **Profile**).

Additional collections are scattered throughout the museum-saturated neighbourhood, including the **Asia Society & Museum** (*see right*), the **China Institute** (*see right*), the **Neue Galerie** (*see p114*) and the **Whitney Museum of American Art** (*see p115*).

Madison Avenue is New York's world-class ultra-luxe shopping strip. Between 57th and 86th Streets, it's packed with top designer names: the usual Euro suspects, such as Gucci, Prada and Chloé, and Americans including Donna Karan, multiple Ralph Lauren outposts and the flagship of Tom Ford's eponymous menswear line (no.845, at 70th Street, 1-212 359 0300, closed Sun). Fashionable department store **Barneys New York** (*see p230*) is stocked with unusual designer finds and features witty, sometimes audacious, window displays.

More than 20 blocks south, near the border with Midtown, lies hugely popular department store **Bloomingdale's** (*see p231*). If you head east on 59th Street, you'll eventually reach the **Queensboro Bridge**, which links to Queens. At Second Avenue you can catch the overhead tram to **Roosevelt Island**. Suspended on a cable, the tram reaches a height of 250 feet (76 metres) above the East River and the fare is the same as a subway ride. The two-mile-long isle between Manhattan and Queens is largely residential. However, from 1686 to 1921, it went by the name of Blackwell's Island, during which time it was the site of an insane asylum, a smallpox hospital and a prison – notable inmates included Mae West, who served eight days here after being moved from the Women's House of Detention in the Village (*see p86*), and Emma Goldman, the anarchist, feminist and political agitator.

Asia Society & Museum

725 Park Avenue, at 70th Street (1-212 288 6400, http://asiasociety.org). Subway 6 to 68th Street-Hunter College. **Open** *Sept-June* 11am-6pm Tue-Thur, Sat, Sun; 11am-9pm Fri. *July, Aug* 11am-6pm Tue-Sun. **Admission** $10; $5-$7 reductions; free under-16s (must be accompanied by an adult). Free to all 6-9pm Fri. **Credit** AmEx, DC, MC, V. **Map** p405 E20.

The Asia Society sponsors study missions and conferences while promoting public programmes in the US and abroad. The headquarters' striking galleries host exhibitions of art from dozens of countries and time periods (from ancient India and medieval Persia to contemporary Japan); some are assembled from public and private collections, including the permanent Mr and Mrs John D Rockefeller III collection of Asian art. A spacious, atrium-like café, with a pan-Asian menu, and an attractive gift shop, help to make the society a one-stop destination for anyone with even a passing interest in Asian culture.

China Institute

125 E 65th Street, between Park & Lexington Avenues (1-212 744 8181, www.chinainstitute.org). Subway F to Lexington Avenue-63rd Street; 6 to 68th Street-Hunter College. **Open** varies. *Gallery* 10am-5pm Mon, Wed, Fri-Sun; 10am-8pm Tue, Thur. **Admission** $7; $4 reductions; free under-12s. Free to all 6-8pm Tue, Thur. **Credit** AmEx, DC, Disc, MC, V. **Map** p405 E21.

Cooper-Hewitt, National Design Museum.

Consisting of just two small galleries, the China Institute is somewhat overshadowed by the nearby Asia Society. But its rotating exhibitions – photographs of modern Beijing, for example, or high-profile collections on loan from Chinese institutions – are compelling. The institute offers lectures and courses on myriad subjects such as calligraphy, contemporary fashion design and traditional dance.

★ Cooper-Hewitt, National Design Museum

2 E 91st Street, at Fifth Avenue (1-212 849 8400, www.cooperhewitt.org). Subway 4, 5, 6 to 86th Street. **Open** 10am-5pm Mon-Fri; 10am-6pm Sat; 11am-6pm Sun. **Admission** $15; $10 reductions; free under-12s. **Credit** AmEx, DC, Disc, MC, V. **Map** p406 E18.

Founded in 1897 by the Hewitt sisters, granddaughters of industrialist Peter Cooper, the only museum in the US solely dedicated to design (both historic and modern) has been part of the Smithsonian since the 1960s. In 1976, it took up residence in the former home of steel magnate Andrew Carnegie: it's worth a look for the impressive mansion as much as for the roster of temporary exhibitions, which include an always-interesting series in which pieces are selected from the permanent collection by a prominent artist or designer. In 2011, the Cooper-Hewitt hosts 'Color Moves: Art and Fashion by Sonia Delaunay' (until 5 June 2011) and 'Design with the other 90%: Cities', an exploration of design and urban growth in the context of the world's population change (autumn 2011). The museum's gift shop is stocked with international design objects (some very affordable) as well as the appropriate books.

El Museo del Barrio

1230 Fifth Avenue, at 104th Street (1-212 831 7272, www.elmuseo.org). Subway 6 to 103rd Street. **Open** 11am-6pm Tue-Sat; 1-5pm Sun. **Admission** *Suggested donation* $9; $5 reductions; free under-12s; free over-65s Wed. Free to all 3rd Sat each mth. **Credit** AmEx, MC, V. **Map** p406 E16.

Founded in 1969 by the artist (and former MoMA curator) Rafael Montañez Ortiz, El Museo del Barrio takes its name from its East Harlem locale. Dedicated to the art and culture of Puerto Ricans and Latin Americans all over the US, El Museo reopened in autumn 2009 following the first phase of a $35 million renovation. The redesigned spaces within the museum's 1921 Beaux-Arts building provide a polished, contemporary showcase for the diversity and vibrancy of Hispanic art. The new galleries allow more space for rotating installations from the museum's 6,500-piece holdings – from pre-Columbian artefacts to contemporary installations – as well as around three temporary shows a year.

In 2011, the museum will unfurl its biennial 'El Museo's Bienal: The (S) Files 2011' (until 21 Aug 2011), dedicated to the art of Latinos working in the New York area.

> **INSIDE TRACK**
> **NIGHT AT THE MUSEUM**
>
> Most of the city's major museums are free or pay what you wish one evening (usually Thursday or Friday) or afternoon of the week. Some enhance the experience with musical and other performances.

★ Frick Collection

1 E 70th Street, between Fifth & Madison Avenues (1-212 288 0700, www.frick.org). Subway 6 to 68th Street-Hunter College. **Open** 10am-6pm Tue-Sat; 11am-5pm Sun. **Admission** $18; $5-$12 reductions (under-10s not admitted). Pay what you wish 11am-1pm Sun. **Credit** AmEx, DC, Disc, MC, V. **Map** p405 E20.

Industrialist, robber baron and collector Henry Clay Frick commissioned this opulent mansion with a view to leaving his legacy to the public. Designed by Thomas Hastings of Carrère & Hastings (the firm behind the New York Public Library) and built in 1914, the building was inspired by 18th-century British and French architecture.

In an effort to preserve the feel of a private residence, labelling is minimal, but you can opt for a free audio guide or pay $2 for a booklet. Works spanning the 14th to the 19th centuries include masterpieces by Rembrandt, Vermeer, Whistler, Gainsborough, Holbein and Titian, exquisite period furniture, porcelain and other decorative objects. Aficionados of 18th-century French art will find two rooms especially enchanting: the panels of the Boucher Room (1750-52) depict children engaged in adult occupations; the Fragonard Room contains the artist's series *Progress of Love* – four of the paintings were commissioned (and rejected) by Louis XV's mistress Madame du Barry. The interior Garden Court is a serene spot to rest your feet and turn your art-saturated gaze to a soothing fountain.

'Picasso's Drawings, 1890 to 1921: Reinventing Tradition' (4 Oct 2011-8 Jan 2012) is certain to be one of the blockbusters on the city's art calendar.

▶ *For the Frick's excellent concert series, see p315.*

Jewish Museum

1109 Fifth Avenue, at 92nd Street (1-212 423 3200, www.thejewishmuseum.org). Subway 4, 5 to 86th Street; 6 to 96th Street. **Open** 11am-5.45pm Mon, Tue, Sat, Sun; 11am-8pm Thur; 11am-4pm Fri. Closed on Jewish holidays. **Admission** $12; $7.50-$10 reductions; free under-12s. Free to all Sat. **Credit** AmEx, MC, V. **Map** p405 E18.

The former home of the financier, collector and Jewish leader Felix Warburg, the Jewish Museum's magnificent French Gothic-style mansion is still gleaming following an exterior spruce-up for its 100th birthday in 2008. Inside, those with an interest in Jewish culture will find a far-reaching collection of

Profile Metropolitan Museum of Art

The mother of all Manhattan museums is an essential stop on any itinerary.

Occupying 13 acres of Central Park, the **Metropolitan Museum of Art** (for listings, *see p114*), which opened in 1880, is impressive in terms both of quality and of scale. Added in 1895 by McKim Mead and White, the neoclassical façade can appear daunting. However, the museum is surprisingly easy to negotiate, particularly if you come early on a weekday and avoid the crowds.

The steep $20 admission price is only a suggested donation (a dollar will gain you entrance without reproachful glares), but it does include access to the Met's blockbuster temporary shows plus, for those with boundless energy, same-day admission to the **Cloisters** in Inwood (*see p124*). It would take many visits to cover all of the Met's huge gallery space, and it's wise to focus on particular collections to save time.

COLLECTIONS

In the ground floor's north wing sits the collection of **Egyptian Art** (all gallery names are given in bold here) and the glass-walled atrium housing the Temple of Dendur, moved en masse from its original Nile-side setting and now overlooking a reflecting pool. Antiquity is also well represented on the southern wing of the ground floor by the halls housing **Greek and Roman Art**, which reopened in 2007 after receiving an elegant makeover. Keep an eye out for the famous 'New York kouros' one of the earliest free-standing marble statues from Greece.

Turning west brings you to the **Arts of Africa, Oceania and the Americas** collection; it was donated by Nelson Rockefeller as a memorial to his son Michael, who disappeared while visiting New Guinea in 1961. A wider-ranging bequest, the two-storey **Robert Lehman Wing** can be found at the western end of the floor. This eclectic collection is housed in a recreation of the Lehman family townhouse and features works by Botticelli (including the artist's celebrated *Annunciation*), Bellini, Ingres and Rembrandt, among others.

Rounding out the ground floor highlights is the **American Wing** on the north-west corner. Its grand, conservatory-style Engelhard Court recently reopened as part of the wing's current revamp. Now more a sculpture court than an interior garden, the light-filled space is flanked by the façade of Wall Street's Branch Bank of the United States (saved when the building was torn down in 1915) and a stunning loggia designed by Louis Comfort Tiffany for his Long Island estate.

From the Great Hall where you originally entered, a grand staircase brings you to the first floor. Veer left – pausing for the **Drawings, Prints and Photographs** galleries, which often hold small yet intriguing temporary exhibitions – and you'll come to the galleries housing **19th Century European Paintings and Sculpture**. These contain some of the Met's most popular rooms, particularly the two-room Monet holdings and a colony of Van Goghs that includes his oft-reproduced *Irises*. This Impressionist hall of fame gives way to – yes, you guessed it – the post-Impressionist section, which includes Modigliani, Matisse, Picasso and Seurat (look out for his pointillist masterpiece *Circus Sideshow*), as well as American masters of the period such as Sargent and Whistler.

The museum's nearby cache of **Modern Art** – which includes works by Pollock, de Kooning and Rothko, to name a few – was boosted in 2006 by a gift of a 63-piece collection of abstract expressionists from collector Muriel Newman.

Retrace your steps westward and you'll reach the **European Paintings** galleries, which hold an amazing reserve of old masters. The Dutch section boasts five Vermeers, the largest collection of the master in the world, and a haunting Rembrandt self-portrait; the jewel of the French rooms is David's riveting *Death of Socrates*; and the Spanish rooms are highlighted by El Grecos and Velázquez's stately *Portrait of Juan de Pareja*.

At the northern wing of the floor, you'll find the sprawling collection of **Asian Art**. It's easy to lose yourself among the Chinese lacquer, Japanese figurines and Indian sculpture, but be sure to check out the ceiling of the Jain Meeting Hall in the South-east Asian gallery. If you're still on your feet, give them a deserved rest in the Astor Court, a tranquil recreation of a Ming Dynasty garden – or head up to the Iris & B Gerald Cantor Roof Garden (open from late May to late October), which showcases large-scale contemporary sculpture by a different artist each year.

SHOWING IN 2011

Don't miss out on the programme of temporary exhibitions; for details, *see p114*.

more than 28,000 works of art, artefacts and media installations, which are all arranged thematically in a two-floor permanent exhibition: 'Culture and Continuity: The Jewish Journey'. This traces the evolution of Judaism from antiquity to the present day.

The excellent temporary shows appeal to a broad audience: 2011 brings 'Maira Kalman: Various Illuminations (of a Crazy World)' (until 31 July 2011), which reveals 30 years of her whimsical drawings and paintings, and 'Collecting Matisse and Modern Masters: The Cone Sisters of Baltimore' featuring around 50 works of art, including paintings by Picasso, Van Gogh and Gauguin (until 25 Sept 2011).

► *The Museum of Jewish Heritage: A Living Memorial to the Holocaust (see p69) and the Museum at Eldridge Street (see p81), both Downtown, further explore Jewish culture.*

★ Metropolitan Museum of Art

1000 Fifth Avenue, at 82nd Street (1-212 535 7710, www.metmuseum.org). Subway 4, 5, 6 to 86th Street. **Open** 9.30am-5.30pm Tue-Thur, Sun; 9.30am-9pm Fri, Sat. **Admission** *Suggested donation* (incl same-day admission to the Cloisters) $20; $10-$15 reductions; free under-12s. **Credit** AmEx, DC, Disc, MC, V. **Map** p405 E19.

For the permanent collection, *see p112* **Profile**.

Scheduled exhibitions at the Met in 2011 include 'Pastel Portraits: Images of 18th-Century Europe' (until 14 Aug 2011); 'Richard Serra Drawing: A Retrospective' (until 28 Aug 2011); 'Modern Tradition: Korean Buncheong Ceramics from the Leeum Collection' (until 31 Aug 2011); and 'Historic Images of the Greek Bronze Age: The Reproductions of E Gillieron & Son' (until 13 Nov 2011).

► *For the Cloisters, which houses the Met's medieval art collection, see p124.*

Museum of the City of New York

1220 Fifth Avenue, between 103rd & 104th Streets (1-212 534 1672, www.mcny.org). Subway 6 to 103rd Street. **Open** 10am-5pm Tue-Sun. **Admission** *Suggested donation* $10; $6 reductions; $20 family; free under-13s. **Credit** AmEx, DC, Disc, MC, V. **Map** p405 E16.

A great introduction to New York, this institution contains a wealth of city history. *Timescapes*, a 25-minute multimedia film that tells NYC's story from 1624 to the present, is shown free with admission every half-hour. A spacious new gallery opened in late 2008 to allow more space for five to seven temporary exhibitions each year, which spotlight the city from different angles.

In 2011, 'The American Style: Colonial Revival and the Modern Metropolis' (7 June-6 Nov 2011) explores New York's role in advancing the colonial revival style in the works of such luminaries as McKim Mead and White, and Tiffany's.

The permanent collection includes exhibits devoted to the city's maritime heritage and interiors: six rooms, among them an original 1906 Park Avenue drawing room sumptuously decorated in the style of the Sala Della Zodiaco in the Ducal Palace, Mantua, chart New York living spaces from 1680 to 1906. But the undoubted jewel is the amazing Stettheimer Dollhouse: it was created in the 1920s by Carrie Stettheimer, whose artist friends reinterpreted their masterpieces in miniature to hang on the walls. Look closely and you'll even spy a tiny version of Marcel Duchamp's famous *Nude Descending a Staircase.*

► *There's more city history at the New-York Historical Society, Lower East Side Tenement Museum (see p80) and Ellis Island Immigration Museum (see p65), among others.*

Neue Galerie

1048 Fifth Avenue, at 86th Street (1-212 628 6200, www.neuegalerie.org). Subway 4, 5, 6 to 86th Street. **Open** 11am-6pm Mon, Thur-Sun; 11am-8pm 1st Fri of the mth. **Admission** (under-16s must be accompanied by an adult; under-12s not admitted) $15; $10 reductions. Free to all 6-8pm 1st Fri of the mth. **Credit** AmEx, MC, V. **Map** p405 E18.

The elegant Neue Galerie is devoted entirely to late 19th- and early 20th-century German and Austrian fine and decorative arts. The creation of the late art dealer Serge Sabarsky and cosmetics mogul Ronald S Lauder, it has the largest concentration of works by Gustav Klimt and Egon Schiele outside of Vienna. Then 2011 sees the presentation of 'Birth of the Modern: Style and Identity in Vienna 1900' (until 27 June 2011). There's also a bookstore, a small design shop and the ultra-refined Café Sabarsky (*see p207*), serving modern Austrian cuisine and ravishing Viennese pastries.

★ Solomon R Guggenheim Museum

1071 Fifth Avenue, between 88th & 89th Streets (1-212 423 3500, www.guggenheim.org). Subway 4, 5, 6 to 86th Street. **Open** 10am-5.45pm Mon-Wed, Fri, Sun; 10am-7.45pm Sat. **Admission** $18; $15 reductions; free under-12s. Pay what you wish 5.45-7.15pm Sat. **Credit** AmEx, DC, MC, V. **Map** p406 E18.

The Guggenheim is as famous for its landmark building, which was designed by architect Frank Lloyd Wright, as it is for its impressive collection and daring temporary shows. The dramatic structure, with its winding, cantilevered curves, was given a major spruce-up for its 50th birthday in 2009. The museum owns Peggy Guggenheim's trove of Cubist, Surrealist and Abstract Expressionist works, along with the Panza di Biumo Collection of American Minimalist and Conceptual art from the 1960s and '70s. As well as works by Manet, Picasso, Chagall and Bourgeois, it includes the largest collection of Kandinskys in the US. In 1992, the addition of a ten-storey tower provided space for a sculpture gallery (with park views), an auditorium and a café.

Museum of the City of New York.

Scheduled exhibitions for 2011 include: 'The Hugo Boss Prize 2010: Hans-Peter Feldmann' (until 5 Sept 2011), a solo exhibit for the German artist who won this prestigious biennial prize awarded by the museum; 'The Harmony of Silence: Kandinsky's Painting with White Border' (21 Oct 2011-15 Jan 2012); and 'Lee Ufan: Marking Infinity' (24 June-28 Sept 2011), a show dedicated to the work of the Korean-born artist and poet.

Whitney Museum of American Art

945 Madison Avenue, at 75th Street (1-212 570 3600, www.whitney.org). Subway 6 to 77th Street. **Open** 11am-6pm Wed, Thur, Sat, Sun; 1-9pm Fri. **Admission** $18; $12 reductions; free under-19s. Pay what you wish 6-9pm Fri. **Credit** AmEx, DC, MC, V. **Map** p405 E20.

Like the Guggenheim, the Whitney is set apart by its unique architecture: it's a Marcel Breuer-designed granite cube with an all-seeing upper-storey 'eye' window. When sculptor and art patron Gertrude Vanderbilt Whitney opened the museum in 1931, she dedicated it to living American artists. Today, the Whitney holds 18,000 pieces by around 2,700 artists, including Willem de Kooning, Edward Hopper (the museum owns his entire collection), Jasper Johns, Georgia O'Keeffe and Claes Oldenburg.

Still, its reputation rests primarily on its temporary shows – particularly the Whitney Biennial, the exhibition that everyone loves to hate. Launched in 1932 and held in even-numbered years, the Biennial is the most prestigious and controversial assessment of contemporary art in America – the 2012 show is on until 30 May.

In 2011, look out for 'Pro Tools', an exhibition devoted to digital artist Cory Arcangel, known for his modifications of computer games (26 May-30 Aug 2011). The Whitney's biggest news for 2011, however, is the breaking ground in May for the Renzo Piano-designed satellite museum alongside the new High Line park (*see p96* **Profile**). The Whitney Downtown is expected to open to the public in 2015.

Yorkville

The atmosphere becomes noticeably less rarefied as you walk east from Central Park, with grand edifices giving way to bland modern apartment blocks and walk-up tenements. Not much remains of the old German and Hungarian immigrant communities that once filled **Yorkville**, the Upper East Side neighbourhood between Third Avenue and the East River, with delicatessens, beer halls and restaurants. However, one such flashback is the 75-year-old **Heidelberg** (1648 Second Avenue, between 85th & 86th Streets, 1-212 628 2332, 11.30am-1am daily), where dirndl-wearing waitresses serve up steins of Spaten and platters of sausages from the wurst-meisters at butcher shop Schaller & Weber a few doors up (1654 Second Avenue, 1-212 879 3047). Second Avenue in the 70s and 80s throbs with rowdy pick-up bars frequented by preppy, twentysomething crowds.

In elegant contrast to this scene, **Gracie Mansion** (*see p116*) stands at the eastern end of 88th Street. The only Federal-style mansion in Manhattan, it's served as New York's official mayoral residence since 1942 – although the current mayor, billionaire Michael Bloomberg, famously eschews this traditional address in favour of his own Beaux Arts mansion at 17 East 79th Street (between Fifth & Madison Avenues). Although Gracie Mansion is fenced off, much of the exterior can be seen from surrounding **Carl Schurz Park**; you can buy provisions for a picnic in this undulating, shady green patch (or on the adjacent East River

INSIDE TRACK ROSEBUD-DHIST

At 331 Riverside Drive, between 105th and 106th Street, lies the Beaux Arts-style New York Buddhist Church, formerly the home of actress Marion Davies, mistress of William Randolph Hearst. The newspaper magnate purportedly nicknamed her 'Rosebud', which Orson Welles used as the name of the sled in Citizen Kane, which was based on Hearst. The large statue of the Buddha outside the church originally stood in Hiroshima and survived the atomic bomb.

Promenade) at sprawling Italian gourmet food shop **Agata & Valentina** (1505 First Avenue, at 79th Street, 1-212 452 0690).

One block from Gracie Mansion, the **Henderson Place Historic District** (at East End Avenue, between 86th & 87th Streets) contains 24 handsome Queen Anne row houses – commissioned by furrier and noted real-estate developer John C Henderson as servants' quarters – with their original turrets, double stoops and slate roofs.

Looking slightly architecturally incongruous in the area, the large **Islamic Cultural Center** (1711 Third Avenue, at 96th Street, 1-212 722 5234), built in 1990, was the city's first major mosque. There are around 150 mosques and masjids throughout the city, ministering to around 600,000 Muslims.

Gracie Mansion

Carl Schurz Park, 88th Street, at East End Avenue (1-212 570 4751). Subway 4, 5, 6 to 86th Street.
Tours 10am, 11am, 1pm, 2pm most Wed. **Admission** $7; $4 reductions; free students. **No credit cards**. **Map** p406 G18.

This green-shuttered yellow edifice was built in 1799 by wealthy Scottish merchant Archibald Gracie as a country house. Today, the stately house is the focal point of tranquil Carl Schurz Park, named in honour of the German immigrant who became a newspaper editor and US senator. When big-bucks mayor Michael Bloomberg declined to move in after taking up office in 2002, Gracie Mansion's living quarters were opened up to public tours for the first time in 60 years. Reservations are required (same-day reservations are not permitted).

SIGHTS

UPPER WEST SIDE

Subway A, B, C, D, 1 to 59th Street-Columbus Circle; B, C to 81st Street-Museum of Natural History; 1, 2, 3 to 72nd Street; 1, 2, 3 to 96th Street.

With a population that's more established than Downtown's but less old-moneyed than the Upper East Side's, this four-mile-long stretch west of Central Park is culturally rich and cosmopolitan. As on the Upper East Side, New Yorkers were drawn here during the late 19th century after the completion of Central Park, the opening of local subway lines and Columbia University's relocation to Morningside Heights. In the 20th century, central Europeans found refuge here, and Puerto Ricans settled along Amsterdam and Columbus Avenues in the 1960s. These days, new real-estate is reducing eye-level evidence of old immigrant life, and the neighbourhood's intellectual, politically liberal spirit has waned a little as apartment prices have risen. Sections of Riverside Drive and Central Park West still rival the grandeur of the East Side's Fifth and Park Avenues.

The gateway to the Upper West Side is **Columbus Circle**, where Broadway meets 59th Street, Eighth Avenue, Central Park South and Central Park West – a rare rotary in a city of right angles. The architecture around it could make anyone's head spin. At the entrance to Central Park, a 700-ton statue of Christopher Columbus goes almost unnoticed under the **Time Warner Center** across the street, which houses offices, apartments, hotel lodgings and Jazz at Lincoln Center's stunning **Frederick P Rose Hall** (*see p312*). The first seven levels of the enormous glass complex are filled with high-end retailers and gourmet restaurants, such as **Per Se** (*see p211*) and **A Voce Columbus** (*see p209*). In 2008, the **Museum of Arts & Design** (*see p118*) opened its new digs in a landmark building on the south side of the circle, itself the subject of a controversial redesign.

If the Upper East Side is the nexus of the city's museums, the Upper West Side's seat of culture is largely concentrated on **Lincoln Center** (*see p312*), a complex of concert halls and auditoriums built in the early 1960s and the home of the New York Philharmonic, the New York City Ballet, the Metropolitan Opera and a host of other notable arts organisations. The big circular fountain in the central plaza is a popular gathering spot – especially in summer, when amateur dancers converge on it to dance alfresco at **Midsummer Night Swing** (*see p264*).

The centre is nearing the completion of a major overhaul that includes a redesign of public spaces, refurbishment of the various halls and a new visitor center, the **David Rubenstein Atrium** (*see p98* **Not Just the Ticket**). The Atrium is the starting point for guided **tours** of the complex (1-212 875 5350, $15, $8-$12 reductions), which, in addition to the hallowed concert halls, contains several notable artworks, including Henry Moore's *Reclining Figure* in the plaza near Lincoln Center Theater, and two massive music-themed paintings by Marc Chagall in the lobby of the

INSIDE TRACK GAZING WITH POE

If you enter Riverside Park at 83rd Street, you can ascend a small rocky outcrop known as Mount Tom. Before the park was landscaped, Edgar Allan Poe, who lived briefly on 84th Street (which has been named after him), was fond of sitting here and gazing across the Hudson River.

Time Warner Center.

Metropolitan Opera House. Nearby is the **New York Public Library for the Performing Arts** (40 Lincoln Center Plaza, at 65th Street, 1-212 870 1630, www.nypl.org, closed Sun); alongside its extraordinary collection of films, letters, manuscripts, videos and sound recordings, it's also a venue for concerts and lectures.

Around Sherman and Verdi Squares (from 70th to 73rd Streets, where Broadway and Amsterdam Avenue intersect), classic early 20th-century buildings stand cheek-by-jowl with newer, often mundane high-rises. The jewel is the 1904 **Ansonia Hotel** (2109 Broadway, between 73rd & 74th Streets). Over the years, Enrico Caruso, Babe Ruth and Igor Stravinsky have lived in this Beaux Arts masterpiece; it was also the site of the Continental Baths, the gay bathhouse and cabaret where Bette Midler got her start, and Plato's Retreat, a swinging 1970s sex club.

The perpetually crowded 72nd Street subway station on Broadway, which opened in 1904, is notable for its Beaux Arts entrance. The splendidly restored rococo **Beacon Theatre** (*see p321*), originally a 1920s movie palace, is now one of New York City's premier mid-size concert venues.

When Central Park was completed, magnificently tall residential buildings rose up along **Central Park West** to take advantage of the views. The first of these great apartment blocks was the **Dakota** (at 72nd Street), so named because its location was considered remote when it was built in 1884. The fortress-like building is known as the setting for *Rosemary's Baby* and the site of John Lennon's murder in 1980 (Yoko Ono still lives here); other residents have included Judy Garland, Rudolph Nureyev, Lauren Bacall and Boris Karloff – but not Billy Joel, who was turned away by the co-op board when he tried to buy an apartment. You might recognise **55 Central Park West** (at 66th Street) from the movie *Ghostbusters*. Built in 1930, it was the first art deco building on the block. Heading north on Central Park West, you'll spy the massive twin-towered **San Remo Apartments** (at 74th Street), which also date from 1930. Rita Hayworth, Steven Spielberg, Tiger Woods and U2's Bono are among the building's many celebrity residents over the years.

A few blocks to the north, the **New-York Historical Society** (*see p118*) is the city's oldest museum, built in 1804. Across the street, at the glorious **American Museum of Natural History** (*see p118*), dinosaur skeletons, a permanent rainforest exhibition and an IMAX theatre lure adults and battalions of school groups.

The sizeable cluster of classic food stores and restaurants lining the avenues of the district's northern end is where the Upper West Side shops, drinks and eats. To see West Siders in their natural habitat, queue at the perpetually jammed smoked fish counter at gourmet market **Zabar's** (*see p250*). Edgar's **Café** (255 W 84th Street, between West End Avenue & Broadway, 1-212 496 6126) is famous for its lavish pastries; **H&H Bagels** (2239 Broadway, at 80th Street, 1-212 595 8000, open 24hrs) is the original location of the city's largest bagel purveyor; and the legendary (if scruffy) restaurant and delicatessen **Barney Greengrass**, the self-styled 'Sturgeon King' (541 Amsterdam Avenue; *see p209*), has specialised in smoked fish, knishes and what may be the city's best chopped liver since 1908.

Designed by Central Park's Frederick Law Olmsted, **Riverside Park** is a sinuous stretch of riverbank that starts at 72nd Street and ends at 158th Street, running between Riverside Drive and the Hudson River. You'll probably see yachts, along with several houseboats, berthed at the **79th Street Boat Basin**. Several sites provide havens for quiet reflection. The **Soldiers' and Sailors' Monument** (89th Street, at Riverside Drive), built in 1902 by

French sculptor Paul EM DuBoy, honours Union soldiers who died in the Civil War; and a 1908 memorial (100th Street, at Riverside Drive) pays tribute to fallen firemen. The stretch of park below 72nd Street, called **Riverside Park South**, is a particularly peaceful city retreat, with a pier, and landscaped patches of grass with park benches.

★ American Museum of Natural History/Rose Center for Earth & Space

Central Park West, at 79th Street (1-212 769 5100, www.amnh.org). Subway B, C to 81st Street-Museum of Natural History. **Open** 10am-5.45pm daily. **Admission** *Suggested donation* $16; $9-$12 reductions; free under-2s. **Credit** AmEx, DC, Disc, MC, V. **Map** p405 C19.

Home to the largest and arguably most fabulous collection of dinosaur fossils in the world, the American Museum of Natural History's fourth-floor dino halls have been blowing minds for decades. The thrills begin when you cross the threshold of the Theodore Roosevelt Rotunda, where you're confronted with a towering barosaurus rearing high on its hind legs to protect its young from an attacking allosaurus – an impressive welcome to the largest museum of its kind in the world. Roughly 80% of the bones on display were dug out of the ground by Indiana Jones types. But during the museum's mid 1990s renovation, several specimens were remodelled to incorporate discoveries made during the intervening years. The Tyrannosaurus rex, for instance, was once believed to have walked upright, *Godzilla*-style; it now stalks prey with its head lowered and tail raised parallel to the ground.

The rest of the museum is equally dramatic. The Hall of Human Origins houses a fine display of our old cousins, the Neanderthals. The Hall of Biodiversity examines world ecosystems and environmental preservation, and a life-size model of a blue whale hangs from the cavernous ceiling of the Hall of Ocean Life. In the Hall of Meteorites, the space's focal point is Ahnighito, the largest iron meteor on display anywhere in the world, weighing in at 34 tons.

The spectacular $210 million Rose Center for Earth & Space – dazzling at night – is a giant silvery globe where you can discover the universe via 3-D shows in the Hayden Planetarium and light shows in the Big Bang Theater. An IMAX theatre screens larger-than-life nature programmes, and the roster of temporary exhibitions are thought-provoking for all ages.

In 2011, 'The World's Largest Dinosaurs' (May 2011-Jan 2012), focusing on sauropods, the largest creatures ever to have roamed the earth, is bound to be a blockbuster. Other shows include 'Brain: The Inside Story' (until 14 Aug 2011) and 'Frogs: A Chorus of Colors' (28 May 2011-8 Jan 2012), which displays over 200 live frogs in their recreated natural habitats.

INSIDE TRACK BOATS & BEER

From late March to October (weather permitting), you can take in the view of the **79th Street Boat Basin** (*see p117*) with a beer and a burger at the no-reservations **Boat Basin Café** (www.boatbasincafe.com). The patio of this extremely popular spot overlooks the marina, but there's also an adjacent covered rotunda.

★ Museum of Arts & Design

2 Columbus Circle, at Broadway (1-212 299 7777, www.madmuseum.org). Subway A, B, C, D, 1 to 59th Street-Columbus Circle. **Open** 11am-6pm Tue, Wed, Fri-Sun; 11am-9pm Thur. **Admission** $15; $12 reductions; free under-13s Pay what you wish 6-9pm Thur. **Credit** AmEx, Disc, MC, V. **Map** p404 C22.

Founded in 1956 as the Museum of Contemporary Crafts, this institution brings together contemporary objects created in a wide range of media – including clay, glass, wood, metal and cloth – with a strong focus on materials and process. And the museum recently crafted itself a new home. Originally designed in 1964 by Radio City Music Hall architect Edward Durell Stone to house the Gallery of Modern Art, 2 Columbus Circle was a windowless monolith that had sat empty since 1998. The new ten-storey building now has four floors of exhibition galleries, including the Tiffany & Co Foundation Jewelry Gallery. Curators are able to display more of the 2,000-piece permanent collection, including porcelain ware by Cindy Sherman, stained glass by Judith Schaechter, basalt ceramics by James Turrell and Robert Arneson's mural *Alice House Wall*.

But the real attractions here are the imaginative temporary shows. In 2011, 'Otherworldly: Artist Dioramas and Small Spectacles' (7 June-18 Sept 2011) turns the tables on virtual reality by displaying small-scale handcrafted works by contemporary artists seeking to depict artificial environments and alternative realities in their own manner. Other exhibits include 'Picasso to Koons: The Artist as Jeweler' (20 Sept 2011-8 Jan 2012) and 'Scent' (8 Nov 2011-19 Feb 2012). You can also watch resident artists create works in studios on the sixth floor, while the ninth-floor American bistro has views over the park.

New-York Historical Society

170 Central Park West, between 76th & 77th Streets (1-212 873 3400, www.nyhistory.org). Subway B, C to 81st Street-Museum of Natural History. **Open** 10am-6pm Tue-Thur, Sat; 10am-8pm Fri; 11am-5.45pm Sun. **Admission** $12; $7-$9 reductions; free under-12s. Pay what you wish 6-8pm Fri. **Credit** AmEx, DC, MC, V. **Map** p405 D20.

Founded in 1804, New York's oldest museum was one of America's first cultural and educational institutions. Highlights in the vast Henry Luce III Center for the Study of American Culture include George Washington's Valley Forge camp cot, a complete series of the extant watercolours from Audubon's *Birds of America* and the world's largest collection of Tiffany lamps.

Temporary offerings in 2011 include 'Making American Taste: Narrative Art for a New Democracy' (11 Nov 2011-1 March 2012) and 'Revolution! The Atlantic World Reborn' (11 Nov 2011-15 Apr 2012). Although the Society is also undergoing an extensive renovation due to finish in November 2011, its galleries will remain open despite the construction. When completed, the airy, newly constructed Great Hall will greet visitors, and the refurbished café will feature the original ceiling panel from Keith Haring's defunct Pop Shop.

MORNINGSIDE HEIGHTS

Subway B, C, 1 to 110th Street-Cathedral Parkway; 1 to 116th Street.

Morningside Heights runs from 110th Street (also known west of Central Park as Cathedral Parkway) to 125th Street, between Morningside Park and the Hudson River. The campus of **Columbia University** exerts a considerable influence over the surrounding neighbourhood, while the Cathedral Church of St John the Divine draws visitors from all over the city.

One of the oldest universities in the US, Columbia was initially chartered in 1754 as King's College (the name changed after the Revolutionary War). It moved to its present location in 1897. If you wander into Columbia's campus entrance at 116th Street, you won't fail to miss the impressive **Low Memorial Building**, modelled on Rome's Pantheon. The former library, completed in 1897, is now an administrative building. The list of illustrious graduates includes Alexander Hamilton, Allen Ginsberg and Barack Obama.

Thanks to the large student population of Columbia and its sister school, Barnard College, the area has an academic feel, with bookshops, inexpensive restaurants and coffeehouses lining Broadway between 110th and 116th Streets. The façade of Tom's Restaurant (2880 Broadway, at 112th Street, 1-212 864 6137) will be familiar to *Seinfeld* aficionados, but the interior doesn't resemble Monk's Café, which was created on a studio set for the long-running sitcom. Better fare can be found at **Community Food & Juice** (2893 Broadway, between 112th & 113th Streets, 1-212 665 2800, closed dinner Sat & Sun).

The **Cathedral Church of St John the Divine** (*see right*) is the seat of the Episcopal Diocese of New York. Subject to a series of construction delays and misfortunes, the enormous cathedral (larger than Paris's Notre Dame) is on a medieval schedule for completion: according to the church, the hammering and chiselling will continue for a couple more centuries, although it has wrapped up work for the time being. Just behind is the green expanse of **Morningside Park** (from 110th to 123rd Streets, between Morningside Avenue & Morningside Drive), while across the street is the **Hungarian Pastry Shop** (1030 Amsterdam Avenue, between 110th & 111th Streets, 1-212 866 4230), a great place for coffee, dessert and engaging graduate students in esoteric discussions as they procrastinate over their theses.

North of Columbia, **General Grant National Memorial** (aka Grant's Tomb), the mausoleum of former president Ulysses S Grant, is located in Riverside Park. Across the street stands the towering Gothic-style **Riverside Church** (490 Riverside Drive, at 120th Street, 1-212 870 6700, www.theriversidechurchny.org), built in 1930. The tower contains the world's largest carillon: 74 bells, played every Sunday at 10.30am.

★ Cathedral Church of St John the Divine

1047 Amsterdam Avenue, at 112th Street (1-212 316 7540, www.stjohndivine.org). Subway B, C, 1 to 110th Street-Cathedral Parkway. **Open** 7am-6pm daily. **Admission** *Suggested donation* $5; $2-$4 reductions. **Credit** Disc, MC, V. **Map** p406 C15.

Construction of this massive house of worship, affectionately nicknamed 'St John the Unfinished', began in 1892 in Romanesque style, was put on hold for a Gothic Revival redesign in 1911, then ground to a halt in 1941, when the US entered World War II. It resumed in earnest in 1979, but a fire in 2001 that destroyed the church's gift shop and damaged two 17th-century Italian tapestries further delayed completion. It's still missing a tower and a north transept, among other things, but the nave has been restored and the entire interior reopened and rededicated. No further work is planned… for now.

In addition to Sunday services, the cathedral hosts concerts and tours. It bills itself as a place for all people – and it certainly means it. Annual events include both winter and summer solstice celebrations, the Blessing of the Animals during the Feast of St Francis, which draws pets and their people from all over the city, and even a Blessing of the Bicycles every spring.

FREE General Grant National Memorial

Riverside Drive, at 122nd Street (1-212 666 1640, www.nps.gov/gegr). Subway 1 to 125th Street. **Open** 9am-5pm daily. **Admission** free. **Map** p407 B14.

Although he was born in Ohio, Civil War hero and 18th president Ulysses S Grant lived in New York for the last five years of his life, and wanted to be buried in the city. More commonly referred to as Grant's Tomb, the neoclassical, granite and marble mausoleum was completed in 1897; his wife, Julia, is also laid to rest here.

HARLEM

In the mythical melting pot that New Yorkers often use to define their city, **Harlem** has long been an integral yet uneasy ingredient. During the Jazz Age, America's most iconic black neighbourhood lured whites to its celebrated nightclubs, only to deter downtowners in the 1960s and '70s with the urban decay and crime of which it became emblematic. Duke Ellington's famous invitation to 'Take the A Train' uptown had lost its appeal, and many visitors (and many native New Yorkers) decline it even today.

The loss is theirs. Although the area isn't spilling over with sights, it has exuberant gospel choirs in historic churches, soul food restaurants serving down-home and upscale fare, markets selling African clothes, and a rejuvenated nightlife and jazz scene.

Few of the city's arteries pulsate like the main drag of 125th Street, where street preachers and mix-tape hawkers vie for the attentions of the human parade. Harlem's buildings maintain the city's eclectic architectural heritage, as a stroll along broad avenues such as Adam Clayton Powell Jr Boulevard (Seventh Avenue) or down the side streets off Convent Avenue readily attest.

The village of Harlem, named by Dutch colonists after their native Haarlem, was annexed by the City of New York in 1873. The extension of the elevated subway two decades later brought eager developers who overbuilt in the suddenly accessible suburb. The consequent housing glut led to cheap rents, and Jewish, Italian and Irish immigrants escaping the tenements of the Lower East Side snapped them up.

Around the turn of the 20th century, blacks joined the procession into Harlem, their ranks swelled by the great migration from the Deep South. By 1914, the black population of Harlem had risen well above 50,000; by the 1920s, Harlem was predominately black and the country's most populous African-American community. This prominence soon attracted some of black America's greatest artists: writers such as Langston Hughes and Zora Neale Hurston and musicians including Duke Ellington, Louis Armstrong and Cab Calloway, an unprecedented cultural gathering known as the Harlem Renaissance. White New York took notice, venturing uptown – where the enforcement of Prohibition was lax – to enjoy the Cotton Club, Connie's Inn, Smalls Paradise and the Savoy Ballroom, which supplied the beat for the city that never sleeps.

The Depression killed the Harlem Renaissance; it deeply wounded Harlem. By the 1960s, the community had been ravaged by middle-class flight and municipal neglect. Businesses closed, racial tensions ran high, and the looting during the 1977 blackout was among the worst the city had seen. However, as New York's economic standing improved in the mid '90s, investment began slowly spilling into Harlem, spawning new businesses and the phalanxes of renovated brownstones that beckon the middle class (white and black). This moneyed influx's co-existence with Harlem's long-standing residents can be tense but it is seldom volatile.

Harlem rises up from the top of Central Park at 110th Street and extends north as far as 155th Street, though the neighbourhood's southern boundary on the West Side is marked by 125th Street. On the East Side, Spanish Harlem begins on 96th Street before petering out before 125th Street. Visitors practising the same common sense they would elsewhere have nothing to fear and will be amply rewarded by one of New York's most distinctive neighbourhoods.

West Harlem

Subway 2, 3 to 125th Street or 135th Street; A, B, C, D to 125th Street

Harlem's main artery, **125th Street** (also known as Martin Luther King Jr Boulevard), beats loudest in West Harlem and most soulfully at the celebrated **Apollo Theater** (*see p321*), which hosts occasional concerts, a syndicated TV show and the classic Amateur Night every Wednesday – James Brown, Ella Fitzgerald, Michael Jackson and Lauryn Hill are among the starry alumni. A block east on 125th is the highly regarded **Studio Museum in Harlem** (*see p122*).

Although new boutiques, restaurants and cafés are scattered around the neighbourhood, especially on Frederick Douglass Boulevard (Eighth Avenue) between 110th and 125th Streets, the recession has slowed Harlem's renewal in other areas, particularly as you head east and north. Yet because redevelopers shunned Harlem for so long, it has managed to retain many of the buildings that went up around the turn of the century. Of particular interest, the **Mount Morris Historic District** (from 119th to 124th Streets, between Malcolm X Boulevard/Lenox Avenue & Mount Morris

Park West) contains charming brownstones and a collection of religious buildings in a variety of architectural styles.

While most tourists wind up at **Sylvia's** (328 Malcolm X Boulevard/Lenox Avenue, between 126th & 127th Streets, 1-212 996 0660), Harlem's best-known soul-food specialist, Harlemites (and visitors in the know) head for **Red Rooster** (310 Malcolm X Boulevard/Lenox Avenue, between 125th & 127th Streets), a gourmet Scandinavian-soulfood hotspot that opened in December 2010, or **Amy Ruth's** (113 W 116th Street; *see p212*), where each dish is named after a prominent African-American – try the President Barack Obama fried chicken. This section of West 116th Street, between St Nicholas Avenue and Morningside Park, is also **'Little Senegal'**, a strip of West African shops and restaurants; we recommend Africa Kine (256 W 116th Street, between Frederick Douglass and Adam Clayton Powell Jr Boulevards, 1-212 666 9400). Continue east along 116th Street West, past the domed **Masjid Malcolm Shabazz** (no.102, 1-212 662 2200), the mosque of Malcolm X's ministry, to the **Malcolm Shabazz Harlem Market** (no.52, 1-212 987 8131; open 10am-8pm daily), an outdoor bazaar that buzzes with vendors, most from West Africa, selling clothes, jewellery and other goods from covered stalls.

No visit to Harlem is complete without a visit to one of the nightspots devoted to the jazz that made the neighbourhood world renowned. The **Lenox Lounge** (*see p330*) is where Billie Holiday sang, John Coltrane played, the young Malcolm X hustled and James Baldwin held court. **Showman's Bar** (375 W 125th Street, between St Nicholas & Morningside Avenues, 1-212 864 8941, closed Sun), is another must for jazz-lovers.

Further north is **Strivers' Row**, also known as the St Nicholas Historic District. On 138th and 139th Streets, between Adam Clayton Powell Jr Boulevard (Seventh Avenue) and Frederick Douglass Boulevard (Eighth Avenue), these harmonious blocks of brick townhouses were developed in 1891 by David H King Jr and designed by three different architects, one of which was Stanford White. The enclave is so well preserved that the alleyway sign advising you to 'walk your horses' is still visible.

Harlem's rich history is stored in the archives of the nearby **Schomburg Center for Research in Black Culture** (*see below*). This branch of the New York Public Library contains more than five million documents, artefacts, films and prints relating to the cultures of peoples of African descent, with a strong emphasis on the African-American experience. A few blocks south, the **Abyssinian Baptist Church** (*see below*) is celebrated for its history, political activism and rousing gospel choir. For more secular inspiration, drop by the Shrine (2271 Adam Clayton Powell Jr Boulevard, between 133rd and 134th Streets, *see p226*) for imaginative cocktails and an ever-changing array of musical acts.

INSIDE TRACK CASTRO COMES TO HARLEM

Although it no longer accepts guests, the Theresa Towers (2090 Adam Clayton Powell Jr Boulevard, at 125th Street) was Harlem's most illustrious hotel until closing in 1966. Known as the 'Waldorf of Harlem,' the **Hotel Theresa** was home away from home to Louis Armstrong, Josephine Baker and Joe Louis, whose fans thronged outside following a victorious bout in 1941. In 1960, Fidel Castro, in New York to address the United Nations, moved the Cuban delegation to the Theresa after a falling out with the Hotel Shelburne downtown. Nehru and Krushchev visited Castro at the Theresa, as did Malcolm X, who conducted meetings of his Organization of Afro-American Unity here.

FREE Abyssinian Baptist Church

132 Odell Clark Place (138th Street), between Malcolm X Boulevard (Lenox Avenue) & Adam Clayton Powell Jr Boulevard (Seventh Avenue) (1-212 862 7474, www.abyssinian.org). Subway 2, 3 to 135th Street. **Services** 7pm Wed; 11am Sun. **Admission** free. **Map** p407 E11.

From the staid gingerbread Gothic exterior, you'd never suspect the energy that charges the Abyssinian when the gospel choir rocks the church every Sunday at 11am and Wednesday at 7pm (get there early, and don't wear shorts or flip-flops). A cauldron of community activism since its Ethiopian elders moved it uptown in the 1920s, the church was under the leadership of legendary civil rights crusader Adam Clayton Powell Jr in the 1930s (there's a modest exhibit about him inside). Today, the pulpit belongs to the Rev Dr Calvin Butts, who carries on the flame.

FREE Schomburg Center for Research in Black Culture

515 Malcolm X Boulevard (Lenox Avenue), between 135th & 136th Streets (1-212 491 2200, www.nypl.org). Subway 2, 3 to 135th Street. **Open** *General Research & Reference Division* noon-8pm Tue-Thur; 10am-6pm Fri, Sat. *Other departments* times vary. **Admission** free. **Map** p407 D12.

Part of the New York Public Library, this institution holds an extraordinary trove of vintage literature and historical memorabilia relating to black culture and the African diaspora, much of which was amassed by notable bibliophile Arturo Alfonso Schomburg, who was curator from 1932 until his death in 1938. (It was posthumously renamed in his honour.) Note that parts of the collection can only be viewed on certain days by appointment; call or refer to detailed hours by department on the NYPL's website. The centre also hosts occasional exhibits, jazz concerts, films, lectures and tours.

Studio Museum in Harlem

144 W 125th Street, between Adam Clayton Powell Jr Boulevard (Seventh Avenue) & Malcolm X Boulevard (Lenox Avenue) (1-212 864 4500, www.studiomuseum.org). Subway 2, 3 to 125th Street. **Open** noon-9pm Thur, Fri; 10am-6pm Sat; noon-6pm Sun. **Admission** *Suggested donation* $7; $3 reductions; free under-13s. Free to all Sun. **No credit cards**. **Map** p407 D13.

The first black fine-arts museum in the United States when it opened in 1968, the Studio Museum is an important player in the art scene of the African diaspora. Under the leadership of director and chief curator Thelma Golden (formerly of the Whitney), the stripped-down three-level space presents shows in a variety of media by black artists from around the world.

► *The new Museum for African Art goes into the art of the African diaspora in more depth.* *See p109* **Profile**.

SIGHTS

East Harlem

Subway 6 to 110th Street or 116th Street.

East of Fifth Avenue is **East Harlem**, commonly called Spanish Harlem but also known to its primarily Puerto Rican residents as El Barrio. North of 96th Street and east of Madison Avenue, El Barrio moves to a different beat. Its main east–west cross street, East 116th Street, shows signs of a recent influx of Mexican immigrants. A slight touch of East Village-style bohemia can be detected in such places as **Camaradas El Barrio** (2241 First Avenue, at 115th Street, 1-212 348 2703, www.camaradaselbarrio.com), a Puerto Rican tapas bar whose wooden benches, exposed brick and modest gallery create a casual hangout for kicking back over a pitcher of sangria or taking in a salsa or jazz show. The modest **Graffiti Hall of Fame** (106th Street, between Madison & Park Avenues) celebrates old- and new-school taggers in a schoolyard. Be sure to check out the recently revamped **El Museo del Barrio** (*see p111*), which has an impressive collection of Latin-American art and a lively programme of cultural events.

Hamilton Heights

Subway A, B, C, D, 1 to 145th Street.

Named after Alexander Hamilton, who owned a farm and estate here, **Hamilton Heights** extends from 125th Street to the Trinity Cemetery at 155th Street, between Riverside Drive and St Nicholas Avenue. Hamilton's 1802 Federal-style house, the **Grange**, now a national memorial, has been moved from 287 Convent Avenue around the corner to Saint Nicholas Park (414 W 141st Street, near Convent Avenue, 1-212 666 1640, www.nps.gov/hagr) and is expected to reopen to visitors in summer 2011.

The former factory neighbourhood developed after the West Side elevated train was built in the early 20th century. Today, it's notable for the elegant turn-of-the-20th-century row houses in the **Hamilton Heights Historic District**, centred on the side streets off scenic **Convent Avenue** between 140th and 145th Streets – just beyond the Gothic Revival-style campus of the **City College of New York** (Convent Avenue, from 135th to 140th Streets). Its main building, Shepard Hall (on Convent Avenue at 138th Street), is striking for its combination of white terra cotta interlaid with black stone that was removed to create the site for the college.

WASHINGTON HEIGHTS & INWOOD

Subway 1 to 157th Street; A, C, 1 to 168th Street; A to 190th Street.

The area from West 155th Street to Dyckman (200th) Street is called **Washington Heights**; venture north of that and you're in Inwood, Manhattan's northernmost neighbourhood, where the Harlem and Hudson Rivers converge. An ever-growing number of artists and young families are relocating to these parts, attracted by the spacious art deco buildings, big parks, hilly streets and (comparatively) low rents.

Washington Heights' main attraction is the **Morris-Jumel Mansion** (*see p125*), a stunning Palladian-style mansion that served as a swanky headquarters for George Washington during the autumn of 1776. But the small and often overlooked **Hispanic Society of America** (*see p125*), featuring a surprising collection of masterworks, is the real gem here.

Since the 1920s, waves of immigrants have settled in Washington Heights. In the post-World War II era, many German-Jewish refugees (among them Henry Kissinger, Dr Ruth Westheimer and Max Frankel, a former executive editor of the *New York Times*) moved to the western edge of the district. Broadway once housed a small Greek population – opera

Harlem.

singer Maria Callas lived here in her youth. But in the last few decades, the southern and eastern parts of the area have become predominantly Spanish-speaking due to a large population of Dominican settlers.

A trek along Fort Washington Avenue, from about 173rd Street to **Fort Tryon Park**, puts you in the heart of what is now called **Hudson Heights** – the posh area of Washington Heights. Start at the **George Washington Bridge**, the city's only bridge across the Hudson River. A pedestrian walkway (also a popular route for cyclists) allows for dazzling Manhattan views. Under the bridge on the New York side is a diminutive lighthouse. To see it up close, look for the footpath on the west side of the interchange on the Henry Hudson Parkway at about 170th Street. If you need to refuel, stop off at the lovely **New Leaf Café** (1 Margaret Corbin Drive, near Park Drive, 1-212 568 5323, closed Mon) within the Frederick Law Olmsted-designed Fort Tryon Park.

At the northern edge of the park is the **Cloisters** (*see p124*), a museum built in 1938 using segments of five medieval cloisters shipped from Europe by the Rockefeller clan. It houses the Metropolitan Museum of Art's permanent medieval art collection.

Inwood stretches from Dyckman Street up to 218th Street, the last residential block in Manhattan. Dyckman buzzes with streetlife from river to river, but, north of that, the island narrows considerably and the parks along the western shoreline culminate in the seclusion of **Inwood Hill Park**, another Frederick Law Olmsted legacy. Some believe that this is the location of the legendary 1626 transaction between Peter Minuit and the Native American Lenapes for the purchase of a strip of land called Manahatta – a plaque at the south-west corner of the ballpark near 214th Street marks the purported spot. The 196-acre refuge contains the island's last swathes of virgin forest and salt marsh. Today, with a bit of imagination, you can hike over the hilly terrain, liberally scattered with massive glacier-deposited boulders (called erratics), and picture Manhattan as it was before development. In recent years, the city's Parks Department has used the densely wooded area as a fledging spot for newly hatched bald eagles.

★ Cloisters

Fort Tryon Park, Fort Washington Avenue, at Margaret Corbin Plaza (1-212 923 3700, www.metmuseum.org). Subway A to 190th Street,

Walk The Harlem Renaissance

Speakeasies, literary lions and all that jazz.

From the end of World War I to the depths if the Depression in the 1930s, African-American musicians, writers and political activists flocked to Harlem, sowing seeds for one of the nation's greatest cultural flowerings. America's largest black neighbourhood experienced this influx because New York had become the country's recording, publishing and artistic capital – yet the city that attracted them kept blacks from living downtown because of segregation. This uneasy social cocktail was topped off by Prohibition, which lured whites uptown in search of the latest dance craze or hippest speakeasy.

Start your walk by getting on the goodfoot with a tour of the **Apollo Theater** (253 West 125th Street, between Frederick Douglass and Adam Clayton Powell Jr Boulevards, *see p321*). While the Apollo's heyday continued into the 1960s, its desegregation in 1934 made it an instant hotspot. One of the first Amateur Nights that year was won by a 17-year-old Ella Fitzgerald (she took home $25), and the legendary Bessie Smith wowed the crowds with a New Year's Eve concert in 1935. Two years later, Count Basie and his Orchestra had his Apollo debut, featuring a young (and very stage-frightened) Billie Holliday.

Head east from the Apollo and turn north on Adam Clayton Powell Jr Boulevard. The restored **Alhambra Ballroom** (2116 Adam Clayton Powell Jr Boulevard, at 126th Street) is now only open for private parties and celebrations but was highly popular from its opening in 1926, featuring such performers as Smith and Jelly Roll Morton and singing waitresses (including Holliday, briefly). Seven blocks north, cast a glance east along the unassuming townhouses of 133rd Street. Although nothing remains, this was once the raunchiest strip in Harlem, known as '**Jungle Alley**' to whites who ventured uptown for its speakeasies and after-hours clubs.

Harlem's nightlife is by no means a thing of the past, and if you're uptown one evening be sure to check out **The Shrine** (2271 Adam Clayton Powell Jr Boulevard, between 133rd and 134th Streets, *see p226*) for its eclectic music shows and inspired cocktails. However, **Small's Paradise** (2294 Adam Clayton Powell Jr Boulevard), a block north on the west side of the street, shuttered years ago. Once one of Harlem's most popular clubs (and employer of Malcolm Little, later Malcolm X, who worked there as a waiter), it is now an International House of Pancakes.

then M4 bus or follow Margaret Corbin Drive north, for about the length of 5 city blocks, to the museum. **Open** *Mar-Oct* 9.30am-5.15pm Tue-Sun. *Nov-Feb* 9.30am-4.45pm Tue-Sun. **Admission** *Suggested donation* (incl admission to Metropolitan Museum of Art on the same day) $20; $10-$15 reductions; free under-12s. **Credit** AmEx, DC, Disc, MC, V. **Map** p409 B3.

Turn east on 135th Street and pass the **Harlem YMCA** (180 W 135th Street), where countless black arrivals denied admission to segregated hotels stayed, including literary lions Langston Hughes, Claude McKay and James Baldwin (the YMCA's Little Theater is said to have launched the career of Paul Robeson). On the north-west corner of Malcolm X Boulevard, the **Schomburg Center for Research into Black Culture** (515 Malcolm X Boulevard, *see p121*) contains most of their work as well as an impressive archive of black history. Be sure to inspect the mosaic 'Rivers' on the floor of the foyer leading to the library's auditorium: the title comes from Hughes's poem 'The Negro Speaks of Rivers'. The poet's ashes are buried beneath it.

Sadly, nondescript highrises have replaced the fabled **Savoy Ballroom** and the **Cotton Club**, which used to pulsate further north along Malcolm X Boulevard (then known as Lenox Avenue). Opening in 1926, the Savoy (between 140th and 141st Streets) boasted an immense 250-foot by 50-foot dance floor that held up to 4,000. The integrated crowd enjoyed 'stompin' at the Savoy' to the syncopated beats of Fletcher Henderson's Rainbow Orchestra. The Cotton Club (at 142nd Street), which opened in 1923, was Mafia owned and did not admit blacks unless performing, but its radio broadcasts brought unprecedented exposure to the Duke Ellington Orchestra (the house band from 1927 to 1931) and Cab Calloway (who led the club's band from 1931 to 1934).

Need to rest those dancing feet? Then repair to the art deco **Lenox Lounge** (288 Malcolm X Boulevard, *see p330*) for a restorative drink and a sultry jazz show. The lounge, where Holliday, Coltrane, and other Harlem luminaries have performed, is a true Harlem landmark and has featured in many films evoking Harlem's past, including *Malcolm X* and the remake of *Shaft*.

Set in a lovely park overlooking the Hudson River, the Cloisters houses the Met's medieval art and architecture collections. A path winds through the peaceful grounds to a castle that seems to have survived from the Middle Ages. It was built a mere 72 years ago, using pieces of five medieval French cloisters. The collection itself is an inspired trove of Romanesque, Gothic and Baroque treasures brought from Europe and assembled in a manner that somehow manages not to clash. Be sure to check out the famous Unicorn Tapestries (c1500), the 12th-century Fuentidueña Chapel and the *Annunciation Triptych* by Robert Campin.

FREE Hispanic Society of America

Audubon Terrace, Broadway, between 155th & 156th Streets (1-212 926 2234, www.hispanicsociety.org). Subway 1 to 157th Street. **Open** 10am-4.30pm Tue-Sat; 1-4pm Sun. **Admission** free. **Map** p408 B9.

Though few people who pass this way seem aware of it, the Hispanic Society boasts the largest assemblage of Spanish art and manuscripts outside Spain. Goya's masterful *Duchess of Alba* greets you as you enter, while several haunting El Greco portraits can be found on the second floor. The collection is dominated by religious artefacts, including 16th-century tombs from the monastery of San Francisco in Cuéllar, Spain. Also on display are decorative art objects and thousands of black and white photographs that document life in Spain and Latin America from the mid 19th century to the present. One of the highlights, Valencian painter Joaquín Sorolla y Bastida's *Vision of Spain*, comprising 14 monumental oils commissioned by the Society in 1911, has recently returned to a renovated gallery after a three-year tour of Spain.

Morris-Jumel Mansion

65 Jumel Terrace, between 160th & 162nd Streets (1-212 923 8008, www.morrisjumel.org). Subway C to 163rd Street-Amsterdam Avenue. **Open** 10am-4pm Wed-Sun. **Admission** $5; $4 reductions; free under-13s. **Credit** AmEx, MC, V. **Map** p408 C8.

Constructed in 1765, Manhattan's only surviving pre-Revolutionary manse was originally the heart of a 130-acre estate that stretched from river to river (on the grounds, a stone marker points south with the legend 'New York, 11 miles'). George Washington planned the Battle of Harlem Heights here in 1776, after the British colonel Roger Morris moved out. The handsome 18th-century Palladian-style villa offers fantastic views. Its former driveway is now Sylvan Terrace, which has the longest continuous stretch (one block in total) of old wooden houses in all of Manhattan.

► *Other 18th-century buildings that are open to visitors include the Fraunces Tavern Museum (see p65) and the Van Cortlandt House Museum (see p147).*

Brooklyn

The second borough is bridging the gap.

Years ago, most tourists who found themselves in Brooklyn were likely to have missed the last subway stop in Manhattan. Recently, however, the second borough has become a destination in its own right. New bars and restaurants continue to proliferate, the music scene is thriving, and even Gray Line is running tours of the area.

Settled by the Dutch in the early 17th century, Breukelen took its name from the Dutch town. It was America's third largest municipality until its amalgamation with the four other boroughs that created New York City in 1898. Its many brownstones are a testament to a large and wealthy merchant class that made its money from the shipping trade. By the end of the 19th century, Brooklyn had become so prosperous, and its view of itself so grandiloquent, it built copies of the Arc de Triomphe (in Grand Army Plaza) and the Champs-Elysées (Eastern Parkway) and a greensward (Prospect Park) to rival Central Park.

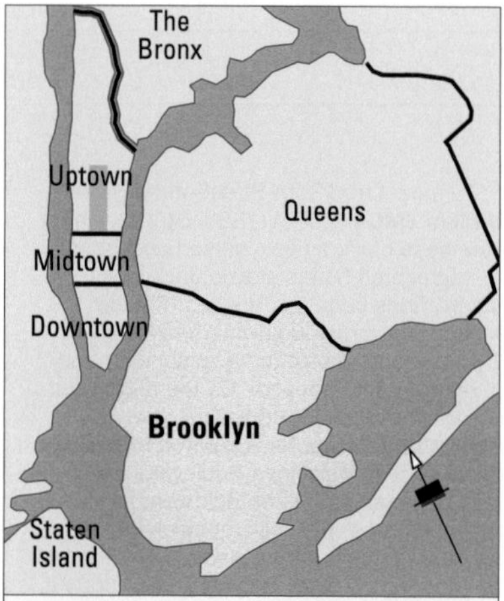

Map pp410-411
Hotels p180
Restaurants & cafés p212
Bars p226

THE CHANGING SCENE

From the arty punks of Bushwick to the Bugaboo-pushing mums of Windsor Terrace, Brooklynites identify themselves by and take great pride in their respective neighbourhoods. It's this precarious small-town-in-a-big-city vibe that gets residents up in arms about impending developments, of which there are many. The biggest and most prominent is the planned 22-acre **Atlantic Yards** complex in Prospect Heights, on the edge of Downtown Brooklyn, encompassing more than 6,000 apartments and the Barclay's Center arena for the New Jersey Nets, which was stalled by local opposition, legal battles and the recession. The original, ambitious plans for the arena by 'starchitect' Frank Gehry have been abandoned as too expensive, but the project moved a step forward in late 2009 when the Court of Appeals ruled that the state could seize residents' property for the developer under compulsory purchase. The first stone was laid in 2010, and the arena's expected to be completed in 2012.

BROOKLYN HEIGHTS & DUMBO

Subway A, C, F to Jay Street-Borough Hall; A, C, G to Hoyt-Schermerhorn; M, R to Court Street; 2, 3, 4, 5 to Borough Hall.

Home to well-to-do families, bankers and lawyers lured by its proximity to Wall Street, **Brooklyn Heights** is where you'll find the idyllic brownstoned, tree-lined streets of Brooklyn legend. Thanks to the area's historic district status, it has many Greek Revival and Italianate row houses dating from the 1820s. Take a stroll down the gorgeous tree-lined streets – try Cranberry, Hicks, Pierrepont and Willow – to see the area at its best.

Given its serenity and easy access to Manhattan, it's not surprising that Brooklyn Heights has been home to numerous illustrious (and struggling) writers. Walt Whitman printed up the first edition of *Leaves of Grass* at 98 Cranberry Street (in a building since demolished); Truman Capote wrote *Breakfast at Tiffany's* at 70 Willow Street; and Thomas Wolfe penned *Of Times and the River* at 5 Montague Terrace. Seven Middagh Street was something of a writers' commune, where Carson McCullers, Paul and Jane Bowles, WH Auden and Richard Wright resided at various times.

Henry and Montague Streets are the prime strips for shops, restaurants and bars. At the end of Montague, the **Brooklyn Heights Promenade** offers spectacular waterfront views of lower Manhattan, New York Harbor and the nearby **Brooklyn Bridge** (*see p130*), a marvel of 19th-century engineering that became the borough's iconic landmark.

For those interested in history of the underground variety, the **New York Transit Museum** (*see p130*) is a must. There are more remnants of bygone Brooklyn at the **Brooklyn Historical Society** building (*see p130*) which, when completed in 1881, was the first structure in New York to feature local terracotta on its façade. The grand **Borough Hall** (209 Joralemon Street, at Court Street), the seat of local government, stands as a monument to Brooklyn's past as an independent municipality. Completed in 1851 but only later crowned with a Victorian cupola, the Greek Revival edifice was renovated in the late 1980s. The building is linked to the **New York State Supreme Court** (360 Adams Street, between Joralemon Street & Tech Place) by **Cadman Plaza** (from Prospect Street to Tech Place, between Cadman Plaza East & Cadman Plaza West).

INSIDE TRACK
DUMBO ART PARTY

Each month, around 25 Dumbo galleries remain open late – some hosting special events – for the **1st Thursday Gallery Walk** (dumboculture411.com/1st-thursday-dumbo-gallery-walk/). On the night, you can pick up a map at 111 Front Street (between Adams & Washington Streets), which houses many of the galleries.

At the turn of the 19th century, **Dumbo** (Down Under the Manhattan Bridge Overpass) was a thriving industrial district; all kinds of manufacturers, including Brillo and Benjamin Moore, were based here, leaving behind a fine collection of factory buildings and warehouses; the most famous of these, the Eskimo Pie Building (100 Bridge Street, at York Street), with its embellished facade, was actually built for the Thomson Meter Company in 1908-09.

In the 1970s and '80s, these warehouses were colonised by artists seeking cheap live/work spaces, but playing out a familiar New York migration pattern, the area is now bursting with million-dollar apartments and high-end design shops. The spectacular views – taking in the Statue of Liberty, the lower Manhattan skyline and the Brooklyn and Manhattan Bridges – remain the same. The best vantage point is below the Brooklyn Bridge at the **Fulton Ferry Landing**, which juts out over the East River at Old Fulton and Water Streets and is

Dumbo.

Walk Tombs with a View

Pay your respects to the great and the good at Brooklyn's landmark cemetery.

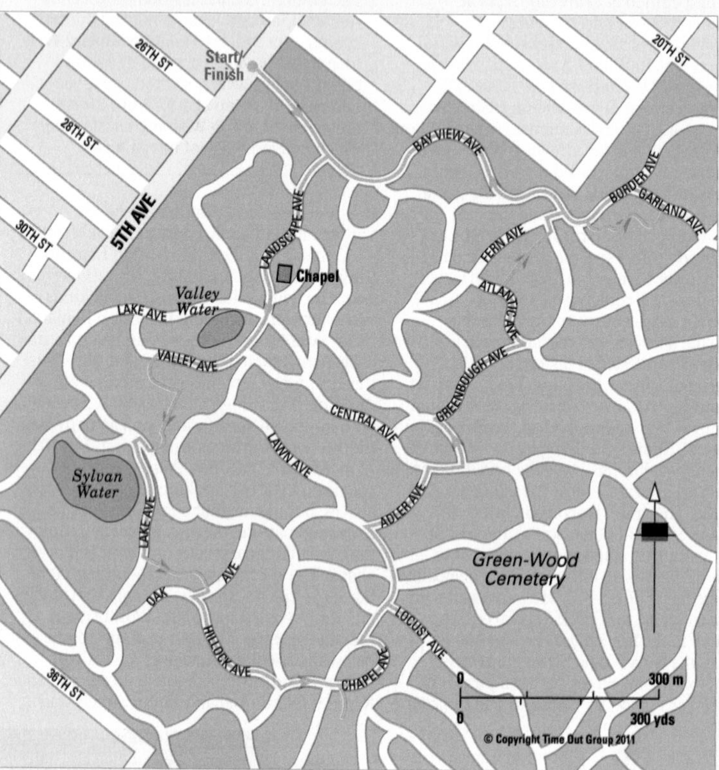

A century ago, Brooklyn's **Green-Wood Cemetery** (*see p134*) vied with Niagara Falls as New York State's greatest tourist attraction. Established in 1838, it's filled with Victorian mausoleums, cherubs and gargoyles. In fact, these winding paths, rolling hills and natural ponds served as the model for Central Park. It remains a beautiful place to spend a few hours, paying your respects to the celebrated and the notorious – among them Jean-Michel Basquiat, Leonard Bernstein and Mae West – who lie at rest in this 428-acre outdoor museum.

Start your walk at the Gothic main gate (Fifth Avenue at 25th Street, Sunset Park, Brooklyn). The spectacular, soaring arches are carved from New Jersey brownstone. That chirping you hear comes from monk parakeets that escaped a shipment to JFK in the 1960s and have nested here ever since.

Bear right and walk down **Landscape Avenue** to the chapel. Built in 1911, it was designed by Warren & Wetmore, the firm that was also responsible for building Grand Central Terminal. Outside, with the creepy Receiving Tomb on your left (this was where bodies were stored when the ground was frozen too hard to dig), head to the corner of Lake Avenue. Graves here belong to Clifton and William Prentiss, brothers who fought on opposite sides of the Civil War. They were both mortally wounded on the same day in 1865 (and both were treated by a nurse named Walt Whitman).

SIGHTS

Follow the pond on Waterside Path to **Valley Avenue**. The monument with the jug on top is the grave of John Eberhard Faber (who first put erasers on pencils). Make a left up Hill Side Path. The grave with the carved figure staring up at scenes from the deceased's life belongs to John Matthews, inventor of the soda fountain.

Cut across the grass and follow **Bluff Side Path** to the stairs down to Sylvan Water. Turn left on Lake, stopping by the tomb of Leonard Jerome, namesake of the Bronx's Jerome Avenue and grandfather of Winston Churchill. Make a left on **Ravine Path**. Up the steep incline, stop at the headstone marked 'Aloi' for a nice view of the Statue of Liberty. At the end of the path, make a right on Oak Avenue (turn around – that green bust is the grave of newspaperman Horace Greeley) and take your first left onto Hillock Avenue.

Make a left on **Landscape Avenue** and you'll find Bill 'The Butcher' Poole (think *Gangs of New York*), behind the huge tree on your left. Otherwise, head up Chapel Avenue and turn right on Thorn Path to the grave of Samuel Morse, inventor of the telegraph. Double back and make a right on **Chapel Avenue**. Walk around the Steinway family mausoleum and bear right. Make a right on Locust Avenue and see disgraced power-monger Boss Tweed's grave (left side), or stay on Chapel past Forest and Vista Avenues and make a right on Alder Avenue.

Next, make a right on Central Avenue and then a left on Sycamore Avenue. Then turn on Greenbough Avenue (you'll pass Henry Raymond, the founder of *The New York Times*), left on Atlantic Avenue and right on Warrior Path. Take the path to the end and climb the staircase to the **Civil War Soldiers' Monument**. The bench behind it has sweet views and it's also the site of the first and largest major battle of the Revolutionary War.

Follow Battle Path to the end, turn left on Garland Avenue. When you're even with the big tree, turn right. You're looking at the grave of Dodgers owner Charles Ebbets and, up the hill behind, the highest point in Brooklyn. Go straight on Garland, left on Border Avenue and right down Battle Avenue to the corner of Bay View Avenue. You'll pass the obelisk honouring the victims of the 1876 Brooklyn Theatre fire on your way back to the main gate.

close to two lovely refurbished parks: **Empire-Fulton Ferry State Park** and **Brooklyn Bridge Park** (riverside, between the Manhattan & Brooklyn Bridges).

Also at the water's edge is a dock for the **New York Water Taxi** (1-212 742 1969, www.nywatertaxi.com), an affordable and picturesque way to travel from Manhattan to Brooklyn and Queens. Along the same pier is the **Brooklyn Ice Cream Factory** (Fulton Ferry Landing, 1 Water Street, 1-718 246 3963, closed Mon Dec-Mar), located in a 1920s fireboat house. Next door, docked at the pier, is one of the borough's great cultural jewels: **Bargemusic** (*see p315*), a 100-foot steel barge that was built in 1899 but has staged chamber music concerts for the last 33 years.

The artists who flocked to the area en masse in the 1970s and '80s maintain a presence in the local galleries, most of which support the work of emerging talent. Among them are non-profit **Smack Mellon** (92 Plymouth Street, at Washington Street, 1-718 834 8761, smackmellon.org, closed Mon, Tue). The **Dumbo Arts Center** (30 Washington Street, between Plymouth & Water Streets, 1-718 694 0831, www.dumboartscenter.org, closed Mon & Tue) promotes artists through its gallery and sponsorship of the **Art Under the Bridge** festival (*see p265*), held in the autumn.

Dumbo is also becoming a performing arts hotspot. You can catch anything from puppet theatre to Lou Reed in concert at **St Ann's Warehouse** (*see p359*). Another artsy venue, which has even more diverse programming – think burlesque, camp variety and contemporary classical – is the **Galapagos Art Space** (*see p322*), which relocated from its Williamsburg birthplace to a gleaming, LEED-certified green space.

If you crave an authentic New York pizza, join the throngs lining up for a coal-fired pie at the famous **Grimaldi's** (19 Old Fulton Street, between Front & Water Streets, 1-718 858 4300). Across the street is the original building of the *Brooklyn Daily Eagle*, where Walt Whitman worked until he was fired for his lefty political leanings. It's now home to luxury condos.

Eating options in the neighbourhood are multifarious. For jumbo lump crab cake and goat's cheese gnocchi, head to **Five Front** (5 Front Street, between Old Fulton & Dock Streets, 1-718 625 5559, closed Mon), tucked under the Brooklyn Bridge. Right at the waterfront, **Bubby's** (1 Main Street, at Water Street, 1-718 222 0666) offers comfort food in a cavernous, kid-friendly setting. **Superfine** (126 Front Street, at Pearl Street, 1-718 243 9005, closed Mon) is a justly popular restaurant and bar that serves a great Sunday brunch. And the **Jacques Torres Chocolate** shop on Water

Street (*see p250*) offers fabulous cocoa and premium chocolates, made on-site (watch through a glass window). Cross the street for exquisite French pastries and espresso at **Almondine** (85 Water Street, between Main & Dock Streets, 1-718 797 5026).

While a good chunk of the retail is furniture shops catering to the loft-dwelling locals, Dumbo has a brace of destination stores for books and records. Also serving as a gallery and performance space, the **Powerhouse Arena** (37 Main Street, at Water Street; *see p271*) is the cavernous retail arm of Powerhouse Books, which produces sumptuous coffee-table tomes on such diverse subjects as rock stars, celebrity dogs and the Brooklyn Navy Yard. **Halcyon** (57 Pearl Street, at Water Street, 1-718 260 9299), one of the city's few surviving DJ-oriented music boutiques, recently celebrated a decade in business.

Head east on Water or Front Street to discover one of Brooklyn's forgotten neighbourhoods. Once a rough and bawdy patch dotted with bars and brothels frequented by sailors and dockworkers, **Vinegar Hill**, between Bridge Street and the Navy Yard, earned the moniker 'Hell's Half Acre' in the 19th century. Only fragments of the enclave remain (parts of it were designated a historic district in the late 1990s). Today, it's considerably quieter. Although inhabited, the isolated strips of early-19th-century row houses and defunct storefronts on Bridge, Hudson and Plymouth Streets, and a stretch of Front, have a ghost-town quality, heightened by their juxtaposition with a Con Edison generating station. The enclave has even gained its first eaterie: cosy, tavern-like **Vinegar Hill House** (72 Hudson Avenue, between Front & Water Streets, 1-718 522 1018, closed lunch Mon-Fri; *see p216*) has become a dining destination, thanks to its weekly changing comfort-food menu.

★ FREE Brooklyn Bridge

Subway A, C to High Street; J, M, Z to Chambers Street; 4, 5, 6 to Brooklyn Bridge-City Hall.
Map p411 S8.

Even if your trip to New York doesn't include a romp in the boroughs, you should try to make it halfway there by walking to the centre of the Brooklyn Bridge along its wide, wood-planked promenade. Stretching across the river's 1,595ft (486m) span, the bridge was constructed in response to the harsh winter of 1867 when the East River froze over, severing connection between Manhattan and what was then the nation's third most populous city. It was the vision of German-born civil engineer John Augustus Roebling, who died before it was completed in 1883. When it opened, the 5,989ft-long (1,825m) structure was the world's longest bridge, and the first bridge in the world to use steel suspension cables. From it, you'll enjoy striking views of the Statue of Liberty, New York Harbor and the skyscrapers of lower Manhattan.

▶ *You can also walk or bike into Brooklyn across the Manhattan or Williamsburg Bridges.*

Brooklyn Historical Society

128 Pierrepont Street, at Clinton Street, Brooklyn Heights (1-718 222 4111, www.brooklynhistory.org). Subway A, C, F to Jay Street-Borough Hall; M, R to Court Street; 2, 3, 4, 5 to Borough Hall.
Open noon-5pm Wed-Fri, Sun; 10am-5pm Sat.
Admission $6; $4 reductions; free under-12s.
Credit AmEx, DC, MC, V. **Map** p411 S9.

Founded in 1863, the BHS resides in a landmark four-storey Queen Anne-style building and presents several permanent and temporary exhibits, including the ongoing 'It Happened in Brooklyn', highlighting local links to crucial moments in American history. A major photo and research library – featuring historic maps and newspapers, notable family histories and archives from the area's abolitionist movement – is accessible by appointment only.

New York Transit Museum

Corner of Boerum Place & Schermerhorn Street, Brooklyn Heights (1-718 694 1600, www.mta.info/mta/museum). Subway A, C, G to Hoyt-Schermerhorn; 2, 3, 4, 5 to Borough Hall. **Open** 10am-4pm Tue-Fri; noon-5pm Sat, Sun. **Admission** $6; $4 reductions; free under-3s; free seniors Wed.
Credit AmEx, DC, MC, V. **Map** p411 S10.

Housed in a historic 1936 IND subway station, this is the largest museum in the United States devoted to urban public transportation history. Exhibits explore the social and practical impact of public transportation on the development of greater New York; among the highlights is an engrossing walk-through display charting the construction of the city's century-old subway system, when fearless 'sandhogs' were engaged in dangerous tunnelling. A line-up of turnstyles shows their evolution from the 1894 'ticket chopper' to the current Automatic Fare Card model. But the best part is down another level to a real platform where you can board an exceptional collection of vintage subway and El ('Elevated') cars, some complete with vintage ads.
Other locations New York Transit Museum

INSIDE TRACK THE TRUCK STOPS HERE

At weekends from May through October, Latin American street vendors descend in vans on the corner of Bay and Clinton Streets, adjacent to the **Red Hook Ballfields**, to serve up some of the finest street food in the city, including Ecuadoran *ceviche*, Salvadoran *papusas*, and Mexican tacos and *huaraches*.

Gallery Annex & Store, Grand Central Terminal, adjacent to stationmaster's office, Main Concourse (1-212 878 0106; *see p105*).

BOERUM HILL, CARROLL GARDENS & COBBLE HILL

Subway A, C, F to Jay Street; F, G to Bergen Street, Carroll Street; 2, 3, 4, 5, M, N, R, W to Court Street-Borough Hall.

A convenient if annoying real estate agents' contraction for these blurred-boundaried 'hoods, BoCoCa is a prime example of gentrification at work. Gone are the bodegas and cheap shoe shops along the stretch of Smith Street that runs from Atlantic Avenue to the Carroll Street subway stop; it's now known as the area's Restaurant Row. Among the strip's hottest spots are the classic bistro **Bar Tabac** (no.128, at Dean Street, Boerum Hill, 1-718 923 0918); new American favourites **The Grocery** (no.288, between Sackett & Union Streets, Carroll Gardens, 1-718 596 3335, closed Mon, Sun); and **Chestnut** (no.271, between DeGraw & Sackett Streets, Carroll Gardens, 1-718 243 0049, closed Mon). Check out the stylish women's clothing at **Bird** (no.220, at Butler Street, Cobble Hill, 1-718 797 3774) and **Dear Fieldbinder** (no.198, between Sackett & Warren Streets, Carroll Gardens, 1-718 852 3620).

Head east on Boerum Hill's **Atlantic Avenue** for a slew of antique and modern furniture stores. Among the best are **City Foundry**, an industrial-chic furniture store (no.365, between Bond & Hoyt Streets, 1-718 923 1786, closed Mon) and **Darr** (no.369, between Bond & Hoyt Streets, 1-718-797-9733), a favourite among stylists and set designers for its taxidermy, industrial cabinets and tamer goods such as horn tableware. The same owners also operate top-notch, neo-rustic menswear emporium **Hollander & Lexer** across the street (no.358, 1-718 797 9190). Browse women's haute designer fashion at the minimalist **Eva Gentry** (no.389, between Bond & Hoyt Streets, 1-718 260 9033) and its more affordable sister store **Eva Gentry Consignment** (no.371, between Hoyt & Bond Streets, 1-718 522 3522).

The mile-long stretch of Atlantic Avenue between Henry and Nevins Streets was once crowded with Middle Eastern restaurants and markets, though gentrification has also taken its toll. One stalwart is the **Sahadi Importing Company** (no.187, between Clinton & Court Streets, Cobble Hill, 1-718 624 4550, closed Sun), a neighbourhood institution that sells olives, spices, cheeses, nuts and other gourmet treats. West of Boerum Hill, **Cobble Hill** has a palpable small-town feel. Here, **Court Street** is dotted with cafés and shops, such as local favourite **Book Court** (no.163, between Pacific & Dean Streets, Cobble Hill, 1-718 875 3677). Be sure to stop by the charming **Sweet Melissa** (no.276, between Butler & Douglass Streets, 1-718 855 3410), which serves lunch, pastries and afternoon tea in a pretty back garden. Walk over the Brooklyn-Queens Expressway to Cobble Hill's industrial waterfront and the corner building housing Mexican bistro **Alma** (187 Columbia Street, at DeGraw Street, 1-718 643 5400). The rooftop dining area (closed Mon-Wed Dec-Mar) has great views of the East River and lower Manhattan.

Further south, you'll cross into the still predominantly Italian-American **Carroll Gardens**. Pick up a prosciutto loaf from the **Caputo Bakery** (329 Court Street, between Sackett & Union Streets, 1-718 875 6871) or an aged soppressata salami from **G Esposito & Sons** (357 Court Street, between President & Union Streets, 1-718 875 6863); then relax in **Carroll Park** (from President to Carroll Streets, between Court & Smith Streets) and watch the old-timers play *bocce* (lawn bowling). Alternatively, a cluster of excellent eateries on Court Street includes casual trattoria **Frankies 457** (no.457, between Lucquer Street & 4th Place, 1-718 403 0033), its Germanic spin-off **Prime Meats** (no.465, 1-718 254 0327) and seasonal American bistro **Buttermilk Channel** (no.524, at Huntington Street; *see p213*).

RED HOOK

Subway F, G to Smith-9th Streets, then B77 bus.

To the south-west of Carroll Gardens, beyond the Brooklyn-Queens Expressway, the formerly rough-and-tumble industrial locale of **Red Hook** has long avoided urban renewal. However, in recent years, the arrivals of gourmet mega-grocer **Fairway** on Van Brunt Street and an immense outpost of Swedish furniture superstore IKEA have served notice that gentrification is slowly moving in.

Luckily for its protective residents, the Hook still feels like a well-kept secret, tucked away on a peninsula. While the area continues to evolve, its time-warp charm is still evident, and its decaying piers make a moody backdrop for massive cranes, empty warehouses and trucks clattering over cobblestone streets. The lack of public transport has thus far prevented it from becoming the next Williamsburg. From the Smith-9th Streets subway stop, it's either a half hour walk south or a transfer to the B77 bus, although the **New York Water Taxi** (*see p59*) has improved the situation by adding stops to Beard Street Pier behind Fairway.

INSIDE TRACK BROOKLYN FLEA MARKET

At weekends from March through November, join meandering Brooklynites at the **Brooklyn Flea** (10am-5pm Sat, 176 Lafayette Avenue, between Clermont & Vanderbilt Avenues; 10am-5pm Sun, 1 Hansen Place, at Flatbush Avenue, www.brooklynflea.com) to browse indie crafts, vintage clothing, artisanal chocolate and perhaps less actual junk than some flea-loving cheapskates would like.

Urban adventurers are rewarded if they make a trip out here. The area offers singular views of the Statue of Liberty and New York Harbor from **Valentino Pier**, and has an eclectic selection of artists' studios, bars and eateries. Retro bar and grill **Hope & Anchor** (347 Van Brunt Street, at Wolcott Street, 1-718 237 0276) opened almost a decade ago, when the stretch was still a culinary wasteland. Similarly pioneering was the **Good Fork** (391 Van Brunt Street, near Coffey Street, 1-718 643 6636, closed Mon), now a local institution, which blends traditional Korean flavours into its trendy American cooking. More recently, the area received a major culinary boost with the arrival of **Fort Defiance** (*see p214*), a vibrant café that draws crowds throughout the day for its breakfasts, new American menu and innovative cocktails. Long-standing dive **Sunny's Bar** (253 Conover Street, between Beard & Reed Streets, 1-718 625 8211) remains keeper of the 'hood's gritty waterfront vibe.

A scattering of quirky local shops includes **Metal & Thread** (398 Van Brunt Street, between Coffey & Dikeman Streets, 1-718 414 9651, Mon-Wed by appointment only), which artfully juxtaposes a mix of locally made and vintage items, and the fastidiously curated antique jewellery shop **Erie Basin** (388 Van Brunt Street, at Dikeman Street, 1-718 554 6147, closed Mon-Wed & Mon-Wed, Sun in July & Aug).

To check out the work of local artists, look for the word 'Gallery' hand-scrawled on the doors of the **Kentler International Drawing Space** (353 Van Brunt Street, between Wolcott & Dikeman Streets, 1-718 875 2098, closed Mon-Wed), or, at weekends, visit the **Brooklyn Waterfront Artists Coalition**'s 25,000-square-foot exhibition space (499 Van Brunt Street, at Beard Street Pier, 1-718 596 2507, www.bwac.org, closed Nov-Feb, Apr, and Mon-Fri May-Oct) in a Civil War-era warehouse on the pier just south of Fairway. BWAC hosts large group shows in the spring and autumn.

PARK SLOPE & PROSPECT HEIGHTS

Subway (Park Slope) F to 7th Avenue, 15th Street-Prospect Park; F, M, R to Fourth Ave-9th Street; M, R to Union Street. (Prospect Heights) B, Q, Franklin Avenue S to Prospect Park; 2, 3 to Eastern Parkway-Brooklyn Museum, Grand Army Plaza; M, R to 25th Street.

Bustling with lively children, baby strollers and the parents who cart them around, **Park Slope** houses hip, young families in Victorian brownstones and feeds them organically from the nation's oldest working food co-operative (only open to members). The neighbourhood's intellectual, progressive-mindedness and lefty political heritage is palpable; local residents include Hollywood actors (Maggie Gyllenhaal, John Turturro and Steve Buscemi, among others) and famous authors (Paul Auster and Jonathan Safran Foer).

Fifth Avenue is the prime locale for restaurants and hip bars. Locals flock to the beloved, always-packed Venetian mainstay **Al Di Là** (*see p212*) and late-night favourites **Blue Ribbon Brooklyn** (no.280, between Garfield Place & 1st Street, 1-718 840 0404) and **Blue Ribbon Sushi Brooklyn** (no.278, between 1st Street & Garfield Place, 1-718 840 0408), part of an acclaimed New York mini-chain. Interesting shops can be found all along Fifth Avenue too, including urban gear depot **Brooklyn Industries** (no.206, at Union Street, 1-718 789 2764); **Matter** (no.227, between President & Carroll Streets, 1-718 230 1150), offering design objects, jewellery, books and a mini art gallery; and the wonderful **Brooklyn Superhero Supply Co.** (no. 372, between 5th & 6th Streets; *see p252*), whose secret identity is a non-profit kids' writing centre.

Park Slope's lesbian community is one of the Big Apple's strongest. You can explore Sapphic lore at the **Lesbian Herstory Archives** (*see p303*), then do field research at **Ginger's Bar** (*see p310*). Park Slope's gay gents frequent **Excelsior** (*see p309*), a low-key bar with a vibrant jukebox and lush back garden. And whether you're straight or gay, boy or girl, you'll want to head off the beaten path to clubby bar **Union Hall** (*see p229*), which has its own indoor *bocce* courts and a live music space downstairs.

The western edge of Prospect Park is a section of the landmarked **Park Slope Historic District**. Brownstones and several fine examples of Romanesque Revival and Queen Anne residences grace these streets. Particularly charming are the brick edifices that line Carroll Street, Montgomery Place and Berkeley Place. Fans of writer-director Noah Baumbach, who grew up in these parts, may

Brooklyn Botanic Garden.

recognise the locale from 2005 hit *The Squid and the Whale*, much of which was set here.

Central Park may be bigger and far more famous, but **Prospect Park** (main entrance at Grand Army Plaza, Prospect Heights, 1-718 965 8999, www.prospectpark.org) has a more rustic quality. By taking a short stroll into its lush green expanse, you may forget you're in the midst of a bustling metropolis. This masterpiece, which designers Frederick Law Olmsted and Calvert Vaux said was more in line with their vision than Central Park, is a great spot for birdwatching, especially with a little guidance from the **Prospect Park Audubon Center at the Boathouse** (park entrance on Ocean Avenue, at Lincoln Road, Prospect Heights, 1-718 287 3400, closed Mon-Wed Apr-mid Dec, Mon-Fri mid Jan-Mar).

Alternatively, you can pretend you've left the city altogether by boating or hiking amid the waterfalls, pools and wildlife habitats of the **Ravine District** (park entrances on Prospect Park West, at 3rd, 9th & 15th Streets, Park Slope). The rolling green park was created with equestrians in mind; you can saddle a horse at the nearby **Kensington Stables** (*see p345*) or hop on a bike and pedal alongside Rollerbladers and runners. Children enjoy riding the hand-carved horses at the park's antique carousel (Flatbush Avenue, at Empire Boulevard) and seeing real animals in the **Prospect Park Zoo** (park entrance on Flatbush Avenue, near Ocean Avenue, Prospect Heights, 1-718 399 7339). A 15-minute walk from Prospect Park is the verdant necropolis of **Green-Wood Cemetery** (*see p128* **Walk**).

Near the main entrance to Prospect Park sits the massive Civil War memorial arch at **Grand Army Plaza** (intersection of Flatbush Avenue, Eastern Parkway & Prospect Park West) and the central branch of the **Brooklyn Public Library** (Grand Army Plaza, Prospect Heights, 1-718 230 2100). The library's central Brooklyn Collection includes thousands of artefacts and photos tracing the borough's history. Around the corner are the tranquil **Brooklyn Botanic Garden** (*see below*) and also the **Brooklyn Museum** (*see p134*), which has a renowned Egyptology collection and a varied roster of temporary exhibitions.

Brooklyn Botanic Garden

1000 Washington Avenue, at Eastern Parkway, Prospect Heights (1-718 623 7200, www.bbg.org). Subway B, Q, Franklin Avenue S to Prospect Park; 2, 3 to Eastern Parkway-Brooklyn Museum. **Open** *Mar-Oct* 8am-6pm Tue-Fri; 10am-6pm Sat, Sun. *Nov-Feb* 8am-4.30pm Tue-Fri; 10am-4.30pm Sat, Sun. **Admission** $8; $4 reductions; free under-12s. Free to all Tue; 10am-noon Sat; Sat, Sun mid Nov-Feb. **Credit** DC, MC, V. **Map** p411 U11.

This 52-acre haven of luscious greenery was founded in 1910. In spring, when Sakura Matsuri, the annual Cherry Blossom Festival, takes place, prize buds and Japanese culture are in full bloom. The restored Eastern Parkway entrance and the Osborne Garden – an Italian-style formal garden – are also worth a peek.

★ Brooklyn Museum

200 Eastern Parkway, at Washington Avenue, Prospect Heights (1-718 638 5000, www.brooklynmuseum.org). Subway 2, 3 to Eastern Parkway-Brooklyn Museum. **Open** 11am-6pm Wed; 11am-10pm Thur, Fri; 11am-6pm Sat, Sun; 11am-11pm 1st Sat of mth (except Sept). **Admission** Suggested donation $10; $6 reductions; free under-12s. Free to all 5-11pm 1st Sat of mth (except Sept). **Credit** AmEx, DC, MC, V. **Map** p411 U11.

While most visitors tend to overlook the Brooklyn Museum, getting their artistic fix from Manhattan's more illustrious collections, the borough's premier institution is one of the city's cultural gems. It presents a tranquil alternative to Manhattan's bigger-name spaces; it's rarely crowded. Among the museum's many assets is the third-floor Egyptian galleries (the entire collection is one of the finest outside of Egypt and numbers more than 8,000 objects). Highlights include the resplendent cartonnage of the priest Nespanetjerenpere; a rare terracotta female figure from 3500-3400 BC; and the Mummy Chamber, an installation of 170 objects related to the post-mortem practice, including human and animal mummies. Also on this level, masterworks by Cézanne, Monet and Degas, part of an impressive European art collection, are displayed in the museum's skylighted Beaux-Arts Court. The Elizabeth A Sackler Center for Feminist Art on the fourth floor is dominated by American artist Judy Chicago's monumental mixed-media installation, *The Dinner Party* (1974-79); its centrepiece is a massive, triangular 'table' with 39 place settings, each representing important women down the ages. The fifth floor is devoted to American works, including Albert Bierstadt's immense *A Storm in the Rocky Mountains, Mt Rosalie*, and the Visible Storage-Study Center, where paintings, furniture and other objects are intriguingly juxtaposed.

Temporary shows in 2011 include 'Youth and Beauty: Art of the American Twenties' (28 October 2011-22 January 2012) and 'Life, Death and Transformation in the Americas' (22 July 2011-27 May 2012), featuring sacred indigenous objects from the museum's collection.

★ FREE Green-Wood Cemetery

Fifth Avenue, at 25th Street, Sunset Park (1-718 768 7300, www.green-wood.com). Subway M, R to 25th Street. **Open** *Sept-May* 8am-5pm daily; *June-Aug* 7am-7pm daily. **Admission** free. **Map** p411 S13.

See p128 **Walk**.

WILLIAMSBURG & BUSHWICK

Subway L to Bedford Avenue; L to Jefferson Street.

With a thriving music scene and an abundance of funky bars, galleries and shops, Williamsburg – or 'Billyburg' as it's affectionately known – channels the East Village (just one stop away on the L train) in its heyday. But the area teeters on the brink of (or, some argue, has already fallen into) hipster cliché. Long before the trendsetters invaded, Williamsburg's waterfront location made it ideal for industry. When the Erie Canal linked the Atlantic Ocean to the Great Lakes in 1825, the area became a bustling port. Companies such as Pfizer and Domino Sugar started here, but businesses had begun to abandon the area's huge industrial spaces by the late 20th century. A sign of the area's rapid gentrification, the Domino refinery finally closed in 2004, though its signature sign is still a local landmark.

Bedford Avenue is the neighbourhood's main thoroughfare. By day, the epicentre of the strip is the **Bedford MiniMall** (no.218, between North 4th & North 5th Streets) – you won't find a Gap or Starbucks here, but you will be able to contemplate a beer selection that will make your head spin at **Spuyten Duyvil Grocery** (1-718 384 1520, closed Mon), browse an exceptionally edited selection of books and magazines at **Spoonbill & Sugartown, Booksellers** (1-718 387-7322) and drink some of the best iced coffee around at the **Verb Café** (1-718 599 0977). The café scene on Bedford is still growing, with arrivals such as the rustic **Blackbird Parlour** (no.197, at North 6th Street, 1-718 599 2707) and organic haven **Ella Café** (no.177, between North 7th & North 8th Streets, 1-718 218 8079), while New York institution **Peter Luger** (*see p215*) grills what most carnivores consider to be the best steak in the city. American bistro **Rye** (*see p216*) has culinary substance as well as style, while **Relish** (225 Wythe Avenue, at North 3rd Street, 1-718 963 4546), housed in a refurbished railcar, serves fancy fare in diner digs. The **Radegast Hall & Biergarten** (113 North 3rd Street, at Berry Street, 1-718 963 3973) is invariably hopping with Billyburgers craving its stellar array of wurst and beer.

You'll find chic shops along North 6th Street, particularly between Wythe and Kent Avenues. Among them are the designer co-op **5 in 1** (no.60, 1-718 384 1990, closed Mon-Thur), housed in a former railcar factory, **Built by Wendy** (no.46, 1-718 384 2882), which offers retro-flavoured threads for both sexes; and innovative home-design emporium **The Future Perfect** (no.115; *see p258*). The 'hood also has more than 30 art galleries (for our pick

Williamsburg.

of the best, *see p299*), which stay open late on the second Friday of every month. Pick up the free gallery guide *Wagmag* at local shops and cafés or visit www.wagmag.org for listings. However, as artists are priced out of the area, more experimental spaces have taken root in the warehouses of Bushwick to the west.

Billyburg is famously band central. From twee emo to stoner psychedelica, local rock bands and touring indie darlings play at **Music Hall of Williamsburg** (*see p327*) and **Pete's Candy Store** (*see p327*). For years, the **McCarren Park Pool** (at Lorimer Street and Driggs Avenue) was a happening outdoor concert venue hosting local and national acts, but its celebrated Pool Parties (www.thepool parties.com) have moved to the Williamsburg waterfront. The park is, however, still home to other events such as June's Renegade Craft Fair (www.renegadecraft.com/brooklyn).

On a different note, the admission price to the **City Reliquary** (370 Metropolitan Avenue, near Havemeyer Street, 1-718 782 4842, open 7-10pm Thur; noon-6pm Sat, Sun) tips you off to its nostalgic bent. A trifling 50 cents gets you into the weekends-only mini-museum of New York history: architectural salvage from renovated landmarks such as the Carlyle Hotel, old subway tokens and Statue of Liberty memorabilia. It also hosts themed temporary exhibitions. Equally beloved is the **Brooklyn Brewery** (79 North 11th Street, between Berry Street & Wythe Avenue, 1-718 486 7422, www.brooklynbrewery.com), which is in a former ironworks. Visit during the happy 'hour' (Fridays 6-11pm) for $4 drafts or take a tour on weekends (hourly 1-5pm Sat; 1-4pm Sun).

With Billyburg approaching hipster saturation point and rents rising accordingly, neighbouring **Bushwick** has caught on as a cheap(er) place for digs as well as a prime nightlife destination. Bounded by Bushwick Avenue to the north-west and Broadway to the south-west, this traditionally Latino neighbourhood has begun to sprout coffee shops and vintage stores over the last few years, not to mention such highly regarded restos as intimate locavore hotspot **Northeast Kingdom** (18 Wyckoff Avenue, at Troutman Street, 1-718 386 3864) and highly acclaimed Italian newcomer **Roberta's** (*see p215*).

Afterwards, get your groove on at the **Beauty Bar** (921 Broadway, at Melrose Street, 1-718 529 0370), where nightly DJs spin punk to funk soundtracks, or slake your thirst in one of the vinyl car-seat booths at the **Wreck Room** (940 Flushing Avenue, at Evergreen Avenue, 1-718 418 6347).

FORT GREENE

Subway B, D, N, Q, R to DeKalb Avenue; B, Q, 2, 3, 4, 5 to Atlantic Avenue; C to Lafayette Avenue; D, M, N, R to Pacific Street; G to Fulton Street, Clinton-Washington Avenues.

With its stately Victorian brownstones and other grand buildings, Fort Greene has undergone a major revival over the past two decades. It has long been a centre of African-American life and business – Spike Lee, Branford Marsalis and Chris Rock have all lived here. **Fort Greene Park** (from Myrtle to DeKalb Avenues, between St Edwards Street & Washington Park) was conceived in 1846 at the behest of poet Walt Whitman (then editor of the *Brooklyn Daily Eagle*); its masterplan was fully realised by Olmsted and Vaux in 1867.

At the centre of the park stands the Prison Ship Martyrs Monument, erected in 1909 (from a design by Stanford White) in memory of 11,000 American prisoners who died on British ships that were anchored nearby during the Revolutionary War.

Despite its name, the 34-floor **Williamsburgh Savings Bank**, located at the corner of Atlantic and Flatbush Avenues, is in Fort Greene, not Williamsburg. The 512-foot (156-metre) structure was long the tallest in the borough and, with its four-sided clocktower, one of the most recognisable features of the Brooklyn skyline. The 1927 building has now been renamed One Hanson Place, and converted into (what else?) luxury condominiums.

Though originally founded in Brooklyn Heights, the **Brooklyn Academy of Music** (*see p311*) moved to its current site on Fort Greene's southern border in 1901. America's oldest operating performing arts centre, BAM was the home of the Metropolitan Opera until

1921; today, it's known for ambitious cultural performances of all varieties that draw big audiences from throughout the metropolitan area. Almost as famous is the cheesecake at nearby **Junior's Restaurant** (386 Flatbush Avenue, at DeKalb Avenue,1-718 852 5257).

Stuart & Wright (85 Lafayette Avenue, between South Elliott Place & South Portland Avenue, 1-718 797 0011) stocks lovely (if pricey) men's and women's clothing by local designers. In addition to some funky shops, a slew of restaurants can be found on or near **DeKalb Avenue**, including South African **i-Shebeen Madiba** (no.195, between Carlton Avenue & Adelphi Street, 1-718 855 9190); lively bistro **Chez Oskar** (no.211, at Adelphi Street, 1-718 852 6250); and French-accented fave **iCi** (no.246, at Vanderbilt Avenue, 1-718 789 2778).

CONEY ISLAND & BRIGHTON BEACH

Subway B, Q to Brighton Beach; D, F, N, Q to Coney Island-Stillwell Avenue; F to Neptune Avenue; F, Q to West 8th Street-NY Aquarium.

Coney Island is on the brink of reinvention (*see below* **New Life at the Old Fairground**).

In the meantime the site is a little desolate, but worth a visit for nostalgics and the atmospheric, three-mile-long boardwalk.

Nathan's Famous hot dog stand (1310 Surf Avenue, at Stillwell Avenue, 1-718 946 2202) is still serving the sizzling, juicy dogs that made its name in 1916. And **Coney Island USA** (1208 Surf Avenue, at W 12th Street, Coney Island, 1-718 372 5159, www.coneyisland.com) keeps the torch burning for 20th-century-style attractions with its **Sideshows by the Seashore**, including legendary freaks such as human pincushion Scott Baker (aka the Twisted Shockmeister) and Heather Holliday, a ravenous sword swallower. Other disturbing appetites are sated every year at **Nathan's Famous Fourth of July Hot Dog Eating Contest** (*see p264*), which always draws a crowd. There's also baseball with **Brooklyn Cyclones** (*see p339*), who play at the seaside **MCU Park**.

If you head left on the boardwalk from Coney Island, a short walk brings you to **Brighton Beach**, New York's Little Odessa. Groups of Russian expats (the display of big hair and garish fashion can be jaw-dropping) crowd semi-outdoor eateries such as **Tatiana** (3152 Brighton 6th Street, at the Boardwalk, 1-718 891 5151) – at night, it morphs into a glitzy club. A better, if less picturesquely placed, bet is **Primorski** (282 Brighton Beach Avenue, 1-718 891 3111), north of the seafront. Buy pickled foodstuffs to take home with you at the enormous **M&I International Foods** (249 Brighton Beach Avenue, 1-718 615 1011).

SIGHTS

New Life at the Old Fairground

Luna Park shoots for the stars.

In its heyday, from the turn of the century until the Second World War, **Coney Island** was New York City's playground drawing millions each year to its seaside amusement parks, Dreamland, Luna Park and Steeplechase Park. The first two were destroyed by fire (Dreamland in 1911 and Luna Park in 1944) and not rebuilt, while Steeplechase Park staggered on until 1964. Astroland was built in 1962 in the euphoria of the World's Fair, went up in flames in 1975 and was rebuilt, only to shutter in 2008.

A few years before, a developer bought about half the area's entertainment district with a view to transforming it into a glitzy, Las Vegas-style resort, with hotels and condos, as well as restaurants, shops and rides. However, a standoff with municipal planners forestalled any progress. Then, in 2009, the city agreed to buy almost seven acres near the boardwalk that would form the core of a 27-acre amusement district, and a new incarnation of Luna Park (www.lunaparknyc.com) opened in the summer of 2010, with such original attractions as the Cyclone, a whiplash-inducing rollercoaster built in 1926, and the 1918 Wonder Wheel – both protected landmarks.

Brooklynites wishing for Coney Island to recapture its popularity hope the new Astroland catches fire – though not literally.

Queens

Enjoy edgy art and every food on the planet.

Let's be honest: Queens is not the first stop for most visitors to New York. In fact, its main claim to fame are probably its airports (around 200,000 people pass through JFK and La Guardia every day) and its curmudgeonly TV characters, yet the city's largest borough is actually the country's most diverse urban area, with almost half its 2.3 million residents hailing from one of nearly 150 different nations. Not for nothing is the elevated 7 subway line nicknamed the 'International Express'.

Queens's ethnic diversity is best sampled at its restaurants. **Astoria** is home to Greek tavernas and Brazilian churrascarias; **Jackson Heights** provides Indian, Thai and South American eateries; and **Flushing** boasts the city's second largest Chinatown and countless Korean barbecues.

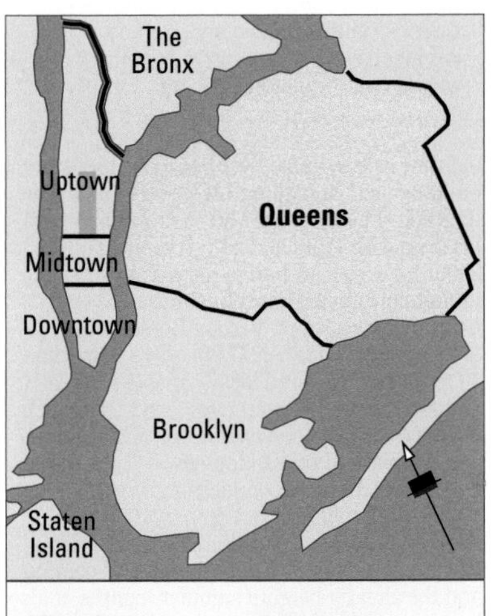

Map p412
Hotels p181
Restaurants & cafés p216
Bars p229

LONG ISLAND CITY

Subway E, M (M on weekdays) to 23rd Street-Ely Avenue; G to 21st Street-Jackson Avenue; 7 to Vernon Boulevard-Jackson Avenue, or 45th Road-Court House Square.

Just across the East River from Manhattan, **Long Island City** has been touted as the 'next Williamsburg' (the hipster Brooklyn enclave; *see p135*) for so long that countless other 'hoods have since claimed and passed on the mantle. In truth, its proximity and easy access – via subway, tunnel and bridge – to Midtown have made LIC more attractive to upscale professionals, who've moved into the modern apartment towers rising on the waterfront, than to hipsters or would-be artists. Nevertheless, the neighbourhood has one of the city's most adventurous museums and a burgeoning art scene.

In the warmer months, begin by taking in the Midtown Manhattan panorama from **Watertaxi Beach** (Borden Avenue, at 2nd Street), a man-made sandy patch with a bar and volleyball courts. If you'd prefer a more sedate setting for gazing at the spectacle, try **Gantry Plaza State Park** (48th Avenue, at Center Boulevard), named after the hulking 19th-century railroad gantries that once transferred cargo from ships to trains. Both are directly across the East River from the United Nations, giving postcard-worthy views of the skyline.

Dining options in the area include the **Waterfront Crabhouse** (2-03 Borden Avenue, at 2nd Street, 1-718 729 4862), an

INSIDE TRACK DRAGON BOAT BLESSINGS

More than 150 boats race on 6 and 7 August from 10am to 5pm at Meadow Lake in Flushing Meadows–Corona Park during the free **Hong Kong Boat Festival**, where land-lubbing spectators play cheerleader and enjoy martial arts demonstrations and music. For more info, check out www.hkdbf-ny.org.

> **INSIDE TRACK**
> **MOVIES ON THE WATERFRONT**
>
> In summer, the East River forms a delightful backdrop for the **Socrates Sculpture Park's Outdoor Cinema** series, which showcases the various cultures of Queens via film, music and food on Wednesdays. For more info, check out out www.socratesculpturepark.org.

old-time saloon and oyster bar in an 1880s brick building, and, signalling LIC's recent culinary upgrade, **Testaccio** (47-30 Vernon Boulevard, between 47th Road and 48th Avenue, 1-718 937 2900), an engaging Italian restaurant serving up Roman cuisine. For refreshments, **Communitea** (47-02 Vernon Boulevard, at 47th Avenue, 1-718 729 7708) offers more than 40 loose-leaf teas (and locally roasted coffee). If you want something stronger, head for **Dutch Kills** (27-24 Jackson Avenue; *see p229*), a cosy and innovative cocktail lounge.

A few blocks east, on Jackson Avenue, stands the **MoMA P.S.1** (*see right*), a progressive museum affiliated with MoMA that highlights the work of the up-and-coming and the already-here. In summer months, it also becomes the city's dance hub with its Saturday-afternoon DJ parties, **P.S.1 Warm Up** (*see p337*). Cross the street for an edgy display of urban art: the graffiti-covered **5 Pointz** (on Jackson Avenue, between Crane and Davis Streets). While the small gallery keeps erratic hours on summer weekends, the façade of the block-long converted warehouse, also visible from the 7 train, affords an ever-evolving tableau of brilliant hues and different tagging styles by graffiti artists from around the world.

As a complete contrast, a well-preserved block of 19th-century houses nearby constitutes the **Hunters Point Historic District** (45th Avenue, between 21st & 23rd Streets). With several artists' studio complexes lodged in Long Island City, a nascent art scene has taken hold. **SculptureCenter** (*see p300*), in a dramatic converted industrial space, is a great place to see new work. For details of open-studio events in the neighbourhood, check out www.licartists.org.

★ MoMA P.S.1

22-25 Jackson Avenue, at 46th Avenue (1-718 784 2084, www.ps1.org). Subway E, M (M on weekdays) to 23rd Street-Ely Avenue; G to 21st Street-Jackson Avenue; 7 to 45th Road-Court House Square. **Open** noon-6pm Mon, Thur-Sun. **Admission** *Suggested donation* $10; $5 reductions. **Credit** AmEx, DC, MC, V. **Map** p412 V5.

In a distinctive Romanesque Revival building, P.S.1 mounts cutting-edge shows and hosts an acclaimed international studio programme. Be sure to peek into the stairwells, as artwork turns up in unexpected corners of the former public school. P.S.1 became an affiliate of MoMA in 1999, and the two institutions sometimes stage collaborative exhibitions, such as the quinquennial 'Greater New York', a survey of innovative artists in the metropolitan area. Call or see website for current exhibits.

ASTORIA

Subway R, M (M on weekdays) to Steinway Street; N, Q to Broadway, 30th Avenue or Astoria-Ditmars Boulevard.

A lively, traditionally Greek and Italian neighbourhood, Astoria has over the last few decades seen an influx of Brazilians, Bangladeshis, Eastern Europeans, Colombians and Egyptians; they've been joined by post-grads sharing row-house digs. A 15-minute downhill hike from Broadway subway station towards Manhattan brings you to the **Noguchi Museum** (*see right*), which shows works by the visionary sculptor. Nearby lies the **Socrates Sculpture Park** (Broadway, at Vernon Boulevard, www.socratessculpturepark.org), a riverfront art space in an industrial setting with great views of Manhattan.

At the end of the subway line (Astoria-Ditmars Boulevard), walk west to **Astoria Park** (from Astoria Park South to Ditmars Boulevard, between Shore Boulevard & 19th Street) for its dramatic views of two bridges: the **Robert F Kennedy Bridge** (formerly the Triborough), Robert Moses's automotive labyrinth connecting Queens, the Bronx and Manhattan; and the 1916 **Hell Gate Bridge**, a steel single-arch tour de force and template for the Sydney Harbour Bridge.

Still New York's Greek-American stronghold, Astoria is well known for Hellenic eateries specialising in impeccably grilled seafood. **Elias Corner** (24-02 31st Street, at 24th Street, 1-718 932 1510) serves meze and a catch of the day in a breezy garden setting, while **Athens Café** (32-07 30th Avenue, between 32nd & 33rd Streets, 1-718 626 2164) is the neighbourhood's social nexus and a terrific place to stop for Greek coffee and pastries. One of the city's last central European beer gardens, **Bohemian Hall & Beer Garden** (29-19 24th Avenue, at 29th Street; *see p229*) offers Czech-style dining and drinking. Arrive early on warm weekends to nab a picnic table in the expansive, linden tree-shaded yard. Cocktail aficionados and local hipsters flock to gastropub **Sweet Afton** (30-09 34th Street, between 30th Avenue and Broadway, 1-718 777 2570), while visitors to the Museum of the Moving Image can enjoy a restorative brew at the nearby modern beer-garden upstart **Studio Square** (35-33 36th Street, between 35th & 36th Avenues, 1-718 383 1001).

South of Astoria Boulevard, you can puff on a shisha – a (legal) hookah pipe – with thick Turkish coffee in the cafés of 'Little Egypt' along Steinway Street, between 28th Avenue and Astoria Boulevard. Over at **Steinway & Sons** (1 Steinway Place, between 19th Avenue & 38th Street, 1-718 721 2600), take a tour (by appointment) of the still-thriving red-brick 1871 piano factory.

★ Noguchi Museum

9-01 33rd Road, between Vernon Boulevard & 10th Street (1-718 204 7088, www.noguchi.org). Subway N, Q to Broadway, then bus Q104 to 11th Street; 7 to Vernon Boulevard-Jackson Avenue, then Q103 bus to 10th Street. **Open** 10am-5pm Wed-Fri; 11am-6pm Sat, Sun. **Admission** $10; $5

MoMA P.S.1.

SIGHTS

Profile Museum of the Moving Image

The definitive modern art form has a worthy museum at last.

In January 2011, the **Museum of the Moving Image** reopened after a major renovation that doubled its size and made it one of the foremost museums in the world dedicated to television, film and video. Housed in one of the buildings of the Astoria Studios complex, which served in the 1920s as the New York production headquarters of Paramount Pictures before talkies moved the industry out to Hollywood, the collection is greatly enhanced by the museum's bold new design, which announces itself at the entrance: a giant frame of transparent and mirrored glass forming the museum's name and suggesting a screen

Upstairs, on the second floor, the MMI's brand-new 264-seat main theatre screams state of the art. It features steep stadium seating and a wraparound screen formed by 1,136 panels along the ceiling and walls – every conceivable format can be screened here, from high-definition 3-D pictures to silent classics (there's even a mini orchestra pit for musical accompaniment). It is complemented by several other new theatres, including an amphitheatre specially designed for videos, as well as a 70-seat digital screening room that is largely devoted to educational programming. Rotating exhibitions are found on the third floor, as well as the educational centre, where aspiring directors can record their own videos and put them up on the internet in the hopes of going viral.

The MMI's highly popular 'Behind the Screen' exhibition, which explores all the nuances of the movie- and TV-programme making process, has been upgraded and now fills a 15,000sq ft (1,400sq m) gallery. An interactive display, it boasts artefacts from more than 1,000 productions (including the super creepy stunt doll used in *The Exorcist*, with full head-rotating capabilities, and the famous diner booth from *Seinfeld*).

To inaugurate the revamped museum, MMI is putting on 'Real Virtuality', an exhibition that will run from 15 January to 12 June 2011. It is composed of five separate installations fusing art and digital technology that enclose the viewer in computer-generated environments that make use of the gallery's new space. Perhaps the most highly anticipated is innovative video artist Bill Viola's 'Night Journey', a video game devised with game designer Tracy Fullerton, which takes the player on an adventure in search of enlightenment, while exploring the technical aspects of the game experience.

Astoria Studios has certainly come a long way from the days of the silent movie.

reductions; free under-12s. Pay what you wish 1st Fri of the mth. No pushchairs/strollers. **No credit cards**. **Map** p412 V3.

The former studio of Japanese-American sculptor Isamu Noguchi (1904-88), who moved to Queens to be nearer to the quarries that supplied the granite and marble for his works, the museum is a monument to the artist's harmonious sensibility. Arranged over two floors, ten galleries and an outdoor space, it showcases his organic, undulating work in granite, marble, bronze and wood, moving seamlessly into the adjoining gardens, laid out by the artist himself, with fountains and small footpaths. Particularly intriguing are his akari works (light fixtures encased by inventive paper shades), as well as a display of his highly imaginative models for playgrounds that, sadly, were rejected by Robert Moses. A shuttle service from Manhattan is available at weekends (call or see the website for more information).

Museum of the Moving Image

35th Avenue, at 36th Street (1-718 784 0077, www.movingimage.us). Subway R, M (M on weekdays) to Steinway Street; N, Q to 36th Avenue. **Open** 10am-3pm Tue-Fri. **Admission** $7; free under-8s. No pushchairs. **Credit** AmEx, DC, MC, V. **Map** p412 W4.

See p140 **Profile**.

JACKSON HEIGHTS

Subway E, F, M, R to Jackson Heights-Roosevelt Avenue; 7 to 74th Street-Broadway.

Dizzying even by Queens standards, Jackson Heights' multiculturalism puts the sanitised display at Disney's Epcot to shame. **Little India** greets you with a swathe of small shops and restaurants. **A to Z Music** (73-09 37th Road, at Broadway, 1-718 429 7179), which specialises in Indian music, also carries an array of Bollywood DVDs. Colourful saris can be had at **India Sari Palace** (37-07 74th Street, at 37th Avenue, 1-718 426 2700) and bracelets and other trinkets at **Mita Jewelers** (37-30 74th Street, between 37th Avenue & 37th Road, 1-718 507 1555), but the main attraction is culinary. The unofficial headquarters of the Indian expat community, **Jackson Diner** (37-47 74th Street, between Roosevelt & 37th Avenues, 1-718 672 1232) serves up sumptuous curries and Hindi soaps on Zee TV. For more intimate dining, try **Mehfil** (76-05 37th Avenue, between 76th & 77th Streets, 1-718 429 3297); its *palak paneer* – a spinach and cheese curry dish – is divine.

Along with adjoining Elmhurst, Jackson Heights has also welcomed waves of Latin American immigrants. Mexicans, Colombians and Argentinians are old-school in these parts: get a taste of Buenos Aires at the exuberant, *fútbol*-themed **Boca Junior Argentinian Steakhouse** (81-08 Queens Boulevard, at 51st Avenue, Elmhurst, 1-718 429 2077), or stop by **Taqueria Coatzingo** (76-05 Roosevelt Avenue, between 76th & 77th Streets, 1-718 424 1977) for meaty tacos (*al pastor*, slow-roasted goat and tongue) with a definite edge over the other holes-in-the-wall under the elevated 7 train. The Thai contingent is reflected in several fine eateries: **Arunee** (37-68 79th Street, between Roosevelt & 37th Avenues, 1-718 205 5559) doesn't hold back with the spices – or the Thai music videos.

The neighbourhood claims a roughly 30-square-block landmark district of mock Tudor and neo-Gothic-style co-op apartment buildings, with attached houses, tree-dotted lawns and park-like courtyards. There are good examples of these 1920s beauties on 70th Street, between 34th Avenue and Northern Boulevard, and on 34th Avenue, between 76th and 77th Streets, and between 80th and 81st Streets.

FLUSHING

Subway 7 to Main Street, 103rd Street-Corona Plaza, 111th Street, or Mets-Willets Point.

Egalitarian Dutchmen staked their claim to 'Vlissingen' in the 1600s and were shortly joined by pacifist Friends, or Quakers, seeking religious freedom in the New World. These religious settlers promulgated the Flushing Remonstrance, a groundbreaking 1657 edict extending 'the law of love, peace and liberty' to Jews and Muslims. It's now regarded as a forerunner of the United States Constitution's First Amendment.

The plain wooden **Old Quaker Meeting House** (137-16 Northern Boulevard, between Main & Union Streets, 1-718 358 9636), built in 1694, creates a startling juxtaposition to the prosperous Chinatown that rings its weathered wooden walls. The neighbourhood has hundreds of temples and churches used by immigrants from Korea, China and south Asia. **St George's Church** (Main Street, between 38th & 39th Avenues, 1-718 359 1171), an

INSIDE TRACK VINTAGE SOUVENIRS

The **Queens Museum of Art** (*see p142*) has an always-changing secret stash of original 1939 and 1964-65 World's Fair memorabilia, such as frosted tumblers, plates, models, hats, aprons, even Unisphere-printed rain capes. Prices range from around $1.50 to $200.

Episcopalian steeple chartered by King George III, was once a dominant site, but now competes for attention with restaurants and shops. The interior is worth a brief visit if only to see the two examples of Queens-made Tiffany stained glass and to hear church services in Caribbean-accented English, Chinese and Spanish. Ambitious explorers will want to make the jaunt south to the **Hindu Temple Society** (45-57 Bowne Street, between Holly & 45th Avenues, 1-718 460 8484), a Ganesh temple whose ornate exterior was hand-carved in India.

The restaurants and dumpling stalls of Flushing's **Chinatown** are another way to commune with the divine. Teenagers tend to love the unique bubble tea – sweet, milky tea loaded with tapioca balls – that you can find in cafés such **Sago** (39-02 Main Street, at 39th Avenue, 1-718 353 2899) or tea specialists **Ten Ren** (135-18 Roosevelt Avenue, between Main & Prince Streets, 1-718 461 9305). If you don't mind tiny dining quarters, head to **White Bear** (135-02 Roosevelt Avenue, entrance on Prince Street, between Roosevelt Avenue & 40th Road, 1-718-961-2322) for an array of exceptional dumplings and wontons.

Flushing Town Hall (137-35 Northern Boulevard, at Linden Place, 1-718 463 7700, www.flushingtownhall.org, closed Mon-Wed), built during the Civil War in the highly fanciful Romanesque Revival style, showcases local arts groups, jazz and chamber music concerts. It also hosts an annual Lunar New Year festival.

The most visited site in Queens is the rambling **Flushing Meadows-Corona Park** (*see below*), where the 1939 and 1964-65 World's Fairs were held. Larger than Central Park, it's home to the **Queens Zoo** (1-718 271 1500, www.queenszoo.com) where natural environments include a lush parrot habitat; **Queens Theatre in the Park**, an indoor amphitheatre designed by Philip Johnson; the **New York Hall of Science** (*see p274*), an acclaimed interactive museum; the **Queens Botanical Garden**, a 39-acre cavalcade of greenery; and the **Queens Museum of Art** (*see right*), which exhibits increasingly avant-garde shows that tie art to the local immigrant experience – fitting enough for the building that was the first home of the United Nations. Also here are **Citi Field**, the new home to the Mets baseball team (*see p339*), and the USTA (United States Tennis Association) National Tennis Center. The US Open (*see p341*) raises an almighty racket at the summer's end, but the general public can play here during the other 11 months of the year.

FREE Flushing Meadows-Corona Park

From 111th Street to Van Wyck Expressway, between Flushing Bay & Grand Central Parkway (1-718 760 6565, 1-718 220 5100, www.nycgovparks.org). Subway 7 to Mets-Willets Point.

Most Manhattanites only venture out to these parts to catch a Mets game or tennis at the US Open, but visitors will also be enticed by the 1964-65 World's Fair sculptures, particularly the iconic 140ft (42m) Unisphere, a mammoth steel globe that was the symbol of the fair (and site of the apocalyptic battle scene between humans and aliens in the first *Men in Black* movie). Also visible are the remnants of the New York State Pavilion, erected by Philip Johnson for the fair. Measuring 350ft by 250ft (106m by 76m), this now-eerie plaza is bordered by 16 100ft (30m) steel columns.

Louis Armstrong House

34-56 107th Street, between 34th & 37th Avenues, Corona (1-718 478 8274, www.satchmo.net). Subway 7 to 103rd Street-Corona Plaza. **Open** 10am-5pm Tue-Fri; noon-5pm Sat, Sun. *Tours* hourly 10am-5pm Tue-Fri; hourly noon-5pm Sat, Sun. **Admission** $8; $6 reductions; free under-4s. **Credit** ($15 min) DC, MC, V.

Pilgrims to the two-storey house where the great 'Satchmo' lived from 1943 until his death in 1971 will find a shrine to the revolutionary trumpet player – as well as his wife's passion for wallpaper. Her decorative attentions extended to the interiors of cupboards, closets – even bathroom cabinets. The 45-minute tour is enhanced by audiotapes of Louis that give much insight into the tranquil domesticity he sought in the then suburban neighbourhood – a far cry from the glamorous life he could have led.

▶ *For more on jazz in New York, see pp48-54.*

★ Queens Museum of Art

New York City Building, park entrance on 49th Avenue, at 111th Street, Flushing Meadows-Corona Park (1-718 592 9700, www.queensmuseum.org). Subway 7 to 111th Street, then walk south on 111th Street, turning left on to 49th Avenue; continue into the park & over Grand Central Parkway Bridge.
Open *Sept-June* 10am-6pm Wed-Sun; *July, Aug* 10am-6pm Mon-Thur, Sat, Sun; 10am-8pm Fri. **Admission** *Suggested donation* $5; $2.50 reductions. **No credit cards.**

In the grounds of the 1939 and 1964-65 World's Fairs, the QMA holds one of the city's most amazing sights: the Panorama of the City of New York, a 9,335sq ft (867sq m), 895,000-building scale model – one inch equals 100ft (30m) – of all five boroughs. A new lighting system mimics the arc of the sun as it passes over NYC, yet despite periodic updates of the model, one part of the Panorama remains decidedly untouched – the Twin Towers still stand proudly (albeit one twelve-hundredth of their actual size). Contemporary and visiting exhibits have grown more bold and inventive in recent years, garnering increasing acclaim.

The Bronx

The Bronx is rising from the ashes of its reputation.

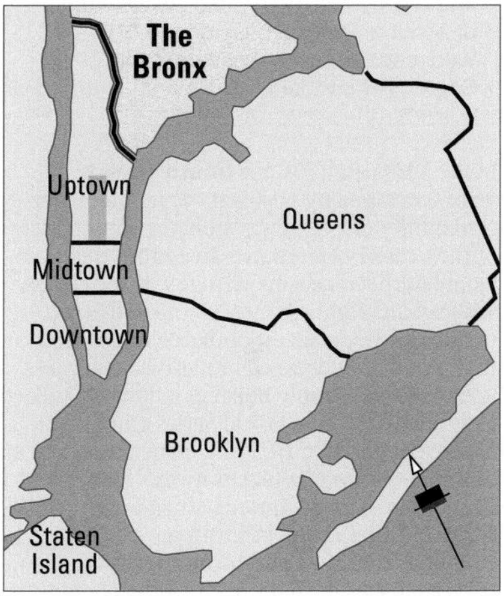

Although the Bronx seems much more remote to most visitors – and, indeed, most Manhattanites – than it really is, it's actually the only borough physically attached to the mainland of America. Much of this perceived distance is due to the **South Bronx**'s global reputation for urban strife, and it isn't helped by the fact that the borough's two best-known visitor attractions – Yankee Stadium and the Bronx Zoo – are generally covered in quick trips in and out.

This is a shame, for the Bronx also glistens with the art deco gems of the **Grand Concourse**, cooks up a storm with its own Little Italy in **Belmont**, enchants the rest of the city's nature-deprived urbanites with its world-class **New York Botanical Garden** and takes pride in one of the most up-and-coming art scenes in the city.

The Bronx
Uptown
Midtown
Downtown
Queens
Brooklyn
Staten Island

THE BRONX IN BRIEF

The Bronx was settled in the 1630s by the family of Jonas Bronck, a Swedish farmer who had a 500-acre homestead in what is now the south-eastern Morrisania section. The area became known as 'the Broncks' farm; although the spelling was altered, the name stuck. Originally part of Westchester County, it was incorporated with the other boroughs into New York City in 1898.

Like Queens and Brooklyn, the Bronx in the early 20th century drew much of its population from the ever-expanding pools of Irish, German, Italian and Eastern European Jewish immigrants who flocked to the area for its cheap rents and open spaces.

After World War II, as the borough became ever more urbanised and transport links improved, the descendants of the European immigrants moved out to the suburbs of Long Island and Westchester, and fresh waves of newcomers, hailing from the Caribbean, Latin America, Africa, the Balkans and Russia, took their places. From the late 1940s until the early 1970s, the Bronx probably witnessed more upheaval than the other areas of the city combined, bearing the brunt of city planner Robert Moses's drastic revamping of the city. Thousands of residents saw their old tenements razed to make room for the Whitestone and Throgs Neck Bridges, the east-to-west Cross Bronx Expressway and the north-to-south Bruckner Boulevard extension of the New England Thruway.

Many areas fell into neglect, a condition exacerbated by the economic and social downturns that plagued the entire city in the 1960s and '70s. The local community felt cut off, forgotten and left to rot, and with good reason. The Bronx became a symbold of urban decay. It's only during the last decade that the area has really started to come alive once more. Visitors should note that although some parts of the Bronx are gentrifying, others, such as the northern swathe of the Grand Concourse, are still very run-down and might make less intrepid urban explorers uncomfortable.

THE SOUTH BRONX

Subway 4 to 161st Street-Yankee Stadium; 6 to Hunts Point Avenue, 138th Street-Third Avenue.

INSIDE TRACK THE BRONX CULTURE TROLLEY

To check out the South Bronx's burgeoning art scene, hop on the free **Bronx Culture Trolley** (www.bronxarts.org/culture_trolley.asp), which stops at about a dozen venues on the first Wednesday of each month, except September and January.

In the 1960s and '70s, the **South Bronx** was so ravaged by post-war 'white flight' and community displacement from the construction of the Cross Bronx Expressway that the neighbourhood became virtually synonymous with urban blight. Crime was rife and arson became widespread, as landlords discovered that renovating decayed property was far less lucrative than simply burning it down to collect insurance. During a World Series game at Yankee Stadium in 1977, TV cameras caught a building on fire just blocks away. 'Ladies and gentlemen,' commentator Howard Cosell told the world, 'the Bronx is burning.'

These days, the South Bronx is rising from the ashes. In 2006, Mayor Bloomberg announced the South Bronx Initiative, aiming to revitalise the area, while eco-sensitive organisations such as Sustainable South Bronx (www.ssbx.org) are converting vacant lots into green spaces such as **Barretto Point Park** (between Tiffany & Barretto Streets) and **Hunts Point Riverside Park** (at the foot of Lafayette Avenue on the Bronx River). In 2005, Hunts Point became the new home to the city's **Fulton Fish Market** (1-718 378 2356, www.newfultonfishmarket.com), which moved from the site it had occupied for 180 years near South Street Seaport to a 400,000 sq ft modern facility that is the largest consortium of seafood retailers in America.

Unsurprisingly, the rejuvenated area has also seen an influx of young professional refugees from overpriced Manhattan and Brooklyn: new condos are sprouting up, old warehouses are being redeveloped, once-crumbling tenements are being refurbished and, inevitably, chain stores are moving in. Young families have been snapping up the renovated townhouses on Alexander Avenue and furnishing them from the thoroughfare's rejuvenated antiques stores, while industrial lofts on Bruckner Boulevard have become homes to creatives. Yet despite developers' hopes for 'SoBro', the area has not quite turned into the Next Big Thing. Yet.

Hunts Point is also becoming a creative live-work hub. In 1994, a group of artists and community leaders converted an industrial building into the **Point** (940 Garrison Avenue, at Manida Street, 1-718 542 4139, www.thepoint.org), an arts-based community development centre with a much-utilized performance space and gallery, studios for dance, theatre and photography, an environmental advocacy group, and lively summer and after-school workshops for neighbourhood children. The Point also leads lively walking tours (phone for reservations) that explore the history of locally born music, such as mambo and hip hop. The nearby **Bronx Academy of Arts & Dance** (BAAD; 2nd Floor, 841 Barretto Street, between Garrison & Lafayette Avenues, 1-718 842 5223, www.bronxacademyofartsanddance.org), located in a renovated 1911 warehouse, provides a platform for dance, theatre and visual arts events, and more than a dozen painters and sculptors work in the academy's studios. It's also the venue for festivals such as Out Like That!, which celebrates works by lesbian, gay, bisexual and transgender artists, and BAAD Ass Women, a showcase for the work of female artists.

Another artistic South Bronx hotbed is simmering further south-west in **Mott Haven**. Here, **Longwood Art Gallery @ Hostos** (450 Grand Concourse, at 149th Street, 1-718 518 6728, www.bronxarts.org/lag.asp), the creation of the Bronx Council on the Arts, mounts top-notch exhibits in a variety of media. Most cultural crawls end up at **Bruckner Bar & Grill** (1 Bruckner Boulevard, at Third Avenue, 1-718 665 2001), which lures locals (and curious Manhattanites) with an eclectic menu, art exhibitions that change bimonthly in its gallery and occasional poetry readings.

Of course, the vast majority of visitors to the South Bronx are just stopping long enough to take in a baseball game at **Yankee Stadium** (*see p340*), at 161st Street and River Avenue. Some of baseball's most famous legends made history on its diamond, from Babe Ruth to Derek Jeter. In April 2009, the Yankees vacated the fabled 'House that Ruth Built' and moved to the brand-new $1.3 billion stadium across the street – and went on to win their first World Series in seven years. **Monument Park**, an open-air museum behind centre field that celebrates the exploits of past Yankee heroes, can be visited, along with the New York Yankees Museum, the dugout, and – when the Yankees are on the road – the clubhouse as part of a tour ($15 adults, $8 reductions; 1-646 977 8687).

THE GRAND CONCOURSE

Subway B, D to 167th Street; B, D, 4 to Kingsbridge Road; 4 to 161st Street-Yankee Stadium.

A few blocks east of Yankee Stadium runs the four-and-a-half-mile **Grand Concourse**, which begins at 138th Street in the South Bronx and ends at Mosholu Parkway just shy of **Van Cortlandt Park** (*see p147*). Once the most prestigious drag in the Bronx, the Grand Boulevard and Concourse (to give the artery its grandiose intended title) is still an absolute must for lovers of art deco. Engineer Louis Risse designed the boulevard in 1892, modelling it on Paris's Champs-Elysées; it was first opened to traffic in 1909, but it wasn't until the arrival of a new subway line in the 1930s that rapid development along the Concourse began in the deco style so popular at the time. For its centennial, the boulevard received a modest facelift with new trees and flowers, street lights, bike lanes and cobblestone sidewalks.

Starting at 161st Street and heading south, look for the permanent street plaques that make up the **Bronx Walk of Fame**, honouring famous Bronxites from Stanley Kubrick and Tony Orlando to Colin Powell and hip hop 'godfather' Afrika Bambaataa. Heading north, the buildings date mostly from the 1920s to the early '40s, and display the country's largest array of art deco housing. Erected in 1937 at the corner of 161st Street, **888 Grand Concourse** has a large concave entrance of gilded mosaic and is topped by a curvy metallic marquee. Inside, the mirrored lobby's central fountain and sunburst-patterned floor could rival those of any hotel on Miami Beach's Ocean Drive. On the south side of **Joyce Kilmer Park**, at 161st Street, is the magnificent white-marble fountain of Lorelei, built in 1893 in Germany in homage to Heinrich Heine, who wrote the poem of the same name. This was intended as the original entrance to the Concourse before it was extended south. The grandest building on the Concourse is the landmark **Andrew Freedman Home**, a 1924 French-inspired limestone palazzo between McClennan and 166th Streets. Freedman, a millionaire subway contractor, left the bulk of his $7 million fortune with instructions to build a poorhouse for the rich – that is, those who had lost their fortunes and were suffering an impecunious old age. It now shelters the Family Preservation Center (FPC), a community-based social service agency. Across the street, the **Bronx Museum of the Arts** (*see p146*), established in 1971 in a former synagogue, exhibits socially conscious, contemporary works largely by Bronx-based artists.

A few blocks north, at **1150 Grand Concourse** at McClellan Place, is a 1937 art deco apartment block commonly referred to as the 'fish building' because of the colourful marine-themed mosaic flanking its doors; pause inside the restored lobby for a glimpse of its two large murals depicting pastoral scenes, which are in sharp contrast with their surroundings. Near the intersection of Fordham Road, keep an eye out for the Italian rococo exterior of the **Paradise Theater** (2403 Grand Concourse, between Elm Place & E 188th Street, 1-718 220 1015, www.paradisetheater events.com), once the largest cinema in the city. To see the elaborate murals, fountains and

SIGHTS

Bronx Museum of the Arts. *See p146.*

grand staircase of the interior, which was restored in 2005, you'll need to buy a ticket for one of the occasional gospel concerts or floor shows it now presents. Just north is the ten-storey **Emigrant Savings Bank**, at 2526 Grand Concourse, worth ducking into for a glimpse of five striking murals by the artist Angelo Manganti depicting scenes of the Bronx's past, including Jonas Bronck buying land from the Indians.

Further north to Kingsbridge Road lies the **Edgar Allan Poe Cottage** (*see below*), a small wooden farmhouse where the writer lived from 1846 to 1849. Moved to the Grand Concourse from its original spot on Fordham Road in 1913, the museum has period furniture and details about Poe and his work.

★ Bronx Museum of the Arts

1040 Grand Concourse, at 165th Street (1-718 681 6000, www.bxma.org). Subway B, D to 167th Street Grand Concourse; 4 to 161st Street-Yankee Stadium. **Open** 11am-6pm Thur, Sat, Sun; 11am-8pm Fri. **Admission** $5; $3 reductions. Free to all Fri. **Credit** AmEx, DC, Disc, MC, V.

Founded in 1971 and featuring more than 800 works, this multicultural art museum shines a spotlight on 20th- and 21st-century artists who are either Bronx-based or of African, Asian or Latino ancestry. In 2011, the museum will present 'Happy Together', featuring art by Asian and Asian-American artists exploring notions of identity in the contexts of community, the family and the larger world until June 6, as well as 'Bronx Calling: The First AIM Biennial', presenting the work of 72 young talents in conjunction with Wave Hill (*see p148*), from 26 June to 5 September 2011. *Photo p145.*

Edgar Allan Poe Cottage

2640 Grand Concourse, at Kingsbridge Road (1-718 881 8900, www.bronxhistoricalsociety.org/poecottage). Subway D or 4 to Kingsbridge Road. **Open** 10am-4pm Sat; 1-5pm Sun. **Admission** $5; $3 reductions. **No credit cards.**

Pay homage to Poe in the house where he spent the last three years of his life and wrote such literary marvels as *Annabel Lee* and *The Bells*. At the time of writing, the cottage was undergoing a major renovation and is expected to reopen in late 2011 with a brand-new visitors' centre complete with sloping shingle roof designed to resemble the wings of the bird from the poet's famous *The Raven*.

BELMONT & BRONX PARK

Subway B, D, 4 to Fordham Road, then Bx12 bus to Arthur Avenue.

Originally settled in the late 19th century by Italian immigrants hired to landscape nearby Bronx Zoo, close-knit Belmont is centred on

New York Botanical Garden.

Arthur Avenue, lined with delis, bakeries, restaurants and stores selling T-shirts proclaiming the locale to be New York's 'real Little Italy'. Still celebrating masses in Italian, neo-classical **Our Lady of Mt Carmel Church** (627 E 187th Street, at Hughes Avenue, 1-718 295 3770) has been serving the community for more than a century. You can get a quick survey of Italian-American history and culture from the modest exhibits at the **Enrico Fermi Cultural Center** (in the Belmont Branch Library, 610 E 186th Street, between Arthur & Hughes Avenues, 1-718 933 6410, closed Sun).

Food, however, is the main reason to visit. **Arthur Avenue Retail Market** (2344 Arthur Avenue, between Crescent Avenue & E 186th Street, closed Sun) is a covered market built in the 1940s when Mayor Fiorello La Guardia campaigned to get the pushcarts off the street. Inside, you'll find **Mike's Deli** (1-718 295 5033), where you can try the trademark Yankee Stadium Big Boy hero sandwich, filled with prosciutto, soppressata, mozzarella, capicola, mortadella, peppers and lettuce. For a full meal, try old-school, red-sauce joints such as **Mario's** (2342 Arthur Avenue, between Crescent Avenue & E 186th Street, 1-718 584 1188, closed Mon), featured in several *Sopranos* episodes and Mario Puzo's novel *The Godfather*; **Dominick's** (2335 Arthur Avenue, between Crescent Avenue & E 186th Street, 1-718 733 2807, closed Tue), where there are no menus (your waiter will guide you course by course through your meal); or the no-frills but charming **Roberto's** (603 Crescent Avenue, between Hughes & Arthur Avenue, 1-718 733 9503, closed Sun).

If you're not too stuffed to continue, Belmont is within easy walking distance of **Bronx Park**, home to two of the borough's most celebrated attractions. Make your way east along 187th Street, then south along Southern Boulevard, and you'll come to the **Bronx Zoo** (*see below*). Opened in 1899 by Theodore Roosevelt, it's the largest urban zoo in the US at 265 acres. A 15-minute walk north of the zoo – and still in Bronx Park – brings you to the serene 250 acres of the **New York Botanical Garden** (*see right*), which offers respite from cars and concrete in the form of 50 different gardens.

★ Bronx Zoo/ Wildlife Conservation Society

Bronx River Parkway, at Fordham Road (1-718 367 1010, www.bronxzoo.org). Subway 2 to Pelham Parkway, then walk two blocks, turn left at Boston Road and bear right to the zoo's Bronxdale entrance; or Metro-North's Harlem Line to Fordham, then take the Bx9 bus south to the zoo entrance, or the Bx12 bus east to Southern Boulevard, and walk east to the zoo entrance. **Open** *Apr-Oct* 10am-5pm Mon-Fri; 10am-5.30pm Sat, Sun. *Nov-Mar* 10am-4.30pm daily. Last entry 30 minutes before zoo closing . **Admission** $16; $12-$14 reductions. Pay what you wish Wed. Some rides & exhibitions cost extra. **Credit** AmEx, DC, Disc, MC, V.

The Bronx Zoo shuns cages in favour of indoor and outdoor environments that mimic the natural habitats of its mammals, birds and reptiles, and there are more than 5,000 of them. Nearly 100 species, including monkeys, leopards and tapirs, live inside the lush, steamy Jungle World, a re-creation of an Asian rainforest inside a 37,000sq ft (3,400sq m) building. The super-popular Congo Gorilla Forest has turned 6.5 acres into a dramatic Central African rainforest habitat. A glass-enclosed tunnel winds through the forest, allowing visitors to get close to the dozens of primate families in residence, including 26 majestic western lowland gorillas. For those who prefer cats, Tiger Mountain has six adult Siberian tigers that look particularly regal on snowy days. Madagascar!, an exhibit focused on the species-rich island off the coast of East Africa, debuted in 2008. Other recent additions at the zoo include an aardvark habitat, an aquatic aviary and a butterfly garden featuring 1,000 colourful flutterers.

▶ *For other zoos, see p108, p133 and p142.*

INSIDE TRACK FERRAGOSTO FESTIVAL

While the eleven-day San Gennaro Festival in Manhattan's Little Italy draws the hordes, Belmont's version, the more intimate **Ferragosto**, on the second Sunday in September, is undoubtedly more authentic. The vendors who gather at 187th Street & Arthur Avenue to serve up Italian delicacies are largely extensions of local restaurant kitchens.

New York Botanical Garden

Bronx River Parkway, at Fordham Road (1-718 817 8700, www.nybg.org). Subway B, D to Bedford Park Boulevard, then take the Bx26 bus to Garden gate; or Metro-North (Harlem Line local) from Grand Central Terminal to Botanical Garden. **Open** 10am-6pm Tue-Sun. **Admission** $20; $10-$18 reductions; free under-2s. *Grounds only* $6; $1-$3 reductions. Free to all (grounds only) Wed, 10am-noon Sat. **Credit** AmEx, DC, MC, V.

The serene 250 acres of the New York Botanical Garden comprise 50 gardens and plant collections, including the Rockefeller Rose Garden, the Everett Children's Adventure Garden and the last 50 original acres of the forest that once covered all of New York City. In spring, the gardens are frothy with pastel blossoms, as clusters of lilac, cherry, magnolia and crab apple trees burst into bloom, followed in autumn by vivid foliage in the oak and maple groves. On a rainy day, stay warm and sheltered inside the Enid A Haupt Conservatory, a striking glass-walled greenhouse – the nation's largest – built in 1902. It contains the World of Plants, a series of environmental galleries that take you on an eco-tour through tropical rainforests, deserts and a palm-tree oasis, as well as seasonal exhibits.

SIGHTS

RIVERDALE & VAN CORTLANDT PARK

Subway D to Norwood-205th Street; 1 to 242nd Street-Van Cortlandt Park.

Riverdale, along the north-west coast of the Bronx, reflects the borough's suburban past; its huge homes perch on narrow, winding streets that meander toward the Hudson River. The only one you can actually visit is **Wave Hill House** (*see p148*), an 1843 stone mansion set on a former private estate that is now both a cultural and environmental centre. The nearby, 1,146-acre **Van Cortlandt Park** (entrance on Broadway, at 242nd Street) occasionally hosts cricket teams largely made up of West and East Indians. You can hike through a 100-year-old forest, play golf on the nation's first municipal course or rent horses at stables in the park.

The oldest building in the Bronx is **Van Cortlandt House Museum** (*see p148*), a pre-Revolutionary Georgian building completed in

1749 and commandeered by both sides during the Revolutionary War. Abutting the park is **Woodlawn Cemetery**, the resting place for such notable souls as Herman Melville, Duke Ellington, Miles Davis, FW Woolworth and Fiorello La Guardia. To help you pay your respects, maps are available at the entrance at Webster Avenue and E 233rd Street. About five blocks south on Bainbridge Avenue, history buffs will also enjoy the Bronx Historical Society's **Museum of Bronx History** (*see below*), set in a lovely 1758 stone farmhouse.

Museum of Bronx History

Valentine-Varian House, 3266 Bainbridge Avenue, between Van Cortlandt Avenue & E 208th Street (1-718 881 8900, www.bronxhistoricalsociety.org/vvhouse). Subway D to Norwood-205th Street. **Open** 10am-4pm Sat; 1-5pm Sun. **Admission** $5; $3 reductions. **No credit cards**.

Operated by the Bronx County Historical Society, the museum's collection of documents and photographs is displayed in the Valentine-Varian House, a Federal-style fieldstone residence built in 1758.

► *The society also offers historical tours of the Bronx neighbourhoods.*

Van Cortlandt House Museum

Van Cortlandt Park, entrance on Broadway, at 246th Street (1-718 543 3344, www.vancortlandthouse.org). Subway 1 to 242nd Street-Van Cortlandt Park. **Open** 10am-3pm Tue-Fri; 11am-4pm Sat, Sun. **Admission** $5; $3 reductions; free under-13s. Free to all Wed. **Credit** ($11 minimum) DC, MC, V.

A one-time wheat plantation that has since been turned into a colonial museum, Van Cortlandt House was alternately used as headquarters by George Washington and British General Sir William Howe during the Revolutionary War.

Wave Hill House

W 249th Street, at Independence Avenue (1-718 549 3200, www.wavehill.org). Metro-North (Hudson Line local) from Grand Central Terminal to Riverdale. **Open** *mid Apr-mid Oct* 9am-5.30pm Tue-Sun. *Mid Oct-mid Apr* 9am-4.30pm Tue-Sun. **Admission** $8; $2-$4 reductions; free under-6s. Free to all 9am-noon Sat; all day Tue Jan-Apr, July, Aug, Nov, Dec; 9am-noon Tue May, June, Sept, Oct. **No credit cards**.

Laze around in these 28 lush acres overlooking the Hudson River at Wave Hill, a Georgian Revival house that was home to Mark Twain, Teddy Roosevelt and conductor Arturo Toscanini. It's now a spectacular nature preserve and conservation centre with cultivated gardens and woodlands commanding excellent views of the river. The small in-house art gallery shows nature-themed exhibits – one such offering is 'Bees in Art' (13 September-28 November 2011). The organisation also presents year-round concerts, performances and other events, and will present 'Bronx Calling: The First AIM Biennial' with the Bronx Museum of the Arts (*see p146*) from 26 June to 5 September 2011.

> **INSIDE TRACK GREEN GOTHAM**
>
> The New York Botanical Garden's (*see p147*) **Holiday Train Show** in the Enid A Haupt Conservatory is a truly amazing family tradition: more than a dozen model railway trains traverse an incredibly detailed retro New York cityscape, including such landmarks as the old Yankee Stadium, the Empire State Building and the original Penn Station, made entirely of natural materials, such as leaves, twigs, bark and berries.

PELHAM BAY PARK

Subway 6 to Pelham Bay Park.

Pelham Bay Park, in the borough's north-eastern corner, is NYC's largest park, once home to the Siwonay Indians. Take a car or a bike if you want to explore the 2,765 acres (11 square kilometres); pick up a map at the Ranger Nature Center, near the entrance on Bruckner Boulevard at Wilkinson Avenue. The **Bartow-Pell Mansion Museum** (*see below*), in the park's south-eastern quarter, overlooks Long Island Sound. The park's 13 miles of coastline skirt the Hutchinson River to the west and the Long Island Sound and Eastchester Bay to the east. In summer, locals hit sandy **Orchard Beach**; set up in the 1930s, this 'Riviera of New York' is that rare beast – a Robert Moses creation not universally lamented.

Bartow-Pell Mansion Museum

895 Shore Road North, at Pelham Bay Park (1-718 885 1461, www.bartowpellmansionmuseum.org). Subway 6 to Pelham Bay Park, then take the Bee-Line bus 45 (ask driver to stop at the Bartow-Pell Mansion; bus does not run on Sun), or take a cab from the subway station. **Open** noon-4pm Wed, Sat, Sun. **Admission** $5; $3 reductions; free under-6s. **Credit** AmEx, DC, MC, V.

Operating as a museum since 1946, this stunning estate dates from 1654, when Thomas Pell bought the land from the Siwonay Indians. It was Robert Bartow, publisher and Pell descendant, who added the 1842 Greek Revival stone mansion, which faces a reflecting pool ringed by gardens.

► *Just east of Pelham Bay Park lies City Island, a rustic fishing village with a New England feel in New York City (see p367).*

Staten Island

Come for the ferry, stay for the greenery.

Staten Island doesn't exactly have a hip reputation. *Saturday Night Live* has pilloried the suburban working-class Italian-American cliché with its skit featuring Blake Lively with a heavy 'Noo Yawk' accent in *Gossip Girl: Staten Island*. Set in a pizza parlour, it made animated references to velour tracksuits and tanning booths. But the caricature is unfair: young creatives have started to infiltrate the borough, which is also home to growing Mexican, Indian, Somali and Sri Lankan populations.

Marketed as a slice of the small town in the big city, Staten Island is easily New York's smallest borough, with a population of 490,000; but with 170 parks, it's also the greenest.

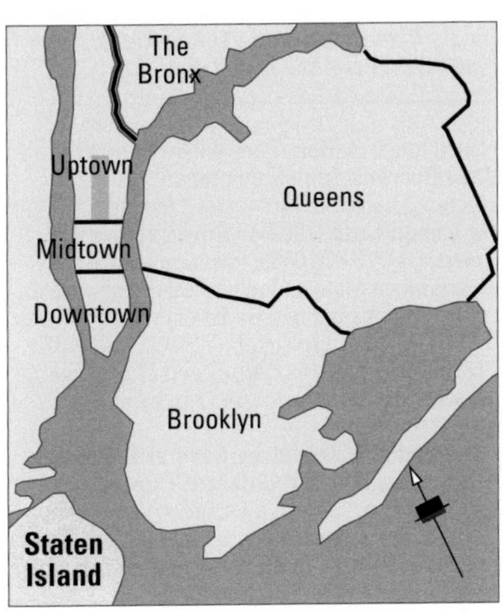

SIGHTS

INTRODUCING STATEN ISLAND

In its early days, Staten Island was an isolated community, until Henry Hudson sailed in and christened it *Staaten Eylandt* (Dutch for 'State's Island', in reference to Holland's Staaten-Generaal, or parliament) in 1609. Early settlers were driven out by Native Americans, the island's first inhabitants, but the Dutch took hold in 1661, establishing shipping and manufacturing enclaves on the northern shore, and farms and hamlets in the south. It became one of the five boroughs in 1898 but remained a backwater until 1964, when the Verrazano-Narrows Bridge joined the island to Bay Ridge in Brooklyn. Many say that's when small-town Staten Island truly vanished.

Still, many quaint aspects remain – not least the free **Staten Island Ferry** (*photo p151*), which links the southern tip of Manhattan with the island's St George terminal (where you can catch the buses noted in this chapter). When you alight, in the St George neighbourhood, head right along the new **Esplanade**, with its stirring views of lower Manhattan across the harbour, to pay your respects at *Postcards*, a memorial to the 274 Staten Islanders lost on 9/11. The fibreglass wings of the sculpture frame the spot where the Twin Towers used to stand.

Across the street from the terminal look for the distinctive clocktower of **Borough Hall** (10 Richmond Terrace); step inside for a peek at the Works Progress Administration murals depicting local history. Exiting the building, turn left to reach the small, 140-year-old **Staten Island Museum** (75 Stuyvesant Place, at Wall Street, 1-718 727 1135, www.statenisland museum.org), devoted to local history, art and natural science.

Walk up Hyatt Street behind Borough Hall for a glimpse of the Spanish baroque-styled lobby of the restored 1920s vaudeville venue **St George Theatre** (35 Hyatt Street, at Central Avenue, 1-718 442 2900, www.stgeorgetheatre.com), which stages family-friendly fare and gigs by stars such as Tony Bennett, Liza Minnelli and Tony Orlando.

If you turn right on to St Marks Place, you will come upon the landmark **St George Historic District**. Covering portions of St Marks and Carroll places, and Westervelt and Hamilton avenues, it features about 80 Queen Anne and Colonial Revival buildings, some from the early 1830s.

Worthwhile eating and drinking options in the area include **Enoteca Maria** (27 Hyatt Street, between Central Avenue & St Marks Place, 1-718 447 2777, www.enotecamaria.com,

INSIDE TRACK
THE STATEN ISLAND RAILWAY

Although it isn't connected to any of the city's other subway lines, the **Staten Island Railway** (S.I.R.) does accept the MetroCard. The railway has one line, which runs from St George to Tottenville on the southern tip of the island.

closed lunch & Mon, Tue), where rotating grandma-chefs from Italy prepare a nightly changing menu. An arty crowd frequents the **Cargo Café** (120 Bay Street, at Slosson Terrace, 1-718 876 0539, www.cargocafe.com, closed lunch Mon), a down-to-earth bar with an eclectic menu, and nearby **Every Thing Goes Thrift & Vintage** (140 Bay Street, 1-718 273 7139, www.etgstores.com, closed Mon & Sun), one of three local businesses run by a local hippie commune.

A short ride west along Richmond Terrace is the **Snug Harbor Cultural Center**, set in the 83-acre grounds of a former sailors' home. The **Staten Island Zoo**, adjacent to the Clove Lakes Park, has a rainforest and one of the East Coast's largest reptile collections.

To explore the island further, take the buses and the single-line Staten Island Railroad that depart from St George for destinations along the eastern half of the island. Along Hylan Boulevard lies photographer **Alice Austen House**, a 15-minute bus ride away. At the east end of Bay Street, **Fort Wadsworth** is one of the oldest military sites in the nation. From here, you can take in views of both the Verrazano Bridge and downtown Manhattan from one of NYC's highest points. Further along the eastern coast runs the two-mile **FDR Boardwalk**: the fourth longest in the world, it runs by South Beach, a sandy strip that's great for picnicking, fishing, beach volleyball and swimming.

For more spiritual calm, head to the centre of the island, to the **Jacques Marchais Museum of Tibetan Art**, a reproduction of a Himalayan mountain temple. Nearby, guides in period garb offer tours of **Historic Richmond Town**, the island's one-time county seat. A stone's throw away, is the 2,800-acre **Greenbelt** network of parks.

Opportunities for good, clean fun abound on the island's south-eastern coast (a 40-minute ride on the S78 bus), where you can swim, picnic and fish at **Wolfe's Pond Park** (Cornelia Avenue, at Hylan Boulevard, 1-718 984 8266). To the west, **Sandy Ground Historical Society** (1538 Woodrow Road, at Bloomingdale Road, 1-718 317 5796, Mar-Aug 1-4pm Tue-Sun, Dec-Feb 1-4pm Tue-Thur, Sun) celebrates the history of America's first settlement of free blacks. A little further south, **Conference House**, site of a failed attempt at peace between the Americans and British in 1776, is now a museum of colonial life.

Alice Austen House

2 Hylan Boulevard, between Bay & Edgewater streets (1-718 816 4506, www.aliceausten.org). S51 bus to Hylan Boulevard. **Open** *Mar-Dec* noon-5pm Tue-Sun. **Admission** *Suggested donation* $2. **No credit cards**.

The beautiful photographs of Alice Austen (1866-1952) are the highlight at this 17th-century cottage: there are no fewer than 3,000 of her glass negative photos here. The restored house and grounds often host concerts and events, and offer breathtaking harbour views.

Conference House (Billopp House)

7455 Hylan Boulevard, at Craig Avenue (1-718 984 0415, www.conferencehouse.org). S78 bus to Craig Avenue and Hylan Boulevard. **Open** *Apr-mid Dec* 1-4pm Fri-Sun. **Admission** $3; $2 reductions. **No credit cards**.

In 1776, Britain's Lord Howe parlayed with John Adams and Benjamin Franklin in this 17th-century house, the only surviving pre-Revolutionary manor in the city, while trying to forestall the American Revolution. Tours point out 18th-century furnishings, decor and daily objects such as quill pens and cookware. The lovely grounds command a terrific view over Raritan Bay, and provide a picturesque setting for free concerts and events.

★ FREE Fort Wadsworth

210 New York Avenue, on the east end of Bay Street (1-718 354 4500, www.nyharborparks.org/visit/fowa). S51 bus to Fort Wadsworth on weekdays, Von Briesen Park on weekends. **Open** dawn-dusk daily. *Visitors' centre* 10am-4.30pm Wed-Sun. **Admission** free.

Explore the fortifications that guarded NYC for almost 200 years at Ford Wadsworth, which was occupied by a blockhouse as far back as the 17th century. You can take one of several free themed tours, such as the popular evening lantern-light events. See the regularly updated Staten Island Unit Program Guide on the National Park Service website or call the visitor centre for the schedule.

FREE Greenbelt

Greenbelt Nature Center *700 Rockland Avenue, at Brielle Avenue (1-718 351 3450, www.sigreenbelt.org). S62 bus to Bradley Avenue, then S57 bus to Brielle & Rockland Avenue.* **Open** *Apr-Oct* 10am-5pm Tue-Sun. *Nov-Mar* 11am-5pm Wed-Sun. **Admission** free.

High Rock Park *200 Nevada Avenue, at Rockland Avenue. S62 bus to Manor Road, then S54 bus to Nevada Avenue.* **Open** dawn-dusk daily.

The Greenbelt Nature Center is the best starting point to explore more than 35 miles of trails in this network of parks (pick up a map or download one from the website). A mile away, at the 90-acre High Rock Park, visitors can hike the mile-long Swamp Trail, climb Todt Hill or explore trails through forests, meadows and wetlands.

Historic Richmond Town

441 Clarke Avenue, between Richmond Road & St Patrick's Place (1-718 351 1611, www.historicrichmondtown.org). S74 bus to St Patrick's Place. **Open** *Sept-June* 1-5pm Wed-Sun. *July, Aug* 11am-5pm Wed-Sun. **Admission** $5; $3.50-$4 reductions; free under-5s. **No credit cards**.

This colonial-era 'living museum' includes residences, public buildings and the oldest schoolhouse in the nation; it dates back to 1695. Tours and activities, from pumpkin picking to quilting, are available.

Jacques Marchais Museum of Tibetan Art

338 Lighthouse Avenue, off Richmond Road (1-718 987 3500, www.tibetanmuseum.org). S74 bus to Lighthouse Avenue. **Open** *Apr-Nov* 1-5pm Wed-Sun. *Dec-Mar* 1-5pm Thur-Sun. **Admission** $6; $4 reductions; free under-6s. **Credit** AmEx, Disc, MC, V.

This tiny museum contains a formidable Buddhist altar, tranquil meditation gardens and an extensive collection of Tibetan art and artefacts: sculptures, paintings, ritual objects and historic photos of the region. The museum hosts meditation workshops and t'ai chi classes; a Tibetan festival is held in October.

Staten Island Ferry. *See p149.*

★ Snug Harbor Cultural Center

1000 Richmond Terrace, between Snug Harbor Road & Tysen Avenue (1-718 448 2500, www.snug-harbor.org). S40 bus to the north gate (tell the bus driver). **Open** *Grounds* dawn-dusk daily.

Stately Greek Revival structures form the nucleus of this former sailors' retirement home. Dating from 1833, the centre has been restored and converted into an arts complex that includes one of the city's oldest concert halls. In addition to the listings below, the **Staten Island Children's Museum** (1-718 273 2060, www.statenislandkids.org, closed Mon) and **Art Lab** (1-718 447 8667, www.artlab.info), a non-profit art school, are also based here.

Newhouse Center for Contemporary Art

1-718 425 3524, www.snug-harbor.org/newhouse. **Open** *mid Mar-Nov* 10am-5pm Tue-Sun. *Nov-mid Mar* 10am-4pm Tue-Sun. **Admission** $3; $2 reductions; free under-13s. **No credit cards**.

Staten Island's premier venue for contemporary art holds several annual exhibitions from leading international sculptors, painters and mixed-media artists in its 15,000sq ft (1,400sq m) gallery.

Noble Maritime Collection *1-718 447 6490, www.noblemaritime.org.* **Open** 1-5pm Thur-Sun. **Admission** $5; $3 reductions; free under-12s. Free to all Sat, Sun.

This museum is dedicated to the artist-seaman John A Noble, who had a 'floating studio' moored in the Kill van Kull, the waterway between Staten Island and New Jersey, for 40 years As well as his maritime-themed paintings, Noble's houseboat is on display, restored to its appearance when the artist was featured in *National Geographic* magazine in 1954. Well worth a look is the recreated dormitory room of the former Sailors' Snug Harbor, circa 1900, upstairs.

Staten Island Botanical Garden *1-718 448 2500, www.snug-harbor.org.* **Open** 10am-4pm Tue-Sun. **Admission** *Chinese Scholar's Garden* $5; $4 reductions. *Grounds & other gardens* free. **Credit** AmEx, DC, MC, V.

Stroll through more than 20 themed gardens, including the traditional Chinese Scholar's Garden, with its pavilions, meandering paths and delicate footbridges, and, in spring and summer, the medieval-style children's Secret Garden, complete with 38-foot-high castle and a maze.

Staten Island Zoo

614 Broadway, between Glenwood Place & Colonial Court (1-718 442 3100, www.statenislandzoo.org). S48 bus to Broadway. **Open** 10am-4.45pm daily. **Admission** $8; $5-$6 reductions; free under-3s. Free to all 2-4.45pm Wed. **Credit** AmEx, DC, Disc, MC, V.

The home of 'Staten Island Chuck', NYC's very own furry Groundhog Day forecaster, also holds a large reptile and amphibian collection.

Consume

Schiller's Liquor Bar. *See p191.*

Hotels

It's a buyer's market for visitors to the Big Apple.

While accommodation is easily more expensive in New York City than the rest of the country, it's the cheapest it's been in years. This is because hotel construction is continuing despite the economic slump, creating more rooms than there is actual demand for. Indeed, by the end of 2011, the hotel industry expects Manhattan alone to have around 78,000 hotel rooms, an increase of almost 10,000 on the number the *entire city* could claim two years ago. Thirty-one new hotels (and an estimated 7,523 rooms) are anticipated between 2010 and 2011. Coupled with the lowest occupancy since the 1980s, this increase has forced many existing hotels to slash rates – the average is currently under $200 a night for a double room. All the better for bargain-hunting travellers.

HOTEL HOT SPOTS

Although Midtown contains the vast majority of hotels, it is by no means the only place to stay in Manhattan. The Financial District around Ground Zero is set to become a boom hotel district as the World Trade Center site redevelopment nears completion. But if you think all these new beds will only be geared towards giving the corporate traveller a good night's rest, think again. Indeed, the stylish Hyatt offshoot **Andaz Wall Street** (*see p155*) is anything but corporate. Andaz isn't the only out-of-towner that's moving into Manhattan. Hip small chains the **Standard** (*see p165*) and **Ace** (*see p168*) have opened up New York properties. The latter has even colonised an area that could emerge as the next hotel hotspot once the World Trade Center site is completed: the Flatiron District. But it's not just new areas that are freshening up the hotel industry: the Midtown scene has been rejuvenated by the opening of **The Chatwal New York** (*see p170*) in the summer of 2010 in a glorious restored Beaux-Arts landmark augmented with art deco touches. It's also worth looking across the river for competitively priced accommodation (*see p176* **Bargains in the Boroughs**).

❶ Red numbers given in this chapter correspond to the location of each hotel on the street maps. *See pp402-412.*

PRICES AND INFORMATION

Over the past couple of years, thousands of new beds have been added to the New York hotel industry. But even though there's no doubt that visitors are currently getting more bang for their buck, rates in the city are higher than in other parts of the country. They can vary wildly within a single property, according to room type and season, and the prices quoted here – obtained from the hotels – reflect that disparity. Unless indicated, the prices given are for a double room, from the cheapest in low season to the most expensive in high season. The prices quoted here are not guaranteed, but they offer a good indication of the hotel's average rack rates – what you would pay if you walked in off the street and asked for a room.

Special deals are often available, and you can frequently shave more off the price by booking on the hotel's website. Locally based discount agency **Quikbook** (www.quikbook.com) has a good selection of the properties listed in this chapter, and more, on their website; **Orbitz** (www.orbitz.com) lets you pick your hotel by stipulating the amenities, location, etc, you desire before offering you a selection to choose from.

For a budget option with a more personal touch, consider a B&B. Artist-run agency **City Sonnet** (1-212 614 3034, www.citysonnet.com) deals in Downtown locations. Expect to pay at least $125 for a double room in a private home. For gay-friendly hotels and B&Bs, *see p303*.

Downtown

FINANCIAL DISTRICT

Expensive

★ Andaz Wall Street
75 Wall Street, between Water Street & Pearl Street, New York, NY 10005 (1-212 590 1234, www.wallstreetandaz.com). Subway 2, 3, 4, 5 to Wall Street. **Rates** $250-$575 double. **Rooms** 253. **Credit** AmEx, DC, Disc, MC, V. **Map** p402 F33 ❶

Although it's a subsidiary brand of global giant Hyatt, Andaz prides itself in giving each property a local flavour. Following launches in London and LA, the first New York outpost (another opened on Fifth Avenue in 2010) occupies the first 13 floors of a former Barclays Bank building, outfitted by David Rockwell. The vibe inside is anything but corporate: upon entering the spacious, bamboo-panelled lobby-lounge, where a barista brews espresso from New York State roaster Gimme! Coffee, you're greeted by a free-range 'host', who acts as combination check-in clerk and concierge. The chic, loft-style rooms (starting at 350sq ft, or 33sq m) are equally casual and user-friendly. A long, blond-wood unit doubles as desk, entertainment console and dressing table (the TV has a vanity mirror on the back); remote-controlled blackout blinds descend to cover the 7ft windows; and non-alcoholic drinks and snacks are free. The local-centric restaurant (Wall & Water), bar and spa are welcome attributes in an area with little action at weekends.

Bar. Concierge. Disabled-adapted rooms. Gym. Internet (wireless, free). No smoking rooms. Restaurant. Room service. Spa. TV: pay movies.

> **INSIDE TRACK TAX NOTICE**
>
> When you're budgeting, don't forget to factor in the hefty 14.75 per cent tax – which includes city, state and hotel-room occupancy tax – plus an additional $3.50 per night for most rooms.

TRIBECA & SOHO

Deluxe

★ Crosby Street Hotel
79 Crosby Street, between Prince & Spring Streets, New York, NY 10012 (1-212 226 6400, www.crosbystreethotel.com). Subway N, R to Prince Street; 6 to Spring Street. **Rates** $495-$715 double. **Rooms** 86. **Credit** AmEx, DC, Disc, MC, V. **Map** p403 E30 ❷

In 2009, Britain's hospitality power couple, Tim and Kit Kemp, brought their super-successful Firmdale

Standard. *See p165.*

CONSUME

formula across the Atlantic with the 11-storey, warehouse-style Crosby Street Hotel – their first outside London. Design director Kit Kemp's signature style – a fresh, contemporary take on classic English decor characterised by an oft audacious mix of patterns, bold colours and judiciously chosen antiques – is instantly recognisable. Like its British cousins, Crosby Street has a carefully selected, predominantly British, art collection, including a giant head by Jaume Plensa and life-size dog sculptures by Justine Smith in the lobby (a canine theme, a noticeable NYC obsession, pervades the property). Other Firmdale imports include a guests-only drawing room as well as a public restaurant and bar, a slick, 100-seat screening room and a verdant garden. The latter inspired the bath products' exclusive scent, created by cult London perfumer Lyn Harris.
Bar. Concierge. Disabled-adapted rooms. Gym. Internet (wireless, free). No smoking floors. Parking ($55). Restaurant. Room service. TV: DVD/pay movies.

★ Greenwich Hotel

377 Greenwich Street, between Franklin & North Moore Streets, New York, NY 10013 (1-212 941 8900, www.thegreenwichhotel.com). Subway 1 to Franklin Street. **Rates** $495-$725 double. **Rooms** 88. **Credit** AmEx, DC, Disc, MC, V. **Map** p402 D31 ❸

'Deluxe guest house' might be a more fitting description of Robert De Niro's latest property, which has the vibe of a large villa located somewhere between Marrakesh and Milan. Rooms are spare and comfortable, appointed with down-filled leather settees, kilims and oriental rugs, and furnished with small libraries of art books. Exquisite Moroccan tile or carrara marble envelops the bathrooms, which have walk-in showers, while the main spaces feature wood-plank floors (beautiful to look at, but unfortunate for those staying under heavy-footed guests). Many rooms overlook the charming courtyard – just off the drawing room, where guests lounge in overstuffed chairs – while suites have perks such as fireplaces. The centrepiece of the subterranean Eastern-inspired Shibui Spa is the low-lit pool, set within the frame of a 250-year-old Kyoto farmhouse.
Bar. Concierge. Disabled-adapted rooms. Internet (wireless, free). No smoking floors. Pool (indoor). Restaurant. Room service. Spa. TV: DVD/pay movies.

▶ *For more on Robert de Niro's Tribeca empire, see p76.*

Mercer

147 Mercer Street, at Prince Street, New York, NY 10012 (1-212 966 6060, 1-888 918 6060, www.mercerhotel.com). Subway N, R to Prince Street. **Rates** $525-$950 double; $1,600-$3,300 suite. **Rooms** 75. **Credit** AmEx, DC, Disc, MC, V. **Map** p403 E29 ❹

Opened in 2001 by trendsetting hotelier André Balazs, Soho's first luxury boutique hotel still has ample attractions that appeal to a celeb-heavy clientele. The lobby, appointed with oversized white couches and chairs, and shelves lined with colourful books, acts as a bar, library and lounge – which is exclusive to hotel guests. The loft-like rooms are large by New York City standards and feature furniture by Christian Liagre, enormous washrooms and Face Stockholm products. The restaurant, Mercer Kitchen, serves Jean-Georges Vongerichten's stylish version of casual American cuisine. Secreted away two levels down is the Submercer lounge.
Bars (3). Concierge. Disabled-adapted rooms. Internet (wireless, free). No smoking rooms. Parking ($55). Restaurant. Room service. TV: DVD/pay movies.

Expensive

Duane Street Hotel

130 Duane Street, at Church Street, New York, NY 10013 (1-212 964 4600, www.duanestreethotel.com). Subway A, C, 1, 2, 3 to Chambers Street. **Rates** $205-$320 double. **Rooms** 45. **Credit** AmEx, DC, Disc, MC, V. **Map** p402 E31 ❺

In a city with a high tolerance for hype, the Duane Street Hotel stands out by laying low and doing the simple things well. Opened on a quiet Tribeca street in 2007, the 45-room boutique takes its cues from its well-heeled residential neighbourhood, offering loft-inspired rooms with 11ft ceilings, oversized windows and hardwood floors. The anonymously modern decor doesn't exactly exude character, but if you appreciate cleanliness and calm (not to mention comfortable beds, free Wi-Fi and rain showerheads), you probably won't mind the lack of designer flair. Affable, unobtrusive staff rounds out the good value – a rare commodity in this part of town.
Bar. Business centre. Concierge. Disabled-adapted rooms. Internet (wireless, free). No smoking. Restaurant. Room service. TV.

The James New York

27 Grand Street, at Thompson Street, New York, NY 10013 (1-888 526 2778, jameshotels.com). Subway A, C, E to Canal Street. **Rates** $399-$899 double. **Rooms** 114. **Credit** AmEx, DC, Disc, MC, V. **Map** p403 D30 ❻

Hotel art displays are usually limited to some eye-catching lobby installations or forgettable in-room prints. Not so at the James, which maintains a substantial showcase of local talent. The corridor of each guest floor is dedicated to the work of an individual artist, selected by a house curator and complete with museum-style notes – which makes waiting for the elevator a lot less tedious. The Chicago-based owners have given the property a distinctly Gotham vibe – even the doorstaff sports rakish uniforms (designed by Andrew Buckler) that

Hotel on Rivington. *See p161.*

look straight out of *Gangs of New York*. Although compact, bedrooms make the most of the available space with high ceilings, wall-spanning windows and glassed-off bathrooms (modesty is preserved by an artist-embellished, remote-controlled screen). Natural materials (wooden floors, linen duvet covers) warm up the clean contemporary lines, beds are piled with eco-friendly pillows, and bathroom products are courtesy of Intelligent Nutrients, the organic line created by Aveda founder Horst Rechelbacher. While the attractions of Soho and Tribeca beckon, the hotel also offers tempting facilities: a three-level 'urban garden' and a rooftop bar that opens on to the (tiny) pool.
Bar. Business centre. Concierge. Disabled-adapted rooms. Gym. No smoking. Internet (wireless, free). Pool. Restaurant. Room service. TV: pay movies.

60 Thompson

60 Thompson Street, between Broome & Spring Streets, New York, NY 10012 (1-212 431 0400, 1-877 431 0400, www.60thompson.com). Subway C, E to Spring Street. **Rates** $599-$875 double. **Rooms** 97. **Credit** AmEx, DC, Disc, MC, V. **Map** p403 E30 ❼

The first property of the nine-hotel-strong boutique chain Thompson Hotel Group remains one of its best. Despite its inauspicious kick-off date of 10 September 2001, this stylish spot has been luring film, fashion and media elites since it opened. Its expansive, somewhat masculine second-floor lobby, done up in dark wood, leather and tasteful shades of beige, brown, cream and grey, sets the tone for the rooms, from the modest doubles to the spectacular duplex, the Thompson Loft, which is often booked for photo shoots. A60, the exclusive guests-only rooftop bar with magnificent city views and a Moroccan-inspired decor, is equally photogenic. The modern rooms are dotted with indulgent details such as pure down duvets and pillows, and Kiehl's products. The hotel's acclaimed restaurant, Kittichai, serves creative Thai cuisine beside a pool filled with floating orchids; in warmer months, request a table on the pavement terrace. For other Thompson hotels, visit the website.
Bars (2). Concierge. Disabled-adapted rooms. Gym. Internet (wireless, $10/day). No smoking floors. Parking ($55). Restaurant. Room service. TV: DVD/pay movies.
Other locations throughout the city.

SoHo Grand Hotel

310 West Broadway, between Canal & Grand Streets, New York, NY 10013 (1-212 965 3000, 1-800 965 3000, www.sohogrand.com). Subway A, C, E, 1 to Canal Street. **Rates** $325-$515 double. **Rooms** 363. **Credit** AmEx, DC, Disc, MC, V. **Map** p403 E30 ❽

Fittingly, this Soho property makes good use of industrial materials such as poured concrete, cast iron and bottle glass (which is used for the staircase). Built in 1996, the Bill Sofield-designed rooms of the hotel (including two spacious penthouse lofts) are in a restrained neutral palette; the designer is currently updating all the rooms, introducing new custom pieces, such as travel-trunk-inspired minibars and natty hound's-tooth tuxedo chairs. The tranquil vibe is fortified by luxe Frette Egyptian cotton bedding and robes, and Malin & Goetz bath products. Bizarrely, you can also boost your soothing in-room experience by requesting a goldfish for the duration of your stay. There are free bicycles in the warmer months if you want to explore the area; alternatively, hole up with a cocktail in the hotel's new Club Room, complete with fireplace and low leather seating.
Bars (3). Business centre. Concierge. Disabled-adapted rooms. Gym. Internet (wireless, free). No smoking. Parking ($55). Restaurants (3). Room service. TV: DVD/pay movies.
Other locations Tribeca Grand Hotel, 2 Sixth Avenue, between Walker & White Streets, Tribeca, New York, NY 10013 (1-877 519 6600).

Moderate

Cosmopolitan

95 West Broadway, at Chambers Street, New York, NY 10007 (1-212 566 1900, 1-888 895 9400, www.cosmohotel.com). Subway A, C, 1, 2, 3 to Chambers Street. **Rates** $125-$179 double. **Rooms** 126. **Credit** AmEx, DC, MC, V. **Map** p402 E31 ❾

Despite the name, you won't find the legendary pink cocktail at this well-maintained hotel in two adjacent 1850s buildings, let alone a bar in which to drink it. The Cosmopolitan is geared towards travellers with little need for extras. Open continuously since the mid 19th century, it remains a tourist favourite for its address, clean rooms and reasonable rates. A wide range of configurations is available, including a room for families and – the best bargain here – cosy duplexes.
Internet (wireless, free). No smoking rooms. TV.

LITTLE ITALY & NOLITA

Moderate

SoHotel

341 Broome Street, between Elizabeth Street & Bowery, New York, NY 10013 (1-212 226 1482, www.thesohotel.com). Subway J, M, Z to Bowery; 6 to Spring Street. **Rates** $99-$239 double. **Rooms** 96. **Credit** AmEx, DC, Disc, MC, V. **Map** p403 F30 ❿

Thanks to new exterior coloured-light effects, this formerly modest hotel at the nexus of Chinatown, Little Italy and Nolita piques the curiosity of passersby. A recent overhaul has given the 1700s establishment's small rooms a quirky punch, including a coat of chartreuse paint, flatscreen TVs and exposed-brick

Greenwich Hotel. *See p157.*

walls. Charming touches such as ceiling fans, hardwood floors, skylights and vaulted ceilings place the SoHotel a rung above similarly priced establishments. Complimentary morning coffee is served in the lobby, and the hotel staff, well aware that the place lacks a lift, are eager to lend a helping hand on your way in and out. SoHotel's many Regency suites ($199-$299), which can accommodate four to five guests, are the best bargain.
Internet (wireless in lobby only, free). No smoking rooms. TV.

LOWER EAST SIDE

Deluxe

Bowery Hotel

335 Bowery, at 3rd Street, New York, NY 10003 (1-212 505 9100, www.theboweryhotel.com). Subway B, D, F, M to Broadway-Lafayette Street; 6 to Bleecker Street. **Rates** $325-$725 double. **Rooms** 135. **Credit** AmEx, DC, Disc, MC, V. **Map** p403 F29 ⓫
This fanciful boutique hotel from prominent duo Eric Goode and Sean MacPherson is the capstone in the gentrification of the Bowery. Shunning minimalism, they have created plush rooms that pair old-world touches (oriental rugs, wood-beamed ceilings, marble washstands) with modern amenities (flatscreen TVs, Wi-Fi, a DVD library). Tall windows offer views of the neighbourhood's historic tenements, and the property includes an antique-looking trattoria, Gemma.
Bar. Concierge. Disabled-adapted rooms. Internet (wireless, free). No smoking rooms. Restaurant. Room service. TV: DVD.

▶ *For the hoteliers' flamboyant take on a boarding house, the Jane, see p167.*

Expensive

Blue Moon

100 Orchard Street, between Delancey & Broome Streets, New York, NY 10002 (1-212 533 9080, www.bluemoon-nyc.com). Subway F to Delancey Street. **Rates** $315-$570 double. **Rooms** 22. **Credit** AmEx, DC, Disc, MC, V. **Map** p403 F30 ⓬
This eight-storey, 22-room hotel housed in a former 19th-century tenement eschews chic modernism in favour of old-world charm. Artist-owner Randy Settenbrino incorporated historic newspaper clippings, ads and photos he discovered during renovation into the decor, complementing original wood mouldings, art nouveau fixtures and touches such as vintage wood-burning stoves. Rooms are enormous for New York standards (325-800sq ft, or 30-74sq m). Continental breakfast (featuring local Kossar's bagels), all-day coffee and a glass of wine upon arrival are among the perks. Some rooms come with balconies, several of which offer stunning views of the nearby Williamsburg Bridge.
Concierge. Internet (wireless, free). No smoking.

THE BEST INDULGENT BOLT-HOLES

For club privileges
Soho House. *See p165.*

For celebrity-chef room service
London NYC. *See p172.*

For the dreamiest bed
Surrey. *See p178.*

▶ *There's more on the extraordinary history of the neighbourhood next door at the Lower East Side Tenement Museum; see p80.*

Hotel East Houston

151 E Houston Street, at Eldridge Street, New York, NY 10002 (1-212 777 0012, www.hoteleasthouston.com). Subway F to Lower East Side-Second Avenue. **Rates** $349-$399 double. **Rooms** 42. **Credit** AmEx, DC, Disc, MC, V. **Map** p403 G29 ⓭
Opened in autumn 2007, this six-storey boutique hotel offers rooms dressed up in rococo-inspired wallpaper and a rich colour palette of golds, chocolate and pomegranate. As enticing as the living quarters are – complete with flatscreen, high-definition TVs – you'll want to spend much of your time soaking up the sun, and exceptional views, on the rooftop patio, which is open (to guests only) round the clock. Rooms are small, but touches such as Bulgari toiletries and a spacious white-clad breakfast room in the basement earn this spot style points.
Business centre. Concierge. Disabled-adapted rooms. Internet (high-speed, wireless, free). No smoking. TV: DVD.

Hotel on Rivington

107 Rivington Street, between Essex & Ludlow Streets, New York, NY 10002 (1-212 475 2600, www.hotelonrivington.com). Subway F to Delancey Street; J, M, Z to Delancey-Essex Streets. **Rates** $229-$595 double. **Rooms** 110. **Credit** AmEx, DC, Disc, MC, V. **Map** p403 G29 ⓮
When the Hotel on Rivington opened in 2005, its ultra-modern glass-covered façade was a novelty on the largely low-rise Lower East Side. Now, with condos popping up on nearly every block, the building (designed by NYC firm Grzywinski & Pons) seems less out of place, but it remains one of the few luxury hotels in the neighbourhood. Rooms are super-sleek, with oh-so-hip black and white decorative touches, including velvet-covered lounge chairs, and floor-to-ceiling windows (even in the shower stalls) that offer views of Manhattan and beyond. A stylish crowd congregates in Thor, the hotel lounge; its brown leather banquettes and rock-star portraits set it apart from the traditional hotel bar. *Photos p158.*

Bars (2). Business centre. Concierge. Disabled-adapted rooms. Gym. Internet (wireless, free). No smoking floors. Parking ($60). Restaurant. TV: pay movies.

Moderate

Off Soho Suites Hotel

11 Rivington Street, between Bowery & Chrystie Street, New York, NY 10002 (1-212 979 9808, 1-800 633 7646, www.offsoho.com). Subway B, D to Grand Street; F to Lower East Side-Second Avenue; J, M, Z to Bowery. **Rates** $159-$299 suite. **Rooms** 38. **Credit** AmEx, DC, MC, V. **Map** p403 F30 ⑮

These no-frills suites have become all the more popular in recent years due to the Lower East Side's burgeoning bar and restaurant scene. The rates are a decent value for the now-thriving location, especially as all have a sitting area and access to a kitchenette. Rooms accommodate either two guests (with two twin beds only, and a shared kitchenette) or four (with a queen bed, plus a sleeper sofa in the lounge area). There's also a handy coin-operated laundry in the basement.

Concierge. Disabled-adapted rooms. Gym. Internet (wireless, free). No smoking rooms.

▶ *For more on the Lower East Side's bar scene, see p218; for its restaurants, including Katz's 'When Harry Met Sally' Delicatessen, see p190.*

CONSUME

EAST VILLAGE

Expensive

Cooper Square Hotel

25 Cooper Square, between 5th & 6th Streets, New York, NY 10003 (1-212 475 5700, www.thecoopersquarehotel.com). Subway N, R to 8th Street-NYU; 6 to Astor Place. **Rates** $300-$700 double. **Rooms** 145. **Credit** AmEx, DC, Disc, MC, V. **Map** p403 F28 ⑯

Carlos Zapata's curved, 21-storey glass tower is hard to miss, but, as you approach the unmarked entrance you'll wonder what it is. A doorman ushers you into a dramatic, double-height lobby, where you should be greeted by staff – in practice this sometimes breaks down. No matter, the charms of the hotel soon make up for any slight disorientation. Checking in over a glass of wine, admire the contemporary lodge-like library-lounge, stocked with diverse reading matter from Housing Works – you can buy the books, benefitting the charity – and furnished by B&B Italia. Rooms start at a compact 250sq ft (23sq m), but the floor-to-ceiling windows and spare furnishings in shades of grey lend a sense of space. If you can stretch to it, get a high corner room (prices rise with the floor level) for spectacular dual-aspect views. Choose from three robes – towelling, silk or cotton kimono – in the minimalist slate-floored bathrooms. Scott Conant's Faustina, which opened in early 2010, is likely to become a destination restaurant.

Bar. Concierge. Disabled-adapted rooms. Internet (wireless, free). No smoking rooms. Restaurant. Room service. TV: DVD/pay movies.

Budget

East Village Bed & Coffee

110 Avenue C, between 7th & 8th Streets, New York, NY 10009 (1-212 533 4175, www.bedandcoffee.com). Subway F to Lower East Side-Second Avenue; L to First Avenue. **Rates** $133-$155 double. **Rooms** 9. **Credit** AmEx, DC, MC, V. **Map** p403 G28 ⑰

Popular with European travellers, this East Village B&B (minus the breakfast) embodies quirky downtown culture. Each of the nine guest rooms has a unique theme: for example, the 'Black and White Room' or the 'Treehouse' (not as outlandish as it sounds: it has an ivory and olive colour scheme, animal-print linens and a whitewashed brick wall). Owner Anne Edris encourages guests to mingle in the communal areas, which include fully equipped kitchens and three loft-like living rooms (bathrooms are also shared). When the weather's nice, sip your complimentary morning java in the private garden.

Internet (wireless, free). No smoking indoors.

Other locations Second Home on Second Avenue, 221 Second Avenue, between 13th & 14th Streets, East Village, New York, NY 10003 (1-212 677 3161).

Hotel 17

225 E 17th Street, between Second & Third Avenues, New York, NY 10003 (1-212 475 2845, www.hotel17ny.com). Subway L to Third Avenue; L, N, Q, R, 4, 5, 6 to 14th Street-Union Square. **Rates** $69-$160 double. **Rooms** 125. **Credit** MC, V. **Map** p403 F27 ⑱

Shabby chic is the best way to describe this East Village hotel a few blocks from Union Square. Past the minuscule but well-appointed lobby, the rooms are a study in contrast, as antique dressers are paired with paisley bedspreads and mismatched vintage wallpaper. Bathrooms are generally shared between two to four rooms, but they're kept immaculately clean. Over the years, the building has been featured in numerous fashion mag layouts and films – including Woody Allen's *Manhattan Murder Mystery* – and has put up Madonna, and, more recently, transsexual downtown diva Amanda Lepore. So there's always that frisson when staying here of wondering who you might bump into on your way to the loo?

Concierge. Internet (wireless, free). No smoking floors. TV.

St Marks Hotel

2 St Marks Place, at Third Avenue, New York, NY 10003 (1-212 674 0100, www.stmarkshotel.net). Subway 6 to Astor Place. **Rates** $120-$180 double. **Rooms** 66. **No credit cards**. **Map** p403 F28 ⑲

Cooper Square Hotel.

Nestled among the tattoo parlours, cheap eateries and souvenir shops of St Marks Place, this small hotel received a much needed facelift in 2007; its modest rooms, which have double beds and private baths, are now bright, clean and understated (if somewhat bland) and offer Wi-Fi and flatscreen TVs. Note that the hotel is in a pre-war building with no lifts.
Bar. Internet (wireless, $10/day). TV: DVD.
► *St Marks is within stumbling distance of dozens of hot East Village bars and restaurants; see p219 and p193, respectively.*

GREENWICH VILLAGE

Moderate

Larchmont Hotel
27 W 11th Street, between Fifth & Sixth Avenues, New York, NY 10011 (1-212 989 9333, www.larchmonthotel.com). Subway F, M to 14th Street; L to Sixth Avenue. **Rates** $119-$145 double. **Rooms** 66. **Credit** AmEx, DC, MC, V. **Map** p403 E28 ⑳

Surrey. *See p178.*

Housed in a 1910 Beaux Arts building, the attractive, affordable Larchmont is great value for this area. The decor (wicker furniture, floral bedspreads) recalls the *Golden Girls*, but with prices this reasonable, you can accept low marks for style. All the bathrooms are shared, but rooms come with a washbasin, bathrobe and slippers.
Internet (wireless, free). No smoking. TV.

Washington Square Hotel

103 Waverly Place, between MacDougal Street & Sixth Avenue, New York, NY 10011 (1-212 777 9515, 1-800 222 0418, www.washingtonsquarehotel.com). Subway A, B, C, D, E, F, M to W 4th Street. **Rates** $187-$385 double. **Rooms** 155. **Credit** AmEx, DC, MC, V. **Map** p403 E28 ㉑

A haven for writers and artists for decades, this hotel is suited to those seeking a quiet bolt-hole in a storied neighbourhood. The hotel's lengthy renovation, which has nearly doubled the lobby size and refurbished the interiors, is nearly complete: rooms are done up with spare art deco furnishings and an odd but pleasant colour scheme of mauve and olive; its ultra-narrow hallways are a quirky reminder of its pre-war beginnings. Rates include a continental breakfast – or you can splurge on the Sunday jazz brunch at North Square, the hotel's restaurant. Get a south-facing room for a glimpse of the park.
Bars (2). Gym. Internet (wireless in lobby only, free). No smoking. Restaurant.

WEST VILLAGE & MEATPACKING DISTRICT

Deluxe

Hotel Gansevoort

18 Ninth Avenue, at 13th Street, New York, NY 10014 (1-212 206 6700, 1-877 426 7386, www.hotelgansevoort.com). Subway A, C, E to 14th Street; L to Eighth Avenue. **Rates** $345-$475 double. **Rooms** 186. **Credit** AmEx, DC, Disc, MC, V. **Map** p403 C28 ㉒

Despite its controversial beginnings (it was strongly opposed by neighbourhood preservationists), the Gansevoort has made a name for itself as a coolhunters' hub. The lobby features four 18ft light boxes that change colour throughout the evening, while simple but elegant rooms offer a more muted colour scheme. The real draw is floor-to-ceiling windows offering incredible views of the Meatpacking District and beyond, but, unfortunately, the glass is not quite thick enough to keep out noise from the street (even on the eighth floor) and can be draughty in winter. But the mini balconies, plush feather beds atop excellent mattresses and Cutler toiletries in the marble bathrooms counterbalance these minor gripes. A visit to the roof is a must in any season: the garden has a heated pool (with underwater music) that is enclosed in winter, a bar (Plunge) and, of course, a 360-degree panorama. Further attractions in the hotel are the Exhale spa and Jeffrey Chodorow's inviting Tanuki Tavern, which serves inventive Japanese small plates.
Bars (2). Business centre. Disabled-adapted rooms. Gym. Internet (wireless, free). No smoking floors. Parking ($40). Pool (indoor/outdoor). Restaurant. Room service. Spa. TV: DVD/pay movies.

★ Soho House

29-35 Ninth Avenue, at W 13th Street, New York, NY 10014 (1-646 253 6122, www.sohohouseny.com). Subway A, C, E to 14th Street; L to Eighth Avenue. **Rates** $495-$950 double. **Rooms** 24. **Credit** AmEx, MC, V. **Map** p403 C27 ㉓

From its origins as a private members' club in London, Soho House is expanding its empire to LA, Miami and Berlin. Designed as a place for creative types to relax, socialise and work, the converted warehouse space is split into six levels, housing a spa, a library, an arthouse cinema, a low-lit bar area and restaurant, and a rooftop pool. You don't have to be a member to stay here, but membership perks apply. The rooms offer the kind of understated luxury you'd actually like to live with: plush rugs on wooden floors, antique chandeliers hanging from wood-beamed ceilings and, in some cases, elaborately carved beds. Showers are stocked with the house spa's divine-smelling Cowshed toiletries, and a selection of things you may have forgotten to pack (hairbrush, dental kit) are thoughtfully supplied, as well as some cheeky extras (love dice, condoms).
Bar. Concierge. Disabled-adapted rooms. Gym. Internet (wireless, free). No smoking. Parking ($45). Pool (outdoor). Restaurant. Room service. Spa. TV: DVD.

Expensive

Standard

848 Washington Street, at 13th Street, New York, NY 10014 (1-212 645 4646, www.standardhotels.com/new-york-city). Subway A, C, E to 14th Street; L to Eighth Avenue. **Rates** $295-$510 double. **Rooms** 337. **Credit** AmEx, DC, Disc, MC, V. **Map** p403 C27 ㉔

André Balazs's lauded West Coast mini-chain arrived in New York in early 2009. Straddling the High Line, the retro 18-storey structure has been configured to give each room an exhilarating view, either of the river or a Midtown cityscape. Quarters are compact (from 230sq ft, or 21sq m) but the combination of floor-to-ceiling windows, curving tambour wood panelling (think old-fashioned roll-top desks) and 'peekaboo' bathrooms (with Japanese-style tubs or huge showerheads) give a sense of space. Eating and drinking options include a chop house, beer garden and a top-floor bar (for hotel guests and members only) with a massive jacuzzi and 180-degree views. *Photo p155.*

What's Old is New

The vintage craze has spread to lodgings.

Jane.

In the sconce-lit lobby, a check-in clerk produces your key from the bank of cubbyholes, and a red-uniformed bellman takes you up in a manually operated lift. But this is no crumbling relic of a bygone era. Welcome to the **Jane** (*see p167*), the latest accommodation from hot hoteliers Eric Goode and Sean MacPherson of the Bowery and the Maritime. The difference is, now they're charging under $100 a night.

Opened in 1907 as the American Seaman's Friend Society Sailors Home, the 14-storey landmark was a residential hotel when the duo took it over (some long-term residents remain). The wood-panelled, 50-square-foot rooms were inspired by vintage train sleeper compartments: there's a single bed with built-in storage and brass hooks for hanging up your clothes – but also iPod docks and wall-mounted 23-inch flatscreen TVs.

If entering the hotel feels like stepping on to a film set, there's good reason. Inspiration came from various celluloid sources, including *Barton Fink*'s Hotel Earle for the lobby. The 'ballroom' (closed at time of writing, but due to reopen soon), decorated with mismatched chairs, oriental rugs and a fireplace topped with a stuffed ram, evokes an eccentric mansion. 'I want it to feel intensely residential and slightly quirky, not like a typical corporate hotel,' says Sean MacPherson. Although he acknowledges an element of escapism in the decor, the main goal was to be true to the building's past. 'As much as it's theatrical and contrived, hopefully you can feel some sense of authenticity, albeit recreated authenticity.'

The owners of the **Ace Hotel** (*see p168*), formerly the 1904 Hotel Breslin, wanted to create the feel of staying with plugged-in friends. They enlisted designers Stephen Alesch and Robin Standefer of Roman & Williams, who have combined custom-made furnishings with pieces from different periods to interesting effect. Double rooms start at under $200; some are equipped with old-school turntables (complete with a small selection of vinyl), retro Smeg fridges and custom-made furniture incorporating plumbing pipes. In the lobby, where 1970s seating mingles with industrial salvage, the bar is housed within a panelled library transplanted from a Madison Avenue apartment, and there's a collection of New York-centric books. 'We found some great pieces of furniture from flea markets and different vendors in various stages of decay,' says Standefer. 'Some we painted and gave a new life to and covered in unexpected industrial felt so they didn't feel too precious. We wanted there to be a real sense of comfort. I hope people do put their legs on the furniture and grab a book from the library and hang out.'

Bars (4). Business centre. Concierge. Disabled-adapted rooms. Gym. Internet (wireless, free). No smoking. Parking ($55). Restaurants (2). Room service. Spa. TV: pay movies.
► *For more about the High Line, see p96* **Profile**.

Moderate

Abingdon Guest House

21 Eighth Avenue, between Jane & 12th Streets, New York, NY 10014 (1-212 243 5384, www.abingdonguesthouse.com). Subway A, C, E to 14th Street; L to Eighth Avenue. **Rates** $159-$259 double. **Rooms** 9. **Credit** AmEx, DC, Disc, MC, V. **Map** p403 D28 ㉕

A charming option in a charming neighbourhood on the Meatpacking District's borders: rooms in the Abingdon's two converted townhouses are done up in plush fabrics and antique furnishings, and sport homespun details such as original 1950s pine floors, hooked rugs, and four-poster or sleigh beds. Although all rooms have private baths, they may not be inside the room. The small back courtyard is lovely on summer mornings or evenings.

Internet (wireless, free). No smoking.

★ Jane

113 Jane Street, at West Street, New York, NY 10014 (1-212 924 6700, www.thejanenyc.com). Subway A, C, E to 14th Street; L to Eighth Avenue. **Rates** $79-$99 single; $250-$300 double. **Rooms** 208. **Credit** AmEx, DC, Disc, MC, V. **Map** p403 D28 ㉖

For review, *see p166* **What's Old is New**.

Bar. Disabled-adapted rooms. Internet (wireless, free). No smoking rooms. Restaurant. Room service. TV: DVD.

Midtown

CHELSEA

Expensive

Maritime Hotel

363 W 16th Street, between Eighth & Ninth Avenues, New York, NY 10011 (1-212 242 4300, www.themaritimehotel.com). Subway A, C, E to 14th Street; L to Eighth Avenue. **Rates** $275-$365 double. **Rooms** 126. **Credit** AmEx, DC, Disc, MC, V. **Map** p403 C27 ㉗

Steve Zissou would feel at home at this nautically themed hotel (the former headquarters of the New York Maritime Union), which is outfitted with self-consciously hip details befitting a Wes Anderson film. Standard rooms are modelled on cruise cabins; lined with teak panelling and sporting a single port-hole window, they're small but well appointed (CO Bigelow products in the bathroom, a Kiki de Montparnasse 'pleasure kit' in the minibar, a well-curated DVD collection available by phone). The hotel's busy Italian restaurant, La Bottega, also supplies room service, and the adjoining bar hosts a crowd of models and mortals, who throng the umbrella-lined patio in warmer weather. In the basement, Matsuri offers sushi, Japanese tapas and the city's only saké sommelier.

Bars (4). Concierge. Disabled-adapted rooms. Gym. Internet (wireless, free). No smoking floors. Restaurants (2). Room service. TV: DVD/pay movies.

Moderate

Hotel Chelsea (aka Chelsea Hotel)

222 W 23rd Street, between Seventh & Eighth Avenues, New York, NY 10011 (1-212 243 3700, www.hotelchelsea.com). Subway C, E, 1 to 23rd Street. **Rates** $149-$269 double. **Rooms** 116. **Credit** AmEx, DC, Disc, MC, V. **Map** p404 D26 ㉘

Built in 1883 as a private apartment building, the Chelsea has a long and infamous past – not surprising considering it's been home to artists and writers of every stripe since it opened a year later. From *Lost Weekend* author Charles R Jackson's suicide to Nancy Spungen's fatal stabbing, it has been the site of several sordid events. The lobby's walls exude history – many of the paintings haven't moved since their installation. Room configurations are diverse, but all are generally large with high ceilings, and amenities – such as flatscreen TVs, washer-dryers and marble fireplaces – vary. In some cases, the bathrooms are shared.

Concierge. Disabled-adapted rooms. Internet (wireless, free). Restaurant. TV.
► *For more on the hotel's extraordinary history and how to go on a guided tour of the premises even if you're not staying there, see p89.*

Inn on 23rd Street

131 W 23rd Street, between Sixth & Seventh Avenues, New York, NY 10011 (1-212 463 0330, www.innon23rd.com). Subway F, M, 1 to 23rd Street. **Rates** $199-$408 double. **Rooms** 14. **Credit** AmEx, DC, Disc, MC, V. **Map** p404 D26 ㉙

This renovated 19th-century townhouse offers the charm of a traditional bed and breakfast with enhanced amenities (a lift, pillow-top mattresses, private bathrooms, white-noise machines). Owners and innkeepers Annette and Barry Fisherman have styled each of the 14 bedrooms with a unique theme, such as Maritime, Bamboo and 1940s. One of its best attributes is the 'library', a cosy jumble of tables and chairs where breakfast is served: it's open 24/7 to guests, should you want to relax with a cup of tea or glass of wine.

Concierge. Disabled-adapted rooms. Internet (wireless, free). No smoking. TV: DVD.

Budget

Chelsea Lodge

318 W 20th Street, between Eighth & Ninth Avenues, New York, NY 10011 (1-212 243 4499, www.chelsealodge.com). Subway C, E to 23rd Street. **Rates** $124 single; $134 double. **Rooms** 26. **Credit** AmEx, DC, MC, V. **Map** p403 D27 ⑳

'Lodge' in this case doesn't denote an Econo-Lodge, but rather the kind you might find out in the woods – despite the inn's situation in a landmark brownstone blocks from the Chelsea gallery district, a rather long way from any arcadian idylls. But the name does serve to make a bit more sense of the, by turns whimsical, hilarious and bizarre, mishmash of Americana – such as rough-hewn duck decoys, cut-out roosters and early 20th-century photos – that adorns the pine panelling of the inn's public spaces. While all of the hotel's mostly tiny rooms come with TVs, showers and seasonal air-conditioning, nearly all share toilets, so it's not for everyone. Still, the low prices and undeniable charm mean that it can fill up quickly. For more privacy, book one of the four suites down the block at 334 West 20th Street ($229), which are decorated by that building's owner, the artist Karl Mann: all are former studio apartments with kitchenettes, and the ones at the back have direct access to a private courtyard.

Concierge. No smoking. TV: DVD.

▶ *For reviews of the many art galleries in Chelsea, see p294.*

FLATIRON DISTRICT & UNION SQUARE

Moderate

★ Ace Hotel

20 W 29th Street, between Fifth & Sixth Avenues, New York, NY 10012 (1-646 214 5742, www.acehotel.com). Subway N, R 28th Street. **Rates** $209-$509 double. **Rooms** 265. **Credit** AmEx, Disc, MC, V. **Map** p404 E26 ㉛

Bourgeois hipsters tired of crashing on couches will appreciate the New York outpost of the cool chainlet that was founded in Seattle by a pair of DJs. The musical influence is clear: many of the rooms in the 1904 building have playful amenities such as functioning turn-tables, stacks of vinyl and gleaming Gibson guitars. And while you'll pay a hefty amount for the sprawling loft spaces, there are reasonable options for those on a lower budget. The respectable 'medium' rooms are outfitted with vintage furniture and original art; even cheaper are the snug bunk-bed set-ups. Should you find the latter lodging stifling, repair to the buzzing hotel lobby to sip coffee from the Stumptown café – the first in the city from the artisan Oregon roasters – or score a table at chef April Bloomfield's massively popular Breslin Bar & Dining Room (*see p201*).

Bars (3). Business centre. Concierge. Disabled-adapted rooms. Gym. Internet (wireless, free). No smoking floors. Parking ($50). Restaurant. Room service. TV: DVD/pay movies.

Budget

Gershwin Hotel

7 E 27th Street, between Fifth & Madison Avenues, New York, NY 10016 (1-212 545 8000, www.gershwinhotel.com). Subway N, R, 6 to 28th Street. **Rates** $39-$60/person in 4- to 8-bed dorm; $109-$309 for 1-3 people in private room. **Rooms** 60 beds in dorms; 145 private. **Credit** AmEx, DC, MC, V. **Map** p404 E26 ㉜

Works by Lichtenstein line the hallways, and an original Warhol soup can painting hangs in the lobby of this pop art-themed budget hotel. Rooms may be less than pristine – especially the hostel-style dorms – but the rates are extremely reasonable for a location just off Fifth Avenue. There are also four suites – the one with screen-printed walls and a sitting room is a favourite of regular guests.

Concierge. Disabled-adapted rooms. Internet (wireless, $10/day). No smoking floors. Parking ($40). Restaurant. Room service.

GRAMERCY PARK & MURRAY HILL

Deluxe

Gramercy Park Hotel

2 Lexington Avenue, at 21st Street, New York, NY 10010 (1-212 475 4320, www.gramercypark hotel.com). Subway 6 to 23rd Street. **Rates** $545-$675 double; suite $900-$2,400. **Rooms** 192. **Credit** AmEx, DC, Disc, MC, V. **Map** p404 F26 ㉝

New Yorkers held their collective breath when hotelier Ian Schrager announced he was revamping the Gramercy Park Hotel, a 1924 gem that had hosted everyone from Humphrey Bogart to David Bowie. They needn't have worried: the redesigned lobby, unveiled in 2006, retains the boho spirit with its stucced walls, red banquettes, an enormous Venetian chandelier and working fireplace, and artwork from Cy Twombly, Andy Warhol, Richard Prince and Julian Schnabel (the hotel's art director). The eclectic elegance continues in the spacious rooms, which include tapestry-covered chairs, hand-tufted rugs, mahogany drinking cabinets and a Pre-Raphaelite colour palette of deep reds and blues. Guests can lounge on the private roof deck, get a facial at the in-house Aerospa, or sip cocktails at the Schnabel-designed Rose and Jade bars. Danny Meyer's new trattoria, Maialino, has bumped up the attractions.

Bars (3). Business centre. Concierge. Disabled-adapted rooms. Gym. Internet (wireless, $16/day). No smoking floors. Parking ($60). Restaurants (2). Room service. Spa. TV: DVD/pay movies.

▶ *For our review of Maialino, see p202.*

Expensive

Marcel at Gramercy

201 E 24th Street, at Third Avenue, New York, NY 10010 (1-212 696 3800, www.themarcelat gramercy.com). Subway 6 to 23rd Street. **Rates** $259-$369 double. **Rooms** 135. **Credit** AmEx, Disc, MC, V. **Map** p404 F26 ㉞

Revamped in early 2008, this fashionable hotel has a hip aesthetic that extends from the lobby, with its marble concierge desk, sprawling leather banquette and in-house library, to the medium-sized rooms, which offer a sleek black and pewter palette, rain-head showers and Frette linens. Complimentary breakfast is served in the tenth-floor guest lounge. For something more substantial, 'inoteca – run by chefs Eric Kleinman and Steve Connaughton (of 'ino and Lupa fame, respectively) – serves inventive takes on classic Italian fare, while master mixologist Tony Abou-Ganim oversees the adjacent bar. Sexy subterranean lounge Polar opened in early 2010.

Bars (2). Business centre. Concierge. Disabled-adapted rooms. Internet (wireless, $12/day). No smoking floors. Restaurant. Room service. TV: DVD/pay movies.

Morgans

237 Madison Avenue, between 37th & 38th Streets, New York, NY 10016 (1-212 686 0300, 1-800 334 3408, www.morganshotel.com). **Rates** $309-$419 double; $519-$939 suite. **Rooms** 113. **Credit** AmEx, DC, Disc, MC, V. **Map** p404 E24 ㉟

New York's original boutique hotel, Morgans opened in 1984. Some 25 years later, the hotel's orginal designer, octogenerian French tastemaker Andrée Putman, returned to officiate over a revamp that has softened its stark monochrome appearance. The boxy 1930s-inspired lobby now features a hypnotic coloured-light ceiling installation by French design collective Trafik (guests can adjust it on a console and save patterns under their name). Unfussy bedrooms, cast in a calming palette of silver, grey, cream and white, are hung with original Robert Mapplethorpe prints; window seats piled with linen cushions encourage quiet reflection. The bathrooms, dressed with classic black and white tiles, offer products made for the hotel group by natural skincare brand Korres. The guests' living room, stocked with coffee and tea, is equally understated, but Philippe Starck's design for the hotel restaurant, Asia de Cuba, all white vinyl and sweeping drapes, looks dated.

Bar. Business centre. Concierge. Disabled-adapted rooms. Internet (wireless, $15/day). No smoking floors. Restaurant. Room service. TV: DVD/pay movies.

Other locations 356 W 58th Street, between Eighth & Ninth Avenues, New York, NY 10019 (1-212 554 6000, www.hudsonhotel.com); Royalton, 44 W 44th Street, between Fifth & Sixth Avenues, Midtown, New York, NY 10036 (1-212 869 4400, 1-800 635 9013).

> **INSIDE TRACK**
> **SECRET GARDEN**
>
> The **Gramercy Park Hotel**'s (*see p168*) greatest amenity is a free key to nearby Gramercy Park (*see p93*) – one of the most exclusive outdoor spaces in the city.

Moderate

Hotel Thirty Thirty

30 E 30th Street, between Madison Avenue & Park Avenue South, New York, NY 10016 (1-212 689 1900, 1-800 804 4480, www.thirtythirty-nyc.com). Subway 6 to 28th Street. **Rates** $129-$269 double. **Rooms** 260. **Credit** AmEx, DC, Disc, MC, V. **Map** p404 E25 ㊱

Rooms vary tremendously in size and configuration in this former residence for single women. Some are tiny, others are oddly, but sometimes felicitously, shaped – such as a double that has an extra seating area – but all are tidy and simply decorated in an inoffensive beige and white colour scheme. The bathrooms vary too, fitted in coloured slate or travertine. Our advice: be guided by the price you're quoted, as it can offer excellent value during certain periods. Facilities include an on-site Mediterranean restaurant and bar, and four internet kiosks in the lobby.

Bar. Business centre. Concierge. Disabled-adapted rooms. Internet (high-speed, $14/day). No smoking rooms. Parking ($30). Restaurant. TV.

Budget

★ Carlton Arms Hotel

160 E 25th Street, at Third Avenue, New York, NY 10010 (1-212 679 0680, www.carltonarms.com). Subway 6 to 23rd Street. **Rates** $110-$130 double. **Rooms** 54. **Credit** DC, MC, V. **Map** p404 F26 ㊲

The Carlton Arms Art Project started in the late 1970s, when a small group of creative types brought fresh paint and new ideas to a run-down shelter. Today, the site is a Bohemian backpackers' paradise and a live-in gallery – every room, bathroom and hallway is festooned with outré artwork. Themed quarters include the Money Room and a tribute to a traditional English cottage. Discounts are offered for students, overseas guests and week-long stays. Most guests share bathrooms; the pricier rooms have a private toilet. Rooms get booked early, so reserve well in advance.

Internet (wireless, $5/day). No smoking rooms.

Murray Hill Inn

143 E 30th Street, at Third Avenue (1-212 683 6900, www.nyinns.com). Subway 6 to 28th Street. **Rates** $89-$149 double. **Rooms** 45. **Credit** AmEx, MC, V. **Map** p404 F25 ㊳

Although many of its rooms now have private bathrooms, this Euro-style inn sacrifices creature comforts for economy. But the location, within walking distance of Madison Square Park and the Empire State Building, is convenient. Be sure to book well in advance, or try the sister locations listed below.
Concierge. Internet (wireless, $7/day). No smoking.
Other locations Amsterdam Inn, 340 Amsterdam Avenue, at 76th Street, Upper West Side, New York, NY 10024 (1-212 579 7500); Central Park Hostel, 19 W 103rd Street, at Central Park West, New York, NY 10025 (1-212 678 0491, www.centralparkhostel.com); Union Square Inn, 209 E 14th Street, between Second & Third Avenues, East Village, New York, NY 10003 (1-212 614 0500).

HERALD SQUARE & GARMENT DISTRICT

Moderate

★ Hotel Metro

45 W 35th Street, between Fifth & Sixth Avenues, New York, NY 10001 (1-212 947 2500, 1-800 356 3870, www.hotelmetronyc.com). Subway B, D, F, M, N, Q, R to 34th Street-Herald Square. **Rates** $191-$395 double. **Rooms** 181. **Credit** AmEx, DC, MC, V. **Map** p404 E25 ㊴
It may not be trendy, but the Metro is that rare thing: a solid, good-value hotel that is extremely well maintained. Every two years, the owners start renovating the rooms, floor by floor, starting at the top; by the time they're finished it's almost time to start again. So even 'old' rooms are virtually new. That said, request a redecorated room if possible, because the latest look – with marble-topped furniture, beige leather-effect headboards and marble bathrooms – is more stylishly contemporary than the previous, art-deco inspired scheme. Unusually for New York, the hotel offers 18 family rooms, consisting of two adjoining bedrooms (one with two beds and a table) and a door that closes. Also rare, a generous continental breakfast buffet is offered in the guests' lounge (or take it to the homey adjoining library), outfitted with several large TVs. The rooftop bar (which is open from April to October) has Empire State Building views.
Bar. Business centre. Concierge. Disabled-adapted rooms. Gym. Internet (wireless, free). No smoking floors. Restaurant. Room service. TV: pay movies.

Budget

Americana Inn

69 W 38th Street, at Sixth Avenue, New York, NY 10018 (1-212 840 6700, www.americanainn.com). Subway B, D, F, M, N, Q, R to 34th Street-Herald Square; B, D, F, M to 42nd Street. **Rates** $85-$145 double. **Rooms** 56. **Credit** AmEx, Disc, MC, V. **Map** p404 E24 ㊵
We're not going pretend otherwise: this is a budget hotel and looks the part, with linoleum floors and fluorescent lighting. But the place is tidy and clean and if you want to be near the Theater District, you won't find cheaper. Bathrooms are shared, but the rooms have sinks and flatscreen TVs.
Disabled-adapted rooms. Internet (high-speed in lobby, $1/10mins). No smoking rooms. TV.

THEATER DISTRICT & HELL'S KITCHEN

Expensive

★ The Chatwal New York

130 W 44th Street, between Sixth Avenue & Broadway, New York, NY 10036 (1-212 764 6200, www.thechatwalny.com). Subway N, Q, R, S, 1, 2, 3 to 42nd St-Times Square. **Rates** $695-$920 double; $1,250-$16,000 suites. **Rooms** 83. **Credit** AmEx, DC, Disc, MC, V. **Map** p404 D24 ㊶
In a city awash with faux deco and incongruous nods to the style, the Chatwal New York opened in August 2010 in a Stanford White building whose interior art deco restoration is pitch perfect. Boutique hotelier Sant Chatwal entrusted the design of this 1905 beaux arts building (formerly the clubhouse for the Lambs Club, America's first professional theatre organisation) to Thierry Despont, who worked on the centennial restoration of the Statue of Liberty and the interiors of the J Paul Getty Museum in Los Angeles. The result is one of the most glamorous hotels in the Theater District, if not the city. The gracious lobby is adorned with murals recalling the hotel's New York roots and theatrical pedigree – past members of the Lamb's Club have included Lionel and John Barrymore, Oscar Hammerstein, Charlie Chaplin, John Wayne, Douglas Fairbanks and Fred Astaire. The theatrical past is further evoked by black-and-white photographs in the hotel's restaurant, the highly acclaimed Lambs Club, which features a stunning floor-to-ceiling 18th-century stone fireplace, originally a gift from Stanford White to the Lambs. The elegant rooms feature vintage Broadway posters as well as hand-tufted Shifman mattresses, 400-thread count Frette linens and custom Asprey toiletries; select rooms have spacious terraces.
Bar. Business Centre. Concierge. Disabled-adapted rooms. Gym. No smoking. Internet (wireless, free). No smoking floors. Pool. Restaurant. Room service. Spa. TV: pay movies.

Flatotel

135 W 52nd Street, between Sixth & Seventh Avenues, New York, NY 10019 (1-212 887 9400, www.flatotel.com). Subway N, R to 49th Street; 1 to 50th Street. **Rates** $255-$509 double. **Rooms** 288. **Credit** AmEx, DC, Disc, MC, V. **Map** p404 D23 ㊷

The Chatwal New York.

Flatotel prides itself on its spacious rooms – hence the 'flat' reference – and it succeeds on that front. A standard room averages 350sq ft (33sq m) and many are substantially larger. On top of that, most come with a fridge and microwave, making it convenient for an extended stay. The overall feel, from the striped chairs in the lobby to the big dishes at the restaurant, is a European take on American proportions. But although it offers reasonable rates in a central location near Rockefeller Center and MoMA, the accommodation has lost a bit of lustre (some of the televisions are old tube-style, carpets show signs of wear and the gym could do with an upgrade).
Bar (2). Business centre. Concierge. Disabled-adapted rooms. Gym. Internet (high-speed, $10/day). No smoking floors. Parking ($47). Restaurant. Room service. TV.

London NYC

151 W 54th Street, between Sixth & Seventh Avenues, New York, NY 10019 (1-866 690 2029, www.thelondonnyc.com). Subway B, D, E to Seventh Avenue. **Rates** $299-$494 double. **Rooms** 561. **Credit** AmEx, DC, Disc, MC, V. **Map** p405 D22 43

This 54-storey high-rise was completely overhauled by David Collins (designer of some of London's most fashionable bars and restaurants) and reopened as the London NYC in early 2007. The designer's sleek, contemporary-British style pervades the rooms, with attractive signature touches such as limed oak parquet flooring, embossed leather travel trunks at the foot of the beds, hand-woven throws and inventive coffee tables that adjust to dining-table heights. But space is perhaps the biggest luxury: the 350-500sq ft (33-46sq m) London Suites (the starting-priced accommodation) are either open-plan or divided with mirrored French doors, and bathrooms feature double rain showerheads. Upper-floor Vista Suites command city views. The London is, appropriately, the site of two eateries from Britain's best-known celebrity chef, the eponymous Gordon Ramsay at the London and the less formal (and less expensive) Maze. The chef also supplies the room-service menu.
Bar. Business centre. Concierge. Disabled-adapted rooms. Gym. Internet (wireless, free). No smoking floors. Parking ($55-$65). Restaurants (2). Room service. Spa. TV: DVD/pay movies.

Stay

157 W 47th Street, between Sixth & Seventh Avenues, 1-212 768 3700, 1-868 950 7829, www.stayhotelny.com). Subway N, R to 49th Street; 1 to 50th Street. **Rates** $159-$340 double. **Rooms** 210. **Credit** AmEx, DC, Disc, MC, V. **Map** p405 D23 44

Hotel mastermind Vikram Chatwal now has a portfolio of four NYC properties – Dream, Night, Time and Stay – with two more due to open this year (for addresses, see www.vikramchatwalhotels.com). Our advice: stay in the newest one, because in our experience, concept hotels don't age well. Stay, which opened in autumn 2008, is also perhaps the most accessible of his properties, but it has several of his signature theatrical lobby flourishes: a huge, tubular tropical fish tank, trippy light effects and snowy seating. In contrast, rooms are sleek but non-statement, decorated in dark wood with copper accents; the Bose Wave radio/iPod docks are a nice detail. Also fitting in with the group's formula, Stay has a striking bar/restaurant/nightclub, the Aspen Social Club, which replicates a slightly surreal log hunting lodge with aged leather seating and an eye-popping antler-themed light installation in the dining area.
Bars. Business centre. Concierge. Disabled-adapted rooms. Internet (wireless in lobby only, free; high-speed, $10/day). No smoking. Parking ($30). Restaurant. Room service. TV: pay movies.
Other locations throughout the city.

W New York-Times Square

1567 Broadway, at 47th Street, New York, NY 10036 (1-212 930 7400, 1-888 627 8680, www.starwoodhotels.com). Subway N, R to 49th Street; 1 to 50th Street. **Rates** $296-$749. **Rooms** 509. **Credit** AmEx, DC, Disc, MC, V. **Map** p404 D23 45

The sleek and modern aesthetic of the W brand is on full display at its entrance – featuring a dimly lit, glassed-in waterfall ceiling – even fuller once you reach the hushed and dramatic seventh-floor lobby and lounge. The attention to atmospheric detail fades a bit in the rooms, though, due to a drab taupe colour scheme punctuated by flimsy furniture and works of art, and discordant purple Lucite bed-stand cubes. Squint, though, and you'll feel cool amid the minimalism, especially thanks to all sorts of clever in-room lighting options and a well-designed bathroom (sans tub, unless you're in a disabled-accessible room or the presidential suite). However, the wonderfully comfortable beds and sparkling Times Square views go quite a long way. Service is friendly and polished, too, and there's a hip in-house fish restaurant, Blue Fin.
Bar. Business centre. Concierge. Disabled-adapted rooms. Gym. Internet (wireless, $17/day). No smoking floors. Parking ($55). Restaurant. Room service. TV: DVD, pay movies.
Other locations throughout the city.

Warwick New York Hotel

65 W 54th Street, at Sixth Avenue, New York, NY 10019 (1-212 247 2700, 1-800 223 4099, www.warwickhotelsny.com). Subway E, M to Fifth Avenue-53rd Street; F to 57th Street. **Rates** $255-$505 double. **Rooms** 426. **Credit** AmEx, DC, MC, V. **Map** p405 D22 46

Built by newspaper baron William Randolph Hearst in 1926, the Warwick is listed by the National Trust for Historic Preservation. You'd never know it from its old-fashioned façade, but it was frequented by Elvis Presley and the Beatles during their tours, and the top-floor suite with wraparound balcony was

CONSUME

once Cary Grant's home. Rooms are exceptionally large by Midtown standards, and have feminine touches such as floral curtains and bedspreads. Check out the historical-themed 1930s wall paintings by illustrator Dean Cornwell in the refurbished Murals on 54 restaurant – they contain images considered obscene at the time (such as an Indian's bare buttocks), which Cornwell included in revenge over a payment dispute.
Bar. Business centre. Concierge. Disabled-adapted rooms. Gym. Internet (wireless, $12/day). No smoking. Parking ($45). Restaurant. Room service. TV: pay movies.

Moderate

Distrikt Hotel

342 W 40th Street, between Eighth & Ninth Avenues, New York, NY 10018 (1-212 706 6100, www.distrikthotel.com). Subway A, C, E to 42nd Street–Port Authority. **Rates** $169-$409 double. **Rooms** 155. **Credit** AmEx, DC, Disc, MC, V. **Map** p404 24C 47

Although it's on an unlovely street alongside Port Authority, this new hotel has much to recommend it. Distrikt's subtle Manhattan theme is conceptual. Each of the 31 guest floors is named after one of the city's beloved 'hoods (Harlem, Soho, Chelsea, etc) and a backlit photo collage created by local artist Chris Rubino adorns the hallways; smaller framed versions liven up the rooms, which are otherwise coolly neutral, with luxury features such as Frette linens and marble in the bathrooms. Request a higher floor for Hudson River or Times Square views—the rates rise accordingly. A 14ft 'living wall' representing Central Park anchors the lobby, but what really impresses is the three big iMacs equipped with free Wi-Fi for guest use.
Bar. Business Centre. Concierge. Disabled-adapted rooms. No smoking. Internet (wireless, free). Restaurant. Room service. TV.

★ 414 Hotel

414 W 46th Street, between Ninth & Tenth Avenues, New York, NY 10036 (1-212 399 0006, www.414hotel.com). Subway A, C, E to 42nd Street-Port Authority. **Rates** $169-$269 double. **Rooms** 22. **Credit** AmEx, DC, MC, V. **Map** p404 C23 48

This is one hotel that truly deserves being described as 'boutique'. Nearly everything about it is exquisite yet unshowy, from its newly power-blasted brick exterior to the modern colour scheme in the rooms that pairs grey and brown furnishings with pale walls and white bedding. The bathrooms are immaculate, and a working gas fireplace in the lobby is a welcoming touch. The 414 is twice as big as it looks, as it consists of two townhouses – one on 45th Street, as well as the one with the entrance – separated by a leafy courtyard, which in warmer months is a lovely place to sip a glass of wine or eat your complimentary breakfast of fresh croissants and bagels. The affordable rates and location in a central, residential neighbourhood, make it even more of a find.
Business centre. Concierge. Disabled-adapted rooms. Internet (wireless, free). No smoking. TV.

> **INSIDE TRACK**
> **NEW IN NOLITA**
>
> Poised to open as we went to press, 55-room boutique property the **Nolitan** (30 Kenmare Street, at Elizabeth Street, 1-212 925 2555, www.nolitanhotel.com) offers nice perks to guests such as free laptop, bike and skateboard loans, discounts at neighbourhood boutiques and bath products from local spa Red Flower.

Hotel Edison

228 W 47th Street, at Broadway, New York, NY 10036 (1-212 840 5000, 1-800 637 7070, www.edisonhotelnyc.com). Subway N, R to 49th Street; 1 to 50th Street. **Rates** $149-$299 double. **Rooms** 800. **Credit** AmEx, DC, Disc, MC, V. **Map** p404 D23 49

This 1931 art deco hotel has enough original touches left – such as gorgeous elevator doors and brass door handles – to evoke old New York. Its affordable rates and proximity to Broadway's theatres seal it as the ideal Gotham hotel for many guests. The no-frills rooms are standard in size and clean, if also devoid of personality. Café Edison, a classic diner just off the lobby, is not to be missed: it's a long-time favourite of Broadway actors and their fans – Neil Simon was so smitten that he put it in one of his plays.
Bar. Business centre. Concierge. Disabled-adapted rooms. Gym. Internet (wireless, $10/day). No smoking. Parking ($34). Restaurants (2). Room service. TV: pay movies.

Hotel 41

206 W 41st Street, between Seventh & Eighth Avenues, New York, NY 10036 (1-212 703 8600, www.hotel41nyc.com). Subway N, Q, R, S, 1, 2, 3, 7 to 42nd Street-Times Square. **Rates** $129-$349 double. **Rooms** 47. **Credit** AmEx, DC, Disc, MC, V. **Map** p404 D24 50

Although its look is starkly modern – especially for the Theater District – this seven-storey boutique hotel is also warm and inviting: reading lamps extend from dark-wood headboards, and triple-glazed windows filter out the cacophony from the streets below. Averaging 100-125sq ft, standard rooms are tiny even by New York standards; superiors have a bit more breathing room, while suites are outfitted with jacuzzis. It's a great place to stay

if you want to be in Times Square without spending a fortune. The cosy Bar 41, which beckons from the reception, serves a complimentary continental breakfast (for guests) as well as lunch and dinner.
Bar-restaurant. Disabled-adapted room. Internet (wireless, free). No smoking. Parking ($32). Room service. TV: DVD.

RoomMate Grace Hotel

125 W 45th Street, between Sixth & Seventh Avenues, New York, NY 10036 (1-212 354 2323, www.room-matehotels.com). Subway N, Q, R, S, 1, 2, 3, 7 to 42nd Street-Times Square. **Rates** $279-$349 double; $195-$425 quad bunk. **Rooms** 139. **Credit** AmEx, DC, MC, V. **Map** p404 D23 51
In 2008, the Spanish RoomMate chain took over André Balazs's Hotel QT but maintained the celebrity hotelier's budget-boutique vibe. Although modestly furnished, the minimalist rooms come with Egyptian cotton linens, 25in flatscreen TVs and bathrooms with rainfall-style showers. Prices are commensurate with the sleek, chic aesthetic but if you're travelling with a posse, quad-bunk rooms, which can comfortably sleep four, offer a more economical option. If you need to move around, take a dip in the hotel pool, complete with bar.
Bar. Gym. Internet (wireless, free). No smoking rooms. Pool (indoor). Spa. TV: DVD.

Hostels

Big Apple Hostel

119 W 45th Street, between Sixth & Seventh Avenues, New York, NY 10036 (1-212 302 2603, www.bigapplehostel.com). Subway B, D, F, M to 42nd Street-Bryant Park; N, Q, R, S, 1, 2, 3, 7 to 42nd Street-Times Square. **Rates** $36-$54 per person in dorm; $110-$154 private room. **Rooms** 30 dorm rooms; 12 private rooms. **Credit** DC, MC, V. **Map** p404 D23 52
Long popular with backpackers, this bare-bones hostel is spotless and cheap for the location. The Big Apple puts you just steps from the Theater District and Times Square. If you want to get away from the crowds, you can take refuge in the breezy back patio, equipped with a grill for summer barbecues. Linens are provided, but remember to pack a towel.
Internet (wireless, free). No smoking. TV (in private rooms only).

FIFTH AVENUE & AROUND

Deluxe

Plaza

768 Fifth Avenue, at Central Park South, New York, NY 10019 (1-212 759 3000, 1-800 759 3000, www.theplaza.com). Subway N, R to Fifth Avenue-59th Street. **Rates** $695-$895 double. **Rooms** 282. **Credit** AmEx, DC, Disc, MC, V. **Map** p405 E22 53
The closest thing to a palace in New York, this 1907 French Renaissance-style landmark reopened in spring 2008 after a two-year, $400 million renovation. Although 152 rooms were converted into private condo units, guests can still check into one of 282 elegantly appointed quarters with Louis XV-inspired furnishings and white-glove butler service. The opulent vibe extends to the bathrooms, which feature mosaic baths, 24-carat gold-plated sink fittings and even chandeliers – perhaps to make the foreign royals feel at home. The property's legendary public spaces – the Palm Court restaurant, the restored Oak Room and Oak Bar, and Grand Ballroom (the setting for Truman Capote's famed Black and White Ball in 1966) – have been designated as landmarks and preserved for the public. The on-site Caudalie Vinothérapie Spa is the French grape-based skincare line's first US outpost.
Bars (3). Business centre. Concierge. Disabled-adapted rooms. Gym. Internet (wireless, $13/day). No smoking rooms. Parking ($65). Restaurants (3). Room service. Spa. TV: DVD/pay movies.

Expensive

Algonquin Hotel

59 W 44th Street, between Fifth & Sixth Avenues, New York, NY 10036 (1-212 840 6800, www.algonquinhotel.com). Subway B, D, F, M to 42nd Street-Bryant Park; 7 to Fifth Avenue. **Rates** $359-$439 double. **Rooms** 174. **Credit** AmEx, DC, Disc, MC, V. **Map** p404 E24 54
Alexander Woollcott and Dorothy Parker swapped bon mots in the famous Round Table Room of this 1902 landmark – and you'll still find writer types holding court on the mismatched armchairs of the sprawling, old-school lobby. The Algonquin certainly trades on its literary past (cartoons from the *New Yorker* cover the hallways, commemorating Harold Ross, who secured funding for the magazine over long meetings at the Round Table), but does it work as a hotel? Yes: the modernised rooms are pleasant and comfortable, if bordering on stark; and amenities such as flatscreen TVs and free Wi-Fi are standard. Skip the impersonal Blue Bar in favour of

THE BEST HOTEL PERKS

For minibar freebies
Andaz Wall Street. *See p155.*

For cult toiletries
Crosby Street Hotel. *See p155.*

For an in-room pet
SoHo Grand Hotel. *See p159.*

For a hot table
Hotel Elysée. *See p175.*

the Oak Room, one of NYC's premier cabaret destinations. Matilda, the hotel's frowsy, free-range cat, evokes some of the old eccentric charm.
Bars (2). Concierge. Disabled-adapted rooms. Gym. Internet (wireless, free). No smoking. Parking ($30). Restaurant. Room service. TV: pay movies.
► *See p333 for details of cabaret performances in the Oak Room.*

Bryant Park Hotel

40 W 40th Street, between Fifth & Sixth Avenues, New York, NY 10018 (1-212 869 0100, www.bryantparkhotel.com). Subway B, D, F, M to 42nd Street-Bryant Park; 7 to Fifth Avenue. **Rates** $219-$595 double. **Rooms** 128. **Credit** AmEx, DC, MC, V. **Map** p404 E24 55

When the shows and the shoots are finished, the fashion and film folk flock to this luxe landing pad that was once, in its days as the American Radiator Building, immortalised by Georgia O'Keefe. Although the exterior (which you can appreciate up-close in one of the many balconied rooms) is gothic art deco, the inside is all soft lighting and blanched hardwood floors, equipped with soothing conveniences such as sleep-aiding sound machines. A section of the room-service menu is devoted to vibrators and other forms of adult recreation, but don't worry, you can also order in from the house restaurant, slick sushi destination Koi.
Bar. Concierge. Disabled-adapted rooms. Gym. Internet (wireless, $10/day). No smoking. Parking (free-$45). Restaurant. Room Service. TV: DVD/pay movies.

MIDTOWN EAST

Deluxe

Four Seasons

57 E 57th Street, between Madison & Park Avenues, New York, NY 10022 (1-212 758 5700, 1-800 332 3442, www.fourseasons.com). Subway N, R to Lexington Avenue-59th Street; 4, 5, 6 to 59th Street. **Rates** $695-$1,195 double. **Rooms** 368. **Credit** AmEx, DC, Disc, MC, V. **Map** p405 E22 56

The New York arm of the global luxury chain, housed in IM Pei's 52-floor tower, is synonymous with dependable luxury. Whether you're staying in a suite or a deluxe room (at around 600sq ft, or 56sq m, it's the most popular accommodation), expect modern, neutral interiors (blond-wood panelling, white high-count linens) and sumptuous, user-friendly design throughout: there's room in the walk-in closet to have a seat and take off your shoes, a TV in the toilet, and the bathtub fills in 60 seconds. If you pay a premium for the park view, you'll be treated to an unsurpassed urban vista. The hotel also houses the L'Atelier de Joël Robuchon, from the superstar French chef. There are no surprises, but that's one of the reasons to stay here.
Bars (2). Business centre. Concierge. Disabled-adapted rooms. Gym. Internet (wireless, $15/day). No smoking floors. Parking ($60). Restaurants (3). Room service. Spa. TV: DVD/pay movies.

Expensive

Hotel Elysée

60 E 54th Street, between Madison & Park Avenues, New York, NY 10022 (1-212 753 1066, www.elyseehotel.com). Subway E, M to Lexington Avenue-53rd Street; 6 to 51st Street. **Rates** $224-$404 double. **Rooms** 100. **Credit** AmEx, DC, Disc, MC, V. **Map** p405 E22 57

Since 1926, this discreet but opulent hotel has attracted luminaries from legendary Russian pianist Vladimir Horowitz (whose grand piano resides in the premier suite) to (an unnamed) modern superstar who stayed for three months preparing to go on tour. You may bump into one on the way from your antique-appointed room to the complimentary wine and cheese served every evening in the sedate second-floor lounge, or in the exclusive Monkey Bar, *Vanity Fair* editor Graydon Carter's restaurant that shares the building. Ask reception to reserve a table and your chances of eating among the power set rise from zilch to good – a few tables are set aside for guests every night.
Bar. Business centre. Concierge. Disabled-adapted rooms. Internet (wireless, free). No smoking. Restaurant. TV: DVD/pay movies.

Library Hotel

299 Madison Avenue, at 41st Street, New York, NY 10017 (1-212 983 4500, www.libraryhotel.com). Subway S, 4, 5, 6, 7 to 42nd Street-Grand Central; 7 to Fifth Avenue. **Rates** $349-$599 double. **Rooms** 60. **Credit** AmEx, DC, MC, V. **Map** p404 E24 58

This bookish boutique hotel is as tall, thin and glossy as a coffee-table tome, with rooms carefully sorted into literary themes. Book nerds flock to the popular Fairy Tales and Paranormal rooms, where motifs are expressed through book selections and wall art; it's more clever than kitsch. Muted colours and luxurious bed linens add to the formal feel, though any librarian would surely wag a finger at the persistently dim lighting. Cocktail shakers adorn every room and nightly receptions dish out wine and cheese – nods to the writerly pastime of tippling. Upstairs in the roof garden, creative libations are inspired by Ernest Hemingway and Harper Lee, and a massive DVD library is on hand to cater for those who simply cannot face reading another word.
Bar. Business centre. Concierge. Disabled-adapted rooms. Internet (wireless, free). No smoking. Restaurant. Room service. TV: DVD/pay movies.
Other locations Hotel Giraffe, 365 Park Avenue South, at 26th Street, Flatiron District, New York, NY 10016 (1-212 685 7700, 1-877 296 0009, www.hotelgiraffe.com).

CONSUME

Bargains in the Boroughs

Visitors are increasingly opting for off-island accommodation.

Nu Hotel.

Although the growing attractions of the outer boroughs, most notably Brooklyn and Queens, have been luring visitors for several years, they haven't been seen as a base for tourists – until now. As ever-rising rents push young creative types out of Manhattan, and formerly diverse areas are homogenised by national chains, visitors in search of New York's Bohemian spirit may find the atmosphere they crave off-island.

In Brooklyn, Williamsburg and Bushwick have adventurous music and art scenes, while Carroll Gardens, Cobble Hill and Park Slope are great for dining and shopping. In Queens, Long Island City is an evolving art destination with a rising number of hip watering holes. Five new hotels are expected to be completed throughout Brooklyn in 2010, while in Queens, the room inventory was boosted by 800 this past year.

Now that apartments in Brooklyn's prime neighbourhoods are fetching millions of dollars, it was inevitable that boutique hotels would follow. The first two opened in late 2007: **Hotel Le Bleu** (*see p181*) has easy access to the cultural and commercial riches of Park Slope, while Williamsburg's **Hotel Le Jolie** (*see p181*) allows indie music fans the chance to spend the night in the hotspot after a gig. Summer 2008 saw the arrival of the **Nu Hotel** (*see p180*) on the edge of Brooklyn Heights. Those who want to experience loft living in Bushwick's cutting-edge art enclave should check into the **New York Loft Hostel** (*see p181*). In summer 2011, look for the **Aloft** (www.alofthotels.com) – a spin-off of the W hotel chain – conveniently located near premier arts hub Brooklyn Academy of Music.

Long Island City, where new-condo construction is rampant, recently acquired its first independent boutique hotel. Although its industrial surroundings are somewhat desolate, **Ravel** (*see p181*), a complete rebuild of an exisiting motel, occupies a prime spot on the waterfront beside the Queensboro Bridge. Perhaps in keeping with its former incarnation, owner Ravi Patel has given the property a vaguely 1960s feel; the lobby is decked out with cream leatherette seating, silver-bubble ceiling lights and a collection of soulful paintings sourced in South America that recall those doe-eyed Spanish girl portraits.

Appealing to a young party set, it's also equipped with a 'virtual' wine bar: buy a card at the front desk and use it at a self-serve bank of more than 18 wines. An 8,000-square-foot (740-square-metre) rooftop restaurant-bar has dazzling views of Midtown and hosts New York-themed film screenings, DJ nights and other events. The majority of the rooms, many of which have private balconies, also face the river – although a Con-Edison training facility directly below is somewhat less than picturesque. While the decor in the rooms isn't anything overly special (touches such as orange faux-ostrich headboards and spacious limestone and granite bathrooms announce them as boutique), like any rental in New York, you get more bang for your buck in the outer boroughs – the open-plan superior rooms are a whopping 550 square feet (51 square metres).

New York Palace Hotel

455 Madison Avenue, between 50th & 51st Streets, New York, NY 10022 (1-212 888 7000, 1-800 697 2522, www.newyorkpalace.com). Subway E, M to Fifth Avenue-53rd Street. **Rates** $369-$819 double. **Rooms** 899. **Credit** AmEx, DC, Disc, MC, V. **Map** p404 E23 59

Modernity literally meets tradition here: a sleek 55-storey tower cantilevers over the landmark 19th-century Villard Houses. The connected mansions, which were built as a residence for railroad magnate Henry Villard, exude Gilded Age splendour, from the sweeping grand staircase to the marble-bedecked lobby. Most of the accommodation, however, conveys more contemporary restraint, with unremarkable, if comfortable, neutral decor. Westward-facing rooms overlook Rockefeller Center, with a bird's-eye view of St Patrick's Cathedral. Service may not be up to one-time owner Leona Helmsley's rigid standards, but to ensure personalised attention, book one of the Tower Suites, which have a separate check-in, dedicated concierge and access to the Executive Lounge, where complimentary light fare and refreshments are set out throughout the day. For a memorable meal, splurge at the hotel's Michelin-starred restaurant, Gilt. In warmer weather, you can also sip cocktails in the charming courtyard.

Bar. Business centre. Concierge. Disabled-adapted rooms. Gym. Internet (wireless, $16/day). No smoking floors. Parking ($50). Restaurants (2). Room service. Spa. TV: DVD/pay movies.

Roger Smith

501 Lexington Avenue, between 47th & 48th Streets, New York, NY 10017 (1-212 755 1400, 1-800 445 0277, www.rogersmith.com). Subway E, M to Lexington Avenue-53rd Street; 6 to 51st Street. **Rates** $249-$349 double. **Rooms** 130. **Credit** AmEx, DC, Disc, MC, V. **Map** p404 F23 60

Who was Roger Smith? Not even the current owners of this 1929 hotel know. Now, it's run by artist James Knowles, whose bronzes adorn the building's exterior and the lobby (there's also an adjacent art space) and the rooms are decorated by his wife. A mishmash of antique and modern, the effect is homey and unpretentious, akin to a European bed and breakfast; many rooms feature old-fashioned four-posters. Each room is different (try to secure a recently upgraded room if you prefer streamlined, modern decor to floral prints), but they're all a good size. The suites, which resemble comfortable private apartments, some featuring (non-operational) fireplaces, are great value for families.

Bar. Concierge. Disabled-adapted rooms. Internet (wireless, free). No smoking floors. Restaurant. Room service. TV: DVD.

Waldorf-Astoria

301 Park Avenue, at 50th Street, New York, NY 10022 (1-212 355 3000, 1-800 925 3673, www.waldorfastoria.com). Subway E, M to

Lexington Avenue-53rd Street; 6 to 51st Street. **Rates** $279-$624 double. **Rooms** 1,416. **Credit** AmEx, DC, Disc, MC, V. **Map** p404 E23 61

As you click across the sparkling marble floor of this 1931 hotel's grandiose lobby, gracious staff will treat you like Princess Grace (a former guest). It's worth visiting this art deco historic landmark just for the history (it's been the accommodation of choice for numerous US presidents; a temporary home to Marilyn Monroe in 1955; and, of course, it's where the Waldorf salad was invented). However, you might find your room doesn't quite live up to its gilded past: our traditionally decorated room had lost a bit of its shine. A luxurious bathroom with water pressure to rival Niagara almost compensated, and total indulgence can be yours in the glamorous Guerlain spa.

Bars (4). Business centre. Concierge. Disabled-adapted rooms. Gym. Internet (wireless, high-speed, $17-$18/day). No smoking floors. Parking ($50). Restaurants (4). Room service. Spa. TV: pay movies.

Budget

Pod Hotel

230 E 51st Street, at Third Avenue, New York, NY 10022 (1-212 355 0300, www.thepodhotel.com). Subway E to Lexington Avenue-53rd Street; 6 to 51st Street. **Rates** $149-$289 double. **Rooms** 347. **Credit** AmEx, DC, MC, V. **Map** p404 F23 62

This surprisingly stylish East Side hotel opened in early 2007, offering tiny but futuristic rooms that are well suited to people who favour convenience and value over elbow room. The 100sq ft single-bed 'pods' have nominal decor and under-bed dressers; baths are shared. The outdoor Pod Café is roomy enough, though, and serves organic yoghurt and baked goods from Balthazar Bakery.

Bar. Concierge. Disabled-adapted rooms. Internet (wireless, free). No smoking. Restaurant. TV: DVD.

Uptown

UPPER EAST SIDE

Deluxe

★ Surrey

20 E 76th Street, between Fifth & Madison Avenues, New York, NY 10021 (1-212 288 3700, 1-800 978 7739, www.thesurreyhotel.com). Subway 6 to 77th Street. **Rates** $499-$999 double. **Rooms** 190. **Credit** AmEx, DC, Disc, MC, V. **Map** p405 E20 63

A stylish addition to an area thin on unstuffy accommodation, the Surrey, in a solid pre-war Beaux Arts building given a $60 million overhaul, pitches at both traditionalists and the trend-driven. Flanked by top chef Daniel Boulud's Café Boulud and his chic cocktail destination, Bar Pleiades, it's also a strong lure for gastronomes on a spree (Boulud's restaurant also supplies the room service). Those seeking a pampering break will appreciate the five-room spa, offering treatments by Darphin. The coolly elegant limestone and marble lobby showcases contemporary art by American conceptualist Jenny Holzer and South African William Kentridge. Rooms are dressed in a refined palette of cream, grey and beige, with luxurious white marble bathrooms featuring products by Italian perfumer Laura Tonatto. But the centrepiece is undoubtedly the incredibly comfortable DUX by Duxiana bed, swathed in luxurious Sferra linens. Coupled with the hotel's quiet location, it practically guarantees your best sleep ever.

Bars. Business centre. Concierge. Disabled-adapted rooms. Gym. Internet (wireless, $15/day). No smoking. Parking ($55). Restaurant. Room service. Spa. TV: pay movies.

► *For our review of Bar Pleiades, see p225.*

Expensive

Wales Hotel

1295 Madison Avenue, at 92nd Street, New York, NY 10128 (1-212 876 6000, www.hotelwalesnyc.com). Subway 4, 5, 6 to 86th Street; 6 to 96th Street. **Rates** $185-$405 double. **Rooms** 89. **Credit** AmEx, DC, Disc, MC, V. **Map** p406 E18 64

Purpose-built as a hotel in the early 1900s, the ten-storey Wales is a comfortable, convenient choice for a culture jaunt due to its proximity to the Museum Mile. Tucked in the quietly affluent Carnegie Hill neighbourhood just above Madison Avenue's prime retail stretch, it's also well placed for a posh shopping spree. Standard double rooms are small, but high ceilings, large windows and an unfussy contemporary-classic style prevents them from seeming cramped. All quarters have recently been redecorated with designer wallpaper, sleek new bathrooms and HD TVs. Higher-floor rooms on the east side have Central Park views, but all guests can enjoy them on the large roof terrace. Unusually, breakfast is included, and two on-site restaurants (Italian spot Paola's and mini-chain Sarabeth's) provide plenty of choice for further meals or snacks.

Business centre. Concierge. Disabled-adapted rooms. Gym. Internet (wireless, high-speed, $13/day). No smoking floors. Parking ($52). Restaurants (2). Room service. TV: DVD.

UPPER WEST SIDE

Expensive

Country Inn the City

270 W 77th Street, between Broadway & West End Avenue, New York, NY 10024 (1-212 580 4183, www.countryinnthecity.com). Subway 1 to 79th Street. **Rates** $210-$350 double. **Rooms** 4. **No credit cards. Map** p405 C19 65

The name of this charming B&B on the West Side is pretty accurate. Spacious, apartment-like rooms with kitchenettes, four-poster beds and flagons of brandy make this intimate inn a special retreat in the middle of the city. Note: they do not accept walk-ins, pets or children under 12; also, there's a three-night minimum. Keep an eye for last-minute specials.
Internet (wireless, free). No smoking.

Moderate

Broadway Hotel & Hostel

230 W 101 Street, at Broadway, New York, NY 10024 (1-212 865 7710, www.broadwayhotelnyc.com). Subway 1, 2, 3 to 96th Street. **Rates** $68-$159 double. **Credit** Disc, MC, V. **Map** p406 C16 66

For those who have outgrown the no-frills backpacker experience but haven't quite graduated to a full-service hotel, the hybrid Broadway Hotel & Hostel, which has been given a 'boutique-style' makeover, fills the gap. On the ground floor, exposed brick, leather sofas and three large flatscreen TVs give the sprawling communal spaces a slick, urban veneer, but they still follow the traditional youth-hostel blueprint: TV room, shared kitchen, plus a computer area with eight credit card-operated terminals (if you have your own gadget, Wi-Fi is free). You won't find six-bed set-ups here, though: the cheapest option, the small, basic 'dormitory-style' rooms, jazzed up with striking color schemes, mass-produced art and ceiling fans (there's AC in the summer too), accommodate a maximum of two in a bunkbed. The good-value 'semi-private' rooms offer a queen bed or two doubles or twins, with luxuries such as down comforters, iPod docks and flatscreen TVs, but you'll have to use the (well-scrubbed) shared bathrooms. En suite quarters are also available. Unlike most hostels, the Broadway provides free linens and towels, daily housekeeping service and 24-hour reception.
Concierge. Internet (wireless, free). No smoking. TV.

Hotel Belleclaire

250 W 77th Street, at Broadway, New York, NY 10024 (1-212 362 7700, www.hotelbelleclaire.com). Subway 1 to 79th Street. **Rates** $106-$429 double. **Rooms** 200. **Credit** AmEx, DC, Disc, MC, V. **Map** p405 C19 67

Housed in a landmark building near Lincoln Center, Central Park and Columbus Circle, the sleek Hotel Belleclaire is a steal for savvy travellers. Rooms feature goose-down comforters, padded headboards and mod lighting fixtures. Each room is equipped with a refrigerator – perfect for chilling your protein shake while you're hitting the state-of-the-art fitness centre.
Concierge. Disabled-adapted rooms. Gym. Internet (wireless, free). No smoking. Room service. TV: pay movies.

Marrakech

2688 Broadway, at 103rd Street, New York, NY 10025 (1-212 222 2954, www.marrakechhotelnyc.com). Subway 1 to 103rd Street. **Rates** $149-$259 double. **Rooms** 127. **Credit** AmEx, DC, Disc, MC, V. **Map** p406 C16 68

Formerly the Hotel Malibu, this Upper West Side accommodation was transformed into a Manhattan take on Morocco by prominent nightclub and restaurant designer Lionel Ohayon. Rooms are warm-toned with diffused lighting and North African decorative touches, such as colourful embroidered cushions. Frills are limited, and there's no lift, but twentysomethings will undoubtedly appreciate the lively Morningside Heights scene nearby.
Bar. Business centre. Concierge. Internet (high-speed, $10/day). No smoking. Restaurant. Room service. TV: pay movies.

On the Ave Hotel

222 W 77th Street, between Broadway & Amsterdam Avenue, New York, NY 10024 (1-212 362 1100, 1-800 497 6028, www.ontheave-nyc.com). Subway 1 to 79th Street. **Rates** $198-$359 double. **Rooms** 282. **Credit** AmEx, DC, Disc, MC, V. **Map** p405 C19 69

Given the affluent area, it's hardly surprising that On the Ave's rooms are stylish, with industrial-style bathroom sinks, HD TVs, ergonomic Herman Miller chairs, plus down comforters and Egyptian cotton sheets. Penthouse suites have fantastic balcony views of Central Park, but all guests have access to the verdant Adirondack balcony on the 16th floor. Although there's no shortage of restaurants in the district, it's worth checking out the hotel's own Fatty Crab (*see p198*).
Bar. Business centre. Concierge. Disabled-adapted rooms. Gym. Internet (wireless, $13/day). No smoking floors. Parking ($50). Restaurants (2). Room service. TV: DVD/pay movies.

Hostels

Hostelling International New York

891 Amsterdam Avenue, at 103rd Street, New York, NY 10025 (1-212 932 2300, www.hinewyork.org). Subway 1 to 103rd Street.

THE BEST CHEAP DIGS

For a deluxe sleeping compartment
Jane. *See p167.*

For a designer dorm
New York Loft Hostel. *See p181.*

For an eye-popping art house
Carlton Arms Hotel. *See p169.*

CONSUME

Rates $29-$45/person in dorm rooms; $135 family rooms; $150 private room with bath. **Rooms** 624 beds in dorms; 6 private rooms. **Credit** AmEx, DC, Disc, MC, V. **Map** p406 C16 70
This budget lodging is actually the city's only 'real' hostel (a non-profit accommodation that belongs to the International Youth Hostel Federation), but it's also one of the most striking. The gabled, Gothic-inspired brick and stone building spans the length of an entire city block, and is much admired by locals as well as those staying there. The interior is somewhat institutional and the immaculate rooms are spare, but they're air-con, and there is a shared kitchen and a large backyard. Linens and towels are free, and the in-house shop sells MetroCards, phone cards, souvenirs and sundries.
Business centre. Disabled-adapted rooms. Internet (wireless, free). No smoking.

Jazz on the Park Hostel

36 W 106th Street, between Central Park West & Manhattan Avenue, New York, NY 10025 (1-212 932 1600, www.jazzhostels.com). Subway B, C to 103rd Street. **Rates** $36-$53/person in 2- to 12-bed dorm; $110-$220 private room with bath. **Beds** 310. **Credit** DC, MC, V. **Map** p406 D16 71
Jazz on the Park is one of the trendiest hostels in the city – the lounge is kitted out like a space-age techno club, and has a piano and pool table. The hostel also has a staffed reception 24 hours a day and no curfew. In summer, the back patio hosts a weekly barbecue. Linens, towels and a continental breakfast are complimentary; lockers come with a surcharge.
Internet (wireless, free). No smoking.
Other locations throughout the city.

West End Studios

850 West End Avenue, at 102nd Street, New York, NY 10025 (1-212 749 7104, www.westendstudios.com). Subway 1 to 103rd Street. **Rates** $23-$27/person in 4- to 6-bed dorm; $34-$65 private room. **Beds** 85. **No credit cards**. **Map** p406 D16 72
This six-storey elevator building on the Upper West Side is a long way from most tourist destinations (although it's within walking distance of Columbia University and Central Park), but visitors enjoy art deco-inspired rooms that are a cut above typical hostel offerings. Fresh linens daily, TVs and alarm clocks all come as standard. The hotel has a basement laundry facility and a front desk open 24/7.
Concierge. Internet (wireless, free). No smoking.

HARLEM

Moderate

102Brownstone

102 W 118th Street, between Malcolm X Boulevard (Lenox Avenue) & Adam Clayton Powell Jr Boulevard (Seventh Avenue), New York, NY 10026 (1-212 662 4223, www.102brownstone.com). Subway 2, 3 to 116th Street. **Rates** $100-$175. **Rooms** 6. **Credit** AmEx, DC, MC, V. **Map** p407 D14 73
Located near Marcus Garvey Park on a landmark, tree-lined street, 102Brownstone features half a dozen substantial suites, all renovated and individually themed by lively proprietor Lizette Lanoue, who owns and lives in the 1892 Greek Revival row house with her husband. You'll like the tranquil Zen and dreamy Luna quarters. Lanoue aims to be unobtrusive and to make guests feel as though they are in their own apartment – an apartment with a jacuzzi, that is.
Concierge. Internet (wireless, free). No smoking. Room service. TV: DVD.

Budget

Harlem Flophouse

242 W 123rd Street, between Adam Clayton Powell Jr Boulevard (Seventh Avenue) & Frederick Douglass Boulevard (Eighth Avenue), New York, NY 10027 (1-212 662 0678, www.harlemflophouse.com). Subway A, B, C, D to 125th Street. **Rates** $100-$135 single/double with shared bath. **Rooms** 4. **Credit** DC, MC, V. **Map** p407 D14 74
The dark-wood interior, moody lighting and lilting jazz music make Rene Calvo's Harlem inn feel more like a 1930s speakeasy than a 21st-century B&B. The airy suites, named for Harlem Renaissance figures such as Chester Himes and Cozy Cole, have restored tin ceilings, glamorous chandeliers and working sinks in antique cabinets.
Concierge. Internet (wireless, free). No smoking.

Brooklyn

BOERUM HILL, CARROLL GARDENS & COBBLE HILL

Moderate

★ Nu Hotel

85 Smith Street, between Atlantic Avenue & State Street, Brooklyn, NY 11201 (1-718 852 8585, www.nuhotelbrooklyn.com). Subway F, G to Bergen Street; A, C, 2, 3, 4, 5 to Jay Street-Borough Hall. **Rates** $199-$329 double. **Rooms** 93. **Credit** AmEx, DC, Disc, MC, V. **Map** p410 T10 75
Conveniently placed for the shops and restaurants of BoCoCa, Nu Hotel has bundled quirky niceties into a classy, eco-friendly package. Cork flooring, organic linens and recycled teak furniture mix it up with 32-inch flatscreen TVs and Sangean audio systems, free Wi-Fi and AV docks for multimedia devices. The minimalist standard rooms are comfortably sized, but Friends Suites have bunk beds,

CONSUME

and the lofty Urban Suites are outfitted with hammocks and a padded-leather sleeping alcove. In the warmer months, cyclists can borrow one of the hotel's loaner bikes to pedal around Brooklyn. Just make sure you eat dinner before you get back; there's no room service, although there's a lovely complimentary continental breakfast buffet in the morning.
Bar. Business centre. Concierge. Disabled-adapted rooms. Gym. Internet (wireless, free). No smoking. Parking ($24). TV.

PARK SLOPE

Moderate

Bed & Breakfast on the Park

113 Prospect Park West, between 6th & 7th Streets, Brooklyn, NY 11215 (1-718 499 6115, www.bbnyc.com). Subway F to Seventh Avenue. **Rates** $155-$325 double. **Rooms** 7. **Credit** MC, V. **Map** p410 T12 76
Staying at this 1895 brownstone, which faces lush Prospect Park, is like taking up residence in the pages of Edith Wharton's *The Age of Innocence.* The parlour floor is crammed with antique furniture, and guest rooms are furnished with love seats and canopy beds swathed in French linens. The Lady Liberty room has a rooftop garden as well as an antique bathtub.
Business centre. Concierge. Internet (wireless, free). No smoking. TV: pay movies.

Hotel Le Bleu

370 Fourth Avenue, between 3rd Street & 5th Street, Brooklyn, NY 11215 (1-718 625 1500, www.hotellebleu.com). Subway F, M, R to 9th Street-Fourth Avenue; R to Union Street. **Rates** $206-$279 double. **Rooms** 48. **Credit** AmEx, Disc, MC, V. **Map** p410 T10 77
The Manhattanisation of Park Slope hit new heights in late 2007, when Andres Escobar's steel and glass hotel popped up on industrial Fourth Avenue. Couples will find the open shower design a plus; more conventional draws include 42-inch plasma TVs, goose-down comforters, iPod docking stations and free Wi-Fi in every room. If you're not keen on wandering the somewhat desolate avenue for sustenance, the two-floor Vue restaurant serves up intercontinental cuisine and views of the Manhattan skyline.
Bar. Concierge. Disabled-adapted rooms. Internet (wireless, free). No smoking. Parking (free). Restaurant. Room service. TV: DVD.

WILLIAMSBURG & BUSHWICK

Moderate

Hotel Le Jolie

235 Meeker Avenue, at Jackson Street, Brooklyn, NY 11211 (1-718 625 2100, www.hotellejolie.com). Subway G, L to Metropolitan Avenue. **Rates** $159-$229 double. **Rooms** 54. **Credit** AmEx, DC, Disc, MC, V. **Map** p411 V8 78
Williamsburg is finally grown up enough to earn a fresh, modern-looking hotel – too bad it's right on top of the Brooklyn-Queens Expressway. Inside, though, 54 well-maintained rooms offer king-size beds (fitted with allergen-free goose-down comforters and Egyptian cotton sheets), ergonomic Aeron desk chairs and 42-inch flatscreen TVs.
Business centre. Concierge. Disabled-adapted rooms. Internet (wireless, free). No smoking. Parking (free). Room service. TV.

Hostels

★ New York Loft Hostel

249 Varet Street, at Bogart Street, Brooklyn, NY 11206 (1-718 366 1351, www.nylofthostel.com). Subway L to Morgan Avenue. **Rates** $35-$40/person in dorm room; $75-$90 private room. **Rooms** 150 beds in dorms; 30 private rooms. **Credit** AmEx, Disc, MC, V. **Map** p411 W9 79
Situated in arty Bushwick, this budget lodging fuses the traditional youth hostel set-up (dorm-style rooms with bunk beds and lockers, communal lounging areas) with a fashionable loft aesthetic. In the former clothing warehouse, linen curtains billow in front of huge windows, and there's plenty of industrial-chic exposed brick and piping. Above the big shared kitchen is a mezzanine equipped with a large flatscreen TV (DVDs can be rented at the front desk). The spacious patio – complete with a seasonal pool – is the site of frequent summer barbecues. Unlike old-school hostels, there's no curfew; an electronically encoded room-key card opens the front door after hours.
Disabled-adapted rooms. Internet (wireless, free; shared terminal, $2/20mins). No smoking. TV (shared).

Queens

LONG ISLAND CITY

Moderate

Ravel

8-08 Queens Plaza South, at Vernon Boulevard, Queens, NY 11101 (1-718 289 6101, www.ravelhotel.com). Subway F to 21st Street-Queensbridge; N, Q, 7 to Queensboro Plaza; E, M, R to Queens Plaza. **Rates** $129-$279 double. **Rooms** 63. **Credit** AmEx, Disc, MC, V. **Map** p412 V4 80
For review, *see p176* **Bargains in the Boroughs**.
Bars (2). Business centre. Disabled-adapted rooms. Internet (wireless, $10/day, free in lobby). No smoking. Parking (free). Restaurant. Room service. TV: pay movies.

Restaurants & Cafés

The world is on your plate in this most cosmopolitan of cities.

New Yorkers have a seemingly insatiable appetite for novel tastes and and different dining experiences. The sheer number and variety of restaurants – approaching 20,000, from high-end food palaces to neighbourhood holes-in-the-wall – means that even long-time residents need never eat at the same place twice. Fierce competition for your cash ensures restaurateurs are always thinking of creative ways to appeal to your tastebuds – and diners are benefiting from special deals and more solicitous service.

THE LOCAL SCENE

One of New York City's most exciting recent openings isn't strictly new. Instead, it's part of a trend that has hit a crescendo: the revival of neglected classics into of-the-moment hotspots. Legendary restaurateur Keith McNally (*see p184* **Profile**), a master of nouveau nostalgia, has put his stamp on storied Greenwich Village literary hangout the **Minetta Tavern** (*see p197*). The interior, with its long wooden bar and vintage murals, attracts a capacity crowd largely for the scene – getting a table is a challenge. The food features solidly executed classics, notably its $28 Black Label burger: a complex, premium custom-beef blend that has upped the city's designer patty ante.

New Yorkers are slaves to fashion, and if a restaurant is hot, chances are they'll want in. Perhaps the most illustrious entrant to the list of impossible-to-get-into places is **Momofuku Ko**. This 13-seat spot, from pork bun wunderkind David Chang, requires diners to snare reservations online – a new day opens for booking each morning – at www.momofuku.com. Suffice to say that it's one of the most sought-after tables (or, in this case, chef's counters) in town, but, luckily, Chang has two other fine options: **Momofuku Ssäm Bar** and **Noodle Bar** (for all three, *see p195*).

> ❶ Blue numbers given in this chapter correspond to the location of each restaurant and café as marked on the street maps. See pp402-412.

The **East Village** has a knack for sprouting reasonably priced eateries that draw cult followings, yet no discussion of New York dining is complete without mention of the second borough, increasingly becoming a first choice for foodies. The farm-to-table movement is perhaps most robust in **Brooklyn**. The DIY spirit and devotion to local purveyors and ingredients are arguably the borough's dining culture's most distinguishing aspects. Enjoy urban-rustic menus and salvaged-wood furnished environments at any of the following notable recent additions: the cosy **Vinegar Hill House** (*see p216*), in the forgotten neighbourhood of the same name; the unpretentious **Buttermilk Channel** (*see p213*), in Carroll Gardens; or nostalgic **Rye** (*see p216*), in Williamsburg.

Elsewhere in the city, there are numerous cheek-by-jowl Asian restaurants in **Chinatown**, while **Koreatown**, the stretch of West 32nd Street between Fifth Avenue and Broadway, is lined with Korean barbecue joints and other eateries. Further afield, **Harlem** offers soul food and African cooking, while the proverbial melting pot that is Queens counts Greek (in **Astoria**) and Indian (in **Jackson Heights**) among its globe-spanning cuisines.

The essentials

Snagging reservations for popular places can be difficult, so be sure to call ahead. Super-trendy spots can be fully booked weeks in advance, although the majority require only a few days' notice (or less). Most restaurants fill up between 7pm and 9pm; if you don't mind eating early (5pm) or late (after 10pm), your chances of getting into a hotspot will improve greatly. Alternatively, you can try to nab a reservation by calling at 5pm on the day you want to dine and hoping for a last-minute cancellation. Dress codes are rarely enforced, but some old-school fancy dining rooms require men to don a jacket and tie. If in doubt, call ahead and ask, but note that you can never really overdress in this town.

Note that prices given for main courses in this chapter are averages. We've used the **$** symbol to indicate operations offering particularly good value: restaurants with main courses for around $10 or less, plus cafés and sandwich stops.

DOWNTOWN

Financial District

$ Financier Pâtisserie

62 Stone Street, between Hanover Square & Mill Lane (1-212 344 5600, www.financierpastries.com). Subway 2, 3 to Wall Street. **Open** 7am-8pm Mon-Fri; 8.30am-6.30pm Sat. **Sandwiches** $7. **Credit** AmEx, MC, V. **Map** p402 F33 ❶ **Café**

Tucked down a cobblestoned street, this sweet gem offers café fare to office workers, tourists and locals seeking a pleasant alternative to the Financial District's ubiquitous pubs and delis. Savoury items, including hot pressed sandwiches (try the croque-monsieur), fresh salads, tarts and quiches are all good, but the pastries are where Financier excels, including classic éclairs, opera cake and miniature *financiers*; the latter are free with each coffee. **Other locations** 35 Cedar Street, at William Street, Financial District (1-212 952 3838); 3-4 World Financial Center, Financial District (1-212 786 3220).

$ Jack's Stir Brew Coffee

222 Front Street, between Beekman Street & Peck Slip (1-212 227 7631, www.jacksstirbrew.com). Subway A, C to Broadway-Nassau Street. **Open** 7am-7pm Mon-Sat; 8am-7pm Sun. **Coffee** $2.50. **No credit cards. Map** p402 F32 ❷ **Café**

Java fiends convene at this award-winning caffeine spot that offers organic, shade-grown beans and a homey vibe. Coffee is served by espresso artisans with a knack for oddball concoctions, such as the super-silky Mountie latte, infused with maple syrup. **Other locations** 138 W 10th Street, between Greenwich Avenue & Waverly Place, West Village (1-212 929 0821).

> **INSIDE TRACK**
> **COUNTER INTELLIGENCE**
>
> Landing a table at the restaurant *du jour*, **Minetta Tavern** (*see p197*) can be well-nigh impossible; the best tactic to get a taste of the atmosphere is to show up for a late-night bite at the bar. You can sometimes score impromptu bar seating at other popular spots, such as **Freemans** (*see p191*).

Tribeca & Soho

Balthazar

80 Spring Street, between Broadway & Crosby Street (1-212 965 1414, www.balthazarny.com). Subway N, R to Prince Street; 6 to Spring Street. **Open** 7.30-11am, noon-5pm, 6pm-midnight Mon-Thur; 7.30-11am, noon-5pm, 6pm-1am Fri; 10am-4pm, 6pm-1am Sat; 10am-4pm, 5.30pm-midnight Sun. **Main courses** $25. **Credit** AmEx, DC, MC, V. **Map** p403 E30 ❸ **French**

At dinner, this iconic eaterie is perennially packed with rail-thin lookers dressed to the nines. But it's not only fashionable – the kitchen rarely makes a false step and the service is surprisingly friendly. The $115 three-tiered seafood platter casts an impressive shadow, and the roast chicken on mashed potatoes for two is *délicieux*.

Bouley Bakery & Market

120 West Broadway, at Duane Street (1-212 219 1011, www.davidbouley.com). Subway A, C, 1, 2, 3 to Chambers Street. **Open** 7.30am-8.30pm daily. **Sandwiches** $9. **Credit** AmEx, DC, Disc, MC, V. **Map** p402 E31 ❹ **American creative/Café**

High-profile chef David Bouley has rejigged his collection of restaurants. Bouley Bakery & Market now occupies the former space of fine-dining room Bouley (which has moved to nearby Duane Street). As well as exquisite loaves and pastries, there's a fine cheese selection. Takeaway and eat-in options include soups and elegant pre-made sandwiches. Less expensive than Bouley proper, Bouley Upstairs now occupies all of Bouley Market's old, bi-level space – got that? Essentially an expanded version of the original second-floor eaterie, it offers a mostly French menu with some small Asian twists (and main courses averaging under $20), and a sushi bar. **Other locations** Bouley Upstairs, 130 West Broadway, at Duane Street, Tribeca (1-212 608 5829); Bouley, 163 Duane Street, at Hudson Street, Tribeca (1-212 964 2525).

► *See p249 for other top city bakeries.*

★ Corton

239 West Broadway, between Walker & White Streets (1-212 219 2777, www.cortonnyc.com). Subway A, C, E to Canal Street; 1 to Franklin Street. **Open** 5.30-10.30pm Mon-Thur; 5.30-11pm Fri, Sat. **3-course prix fixe** $85. **Tasting menu** $145. **Credit** AmEx, DC, Disc, MC, V. **Map** p402 E31 ❺ **French**

Profile Keith McNally

The city's top tastemaker for over 30 years can't put a foot wrong.

How many restaurateurs can claim to be immortalised in fiction? **Schiller's Liquor Bar** and its owner, Keith McNally, inspired the white-hot restaurant Berkmann's and its world-weary proprietor, Harry Steele, in *Lush Life*, Richard Price's raw, stylised portrait of the Lower East Side – proof of this expat's importance in New York culture. Yet despite his fame, McNally keeps a low profile. The British-born restaurateur, who moved to the city in 1975, seems incapable of failure. Each of his restaurants, hotspots at one time or another – the Odeon, Balthazar, Pastis, Schiller's, Minetta Tavern, and more – has managed to capture exactly what New Yorkers want at the moment.

His first restaurant was the **Odeon**, the comfortable yet buzzy brasserie that he opened in 1980 with his now ex-wife, Lynn Wagenknecht, and brother, Brian, in Tribeca, then a frontier neighbourhood. It established the restaurateur as an arbiter of cool. The bistro-cum-diner, which is still open but no longer owned by McNally, was a nucleus of Downtown artistic activity, with such regulars as Andy Warhol, Jean-Michel Basquiat and David Byrne.

All of McNally's ventures are characterised by an appealing worn-in casualness that feels somehow familiar – there isn't a single fine dining establishment among them. Many have said that **Balthazar** and **Pastis**, with their aged mirrors, tiled floors and Francophile memorabilia, are more French than their Parisian counterparts.

Although McNally's restaurants aren't really for foodies – the menus generally feature comfort staples with enough finesse to please the crowds – he has a talent for turning an emerging neighbourhood into a bona fide destination. That's what he accomplished for Tribeca with the Odeon, for the Meatpacking District with Pastis in 2000, and for the Lower East Side with Schiller's Liquor Bar in 2003, another boisterous, constantly packed brasserie, this time with a few nods on the menu and in the decor to its old Jewish tenement neighbourhood.

His most recent restaurant, **Minetta Tavern**, is a revival of a storied Greenwich Village literary hangout that's been serving the Village since 1937. Now, there's a doorman at the entrance, and the place serves people such as Madonna and Uma Thurman $28 burgers. And the McNally legend continues: this past year, he opened a pizzeria, **Pulino's**, at 282 Bowery on the Lower East side (1-212 226 1966), with San Francisco chef Nate Appleman.

THREE TO TASTE

Raw bar tower at **Balthazar**. *See p183.*

Sticky toffee pudding at **Schiller's Liquor Bar**. *See p191.*

Black Label burger at **Minetta Tavern**. *See p197.*

Pastis.

When it opened in 2008, Corton was given the highest possible star rating by *Time Out New York*'s critics. A meal here is an extraordinary experience. Restaurateur Drew Nieporent's white-on-white sanctuary focuses all attention on chef Paul Liebrandt's finely wrought food. The presentations, in the style of the most esteemed modern kitchens of Europe, are Photoshop flawless: sweet bay scallops, for example, anchor a visual masterpiece featuring wisps of radish, marcona almonds and sea urchin.

Landmarc Tribeca

179 West Broadway, between Leonard & Worth Streets (1-212 343 3883, www.landmarc-restaurant.com). Subway 1 to Franklin Street. **Open** noon-2am Mon-Fri; 9am-2am Sat, Sun. **Main courses** $26. **Credit** AmEx, DC, Disc, MC, V. **Map** p402 E31 ❻ **Eclectic**

This Downtown dining destination quickly distinguished itself among its Tribeca competitors by serving heady bistro dishes (bone marrow, crispy sweetbreads) until 2am, and stocking the wine list with reasonably priced half bottles. Chef-owner Marc Murphy focuses on the tried-and-trusted: *frisée aux lardons*, boudin noir and several types of mussels. Metal beams and exposed brick add an unfinished edge to the elegant bi-level space. Those who have little restraint when it comes to sweets will appreciate the dessert menu: miniature portions cost just $4 a pop and a tasting of six goes for $16.

Other locations 3rd Floor, Time Warner Center, 10 Columbus Circle, at Eighth Avenue, Upper West Side (1-212 823 6123).

La Sirene

558 Broome Street, between Sixth Avenue & Varick Street (1-212 925 3061, lasirenenyc.com). Subway C, E to Spring Street. **Open** 5-11.30pm daily. **Main courses** $26. **No credit cards**. **Map** p403 E30 ❼ **French**

Fishing nets and posters of the Côte d'Azur may not entice you into this French bistro, but the exuberant cooking of Marseille-born chef-owner Didier Pawlicki should. The chef lavishes his mussels with curried cream and apples, and his garlicky, ruby-red slices of rare hanger steak are served with a sensuous trio of sides (carrot purée, potato gratin in a cheesy veil, and a pot of zucchini flan). A dessert of fluffy profiteroles will have you moaning – very French indeed.

★ Locanda Verde

377 Greenwich Street, at North Moore Street (1-212 925 3797, www.locandaverdenyc.com). Subway 1 to Franklin Street. **Open** 8-11am, 11.30am-3pm, 5.30-11pm Mon-Fri; 8am-3pm, 5.30-11pm Sat, Sun. **Main courses** $21. **Credit** AmEx, MC, V. **Map** p402 D31 ❽ **Italian**

Owner Robert De Niro hired Daniel Boulud protegé Andrew Carmellini to take the helm of his latest culinary venture. Carmellini's bold family-style fare is best enjoyed as a bacchanalian banquet. A single charred octopus tentacle served with tangy romesco won't last long in the middle of the table. Nor will the chef's ravioli – as delicate as silk and oozing pungent robiola. Locanda is the rare Italian restaurant with desserts worth saving room for: try the rich, crumbly brown-butter plum cake.

Megu

62 Thomas Street, between Church Street & West Broadway (1-212 964 7777, www.megunyc.com). Subway A, C, 1, 2, 3 to Chambers Street. **Open** 5.30-11pm Mon-Wed, Sun; 5.30pm-midnight Thur-Sat. **Main courses** $30. **Omakase tasting menu** $125. **Credit** AmEx, DC, Disc, MC, V. **Map** p402 E31 ❾ **Japanese**

Since the day this awe-inspiring temple of Japanese cuisine opened in 2004, diners have criticised its overblown prices and unwieldy, complicated menu. But critics often forget to mention that this is one of the most thrilling meals you'll find in New York. Opt for the tasting menu: a parade of ingenious little bites and surprising presentations.

Other locations Trump World Tower, 845 UN Plaza, First Avenue, between 47th & 48th Streets, Midtown East (1-212 964 7777).

Nobu

105 Hudson Street, at Franklin Street (1-212 219 0500, www.noburestaurants.com). Subway 1 to Franklin Street. **Open** 11.45am-2pm, 5.45-10.15pm Mon-Fri; 5.45-10.15pm Sat, Sun. **Sushi dinner** $32. **Omakase tasting menu** from $100. **Credit** AmEx, DC, Disc, MC, V. **Map** p402 E31 ❿ **Japanese**

Since opening in 1994, the original Nobu has promised impeccable fish and serious stargazing – and it still delivers both: luscious fluke sashimi with crunchy, salty bits of dried miso at your table, Martha Stewart at the next. While chef Nobu Matsuhisa and his partners have taken Nobu worldwide (and opened a showy outpost on 57th Street), they've left this Tribeca mainstay in its slightly weathered but beloved form. Nobu Next Door, at the same address, offers later dining (until 11pm Mon-Thur, Sun; midnight Fri, Sat), drop-in seating between 7pm and 9pm and food to go.

Other locations Nobu Fifty Seven, 40 W 57th Street, between Fifth & Sixth Avenues, Midtown (1-212 757 3000).

INSIDE TRACK DIY BBQ

Many of the Asian barbecue joints in **Koreatown**, the block-long strip of 32nd Street between Broadway and Fifth Avenue, give you the option of cooking your own meat on a gas grill built into the table... although you can also ask the server to do it for you.

Savoy

70 Prince Street, between Crosby Street & Lafayette Street (1-212 219 8570, www.savoynyc.com). Subway N, R to Prince Street; 6 to Spring Street. **Open** noon-10pm Mon-Thur; noon-10.30pm Fri, Sat; 6-10pm Sun. **Main courses** $28. **Credit** AmEx, MC, V. **Map** p403 E29 ⓫ **American creative**

Chef Peter Hoffman maintains his reputation as one of the godfathers of the local foods movement at this comfortable Soho stalwart, outfitted with a wood-burning fireplace (in use during colder months) and a congenial, semicircular bar. Hoffman makes daily pilgrimages to the Union Square Greenmarket to assemble Savoy's farm-forward, aggressively seasonal menus, which may include such dishes as flaky halibut, perched over a verdant fava bean purée; or duck, vibrantly pink within and sporting a slightly crunchy, salted crust.

► *See p250 for the Union Square Greenmarket.*

Little Italy & Nolita

$ Café Habana

17 Prince Street, between Elizabeth Street & Mott Street (1-212 625 2001, www.ecoeatery.com). Subway N, R to Prince Street; 6 to Spring Street. **Open** 9am-midnight daily. **Main courses** $10. **Credit** AmEx, DC, MC, V. **Map** p403 F29 ⓬ **Cuban**

Trendy Nolita types storm this chrome corner fixture for the addictive grilled corn: golden ears doused in fresh mayo, chargrilled, and generously sprinkled with chilli powder and grated cotija cheese. Staples include a Cuban sandwich of roasted pork, ham, melted swiss and sliced pickles, and crisp beer-battered catfish with spicy mayo. At the takeaway annexe next door (open May-Oct), you can get that corn-on-a-stick to go. There's also a sprawling seasonal outdoor branch in Brooklyn, Habana Outpost (open Apr-Oct).

Other locations 757 Fulton Street, at South Portland Avenue, Fort Greene, Brooklyn (1-718 858 9500).

Ed's Lobster Bar

222 Lafayette Street, between Kenmare Street & Spring Street (1-212 343 3236, www.lobsterbarnyc.com). Subway B, D, F, M to Broadway-Lafayette Street. **Open** noon-3pm, 5-11pm Mon-Thur; noon-3pm, 5pm-midnight Fri; noon-midnight Sat; noon-9pm Sun. **Main courses** $21. **Credit** AmEx, DC, MC, V. **Map** p403 E30 ⓭ **Seafood**

If you secure a place at the 25-seat marble seafood bar or one of the few tables in the whitewashed eaterie, expect superlative raw-bar eats, delicately fried clams and lobster served every which way: steamed, grilled, broiled, chilled, stuffed into a pie and – the crowd favourite – the lobster roll. Here, it's a buttered bun stuffed with premium chunks of meat and just a light coating of mayo.

La Esquina

106 Kenmare Street, at Cleveland Place (1-646 613 7100, www.esquinanyc.com). Subway 6 to Spring Street. **Open** *Taqueria* 8am-5am Mon-Fri; noon-5am Sat, Sun. *Café* noon-midnight Mon-Fri; 11am-midnight Sat, Sun. *Restaurant* 6pm-2am daily. **Main courses** $21. **Credit** AmEx, DC, MC, V. **Map** p403 E30 ⓮ **Mexican**

This cabbie-pit-stop-turned-taco-stand comprises three dining and drinking areas: first, a street-level taqueria, serving a short-order menu of fish tacos and Mexican tortas. Around the corner is a 30-seat café, its shelves stocked with books and old vinyl. Lastly, there's a dungeonesque restaurant and lounge accessible through a back door of the taqueria (to enter, you have to confirm that you have a reservation). It's worth the hassle: a world of Mexican murals, fine tequilas, *huitlacoche* (Mexican truffle) quesadillas and crab tostadas awaits.

Lombardi's

32 Spring Street, between Mott & Mulberry Streets (1-212 941 7994, www.firstpizza.com). Subway 6 to Spring Street. **Open** 11.30am-11pm Mon-Thur, Sun; 11.30am-midnight Fri, Sat. **Pizzas** $19.50. **No credit cards. Map** p403 F30 ⓯ **Pizza**

There may be hotter contenders for New York City's best pizzeria, but Lombardi's is the oldest, established in 1905. It still bakes tasty thin-crust pies in a coal-fired oven – try one topped with its speciality meatballs. An expansion has reduced waiting times, but try to snag a seat in the original, narrow dining room with its old wooden booths and red and white check tablecloths.

► *The new wave of top pizzerias in town includes Co (see p199) and Kesté Pizza & Vino (see p198).*

Peasant

194 Elizabeth Street, between Prince & Spring Streets (1-212 965 9511, www.peasantnyc.com). Subway B, D, F, M to Broadway-Lafayette Street; 6 to Bleecker Street. **Open** 6-11pm Tue-Sun. **Main courses** $27. **Credit** AmEx, DC, MC, V. **Map** p403 E29 ⓰ **Italian**

The dining room at Peasant, one of Downtown's most celebrated Italian restaurants, is equal parts rustic and urban chic. Cement floors and metal chairs give the place an unfinished edge, while the gaping brick oven and lengthy wooden bar provide the tell-tale old-world notes. Dishes that emerge from the fire are particularly good, including gooey speck-wrapped *bocconcini* (mozzarella).

Public

210 Elizabeth Street, between Prince & Spring Streets (1-212 343 7011, www.public-nyc.com). Subway N, R to Prince Street; 6 to Spring Street. **Open** 6-11.30pm Mon-Thur; 6pm-midnight Fri; 11am-3.30pm, 6pm-midnight Sat, Sun. **Main courses** $25. **Credit** AmEx, DC, Disc, MC, V. **Map** p403 E29 ⓱ **Eclectic**

CONSUME

the CORNER DELI
est. 1932
114 Kenmare
TACOS
BURGE S
BREAKF S T UNCH
ENSALADAS
TORTAS
SOPAS
POZOLE
H&M

La Esquina.

Hard Roc
CAFE

This sceney restaurant in a former bakery is moodily lit and industrially chic. The mastermind behind the globally inspired cuisine is British-trained Brad Farmerie, whose travels have left a cosmopolitan mark on his culinary concoctions. Reflecting pan-Pacific, Middle Eastern and South-east Asian influences, the clipboard menu offers creative dishes such as grilled kangaroo on a coriander falafel, or snail and oxtail ravioli, all paired with interesting wines.

Chinatown

★ Dim Sum Go Go

5 East Broadway, at Catherine Street (1-212 732 0797). Subway F to East Broadway. **Open** 10am-10.30pm daily. **Dumplings** $4 for 3 or 4. **Credit** AmEx, MC, V. **Map** p402 F31 ⓲ **Chinese**

A red and white colour scheme spruces up this Chinatown dim sum restaurant, where dumplings (more than 24 types) are the focus. A neophyte-friendly menu is divided into categories that include 'fried', 'baked' and 'steamed'. To avoid tough decisions, order the dim sum platter, whose artful array of ten items includes juicy steamed duck and mushroom dumplings, and the offbeat, slightly sweet pan-fried dumplings filled with pumpkin. Prices are a little higher than at your average dim sum emporium.

$ Doyers Vietnamese Restaurant

11 Doyers Street, between Bowery & Pell Street (1-212 513 1521). Subway J, M, N, Q, R, Z, 6 to Canal Street. **Open** 11am-10pm Mon-Thur, Sun; 11am-11pm Fri, Sat. **Main courses** $9. **Credit** AmEx. **Map** p402 F31 ⓳ **Vietnamese**

Hidden in a basement on a zigzagging Chinatown alley, this bare-bones joint features a menu that requires (and rewards) exploration. The long appetisers list includes sweet-and-smoky sugarcane wrapped with grilled shrimp, and a delicious Vietnamese crêpe crammed with shrimp and pork. In the winter, hotpot soups (served on a tabletop stove) feature the same exceptional broth base and come packed with vegetables, no matter the add-in. There's no beer or wine on the menu, but you can bring your own for a corkage fee of $5 per person.

Peking Duck House

28 Mott Street, between Mosco & Pell Streets (1-212 227 1810, www.pekingduckhousenyc.com). Subway J, M, N, Q, R, Z, 6 to Canal Street. **Open** 11.30am-10pm Mon-Thur, Sun; 11.30am-11pm Fri, Sat. **Main courses** $23. **Credit** AmEx, MC, V. **Map** p402 F31 ⓴ **Chinese**

Unlike some establishments, Peking Duck House doesn't require you to order the namesake speciality in advance; a chef will slice the aromatic, crisp-skinned, succulent meat at your table. Select the 'three-way' and your duck will yield the main course, a vegetable stir-fry with leftover bits of meat, and a cabbage soup made with the remaining bone.

Ping's

22 Mott Street, between Mosco & Pell Streets (1-212 602 9988). Subway J, M, Z, N, Q, R, 6 to Canal Street. **Open** 10am-midnight daily. **Main courses** $25. **Credit** MC, V. **Map** p402 F31 ㉑ **Chinese**

The bank of fish tanks near the entrance suggests the category. Go for something you haven't tried: spiced baby silvery fish are bite-sized pieces of boneless smelt deep-fried to a golden yellow; ask for pepper salt (a mix of Szechuan peppercorns and salt) to boost the mild flavour. Big steamed oysters benefit from a splash of Ping's celebrated homemade XO sauce – a spicy condiment made of dried shrimp, scallops and garlic. The sliced sautéed conch is set off by snappy snow peas and a tangy fermented shrimp sauce. Those exotic flavours, plus touches like tablecloths, justify prices that are a notch above the Chinatown norm.

$ Super Taste Restaurant

26 Eldridge Street, at Canal Street (1-212 625 1198). Subway F to East Broadway. **Open** 10.30am-10.30pm daily. **Main courses** $5. **No credit cards. Map** p403 F30 ㉒ **Chinese**

In a sea of cheap Chinatown noodle bars, Super Taste stands out. Watch the cook hand pull your Lanzhou-style *la mian*, the Chinese relative of Japanese ramen, which is served in a soup with a choice of toppings that vary from beef tendon to eel – at around a fiver for a bowl.

Lower East Side

Clinton Street Baking Company

4 Clinton Street, between Houston & Stanton Streets (1-646 602 6263, www.clintonstreetbaking.com). Subway F to Delancey Street; J, M, Z to Delancey-Essex Streets. **Open** 8am-4pm, 6-11pm Mon-Fri; 9am-4pm, 6-11pm Sat; 9am-4pm Sun. **Main courses** $14. **Credit** (evenings only) AmEx, DC, MC, V. **Map** p403 G29 ㉓ **Café**

The warm buttermilk biscuits and fluffy plate-size pancakes at this pioneering little eaterie are reason enough to face the brunch-time crowds. If you want

> **INSIDE TRACK**
> **PRIX FIXE TRICKS**
>
> To make your money stretch further, consider timing your visit to coincide with the biannual **Restaurant Week** (*see p264*), when you can dine at notable restaurants around town for around $25 and $35 for a three-course lunch and dinner, respectively. Affordable prix fixe lunches are also a great way to experience some of the city's fine-dining establishments.

Schiller's Liquor Bar.

to avoid the onslaught, the homey place is just as reliable for both lunch and dinner. Try the $12 beer and burger special (6-8pm Mon-Thur): eight ounces of Black Angus topped with swiss cheese and caramelised onions, served with a Brooklyn Lager.

Les Enfants Terribles

37 Canal Street, at Ludlow Street (1-212 777 7518, www.lesenfantsterriblesnyc.com). Subway F to East Broadway. **Open** 10am-midnight daily. **Main courses** $20. **Credit** AmEx. **Map** p403 G30 ㉔ **French-African**

Worn-in brown leather banquettes and a sepia-toned colour scheme foster a Bohemian vibe at this lively hangout. Although the menu claims French-African influences, the best items come straight from the bistro, such as steak frites, dripping with juices and served with a side of aggressively seasoned fries.

Freemans

2 Freeman Alley, off Rivington Street, between Bowery & Chrystie Street (1-212 420 0012, www.freemansrestaurant.com). Subway F to Lower East Side-Second Avenue; J, M, Z to Bowery. **Open** 11am-4pm, 6-11.30pm Mon-Fri; 10am-4pm, 6-11.30pm Fri, Sat. **Main courses** $23. **Credit** AmEx, DC, Disc, MC, V. **Map** p403 F29 ㉕ **American**

At the end of a graffiti-marked alley, Freemans' colonial tavern meets hunting lodge style is an enduring hit with retro-loving New Yorkers. Garage-sale oil paintings and moose antlers serve as backdrops to a curved zinc bar, while the menu recalls a simpler time – devils on horseback (prunes stuffed with stilton cheese and wrapped in bacon); rum-soaked ribs, the meat falling off the bone with a gentle nudge of the fork; and stiff cocktails that'll get you good and sauced.

★ Katz's Delicatessen

205 E Houston Street, at Ludlow Street (1-212 254 2246, www.katzdeli.com). Subway F to Lower East Side-Second Avenue. **Open** 8am-9.45pm Mon, Tue; 8am-10.35pm Wed, Thur, Sun; 8am-2.45am Fri, Sat. **Sandwiches** $15. **Credit** AmEx, DC, Disc, MC, V. **Map** p403 F29 ㉖ **American**

A visit to Gotham isn't complete without a stop at a quintessential New York deli, and this Lower East Side survivor is the real deal. You might get a kick out of the famous faces plastered to the panelled walls, or the spot where Meg Ryan faked it in *When Harry Met Sally*..., but the real stars of this cavernous cafeteria are the thick-cut pastrami sandwiches and the crisp-skinned all-beef hot dogs – the latter are a mere $3.10.

► *See p79 for more local kosher nosh.*

Oliva

161 E Houston Street, at Allen Street (1-212 228 4143, www.olivanyc.com). Subway F to Lower East Side-Second Avenue. **Open** 5.30pm-midnight Mon-Thur, Sun; 5.30pm-1am Fri, Sat. **Main courses** $16. **Tapas** $8. **Credit** AmEx. **Map** p403 F29 ㉗ **Spanish**

With a Cuban salsa band playing most nights of the week, this spirited sangria and tapas place often gets as loud as the corner of Houston and Allen outside. Oliva primarily peddles traditional tapas, from a fat wedge of tortilla and warm or ham-flecked croquettes to plump olives. The buzzy, tightly packed room is lined with wooden tables spray-painted with images of red bulls. *¡Olé!*

Schiller's Liquor Bar

131 Rivington Street, at Norfolk Street (1-212 260 4555, www.schillersny.com). Subway F to Delancey Street; J, M, Z to Delancey-Essex Streets. **Open** 11am-1am Mon-Wed; 11am-2am Thur; 11am-3am Fri; 10am-3am Sat; 10am-1am Sun. **Main courses** $18. **Credit** AmEx, DC, MC, V. **Map** p403 G29 ㉘ **Eclectic**

At this artfully reconstructed faux-vintage hangout, the menu is a mix of French bistro (steak frites), British pub (fish and chips) and good ol' American (cheeseburger), while the wine menu famously hawks a down-to-earth hierarchy: Good, Decent, Cheap. As at Keith McNally's other establishments (*see p184* **Profile**), folks pack in for the scene, triple-parking at the curved central bar for elaborate cocktails and star sightings.

Sorella

95 Allen Street, between Broome & Delancey Streets (1-212 274 9595, www.sorellanyc.com). Subway F to Delancey Street; J, M, Z to Delancey-Essex Streets. **Open** 6pm-2am Tue-Sat; 5.30pm-midnight Sun. **Small plates** $12. **Credit** AmEx, MC, V. **Map** p403 F30 ㉙ **Italian**

Despite its culinary significance, few of New York's Italian restaurants spotlight Piedmont. This small, sleek space serves spunky renditions of traditional dishes that do justice to the region's pedigree – and then some. Small plates include *vitello tonnato* (veal with tuna sauce) reworked as a refreshing salad of shredded chicken, veal tongue and beets in a tuna-mayonnaise dressing. Some pastas are also given delectable updates – the thin egg-noodle *tajarin* is tossed with a minty, pistachio-studded lamb *ragù*

THE BEST MODERN MELTING POT

For cool Korean
Momofuku Ssäm Bar. *See p195.*

For upscale Malaysian
Fatty Crab. *See p198.*

For Portuguese chic
Aldea. *See p201.*

CONSUME

and topped with black-pepper ricotta. This is hefty fare (you're better off ordering less), but enjoyed with a glass of barbera, it goes down just fine.

East Village

Back Forty

190 Avenue B, between 11th & 12th Streets (1-212 388 1990, www.backfortynyc.com). Subway L to First Avenue. **Open** 6-11pm Mon-Thur; 6pm-midnight Fri, Sat; noon-3.30pm, 6-10pm Sun. **Main courses** $15. **Credit** AmEx, DC, MC, V. **Map** p403 G28 ㉚ **American**

Chef-restaurateur Peter Hoffman (Savoy, *see p186*) is behind this East Village seasonal-eats tavern, where pared-down farmhouse chic prevails in the decor and on the menu. House specialities include juicy grass-fed burgers, stout floats made with beer from New York-area breweries, and golden pork-jowl nuggets. The spacious back garden, open in warmer months, is a bonus.

$ Baoguette

37 St Marks Place, at Second Avenue (1-212 380 1487, www.baoguettecafe.com). Subway 6 to Astor Place. **Open** 11am-midnight Mon-Thur, Sun; 11am-2am Fri, Sat. **Sandwiches** $6. **No credit cards. Map** p403 F28 ㉛ **Vietnamese**

If the Vietnamese *banh mi* is a study in contrasts, then Baoguette's signature is the definitive text. Three forms of sweet and juicy pork (pâté, terrine and pulled) are stuffed into a crusty French loaf, their fatty flavour offset by bright strands of pickled carrot and daikon radish, enhanced by fresh cilantro (coriander), garlicky aïoli and hot sriracha sauce. Other variations include a veggie version. Husband-and-wife team Thao Nguyen and Michael 'Bao' Huynh have expanded to several locations, but this outpost has a larger repertoire, including some exceptional soups.

Other locations throughout the city.

$ Caracas Arepa Bar

91 E 7th Street, between First Avenue & Avenue A (1-212 228 5062, www.caracasarepabar.com). Subway F to Lower East Side-Second Avenue; 6 to Astor Place. **Open** noon-11pm Tue-Sat; noon-10pm Sun. **Arepas** $7. **Credit** AmEx, DC, Disc, MC, V. **Map** p403 F28 ㉜ **Venezuelan**

This endearing spot, with flower-patterned, vinyl-covered tables, zaps you straight to Caracas. Each *arepa* is made from scratch daily; the pitta-like pockets are stuffed with a choice of 18 fillings, such as chicken and avocado, or mushrooms with tofu. Top off your snack with a *cocada*, a thick and creamy milkshake made with freshly grated coconut and cinnamon.

$ Crif Dogs

113 St Marks Place, between First Avenue & Avenue A (1-212 614 2728). Subway L to First Avenue; 6 to Astor Place. **Open** noon-2am Mon-Fri; noon-4am Fri, Sat; noon-1am Sun. **Hot dogs** $4. **Credit** AmEx, MC, V. **Map** p403 F28 ㉝ **American**

You'll recognise this place by the giant hot dog outside, bearing the come-on 'Eat me'. Crif offers the best Jersey-style dogs this side of the Hudson: handmade smoked-pork tube-steaks that are deep-fried until they're bursting out of their skins. While they're served in various guises, including the Spicy Redneck (bacon-wrapped and covered in chilli, coleslaw and jalapeños) and the Chihuahua (bacon-wrapped with sour cream and avocado), the classic with mustard and kraut is most popular. If you're wondering why there are so many people hanging around near the public phone booth at night, it's because there's a trendy cocktail bar, PDT (*see p221*), concealed behind it.

Back Forty.

INSIDE TRACK QUICK TIP

Tipping etiquette can be a nightmare if you don't know what you're doing. However, things are simple here. Few restaurants add service to the bill for parties under six; it's customary to give between 15 and 20 per cent. The easiest way to figure out the amount is to double the sales tax. Bartenders also get tipped – $1 a drink should ensure friendly pours.

Diffusion Dining

Top chefs offer more-affordable spin-offs from their famous flagships.

HUNGER FOR... Per Se (*see p211*)
When this restaurant from superchef Thomas Keller breezed into town in 2005, it quickly became one of Manhattan's most lauded (and toughest to reserve) haute-cuisine experiences. The $275 tasting menu ($175 for lunch) can bring delights such as Keller's signature oysters-and-caviar starter, as well as dazzling iterations of such down-to-earth pairings as steak with potatoes, and chocolate with coffee.

THEN TRY... Bouchon Bakery (*see p209*)
Keller's café, in the same mall as his fine-dining room, certainly wants for ambience, and the tartines, soups and salads are a bit basic. The prices are more palatable though, with sandwiches such as the Fluffernutter – cashew butter with Italian meringue, bananas and side of Nutella pudding – for around a tenner. So focus on the bakery. French classics and Keller's takes on American ones – Oreo cookies and Nutter Butters – are the real highlights.

HUNGER FOR... Babbo (*see p196*)
Good luck getting a table at Mario Batali's flagship operation. The celebrity chef's town-house restaurant is one of NYC's toughest tables to score. Would it make you feel better if we said it wasn't worth the trouble? On our most recent visit, the sauce coating our goose liver ravioli was reduced almost to the point of being burnt, and other dishes, while serviceable, did not live up to the hype.

THEN TRY... Lupa (*see p197*)
Batali's convivial West Village trattoria offers communal dining, reasonably priced wines and hit-the-spot comfort foods. Come for classic Roman fare including punchy orecchiette with greens and sausage, and gumdrop-shaped ricotta gnocchi. A favourite for late-night diners, it offers such specials as three courses for $26 (including a glass of wine; 10.30pm-midnight Sun-Thur).

HUNGER FOR... Daniel (*see p209*)
It's official: Daniel Boulud is New York City's fine-dining king. His recently (and subtly) refurbished flagship achieved perfect ratings from the *New York Times* and *Time Out New York* magazine. The prix fixe dinner – $105 for three courses – is ceremoniously served in a hushed two-tiered dining room. Choose a classic Boulud dish, such as the black truffle and scallops in puff pastry. Or visit the less formal lounge for à la carte options.

THEN TRY... DBGB Kitchen & Bar (*see p195*)
In a continuous attempt to soften his upscale image, Daniel Boulud recently opened this Bowery meat mecca, known for its international array of sausages (made by the charcutiers at Bar Boulud), copious beers on tap and indulgent burgers and sundaes. The industrial interior – cement floors and all – doesn't hide the fact that this is a gourmand's take on casual food. The Beaujolais sausage, at once refined yet deeply porky, is among the best in the city.

HUNGER FOR... Momofuku Ko (*see p196*)
Turning the usual formula on its head, David Chang opened the exclusive jewel in his culinary crown after the success of his more casual Momofuku Noodle Bar and Momofuku Ssäm Bar. Reservations can only be made online, but if you score a coveted seat at the 12-stool counter, you'll be privy to eight or so eye-opening courses that may include raw fluke coated in buttermilk, poppy seeds and sriracha, or a frozen foie gras torchon shaved into snowy flakes.

THEN TRY... Momofuku Noodle Bar (*see p196*)
This is where David Chang's legacy began, and the Noodle Bar still satisfies. Order the signature pork buns, succulent slices of belly folded into a steamed roll. Although the hipster atmosphere may not be to everyone's taste, sitting at the long bar or on a bench at a communal table, you'll certainly feel in the centre of the action. Soft-serve ice-cream in imaginative flavours (Graham cracker, salted pistachio) also displays Chang's trendsetting talent.

DBGB Kitchen & Bar

299 Bowery, at 1st Street (1-212 933 5300, www.danielnyc.com). Subway B, D, F, M to Broadway-Lafayette Street; 6 to Bleecker Street. **Open** 5.30pm-midnight Mon; noon-midnight Tue-Thur; 11am-1am Fri, Sat; 11am-11pm Sun. **Main courses** $19. **Credit** AmEx, DC, MC, V. **Map** p403 F29 ㉞ **French**

Even in a city awash in unruly menus, the one at DBGB – chef Daniel Boulud's most populist venture – stands out for its kitchen-sink scope. There's high-end junk food in the form of sausages (the best of the bunch is the Beaujolaise, infused with red wine, bacon and mushrooms). And there's haute bistro fare such as pink duck breast with boozy cherries and marcona almonds. The best way to get your head around the schizophrenic enterprise is to bring a large group and try to sample as much of the range as possible – including a sundae, layered with cherry-flavoured kriek beer ice-cream and speculoos cookies, for dessert.

▶ *For more of Daniel Boulud's output, see p209.*

Dirt Candy

430 E 9th Street, between First Avenue & Avenue A (1-212 228 7732, www.dirtcandynyc.com). Subway L to First Avenue; 6 to Astor Place. **Open** 5.30-11pm Tue-Sat. **Main courses** $18. **Credit** AmEx, MC, V. **Map** p403 F28 ㉟ **Vegetarian**

The shiny, futuristic environment here looks more like a chic nail salon than a restaurant. Chef-owner Amanda Cohen has created an unlikely space to execute her less-likely ambition: to make people crave vegetables. She mostly succeeds. Elaborate dishes might include a spicy asparagus paella served with a crisped-rice cake on top, or a pungent portobello mousse accompanied by shiitake mushrooms and fennel-peach compote. Although some dishes miss the mark (the kimchi doughnuts were neither crispy nor spicy), Cohen has created a vegetarian menu suitable for omnivores.

▶ *For Amanda Cohen's earlier veggie enterprise, Pure Food & Wine, see p203.*

Five Points

31 Great Jones Street, between Lafayette Street & Bowery (1-212 253 5700, www.fivepointsrestaurant.com). Subway B, D, F, M to Broadway-Lafayette Street; 6 to Bleecker Street. **Open** noon-3pm, 5.30pm-midnight Mon-Fri; 11am-3pm, 6pm-midnight Sat; 11am-3pm, 5.30-10pm Sun. **Main courses** $23. **Credit** AmEx, DC, MC, V. **Map** p403 F29 ㊱ **American**

Five Points is one of those rare places where grown-ups and scenesters, romantics and power brokers, can all coexist happily. The vaguely country-style dining room bustles nightly the way a great neighbourhood restaurant should. Chef-owner Marc Meyer's ever-changing seasonal menu might include a side dish of roasted corn, a salad of fresh figs, or scallops with deliciously sweet corn chowder.

★ Ippudo NY

65 Fourth Avenue, between 9th & 10th Streets (1-212 388 0088). Subway 6 to Astor Place. **Open** 11am-3.30pm, 5-11.30pm Mon-Thur; 11am-3.30pm, 5pm-12.30am Fri, Sat; 11am-10.30pm Sun. **Ramen** $13. **Credit** AmEx, MC, V. **Map** p403 F28 ㊲ **Japanese**

This sleek outpost of a Japanese ramen chain is packed mostly with Nippon natives who queue up for a taste of 'Ramen King' Shigemi Kawahara's *tonkotsu*– a pork-based broth. The house special, Akamaru Modern, is a smooth, buttery soup topped with scallions, cabbage, a slice of roasted pork and pleasantly elastic noodles. Avoid non-soup dishes like the oily fried-chicken nuggets coated in a sweet batter. Long live the Ramen King– just don't ask him to move beyond his speciality.

Kyo Ya

94 E 7th Street, between First Avenue & Avenue A (1-212 982 4140). Subway 6 to Astor Place. **Open** 5.30-11.30pm Tue-Sat; 5.30-10.30pm Sun. **Main courses** $20. **Credit** AmEx, Disc, MC, V. **Map** p403 F28 ㊳ **Japanese**

The city's most ambitious Japanese speakeasy is marked only by an 'Open' sign, but in-the-know diners still find their way inside. The food, presented on beautiful handmade plates, is gorgeous: maitake mushrooms are fried in the lightest tempura batter and delivered on a polished stone bed. Sushi is pressed with a hot iron on to sticky vinegared rice. The few desserts – including an extra-silky crème caramel – are just as ethereal as the savoury food.

$ Little Veselka

First Park, First Avenue, at 1st Street (1-347 907 3317, www.veselka.com). Subway F to Second Avenue-Lower East Side. **Open** 7am-8.30pm daily. **Main courses** $8. **No credit cards. Map** p403 F29 ㊴ **Eastern European**

For review, *see p209* **Eating and Drinking on the Green**.

Momofuku Ssäm Bar

207 Second Avenue, at 13th Street (1-212 254 3500, www.momofuku.com). Subway L to First or

> **THE BEST NYC INSTITUTIONS**
>
> For simply delicious burgers
> **Corner Bistro**. *See p197.*
>
> For bivalves & beer
> **Grand Central Oyster Bar & Restaurant**. *See p207.*
>
> For an honest steak
> **Peter Luger**. *See p215.*

CONSUME

Third Avenues; L, N, Q, R, 4, 5, 6 to 14th Street-Union Square. **Open** 11.30am-midnight Mon-Thur, Sun; 11.30am-2am Fri, Sat. **Main courses** $16. **Credit** AmEx, MC, V. **Map** p403 F27 ⓴ **Korean**

At chef David Chang's second modern Korean restaurant, waiters hustle to noisy rock music in the 50-seat space, which feels expansive compared with its Noodle Bar predecessor's crowded counter dining. Try the wonderfully fatty pork-belly steamed bun with hoisin sauce and cucumbers, or one of the ham platters. But you'll need to come with a crowd to sample the house speciality, *bo ssäm* (a slow-roasted hog butt that is consumed wrapped in lettuce leaves, with a dozen oysters and other accompaniments); it serves six to eight people and must be ordered in advance. David Chang has further expanded his E Vill empire with a sweet annexe at this location, Momofuku Bakery & Milk Bar.

Other locations Momofuku Ko, 163 First Avenue, at 10th Street, East Village (no phone); Momofuku Noodle Bar, 171 First Avenue, between 10th & 11th Streets, East Village (1-212 777 7773).

★ $ Porchetta

110 E 7th Street, between First Avenue & Avenue A (1-212 777 2151, www.porchettanyc.com). Subway F to Lower East Side-Second Avenue; L to First Avenue; 6 to Astor Place. **Open** 11.30am-10pm Mon-Thur, Sun; 11.30am-11pm Fri, Sat. **Sandwiches** $9. **Credit** MC, V. **Map** p403 F28 ㊶ **Café**

This small, subway-tiled space has a narrow focus: central Italy's classic boneless roasted pork. The meat – available as a sandwich or a platter – is amazingly moist and tender, having been slowly roasted with rendered pork fat, seasoned with fennel pollen, herbs and spices, and flecked with brittle shards of skin. The other menu items (a mozzarella sandwich, humdrum sides) seem incidental; the pig is the point.

Veselka

144 Second Avenue, at 9th Street (1-212 228 9682, www.veselka.com). Subway L to Third Avenue; 6 to Astor Place. **Open** 24hrs daily. **Main courses** $15. **Credit** AmEx, DC, Disc, MC, V. **Map** p403 F28 ㊷ **Eastern European**

THE BEST MEMORABLE MEALS

For the food
Ouest. *See p210.*

For the scene
Minetta Tavern. *See p197.*

For a major blow-out
Breslin Bar & Dining Room. *See p201.*

Momofuku Ssäm Bar. *See p195.*

When you need food to soak up the mess of drinks you've consumed in the East Village in the early hours, it's worth remembering Veselka: a relatively inexpensive Eastern European restaurant with plenty of seats that's open 24 hours a day. Hearty appetites can get a platter of classic Ukrainian grub: goulash, kielbasa, beef stroganoff or *bigos* stew. For dessert, try the *kutya* (traditional Ukrainian pudding made with berries, walnuts, poppy seeds and honey).

▶ *For more on Ukrainian culture in the East Village, see 82. For its Little Veselka outpost in tiny First Park, see p209 Eating and Drinking on the Green.*

Greenwich Village

Babbo

110 Waverly Place, between MacDougal Street & Sixth Avenue (1-212 777 0303, www.babbonyc.com). Subway A, B, C, D, E, F, M to W 4th Street. **Open** 5.30-11.30pm Mon-Sat; 5-11pm Sun. **Main courses** $28. **Credit** AmEx, MC, V. **Map** p403 E28 ㊸ **Italian**

See p194 **Diffusion Dining**.

Blue Hill

75 Washington Place, between Washington Square West & Sixth Avenue (1-212 539 1776, www.bluehillnyc.com). Subway A, B, C, D, E, F, M to W 4th Street. **Open** 5.30-11pm Mon-Sat; 5.30-10pm Sun. **Main courses** $28. **Credit** AmEx, DC, MC, V. **Map** p403 E28 ㊹ **American**

More than a mere crusader for sustainability, Dan Barber is also one of the most talented cooks in town, building his menu around whatever's at its peak on his Westchester farm (home to a sibling restaurant). During fresh pea season, bright green infuses every inch of the menu, from a velvety spring pea soup, to sous-vide duck breast as soft as sushi fanned over a slivered bed of sugar snap peas. Thanks to the 2009 visit from the Obamas, the restaurant's popularity is unlikely to wane any time soon.

$ Cake&Shake

Washington Square Park, enter at La Guardia Place & W 4th Street (1-718 383 0046, www.cakeandshakeny.com). Subway A, B, C, D, E, F, M to West Fourth Street-Washington Square. **Open** 11am-9pm daily. **Main courses** $3. **No credit cards. Map** p403 E28 ㊺ **Café**

For review, *see p209* **Eating and Drinking on the Green**.

Lupa

170 Thompson Street, between Bleecker & Houston Streets (1-212 982 5089, www.luparestaurant.com). Subway A, B, C, D, E, F, M to W 4th Street. **Open** noon-midnight daily. **Main courses** $18. **Credit** AmEx, MC, V. **Map** p403 E29 ㊻ **Italian**

No mere 'poor man's Babbo' (Mario Batali's pricier restaurant around the corner), this convivial trattoria offers communal dining, reasonably priced wines and hit-the-spot comfort foods. Come for classic Roman fare such as punchy orecchiette with greens and sausage, or gumdrop-shaped ricotta gnocchi.

▶ *For a comparison, see p194 Diffusion Dining.*

★ Minetta Tavern

113 MacDougal Street, between Bleecker & W 3rd Streets (1-212 475 3850, www.minettatavernny.com). Subway A, B, C, D, E, F, M to W 4th Street. **Open** 5.30pm-1am Mon-Thur, Sun; 5.30pm-2am Fri, Sat. **Main courses** $25. **Credit** AmEx, Disc, MC, V. **Map** p403 E29 ㊼ **Eclectic**

Thanks to restaurateur extraordinaire Keith McNally's spot-on restoration, this former literati hangout, once frequented by Hemingway and Fitzgerald, is as buzzy now as it must have been in its mid 20th-century heyday. The big-flavoured bistro fare is as much of a draw as the scene and includes classics such as roasted bone marrow, trout meunière topped with crabmeat, and an airy Grand Marnier soufflé for dessert. But the most illustrious thing on the menu is the Black Label burger. You might find the $28 price tag a little hard to swallow, but the superbly tender sandwich – essentially chopped steak in a bun smothered in caramelised onions – is worth every penny.

▶ *For more on Minetta's most hyped dish – and other nominations for NYC's best burger – see p211 Essentially New York.*

West Village & Meatpacking District

Barbuto

775 Washington Street, at W 12th Street (1-212 924 9700, www.barbutonyc.com). Subway A, C, E to 14th Street; L to Eighth Avenue. **Open** noon-11pm Mon-Wed; noon-midnight Thur-Sat; noon-10pm Sun. **Main courses** $20. **Credit** AmEx, MC, V. **Map** p403 C28 ㊽ **Italian**

The earthy, season-driven cooking in this raw, cement-floored space is top-notch – for example, marvellously light calamares in lemon-garlic sauce; pasta with walnuts, garlic, olive oil and parmesan; and fried Vermont veal. In the summer, the garage doors go up and the crowd of stylists, assistants, yuppies and West Village whatevers mob the corner from breakfast until last orders.

Cabrito

50 Carmine Street, at Bedford Street (1-212 929 5050, www.cabritonyc.com), West Village. Subway A, B, C, D, E, F, M to W 4th Street; 1 to Christopher Street-Sheridan Square. **Open** noon-11pm Mon, Sun; noon-midnight Tue, Wed; noon-2am Thur-Sat. **Main courses** $19. **Credit** AmEx, Disc, MC, V. **Map** p403 D29 ㊾ **Mexican**

This artfully scuffed roadhouse, done up with Mexican wall tiles and bare filament bulbs, traffics in big, offbeat flavours. Chef David Schuttenberg favours authenticity over crowd-pleasing Tex-Mex: *jalapeños rellenos* stuffed with shredded snapper, raisins, capers and pumpkin seeds were a fiery starter; and the namesake *cabrito*, served on a banana leaf with a side of flour tortillas, offered the slow-cooked richness of a pit-roasted goat. You may find South of the Border fare this good on an outer-borough street corner, but Cabrito is a far more comfortable place to enjoy it.

$ Corner Bistro

331 W 4th Street, at Jane Street (1-212 242 9502). Subway A, C, E to 14th Street; L to Eighth Avenue. **Open** 11.30am-4am Mon-Sat; noon-4am Sun. **Burgers** $6. **No credit cards. Map** p403 D28 ㊿ **American**

There's only one reason to come to this legendary pub: it serves what some New Yorkers believe are the city's best burgers – plus the beer is just $2.50 a mug. The prime patties are no-frills and served on a flimsy paper plate. To get one, you may have to queue for a good hour, especially on weekend nights; if the wait is too long for a table, try to slip into a space at the bar.

▶ *For more about NYC's best burgers, see p211 Essentially New York.*

EN Japanese Brasserie

435 Hudson Street, at Leroy Street (1-212 647 9196, www.enjb.com). Subway 1 to Houston Street. **Open** noon-2.30pm, 5.30-11pm Mon-Thur;

noon-2.30pm, 5.30pm-midnight Fri, Sat; 5.30-11pm Sun. **Main courses** $15. **Credit** AmEx, MC, V. **Map** p403 D29 51 **Japanese**
Sibling restaurateurs Bunkei and Reika Yo evoke a sense of Japanese living in this multi-level space. On the ground floor are *tatami*-style rooms; on the mezzanine are recreations of a living room, dining room and library of a Japanese home from the Meiji era. But the main dining room is where the action is. Chef Koji Nakano offers handmade miso paste, tofu and yuba in dishes such as Berkshire pork belly braised in sansho miso; and foie gras and poached daikon steak with white miso vinegar. Try the saké and shochu flights (or wonderful cocktails) for an authentic Asian buzz.

Fatty Crab

643 Hudson Street, between Gansevoort & Horatio Streets (1-212 352 3592, fattycrab.com). Subway A, C, E to 14th St; L to Eighth Avenue. **Open** noon-midnight Mon-Wed, Thur; noon-2am Fri; 11am-2am Sat; 11am-midnight Sun. **Main courses** $19. **Credit** AmEx, Disc, MC, V. **Map** p403 C28 52 **Malaysian**
This Malaysian-inspired eaterie reflects chef Zak Pelaccio's cunning take on South-east Asian cuisine: Who knew you could squeeze sambal mayo and pork belly between slices of Pepperidge Farm bread for a killer tea sandwich? The classic Malaysian chilli crab makes an appearance, but expect to pay quite a bit more for it: 'market price' can mean $40 for a single Dungeness swimming in an admittedly excellent tomato chilli sauce. Far better bang for your buck is the short rib *rendang*, an unbelievably tender chunk of meat braised in coconut and kaffir lime. This packed spot takes no reservations, but turnover is quick – hard wooden chairs squeezed behind tiny tables in the single red-walled room don't encourage tarrying.

★ Kesté Pizza & Vino

271 Bleecker Street, between Cornelia & Jones Streets (1-212 243 1500, www.kestepizzeria.com). Subway 1 to Christopher Street-Sheridan Square. **Open** noon-3.30pm, 5-11pm Mon-Sat; noon-3.30pm, 5-10pm Sun. **Pizzas** $15. **Credit** AmEx, DC, MC, V. **Map** p403 D29 53 **Pizza**
If anyone can claim to be an expert on Neapolitan pizza, it's Kesté's Roberto Caporuscio: as president of the US branch of the Associazione Pizzaiuoli Napoletani, he's top dog for the training and certification of *pizzaioli*. At his intimate, 46-seat space, it's all about the crust – blistered, salty and elastic, it could easily be eaten plain. Add ace toppings such as sweet-tart San Marzano tomato sauce, milky mozzarella and fresh basil, and you have one of New York's finest pies.

Moustache

90 Bedford Street, between Barrow & Grove Streets (1-212 229 2220). Subway 1 to Christopher Street-Sheridan Square. **Open** noon-midnight daily. **Main courses** $13. **No credit cards**. **Map** p403 D29 54 **Middle Eastern**
Located on a leafy, brownstone-lined street, this beloved cheap-eats haven serves some of the city's best Middle Eastern food. The small, exposed-brick dining room packs in a neighbourhood crowd nightly and, as it doesn't take reservations, it's not unusual to see a queue outside. It's worth the wait; the freshly baked pittas, still puffed up with hot air when served, are perfect for scooping up smoky baba ganoush. More elaborate offerings include *ouzi*: rice, chicken, vegetables and raisins cooked in filo.
Other locations 265 E 10th Street, between First Avenue & Avenue A, East Village (1-212 228 2022); 1621 Lexington Avenue, at 102 Street, East Harlem (1-212 828 0030).

★ Pearl Oyster Bar

18 Cornelia Street, between Bleecker & W 4th Streets (1-212 691 8211, www.pearloysterbar.com). Subway A, B, C, D, E, F, M to W 4th Street. **Open** noon-2.30pm, 6-11pm Mon-Fri; 6-11pm Sat. **Main courses** $24. **Credit** MC, V. **Map** p403 D29 55 **Seafood**
There's a good reason this convivial, no reservations, New England-style fish joint always has a queue – the food is outstanding. Signature dishes include the lobster roll – sweet, lemon-scented meat laced with mayonnaise on a butter-enriched bun – and a contemporary take on bouillabaisse: a briny lobster broth packed with mussels, cod, scallops and clams, topped with an aïoli-smothered croûton.

$ 'sNice

45 Eighth Avenue, at W 4th Street & Jane Street (1-212 645 0310). Subway A, C, E to 14th Street; L to Eighth Avenue. **Open** 7.30am-10pm Mon-Fri; 8am-10pm Sat, Sun. **Sandwiches** $8. **No credit cards**. **Map** p403 D28 56 **Café/Vegetarian**
If you're looking for a laid-back place to read a paper, do a little laptopping, and enjoy cheap, simple and satisfying veggie fare, then 'sNice is nice indeed. Far roomier than it appears from its corner windows, the exposed-brick café has what may well be the largest menu in the city, scrawled on the wall, giving carefully wrought descriptions of each sandwich and salad.
Other locations 315 Fifth Avenue, at 3rd Street, Park Slope, Brooklyn (1-718 788 2121).

Spotted Pig

314 W 11th Street, at Greenwich Street (1-212 620 0393, www.thespottedpig.com). Subway A, C, E to 14th Street; L to Eighth Avenue. **Open** noon-3pm, 5.30pm-2am Mon-Fri; 11am-3pm, 5.30pm-2am Sat, Sun. **Main courses** $21. **Credit** AmEx, DC, MC, V. **Map** p403 D28 57 **Eclectic**
With a creaky interior that recalls an ancient pub, this Anglo-Italian hybrid is still hopping – and even

after it opened more seating upstairs, a wait can always be expected. Some might credit the big names involved (Mario Batali consults and April Bloomfield, of London's River Café, is in the kitchen). The burger is a must-order: a top-secret blend of ground beef grilled rare (unless otherwise specified) and covered with gobs of pungent roquefort. It arrives with a tower of crispy shoestring fries tossed with rosemary. But the kitchen saves the best treat for dessert: a delectable slice of moist orange and bourbon chocolate cake.

Standard Grill

846 Washington Street, between Little W 12th & 13th Streets (1-212 645 4100, www.standardhotels.com). Subway A, C, E to 14th Street; L to Eighth Avenue. **Open** 7-11am, 11.30am-4pm, 5.30pm-2am Mon-Fri; 11am-4pm, 5.30pm-2am Sat, Sun. **Main courses** $19. **Credit** AmEx, DC, Disc, MC, V. **Map** p403 C28 (58) **American creative**

Now that the High Line has the Meatpacking District once again on the tips of New Yorkers' tongues, the Standard Grill is drawing fashionable diners back to the neighbourhood. But even more than the clientele, it's the modelesque waitstaff who turn heads at dinner. Checked tablecloths and bread baskets fashioned from brown paper bags make dinner here feel like a sort of urban picnic – particularly if you order family-style dishes such as the golden 'Million Dollar' roasted chicken, or a richly marbled steak, delivered in thick, charred slices. Playful, homey desserts – such as a flaky slice of rhubarb 'humble pie' – capture this new phase of Meatpacking chic.

► *For more about the transformation of the High Line, see p96 Profile.*

$ Sweet Revenge

62 Carmine Street, between Bedford Street & Seventh Avenue (1-212 242 2240, www.sweetrevengenyc.com). Subway A, B, C, D, E, F, M to W 4th Street; 1 to Christopher Street-Sheridan Square. **Open** 8am-11pm Mon-Thur; 8am-12.30am Fri; 11am-12.30am Sat; 11am-9pm Sun. **Cupcakes** $3.50. **Credit** MC, V. **Map** p403 D29 (59) **Café**

Baker Marlo Scott steamrollered over the Magnolia Bakery-model cupcake's innocent charms: at her café/bar, she pairs her confections with wine; where there were pastel swirls of frosting, there are now anarchic spikes of peanut butter, cream cheese and milk-chocolate icing. In the process, she saved the ubiquitous treat from becoming a cloying cliché. Gourmet sandwiches and other plates means it's not strictly for sweet-tooths.

THE BEST HIDDEN GEMS

For tucked-away tranquillity
Convivio. *See p206.*

For secret sushi
Kyo Ya. *See p195.*

For a private-home vibe
Vinegar Hill House. *See p216.*

MIDTOWN

Chelsea

Co

230 Ninth Avenue, at 24th Street (1-212 243 1105, www.co-pane.com). Subway C, E to 23rd Street. **Open** 5-11pm Mon; 11.30am-11pm Tue-Sat; 11am-10pm Sun. **Pizzas** $16. **Credit** AmEx, MC, V. **Map** p404 C26 (60) **Pizza**

This unassuming pizzeria is the restaurant debut of Jim Lahey, whose Sullivan Street Bakery supplies many of the city's top restaurants. Lahey's crust is so good, in fact, it doesn't need any toppings (try the pizza bianca, dusted with sea salt and rosemary). The most compelling individual-sized pies come from non-traditional sources, such as the ham and cheese, essentially a croque-monsieur in pizza form.

Cookshop

156 Tenth Avenue, at 20th Street (1-212 924 4440, www.cookshopny.com). Subway C, E to 23rd Street. **Open** 8-11am, 11.30am-3pm, 5.30-11.30pm Mon-Fri; 11am-3pm, 5.30-11.30pm Sat; 11am-3pm, 5.30-10pm Sun. **Main courses** $24. **Credit** AmEx, DC, MC, V. **Map** p403 C27 (61) **American**

Chef Marc Meyer and his wife/co-owner Vicki Freeman want Cookshop to be a platform for sustainable ingredients from independent farmers. True to the restaurant's mission, the ingredients are consistently top-notch, and the menu changes daily. While organic ingredients alone don't guarantee a great meal, Meyer knows how to let the natural flavours speak for themselves, and Cookshop scores points for getting the house-made ice-cream to taste as good as Ben & Jerry's.

RUB

208 W 23rd Street, between Seventh & Eighth Avenues (1-212 524 4300, www.rubbbq.net). Subway C, E to 23rd Street. **Open** 11.30am-11pm Mon-Thur; 11.30am-midnight Fri, Sat; 11.30am-10pm Sun. **Main courses** $16. **Credit** AmEx, DC, Disc, MC, V. **Map** p404 D26 (62) **Barbecue**

The name stands for 'Righteous Urban Barbecue', and that's not all that's cocky about this barbecue joint. RUB takes no reservations and it doesn't apologise – even for the paper plates and paper towels. The message: our barbecue is so good, nothing else matters. Paul Kirk, a seven-time world barbecue champion, is the man behind the mission, and while the grub ain't flawless by Kansas City Barbecue Society standards, less discerning eaters will find much to praise. Ribs are lean and tender, and the details are just right: Wonder Bread comes with each platter, and sides include baked beans studded with bits of brisket.

Tía Pol

205 Tenth Avenue, between 22nd & 23rd Streets (1-212 675 8805, www.tiapol.com). Subway C, E to 23rd Street. **Open** 5.30-11pm Mon; 11am-3pm, 5.30-11pm Tue-Thur; 11am-3pm, 5.30pm-midnight Fri; 11am-3pm, 6pm-midnight Sat; 11am-3pm, 6-10.30pm Sun. **Tapas** $8. **Credit** AmEx, MC, V. **Map** p404 C26 ⑬ **Spanish**

Reaching crowd capacity at this tapas spot isn't hard: it's as slender as the white asparagus that garnishes some of its dishes. Seating is on high stools, with spill-over at the bustling bar, where handsome diners stand cheek by jowl while guzzling fruity sangria. The memorable menu is one part classical, two parts wholly original: munch on superb renditions from the tapas canon – springy squid '*en su tinta*' (in its own ink); *patatas bravas* topped with spicy aïoli – and then delve into eclectic treats that are eyebrow-raising on paper and delicious on the tongue, such as chorizo with bittersweet chocolate.

Tipsy Parson

156 Ninth Avenue, between 19th & 20th Streets (1-212 620 4545, www.tipsyparson.com). Subway

Aldea.

C, E to 23rd Street. **Open** 8am-11.30pm Mon-Thur; 8am-midnight Fri; 10am-midnight Sat; 10am-11pm Sun. **Main courses** $22. **Credit** AmEx, MC, V. **Map** p403 C27 ⓸ **American regional**
Tasha Gibson and Julie Wallach's Chelsea restaurant channels the experience of dining at home – if home happens to be a charming cottage in the country stocked with grandmotherly knick-knacks. The nostalgic food is grounded firmly in the deep South. A tasty burger comes with batter-fried pickles and crispy bacon, plus a smear of pimento cheese. Macaroni and cheese features a complex medley of Grafton cheddar, gruyère and grana padano, with crumbled corn bread and fresh cavatelli. For dessert, try the namesake Tipsy Parson – a boozy trifle served in a stemmed parfait glass.

Flatiron District & Union Square

Aldea

31 W 17th Street, between Fifth & Sixth Avenues (1-212 675 7223, www.aldearestaurant.com). Subway F to 14th Street; L to Sixth Avenue. **Open** 11.30am-2pm, 5.30-11pm Mon-Thur; 11.30am-2pm, 5.30pm-midnight Fri; 5.30pm-midnight Sat. **Main courses** $25. **Credit** AmEx, MC, V. **Map** p403 E27 ⓹ **Portuguese**
Aldea is a low-key stage for one of New York City's most original chefs: George Mendes. And while the minimalist space is restrained, the food certainly isn't. Tender baby cuttlefish was the centrepiece of a complex starter featuring caramelised lychee, *mentaiko* (pollock fish roe) and squid ink. More traditional fare also gets a haute spin. Beautiful garlicky shrimp *alhinho* are finished with an intense shrimp and brandy reduction.

Bar Breton

254 Fifth Avenue, between 28th & 29th Streets (1-212 213 4999, www.barbreton.com). Subway N, R to 28th Street. **Open** 11am-10.40pm Mon-Fri; 10am-10.40pm Sat, Sun. **Main courses** $21. **Credit** AmEx, MC, V. **Map** p404 E25 ⓺ **French**
Located in the restaurant-starved area near the Empire State Building, this clean-lined French eaterie touts the buckwheat crêpes – galettes – for which Brittany is known. Try the classic version – an egg with gruyère and Black Forest ham – washed down with that other Breton delicacy, hard cider. Though the pancakes get top billing, other successes included an elegantly rendered beef bourguignon, and a duck confit salad: romaine lettuce with bits of duck flesh, fat and skin folded in.

★ Breslin Bar & Dining Room

Ace Hotel, 20 W 29th Street, at Broadway (1-212 679 1939). Subway B, D, F, M, N, Q, R to 34th Street-Herald Square. **Open** 7am-midnight daily. **Main courses** $29. **Credit** AmEx, DC, Disc, MC, V. **Map** p404 E26 ⓻ **Eclectic**
The third project from restaurant savant Ken Friedman and Anglo chef April Bloomfield, the Breslin breaks gluttonous new ground. Expect a wait at this no-reservations hotspot – quell your appetite at the bar with an order of scrumpets (fried strips of lamb belly). The overall ethos might well be described as late-period Henry VIII: groaning boards of house-made terrines feature thick slices of guinea hen, rabbit and pork. The pig's foot for two – half a leg, really – could feed the full Tudor court. Amped-up classic desserts, such as sticky-toffee pudding, would befit a Dickensian Christmas feast. *Photos p203.*

★ City Bakery

3 W 18th Street, between Fifth & Sixth Avenues (1-212 366 1414, www.thecitybakery.com). Subway L, N, Q, R, 4, 5, 6 to 14th Street-Union Square. **Open** 7.30am-7pm Mon-Fri; 8am-7pm Sat; 10am-6pm Sun. **Salad bar** $14/lb. **Credit** AmEx, MC, V. **Map** p403 E27 ⓼ **Café**
Pastry genius Maury Rubin's loft-size City Bakery is jammed with shoppers loading up on unusual salad bar choices (grilled pineapple with ancho chilli, or beansprouts with smoked tofu, for example). There's also a small selection of soups, pizzas and hot dishes. But never mind all that: the thick, incredibly rich hot chocolate with fat house-made marshmallows is justly famed, and the moist 'melted' chocolate-chip cookies are divinely decadent.

Eataly

200 Fifth Avenue, between 23rd & 24th Streets (1-212 229 2560, www.eataly.com). Subway F, M, N, R to 23rd Street. **Open** 7am-11pm daily. **Main courses** $20. **Credit** AmEx, Disc, MC, V. **Map** p404 E26 ⓽ **Italian**
This massive food and drink complex, from Mario Batali and Joe and Lidia Bastianich, sprawls across 42,500sq ft in the Flatiron District. A spin-off of an operation by the same name just outside Turin, Italy, the store's retail maze and six full-service restaurants include a rotisserie with the city's best flame-roasted chickens, an awe-inspiring display of hard-to-find produce (plus an in-house 'vegetable butcher') and the meatcentric white-tablecloth joint Il Manzo, which serves a gorgeous tartare of Montana-raised Piedmontese-breed beef.

★ Hill Country

30 W 26th Street, between Broadway & Sixth Avenue (1-212 255 4544, www.hillcountryny.com). Subway N, R to 28th Street. **Open** noon-10pm Mon-Wed, Sun; noon-11pm Thur-Sat. **Main courses** $18. **Credit** AmEx, DC, MC, V. **Map** p404 E26 ⓾ **Barbecue**
The guys behind Hill Country are about as Texan as Mayor Bloomberg in a stetson, but the cooking is an authentic, world-class take on the restaurant's namesake region. It includes sausage imported from barbecue stalwart Kreuz Market of Lockhart, Texas, and two options for brisket: go for the

CONSUME

'moist' (read: fatty) version for full flavour. Beef shoulder emerges from the smoker in 20-pound slabs, and show-stealing tips-on pork ribs are hefty with just enough fat to imbue proper flavour. Desserts, such as jelly-filled cupcakes with peanut butter frosting, live out some kind of *Leave It to Beaver* fantasy, but June Cleaver wouldn't approve of the two dozen tequilas and bourbons.

$ Shake Shack

Madison Square Park, 23rd Street, at Madison Avenue (1-212 889 6600, shakeshack.com). Subway N, R to 23rd Street. **Open** 11am-9pm daily. **Main courses** $6. **Credit** AmEx, MC, V. **Map** p404 E26 ⑦① **American**

For review, *see p208* **Eating and Drinking on the Green**.

Union Square Café

21 E 16th Street, between Fifth Avenue & Union Square West (1-212 243 4020, www.unionsquarecafe.com). Subway L, N, Q, R, 4, 5, 6 to 14th Street-Union Square. **Open** noon-4pm, 5.30-10pm Mon-Thur, Sun; noon-4pm, 5.30-11pm Fri, Sat. **Main courses** $31. **Credit** AmEx, Disc, MC, V. **Map** p403 E27 ⑦② **American**

The Union Square Café's art collection and floor-to-ceiling murals have been here as long as the tuna filet mignon has been on the menu. That 1980s throwback remains hugely popular despite being relegated to a weekly special along with the restaurant's other signature standbys. However, novelty is not what keeps this place packed year after year. Danny Meyer's first New York restaurant – and a pioneer in Greenmarket cooking – remains one of the city's most relaxed fine dining establishments. Chef Carmen Quagliata has wisely kept the USC standards on the menu while making his own mark with lusty Italian additions, such as outstanding house-made pastas.

► *See p250 for information about the nearby Union Square Greenmarket.*

Gramercy Park & Murray Hill

Artisanal

2 Park Avenue, at 32nd Street (1-212 725 8585, www.artisanalbistro.com). Subway 6 to 33rd Street. **Open** 11.45am-11pm Mon-Sat; 11am-10pm Sun. **Main courses** $24. **Credit** AmEx, DC, Disc, MC, V. **Map** p404 E25 ⑦③ **French**

As New York's bistros veer towards uniformity, Terrance Brennan's high-ceilinged deco gem makes its mark with an all-out homage to fromage. Skip the appetisers and open with fondue, which comes in three varieties. Familiar bistro fare awaits, with such dishes as steak frites and a delectable glazed Scottish salmon, but the curd gets the last word with the cheese and wine pairings. These selections of three cheeses – chosen by region, style or theme (for example, each one produced in a monastery) – are matched with three wines (or beers or even sakés) for a sumptuous and intriguing finale. One of the most interesting places to eat in New York.

Blue Smoke

116 E 27th Street, between Park Avenue South & Lexington Avenue (1-212 447 7733, www.bluesmoke.com). Subway 6 to 28th Street. **Open** 11.30am-10pm Mon, Sun; 11.30am-11pm Tue-Thur; 11.30am-1am Fri, Sat. **Main courses** $20. **Credit** AmEx, DC, Disc, MC, V. **Map** p404 E26 ⑦④ **Barbecue**

St Louis native Danny Meyer's barbecue joint tops the short list of Manhattan's best 'cue contenders. Chef Kenny Callaghan knows his wet sauces and dry rubs: the menu includes traditional Texas salt and pepper beef ribs, Memphis baby backs and Kansas City spare ribs. The atmosphere is sports-heavy and includes a prominent bourbon bar and galvanised metal buckets for your bones.

★ Casa Mono

52 Irving Place, at 17th Street (1-212 253 2773, www.casamononyc.com). Subway L to Third Avenue; N, Q, R, 4, 5, 6 to 14th Street-Union Square. **Open** noon-midnight daily. **Tapas** $12. **Credit** AmEx, DC, MC, V. **Map** p403 F27 ⑦⑤ **Spanish**

Offal-loving consulting chef Mario Batali and protégé Andy Nusser go where many standard Manhattan tapas restaurants fear to tread: cocks' combs with ceps, pigs' feet with caper aïoli, and sweetbreads dusted with almond flour and fried. There are equally intriguing options for non-organ lovers, which might include juicy skirt steak atop onion marmalade, or the fried duck egg, a delicately flavoured breakfast-meets-dinner dish topping a mound of sautéed fingerling potatoes and salt-cured tuna loin. For a cheaper option, head to the attached Bar Jamón (125 E 17th Street), which doesn't open until 5pm during the week but stays open until 2am daily, and serves a more casual menu of treasured Ibérico hams, bocaditos and Spanish cheeses.

Maialino

Gramercy Park Hotel, 2 Lexington Avenue, between E 21st & E 22nd Streets (1-212 777 2410, www.maialinonyc.com). Subway 6 to 23rd Street. **Open** 7.30am-10.30pm Mon-Thur; 7.30am-11pm Fri; 10am-11pm Sat; 10am-10.30pm Sun. **Main courses** $26. **Credit** AmEx, DC, Disc, MC, V. **Map** p404 F26 ⑦⑥ **Italian**

Danny Meyer's first full-fledged foray into Italian cuisine is a dedicated homage to the neighbourhood trattorias that kept him well fed as a 20-year-old tour guide in Rome (the name itself is a corruption of his nickname when he was working in the Eternal City: 'Meyerino'). Salumi and bakery stations between the front bar and the wood-beamed dining room – hog jowls and sausages dangling near shelves stacked with crusty loaves of bread –

mimic a market off the Appian Way. Chef Nick Anderer's menu offers exceptional facsimiles of dishes specific to Rome: carbonara, braised tripe and suckling pig, among others.

Pure Food & Wine

54 Irving Place, between 17th & 18th Streets (1-212 477 1010, www.purefoodandwine.com). Subway L, N, Q, R, 4, 5, 6 to 14th Street-Union Square. **Open** noon-3pm, 5.30-11pm daily. **Main courses** $25. **Credit** AmEx, DC, MC, V. **Map** p403 F27 ⑰ **Vegetarian**

The dishes delivered to your table – whether out on the leafy patio or inside the ambient dining room – are minor miracles, not only because they look gorgeous and taste terrific, but because they come from a kitchen that lacks a stove. Everything at Pure is raw and vegan – from the pad thai appetiser to the lasagne (a rich stack of courgette, pesto and creamy 'cheese' made from cashews). Wines, most of which are organic, are top-notch, as are the desserts, especially the confoundingly fudgy chocolate layer cake.

$ 71 Irving Place Coffee & Tea Bar

71 Irving Place, between 18th & 19th Streets (1-212 995 5252, www.irvingfarm.com). Subway L, N, Q, R, 4, 5, 6 to 14th Street-Union Square. **Open** 7am-11pm Mon-Fri; 8am-11pm Sat. **Coffee** $2.50. **Credit** AmEx, DC, Disc, MC, V. **Map** p403 E27 ⑱ **Café**

Irving Farm's beans are roasted in a 100-year-old carriage house in the Hudson Valley; fittingly, its Gramercy Park café, which occupies the ground floor of a stately brownstone, also has a rustic edge. Breakfast (granola, oatmeal, waffles, bagels), sandwiches and salads accompany the excellent java.

Herald Square & Garment District

$ Mandoo Bar

2 W 32nd Street, between Fifth Avenue & Broadway (1-212 279 3075). Subway B, D, F, M, N, Q, R to 34th Street-Herald Square. **Open** 11am-11pm daily. **Main courses** $13. **Credit** AmEx, DC, MC, V. **Map** p404 E25 ⑲ **Korean**

Breslin Bar & Dining Room. *See p201.*

CONSUME

Food Walking Tours

Sample world cuisine while exploring new neighbourhoods on these walking tours throughout New York.

New York is a food-lover's dream, filled with a cornucopia of cuisines from all over the globe. All it takes is a healthy appetite, a sense of adventure and comfortable shoes to discover new taste sensations all over the city.

ASTORIA, QUEENS, WALKABOUT
Although the tour is billed as 'Around the World in 80 Minutes', its creator, Susan Birnbaum, doesn't like to be a stickler for the clock when visiting Greek, Italian, Colombian, Egyptian, and Lebanese restaurants and shops along 30th Avenue. The eight-stop trip is popular with adventurous tourists and locals who don't know that Astoria offers more than Greek treats.

SusanSez NYC Walkabouts
Meet *30th Avenue at 31st Street, Astoria, Queens (1-917 509 3111, www.susansez.com).* **Cost** $40.

BOWERY LANE CHOCOLATE TOUR
The sugar high that comes from visiting five haute chocolate spots along the Bowery is significant, but this two-hour walking tour is meant to work it off along the way. Taste confections flavoured with chili, paprika, ginger, wasabi, tequila, Cuban rum and even absinthe.

New Chocolate Tours
Meet *63 E 4th Street, between Bowery & Second Avenue (1-917 292 0680, sweetwalks.com).* **Cost** $50 in advance.

CHINATOWN, BROOKLYN
Liz Young's four-hour marathon tour treks through Brooklyn to explore a lesser-known culinary enclave straddling Sunset Park and Bay Ridge. The Chinese food is mostly Cantonese, notable for what she calls 'refined, delicate flavours'. The tour starts with Hong Kong-style dim sum, with curious eaters noshing on dumplings, Chinese tarts and stuffed buns, rice porridge, bubble tea, scallion pancakes and, for the truly adventurous, chicken feet or fin soup.

Liz Young Culinary Tours
(1-646 286 8065, lizyoungtours.com). **Tours** 10am-2pm Mon-Fri; 9am-1pm Sat, Sun, or by request. **Cost** $125.

Bowery Lane Chocolate Tour.

A TASTE OF HELL
On this seven-stop, three-hour tour through Hell's Kitchen, expect a midtown melting pot of eats, including empanadas, milk shakes, secret-spot chorizo tacos, pork buns, biscotti and apple pie. Bonus: on cold days, local tour guide Moira Campbell swings by the little-known 414 Hotel, a bed-and-breakfast where you can rest your legs by a cosy fireplace.

Rum & Blackbird Tasting Tours
(1-212 209 3370, www.rumand blackbird.com). **Tours** noon-3pm Sat, Sun. **Cost** $49.

TASTE OF HARLEM TOUR
'I feel sometimes like I'm Mr UN,' says tour leader Neal Shoemaker, who guides school kids and tourists through Harlem. 'I mean, Kentucky kids eating authentic African food? It's so cool! They're not going to get that in Louisville'. The mix of African, African-American, Spanish and Jamaican edibles won't merely fill the stomach, he promises; they'll help to illustrate Harlem's diverse culture as well.

Harlem Heritage Tours
Meet *104 Malcolm X Boulevard (Lenox Avenue), between 115th & 116th Streets (1-212 280 7888, www.harlemheritage.com).* **Cost** $39.

CONSUME

If the staff painstakingly filling and crimping dough squares in the front window don't give it away, we will – this wood-wrapped industrial-style spot elevates *mandoo* (Korean dumplings) above mere appetiser status. Six varieties of the tasty morsels are filled with such delights as subtly piquant kimchi, juicy pork, succulent shrimp and vegetables. Try them miniaturised, as in the 'baby mandoo', swimming in a soothing beef broth or atop springy, soupy ramen noodles.

New York Kom Tang Kalbi House

32 W 32nd Street, between Fifth Avenue & Broadway (1-212 947 8482). Subway B, D, F, M, N, Q, R to 34th Street-Herald Square. **Open** 24hrs Mon-Sat. **Main courses** $17. **Credit** AmEx, MC, V. **Map** p404 E25 ⑧⓪ **Korean**

Tender *kalbi* (barbecued short ribs) are indeed the stars here; their signature smoky flavour comes from being cooked over *soot bul* (wood chips). The city's oldest Korean restaurant also makes crisp, seafood-laden *haemool pajun* (pancakes); sweet, juicy *yuk hwe* (raw beef salad); and garlicky *bulgogi*. *Kom tang*, or 'bear soup', is a milky beef broth that's deep and soothing.

Theater District & Hell's Kitchen

Aureole

135 W 42nd Street, between Broadway & Sixth Avenue (1-212 319 1660, www.charliepalmer.com). Subway B, D, F, M to 42nd Street-Bryant Park; 7 to Fifth Avenue. **Open** noon-2.30pm, 5-10.30pm Mon-Sat; 5-10pm Sun. **3-course prix fixe** $84. **Credit** AmEx, Disc, MC, V. **Map** p404 D24 ⑧① **American**

Chef Charlie Palmer tapped rising talent Christopher Lee to run the new Times Square incarnation of his American classic, which moved from an Upper East Side townhouse to a spiffy modern tower with high ceilings, tall windows and a showcase wine vault. Lee's complex food strikes a fine balance between big-ticket opulence and homespun inclinations; this ethos can be seen in a foie gras starter, with buttery corn bread, smoked corn coulis and tart blueberries, and a surf and turf dish that presents side-by-side renditions of butter-poached lobster and barbecued pork.

Virgil's Real BBQ

152 W 44th Street, between Sixth Avenue & Broadway (1-212 921 9494, www.virgilsbbq.com). Subway B, D, F, M to 42nd St–Bryant Park; 7 to Fifth Avenue. **Open** 11.30am-11pm Mon; 11.30am-midnight Tue-Fri; 11am-midnight Sat; 11am-11pm Sun. **Main courses** $18. **Credit** AmEx, DC, Disc, MC, V. **Map** p404 D24 ⑧② **Barbecue**

As befits its Times Square location, perennially crowded Virgil's is the Epcot Center of barbecue: paper placemats present a map of the country's barbecue-producing regions and their specialities, from Texas beef brisket to Memphis pork ribs to vinegary Carolina pulled pork – all of which are on the menu, along with oddities like Oklahoma State Fair corndogs, served with a jalapeño 'mustard'. The dessert selection is a schizophrenic sugar rush, with peanut butter pie sharing a dessert sampler plate with key lime pie and fluffy banana pudding, among others. The Memphis pork ribs – dry-rubbed and slow-smoked, like the rest of Virgil's meats, with a mix of hickory, oak and fruit woods – are but a hair's-breadth from being too tender.

Midtown West

Adour Alain Ducasse

St Regis New York, 2 E 55th Street, between Fifth & Madison Avenues (1-212 710 2277, www.adour-stregis.com). Subway E, M to Fifth Avenue-53rd Street; F to 57th Street. **Open** 6-10pm Mon-Thur, Sun; 6-10.30pm Fri, Sat. **Main courses** $45. **Credit** AmEx, DC, Disc, MC, V. **Map** p405 D22 ⑧③ **French**

Legendary chef-restaurateur Alain Ducasse opened this temple of fine dining (and drinking) in the former L'Espinasse space in 2008. Here, wine is the muse (the list includes 118 under-$50 selections among its 1,500-strong list), and executive chef Joel Dennis's seasonally driven menu is equally decadent. Main dishes, such as lobster poached in butter with royal trumpet mushrooms and a champagne emulsion, or prime beef ribeye with chanterelles and potato soufflé, are rich without being heavy. Ditto the desserts, which include a chocolate 'sorbet' – a cold chocolate core ringed by a coating of pudding, coffee granita, vanilla cream and, in a Ducasse-worthy flourish, a gold-leafed chocolate disc. *Photo p207.*

Bar Room at the Modern

9 W 53rd Street, between Fifth & Sixth Avenues (1-212 333 1220, www.themodernnyc.com). Subway E, M to Fifth Avenue-53rd Street. **Open** 11.30am-3pm, 5-10.30pm Mon-Thur; 11.30am-3pm, 5-11pm Fri, Sat; 11.30am-3pm, 5-9.30pm Sun. **Main courses** $22. **Credit** AmEx, DC, Disc, MC, V. **Map** p405 E22 ⑧④ **American creative**

Those who can't afford to drop a pay cheque at award-winning chef Gabriel Kreuther's formal

INSIDE TRACK
CHEAP THEATRELAND EATS

The area surrounding Times Square is notoriously thin on decent pre- or post-theatre options. Locals skip the expensive, largely tourist-targeted places on Restaurant Row (46th Street, between Eighth & Ninth Avenues) and head for the multi-ethnic cheap-eats line-up on **Ninth Avenue** in the 40s and 50s.

CONSUME

MoMA dining room, the Modern, should drop into the equally stunning and less pricey Bar Room at the front (which shares the same kitchen). The Alsatian-inspired menu is constructed of 30 small and medium-sized plates (for example, pancetta-wrapped baby squid with eggplant 'caviar'; country sausage with sauerkraut and mustard sauce; and dry-aged steak with spätzle and beluga lentils), which can be mixed and shared. Desserts come courtesy of pastry chef Marc Aumont, and the wine list is extensive to say the least.

▶ *For the Museum of Modern Art itself, see p102.*

Carnegie Deli

854 Seventh Avenue, at 55th Street (1-212 757 2245, www.carnegiedeli.com). Subway B, D, E to Seventh Avenue; N, Q, R to 57th Street. **Open** 6.30am-4am daily. **Sandwiches** $15. **No credit cards. Map** p405 D22 ⑮ **American**

If the Carnegie Deli didn't invent schmaltz, it has certainly perfected it. All of the gargantuan sandwiches have punning names: Bacon Whoopee (BLT with chicken salad), Carnegie Haul (pastrami, tongue and salami). A waiter sings the deli's virtues in a corny video loop, and more than 600 celebrity glossies crowd the walls. This sexagenarian legend is a time capsule of the bygone Borscht Belt-era, when shtick could make up for cramped quarters, surly waiters and shabby tables – and tourists still eat it up. But when you're craving a deli classic, you can't do much better than the Carnegie's obscenely stuffed pastrami and corned beef sandwiches on rye.

CONSUME

★ Marea

240 Central Park South, between Seventh Avenue & Broadway (1-212 582 51000, www.marea-nyc.com). Subway A, B, C, D, 1 to 59th Street-Columbus Circle. **Open** noon-2.30pm, 5.30-11pm Mon-Thur; noon-2.30pm, 5-11.30pm Fri; 5-11.30pm Sat; 5-10.30pm Sun. **Main courses** $35. **Credit** AmEx, MC, V. **Map** p405 D22 ⑯ **Italian/Seafood**

Chef Michael White's shrine to the Italian coastline seems torn between its high and low ambitions. You might find lofty items such as an unorthodox starter of cool lobster with creamy burrata, while basic platters of raw oysters seem better suited to a fish shack. Seafood-focused pastas are the meal's highlight: you'll love the sedanini (like ridgeless rigatoni) in a smoky cod-chowder sauce with potatoes and speck. But the desserts – such as a chocolate-hazelnut Kit Kat – confirm a split identity that a little editing could easily fix.

Russian Tea Room

150 W 57th Street, between Sixth & Seventh Avenues (1-212 581 7100, www.russiantearoom nyc.com). Subway F, N, Q, R to 57th Street. **Open** 11.30am-3pm, 4.45-11pm Mon-Fri; 11am-11pm Sat, Sun. **Main courses** $40. **Credit** AmEx, DC, MC, V. **Map** p405 D22 ⑰ **Russian**

This refurbished 1920s icon has never looked better. Nostalgia buffs will be happy to hear that nothing's happened to the gilded-bird friezes or the famously tacky crystal-bear aquarium, although the food has not been frozen in time. Chef Mark Taxiera has at once modernised the menu – adding signature novelties such as sliders (mini burgers) – and brought back waylaid classics such as beef stroganoff and chicken kiev. In truth, however, the main reason to make for this tourist magnet is to luxuriate in the opulent setting.

Midtown East

Bryant Park Café & Grill

25 W 40th Street, between Fifth & Sixth Avenues (1-212 840 6500, www.arkrestaurants.com). Subway B, D, F, M to 42nd St–Bryant Park; 7 to Fifth Ave. **Open** 11.30am-3.30pm; 5-10pm daily. **Main courses** $24. **Credit** AmEx, DC, Disc, MC, V. **Map** p404 E24 ⑱ **American**

For review, *see p208* **Eating and Drinking on the Green**.

Convivio

45 Tudor City Place, at 43rd Street (1-212 599 5045, www.convivionyc.com). Subway S, 4, 5, 6, 7 to 42nd Street-Grand Central. **Open** noon-2.15pm, 5.30-10.15pm Mon-Thur; noon-2.15pm, 5.30-11.15pm Fri; 5.30-11.30pm Sat; 5-9.30pm Sun. **Main courses** $25. **4-course prix fixe** $62. **Credit** AmEx, DC, MC, V. **Map** p404 F24 ⑲ **Italian**

Adour Alain Ducasse. *See p205.*

At this tucked-away spot in peaceful residential microcosm Tudor City, the emphasis is squarely on southern Italy. Antipasti might include country bread slathered with chicken liver mousse, while the pastas – saffron gnocchetti with crabmeat, sea urchin, chilli flakes, scallion and garlic, to give one example – are hauntingly good. The quality carries through to dessert: a moist chocolate cake was flavourful not cloying.

Grand Central Oyster Bar & Restaurant

Grand Central Terminal, Lower Concourse, 42nd Street, at Park Avenue (1-212 490 6650, www.oysterbarny.com). Subway S, 4, 5, 6, 7 to 42nd Street-Grand Central. **Open** 11.30am-9.30pm Mon-Fri; noon-9.30pm Sat. **Main courses** $25. **Credit** AmEx, DC, Disc, MC, V. **Map** p404 E24 90 **Seafood**

At the legendary 98-year-old Grand Central Oyster Bar, located in the epic and gorgeous hub that shares its name, the surly countermen at the mile-long bar (the best seats in the house) are part of the charm. Avoid the more complicated fish concoctions and play it safe with a reliably awe-inspiring platter of iced, just-shucked oysters (there can be a whopping three-dozen varieties to choose from at any given time, from Baja to Plymouth Rock).

► *For more on the iconic transport hub, see p104.*

Quality Meats

57 W 58th Street, between Fifth & Sixth Avenues (1-212 371 7777, www.qualitymeatsnyc.com). Subway F to 57th St; N, R to Fifth Ave-59th Street. **Open** 11.30am-3pm, 5-10.30pm Mon-Wed; 11.30am-3pm, 5-11.30pm Thur-Sat; 5-10pm Sun. **Main courses** $35. **Credit** AmEx, MC, V. **Map** p405 D22 91 **Steakhouse**

Michael Stillman – son of the founder of landmark steakhouse Smith & Wollensky – shuttered Manhattan Ocean Club, a 22-year-old seafood palace in midtown, and replaced it with this highly stylised industrial theme park complete with meat-hook light fixtures, wooden butcher blocks, white tiles and exposed brick. Lespinasse-trained chef Craig Koketsu nails the steaks (including a $110 double-rib steak) and breathes new life into traditional side dishes. Pudding-like corn crème brûlée and the airy 'gnocchi & cheese', a clever take on mac and cheese, are terrific. High-concept desserts are best exemplified by the outstanding coffee-and-doughnuts ice cream crammed with chunks of the fritters and crowned with a miniature doughnut.

UPTOWN

Upper East Side

★ Café Sabarsky

Neue Galerie, 1048 Fifth Avenue, at 86th Street (1-212 288 0665, www.cafesabarsky.com). Subway 4, 5, 6 to 86th Street. **Open** 9am-6pm Mon, Wed; 9am-9pm Thur-Sun. **Main courses** $22. **Credit** AmEx, DC, Disc, MC, V. **Map** p406 E18 92 **Austrian/Café**

Purveyor of indulgent pastries and whipped cream-topped *einspänner* coffee for Neue Galerie patrons

Eating and Drinking on the Green

The top spots for refuelling in the city's green spaces.

New York may be the ultimate urban destination, but even the most committed metropolitan can come to crave some greenery. These are some places where you can combine eating with recharging in relatively natural surroundings.

Shake Shack.

Bryant Park Café & Grill
For listings, *see p207.*
The casual outdoor café in this convenient setting for brunch or an after-work drink has a standard American menu loaded with dishes like sweet-potato fries ($6.95) and eggs Benedict ($17). Sip a glass from the California-centric wine list while taking shade under Bryant Park's canopy of trees.

Cake&Shake
For listings, *see p197.*
Dash over to this robin's-egg-blue cart for inventive, elaborate milk shakes ($5) and cupcakes ($3) in flavours inspired by owner Gina Ojile's Minnesota dairy-country, like the Hot Tottie. There's always a vanilla shake on the menu, alongside three other daily flavours (such as salted caramel or huckleberry), and a 20-strong cupcake roster.

Little Veselka
For listings, *see p195.*
Beloved Eastern European eatery Veselka (*see p196*) opened this tiny outpost in equally minuscule First Park. The pagoda-like stand has outdoor seating, so you can sit and enjoy an early-morning plate of sweet-cheese-filled blintzes (one $5.95, two for $9.95). Come lunchtime, grab a filling Baczynski sandwich, made with sliced ham, Ukrainian salami, pickled vegetable relish and a mild Polish cheese, stuffed between two slices of fluffy potato bread ($8.95).

Cake&Shake.

Public Fare
For listings, *see p212.*
Feast on albacore tuna salad mixed with cured black olives on multigrain bread ($8.50), lemon whoopie pies ($3), and a small selection of draft beer and wine at this delightful cafe by the Public Theater. The café stays open late and for the entirety of the performances (visit publictheater.org for a schedule), so sate your hunger while listening to the Bard's banter.

Shake Shack
For listings, *see p202.*
You'll probably wait upwards of an hour to sink your teeth into a juicy burger topped with melted American cheese and a creamy special sauce (single $4.75) from celebrity chef Danny Meyer's quintessential fast-food throwback. But once you're full, the lines never seem like they were much of an inconvenience in the first place. *See p212* for a review of Shake Shack, the restaurant on the Upper West Side.

by day, this sophisticated, high-ceilinged room becomes an upscale restaurant four nights a week. Appetisers are most adventurous – the creaminess of the spätzle is a perfect base for sweetcorn, tarragon and wild mushrooms – while main course specials, such as the Wiener schnitzel tartly garnished with lingonberries, are capable yet ultimately feel like the calm before the Sturm und Drang of dessert. Try the Klimttorte, which masterfully alternates layers of hazelnut cake with chocolate.

Daniel

60 E 65th Street, between Madison & Park Avenues (1-212 288 0033, www.danielnyc.com). Subway F to Lexington Avenue-63rd Street; 6 to 68th Street-Hunter College. **Open** 5.30-11pm Mon-Sat. **3-course prix fixe** $105. **Credit** AmEx, DC, MC, V. **Map** p405 E21 (93) **French**

The revolving door off Park Avenue and the elegant, Adam Tihany-designed interior announce it: welcome to fine dining. The cuisine at Daniel Boulud's flagship is rooted in French technique, with *au courant* flourishes such as fusion elements and an emphasis on local produce. Although the seasonally changing menu always includes a few signature dishes – Boulud's black truffle and scallops in puff pastry remains a classic – it's the chef's new creations that keep the food as fresh as the decor.

Other locations Café Boulud, 20 E 76th Street, between Fifth & Madison Avenues, Upper East Side (1-212 772 2600); Bar Boulud, 1900 Broadway, between 63rd & 64th Streets, Upper West Side (1-212 595 0303); DBGB Kitchen & Bar (*see p195*).

★ Park Avenue Summer

100 E 63rd Street, between Park & Lexington Avenues (1-212 644 1900, www.parkavenyc.com). Subway F to Lexington Avenue-63rd Street. **Open** 11.30am-3pm, 5.30-10pm Mon-Thur; 11.30am-3pm, 5.30-11pm Fri; 11am-3pm, 5.30-11pm Sat; 11am-3pm, 5-9pm Sun. **Main courses** $34. **Credit** AmEx, DC, Disc, MC, V. **Map** p405 E21 (94) **American creative**

Design firm Avroko and chef Craig Koketsu conceived this ode to seasonal dining: the design, the staff uniforms and the very name (yes, it's Park Avenue Autumn, Winter and Spring too) rotates along with the menu. 'Summer' means sunny wall panels and clusters of flowers to go with the warm-weather foods. Appetisers showcase produce (baby beet salad, corn soup) and seafood (peekytoe crab salad, fluke sashimi), often mixing both with winning results, while pastry chef Richard Leach, a James Beard Award winner, dazzles with sweet confections such as moist chocolate cake and whipped mascarpone.

Upper West Side

A Voce Columbus

3rd Floor, 10 Columbus Circle, at Broadway (1-212 823 2523, www.avocerestaurant.com). Subway A, B, C, D, 1 to 59th Street-Columbus Circle. **Open** 11.30am-2.30pm, 5-10pm Mon-Wed; 11.30am-2.30pm, 5-11.30pm Thur, Fri; 11am-3pm, 5-11.30pm Sat; 11am-3pm, 5-10pm Sun. **Main courses** $27. **Credit** AmEx, Disc, MC, V. **Map** p405 D22 (95) **Italian**

Want views over Columbus Circle and the park without paying Per Se prices? A Voce's sleek new Uptown outpost also has a solid menu and impeccable service. Brick-flattened chicken, infused with roasted garlic, lemon and dried Calabrian chillies and served with tuscan kale, enormous white beans and potatoes, is a comfort-food triumph. The owner's art collection, including a massive Frank Stella mixed-media piece that hangs near the host stand, is a feast for the eyes.

★ Barney Greengrass

541 Amsterdam Avenue, between 86th & 87th Streets (1-212 724 4707, www.barneygreengrass.com). Subway B, C, 1 to 86th Street. **Open** 8.30am-4pm Tue-Fri; 8.30am-5pm Sat, Sun. **Main courses** $15. **No credit cards. Map** p406 C18 (96) **American**

Despite decor that Jewish mothers might call 'schmutzy', this legendary deli is a madhouse at breakfast and brunch. Enormous egg platters come with the usual choice of smoked fish (such as sturgeon or Nova Scotia salmon). Prices are on the high side, but portions are large, and that goes for the sandwiches too. Or try the less costly dishes: matzo-ball soup, creamy egg salad or cold pink borscht served in a glass jar.

$ Bouchon Bakery

3rd Floor, Time Warner Center, 10 Columbus Circle, at Broadway (1-212 823 9366, www.bouchonbakery.com). Subway A, B, C, D, 1 to 59th Street-Columbus Circle. **Open** 11.30am-9pm Mon-Sat; 11.30am-7pm Sun. **Pastries** $9. **Credit** AmEx, DC, MC, V. **Map** p405 D22 (97) **Café**

The appeal is obvious: sample Thomas Keller's food for a fraction of the cost of a meal at Per Se. The reality is that you will have to eat in an open café setting in the middle of a mall, under a giant Samsung sign, and choose from a limited selection of sandwiches, salads, quiches and spreadable delights (pâté, foie gras and so on). That said, this is a great place for lunch. The sandwiches are impeccably plated, although portions can be small.

▶ *For a comparison with Per Se, see p194 Diffusion Dining.*

Café Luxembourg

200 W 70th Street, between Amsterdam & West End Avenues (1-212 873 7411, www.cafeluxembourg.com). Subway B, C, 1, 2, 3 to 72nd Street. **Open** 8am-11pm Mon, Tue; 8am-midnight Wed-Fri; 9am-midnight Sat; 9am-11pm Sun. **Main courses** $27. **Credit** AmEx, DC, MC, V. **Map** p405 C20 (98) **French**

Buttermilk Channel. *See p212.*

Café Luxembourg thankfully isn't trying to be anything other than what it is – a comfortable neighbourhood bistro that makes its money successfully executing uncomplicated French-American fare. Seasonal starters and desserts punctuate a short menu of steak frites, grilled fish and crème brûlée. It all adds up to an atmosphere of relaxed elegance that keeps the local regulars (both celebrities and ordinary joes) coming back time and again.

Celeste

502 Amsterdam Avenue, between 84th & 85th Streets (1-212 874-4559). Subway 1 to 86th Street. **Open** 5-11pm Mon-Thur; 5-11.30pm Fri; noon-3.30pm, 5-11.30pm Sat; noon-3.30pm, 5-10.30pm Sun. **Main courses** $15. **No credit cards. Map** p406 C18 (99) **Italian**

This highly popular spot offers authentic fare in a country setting, and has a large fan club. It's become extremely popular, so a wait is to be expected, but you can call ahead to see how long it's likely to be. Once you're in, start with *carciofi fritti*, fried artichokes that are so light, they're evanescent. Three home-made pastas are prepared daily by chef Giancarlo Quadalti; the tagliatelle with shrimp, cabbage and pecorino stands out. Carbohydrate watchers are offered dishes like chicken cutlet with crushed almonds. Those who can manage a few more bites are advised to try the *pastiera*, a grain-and-ricotta cake flavoured with candied fruit and orange-blossom water.

Jean Georges

Trump International Hotel & Tower, 1 Central Park West, at Columbus Circle (1-212 299 3900, www.jeangeorges.com). Subway A, B, C, D, 1 to 59th Street-Columbus Circle. **Open** noon-2.30pm, 5.30-11pm Mon-Thur; noon-2.30pm, 5.15-11pm Fri; 5.15-11pm Sat. **3-course prix fixe** $98. **7-course prix fixe** $148. **Credit** AmEx, DC, MC, V. **Map** p405 D22 (100) **French**

Unlike so many of its vaunted peers, the culinary flagship of celebrated chef Jean-Georges Vongerichten has not become a shadow of itself: the top-rated food is still breathtaking. A velvety foie gras terrine with spiced fig jam was coated in a thin brûlée shell; a more ascetic dish of green asparagus with rich morels showcased the vegetables' essence. Pastry chef Johnny Iuzzini's inventive seasonal quartets, comprising four mini desserts, are always a delight. The more casual, on-site Nougatine café provides a less expensive option, but still provides a taste of its big brother.

Ouest

2315 Broadway, between 83rd & 84th Streets (1-212 580 8700, www.ouestny.com). Subway 1 to 86th Street. **Open** 5-10.30pm Mon-Thur; 5-11.30pm Fri, Sat; 5-9.30pm Sun. **Main courses** $28. **Credit** AmEx, DC, Disc, MC, V. **Map** p406 C19 (101) **American creative**

Essentially New York Burgers

The foodies' favourites.

FRANK BRUNI, FORMER NEW YORK TIMES RESTAURANT CRITIC: 'I have to say **Shake Shack** (*see p202*). This is clearly a New York success story and a New York fetish of epic proportions. The Black Label burger wouldn't be my choice, because at $28, it's a burger of the elite. It's essential to a certain subset of New York that is a very, very prominent and legendary aspect of this city, whereas the Shake Shack burger, while not inexpensive, is the people's burger.'

ANITA LO, TOP CHEF MASTERS ALUMNUS, FOUNDER OF RICKSHAW DUMPLINGS: 'For the classic burger, I like my old standby, the Bistro Burger at **Corner Bistro** (*see p197*). The meat is deliciously loose and juicy, with all my favourite garnishes – bacon, american cheese, lettuce, tomato and raw onion. And it's just a few blocks from my apartment, making it accessible, everyday and comforting – just what a classic burger should be.'

NICK SOLARES, ROVING REPORTER FOR A HAMBURGER TODAY BLOG: 'The **Shake Shack** [burger] is a good egalitarian answer. Minetta Tavern's burger is my favourite in the world, but it's not essential New York, because it's unimportant to so many New Yorkers who will never have a chance to eat it. Anybody can go to Shake Shack: it doesn't require anything more than $5 and an hour of time.'

TOM COLICCHIO, TOP CHEF STAR, FOUNDER OF CRAFT RESTAURANTS: 'The **Spotted Pig** (*see p198*) for its great beef flavour; love the blue-cheese-roast-onion combo.'

A prototypical local clientele calls chef Tom Valenti's Uptown stalwart – one of the neighbourhood's most celebrated restaurants – its local canteen. And why not? The friendly servers ferry pitch-perfect cocktails and rich, Italian-inflected cuisine from the open kitchen to immensely comfortable round red booths. Valenti adds some unexpected flourishes to the soothing formula: salmon gravadlax are served with a chick-pea pancake topped with caviar and potent mustard oil, whereas the house-smoked sturgeon presides over frisée, lardons and a poached egg.

Per Se

4th Floor, Time Warner Center, 10 Columbus Circle, at Broadway (1-212 823 9335, www.perseny.com). Subway A, B, C, D, 1 to 59th Street-Columbus Circle. **Open** 5.30-10pm Mon-Thur; 11.30am-1.30pm, 5.30-10.30pm Fri-Sun. **Main courses** (in lounge) $36. **5-course prix fixe** $175 (Fri-Sun only). **9-course tasting menu** $275. **Credit** AmEx, MC, V. **Map** p405 D22 **102** **French**

Expectations are high at Per Se – and that goes both ways. You're expected to wear the right clothes, pay a non-negotiable service charge, and pretend you aren't eating in a shopping mall. The restaurant, in turn, is expected to deliver one hell of a tasting menu for $275. And it does. Dish after dish is flawless, beginning with Thomas Keller's signature salmon tartare cone. Have you tasted steak with mashed potatoes and swiss chard, or chocolate brownies with coffee ice-cream? Possibly. Have you had them this good? Unlikely. In the end, it's worth every penny. Avoid the new à la carte option in the lounge, however, which offers miserly portions at high prices, making it less of a deal than the celebrated tasting menu in the formal dining room.

$ Public Fare
The Delacorte Theater, Central Park, enter at W 81st Street & Central Park West (1-646 747 5354, www.publicfarenyc.com). Subway B, C to 81st St–Museum of Natural History. **Open** 8am-9pm Wed-Sun; closed winter. **Main courses** $8. **No credit cards. Map** p405 D19 **103 American**
For review, *see p208* **Eating and Drinking on the Green**.

Recipe
452 Amsterdam Avenue, between 81st & 82nd Streets (1-212 501 7755, www.recipenyc.com). Subway B, C to 81st Street-Museum of Natural History; 1 to 79th Street. **Open** noon-3.30pm, 5-10.30pm Mon-Thur; noon-3.30pm, 5pm-2am Fri; 11am-3.30pm, 5pm-2am Sat; 11am-3.30pm, 5-10.30pm Sun. **Main courses** $18. **Credit** MC, V. **Map** p405 C19 **104 American**
This tiny Upper West Side restaurant would be at home among Brooklyn's beloved farm-forward eateries. Chef Shawn Dalziel executes homespun, 'locavore' (made with locally sourced ingredients) dishes with sophistication. A lush foie gras terrine was presented as a jar of duck liver in a seal of its own fat, layered over apricot-fig jam. A special of seared scallops was surrounded by tender kabocha-squash gnocchi and seasonal vegetables. The strength of the meal persisted through dessert: buttermilk panna cotta was perfumed with potent Tahitian vanilla and anointed with rooftop honey.

★ $ Shake Shack
366 Columbus Avenue, at 77th Street (1-646 747 8770, www.shakeshacknyc.com). Subway 1 to 79th Street. **Open** 10.45am-11pm daily. **Burgers** $4.75. **Credit** AmEx, Disc, MC, V. **Map** p405 C19 **105 American**
The spacious offspring of Danny Meyer's wildly popular Madison Square Park concession stand, Shake Shack gets several local critics' votes for New York's best burger. Sirloin and brisket are ground daily for the prime patties, and the franks are served Chicago-style on poppy seed buns with a 'salad' of toppings and a dash of celery salt. Frozen-custard shakes hit the spot, and there's beer and wine if you want something stronger.
Other locations Madison Square Park, 23rd Street, at Madison Avenue, Flatiron District (1-212 889 6600).
► *For other nominations for NYC's best burger, see p211 Essentially New York.*

Harlem

Amy Ruth's
113 W 116th Street, between Malcolm X Boulevard (Lenox Avenue) & Adam Clayton Powell Jr Boulevard (Seventh Avenue) (1-212 280 8779, www.amyruthsharlem.com). Subway 2, 3 to 116th Street. **Open** 11.30am-11pm Mon; 8.30am-11pm Tue-Thur, Sun; 24hrs Fri, Sat. **Main courses** $14. **No credit cards. Map** p407 D14 **106 American regional**
This perpetually packed, no-reservations spot is the place for soul food. Delicately fried okra is delivered without a hint of slime, and the mac and cheese is gooey inside and crunchy-brown on top. Dishes take their names from notable African-Americans; be patriotic and vote for the President Barack Obama (fried, smothered, baked or barbecued chicken).
► *For more about the West Harlem neighbourhood around Amy Ruth's, see p121.*

Country Panfried Chicken
2841 Frederick Douglass Boulevard (Eighth Avenue), between 151st & 152nd Streets (1-212 281 1800). Subway B, D to 155th Street. **Open** 11am-11pm Mon-Thur; 11am-1am Fri, Sat; 11am-9pm Sun. **Main courses** $13. **No credit cards. Map** p408 D10 **107 American regional**
Fried chicken has made quite the comeback, and the guru of moist flesh and crackly skin, Charles Gabriel, has also made a triumphant return to Harlem with his resurrected restaurant. In addition to the poultry, you can feast on barbecued ribs, mac and cheese, yams and other Southern favourites.

BROOKLYN

Al di là
248 Fifth Avenue, at Carroll Street, Park Slope (1-718 783 4565, www.aldilatrattoria.com). Subway M, R to Union Street. **Open** 6-10.30pm Mon; noon-3pm, 6-10.30pm Wed, Thur; noon-3pm, 6-11pm Fri; noon-3.30pm, 5.30-10.30pm Sat; noon-3.30pm, 5-10pm Sun. **Main courses** $16. **Credit** MC, V. **Map** p410 T11 **108 Italian**
A fixture on the Slope's Fifth Avenue for more than a decade, this convivial, no-reservations restaurant is still wildly popular. Affable owner Emiliano Coppa orchestrates the inevitable wait with panache. Coppa's wife, co-owner and chef Anna Klinger, produces northern Italian dishes with a Venetian slant. It would be hard to improve upon her braised rabbit with black olives atop polenta, and even simple pastas, such as the home-made tagliatelle al ragù, are superb.
Other locations Al di là vino, 607 Carroll Street, at Fifth Avenue, Park Slope, Brooklyn (1-718 783 4565).

Buttermilk Channel
524 Court Street, at Huntington Street, Carroll Gardens (1-718 852 8490, www.buttermilkchannelnyc.com). Subway F, G to Smith-9th Streets. **Open** 5-11pm Mon-Thur, Sun; 5pm-midnight Fri, Sat. **Main courses** $17. **Credit** AmEx, Disc, MC, V. **Map** p410 S11 **109 American**
This bright, charming restaurant won *Time Out New York*'s Eat Out Readers' Choice award for best new Brooklyn restaurant in 2009, and the menu

CONSUME

Fette Sau. *See p214.*

emphasises its hometown flavour. New York State dominates the taps and the wine list; and a first-rate starter layers vibrant local delicata squash with tart house-made ricotta. Comfort-food innovations also hit close to home, such as duck meat loaf, packed with caramelised onions and raisins, and one of the best sundaes around: pecan pie layered with organic butter-pecan ice-cream from nearby Blue Marble. *Photos p210.*

Dressler

149 Broadway, between Bedford & Driggs Avenues, Williamsburg (1-718 384 6343). Subway J, M, Z to Marcy Avenue. **Open** 6-11pm Mon-Thur; 6pm-midnight Fri, Sat; 11.30am-3.30pm, 5.30-10.30pm Sun. **Main courses** $22. **Credit** AmEx, MC, V. **Map** p411 U8 110 American

The team behind popular local eateries Dumont and Dumont Burger recognised that they could launch a fancier spot in a neighbourhood that already has a culinary landmark. The short menu bridges two worlds; this is a brasserie with creative American flourishes. The emphasis is on seasonal ingredients. Frankly, everything sounds good, but the star behind the fish-and-veggie-heavy appetisers has to be the produce purveyor. The chilled spring pea soup with lobster meat topping has a powerhouse broth that packs more flavour than any pea has the right to. And the crispy artichoke-and-white-bean salad is alternately crunchy, tender, hot and cold. The seared sea bass is expertly paired with a cream sauce containing a classic cockles-bacon-leek combination, while the roasted duck breast comes with sweet, braised duck leg and spicy duck sausage – an onslaught that makes each bite exciting.

★ Fette Sau

354 Metropolitan Avenue, between Havemeyer & Roebling Streets, Williamsburg (1-718 963 3404). Subway L to Lorimer Street; G to Metropolitan Avenue. **Open** 5-11pm daily. **Main courses** $15. **Credit** AmEx, Disc, MC, V. **Map** p411 U8 111 Barbecue

Communal picnic tables and gallon-size glass jugs of beer foster a casual party vibe at this cavernous former auto body shop. It ain't called 'Fat Pig' for nothing: load up on glistening cuts of beef and pork sold by the pound at the deli-style barbecue station, then mosey over to the bar to choose your poison – connoisseurs of the hard stuff will appreciate the 200-plus bourbon list. A late-night menu is often on offer at the bar after the kitchen closes. *Photo p213.*

Fort Defiance

365 Van Brunt Street, at Dikeman Street, Red Hook, Brooklyn (1-347 453 6672, http://fortdefiancebrooklyn.com). Subway F, G to Smith–9th Streets, then take the B77 bus to Dikeman and Van Brunt Streets. **Open** 7am-midnight Mon, Wed, Thur; 7am-2.30pm Tue;

The Kitchen at Brooklyn Labs.

7am-2am Fri; 8am-2am Sat; 8am-midnight sun. **Main courses** $14. **No credit cards. Map** p410 R11 **112 American**
With every meal covered, this café-bar has become Red Hook's culinary and social epicentre since opening in 2009. Breakfast – so cheap it seems subsidised – is among the best in the city: the egg sandwich (Berkshire ham, Emmentaler and fried egg on a Balthazar bun) a truly superior breed. Lunch is crowned with a muffaletta sandwich worthy of New Orleans, while dinner is subject to a changing, southern-accented menu devised by Bobby Duncan, formerly of Dylan Prime and Gramercy Tavern. The bar is always hopping, thanks to cocktails that rank among the best in the borough: the Journalist, made with gin and vermouth, is as clean and crisp as a classic Manhattan. Red Hook may be hard to reach, but at Fort Defiance there's little cause to leave.

★ The Kitchen at Brooklyn Labs

200 Schermerhorn Street, at Hoyt Street, Downtown Brooklyn (1-718 243 0050). Subway A, C, G to Hoyt–Schermerhorn; B, N, Q, R to DeKalb Ave; 2, 3 to Hoyt St; 2, 3, 4, 5 to Nevins Street. **Open** *One seating* 7pm Tue-Sat. **Prix fixe** $115. **Credit** AmEx, MC, V. **Map** p410 T10 **113** **Eclectic**
Chef César Ramirez spends his days preparing delicase items at the Brooklyn Fare supermarket – and one luxurious, 15-course meal in the store's kitchen each night, which is some of New York's best small-plate cuisine. The dinner-party vibe is convivial: Diners perch on stools around a prep table, the menu changes daily, and wine is BYOB. A Kumamoto oyster reclines on crème fraîche and *yuzu gelée*; halibut is served in a miraculous broth of dashi and summer truffles. For dessert: an airy parfait layering mango mousse, coconut froth, candied cashews and rum-soaked brioche.

Marlow & Sons

81 Broadway, between Berry Street & Whythe Avenue, Williamsburg (1-718 384 1441, www.marlowandsons.com). Subway J, M, Z to Marcy Avenue. **Open** 8am-midnight daily. **Main courses** $20. **Credit** AmEx, MC, V. **Map** p411 U8 **114 American creative**
This popular place serves as an old-time oyster bar, quaint general store and daytime café. Seated in the charming front-room shop, diners survey the gourmet olive oils and honeys while wolfing down market-fresh salads, succulent brick chicken and the creative crostini of the moment (such as goat's cheese with flash-fried strawberries). In the back room, an oyster shucker cracks open the catch of the day, while the bartender mixes the kind of potent drinks that helped to make the owners' earlier ventures (including next-door Diner, a tricked-out 1920s dining car) successes.

★ Peter Luger

178 Broadway, at Driggs Avenue, Williamsburg (1-718 387 7400, www.peterluger.com). Subway J, M, Z to Marcy Avenue. **Open** 11.45am-10pm Mon-Thur; 11.45am-11pm Fri, Sat; 12.45-10pm Sun. **Steak for two** $85. **No credit cards. Map** p411 U8 **115 Steakhouse**
At Luger's old-school steakhouse, the choice is limited, but the porterhouse is justly famed. Choose from various sizes, from a small single steak to 'steak for four'. Although a slew of Luger copycats have prospered in the last several years, none has captured the elusive charm of this stucco-walled, beer-hall-style eaterie, with worn wooden floors and tables, and waiters in waistcoats and bow ties.

Roberta's

261 Moore Street, between Bogart & White Streets, Bushwick, Brooklyn (1-718 417 1118). Subway L to Morgan Avenue. **Open** noon-midnight Mon-Fri; 11am-midnight Sat, Sun. **Average pizza** $12. **No credit cards. Map** p411 W8 **116 Italian**
Buzzing with urban-farming fund-raisers, local brewers pouring their ales and food-world luminaries fresh off interviews at the indie Heritage Radio station, this sprawling hangout has become the unofficial meeting place for Brooklyn's sustainable-food movement. Opened in 2008 by a trio of friends, Roberta's features its own rooftop garden, a food-focused Internet-radio station and a kitchen that turns out excellent, locally sourced dishes, such as

delicate bibb lettuce with red-cherry vinaigrette or linguine carbonara made with lamb pancetta. It also doesn't hurt that the pizzas – like the Cheesus Christ, topped with mozzarella, Taleggio, Parmesan, black pepper and cream – are among Brooklyn's finest.

Rye

247 South 1st Street, between Havemeyer & Roebling Streets, Williamsburg (1-718 218 8047, www.ryerestaurant.com). Subway L to Bedford Avenue. **Open** 6-11.30pm Mon-Thur, Sun; 6pm-midnight Fri, Sat. **Main courses** $18. **Credit** AmEx, Disc, MC, V. **Map** p411 U8 **117 American**

The whiff of the hipster is undeniable – note the turn-of-the-20th-century decor and signless exterior – but this American bistro is unexpectedly egalitarian. The food is delicious and affordable: one starter featured grilled sardines over zingy preserved tomatoes on a slice of country bread. A butter-poached lobster special arrived with citrusy corn salsa, sweet corn flan and avocado mousse. Cocktails, meanwhile, feature both classic and original concoctions worthy of the antique setting.

Vinegar Hill House

72 Hudson Avenue, between Front & Water Streets, Dumbo (1-718 522 1018, www.vinegarhillhouse.com). Subway A, C to High Street; F to York Street. **Open** 6-11pm Mon-Thur; 11am-3.30pm, 6-11.30pm Sat; 11am-3.30pm, 5.30-11pm Sun. **Main courses** $16. **Credit** AmEx, Disc, MC, V. **Map** p411 T9 **118 American**

As it's hidden in a residential street in the forgotten namesake neighbourhood (now essentially part of Dumbo), tracking down Vinegar Hill House engenders a treasure-hunt thrill. Chef and co-owner Jean Adamson, who worked at equally tucked-away Lower East Side success story Freemans, offers a weekly changing comfort-food menu. A tender butternut-squash tart with robust farmstead blue cheese was made memorable by golden, flaky pastry; wispy ribbons of pappardelle were coated with a sweet rabbit-and-bacon ragù.

► *For a review of Freemans, see p191.*

QUEENS

$ Jackson Diner

37-47 74th Street, between 37th Avenue & 37th Road, Jackson Heights (1-718 672 1232, www.jacksondiner.com). Subway E, F, M, R to Jackson Heights-Roosevelt Avenue; 7 to 74th Street-Broadway. **Open** 11.30am-10pm Mon-Thur, Sun; 11.30am-10.30pm Fri, Sat. **Main courses** $13. **Credit** AmEx, DC, Disc, MC, V. **Map** p412 Y5 **119 Indian**

Harried waiters and Formica-topped tables complete the diner experience at this weekend meet-and-eat headquarters for New York's Indian expat community. Watch Hindi soaps on Zee TV while enjoying *samosa chat* topped with chick peas, yoghurt, onion, tomato, and a sweet-spicy mix of tamarind and mint chutneys. Specials such as *murgh tikka makhanwala*, tender pieces of marinated chicken simmered in curry and cream, are fiery and flavourful – ask for mild if you're not immune to potent chillies.

► *For more on Little India, see p141.*

Mezzo-Mezzo

31-29 Ditmars Boulevard, at 33rd Street, Astoria (1-718 278 0444, mezzomezzony.com). Subway N, Q to Astoria–Ditmars Boulevard. **Open** 11am-midnight Mon-Fri, Sun; 11am-1am Sat. **Main courses** $18. **Credit** AmEx, Disc, MC, V. **Map** p412 X3 **120 Greek**

This taverna beckons with a stone-walled rustic atmosphere and service befitting much pricier joints. Belly dancers and Middle Eastern musicians add weekend bounce. Even more uplifting is the chef's instinct for Greek standards and Mediterranean classics. Lemony stuffed squid oozes with herbed feta; lamb kebabs flaunt hunks of deftly grilled meat; and garlic-tossed seafood pasta is studded with shrimp, squid, clams and salmon, all cooked to tender perfection. Mezzo-mezzo might mean 'half and half', but this place gets the whole Hellenic taverna thing right.

★ $ Sripraphai

64-13 39th Avenue, between 64th & 65th Streets, Woodside (1-718 899 9599, www.sripraphairestaurant.com). Subway 7 to 61st Street-Woodside. **Open** 11.30am-9.30pm Mon, Tue, Thur-Sun. **Main courses** $10. **No credit cards**. **Map** p412 Y5 **121 Thai**

Woodside's destination eaterie offers distinctive, traditional dishes such as catfish salad or green curry with beef: a thick, piquant broth filled out with roasted Thai eggplant. The dining areas, which sprawl over two levels and a garden (open in summer), are packed with lip-smacking Manhattanites who can be seen eyeing the plates enjoyed by the Thai regulars, mentally filing away what to order the next time.

Zenon Taverna

34-10 31st Avenue, at 34th Street, Astoria (1-718 956 0133, www.zenontaverna.com). Subway N, Q to Broadway. **Open** 11am-11pm daily. **Main courses** $14. **No credit cards**. **Map** p412 W4 **122 Greek**

The faux-stone entryway and murals of ancient ruins don't detract from the Mediterranean charm of this humble place that's been serving Greek and Cypriot food for more than 20 years. The broad menu rotates daily, embracing all the classics – stuffed vine leaves, *keftedes* (Cypriot meatballs), *spanakopita* (spinach pie) – and less ubiquitous dishes such as rabbit stew and plump *loukaniko* (pork sausages). Filling sweets, such as *galaktopoureko* (syrupy layers of filo baked with custard cream), merit a taste, if your stomach isn't already bursting.

Bars

The city that never sleeps has a bar to slake every thirst.

Sophisticated wine bars, subterranean dives, faux speakeasies, rooftop havens, whiskey joints, fastidious cocktail lounges, gastropubs, old-school taverns, artisanal beer gardens – just choosing your watering hole can be more difficult than choosing a drink once you get there. Location, location, location generally influences most choices, with the downtown 'hoods of Tribeca, Soho, the Lower East Side and the East Village traditionally luring most drinkers. However, in the last few years, Brooklyn – particularly Williamsburg – has thrown down the gauntlet as a major drinking destination, and even the most dyed-in-the-wool Manhattanites have found themselves crossing the river to gawk at the range of microbrews at **Spuyten Duyvil** or to sample the sumptuous cocktails at the **Huckleberry Bar**.

The drinking scene evolves like the city, but it's always worth checking out some of the classic New York bars, like the art deco **Lenox Lounge** in Harlem or the muralled **Bemelmans Bar** on the Upper East Side, for a glimpse of the city's cosmopolitan tippling past.

DOWNTOWN

Tribeca & Soho

B Flat

277 Church Street, at White Street (1-212 219 2970, www.bflat.info). Subway 1 to Franklin Street. **Open** 5pm-2am Mon-Wed; 5pm-3am Thur-Sat; 5pm-1am Sun. **Average drink** $12. **Credit** AmEx, DC, MC, V. **Map** p402 E31 ❶

Slink underground to this red-lit rathskeller for Far East-influenced potions, such as the Groovy (shiso-infused vodka and yuzu juice) or the Giant Steps (wasabi-infused vodka and saké). Couples take to the booths for the delectable Japanese nibbles – scallop carpaccio, or sautéed shrimp with anchovy garlic sauce, for example.

M1-5

52 Walker Street, between Broadway & Church Street (1-212 965 1701, www.m1-5.com). Subway J, M, N, Q, R, Z, 6 to Canal Street. **Open** 4pm-4am Mon-Fri; 8pm-4am Sat; 11am-midnight Sun. **Average drink** $9. **Credit** AmEx, DC, Disc, MC, V. **Map** p402 E31 ❷

The name of this huge, red-walled hangout refers to Tribeca's zoning ordinance, which permits trendy restaurants to coexist with warehouses. The mixed-use concept also applies to M1-5's crowd: suited brokers, indie musicians and baby-faced screenwriters play pool and order from the full, well-stocked bar specialising in stiff martinis.

★ Pegu Club

77 W Houston Street, at West Broadway (1-212 473 7348, www.peguclub.com). Subway B, D, F to Broadway-Lafayette Street; N, R to Prince Street. **Open** 5pm-2am Mon-Wed, Sun; 5pm-3am Thur; 5pm-4am Fri, Sat. **Average drink** $15. **Credit** AmEx, Disc, MC, V. **Map** p403 E29 ❸

Audrey Saunders, the drinks maven who turned Bemelmans Bar (*see p225*) into one of the city's most respected cocktail lounges, is behind this sleek liquid destination. It has just the right element of secrecy without any awkward faux-speakeasy trickery. Tucked away on the second floor, this sophisticated spot was inspired by a British officers' club in Burma. The cocktail list features classics culled from decades-old booze bibles. Gin is the key ingredient; these are serious drinks for grown-up tastes.

❶ Green numbers given in this chapter correspond to the location of each bar on the street maps. *See pp404-412.*

THE BEST BARS WITH GARDENS

For vintage class
Soda Bar. *See p229.*

For rickety-dive charm
Bohemian Hall & Beer Garden. *See p229.*

For art deco perfection
d.b.a. *See p219.*

Pravda

281 Lafayette Street, between E Houston & Prince Streets (1-212 226 4944, www.pravdany.com). Subway B, D, F to Broadway–Lafayette Street; N, R to Prince Street; 6 to Spring Street. **Open** 5pm-1am Mon-Wed; 5pm-2am Thur; 5pm-3am Fri, Sat; 6pm-1am Sun. **Average drink** $23. **Credit** AmEx, MC, V. **Map** p403 F29 ❹

The staircase opens into a cavernous subterranean brasserie that recalls a Cold War-era movie set – cement ceiling, stainless-steel toilet seats, all in a Keith McNally style. Chic couples and the Soho working class sit in curved red banquettes and leather armchairs, sipping colorful martinis and sampling Soviet snacks like spinach-and-cheese piroshki and smoked sturgeon scattered with dill and a dollop of crème fraîche. Caviar is, of course, found in various guises, including a Wolfgang Puck-like application atop smoked-salmon pizza. The White Russian profiteroles, made with Kahlúa ice cream, are hard to say *nyet* to.

Lower East Side

Back Room

102 Norfolk Street, between Delancey & Rivington Streets (1-212 228 5098). Subway F, J, M, Z to Delancey-Essex Streets. **Open** 7.30pm-3am Tue-Thur, Sun; 7.30pm-4am Fri, Sat. **Average drink** $9. **Credit** AmEx, DC, MC, V. **Map** p403 G30 ❺

For access to this ersatz speakeasy, look for a sign that reads 'The Lower East Side Toy Company'. Pass through the gate, walk down an alleyway, up a metal staircase and open an unmarked door to find a convincing replica of a 1920s watering hole. Cocktails are poured into teacups, and bottled beer is brown-bagged before being served. A trick bookcase leads to the real 'back room', a VIP-only lounge. Patrons must be 25 or older on Fridays and Saturdays.

Botanica

47 E Houston Street, between Mott & Mulberry Streets (1-212 343 7251). Subway B, D, F to Broadway-Lafayette Street; 6 to Bleecker Street. **Open** 5pm-4am Mon-Fri; 6pm-4am Sat, Sun. **Average drink** $5. **Credit** AmEx, DC, Disc, MC, V. **Map** p403 F29 ❻

The thrift-store decor (mismatched chairs with sagging seats, statues of the Virgin Mary and a faux fireplace) makes for a charmingly shabby backdrop at this Downtown dive, a favourite among laid-back creative types and the occasional gaggle of NYU students. Libations range from basic brews (eight on tap) to house cocktails such as the Mean Bean martini, made with vodka and spicy green beans from Rick's Picks. DJs spin every night (except Monday), providing a sultry soundtrack for the singles lounging in the conversation-friendly back room.

Happy Ending Lounge

302 Broome Street, between Eldridge & Forsyth Streets (1-212 334 9676, www.happyendinglounge.com). Subway B, D to Grand Street; J, M, Z to Bowery. **Open** 10pm-4am Tue; 7pm-4am Wed-Sat. **Average drink** $8. **Credit** AmEx, DC, MC, V. **Map** p403 F30 ❼

The racy name refers to *that* kind of happy ending – the two-storey space was once home to a massage parlour that went all the way. Traces of its sordid past remain (shower knobs poking out from the walls), but these days the only lubricants on the premises are cocktails – try the spicy, frothy Mr Ginger, made with ginger ale and house-infused ginger vodka.

Loreley

7 Rivington Street, between Bowery & Chrystie Street (1-212 253 7077, www.loreleynyc.com). Subway J, M, Z to Bowery. **Open** noon-1am Mon, Tue, Sun; noon-2am Wed, Thur; noon-4am Fri, Sat. **Average drink** $9. **Credit** AmEx, DC, Disc, MC, V. **Map** p403 F30 ❽

Perhaps bar owner Michael Momm, aka DJ Foosh, wanted a place where he could spin to his heart's content. Maybe he missed the *biergartens* of his youth in Cologne. Whatever. Just rejoice that he opened Loreley. Twelve draughts and eight bottled varieties of Germany's finest brews are available, along with wines from the country's Loreley region and a full roster of spirits. Avoid drinking the fearsome schnapps straight; sample it in the Black German instead, a combination of blackberry schnapps, vodka and champagne served in a martini glass.

★ Spitzer's Corner

101 Rivington Street, at Ludlow Street (1-212 228 0027, www.spitzerscorner.com). Subway F to Delancey Street; J, M, Z to Delancey-Essex Streets. **Open** 4pm-3am Mon, Tue; 4pm-4am Wed, Thur; noon-4am Fri; 10am-4am Sat; 10am-3am Sun. **Average drink** $7. **Credit** AmEx, MC, V. **Map** p403 G29 ❾

Referencing the Lower East Side's pickle-making heritage, the walls at this rustic gastropub are made from salvaged wooden barrels. The formidable beer list – 40 ever-rotating draughts – includes

Bear Republic's fragrant Racer 5 IPA. Mull over your selection, with the help of appetising tasting notes, at one of the wide communal tables. The gastro end of things is manifest in the menu of quality pub grub – pan-seared foie gras, for example, or panko-encrusted asparagus.

East Village

★ Angel's Share

8 Stuyvesant Street, between Second & Third Avenues (1-212 777 5415). Subway L to Third Ave; N, R to 8th Street–NYU; 6 to Astor Place. **Open** 6pm-1.30am Mon-Wed, Sun; 6pm-2am Thur; 6pm-2.30am Fri, Sat. **Average drink** $8. **Credit** AmEx, DC, Disc, MC, V. **Map** p403 F28 ⑩

Walk through an unmarked side door at the front of Japanese restaurant Village Yokocho, and you'll find yourself in perhaps the classiest joint to be found in the East Village. Angel's Share still remains completely unknown to some of its neighbours; that duality is part of its charm. Standing around and groups of four or more are not allowed – but this is primarily the sort of place to take a date anyway, offering a stellar view of Stuyvesant Square, tuxedoed bartenders and excellent cocktails, including one of the city's best grasshoppers.

Blue Owl

196 Second Avenue, between 12th & 13th Streets (1-212 505 2583, www.blueowlnyc.com). Subway L to First or Third Avenue. **Open** 5pm-2am Mon-Wed, Sun; 5pm-4am Thur-Sat. **Average drink** $10. **Credit** AmEx, MC, V. **Map** p403 F28 ⑪

Creatures of the night come to perch at this subterranean bar, where the lights are low, the patrons well heeled and the drinks properly stiff. Stake out one of the stylish pressed-tin tables, nibble on house-marinated olives and sip a Blue Owl – a sultry mix of Miller's gin, maraschino liqueur and lemon juice.

Bourgeois Pig

111 E 7th Street, between First Avenue & Avenue A (1-212 475 2246, www.bourgeoispigny.com). Subway F to Lower East Side-Second Avenue; 6 to Astor Place. **Open** 6pm-2am daily. **Average drink** $12. **Credit** AmEx, DC, MC, V. **Map** p403 F28 ⑫

Ornate mirrors and antique chairs give this small, red-lit wine and fondue joint a decidedly decadent feel. The wine list is well chosen, and although the hard stuff is verboten here, mixed concoctions based on wine, champagne or beer – such as the thick Flip, or the Tannat, featuring egg, strawberry, tannat and heavy cream – cater to cocktail aficionados.

★ d.b.a

41 First Avenue, between 2nd & 3rd Streets (1-212 475 5097, www.drinkgoodstuff.com). Subway F to Lower East Side–Second Avenue. **Open** 1pm-4am daily. **Average drink** $7.**Credit** AmEx, MC, V. **Map** p403 F29 ⑬

Though this East Village bar is held hostage by fraternity types at weekends, there's plenty of elbow

CONSUME

Spitzer's Corner.

room among the locals during the week. It's a beer-lover's mecca – 250 brews (20 on tap), from the expensive (a Belgian *kriek*, or sour-cherry beer, goes for $25 per bottle) to the unpronounceable (Schlenkerla Rauchbier). Paralyzed by indecision? Think it over in the back garden (it's open year-round).

Death & Company

433 E 6th Street, between First Avenue & Avenue A (1-212 388 0882, www.deathandcompany.com). Subway F to Lower East Side-Second Avenue; 6 to Astor Place. **Open** 6pm-1am Mon-Thur, Sun; 6pm-2am Fri, Sat. **Average drink** $13. **Credit** AmEx, MC, V. **Map** p403 F28 ⓮

The nattily attired mixologists at Death & Company are deadly serious about drinks at this pseudo speakeasy with gothic flair (don't be intimidated by the imposing wooden door). Black walls and cushy booths combine with chandeliers to set the luxuriously sombre mood. Patrons bored by the

The Sky's the Limit

Rise above it all at these rooftop lounges.

Bookmarks Rooftop Lounge.

After a day of pounding the pavement and gawking at the skyscrapers, there's nothing like taking in some booze with views.

Dig out your cravat when hitting the **Bookmarks Rooftop Lounge** (299 Madison Avenue, at 41st Street, 14th floor, 1-212 204 5498, www.hospitalityholdings.com) at the **Library Hotel** (*see p175*). Not only is this upscale, literary-themed bar intolerant of athletic attire, you'll also want to look the part when quoting Dostoyevsky in a wicker chair in one of two greenhouses or on the outdoor terrace. Order a Hemingway Cocktail with aged rum, lime juice, mint and champagne ($13.50), dig into the book collection, and let your imagination soar.

While the music pounds downstairs, the rooftop at the **Delancey** (168 Delancey Street, between Attorney & Clinton Streets, 1-212 254 9920, www.thedelancey.com) offers a palm-studded oasis with white chaise longues and a fountain. On Wednesdays, an all-you-can-eat barbecue for $5 packs them in, but on Saturdays between 10pm and 1am the spot is virtually shut down with large group reservations. Head there before or after to enjoy the $8 frozen margaritas.

Among the swanky midtown rooftop set, **Mé Bar** (17 W 32nd Street, between Fifth and Sixth Avenues, 14th floor, 1-212 290 2460, www.mebarnyc.com) is a refreshing oddity, serving reasonably priced drinks on a plain patio above the La Quinta hotel with no doorman to negotiate. The view may not be anything special, but the Empire State Building towering above you certainly is.

Boasting stunning views of the towering Chrysler and Empire State Buildings, the **Rare Bar and Grill** (303 Lexington Avenue, at 37th Street, 16th floor, 1-212 481 8439, www.rarebarandgrill.com) draws in an after-work crowd with DJs and dancing every Wednesday and Thursday. The tiled terrace with strings of lights make it a delightful spot when the sun goes down, and it never feels oppressively stylish as the pricey drinks are served in plastic cups.

city's shot-and-beer bars can sample the inventive cocktails as well as top-notch food, which includes bacon-swaddled filet mignon bites.

Elsa

217 E 3rd Street, between Avenues B & C (1-917 882 7395). Subway F to Lower East Side-Second Avenue. **Open** 6pm-2am Mon-Thur, Sun; 6pm-4am Fri, Sat. **Average drink** $10. **Credit** AmEx, MC, V. **Map** p403 G29 ⑮

At this stylish boîte, named for the iconoclastic 1930s clothing designer Elsa Schiaparelli, nods to couture include framed fashion sketches and three tap lines that flow through a vintage sewing machine. White wooden banquettes are the sole perches from which to enjoy speciality cocktails such as the Earhart (rye, St Germain, lemon and cloves).

★ Mayahuel

304 E 6th Street, between First & Second Avenues (1-212 253 5888). Subway F to Lower East Side-Second Avenue; 6 to Astor Place. **Open** 6pm-2am Mon-Sat; 11am-4pm, 6pm-2am Sun. **Average drink** $13. **Credit** AmEx, MC, V. **Map** p403 F28 ⑯

Barkeep Phil Ward focuses on tequila and its cousin, mescal, at this haute cantina. His wonderful menu features cool-as-marble Cinquenta Cinquenta – a pairing of chamomile-infused *reposado* tequila and white vermouth that goes down like iced tea. The Slynx cocktail is a liquid campfire of aged tequila, applejack, bitters and a smoky rinse of mescal. The craftsmanship in the drinks is equalled in the bar menu, featuring juicy pork bellies. Despite its many strengths, Mayahuel wears its ambitions lightly. With so many of today's top-tier cocktail bars lousy with vanity, that humility is entirely welcome.

Mayahuel.

★ PDT

113 St Marks Place, between First Avenue & Avenue A (1-212 614 0386). Subway L to First Avenue; 6 to Astor Place. **Open** 6pm-2am Mon-Thur, Sun; 6pm-4am Fri, Sat. **Average drink** $14. **Credit** AmEx, MC, V. **Map** p403 F28 ⑰

Word has got out about 'Please Don't Tell', the faux speakeasy inside gourmet hot dog joint Crif Dogs (*see p193*), so it's a good idea to reserve a booth in advance. Once you arrive, you'll notice people lingering outside an old wooden phonebooth near the front. Slip inside, pick up the receiver and the host opens a secret panel to the dark, narrow space. The serious cocktails surpass the gimmicky entry: try the house old-fashioned, made with bacon-infused bourbon, which leaves a smoky aftertaste.

Summit Bar

133 Avenue C, between 8th & 9th Streets (no phone, www.thesummitbar.net). Subway L to First Avenue; 6 to Astor Place. **Open** 5.30pm-3am Mon, Sun; 5.30pm-4am Tue-Sat. **Average drink** $11. **Credit** AmEx, MC, V. **Map** p403 G28 ⑱

In a rebuttal to the clandestine posturing that defines the city's cocktail revival, no secret buzzer is needed to enter this democratic lounge. Opened by Greg Seider, the mixologist who designed Minetta Tavern's cocktails, it is a handsome space with blue-velvet banquettes, a black-granite bar and chandeliers turned low. The drinks are presented in two categories: 'Classic' features spot-on standards, including an old-fashioned owing its peppery kick to Rittenhouse Rye, and a whiskey sour bright with fresh lemon juice; while 'Alchemist' highlights Seider's creative impulses. *Photo p222.*

Terroir

413 E 12th Street, between First Avenue & Avenue A (no phone, www.wineisterroir.com). Subway L to First Avenue; L, N, Q, R, 4, 5, 6 to 14th Street-Union Square. **Open** 5pm-2am Mon-Sat; 5pm-midnight Sun. **Average drink** $13. **Credit** AmEx, DC, MC, V. **Map** p403 F28 ⑲

The surroundings are stripped-back basic at this wine-bar offspring of nearby restaurant Hearth – the focus is squarely on the drinks. Co-owner and oeno-evangelist Paul Grieco preaches the powers of *terroir* – grapes that express a sense of place –

Summit Bar. See p221.

and the knowledgeable waitstaff deftly helps patrons to navigate approximately 45 by-the-glass options. Pair the stellar sips with their restaurant-calibre small plates.

Greenwich Village

124 Rabbit Club

124 MacDougal Street, between Bleecker & W 3rd Streets (1-212 254 0575). Subway A, B, C, D, E, F to W 4th Street. **Open** 6pm-2am Mon-Thur; 6pm-4am Fri, Sat. **Average drink** $8. **No credit cards. Map** p403 E29 (20)

European suds get the speakeasy treatment at this murky, unmarked cellar that could double as an S&M dungeon with its coarse brick walls and votives sheathed in broken bottles. Serious beer geeks can sample 70-odd imported quaffs at the brass bar, such as the tart Belgian ale Rodenbach. Be sure to visit the loo: appropriately, it features a recreation of Brussels' legendary peeing-boy statue.

Vol de Nuit Bar (aka Belgian Beer Bar)

148 W 4th Street, between Sixth Avenue & MacDougal Street (1-212 982 3388, www.voldenuitbar.com). Subway A, B, C, D, E, F to W 4th Street. **Open** 4pm-midnight Mon-Wed; 4pm-1am Thur; 4pm-2.30am Fri, Sat; 4pm-11.30pm Sun. **Credit** AmEx, DC, Disc, MC, V. **Map** p403 E29 (21)

Duck through an unmarked doorway on a busy stretch of West 4th Street and find yourself in a red-walled Belgian bar that serves brews exclusively from the motherland. Clusters of European grad students knock back glasses of De Konick and La Chouffe, just two of 13 beers on tap and 17 by the bottle. Moules and frites are the only eats.

West Village & Meatpacking District

★ Employees Only

510 Hudson Street, between Christopher & W 10th Streets (1-212 242 3021, www.employeesonlynyc.com). Subway 1 to Christopher Street-Sheridan Square. **Open** 6pm-4am daily. **Average drink** $13. **Credit** AmEx, MC, V. **Map** p403 D29 (22)

This Prohibition-themed bar cultivates an exclusive vibe, but there's no cover and no trouble at the door. Pass by the palm reader in the window (it's a front) and you'll find an amber-lit art deco interior where formality continues to flourish: servers wear custom-designed frocks and bartenders don waitstaff whites. The real stars are cocktails such as the West Side, a lethal mix of lemon vodka, lemon juice, mint and club soda.

Highlands

150-152 W 10th Street, between Greenwich Avenue & Waverly Place (1-212 229-2670). Subway A, C, E, B, D, F to W 4th Street. **Open** 6pm-2am Mon-Thur; 5pm-3am Fri; 11am-3am Sat, Sun. **Average drink** $10. **Credit** AmEx, MC, V. **Map** p403 D28 (23)

This buzzing barroom marks the overdue arrival of a stylish Scottish tavern in NYC. The look is urban drawing room: furnishings include stag heads, and the charming staff sports tartan ties. Scotch is the thing – sip from a collection of 100 whiskeys, or try one of the smart cocktails, which provide a perfect introduction to the spirit. You'll like the citrusy Blood and Sand, made with 12-year-old Highland Park, Cherry Heering, orange juice and bitters. It's worth bringing an appetite for the gastropub fare, too: lamb sausage rolls with *harissa aioli* make for a topflight drinking snack.

★ Little Branch

20 Seventh Avenue South, at Leroy Street (1-212 929 4360). Subway 1 to Houston Street. **Open** 7pm-3am daily. **Average drink** $13. **No credit cards. Map** p403 D29 (24)

Sasha Petraske's members-only Lower East Side bar, Milk & Honey (134 Eldridge Street, between Broome & Delancey Streets, www.mlkhny.com), may require a referral, but Little Branch, his clubby, low-ceilinged Village rathskeller, retains an open-door policy. As befits Petraske's liquid legacy, the drinks – such as a velvety-smooth, mildly spiced hot buttered rum – are nigh perfect. If you choose to deviate from the menu, just give the neatly attired, polite bartenders a base liquor and a hint of your mood, and they can tailor a drink on the fly.

► *Sasha Petraske's reach has extended to Queens with cocktail bar Dutch Kills* *(see p229).*

Otheroom

143 Perry Street, between Greenwich & Washington Streets (1-212 645 9758, www.the otheroom.com). Subway 1 to Christopher Street-Sheridan Square. **Open** 5pm-2am Mon, Sun; 5pm-4am Tue-Sat. **Average drink** $7. **Credit** AmEx, DC, Disc, MC, V. **Map** p403 D28 25

This gallery moonlights as a lounge, where a civilised crowd drinks amid the work of up-and-coming artists. You won't find any hard liquor, but rather a (fittingly) well-curated selection of New World wines by the glass. Those more given to hops can choose among 50 microbrews (ten taps, 40 bottles) while mulling over the changing art display.

Other locations Anotheroom, 249 West Broadway, between Ericsson Place & Walker Street, Tribeca (1-212 226 1418); Room, 144 Sullivan Street, between Houston & Prince Streets, Soho (1-212 477 2102).

Rusty Knot

425 West Street, at 11th Street (1-212 645 5668). Subway 1 to Christopher Street-Sheridan Square. **Open** 4pm-4am Mon-Fri; noon-4am Sat, Sun. **Average drink** $10. **Credit** AmEx, MC, V. **Map** p403 C28 26

This Hudson River-hugging nautical 'dive bar' from Taavo Somer (Freemans) and Ken Friedman (the Spotted Pig) is a confusing, but successful, high-low hybrid. Faux Tiffany lamps and neon beer signs clash with the elaborate tiki cocktails (devised by Milk & Honey vet Toby Maloney), and with the foppish hordes who queue up outside the place. You'd never find the eponymous Rusty Knot – a refreshing, blender-whirred mix of rum, ice and mint – or food such as a luxe bacon and chicken liver sandwich at a grimy pub. But you would find three-buck pints of Busch and 50¢ rounds of pool. Happily, the Knot has those bases covered too.

MIDTOWN

Chelsea

Half King

505 W 23rd Street, between Tenth & Eleventh Avenues (1-212 462 4300, www.thehalfking.com). Subway C, E to 23rd Street. **Open** 11am-4am Mon-Fri; 9am-4am Sat, Sun. **Average drink** $9. **Credit** MC, V. **Map** p404 C26 27

Don't let their blasé appearance fool you – the creative types gathered at the Half King's yellow pine bar are probably as excited as you are to catch a glimpse of the part-owner, author Sebastian Junger. While you're waiting, order one of the 14 draught beers – which include Lagunitas, IPA and a cloudy *hefeweizen* – or a speciality cocktail (try the Parisian: Hendrick's Gin, sauvignon blanc and elderflower liquor).

Tillman's

165 W 26th Street, between Sixth & Seventh Avenues (1-212 627 8320, www.tillmansnyc.com). Subway F, 1 to 23rd Street. **Open** 5pm-2am Mon-Wed; 5pm-4am Thur, Fri; 7pm-4am Sat. **Average drink** $12. **Credit** AmEx, DC, MC, V. **Map** p404 D26 28

Sepia images of jazz, funk and soul legends line the walls at this warm, earth-toned cocktail emporium. Waitresses glide amid crescent-shaped leather booths, and it's likely that you'll hear Coltrane oozing from the speakers – if not live music, which is on tap Wednesdays and Thursdays. Given the old-fashioned aesthetic, a classic cocktail is the way to go: try a well-crafted negroni or a bracing dark & stormy (dark rum, ginger beer and lime juice).

Flatiron District & Union Square

Cibar

56 Irving Place, between 17th & 18th Streets (1-212 460 5656). Subway L, N, Q, R, 4, 5, 6 to 14th Street-Union Square. **Open** 5pm-1am Mon, Tue, Sun; 5pm-2am Fri, Sat. **Average drink** $13. **Credit** AmEx, MC, V. **Map** p403 F27 29

Socialising at this bar beneath the posh Inn at Irving Place makes even jeans-clad tipplers feel swishy. Everything here is plush: pink walls, sleek black couches and modern chandeliers, not to mention the sharp-looking group of post-work revellers. The speciality here is elegant cocktails, like an elderflower, vodka and lychee martini. DJs spin nightly (except Monday), and there's a small, smoking-permitted backyard patio outfitted with bamboo and cushioned benches.

Flatiron Lounge

37 W 19th Street, between Fifth & Sixth Avenues (1-212 727 7741, www.flatironlounge.com). Subway F, N, R to 23rd Street. **Open** 5pm-2am

INSIDE TRACK
WHERE THERE'S SMOKE

Despite the strict city-wide smoking ban, you can still indulge your habit in establishments that could prove a percentage of their income came from selling tobacco products when the ban was enforced. Among them are **Circa Tabac** (32 Watts Street, between Sixth Avenue & Thompson Street, Soho, 1-212 941 1781, www.circatabac.com) and **Hudson Bar & Books** (636 Hudson Street, at Horatio Street, 1-212 229 2642, www.barandbooks.cz), which also has a smoke-friendly Upper East Side location (1020 Lexington Avenue, at 73rd Street, 1-212 717 3902).

Mon-Wed, Sun; 5pm-3am Thur; 5pm-4am Fri, Sat. **Average drink** $13. **Credit** AmEx, MC, V. **Map** p403 E27 30

Red leather booths, mahogany tables and globe-shaped lamps amp up the vintage vibe at this art deco space. Julie Reiner's notable mixology skills have made the bar a destination, and her Beijing Peach (jasmine-infused vodka and white peach purée) is not to be missed. The 30ft bar, built in 1927, stays packed well into the wee hours.

Raines Law Room

48 W 17th Street, between Fifth & Sixth Avenues (no phone). Subway F to 14th Street; L to Sixth Avenue. **Open** 5pm-2am Mon-Thur; 5pm-3am Fri; 7pm-3am Sat; 8pm-2am Sun. **Average drink** $13. **Credit** AmEx, MC, V. **Map** p403 E27 31

There's no bar to belly up to at this louche lounge. In deference to its name (which refers to an 1896 law designed to curb liquor consumption), drinks are prepared in a half-hidden back room. While this reduces the noise level in the plush, upholstered space, it robs you of the opportunity to watch the barkeep at work. The cocktail list includes classics such as the manhattan and negroni, and variations thereof. The Gold Rush, a honey-and-lemon-laced bourbon drink, tastes like a delectable cold remedy, while the Old Cuban (rum, champagne, mint and bitters) smacks of a mojito with something to celebrate.

★ Rye House

11 W 17th Street, between Fifth & Sixth Avenues (1-212 255 7260, www.ryehousenyc.com). Subway F to 14th Street; L to Sixth Avenue. **Open** noon-2am Mon-Fri; 11am-4pm, 5pm-2am Sat, Sun. **Average drink** $12. **Credit** AmEx, MC, V. **Map** p403 E27 32

As the name suggests, American spirits are the emphasis at this dark, sultry bar. Along with a selection of bourbons and ryes, there are gins, vodkas and rums, all distilled in the States. Top-notch mixed drinks include chai-infused rye, and the Creole Daiquiri, which combines New Orleans rum with chorizo-flavoured mescal (it's a bit like sipping a taco, in a good way). While the focus is clearly on drinking, there's excellent upscale pub grub; we liked the fiery fried buffalo sweetbreads.

THE BEST BAR SNACKS

For gourmet pairings
Ardesia. *See above.*

For top-chef canapés
Bar Pleiades. *See p225.*

For refined pub grub
Spitzer's Corner. *See p218.*

230 Fifth

230 Fifth Avenue, between 26th & 27th Streets (1-212 725 4300, www.230-fifth.com). Subway N, R to 28th Street. **Open** 4pm-4am daily. **Average drink** $11. **Credit** AmEx, Disc, MC, V. **Map** p404 E26 33

The 14,000sq ft (1,300sq m) roof garden dazzles with truly spectacular views, including a close-up of the Empire State Building, but the glitzy indoor lounge – with its ceiling-height windows, wrap-around sofas and bold lighting – shouldn't be overlooked. While the sprawling outdoor space gets mobbed on sultry nights, it's less crowded in the cooler months when heaters, fleece robes and hot ciders make it a winter hotspot.

Theater District & Hell's Kitchen

★ Ardesia

510 W 52nd Street, between Tenth & Eleventh Avenues (1-212 247 9191, www.ardesia-ny.com). Subway C, E to 50th Street. **Open** 5pm-midnight Mon, Tue; 5pm-2am Wed-Fri; noon-2am Sat; noon-midnight Sun. **Average glass of wine** $10. **Credit** AmEx, Disc, MC, V. **Map** p404 C23 34

Le Bernardin vet Mandy Oser's iron-and-marble gem offers superior wines in a relaxed setting. The 75-strong collection of international bottles is a smart balance of Old and New World options that pair beautifully with the varied selection of small plates. A grüner veltliner – a dry, oaky white from the Knoll winery in Wachau, Austria – had enough backbone to stand up to a duck *banh mi* layered with house-made pâté and duck prosciutto. A blended red from Spain's Cellar Can Blau, meanwhile, was a spicy, velvety match for coriander-rich home-made mortadella. One for the serious oenophile.

Pony Bar

637 Tenth Avenue, at 45th Street (1-212 586 2707, www.theponybar.com). Subway A, C, E to 50th Street. **Open** 3pm-4am Mon-Fri; noon-4am Sat, Sun. **Average drink** $5. **Credit** AmEx, Disc, MC, V. **Map** p404 C24 35

Hell's Kitchen has long been a dead zone for civilised bars, but this sunny paean to American microbrews is an oasis. There are 20 beers on tap and two cask ales artfully listed on signboards according to provenance and potency. The thoughtful selections include Dogfish Head's peachy Berliner Weisse-style Festina Pêche and Victory's Bags Packed Porter, a toasty treat rich with coffee and chocolate. The low prices (all beers served cost $5) and expert curation suggest that the drought may finally be easing.

Russian Samovar

256 W 52nd Street, between Broadway & Eighth Avenue (1-212 757 0168, www.russiansamovar.com). Subway C, E, 1 to 50th Street. **Open** 5pm-4am daily. **Average drink** $9. **Credit** AmEx, Disc, MC, V. **Map** p404 D23 36

INSIDE TRACK PROVE YOURSELF

Don't forget to carry photo ID, such as a driver's licence or passport, at all times. Even those who look well over the legal drinking age of 21 may well get 'carded' when trying to order drinks at the bar.

At this Russki haven, house-infused vodkas are the poison of choice. Impress your friends by sampling the eye-opening pepper vodka, or (for $20), you can choose three of more than 20 seasonal varieties, which can include raspberry, apple-cinnamon, ginger or tarragon. If you don't want to drink on an empty stomach – and it's probably not a good idea to do so, given the strength of the vodkas on offer – try a satisfying bowl of borscht or the toothsome beef stroganoff.

Midtown East

★ Bill's Gay Nineties

57 E 54th Street, between Madison Avenue & Park Avenue (1-212 355 0243). Subway E to Fifth Avenue-53rd Street. **Open** 11.30am-1am Mon-Fri; 5pm-2am Sat. **Average drink** $8. **Credit** AmEx, DC, Disc, MC, V. **Map** p405 E22 37

The pseudo speakeasies beloved by today's cocktail set have nothing on Bill's – a genuine throwback to Prohibition. Down a small flight of stairs in an ancient brownstone you'll find this low-ceilinged gem, lined with photos of Ziegfeld girls, boxers and thoroughbreds. Rye manhattans go down smooth, and the piano can be heard most nights.

UPTOWN

Upper East Side

★ Bar Pleiades

The Surrey, 20 E 76th Street, between Fifth & Madison Avenues (1-212 772 2600, www.danielnyc.com). Subway 6 to 77th Street. **Open** noon-midnight daily. **Average drink** $18. **Credit** AmEx, MC, V. **Map** p405 E20 38

Designed as a nod to Coco Chanel, Daniel Boulud's bar – across the hotel lobby from Café Boulud – is framed in black lacquered panels that recall an elegant make-up compact. The luxe setting and monied crowd might seem a little stiff, but the drinks are so exquisitely executed, you won't mind sharing your banquette with a suit – try La Terre, an earthy, complex blend of red vermouth, Aperol, grapefruit juice and house-infused beet gin. All of this refinement will cost you: canapés (made at Café Boulud next door) are $28 for four people, and cocktails average out at $18.

Bemelmans Bar

The Carlyle, 35 E 76th Street, at Madison Avenue (1-212 744 1600, www.thecarlyle.com). Subway 6 to 77th Street. **Open** noon-1am Mon-Thur, Sun; noon-1.30am Fri, Sat. **Average drink** $19. **Credit** AmEx, DC, Disc, MC, V. **Map** p405 E20 39

The Plaza may have Eloise, but the Carlyle has its own children's book connection – the wonderful 1947 murals of Central Park by *Madeline* creator Ludwig Bemelmans in this, the quintessential classy New York bar. A jazz trio adds to the atmosphere most nights (a cover charge of $10-$25 applies from 9.30pm, when they take up residence).

Upper West Side

Clo Wine Bar

4th Floor, Time Warner Center, 10 Columbus Circle, at Broadway (1-212 823 9898, www.clowines.com). Subway A, B, C, D, 1 to 59th Street-Columbus Circle. **Open** 4pm-midnight Mon-Thur; 4pm-1am Fri, Sat; 3-11pm Sun. **Average drink** $11. **Credit** AmEx, DC, Disc, MC, V. **Map** p405 D22 40

This futuristic spot is what we imagine a wine bar aboard the starship *Enterprise* might look like. The mechanised set-up is challenging at first, but ultimately liberating: you exchange a credit card for a glass and a smart card, which you insert before pressing a button for your chosen wine to be dispensed from a metal spigot. A tabletop touch screen displays tasting notes for each selection. The tech doesn't come cheap – glasses under $10 are few and far between.

Ding Dong Lounge

929 Columbus Avenue, between 105th Street & 106th Street (Duke Ellington Boulevard) (1-212 663 2600, www.dingdonglounge.com). Subway B, C to 103rd Street. **Open** 4pm-4am daily. **Average drink** $6. **Credit** MC, V. **Map** p406 C16 41

Goth chandeliers and kick-ass music mark this dark dive as punk – with broadened horizons. The tap pulls, dispensing Stella Artois, Guinness and Bass, are sawn-off guitar necks, and the walls are covered with vintage concert posters (from Dylan to the Damned). The affable local clientele and mood-lit conversation nooks make it surprisingly accessible (even without a working knowledge of Dee Dee Ramone).

Harlem

Lenox Lounge

288 Malcolm X Boulevard (Lenox Avenue), between 124th & 125th Streets (1-212 427 0253, www.lenoxlounge.com). Subway 2, 3 to 125th Street. **Open** noon-4am daily. **Average drink** $8. **Credit** AmEx, DC, MC, V. **Map** p407 D13 42

This is where a street hustler named Malcolm worked before he found religion and added an X to his name.

Now the famous Harlem lounge and jazz club welcomes a mix of old-school cats, unobtrusive tipplers and jazz-loving tourists. Settle into the gorgeously restored 1939 art deco bar at the front, or retire to the illustrious Zebra Room in the back (a cover charge sometimes applies), where the likes of Miles Davis, Billie Holiday and John Coltrane have all worked their elusive brand of magic.

► *For more on music at the Lenox, see p330.*

Nectar Wine Bar

2235 Frederick Douglass Boulevard (Eighth Avenue), between 120th & 121st Streets (1-212 961 9622). Subway A, B, C, D to 125th Street. **Open** 5pm-midnight Mon-Thur; 5pm-1am Fri, Sat; 3-11pm Sun. **Average drink** $10. **Credit** AmEx, Disc, MC, V. **Map** p407 D14 43

The offshoot of the beloved pioneering Harlem Vintage wine shop next door, chic Nectar Wine Bar continues the store's legacy with hands-on service and a well-curated wine list. Europe- and California-heavy selections (36 by the glass) are well priced at around $10. Servers ably match the wines to appropriate charcuterie and cheese.

★ The Shrine

2271 Adam Clayton Powell Jr Boulevard (Seventh Avenue), between 133rd & 134th Streets (1-212 690 7807, www.shrinenyc.com). Subway B, C, 2, 3 to 135th Street. **Open** 4pm-4am daily. **Average drink** $9. **Credit** AmEx. **Map** p407 D12 44

Playfully adapting a sign left over from the previous tenants (the Black United Foundation), the Shrine advertises itself as a 'Black United Fun Plaza'. The interior is tricked out with African art and vintage album covers, and actual vinyl adorns the ceiling. Harlemites and downtowners pack the Shrine for nightly concerts, which might feature indie rock, jazz, reggae or DJ sets. The cocktail menu aspires to similar diversity: drinks range from a smooth mango mojito to signature tipples like a snappy Afro Trip (a lime and ginger concoction enhanced by Jamaican or Brazilian rum), and a sweet vodka-and-Bailey's driven Muslim Jew.

BROOKLYN

Abilene

442 Court Street, at 3rd Place, Carroll Gardens (1-718 522 6900, www.abilenebarbrooklyn.com). Subway F, G to Carroll Street. **Open** noon-4am Mon-Fri; 11am-4am Sat, Sun. **Average drink** $6. **Credit** AmEx, Disc, MC, V. **Map** p410 S11 45

Leah Allen, a Carroll Gardens artist, has decorated her watering hole with thrift store scores, a rescued church pew, a 27-foot-long bar and painted grass-like patterns. The spot is laid-back and dimly lit. Chatting up the friendly bartenders is easy, as is getting an impromptu game of Scrabble going. Take advantage of happy hour (4-7pm and midnight-1am Mon-Fri; 4-7pm Sat, Sun), when all drafts are $4.

★ Clover Club

210 Smith Street, between Baltic & Butler Streets, Cobble Hill (1-718 855 7939, www.cloverclubny.com). Subway F, G to Bergen Street. **Open** 5pm-2am Mon-Wed; 5pm-3am Thur; 5pm-4am Fri; 11am-4am Sat; 11am-midnight Sun. **Average drink** $10. **Credit** AmEx, MC, V. **Map** p410 S10 46

This Victorian-styled cocktail parlour from mixology maven Julie Reiner (Flatiron Lounge) joins Brooklyn's recent spate of serious drinking establishments. Classic cocktails are the Club's signature drink: sours, fizzes, mules, punches and cobblers all get their latter-day due at the 19th-century mahogany bar. Highbrow snacks (fried oysters, steak tartare) and tipples, like a Market Street Julep (pisco, pineapple and mint) or the ginger-packed Pimms Punch, should absolve you of the folly of your appletini days. *Photos p228.*

★ Dram

177 South 4th Street, between Driggs Avenue & Roebling Street, Williamsburg (1-718 486 3726). Subway J, Z, M to Marcy Avenue. **Open** 4pm-4am daily. **Average drink** $9. **Credit** AmEx, Disc, MC, V. **Map** p411 U8 47

This airy Williamsburg bar is New York's first truly progressive cocktail joint: a casual mixology haven with stools to spare for drinkers of all persuasions. The lighthearted but exquisitely executed menu changes according to the whims of Dram's precocious barkeeps. The Mighty Tux is a botanical balancing act, with crisp gin, bittersweet maraschino liqueur, and both dry and sweet vermouth lending body and depth. There are classics, too – like a beautifully integrated Sazerac – but you can also take your boozing cues from the neighbourhood dudes, busily draining $4 Porkslap ales or sipping from a smart collection of international wines. It's this egalitarian tack that will serve to keep the place packed well into the future – whether or not its patrons appreciate Italian bitters and Kold-Draft ice cubes.

Floyd, NY

131 Atlantic Avenue, between Clinton & Henry Streets, Cobble Hill (1-718 858 5810, www.floydny.com). Subway M, R to Court Street; 2, 3, 4, 5 to Borough Hall. **Open** 5pm-4am Mon-Fri; 1pm-4am Sat, Sun. **Average drink** $4. **No credit cards**. **Map** p410 S10 48

Floyd, NY, is modelled on the taverns in Floyd, Iowa, which was owner Pam Carden's hometown. She and her husband have added rural elements – and Floyd, Iowa really is rural – like a jukebox stocked with Hank Williams and the Bad Livers; tin ceilings; vintage signs; a salvaged 1870s bar; and nice bartenders. It looks like a joint that's been around for ages – not the renovated liquor store that it is. Schlitz beer and Kentucky beer cheese complete the theme. The indoor *bocce* court is a little incongruous but works nonetheless.

CONSUME

Hometown Hooch

Three distilleries grow in Brooklyn.

Brooklyn isn't short on local libations. First it was lager and ale from the Brooklyn Brewery, Sixpoint and Kelso. Then in 2009, the Red Hook Winery uncorked its first vintage. Now, thanks to recently relaxed liquor laws allowing New York State distillers to sell directly to consumers, handcrafted hard stuff has entered the mix via three outfits in Kings County.

Recovering Wall Streeter turned artisan-booze-maker Brad Estabrooke founded **Breuckelen Distilling** (77 19th Street, at Third Avenue, Sunset Park, Brooklyn, 1-347 725 4985, www.brkgin.com) in a bare-bones space in 2009. Along with girlfriend Liz O'Connell, he installed a gorgeous, custom-made copper still from Germany and started experimenting with gin. His product – distilled from upstate grain and infused with botanicals such as juniper, grapefruit peel, ginger and rosemary – is rich, balanced and slightly sweet. It's as good with a splash of fizzy tonic as it is straight with a lemon twist. Savour it at **Abilene** (*see p226*), **Fort Defiance** (*see p214*) or drop by the distillery for a free tour (1-5pm Sat, Sun) or tasting (2-8pm Thur, Fri; noon-6pm Sat, Sun).

Joining Breuckelen is the scrappier **Kings County Distillery** (35 Meadow Street, at Bogart Street, Williamsburg, Brooklyn, kingscountydistillery.com), which operates out of a cramped Williamsburg loft. Co-founders David Haskell and Colin Spoelman make do with five eight-gallon stills they bought online. The pair's first release is a fiery yet smooth un-aged corn whiskey – what Jed Clampett might call white lightning. Try it at Billyburg stalwart **The Richardson** (451 Graham Avenue, at Richardson Street, 1-718 389 0839) or Cobble Hill's **Henry Public** (329 Henry Street, between Atlantic Avenue & Pacific Street, 1-718 852 8630).

At the time of writing, Brooklyn Brewery co-founder Tom Potter and spirits guru Allen Katz are planning to open the **New York Distilling Co.** (405 Leonard Street, at Bayard Street, Williamsburg, Brooklyn, 1-718 369 3749, nydistilling.com) in what amounts to a rusty metal box near McCarren Park. A 1,000-litre handmade copper still will be shipped from Germany as soon as the space is ready, and they expect to have gin available by the beginning of 2011 and a rye soon after.

Breuckelen Distilling.

Clover Club. *See p226.*

CONSUME

★ Huckleberry Bar

588 Grand Street, between Leonard & Lorimer Streets, Williamsburg (1-718 218 8555, www.huckleberrybar.com). Subway L to Lorimer Street; G to Metropolitan Avenue. **Open** 4pm-2am Mon-Thur; 4pm-4am Fri; 2pm-4am Sat; 2pm-2am Sun. **Average drink** $9. **Credit** AmEx, MC, V. **Map** p412 V8 49

East Billyburg's upscaling continues apace at this baroque cocktail boutique that comes from the Danny Meyer-pedigreed Stephanie Schneider (Gramercy Tavern) and Andrew Boggs (Union Square Café, *see p202*). Aim to claim an intimate table in the expansive, old-world room and ask the barkeeps to muddle a pitch-perfect classic vodka gimlet or a speciality tipple such as summer's Article 57, a house-infused citric vodka, or autumn's Edward Bulwer-Lytton, concocted with ginger-infused rum.

Soda Bar

629 Vanderbilt Avenue, between Prospect Place & St Marks Avenue, Prospect Heights (1-718 280 8393). Subway B, Q to Seventh Avenue; 2, 3 to Grand Army Plaza. **Open** noon-2am Mon-Thur, Sun; noon-4am Fri, Sat. **Average drink** $6. **Credit** AmEx, DC, MC, V. **Map** p410 U11 50

Prospect Heights's nightlife swirls around Soda Bar, a former ice-cream sundae shop where locals congregate for killer happy hours and bulging burgers. Punch up some indie rock on the jukebox, then relax in the lounge or on the summer perfect patio.

★ Spuyten Duyvil

359 Metropolitan Avenue, at Havermeyer Street, Williamsburg (1-718 963 4140, www.spuytenduvilnyc.com). Subway L to Bedford Avenue; G to Metropolitan Avenue. **Open** 5pm-

2am Mon-Thur; 5pm-4am Fri; 1pm-4am Sat; 1pm-2am Sun. **Average drink** $9. **Credit** AmEx, Disc, MC, V. **Map** p411 U8 51
Don't arrive thirsty. It takes at least ten minutes to choose from roughly 150 quaffs, a list that impresses even microbrew mavens. Most selections are middle-European regionals, and bartenders are eager to explain the differences among them. The cosy interior is chock-full of flea market finds, most of which are for sale. There's also a tasty bar menu of smoked meats, pâtés, cheeses and terrines.

Tandem
236 Troutman Street, between Knickerbocker & Wilson Avenues, Bushwick (1-718 386-2369, www.tandembar.net). Subway L to Jefferson Street. **Open** 6pm-4am Mon-Fri; 11am-4am Sat, Sun. **Average drink** $7. **Credit** AmEx, MC, V. **Map** p411 W9 52
Shunning by-the-books trendiness, Tandem is a true original: sister owners Jane and Cathy Virga either sourced or crafted nearly every piece of the interior, and the quirky drinks are just as special. The herbaceous Masten Lake is a highlight of the seasonal cocktail list, combining gin, seltzer, lemon and basil plucked from the rooftop garden. The mostly local drafts, meanwhile, are siphoned into home-made ceramic pint glasses. Tandem's many charms have drawn in the 'hood's ultrahip, who take to the rear dancefloor on Fridays and Saturdays. You might join them too.

Union Hall
702 Union Street, between Fifth & Sixth Avenues, Park Slope (1-718 638 4400, www.unionhallny.com). Subway M, R to Union Street. **Open** 4pm-4am Mon-Fri; noon-4am Sat, Sun. **Average drink** $6. **Credit** AmEx, DC, MC, V. **Map** p412 T11 53
Upstairs at Union Hall, couples chomp on mini burgers and sip microbrews in the gentlemen's club anteroom (decorated with Soviet-era globes, paintings of fez-capped men, fireplaces) – before battling it out on the clay *bocce* courts. Downstairs, in the taxidermy-filled basement, the stage hosts bands, comedians and offbeat events.
▶ *For more on the entertainment here, see p328.*

Union Pool
484 Union Avenue, at Meeker Avenue, Williamsburg (1-718 609 0484). Subway L to Lorimer Street; G to Metropolitan Avenue. **Open** 5pm-4am daily. **Average drink** $6. **Credit** AmEx, Disc, MC, V. **Map** p412 V8 54
This former pool-supply outlet now supplies booze to scruffy Williamsburgers, who pack the tin-walled main room's half-moon booths and snap saucy photo-kiosk pics. Bands strum away on the adjacent stage, while a spacious courtyard is packed with wooden benches to lure smokers. Arrive early to kick back $3 PBRs or $7 Jack-and-Cokes (a buck off from 5 to 8pm).

QUEENS

★ Bohemian Hall & Beer Garden
29-19 24th Avenue, between 29th & 30th Streets, Astoria (1-718 274 4925, www.bohemianhall.com). Subway N, Q to Astoria Boulevard. **Open** 5pm-2am Mon-Thur; 5pm-3am Fri; noon-3am Sat, Sun. **Average drink** $5. **Credit** DC, MC, V. **Map** p412 X3 55
This authentic Czech beer garden features plenty of mingle-friendly picnic tables, where you can sample cheap, robust platters of sausage, $5 Stolis and $5 Spaten Oktoberfests. Though the huge, tree-canopied garden is open year-round (in winter, the area is tented and heated), summer is prime time to soak up some rays over a pint.

Dutch Kills
27-24 Jackson Avenue, at Dutch Kills Street, Long Island City (1-718 383 2724, www.dutchkillsbar.com). Subway E, R to Queens Plaza. **Open** 5pm-2am daily. **Average drink** $10. **No credit cards. Map** p412 V5 56
What separates Dutch Kills from the rest of the mixology temples dotting the city is the easy access and abundance of elbow room, from the deep, dark-wood booths up front to the sawdust-strewn piano room in the back, which adds to the 19th-century saloon atmosphere. Cocktails nod to the borough, with tipples such as the Astoria and the Steinway Punch, and prices are slightly lower than the norm.

Sweet Afton
30-09 34th Street, at 30th Avenue, Astoria (1-718 777 2570, www.sweetafton.com). Subway N, Q to 30th Avenue. **Open** 4pm-3.30am Mon-Fri; 1pm-3.30am Sat, Sun. **Average beer** $7. **Credit** AmEx, V. **Map** p412 X3 57
This Queens gastropub combines an industrial feel – lots of concrete and massive beams – with the dim, dark-wood cosiness of an Irish pub. The bar's smartly curated array of reasonably priced suds includes strong selections from craft breweries like Kelso, Fire Island and Captain Lawrence, but the unpretentious bartender will just as happily crack open a cheap everyman ale like Amstel or Miller. The satisfying food menu is highlighted by the beer-battered McClure's pickles – an epic bar snack.

THE BEST SPEAKEASIES

For an authentic Prohibition vibe
Angel's Share. *See p219.*

For the most ingenious front
PDT. *See p221.*

For a twist on the theme
Raines Law Room. *See p224.*

CONSUME

Shops & Services

You want it? New York's got it.

Although American shopping culture has taken a hit from the recession, New York City remains the country's retail capital. As well as the famous department stores and global flagships, Gotham retains a large number of unusual, independently run businesses. A silver-lined effect of the increase in empty storefronts is a dip in rents, luring young designers and boutique-owners back from the outer boroughs to Manhattan.

Whatever you're looking for – big-name fashion or one-off items from local artisans, cut-price CDs or rare vinyl, fresh-from-the-studio home design or market bric-a-brac – you won't be disappointed. The only pitfall is exhaustion if you attempt to cover too much ground at once. We recommend taking it slowly and arranging your retail excursions by neighbourhood; for a guide, *see p232* **Where to Shop**.

THE SHOPPING SCENE

New York is fertile bargain-hunting territory. The traditional post-season sales (which usually start just after Christmas and in early to mid June) have given way to frequent markdowns throughout the year: look for sale racks in boutiques, chain and department stores. The twice-a-year Barneys Warehouse Sale (*see right*) is an important fixture on the bargain hound's calendar, but as the city is the centre of the American fashion industry, every week sees several designer sample sales. To find out what's on, consult the Shopping & Style section of *Time Out New York* magazine. **Top Button** (www.topbutton.com) and **Clothing Line** (1-212 947 8748, www.clothingline.com), which holds sales for a variety of labels – from J Crew and Theory to Tory Burch and Rag & Bone – at its Garment District showroom (2nd Floor, 261 W 36th Street, between Seventh & Eighth Avenues) – are also good resources.

While many shops in the city keep late hours most nights of the week, Thursday is generally the unofficial shop-after-work night, when most places remain open until at least 8pm. Stores downtown generally stay open an hour or so later than those uptown. Note that some of the shops listed in this chapter have more than one location; we have detailed up to three other branches below the review. For the bigger chains, check individual shop websites or consult the business pages in the telephone book for more addresses across the city.

Sales tax in the city is 8.875 per cent, though there are exemptions. For details, *see p380*.

INSIDE TRACK
STRIP FOR BARGAINS

Sample sales are usually held in the designers' shops, showrooms or rented loft spaces, and are known to get seriously heated. Most lack changing rooms, so bring a courageous spirit (and plenty of cash) and remember to wear appropriate undergarments to avoid embarrassment.

General

DEPARTMENT STORES

★ Barneys New York

660 Madison Avenue, at 61st Street, Upper East Side (1-212 826 8900, www.barneys.com). Subway N, R to Fifth Avenue-59th Street; 4, 5, 6 to 59th Street. **Open** 10am-8pm Mon-Fri; 10am-7pm Sat; 11am-6pm Sun. **Credit** AmEx, DC, MC, V. **Map** p405 E22.

Barneys has a reputation for spotlighting less ubiquitous designer labels than other upmarket department stores, and has its own quirky-classic line. Its funky Co-op boutiques (see website for locations) carry threads by up-and-comers and the latest hot denim lines. Every February and August, the Chelsea Co-op hosts the Barneys Warehouse Sale, when prices are slashed by 50-80%.
Other locations Co-ops throughout the city.

Bergdorf Goodman

754 Fifth Avenue, between 57th & 58th Streets, Midtown (1-212 753 7300, www.bergdorfgoodman.com). Subway E, M to Fifth Avenue-53rd Street; N, R to Fifth Avenue-59th Street. **Open** 10am-8pm Mon-Fri; 10am-7pm Sat; noon-6pm Sun. **Credit** AmEx, DC, MC, V. **Map** p405 E22.

Synonymous with understated luxury, Bergdorf's is known for its designer clothes (the fifth floor is dedicated to younger, trend-driven labels) and accessories – seek out the wonderful vintage-jewellery cache on the ground floor. Descend to the basement for the wide-ranging beauty department. The men's store is across the street at 745 Fifth Avenue.

Bloomingdale's

1000 Third Avenue, at 59th Street, Upper East Side (1-212 705 2000, www.bloomingdales.com). Subway N, R to Lexington Avenue-59th Street; 4, 5, 6 to 59th Street. **Open** 10am-8.30pm Mon-Fri; 10am-7pm Sat; 11am-7pm Sun. **Credit** AmEx, DC, MC, V. **Map** p405 F22.

Ranking among the city's top tourist attractions, Bloomie's is a gigantic, glitzy department store stocked with everything from handbags to beauty

Brooklyn flea market. *See p232.*

CONSUME

products, home furnishings to designer duds. The beauty hall, complete with an outpost of globe-spanning apothecary Space NK and a Bumble & Bumble dry-styling bar, recently got a glam makeover. The hipper, compact Soho outpost concentrates on young fashion, denim and cosmetics.
Other locations 504 Broadway, between Broome & Spring Streets, Soho (1-212 279 5900).

Henri Bendel

712 Fifth Avenue, at 56th Street, Midtown East (1-212 247 1100, www.henribendel.com). Subway E, M to Fifth Avenue-53rd Street; N, R to Fifth Avenue-59th Street. **Open** 10am-8pm Mon-Sat; noon-7pm Sun. **Credit** AmEx, DC, Disc, MC, V. **Map** p405 E22.
While the merchandise (a mix of mid-price and designer clothes, fashion accessories and big-brand cosmetics) and prices are comparable to those of other upscale stores, the goods at Bendel's somehow seem more desirable seen in its opulent premises, a conglomeration of three 19th-century townhouses – and those darling brown-striped shopping bags don't hurt, either. Bendel's is also the home of celebrity hairdresser Frédéric Fekkai's flagship salon.

Jeffrey New York

449 W 14th Street, at Tenth Avenue, Meatpacking District (1-212 206 1272, www.jeffreynewyork.com). Subway A, C, E to 14th Street; L to Eighth Avenue. **Open** 10am-8pm Mon-Wed, Fri; 10am-9pm Thur; 10am-7pm Sat; 12.30-6pm Sun. **Credit** AmEx, DC, MC, V. **Map** p403 C27.
Jeffrey Kalinsky, a former Barneys shoe buyer, was a Meatpacking District pioneer when he opened his namesake store in 1999. Designer clothing abounds here – by Yves Saint Laurent, Halston, L'Wren Scott, Céline and young British star Christopher Kane, among others. But the centrepiece is without doubt the shoe salon, which features the work of Manolo Blahnik, Prada and Christian Louboutin, as well as newer names to watch.

Where to Shop

New York's best shopping neighbourhoods in brief.

SOHO
Although it's been heavily commercialised, especially the main thoroughfares, this once edgy, arty enclave still has some idiosyncratic survivors and numerous top-notch shops. Urban fashion abounds on Lafayette Street, while Broome Street is becoming a burgeoning enclave for chic home design.

NOLITA
This area has been colonised by indie designers, especially along Mott and Mulberry Streets.

LOWER EAST SIDE
Once the centre of the rag trade, this old Jewish neighbourhood was associated with bargain outlets and bagels. Now a bar- and boutique-rich patch, it's especially good for vintage, streetwear and local designers. Orchard, Ludlow and Rivington Streets have the highest concentration of retail.

WEST VILLAGE & MEATPACKING DISTRICT
On the other side of the island, the once-desolate wholesale meat market stretching south from 14th Street has become a high-end consumer playground, its warehouses now populated by a clutch of international designers, including Diane von Furstenberg, Stella McCartney and Yigal Azrouël. The western strip of Bleecker Street is lined with a further cache of designer boutiques.

EAST VILLAGE
Although the shops are more scattered here than in the LES, you'll find a highly browsable mix of vintage clothing, streetwear, records, stylish homewares and children's goods.

FIFTH AVENUE & UPPER EAST SIDE
Most of the city's famous department stores can be found on Fifth Avenue between 42nd and 59th Streets, in the company of big-name designer flagships and chain stores. The exceptions are Bloomingdale's and Barneys, which are both on the Upper East Side. Here, Madison Avenue has long been synonymous with the crème de la crème of international fashion.

BROOKLYN
Williamsburg, one subway stop from Manhattan, abounds with hip retail and an excellent flea market. As well as the main drag, Bedford Avenue, North 6th and Grand Streets are good hunting grounds for vintage clothes, arty homewares and record stores. There are further treasures in Cobble Hill, Carroll Gardens and Boerum Hill (especially on Court and Smith Streets, and Atlantic Avenue).

Macy's

151 W 34th Street, between Broadway & Seventh Avenue, Garment District (1-212 695 4400, www.macys.com). Subway B, D, F, M, N, Q, R to 34th Street-Herald Square; 1, 2, 3 to 34th Street-Penn Station. **Open** 10am-9.30pm Mon-Sat; 11am-8.30pm Sun. **Credit** AmEx, DC, Disc, MC, V. **Map** p404 D25.

It may not be as glamorous as New York's other famous stores, but for sheer breadth of stock, the 34th Street behemoth is hard to beat. You won't find exalted labels here, though – mid-price fashion and designers' diffusion lines for all ages are its bread and butter, along with all the big beauty names. Among the largely mainstream refreshment options (McDonald's, Starbucks) is a Ben & Jerry's outpost.

▶ *There's a branch of the Metropolitan Museum of Art (see p114) gift shop here.*

Saks Fifth Avenue

611 Fifth Avenue, between 49th & 50th Streets, Midtown (1-212 753 4000, www.saksfifthavenue.com). Subway E, M to Fifth Avenue-53rd Street. **Open** 10am-8pm Mon-Sat; noon-6pm Sun. **Credit** AmEx, DC, Disc, MC, V. **Map** p404 E23.

Although Saks maintains a presence in 25 states, the Fifth Avenue location is the original, established in 1924 by New York retailers Horace Saks and Bernard Gimbel. The store features all the big names in fashion, from Armani to Yves Saint Laurent, including an expansive shoe salon that shares the eighth floor with a shop/café from deluxe chocolatier Charbonnel et Walker. The opulent beauty hall is fun to peruse, although some might find the aggressive tactics of the sales staff a bit off-putting.

MALLS

Shops at Columbus Circle

Time Warner Center, 10 Columbus Circle, at 59th Street, Upper West Side (1-212 823 6300, www.shopsatcolumbuscircle.com). Subway A, B, C, D, 1 to 59th Street-Columbus Circle. **Open** 10am-9pm Mon-Sat; 11am-7pm Sun (hours vary for some shops, bars and restaurants). **Credit** varies. **Map** p405 D22.

Classier than your average mall, the retail contingent of the 2.8 million sq ft (260,000sq m) Time Warner Center features upscale stores such as Coach and Cole Haan for accessories and shoes, Bose home entertainment, the fancy kitchenware purveyor Williams-Sonoma and True Religion jeans, as well as national shopping centre staples Aveda, J Crew and Borders. There's an outpost of Whole Foods Market in the basement. Some of the city's top restaurants, including Per Se (*see p211*) and a branch of A Voce (*see p209*) have made it a dining destination that transcends the stigma of eating at the mall.

▶ *Next door is the new Museum of Arts & Design; see p118.*

Specialist

BOOKS & MAGAZINES

New York is so saturated with **Barnes & Noble** branches (www.barnesandnoble.com) that some neighbourhoods seem to have a megastore every few blocks. While the stock varies little from branch to branch, several feature readings by authors. **Borders** (www.borders.com), a smaller national chain, also provides under-one-roof browsing, as does **Shakespeare & Co** (www.shakeandco.com), an independent alternative with four stores. Grand Central Terminal's well-stocked **Posman Books** (www.posmanbooks.com) has been a godsend for commuters for a decade and recently opened a second outpost in Chelsea Market (*see p250*). For details of shops and venues that host readings, *see pp269-271.* Weekly listings of such events can be found in *Time Out New York* magazine.

General

Book Culture

536 W 112th Street, between Amsterdam Avenue & Broadway, Upper West Side (1-212 865 1588, www.bookculture.com). Subway 1 to 110th Street-Cathedral Parkway. **Open** 9am-10pm Mon-Fri; 10am-8pm Sat; 11am-7pm Sun. **Credit** AmEx, DC, Disc, MC, V. **Map** p406 C15.

Ostensibly catering to the Columbia University community, two-storey Book Culture lures bibliophiles uptown with stellar fiction and scholarly book collections, as well as its various discount tables sure to yield surprises. A welcoming places to browse. **Other locations** 114th Street, at Broadway, Morningside Heights (1-646 403 3000).

McNally Jackson

52 Prince Street, between Lafayette & Mulberry Streets, Nolita (1-212 274 1160, www.mcnallyjackson.com). Subway N, R to Prince Street; 6 to Spring Street. **Open** 10am-10pm Mon-Sat; 10am-9pm Sun. **Credit** AmEx, DC, Disc, MC, V. **Map** p403 F29.

The New York outpost of Canada's excellent and expanding chain, McNally Jackson (formerly McNally Robinson) has a good selection of novels, non-fiction titles and also magazines. A diverse range of writers present readings in the shop's comfortable café.

192 Books

192 Tenth Avenue, between 21st & 22nd Streets, Chelsea (1-212 255 4022, www.192books.com). Subway C, E to 23rd Street. **Open** noon-7pm Mon, Sun; 11am-7pm Tue-Sat. **Credit** AmEx, MC, V. **Map** p404 C26.

In an era when many an indie bookshop has closed its doors, this youngster, open since 2003, is proving

Discover the city from your back pocket

Essential for your weekend break, over 30 top cities available.

that quirky boutique booksellers can make it after all. Owned and 'curated' by art dealer Paula Cooper and her husband, editor Jack Macrae, 192 offers a strong selection of art books and literature, as well as books on gardening, history, politics, design, music and memoirs.

▶ *For information about readings at the shop, see p270.*

St Mark's Bookshop

31 Third Avenue, between 8th & 9th Streets, Greenwich Village (1-212 260 7853, www.stmarksbookshop.com). Subway N, R to 8th Street; 6 to Astor Place. **Open** 10am-midnight Mon-Sat; 11am-midnight Sun. **Credit** AmEx, DC, Disc, MC, V. **Map** p403 F28.

Students, academics and arty types gravitate to this esteemed East Village bookseller, which maintains strong inventories on cultural theory, graphic design, poetry and film, as well as numerous avant-garde journals and zines. The fiction section is one of the finest in the city.

Specialist

Books of Wonder

18 W 18th Street, between Fifth & Sixth Avenues, Flatiron District (1-212 989 3270, www.booksofwonder.com). Subway F, M to 14th Street; L to Sixth Avenue; 1 to 18th Street. **Open** 10am-7pm Mon-Sat; 11am-6pm Sun. **Credit** AmEx, Disc, MC, V. **Map** p403 E27.

The only independent children's bookstore in the city features titles new and old (rare and out-of-print editions), plus a special collection of Oz books. The store also always has a good stock of signed books, and the on-site Cupcake Café makes a visit even more of a treat.

▶ *For more things to do with the kids, see p272.*

Forbidden Planet

840 Broadway, at 13th Street, Greenwich Village (1-212 475 6161, www.fpnyc.com). Subway L, N, Q, R, 4, 5, 6 to 14th Street-Union Square. **Open** 10am-10pm Mon, Tue, Sun; 9am-midnight Wed; 10am-midnight Thur-Sat. **Credit** AmEx, Disc, MC, V. **Map** p403 E27.

Embracing both pop culture and the cult underground, the Planet takes comics seriously. You'll also find graphic novels, manga, action figures, DVDs and more.

Hue-Man Bookstore & Café

2319 Frederick Douglass Boulevard (Eighth Avenue), between 124th & 125th Streets, Harlem (1-212 665 7400, www.huemanbookstore.com). Subway A, B, C, D to 125th Street. **Open** 10am-8pm Mon-Sat; 11am-7pm Sun. **Credit** AmEx, DC, Disc, MC, V. **Map** p407 D13.

Focusing on African-American non-fiction and fiction, this superstore-sized Harlem indie also stocks bestsellers and general interest books. It hosts readings, as well as in-store appearances by authors such as Chris Abani and Marlon James.

Idlewild

12 W 19th Street, between Fifth & Sixth Avenues, Flatiron District (1-212 414 8888, www.idlewildbooks.com). Subway F, M to 14th Street; L to Sixth Avenue. **Open** 11.30am-8pm Mon-Fri; noon-7pm Sat, Sun. **Credit** AmEx, Disc, MC, V. **Map** p403 E27.

Opened by a former United Nations press officer, Idlewild stocks travel guides to more than 100 countries and all 50 states, which are grouped with related works of fiction and non-fiction. Fun fact: Idlewild was the original name for JFK Airport before it was renamed to honour the assassinated president in 1963.

Printed Matter

195 Tenth Avenue, between 21st & 22nd Streets, Chelsea (1-212 925 0325, www.printedmatter.org). Subway C, E to 23rd Street. **Open** 11am-6pm Tue, Wed; 11am-7pm Thur-Sat. **Credit** AmEx, Disc, MC, V. **Map** p404 C26.

This non-profit organisation is devoted to artists' books – from David Shrigley's deceptively naive illustrations to provocative photographic self-portraits by Matthias Herrmann – and operates a public reading room as well as a shop. Works by unknown and emerging artists share shelf space with those of veterans such as Yoko Ono and Edward Ruscha.

Used & antiquarian

★ Housing Works Bookstore Café

126 Crosby Street, between Houston & Prince Streets, Soho (1-212 334 3324, www.housingworksbookstore.org). Subway B, D, F, M to Broadway-Lafayette Street; N, R to Prince Street; 6 to Bleecker Street. **Open** 10am-9pm Mon-Fri; noon-7pm Sat, Sun. **Credit** AmEx, MC, V. **Map** p403 E29.

This endearing two-level space – which stocks a range of literary fiction, non-fiction, rare books and collectibles – is a peaceful spot to relax over coffee or wine. All proceeds go to providing support services for people living with HIV/AIDS.

▶ *For information on the store's literary events, see p269.*

Strand Book Store

828 Broadway, at 12th Street, East Village (1-212 473 1452, www.strandbooks.com). Subway L, N, Q, R, 4, 5, 6 to 14th Street-Union Square. **Open** 9.30am-10.30pm Mon-Sat; 11am-10.30pm Sun. **Credit** AmEx, DC, Disc, MC, V. **Map** p403 E28.

Boasting 18 miles of books, the Strand has a mammoth collection of more than two million discount volumes (both new and used), and the store is made all the more daunting by its chaotic, towering shelves and sometimes crotchety staff. Reviewer discounts are in the basement, while rare volumes lurk upstairs. If you spend enough time here you can find just about anything, from that out-of-print Victorian book on manners to the kitschiest of sci-fi pulp.

CHILDREN

Fashion

Babesta Threads

66 West Broadway, between Murray & Warren Streets, Tribeca (1-212 608 4522, www.babesta.com). Subway 1, 2, 3 to Chambers Street. **Open** 11am-7pm Mon-Fri; noon-6pm Sat, Sun. **Credit** AmEx, DC, Disc, MC, V. **Map** p402 E32.

Husband and wife team Aslan and Jenn Cattaui fill their cosy 450sq ft (42sq m) store with the stuff kids love – Junk Food concert tees, Uglydolls and vintage wear that'll make parents envious. The shop largely focuses on the under-six set, but there are also pieces for children aged up to 12 from popular lines such as Kaos Recycled.

Egg

72 Jay Street, between Front & Water Streets, Dumbo, Brooklyn (1-718 422 7811, www.egg-baby.com). Subway A, C to High Street; F to York Street. **Open** 10am-6pm Mon-Fri; noon-5pm Sun. **Credit** AmEx, MC, V. **Map** p411 T9.

Set in the old HQ of the Grand Union Tea Company, designer Susan Lazar's flagship has a retro garment-factory vibe. Among her seasonally changing creations for babies and kids up to six you might find boys' peacoats, sophisticated Empire-waist cashmere dresses and pastel infant bodysuits. Lazar uses organic cotton whenever possible, particularly in her Purely Peru line – inspired by the craftsmanship she encountered on travels in South America. There's also a chic maternity collection.

Toys

★ FAO Schwarz

767 Fifth Avenue, at 58th Street, Midtown (1-212 644 9400, www.fao.com). Subway N, R to Lexington Avenue-59th Street; 4, 5, 6 to 59th Street. **Open** 10am-7pm Mon-Thur; 10am-8pm Fri, Sat; 11am-6pm Sun. **Credit** AmEx, Disc, MC, V. **Map** p405 E22.

Although it's now owned by the ubiquitous Toys 'R' Us company, this three-storey emporium is still the ultimate NYC toy box. Children will marvel at the giant stuffed animals, and the detailed and imaginative Lego figures, and there are lots of fun opportunities to create custom playthings at the Madame Alexander Doll Factory, Styled by Me Barbie area (complete with revolving dolls' catwalk) and Muppet Whatnot Workshop.

Mary Arnold Toys

1010 Lexington Avenue, between 72nd & 73rd Streets, Upper East Side (1-212 744 8510). Subway 6 to 77th Street. **Open** 9am-6.20pm Mon-Fri; 10am-5pm Sun. **Credit** AmEx, Disc, MC, V. **Map** p405 E20.

This charming speciality toy shop carries unusual, hard-to-find playthings, such as a flat-car racing set. Also head here if you're looking for Madame Alexander dolls, Jellycat animals and other kid (and grown-up) classics.

Pumpkin

334 Bleecker Street, between Christopher & 10th Streets, West Village (1-212 352 0109). Subway 1 to Christopher Street-Sheridan Square. **Open** 11am-7pm Mon-Sat; noon-6pm Sun. **Credit** AmEx, DC, Disc, MC, V. **Map** p403 D28.

Don't expect to find mass-produced playthings at this quirky emporium, which also sells clothing for children ages newborn to six years. Instead, you'll spot innovative items that other stores don't carry. We love the Ecolights colouring book pages that look like stained glass when held up to a window.

ELECTRONICS & PHOTOGRAPHY

iPod junkies can get their fix 24/7 at the **Apple Store**'s Fifth Avenue, open-all-hours flagship (no.767, between 58th & 59th Streets, 1-212 336 1440, www.apple.com), which is marked by a dramatic 32-foot glass entrance. There are further branches at 103 Prince Street, between Greene & Mercer Streets, in Soho; 401 W 14th Street, at Ninth Avenue, in the Meatpacking District; and 1981 Broadway, at 67th Street, on the Upper West Side. All are equipped with Genius Bars, offering technical help for Mac users as well as repairs; well-regarded Apple specialist **Tekserve** (119 W 23rd Street, between Sixth & Seventh Avenues, Chelsea, 1-212 929 3645, www.tekserve.com) is another trusted resource. For PCs, **New York Computer Help** (3rd Floor, 53 E 34th Street, between Madison & Park Avenues, 1-212 599 0339, www.newyorkcomputerhelp.com) provides a free diagnostic service, and also does repairs ($85 per hour).

Mobile phones can be hired on a weekly or daily basis from **Roberts Rent-a-phone** (1-800 964 2468, www.roberts-rent-a-phone.com), which delivers to any US address within 24 hours. However, it may be cheaper to buy a phone (for as little as $15) and a pay-as-you-go card from one of the ubiquitous main service providers. For more on mobile phones, *see p382*.

B&H

420 Ninth Avenue, at 34th Street, Garment District (1-212 444 5040, www.bhphotovideo.com).

Subway A, C, E to 34th Street-Penn Station. **Open** 9am-7pm Mon-Thur; 9am-1pm Fri; 10am-6pm Sun. **Credit** AmEx, Disc, MC, V. **Map** p404 C25.

In this huge, busy store, goods are transported from the stock room via an overhead conveyor belt. It's the place to come to for the latest and rarest photo, video and audio equipment at the lowest prices. Note that due to the largely Hasidic Jewish staff, the store is closed on Saturdays and other Jewish holidays (see website for specifics).

J&R Music & Computer World

23 Park Row, at Beekman Street, Financial District (1-212 238 9000, www.jr.com). Subway A, C to Broadway-Nassau. **Open** 9am-7.30pm Mon-Sat; 10.30am-6.30pm Sun. **Credit** AmEx, Disc, MC, V. **Map** p402 E32.

Established in 1971, this block-long electronics emporium is still family run. As well as a plethora of electronic and electrical goods – from MP3 players and TVs to kitchen appliances – there's an extensive CD section.

FASHION

Designer

We've listed some of the hottest independent designers to be found in Manhattan, but if you're looking for the big international names, then head for Madison Avenue, in between the 60s and 70s cross streets, or Fifth Avenue in between the 40s and 50s cross streets. Outside of these two key areas, there is also a growing number of designer stores in Soho, on Bleecker Street in the West Village (where Marc Jacobs and Ralph Lauren seem engaged in a smackdown for ownership of the strip) and in the Meatpacking District.

Late-night Shopping

As these indie shops attest, the megachains aren't the only stores keeping the lights on late.

Babeland

94 Rivington Street, at Ludlow Street (1-212 375 1701, www.babeland.com). Subway F to Second Avenue-Lower East Side. **Open** noon-10pm Mon-Wed, Sun; noon-11pm Thur-Sat. **Credit** AmEx, Disc, MC, V. **Map** p403 G29.

The flagship of this sex shop minichain is not only open late, it also offers free private appointments after regular business hours every day, so you can loot through organic lube and lifelike dildos on your own time.

By Robert James

72 Orchard Street, between Broome & Grand Streets (1-212 253 2121, www.byrobertjames.com). Subway F to Second Avenue-Lower East Side. **Open** noon-8pm Mon-Sat; noon-6pm Sun. **Credit** AmEx, DC, Disc, MC, V. **Map** p403 G30.

Though technically closed at 8pm, this men's boutique's tailored button-down shirts, wool jackets and hand-printed tees aren't reserved for early birds, thanks to the designer's workaholic – and accommodating – tendencies. 'I'm here late most nights making clothes,' says James. 'If you come knocking, I'll let you in.'

Forbidden Planet

For listings, *see p235*.

Archie and *Batman* are scattered among more novel titles, such as *Puppy Power: Bo, Adventures from the White House*. So is the largest manga selection in the city. After perusing, slip out into the shadows of the night.

St Mark's Bookshop

For listings, *see p235*.

You may never make the 7.30pm readings, but you can enjoy the signed tomes from the authors who give them.

Search & Destroy

25 St Marks Place, between Second & Third Avenues (1-212 358 1120). Subway N, R to 8th Street; 6 to Astor Place. **Open** 1-10pm daily. **Credit** AmEx, DC, Disc, MC, V. **Map** p403 F28.

Punk lives on at this vintage clothing shop rife with Sex Pistols T-shirts, leather bomber jackets, studded belts, and clothing festooned with patches and safety pins.

Village Scandal

19 E 7th Street, between Second & Third Avenues (1-212 460 9358). Subway N, R to 8th Street; 6 to Astor Place. **Open** noon-midnight Mon-Wed, Sun; noon-1.30am Thur-Sat. **Credit** AmEx, Disc, MC, V. **Map** p403 F28.

Change it up mid-barhop with a vintage pillbox hat, a sequined beret or a close-fitting cloche – who knows what will turn up in the $10 hat bin.

Dear: Rivington. *See p240.*

Built by Wendy

7 Centre Market Place, at Grand Street, Soho (1-212 925 6538, www.builtbywendy.com). Subway B, D to Grand Street; J, M, N, Q, R, Z, 6 to Canal Street. **Open** noon-7pm Mon-Sat; noon-6pm Sun. **Credit** AmEx, MC, V. **Map** p403 F30.

Chicago-bred designer and author Wendy Mullin started selling handmade clothes and guitar straps out of record stores in 1991. Today, her youthful men's and women's garb still maintains a homespun look and down-home Midwestern vibe, via men's plaid flannel shirts and girlish dresses, as well as cool graphic T-shirts.

Other locations 46 North 6th Street, at Kent Avenue, Williamsburg, Brooklyn (1-718 384 2882).

Kirna Zabete

96 Greene Street, between Prince & Spring Streets, Soho (1-212 941 9656, www.kirnazabete.com). Subway C, E to Spring Street; N, R to Prince Street. **Open** 11am-7pm Mon-Sat; noon-6pm Sun. **Credit** AmEx, DC, MC, V. **Map** p403 E30.

The clothes and accessories provide the colour at this all-white, bi-level, boutique. The designers stocked here – big hitters such as Balenciaga, Lanvin and Balmain and younger names such as Alexander Wang, Thakoon and Jason Wu – may be exclusive, but the staff is friendly and the vibe unintimidating. The laid-back air is reinforced by a selection of art books and fun gifts.

Lisa Perry

976 Madison Avenue, between 76th & 77th Streets, Upper East Side (1-212 431 7467, www.lisaperrystyle.com). Subway 6 to 77th Street. **Open** 10am-7pm Mon-Sat; 11am-6pm most Suns. **Credit** AmEx, MC, V. **Map** p405 E19.

You don't have to be a flower child to appreciate Lisa Perry's vivid shift dresses, geometric-shaped home goods and bright baubles. The FIT (*see p89*) graduate's new 4,000sq ft (370sq m) concept store carries her '60s-inspired wares; you'll find technicolour duffel bags, flower-print throw pillows and clothing. Customers can also browse a rotating selection of Perry's rare vintage pieces from Pierre Cardin, André Courrèges, Emilio Pucci, Rudi Gernreich and more.

Phillip Lim

115 Mercer Street, between Prince & Spring Streets, Soho (1-212 334 1160, www.31philliplim.com). Subway N, R to Prince Street; 6 to Spring Street. **Open** 11am-7pm Mon-Sat; noon-6pm Sun. **Credit** AmEx, MC, V. **Map** p403 E29.

Since Phillip Lim debuted his collection in 2005, he has amassed a devoted international following for his simple yet strong silhouettes and beautifully constructed tailoring-with-a-twist. His boutique gathers together his award-winning womens- and menswear, plus accessories and a children's line, under one roof.

★ Rag & Bone

100 & 104 Christopher Street, between Bedford & Bleecker Streets, West Village (1-212 727 2999, 1-212 727 2990, www.rag-bone.com). Subway 1 to Christopher Street-Sheridan Square. **Open** 11am-7pm Mon-Sat; noon-6pm Sun. **Credit** AmEx, MC, V. **Map** p403 D28.

Born out of its founders' growing frustrations with mass-produced jeans, what began as a denim line in 2002 has expanded to cover clothing for both men and women. All Rag & Bone's clothes come with an emphasis on craftsmanship. The designs, in substantial, luxurious fabrics such as cashmere and tweed, nod towards tradition (riding jackets, greatcoats) while exuding an utterly contemporary vibe. This aesthetic is reflected in its elegant, industrial-edged his 'n' hers stores; the new Soho outpost caters to both sexes.

Other locations 119 Mercer Street, between Prince & Spring Streets, Soho (1-212 219 2204).

★ Thecast

71 Orchard Street, between Broome & Grand Streets, Lower East Side (1-212 228 2020, www.thecast.com). Subway F to Second Avenue-Lower East Side. **Open** 11am-8pm Mon-Sat; noon-7pm Sun. **Credit** AmEx, DC, Disc, MC, V. **Map** p403 F30.

Owner Chuck Guarino has traded his (literally) underground location for a weathered sliver of a storefront on Orchard Street, but the new shop maintains the neo-gothic vibe with signature ghoulish knick knacks, such as a human skull (bought on eBay). At the core of the unabashedly masculine collection is the trinity of well-cut denim, superior leather jackets based on classic motorcycle styles, and the artful T-shirts that launched the label in 2004. Model and Brit 'it' girl Agyness Deyn was so smitten she bought some pieces for herself, but this spring the ladies get their own line, Aloha From Hell, covering similar ground.

Discount

★ Century 21

22 Cortlandt Street, between Broadway & Church Street, Financial District (1-212 227 9092, www.c21stores.com). Subway N, R to Cortlandt Street. **Open** 7.45am-9pm Mon-Wed; 7.45am-9.30pm Thur, Fri; 10am-9pm Sat; 11am-8pm Sun. **Credit** AmEx, Disc, MC, V. **Map** p402 E32.

A Gucci men's suit for $300? A Marc Jacobs cashmere sweater for less than $200? Stella McCartney sunglasses for a scant $40? No, you're not dreaming – you're shopping at Century 21. You may have to rummage to unearth a treasure, but with savings from 25% to 75% off regular store prices, this is a goldmine for less-minted fashion addicts.

Other locations 472 86th Street, between Fourth & Fifth Avenues, Bay Ridge, Brooklyn (1-718 748 3266).

Daffy's

462 Broadway, between Broome & Grand Streets, Soho (1-212 334 7444, www.daffys.com). Subway J, M, N, Q, R, Z, 6 to Canal Street. **Open** 10am-8pm Mon-Sat; noon-7pm Sun. **Credit** AmEx, DC, Disc, MC, V. **Map** p403 E30.

Daffy Dan's Bargain Town started off as a modest discount store in New Jersey in 1961; today it has eight NYC outposts. Stock varies from store to store, and new merchandise comes in every week, so scoring that coveted haute loot might require a little patience, or just luck. But it's worth it when you unearth super-cheap Tracy Reese or DKNY garb.

Other locations throughout the city.

Gabay's

225 First Avenue, between 13th & 14th Streets, East Village (1-212 254 3180, gabaysoutlet.com). Subway L to First Avenue. **Open** 10am-6.30pm Mon-Sat; 11am-6pm Sun. **Credit** AmEx, Disc, MC, V. **Map** p403 F27.

This family-run shoe and bag specialist gets most of its goods from fine department stores' surpluses (the likes of Yves Saint Laurent, Marc Jacobs and Chanel) and slaps them with 50-80% discounts. Get on the mailing list to be notified of big deliveries.

Loehmann's

101 Seventh Avenue, at 16th Street, Chelsea (1-212 352 0856, www.loehmanns.com). Subway A, C, E to 14th Street; L to Eighth Avenue; 1 to 18th Street. **Open** 9am-9pm Mon-Sat; 11am-7pm Sun. **Credit** AmEx, Disc, MC, V. **Map** p403 D27.

Although this venerable discount emporium is often crowded and cramped, its five floors offer major markdowns on current and off-season clothes (make a beeline upstairs for the 'Back Room' for big names such as Valentino, Prada and Armani) and accessories, as well as fragrances and homewares.

Other locations 2101 Broadway, between 73rd & 74th Streets (1-212 882 9990).

General

National chains J Crew, Banana Republic and Gap, offering good-value basics for both sexes, are all over town; European behemoths Zara, Mango and H&M were joined in 2009 by British fashion giant **Topshop** (478 Broadway, at Broome Street, Soho, 1-212 966 9555, www.topshop.com). Hip girls' boutique chains **Intermix** (www.intermixonline.com) and **Scoop** (www.scoopnyc.com) combine lofty labels with denim and 'it' accessories.

BBlessing

181 Orchard Street, between Houston & Stanton Streets, Lower East Side (1-212 378 8005, www.bblessing.com). Subway F to Lower East Side-Second Avenue. **Open** noon-8pm daily. **Credit** AmEx, DC, Disc, MC, V. **Map** p403 F29.

The interior of this men's shop, which frequently doubles as a gallery space, is as elegant as the clothing displayed within it. New York designers who put a current spin on classic American style – Thom Browne, Patrik Ervell and the store's own line – are the central focus. You can also pick up CDs, DVDs and accessories that reflect owner Nicholas Kratochvil's enviable aesthetic.

Castor & Pollux

238 W 10th Street, between Bleecker & Hudson Streets, West Village (1-212 645 6572, www.castorandpolluxstore.com). Subway A, B, C, D, E, F, M to W 4th Street; 1 to Christopher Street-Sheridan Square. **Open** noon-7pm Tue-Sat; 1-6pm Sun. **Credit** AmEx, MC, V. **Map** p403 D28.

This beloved Brooklyn-born boutique unites European and New York labels in a stylish yet relaxed setting. Owner Kerrilynn Pamer sleuths out such breakout stars as Macedonian-born Risto Bimbiloski, the Louis Vuitton knitwear designer who launched his own womenswear label, and Caron Callahan, formerly of Derek Lam, whose beautifully simple line, Standard Finery, is made in New York's Garment District. Unusual accessories are a constant feature – look for exquisitely handcrafted Reece Hudson lambskin bags by recent Parsons graduate Reece Solomon, and Katie Finn's delicate Elizabeth Street gold and gem jewellery.

Dave's Quality Meat

7 E 3rd Street, between Bowery & Second Avenue, East Village (1-212 505 7551, www.davesqualitymeat.com). Subway F to Lower East Side-Second Avenue. **Open** 11.30am-7.30pm Mon-Sat; 11.30am-6.30pm Sun. **Credit** AmEx, Disc, MC, V. **Map** p403 F29.

Dave Ortiz – formerly of ghetto urban threads label Zoo York – and professional skateboarder Chris Keefe stock a range of top-shelf streetwear in their wittily designed shop, complete with butcher-block counter. As well as a line-up of the latest sneaks by Adidas, Nike and Vans, DQM sells its own-label graphic print tees and hoodies.

★ Dear: Rivington

95 Rivington Street, between Ludlow & Orchard Streets, East Village (1-212 673 3494, www.dearrivington.com). Subway F to Delancey Street; J, M, Z to Delancey-Essex Streets. **Open** noon-7pm daily. **Credit** AmEx, DC, Disc, MC, V. **Map** p403 G29.

The glass storefront is a stage for Moon Rhee and Hey Ja Do's art installation-like displays; inside the white bi-level space, head downstairs for their own Victorian-inspired line and select pieces by avant-garde Japanese labels such as Comme des Garçons and Yohji Yamamoto. Upstairs is a fascinating archive of vintage homewares, objects and contemporary art, including framed antique silhouettes, old globes and tins. *Photos p238.*

One-Stop Shops

Nosh, drink, craft and get your nails done while you browse the wares at these multitasking hybrids.

The Dressing Room.

Black Gold Records
461 Court Street, between Luquer Street & 4th Place, Carroll Gardens, Brooklyn (1-347 227 8227, http://blackgoldbrooklyn.com). Subway F or G to Smith & 9th Street. **Open** 6am-9pm Tue, Wed; 6am-9pm Thur, Fri; 10am-9pm Sat; 10am-5pm Sun. **Credit** AmEx, MC, V. **Map** p410 S11.
Coffee, records, antiques. What more could you want? It's ideal for people watching, with a cup of New Jersey's Rook coffee, or browse through bins of post-1960 45s and LPs. The constantly evolving collection mostly features rock, soul and jazz albums. Antique antlers ($100), framed crucifix prints ($80) and eerie black-and-white photo portraits ($70-$100) strike the right note.

The Dressing Room
For listings, *see p243*.
It's hard not to love a spot that combines drinking and shopping. On the street level of the two-floor emporium you'll find a co-op boutique for emerging local designers. The top floor is where you'll also find the charming dark oak bar. Check out the basement level clothing exchange, which features a maze of second-hand and vintage pieces at seriously good prices.

Martier
1010-1014 Second Avenue, between 53rd & 54th Streets (1-212 758 5370, martierusa.com). Subway E, M to Lexington Avenue-53rd Street. **Open** *Boutique* 10.30am-9pm daily. *Spa* 11am-8pm Tue, Wed; 11am-11pm Thur, Fri; 10am-8pm Sat; 11am-7pm Sun. *Café* 7am-9pm Mon-Fri; 8am-9pm Sat; 8am-9pm Sun. **Credit** AmEx, DC, Disc, MC, V. **Map** p405 F22.
The fun starts downstairs at the ritzy, just-opened spa. Savour the Continental bistro fare served at the upstairs restaurant delivered to you in the elegant spa lounge, or fuel up in the long dining room with plush leather benches. Nearly all the contemporary designer pieces in the super-sleek adjacent women's boutique are big-night-out-appropriate.

Valley/Portia and Manny
198 Elizabeth Street, at Prince Street (1-212 219 6400, www.portiaandmanny.com). Subway N, R to Prince Street. **Open** noon-7.30pm Mon-Sat; noon-6pm Sun. **Credit** AmEx, Disc, MC, V. **Map** p403 F29.
Fashionistas and beauty fiends flock to this vintage store-salon combo for one-of-a-kind duds and artistic manicures in a quaint, kitschy-cool setting. On the Portia & Manny side, browse the well-curated racks of mostly '60s and '70s fashions. Try the signature facial ($130-$300) with skin-care specialist Emma Graves, who created the holistic, organic product line Between You and the Moon ($22-$128) especially for Valley customers.

Earnest Sewn.

D/L Cerney

13 E 7th Street, between Second & Third Avenues, East Village (1-212 673 7033). Subway N, R to 8th Street-NYU; 6 to Astor Place. **Open** noon-8pm daily. **Credit** AmEx, MC, V. **Map** p403 F28.

Duane Cerney and his wife Linda St John branched out of their vintage clothing business by creating their own nostalgic designs; now the D/L Cerney line forms the bulk of the stock in this narrow shop: neat, figure-skimming dresses and nipped-in jackets for women, gabardine shirts and dapper suits for men – some in 1940s and '50s fabrics scored from a retiring Brooklyn tailor. Price points are reasonable: from around $150 for a dress, $225 and up for a gent's jacket. The selection of mint-condition vintage accessories is a remnant of the shop's earlier incarnation.

Dressing Room

75A Orchard Street, between Broome & Grand Streets, Lower East Side (1-212 966 7330, www.thedressingroomnyc.com). Subway B, D to Grand Street; F to Delancey Street. **Open** 1pm-midnight Sun, Tue, Wed; 1pm-2am Thur-Sat. **Credit** AmEx, MC, V. **Map** p403 F30.

At first glance, the Dressing Room may look like any Lower East side lounge, thanks to a handsome wood bar, but stylist and designer Nikki Fontanella's quirky co-op cum watering hole rewards the curious. The adjoining room displays designs by indie labels, which rotate every four months, while downstairs is a vintage and second-hand clothing exchange.

★ Earnest Sewn

821 Washington Street, between Gansevoort & Little West 12th Streets, Meatpacking District (1-212 242 3414, www.earnestsewn.com). Subway A, C, E to 14th Street; L to Eighth Avenue. **Open** 11am-7pm Mon-Sat; 11am-6pm Sun. **Credit** AmEx, MC, V. **Map** p403 C28.

Established by former Paper Denim & Cloth designer Scott Morrison, this culty jeans label marries vintage American style with old-school workmanship. Shirts and T-shirts for both genders, and select accessories, are also sold in the rustic, brick-walled space.

Other locations 90 Orchard Street, at Broome Street, Soho (1-212 979 5120).

Honey in the Rough

161 Rivington Street, between Clinton & Suffolk Streets, Lower East Side (1-212 228 6415, www.honeyintherough.com). Subway F to Delancey Street; J, M, Z to Delancey-Essex Streets. **Open** noon-8pm Mon-Sat; noon-7pm Sun. **Credit** AmEx, DC, Disc, MC, V. **Map** p403 G29.

Looking for something sweet and charming? Hit this cosy, ultra-femme boutique. Owner Ashley Hanosh fills the well-worn spot with an excellent line-up of local indie labels, including Samantha Pleet, Thread Social and Nomia, alongside carefully selected accessories, some of which are exclusive to the shop. In the downstairs beauty studio, Rosie Rodriguez offers eyebrow sculpting, make-up application and more.

Market NYC

268 Mulberry Street, between Houston & Prince Streets, Nolita (no phone, www.themarketnyc.com). Subway B, D, F, M to Broadway-Lafayette Street; N, R to Prince Street; 6 to Bleecker Street. **Open** 11am-7pm Sat, Sun. **No credit cards**. **Map** p403 F29.

Every weekend, independent clothing and accessories designers set up shop in the gymnasium of a church's youth centre (complete with basketball hoop), giving punters the chance to buy a variety of unique wares direct from the makers.

Nepenthes

307 W 38th Street, between Eighth & Ninth Avenues, Garment District (1-212 643 9540, nepenthesny.com). Subway A, C, E, 1, 2, 3 to 34th St–Penn Station. **Open** noon-7pm Mon-Fri; noon-5pm Sat, Sun. **Credit** AmEx, Disc, MC, V. **Map** p404 C24.

Well-dressed dudes with an eye on the Japanese style scene will already be familiar with this Tokyo fashion retailer. But with its first US location in the Garment District, Nepenthes's followers can finally get the store's urban rustic threads on their home turf. The large, high-ceilinged space holds an eclectic mix of well-designed, expertly crafted menswear including pieces from house label Engineered Garments, such as plaid flannel work shirts ($167), hooded knee-length ponchos ($460) and knit wool cardigans ($385). A rack in the back holds items from FWK, a female version of the Engineered Garments line ($154-$575).

Nom de Guerre

640 Broadway, at Bleecker Street, Greenwich Village (1-212 253 2891, www.nomdeguerre.net). Subway 6 to Bleecker Street. **Open** noon-8pm Mon-Sat, noon-7pm Sun. **Credit** AmEx, MC, V. **Map** p403 E29.

INSIDE TRACK FINE VINTAGE

Three times a year, the **Manhattan Vintage Clothing Show** touches down at Chelsea's Metropolitan Pavilion (125 W 18th Street, between Sixth & Seventh Avenues, 1-518 434 4312, www.manhattanvintage.com). With around 90 exhibitors from across the country (and beyond), selling garb from the 19th century through the 1980s, it attracts vintage aficionados as well as the fashion crowd (Ralph Lauren often sends a posse of scouts for inspiration). Admission is $20.

Fitting in nicely with its revolutionary name, this upscale streetwear label's Noho flagship is designed to resemble a bunker; the average shopper would have to be sleuth-level perceptive to spot the faded stencil on the sidewalk in front of the forbidding caged metal staircase that leads down to the store. A design collective founded by four New Yorkers, the understated line has a rugged, utilitarian look, encompassing military-inspired jackets, tailored sportswear, classic shirts and knitwear.

Odin

199 Lafayette Street, between Broome & Kenmare Streets, Soho (1-212 966 0026, www.odinnewyork.com). Subway 6 to Spring Street. **Open** 11am-8pm Mon-Sat; noon-7pm Sun. **Credit** AmEx, MC, V. **Map** p403 E30.
The Norse god Odin is often portrayed sporting an eye patch and an array of shabby robes to complement his dour, bearded visage. That may have been fashionable in medieval Scandinavia, but to make it in NYC, he'd have to pick up some Engineered Garments, Rag & Bone or Comme des Garçons from this upscale men's boutique bearing his name. Also look out for the Edward line of classic shirts and tailoring – the store's collaboration with West Village design duo Duckie Brown.
Other locations 328 E 11th Street, between First & Second Avenues (1-212 475 0666).

Opening Ceremony

35 Howard Street, between Broadway & Lafayette Street, Soho (1-212 219 2688, www.openingceremony.us). Subway J, M, N, Q, R, Z, 6 to Canal Street. **Open** 11am-8pm Mon-Sat; noon-7pm Sun. **Credit** AmEx, MC, V. **Map** p403 E30.
The name references the Olympic Games; each year the store assembles hip US designers (Band of Outsiders, Alexander Wang, Patrik Ervell, Rodarte) and pits them against the competition from abroad in its chandelier-lit warehouse-size space. While the next theme has yet to be announced, the store is currently focusing on high-profile collaborations, including Chloë Sevigny's line, which channels preppy style.

Voz.

Reed Space

151 Orchard Street, between Rivington & Stanton Streets, Lower East Side (1-212 253 0588, www.thereedspace.com). Subway F, J, M, Z to Essex Street-Delancey. **Open** 1-7pm Mon-Fri; noon-7pm Sat, Sun. **Credit** AmEx, MC, V. **Map** p403 F29.
Reed Space is the brainchild of Jeff Staple (Staple Design), who has worked on product design and branding with the likes of Nike, Timberland and New Era. It displays a collection of local and international urban menswear brands (10.Deep, Mishka, Crooks & Castle), footwear (including exclusive Staple collaborations), and hard-to-get accessories, such as Japanese Head Porter nylon bags and

pouches. Art books and culture mags are shelved on an eye-popping 'chair wall' – four stacked rows of white chairs fixed to one wall.

Suite Orchard

145A Orchard Street, at Rivington Street, Lower East Side (1-212 533 4115, www.suiteorchard.com). Subway F to Second Avenue-Lower East Side; J, M, Z to Delancey Street. **Open** noon-7pm Tue, Wed, Fri, Sun; noon-8pm Thur, Sat. **Credit** AmEx, DC, MC, V. **Map** p403 F29.

Fashion veterans and sisters Cindy and Sonia Huang worked at Diane von Furstenberg and Chloé, respectively, before joining forces to make their mark on the Lower East Side. Adorned with grey and white striped walls, this boudoir-inspired spot pays tribute to their well-honed aesthetic via gamine pieces from an international cast of designers, including Alexander Wang, Sonia by Sonia Rykiel, Hanii Y and Karen Walker.

Voz

618 E 9th Street, between Avenues B & C, East Village (1-646 845 9618, www.voznewyork.com). Subway L to First Avenue. **Open** 2-8pm Tue-Fri. **Credit** AmEx, MC, V. **Map** p403 G28.

This artistically presented shop is a pleasure to browse – loose pages from a 1950s Webster's dictionary are pressed and sealed into the floors, and the stock spans fashion, mid-century Danish and modern furniture, paintings and pottery. Owners Alex de Laxalt and Naoko Ito believe a woman's wardrobe should be equally eclectic, so they've rounded up a mix of labels – including Gary Graham, Givenchy and Lolita Lempicka – from different countries and at different price points, and vintage pieces by the likes of Yves Saint Laurent and Sonia Rykiel. The duo hope to launch their own label, Ito de Laxalt, soon.

Used & vintage

Allan & Suzi

416 Amsterdam Avenue, at 80th Street, Upper West Side (1-212 724 7445, www.allanandsuzi.net). Subway 1 to 79th Street. **Open** 12.30-7pm Mon-Sat; noon-6pm Sun. **Credit** AmEx, Disc, MC, V. **Map** p405 C19.

Models and celebs drop off worn-once Gaultiers, Muglers, Pradas and Manolos here. The platform shoe collection is flashback-inducing and incomparable, as is the selection of vintage jewellery.

Beacon's Closet

88 North 11th Street, between Berry Street & Wythe Avenue, Williamsburg, Brooklyn (1-718 486 0816, www.beaconscloset.com). Subway L to Bedford Avenue. **Open** 11am-9pm Mon-Fri; 11am-8pm Sat, Sun. **Credit** AmEx, DC, Disc, MC, V. **Map** p411 U7.

Some vintage boutiques have prices more akin to major fashion labels. Not so at this bustling Brooklyn favourite, where not only are the prices great, but so is the Williamsburg-appropriate clothing selection – from iconic T-shirts and party dresses to sneakers, leathers and denim.

Chelsea Girl Couture

186 Spring Street, between Sullivan & Thompson Streets, Soho (1-212 343 7090, www.chelsea-girl.com). Subway A, C, E, 1 to Canal Street. **Open** noon-7pm daily. **Credit** AmEx, MC, V. **Map** p403 E30.

Owner Elisa Casas fills her jewel box of a space with pristine, on-trend, upscale garb from the '20s through '80s, including YSL, Diane Von Furstenberg and Pucci. No matter what your period proclivity, glam girls can find everything from 1950s Doris Day-style prom dresses to a ruched leopard-print frock fit for Alexis Carrington.

Edith Machinist

104 Rivington Street, between Essex & Ludlow Streets, Lower East Side (1-212 979 9992). Subway F to Delancey Street; J, M, Z to Delancey-Essex Streets. **Open** 1-8pm Mon-Fri; noon-8pm Sat; noon-7pm Sun. **Credit** AmEx, DC, Disc, MC, V. **Map** p403 G29.

An impeccable assemblage of leather bags, shoes and boots is the main draw here, but you'll also find a whittled-down collection of clothes, including a small men's section.

INA

15 Bleecker Street, between Bowery & Lafayette Street, Greenwich Village (1-212 228 8511, www.inanyc.com). Subway 6 to Bleecker Street; B, D, F, M to Broadway-Lafayette Street. **Open** noon-8pm Mon-Sat; noon-7pm Sun. **Credit** AmEx, MC, V. **Map** p403 F29.

For more than 20 years, INA has been a leading light of the designer-resale scene. A string of five consignment shops offers immaculate, bang-on-trend items (Christian Louboutin and Manolo Blahnik shoes, Louis Vuitton and Marc Jacobs bags, clothing by Alexander McQueen and Marni) at a fraction of their original prices. This branch caters to both sexes; others (check the website for details of locations) are for men or women only.

Other locations throughout the city.

Laurel Canyon

63 Thompson Street, between Broome & Spring Streets, Soho (1-212 343 1658). Subway A, C, E, 1 to Canal Street. **Open** noon-7pm daily. **Credit** AmEx, MC, V. **Map** p403 E30.

In this shrine to the 1970s, the days of Joni Mitchell, the Mamas and the Papas, and the Eagles will never die. Expect an impressive array of men's Western-style shirts, worn-in cowboy boots and a standout collection of romantic Victorian-style, long tiered dresses that are way sexier than anything ever worn on *Little House on the Prairie*.

Marmalade

172 Ludlow Street, between Houston & Stanton Streets, Lower East Side (1-212 473 8070, www.marmaladevintage.com). Subway F to Lower East Side-Second Avenue. **Open** noon-8pm daily. **Credit** AmEx, MC, V. **Map** p403 G29.
Containing a kaleidoscope of covetable colours and patterns, Marmalade has some of the hottest 1970s and '80s threads to be found below Houston Street, including a rainbow of retro shoes.

New & Almost New

166 Elizabeth Street, at Kenmare Street, Nolita (1-212 226 6677, www.newandalmostnew.com). Subway 6 to Spring Street; B, D to Grand Street. **Open** 12.30-6.30pm Tue-Sat; 1-5pm Sun. **Credit** AmEx, Disc, MC, V. **Map** p403 F30.
Germophobe label-lovers, rejoice: 40% of the merchandise at this resale shop is brand new. Owner Maggie Chan hand selects each and every piece, ensuring its quality and authenticity. Among the items hanging on the colour-coded racks are lofty labels such as Prada, Chanel and Hermès (prices from $15 to $600).

FASHION ACCESSORIES & SERVICES

Cleaning & repairs

There are numerous dry-cleaners and shoe-repair shops in most neighbourhoods, but the following come recommended if you're looking for a particularly difficult job to be done.

New Erotica Boutiques

Get your rocks off at three nouveau sex emporiums.

Coco de Mer

236 Elizabeth Street, between E Houston & Prince Streets (1-212 966 9069, www.cocodemerusa.com). Subway 6 to Spring Street. **Open** noon-6pm Mon, Tue, Sun; noon-8pm Wed-Sat. **Credit** AmEx, DC, Disc, MC, V. **Map** p403 F29.
The first NYC outpost of this eight-year-old British boutique, founded by Justine and Samantha Roddick, puts the ass in class. Think: racy lingerie by Stella McCartney, sustainable-wood paddles, comics (*Anal Intruders from Uranus!*) and dog masks. Dressing rooms share a confessional-style partition, and one is equipped with a digital camera (use your imagination).

Museum of Sex Gift Shop

233 Fifth Avenue, betweem 27th & 28th Streets (1-212 689 6337, ext 116, www.museumofsex.com). Subway N, R, 6 to 28th Street. **Open** 11am-6.30pm Mon-Fri, Sun; 11am-8pm Sat. **Credit** AmEx, MC, V. **Map** p404 E26.
The Museum of Sex's recently overhauled gift shop is now twice the size. 'We wanted the store to be a destination shop,' says creative director Mark Snyder. 'We're looking at products for their art, their design and their technology.' Such lofty merchandise includes the Dirty Flirty Novelty Company's festive glass 'pornaments' and Matteo Cibic's functional fishbowl dildo.

Shag Brooklyn

108 Roebling Street, at North 6th Street, Williamsburg, Brooklyn (1-347 721 3302, weloveshag.com). Subway L to Bedford Avenue. **Open** noon-8pm Tue-Thur, Sun; noon-10pm Fri, Sat. **Credit** AmEx, DC, Disc, MC, V. **Map** p411 U8.
Samantha Bard and Ashley Montgomery-Pulido's spankin'-new shop boasts a top-rate selection of toys, including wood and marble dildos, plus hats, jewellery, home goods, fine art and even vagina doorknobs.

Shag Brooklyn.

CONSUME

Acme Cleaners

508 Hudson Street, between Christopher & W 10th Streets, West Village (1-212 255 4702). Subway 1 to Christopher Street. **Open** 7am-7pm Mon-Fri; 8am-6pm Sat. **Credit** AmEx, MC, V. **Map** p403 D29.

In an area populated by posh boutiques, this highly regarded drycleaners gets referrals from its fashionable neighbours. But the prices are still down to earth: from $4.50 for a top; $7 for a jacket or trousers.

Leather Spa

10 W 55th Street, between Fifth & Sixth Avenues, Midtown (1-212 262 4823, www.leatherspa.com). Subway E, M to Fifth Avenue-53rd Street. **Open** 8am-7pm Mon-Fri; 10am-6pm Sat. **Credit** AmEx, Disc, MC, V. **Map** p405 E22.

Recommended by glossy mags and posh shoe shops, the crème de la crème of cobblers can rejuvenate even the most faded footwear and handbags – at a price. As well as standard repairs (from $12 for a women's reheel), a cleaning and reconditioning service is offered (from $35).

Clothing hire

New York Vintage

17 W 25th Street, between Sixth & Seventh Avenues, Flatiron District (1-212 647 1107, www.newyorkvintage.com). Subway F, M, 1 to 23rd Street. **Open** noon-6.30pm Mon-Wed, Fri-Sun; or by appt. **Credit** AmEx, MC, V. **Map** p404 D26.

Vogue photographs featuring the store's antique garb line the walls at this living-history reservoir, where everything from 19th-century walking suits to neon Vivienne Westwood platforms is neatly arranged by era. Walk-ins are welcome at the shop/rental agency, but it's worth calling ahead to peruse the appointment-only upstairs area. There, you'll find a priceless ostrich-hemmed 1920s gold lamé gown by designer Charles Frederick Worth, a 1960s chain-link Paco Rabanne vest and Josephine Baker's rhinestone-encrusted 1920s bra (recently rented by Lady Gaga). Pricing depends on the item and length of rental; there is a minimum fee of $200.

Hats

★ JJ Hat Center

310 Fifth Avenue, at 32nd Street, Flatiron District (1-212 239 4368, www.jjhatcenter.com). Subway B, D, F, M, N, Q, R to 34th Street-Herald Square. **Open** 9am-6pm Mon-Fri; 9.30am-5.30pm Sat. **Credit** AmEx, DC, Disc, MC, V. **Map** p404 E25.

Trad hats are back in fashion, but this venerable shop, in business since 1911, is oblivious to passing trends. Dapper gents sporting the shop's wares will help you choose from more than 2,000 fedoras, pork pies, caps and other styles on display in the splendid, chandelier-illuminated, wood-panelled showroom. The store's prices start at $35 for a wool-blend cap.

INSIDE TRACK DISCOUNT EXCURSION

Although there's no shortage of bargain emporia in Manhattan, a trip upstate to **Woodbury Common Premium Outlets** (1-845 928 4000, www.premiumoutlets.com), about two hours from Midtown, is a fun excursion. The place looks like a colonial village, except the houses are occupied by more than 200 designer shops, including Barneys New York, Balenciaga, Chloé and Ralph Lauren – all offering big discounts. Hampton Luxury Liner (1-631 567 5100, www.hamptonluxuryliner.com) offers daily coach service for $42 round-trip from various Manhattan locations.

Still Life

77 Orchard Street, between Broome & Grand Streets, Little Italy (1-212 575 9704, www.stilllifenyc.com). Subway F to Delancey Street; J, M, Z to Delancey-Essex Streets. **Open** noon-7pm daily. **Credit** AmEx, DC, MC, V. **Map** p403 F30.

Biggie and Tupac's portraits share wall space at this chapeau shop, and if the rappers couldn't make peace in life, at least they can posthumously agree on the virtue of a well-made hat. Owner Frenel Morris's natty men's headwear pieces ($75-$300) are definitely not dusty throwbacks. He often scours the city for artful ribbon and feathers to finish his creations (custom hats are a mere $50 more). A range of Kanye-style vintage sunglasses ($150-$500) and a small selection of men's clothing are also sold.

Victor Osborne

160 Orchard Street, between Rivington & Stanton Streets, Lower East Side (1-212 677 6254, www.victorosborne.com). Subway F to Second Ave-Lower East Side. **Open** noon-8pm daily. **Credit** AmEx, Disc, MC, V. **Map** p403 F29.

Victor Osborne's Lower East Side shop and atelier opened its doors in 2009 with an ample selection of handmade hats for men and women. In addition to collaborations with Diesel Black Gold, Trovata, Andrew Buckler and the Blonds, Osborne recently partnered with Opening Ceremony on a capsule collection of spring pieces. Non-custom hats range in price from $159 for a satin turban cap to $200 for a Trilby, cloche or fedora.

Jewellery

Alexis Bittar

465 Broome Street, between Greene & Mercer Streets, Soho (1-212 625 8340, www.alexisbittar.com). Subway N, R to Prince Street; 6 to Spring Street. **Open** 11am-7pm Mon-Sat; noon-6pm Sun. **Credit** AmEx, DC, Disc, MC, V. **Map** p403 E30.

The jewellery designer who started out selling his designs from a humble Soho street stall now has two shops to show off his art-object designs, including his trademark sculptural Lucite cuffs and oversized crystal-encrusted earrings. All are handcrafted in his Brooklyn atelier.
Other locations 353 Bleecker Street, between Charles & 10th Streets, West Village (1-212 727 1093).

★ Doyle & Doyle

189 Orchard Street, between Houston & Stanton Streets, Lower East Side (1-212 677 9991, www.doyledoyle.com). Subway F to Lower East Side-Second Avenue. **Open** 1-7pm Tue, Wed, Fri; 1-8pm Thur; noon-7pm Sat, Sun. **Credit** AmEx, MC, V. **Map** p403 F29.
Whether your taste is art deco or nouveau, Victorian or Edwardian, gemologist sisters Pam and Elizabeth Doyle, who specialise in estate and antique jewellery, will have that one-of-a-kind item you're looking for, including engagement and eternity rings. The artfully displayed pieces within wall-mounted wooden framed cases are just a fraction of what's in stock.

Lingerie & underwear

Bloomingdale's has an encyclopaedic lingerie department, but **Victoria's Secret** (www.victoriassecret.com) remains the choice of the masses for their inexpensive yet pretty unmentionables.

See also p246 **New Erotica Boutiques**.

Bra Smyth

905 Madison Avenue, between 72nd & 73rd Streets, Upper East Side (1-212 772 9400, www.brasmyth.com). Subway 6 to 77th Street. **Open** 10am-6.30pm Mon-Sat; noon-5pm Sun. **Credit** AmEx, Disc, MC, V. **Map** p405 E20.
This shop stocks sizes to suit all cleavages, and the employees are so experienced that they can guess your bust measurements the second you walk in the door (they're usually right). On-site seamstresses can alter your purchase for a customised fit.
Other locations 2177 Broadway, at 77th Street (1-212 721 5111).

★ Kiki de Montparnasse

79 Greene Street, between Broome & Spring Streets, Soho (1-212 965 8150, www.kikidm.com). Subway N, R to Prince Street; 6 to Spring Street. **Open** 11am-7pm Mon, Sun; 11am-8pm Tue-Sat. **Credit** AmEx, Disc, MC, V. **Map** p403 E30.
This erotic luxury boutique channels the spirit of its namesake, a 1920s sexual icon and Man Ray muse, with a posh array of tastefully provocative contemporary lingerie in satin and French lace, including such novelties as cotton tank tops with built-in garters and knickers embroidered with saucy legends. Bedroom accoutrements, such as molten crystal 'dilettos' and tastefully packaged 'intimacy kits', give new meaning to the term 'satisfied customer'.

Luggage

Flight 001

96 Greenwich Avenue, between Jane & 12th Streets, Meatpacking District (1-212 989 0001, www.flight001.com). Subway A, C, E to 14th Street; L to Eighth Avenue. **Open** 11am-8pm Mon-Sat; noon-6pm Sun. **Credit** AmEx, DC, Disc, MC, V. **Map** p403 D28.
As well as a tasteful selection of luggage by the likes of Mandarina Duck, Rimowa and Hideo Wakamatsu, this one-stop shop carries everything for the chic jet-setter, including fun travel products such as Redeye Pak in-flight survival kits, eye masks, emergency totes that squash down to tennis ball size and 'essentials' such as expanding toilet tissue tablets and single-use packets of Woolite.
Other locations 132 Smith Street, between Bergen & Dean Streets, Boerum Hill, Brooklyn (1-718 243 0001).

Shoes

★ Alife Rivington Club

158 Rivington Street, between Clinton & Suffolk Streets, Lower East Side (1-212 375 8128, www.rivingtonclub.com). Subway F to Delancey Street; J, M, Z to Delancey-Essex Streets. **Open** noon-7pm daily. **Credit** AmEx, MC, V. **Map** p403 G29.
Whether you're looking for a simple white trainer or a trendy graphic style, you'll want to gain entry to this 'club', which stocks a wide range of major brands including Nike, Adidas and New Balance, along with less mainstream names. Shoes that get sneaker freaks salivating include retro styles such as Warrior Footwear, an athletic-shoe line that originated in China in the 1930s, and the Nike Air Jordan 1.

Moo Shoes

78 Orchard Street, between Broome & Grand Streets, Lower East Side (1-212 254 6512, www.mooshoes.com). Subway F to Delancey Street; J, M, Z to Delancey-Essex Streets. **Open** 11.30am-7.30pm Mon-Sat; noon-6pm Sun. **Credit** AmEx, DC, Disc, MC, V. **Map** p403 G30.
Cruelty-free footwear is far more fashionable than it once was (Stella McCartney's non-leather line is a case in point). Moo stocks a variety of brands for men and women, such as Vegetarian Shoes and Novacas, plus styles from independent designers such as Elizabeth Olsen, whose arty line of high heels and handbags is anything but hippyish.

Shoe Woo

750 Lexington Avenue, between 59th & 60th Streets, Upper East Side (1-212 486 8094, www.shoewoo.com). Subway N, R to Lexington

Avenue-59th Street; 4, 5, 6 to 59th Street. **Open** 10am-8pm Mon-Sat; 11am-7pm Sun. **Credit** AmEx, Disc, MC, V. **Map** p405 E22.
A fun alternative to the women's shoe section of a department store, this spacious footwear flagship brings together numerous mid-range lines such as Enzo Angiolini, Circa and Joan & David in a whimsical two-level space. Part *Alice in Wonderland*, part fantasy shoe shrine, it has a giant stiletto adorning one wall, heels posed on pedestals, and plush sofas and seating around every corner.

Sigerson Morrison

19 71st Street, between Fifth & Madison Avenues, Upper East Side (1-212 734 2100, www.sigersonmorrison.com). Subway 6 to 68th Street. **Open** 10am-6pm Mon-Sat. **Credit** AmEx, MC, V. **Map** p405 E20.
Keri Sigerson and Miranda Morrison's footwear brand may have a Downtown vibe, but their latest venture is a concept store (which doubles as an art gallery) on the posh Upper East Side. Alongside the sleek – often 1960s or '70s-inspired – boots and pixie-like flats (from around $350) you'll find accessories such as bags and gloves, plus goods from SM-approved vendors, such as Maria Beaulieu's coral-inspired earrings or the intoxicating 06130 French perfumes. The duo's Belle line is more affordable.
Other locations 28 Prince Street, between Elizabeth & Mott Streets, Nolita (1-212 219 3893); Belle, 242 Mott Street, between Houston & Prince Streets, Nolita (1-212 941 5404).

FOOD & DRINK

Bakeries

Amy's Bread

672 Ninth Avenue, between 46th & 47th Streets, Hell's Kitchen (1-212 977 2670, www.amysbread.com). Subway C, E to 50th Street; N, R to 49th Street. **Open** 7.30am-11pm Mon-Fri; 8am-11pm Sat; 9am-6pm Sun. **Credit** AmEx, Disc, MC, V. **Map** p404 C23.
Whether you want sweet (double-chocolate pecan Chubbie cookies) or savoury (hefty French sourdough *boules*), Amy's never disappoints. Breakfast and snacks such as the grilled cheese sandwich (made with New York State cheddar) are also served.
Other locations Chelsea Market, 75 Ninth Avenue, between 15th & 16th Streets, Chelsea (1-212 462 4338); 250 Bleecker Street, at Leroy Street, West Village (1-212 675 7802).

Billy's Bakery

184 Ninth Avenue, between 21st & 22nd Streets, Chelsea (1-212 647 9956, www.billysbakerynyc.com). Subway C, E to 23rd Street. **Open** 8.30am-11pm Mon-Thur; 8.30am-midnight Fri, Sat; 9am-10pm Sun. **Credit** AmEx, Disc, MC, V. **Map** p404 C26.
Amid super-sweet retro delights such as coconut cream pie, cupcakes, Hello Dollies (indulgent graham cracker treats) and Famous Chocolate Icebox Cake, you'll find friendly service in a setting that will remind you of grandma's kitchen – or, at least, it will if your grandmother was Betty Crocker.
Other locations 75 Franklin Street, between Broadway & Church Street, Tribeca (1-212 647 9958).

Levain Bakery

167 W 74th Street, between Columbus & Amsterdam Avenues, Upper West Side (1-212 874 6080, www.levainbakery.com). Subway 1 to 79th Street. **Open** 8am-7pm Mon-Sat; 9am-7pm Sun. **Credit** AmEx, MC, V. **Map** p405 C20.
Forget the Big Apple – a Big Cookie is much tastier. Levain's are a full 6oz, and the massive mounds stay gooey in the middle. The lush, brownie-like double-chocolate variety, made with extra-dark French cocoa and semi-sweet chocolate chips, is a truly decadent treat.

Drinks

Astor Wines & Spirits

399 Lafayette Street, at 4th Street, East Village (1-212 674 7500, www.astorwines.com). Subway 6 to Astor Place; N, R to 8th Street-NYU. **Open** 9am-9pm Mon-Sat; noon-6pm Sun. **Credit** AmEx, DC, Disc, MC, V. **Map** p403 F28.
An oenophile's delight, high-ceilinged, wide-aisled Astor Wines is a terrific place to browse for wines of every price range, vineyard and year – which makes it a favourite hunting ground for the city's top sommeliers. Sakés and spirits are also well represented.

Porto Rico Importing Co

201 Bleecker Street, at Sixth Avenue, Greenwich Village (1-212 477 5421, www.portorico.com). Subway A, B, C, D, E, F, M to W 4th Street. **Open** 8am-9pm Mon-Fri; 9am-9pm Sat; noon-7pm Sun. **Credit** AmEx, Disc, MC, V. **Map** p403 E29.
This small, family-run store has earned a large following with a terrific range of coffees as well as its own prepared blends. Prices are reasonable and the selection of teas warrants exploration.

THE BEST LOCALLY MADE GOODS

For handcrafted hats
Still Life. *See p247.*

For scents of the city
CB I Hate Perfume. *See p255.*

For arty bonbons
Bond Street Chocolates. *See p250.*

Other locations 107 Thompson Street, between Prince & Spring Streets, Soho (1-212 966 5758); 40½ St Marks Place, between First & Second Avenues, East Village (1-212 533 1982); 636 Grand Street, between Manhattan Avenue & Leonard Street, Williamsburg, Brooklyn (1-718 782 1200).

General

New York City now has six branches of natural food giant **Whole Foods Market** (www.wholefoodsmarket.com), a reliable bet for ready-prepared meals as well as organic produce, baked goods and toiletries. Longtime Soho gourmet grocer **Dean & DeLuca** (www.deananddeluca.com) operates several stores and cafés throughout the city.

Eataly

200 Fifth Avenue, between 23rd & 24th Streets Flatiron District (1-212 229 2560, www.eataly.com). Subway F, M, N, R to 23rd Street. **Open** 7am-11pm daily. **Credit** AmEx Disc, MC, V. **Map** p404 E26.

Going big can be a blessing or a curse in this town, but celebrity chef Mario Batali got it right. His massive shrine to Italian cuisine is a haven for foodies, encompassing four proper eateries, each devoted to a particular food group. Adjacent retail areas offer gourmet provisions – Piedmontese hamburger patties ($8.80 per lb), live Scottish langoustines ($32.80 per lb), imported cheeses infused with fresh truffles ($19.80 per lb) and more – so you can cook your own Italian feasts at home.

Zabar's

2245 Broadway, at 80th Street, Upper West Side (1-212 787 2000, www.zabars.com). Subway 1 to 79th Street. **Open** 8am-7.30pm Mon-Fri; 8am-8pm Sat; 9am-6pm Sun. **Credit** AmEx, MC, V. **Map** p405 C19.

Zabar's is more than just a market – it's a genuine New York City landmark. It began in 1934 as a tiny storefront specialising in Jewish 'appetising' delicacies and has gradually expanded to take over half a block of prime Upper West Side real estate. What never ceases to surprise, however, is its reasonable prices – even for high-end foods. Besides the famous smoked fish and rafts of delicacies, Zabar's has fabulous bread, cheese, olives and coffee – and an entire floor dedicated to gadgets and homewares.

Markets

More than 40 open-air **Greenmarkets**, run by a non-profit programme of the Council on the Environment of NYC, operate in various locations on different days. The largest and best known is at **Union Square**, where small producers of cheese, flowers, herbs, fruits and vegetables hawk their goods on Mondays, Wednesdays, Fridays and Saturdays (8am-6pm). Arrive early, before the prime stuff sells out. For other venues, contact Greenmarket (1-212 788 7476, www.cenyc.org/greenmarket).

The indoor **Chelsea Market** (75 Ninth Avenue, at 16th Street, www.chelseamarket.com, open 7am-10pm Mon-Sat; 8am-8pm Sun) is a one-stop gastronomic shopping playground. It has a number of high-quality stores selling flowers, fish, fruit, baked goods, meat and alcohol.

Specialist

★ Bond Street Chocolates

63 E 4th Street, between Bowery & Second Avenue, East Village (1-212 677 5103, www.bondstchocolate.com). Subway 6 to Bleecker Street. **Open** noon-8pm Tue-Sat. **Credit** MC, V. **Map** p403 F29.

Former pastry chef Lynda Stern's East Village spot is a grown-up's candy store, with quirky chocolate confections in shapes ranging from gilded Buddhas (and other multi-secular deities) to skulls, and flavours from elderflower to bourbon.

Jacques Torres Chocolate

350 Hudson Street, between Charlton & King Streets, entrance on King Street, Soho (1-212 414 2462, www.mrchocolate.com). Subway 1 to Houston Street. **Open** 9am-7pm Mon-Sat; 10am-6pm Sun. **Credit** ($10 min) AmEx, MC, V. **Map** p403 D29.

Walk into Jacques Torres's glass-walled shop and café, and you'll be surrounded by a Willy Wonka-esque factory that turns raw cocoa beans into luscious chocolate goodies before your eyes. As well as selling the usual assortments, truffles and bars (plus more unusual delicacies such as chocolate-covered cornflakes), the shop serves deliciously rich hot chocolate, steamed to order.

Other locations 66 Water Street, between Dock & Main Streets, Dumbo, Brooklyn (1-718 875 1269); 285 Amsterdam Avenue, between 73rd & 74th Streets, Upper West Side (1-212 787 3256).

Murray's Cheese

254 Bleecker Street, between Sixth & Seventh Avenues, Greenwich Village (1-212 243 3289, www.murrayscheese.com). Subway A, B, C, D, E, F, M to W 4th Street. **Open** 8am-8pm Mon-Sat; 10am-7pm Sun. **Credit** AmEx, MC, V. **Map** p403 D29.

For the last word in curd, New Yorkers have been flocking to Murray's since 1940 to sniff out the best international and domestic cheeses. The helpful staff will guide you through hundreds of stinky, runny, washed rind and aged cheesy comestibles.

★ Russ & Daughters

179 E Houston Street, between Allen & Orchard Streets, Lower East Side (1-212 475 4880, www.russanddaughters.com). Subway F to Lower

Smile. *See p252.*

East Side-Second Avenue. **Open** 8am-8pm Mon-Fri; 9am-7pm Sat; 8am-5.30pm Sun. **Credit** AmEx, Disc, MC, V. **Map** p403 F29.

The daughters in the name have given way to great-grandchildren, but this Lower East Side survivor, established in 1914, is still run by the same family. Specialising in smoked and cured fish and caviar, it sells ten varieties of smoked salmon, eight types of herring (pickled, salt-cured, smoked, etc) and many other Jewish-inflected Eastern European delectables. Bagels are available to take away (or eat standing up on the premises); the amazing Super Heebster is filled with fluffy whitefish salad, horseradish cream cheese and wasabi-flavoured flying-fish roe.

Yonah Schimmel Knish Bakery

137 E Houston Street, between First & Second Avenues, Lower East Side (1-212 477 2858, www.yonahschimmel.com). Subway F to Lower East Side-Second Avenue. **Open** 9am-7pm Mon-Thur, Sun; 9am-9pm Fri, Sat. **Credit** AmEx, DC, Disc, MC, V. **Map** p403 F29.

This 'knishery' has been doling out its carborific goodies since 1910. Traditional potato, kasha and spinach knishes are the most popular, but sweet potato and blueberry fillings are also available. The latkes (potato pancakes) are a city secret.

CONSUME

GIFTS & SOUVENIRS

★ Bowne & Co Stationers

South Street Seaport Museum, 211 Water Street, at Fulton Street, Financial District (1-212 748 8651). Subway A, C, J, M, Z to Broadway-Nassau Street. **Open** 10am-6pm daily. **Credit** AmEx, DC, MC, V. **Map** p402 F32.

South Street Seaport Museum's recreation of an 1870s-style print shop, Bowne & Co Stationers, doesn't just look the part: the 19th-century platen presses – hand-set using antique type and powered by a treadle – turn out everything from art prints to business cards (from $165 for 100) using classic Crane & Co stationery.

Brooklyn Superhero Supply Company

372 Fifth Avenue, between 5th & 6th Streets, Park Slope, Brooklyn (1-718 499 9884, www.superherosupplies.com). Subway F, R to 4th Avenue-9th Street. **Open** 11am-5pm daily. **Credit** AmEx, DC, Disc, MC, V. **Map** p410 T11.

This mysterious shop – where you can buy such novelties as capes, X-ray goggles and gallon tins of Immortality – is actually a front (and money-earner) for the non-profit 826 NYC kids' writing centre (a chapter of the San Francisco centre founded by novelist Dave Eggers), hidden behind a concealed door.

★ Kiosk

95 Spring Street, between Broadway & Mercer Street, Soho (1-212 226 8601, www.kioskkiosk.com). Subway 6 to Spring Street. **Open** 11am-7pm Mon-Sat. **Credit** AmEx, MC, V. **Map** p403 E30.

Don't be put off by the unprepossessing, graffiti-covered stairway that leads up to this gem of a shop in Soho. Alisa Grifo has collected an array of inexpensive items – mostly simple and functional but with a strong design aesthetic – from around the world, such as Finnish chalk, colourful net bags from Germany and hairpins in a cool retro box from Mexico. Wonderful for browsing.

Smile

26 Bond Street, at Lafayette Street, East Village (1-646 329 5836). Subway B, D, F, M to Broadway-Lafayette Street; 6 to Bleecker Street. **Open** 8am-midnight Mon-Fri; 10am-midnight Sat, Sun. **Credit** AmEx, DC, Disc, MC, V. **Map** p403 F29.

The artfully weathered sign, mullioned windows and benches outside make this mixed-use enterprise look like a cross between a tavern and a general store. In the rustic, stone-walled space – the brainchild of Carlos Quirarte (formerly of Earnest Sewn) and Matt Kliegman – wooden shelves display disparate yet discerningly chosen goods: scarves and ties made of dead-stock chambray by Brooklyn-based company the Hill-Side; Moscot sunglasses; hip knitting kits; toiletries by Santa Maria Novella; coffee from New York State roastery Plowshares; and teas by Mariage Frères – the latter two can be sipped in the restaurant, which serves breakfast, lunch (brunch at weekends) and dinner. *Photos p251.*

Sustainable NYC

139 Avenue A, at 9th Street, East Village (1-212 254 5400, www.sustainable-nyc.com). Subway L to First Avenue; 6 to Astor Place. **Open** 8am-10pm Mon-Wed; 8am-11pm Thur, Fri; 9am-11pm Sat; 9am-10pm Sun. **Credit** AmEx, Disc, MC, V. **Map** p403 G28.

This gift-centric shop houses a wealth of eco-minded goods within its green walls: organic shampoos and beauty products; fair-trade jewellery and chocolate; clutch bags and other gifts made from recycled materials; and sun-fuelled BlackBerry chargers.

HEALTH & BEAUTY

Complementary medicine

Body Central

Suite 505, 39 W 14th Street, between Fifth & Sixth Avenues, Union Square (1-212 677 5633, www.bodycentralnyc.com). Subway F, M to 14th Street; L, N, Q, R, 4, 5, 6 to 14th Street-Union Square. **Open** 12.30-6.45pm Mon, Wed; 8.30am-3.15pm Tue, Thur; 8.30-11.45am Fri. **Credit** AmEx, MC, V. **Map** p403 E28.

Under the direction of Dr JoAnn Weinrib, Body Central offers a range of health and wellness services including chiropractic, tension easing treatments for temporomandibular joint disorder (TMJ) and sinus pressure, and various forms of massage, including reflexology, shiatsu and deep-tissue.

Hairdressers & barbers

The styling superstars at **Frédéric Fekkai** (www.fredericfekkai.com, 4th Floor, Henri Bendel; *see p232*), **John Barrett Salon** (www.johnbarrett.com, 9th Floor, Bergdorf Goodman; *see p231*) and **Sally Hershberger Downtown** (2nd Floor, 423-425 W 14th Street, between Ninth & Tenth Avenues, 1-212 206 8700, www.sallyhershberger.com, closed Sun & Mon) are top-notch, but they tend to charge hair-raising prices.

Astor Place Hairstylist

2 Astor Place, at Broadway, East Village (1-212 475 9854). Subway N, R to 8th Street-NYU; 6 to Astor Place. **Open** 8am-8pm Mon, Sat; 8am-10pm Tue-Fri; 9am-6pm Sun. **No credit cards. Map** p403 E28.

The army of barbers here does everything from neat trims to more complicated and creative shaved designs. You can't make an appointment: just take a number and wait outside with the crowd. Sunday mornings are usually quieter. Cuts start at $15.

Blow

342 W 14th Street, between Eighth & Ninth Avenues, Meatpacking District (1-212 989 6282, www.blowny.com). Subway A, C, E to 14th Street. **Open** 8am-8pm Mon-Fri; 10am-8pm Sat; noon-6pm Sun. **Credit** AmEx, MC, V. **Map** p403 C27.

Launched as a scissor-free 'blow-dry bar', this award-winning salon now offers cuts, colour and select beauty services as well as expertly executed blow-outs ($40-$60, depending on length and texture). For curling- or flat-irons, add $10-$20.

Other locations 2nd Floor, 843 Lexington Avenue, between 64th & 65th Streets, Upper East Side (1-212 452 0246).

John Masters Organics

77 Sullivan Street, between Spring & Broome Streets, Soho (1-212 343 9590, www.johnmasters.com). Subway C, E to Spring Street; N, R to Prince Street. **Open** 10.30am-6.30pm Mon-Fri; 10am-6pm Sat. **Credit** AmEx, DC, MC, V. **Map** p403 E30.

A visit to this environmentally friendly salon, which is powered by wind energy, is like visiting an intoxicating botanical garden: the organic shiatsu scalp treatment ($80) will send you into relaxed oblivion, and ammonia-free, herbal-based colour treatments will appeal to your inner purist. Cuts or colour start at around $100, but even if you don't need a restyle, it's worth stopping in for John Masters Organics chic apothecary line.

Paul Molé Barber Shop

1031 Lexington Avenue, at 74th Street, Upper East Side (1-212 535 8461, www.paulmole.com). Subway 6 to 6th Street. **Open** 7.30am-8pm Mon-Fri; 7.30am-6pm Sat; 8am-4pm Sun. **No credit cards. Map** p405 E20.

Best known for its precise shaves, this nostalgic barbers' has been grooming men since 1913 (John Steinbeck used to come here to be debearded). As well as its signature Deluxe Open Razor Shave ($35), you can get a haircut (from $32) and add other services such as a scalp massage ($10).

Whittemore House

45 Grove Street, between Bleecker & Bedford Streets, West Village (1-212 242 8880, www.whittemorehousesalon.com). Subway 1 to Christopher Street-Sheridan Square. **Open** 9.30am-6pm Mon; 9.30am-8pm Tue, Wed; 9.30am-9pm Thur, Fri; 10am-6pm Sat. **Credit** AmEx, DC, Disc, MC, V. **Map** p403 D28.

Victoria Hunter and Larry Raspanti, who each spent more than 15 years dressing tresses at Bumble & Bumble, opened this new salon in the garden level of an 1830s mansion (one of the three oldest buildings in the city). The antithesis of streamlined minimalism, the decor features artfully aged woods, faux-decayed stencilled walls and big, comfy boudoir chairs. Cuts (starting at $90) and colour (a full head of foils starts at $150) come courtesy of a bevy of New York's best stylists, while soy-based mani-pedis, minifacials and waxing are administered by Rose Woo of Rescue Beauty Lounge.

★ Woodley & Bunny

490 Driggs Avenue, between North 9th & North 10th Streets, Williamsburg, Brooklyn (1-718 218 6588, www.woodleyandbunny.com). Subway L to Bedford Avenue; G to Nassau. **Open** 10am-9pm Mon-Fri; 9am-8pm Sat; 11am-7pm Sun. **Credit** Disc, MC, V. **Map** p411 U7.

With a prime Williamsburg location, Woodley & Bunny is where to get the most cutting-edge crop (from $75 for women, from $55 for men) or colour, but there's a welcome emphasis on individuality at this laid-back beauty spot. Part salon, part apothecary, it also offers treatments such as facials and waxing. And while you're getting shorn, you can sip local El Beit coffee, or something stronger, while listening to cool new music.

Opticians

A former flea market stall, **Fabulous Fanny's** (335 E 9th Street, between First & Second Avenues, East Village, 1-212 533 0637, www.fabulousfannys.com) has been the city's premier source of period frames for two decades, with more than 30,000 pairs of spectacles on offer, some them dating back to the 1700s.

Morgenthal Frederics

399 W Broadway, at Spring Street, Soho (1-212 966 0099, www.morgenthalfrederics.com). Subway C, E to Spring Street. **Open** 10am-7pm Mon-Fri; 11am-7pm Sat; noon-6pm Sun. **Credit** AmEx, Disc, MC, V. **Map** p403 E30.

The house-designed, handmade frames displayed in Morgenthal Frederics' David Rockwell-designed shops exude quality and subtly nostalgic style. Frames start from around $300 for plastic, but the buffalo horn and gold ranges are more expensive; you can even have a pair accented with tiny diamonds for around $2,000.

Other locations throughout the city.

Selima Optique

59 Wooster Street, at Broome Street, Soho (1-212 343 9490, www.selimaoptique.com). Subway C, E, 6 to Spring Street. **Open** 11am-8pm Mon-Sat; noon-7pm Sun. **Credit** AmEx, MC, V. **Map** p403 E30.

Eyewear designer Selima Salaun's spacious flagship stocks her full range of frames alongside other brands and vintage eyewear. Nostalgic styles, including square and curvy cat-eye 1950s-inspired shapes and 1970s-vibe large rounded frames, come in a variety of eye-catching colour combinations. You can have your prescription filled on-site (an optician is available for appointments on Fridays).

Other locations throughout the city.

Pharmacies

The fact that there's a **Duane Reade** pharmacy on almost every corner of Manhattan is lamented among chain-deriding locals; however, it's convenient if you need an aspirin pronto. Several branches, including the one at 250 W 57th Street, at Broadway (1-212 265 2101, www.duanereade.com), are open 24 hours. Competitor **Rite Aid** (with one of several 24-hour branches at 301 W 50th Street, at Eighth Avenue, 1-212 247 8736, www.riteaid.com) is also widespread.

CO Bigelow Chemists

414 Sixth Avenue, between 8th & 9th Streets, Greenwich Village (1-212 473 7324, www.bigelowchemists.com). Subway A, B, C, D, F, M to W 4th Street; 1 to Christopher Street. **Open** 7.30am-9pm Mon-Fri; 8.30am-7pm Sat; 8.30am-5.30pm Sun. **Credit** AmEx, Disc, MC, V. **Map** p403 D28.

Established back in 1838, Bigelow is the oldest apothecary in America. Its simply packaged and appealingly old-school line of toiletries include such tried-and-trusted favourites as Mentha Lip Shine, Barber Cologne Elixir Red No. 1584 and Lemon Body Cream. The spacious, chandelier-lit store is packed with natural remedies, organic skincare products and drugstore essentials – and they still fill prescriptions.

Shops

Aedes de Venustas

9 Christopher Street, at Sixth Avenue, West Village (1-212 206 8674, www.aedes.com). Subway A, B, C, D, F, M to W 4th Street; 1 to Christopher Street. **Open** noon-8pm Mon-Sat; 1-7pm Sun. **Credit** AmEx, Disc, MC, V. **Map** p403 D28.

Kiehl's.

Decked out like a 19th-century boudoir, this perfume collector's palace devotes itself to ultra-sophisticated fragrances and high-end skincare lines, such as Diptyque, Santa Maria Novella and its own glamorously packaged range of fragrances, candles and room sprays. Hard-to-find scents, such as Eau d'Italie's Umbrian-wood-accented sprays and Serge Lutens perfumes, line the walls.

Bond No.9

9 Bond Street, between Broadway & Lafayette Street, East Village (1-212 228 1732, www.bondno9.com). Subway B, D, F, M to Broadway-Lafayette Street; 6 to Bleecker Street. **Open** 11am-8pm Mon-Sat; noon-6pm Sun. **Credit** AmEx, DC, MC, V. **Map** p403 E29.

The collection of scents here pays olfactory homage to New York City. Choose from 41 'neighbourhoods' and 'sensibilities', including Wall Street, Park Avenue, Eau de Noho – even Chinatown (but don't worry, it smells of peach blossoms, gardenia and patchouli, not fish stands). A scent celebrating NYC's newest park, the High Line, made its debut in 2010. The arty bottles and neat, colourful packaging are particularly gift friendly.

Other locations 680 Madison Avenue, at 61st Street, Upper East Side (1-212 838 2780); 897 Madison Avenue, at 73rd Street, Upper East Side (1-212 794 4480); 399 Bleecker Street, at 11th Street, West Village (1-212 633 1641).

CB I Hate Perfume

93 Wythe Avenue, between North 10th & North 11th Streets, Williamsburg, Brooklyn (1-718 384 6890, www.cbihateperfume.com). Subway L to Bedford Avenue. **Open** noon-6pm Tue-Sat. **Credit** AmEx, DC, Disc, MC, V. **Map** p411 U7.

Contrary to his shop's name, Christopher Brosius doesn't actually hate what he sells; he just despises the concept of mass-produced fragrances. Although there's currently a year's waiting list to collaborate with him on a signature scent of your own, you can choose from 35 evocative, ready-made fragrances, such as Gathering Apples or At the Beach 1966.

Kiehl's

109 Third Avenue, between 13th & 14th Streets, East Village (1-212 677 3171, www.kiehls.com). Subway L to Third Avenue; N, Q, R, 4, 5, 6 to 14th Street-Union Square. **Open** 10am-8pm Mon-Sat; 11am-6pm Sun. **Credit** AmEx, DC, Disc, MC, V. **Map** p403 F27.

The apothecary founded on this East Village site in 1851 has morphed into a major, world-renowned skincare brand widely sold in upscale department stores, but the products, in their minimal-frills packaging, are still good value and produce great results. The lip balms and thick-as-custard Creme de Corps are cult classics.

Other locations 150 Columbus Avenue, between 66th & 67th Streets, Upper West Side (1-212 799 3438).

Spas & salons

Many of the city's luxury hotels are equipped with indulgent spas: those at the **Plaza** (*see p257* **Caudalie Vinothérapie Spa**), the **Surrey** (*see p178*) and **Waldorf-Astoria** (*see p177*) are especially recommended, as are the ones listed over leaf.

Fishs Eddy. *See p258.*

Caudalie Vinothérapie Spa
4th Floor, 1 W 58th Street, at Fifth Avenue, Midtown (1-212 265 3182, www.caudalie-usa.com). Subway N, R to Fifth Avenue-59th Street. **Open** noon-6pm Mon; 11am-7pm Tue, Wed; 11am-8pm Thur, Fri; 10am-7pm Sat; 11am-6pm Sun. **Credit** AmEx. MC, V. **Map** p405 E22.
The first Vinothérapie outpost in the US, and the first not attached to a European vineyard, this original spa harnesses the antioxidant power of grapes and vine leaves. The 8,000sq ft (740sq m) facility in the Plaza (*see p174*) offers such treatments as a Red Vine bath ($75) in one of its cherrywood 'barrel' tubs. In the wine lounge, relax with artisanal tipples from its French vineyard, cheeses and foie gras.

★ Great Jones Spa
29 Great Jones Street, at Lafayette Street, East Village (1-212 505 3185, www.greatjonesspa.com). Subway 6 to Astor Place. **Open** 9am-10pm daily. **Credit** AmEx, Disc, MC, V. **Map** p403 F29.
Based on the theory that water brings health, Great Jones is outfitted with a popular water lounge complete with subterranean pools, saunas, steam rooms and a three-and-a-half-storey waterfall. Enjoy the serenity of the 15,000sq ft (1,400sq m) paradise before a haircut ($90 and up), or treat yourself to a Coconut Paradise Manicure ($40). Access to the water lounge is complimentary with services over $100; alternatively, a three-hour pass is available for $50. Note that the spa is closed for maintenance some Monday mornings, so call before visiting.

Homme Spa
465 Lexington Avenue, between 45th & 46th Streets, Midtown East (1-212 983 0033, www.hommespa.com). Subway S, 4, 5, 6, 7 to 42nd Street-Grand Central. **Open** 11am-3am Mon-Fri; noon-midnight Sat, Sun. **Credit** AmEx, Disc, MC, V. **Map** p404 F24.
The ingenious idea of prefacing a signature hot-towel massage with a spell in a recliner, watching TV sports, is metrosexual nirvana. This bi-level space (which offers services for women, too) includes a sealed steam area, a sauna, a spacious lounge and softly lit treatment rooms.

Juvenex
5th Floor, 25 W 32nd Street, between Fifth Avenue & Broadway, Garment District (1-646 733 1330, www.juvenexspa.com). Subway B, D, F, M, N, Q, R to 34th Street-Herald Square. **Open** 24hrs daily. **Credit** AmEx, MC, V. **Map** p404 E25.
This huge, bustling Koreatown relaxation hub may be slightly rough around the edges (frayed towels, dingy sandals), but it retains appeal for its bathhouse meets Epcot feel (igloo saunas, tiled 'soaking ponds', and a slatted bridge), and 24hr availability (women only before 5pm). The Basic Purification Program – including soak and sauna, face, body and hair cleansing, and a salt scrub – is great value at $115.

Tattoos & piercings

Invisible NYC
148 Orchard Street, between Stanton & Rivington Streets, Lower East Side (1-212 228 1358, www.invisiblenyc.com). Subway F to Lower East Side-Second Avenue. **Open** 1-9pm daily. **No credit cards. Map** p403 F29.
At this tattoo salon specialising in large-scale Japanese body art, human canvases are adorned in the back and contemporary paintings are sold in the front gallery. The five inkers at Invisible NYC have waiting lists ranging from a couple of weeks to a few months, but the doodles are all custom-made, so your $180/hour artwork is guaranteed to be one of a kind.

HOUSE & HOME

Antiques

Antiques Garage
112 W 25th Street, between Sixth & Seventh Avenues, Chelsea (1-212 243 5343, www.annexmarkets.com). Subway F, M to 23rd Street. **Open** 9am-5pm Sat, Sun. **No credit cards. Map** p404 D26.
Designers (and the occasional celebrity) hunt regularly at this flea market in a vacant parking garage. Specialities include old prints, vintage clothing and household paraphernalia. The weekend outdoor Hell's Kitchen Flea Market, run by the same people, features a mix of vintage clothing and textiles, furniture and miscellaneous bric-a-brac.
Other locations 39th Street, between Ninth & Tenth Avenues, Hell's Kitchen.

★ Mantiques Modern
146 W 22nd Street, between Sixth & Seventh Avenues, Chelsea (1-212 206 1494, www.mantiquesmodern.com). Subway 1 to 23rd Street. **Open** 10.30am-6.30pm Mon-Fri; 11am-7pm Sat, Sun. **Credit** MC, V. **Map** p404 D26.
Walking into this bi-level shop is a little like stumbling upon the private collection of some mad professor. Specialising in industrial and modernist furnishings and art from the 1880s to the 1980s, Mantiques Modern is a fantastic repository of beautiful and bizarre items, from kinetic sculptures and early-20th-century wooden artists' mannequins to a Russian World War II telescope and a rattlesnake frozen in a slab of Lucite. Pieces by famous designers such as Hermès sit side by side with natural curiosities, and skulls (in metal or Lucite), crabs, animal horns and robots are all recurring themes.

Showplace Antique & Design Center
40 W 25th Street, between Fifth & Sixth Avenues, Flatiron District (1-212 633 6063, www.nyshowplace.com). Subway F, M to 23rd Street. **Open** 10am-6pm Mon-Sat; 8.30am-5.30pm Sun. **Credit** varies. **Map** p404 E26.

Set over four expansive floors, this indoor market houses more than 200 high-quality dealers selling everything from vintage designer wear to Greek and Roman antiquities. Among the highlights are Joe Sundlie Vintedge's colourful, spot-on-trend vintage pieces from Lanvin and Alaïa on the ground floor, and Waves LLC (on the ground and second levels) for early radios and phonographs. But our favourite is Mood Indigo – arguably the best source in the city for collectible bar accessories and dinnerware. The array of Bakelite jewellery and table accessories, Fiestaware, and novelty cocktail glasses is dazzling, and it's a wonderful repository of art deco cigarette cases, lighters and New York memorabilia.

General

★ ABC Carpet & Home

888 Broadway, at 19th Street, Flatiron District (1-212 473 3000, www.abchome.com). Subway L, N, Q, R, 4, 5, 6 to 14th Street-Union Square. **Open** 10am-7pm Mon-Sat; 11am-6.30pm Sun. **Credit** AmEx, Disc, MC, V. **Map** p403 E27.

Most of ABC's 35,000-strong carpet range is housed in the store across the street at no.881 – except the rarest rugs, which reside on the sixth floor of the main store. Browse everything from organic soap to hand-beaded lampshades on the bazaar-style ground floor. On the upper floors, furniture spans every style, from slick European minimalism to antique oriental and mid-century modern, and the Conran Shop just relocated from its Upper East Side store to the basement. The massive Bronx warehouse outlet (its address is below) offers discounted furnishings, but don't expect incredible bargains as prices are still steep.

Other locations ABC Carpet & Home Warehouse, 1055 Bronx River Avenue, between Bruckner Boulevard & Westchester Avenue, Bronx (1-718 842 8772).

Domus

413 W 44th Street, between Ninth & Tenth Avenues, Hell's Kitchen (1-212 581 8099, www.domusnewyork.com). Subway A, C, E to 42nd Street-Port Authority. **Open** noon-8pm Tue-Sat; noon-6pm Sun. **Credit** AmEx, MC, V. **Map** p404 C24.

Scouring the globe for unusual design products is nothing new, but owners Luisa Cerutti and Nicki Lindheimer take the concept a step further; each year they visit a far-flung part of the world to forge links with and support co-operatives and individual craftspeople. The beautiful results reflect a fine attention to detail and a sense of place. With their vivid colours and swirling abstract patterns, baskets woven from telephone wire by South African Zulu tribespeople ($29-$335) would look fantastic in a modern apartment. Some items are sourced closer to home, such as Hell's Kitchen cabinet-maker Beau Van Donkelaar's one-of-a-kind cheese boards made of different-coloured wood offcuts. A great place to find reasonably priced gifts, from handmade Afghan soaps ($8.25) to Italian throws (from $69), plus cushions, glassware, toys and much more.

Fishs Eddy

889 Broadway, at 19th Street, Flatiron District (1-212 420 9020, www.fishseddy.com). Subway N, R to 23rd Street. **Open** 10am-9pm Mon; 9am-9pm Tue-Sat; 10am-8pm Sun. **Credit** AmEx, DC, Disc, MC, V. **Map** p403 E27.

Penny-pinchers frequent this barn-like space for sturdy dishware and glasses – surplus stock or recycled from restaurants, ocean liners and hotels (plain white side plates are a mere 99¢). But there are plenty of affordable, freshly minted kitchen goods too. Add spice to mealtime with glasses adorned with pole-dancers ($5 and up), platters printed with the Brooklyn skyline for under $20 and Floor Plan dinnerware (from $8 for a 'studio' side plate). *Photo p256.*

Future Perfect

115 North 6th Street, between Berry Street & Bedford Avenue, Williamsburg, Brooklyn (1-718 599 6278, www.thefutureperfect.com). Subway L to Bedford Avenue. **Open** noon-7pm daily. **Credit** AmEx, Disc, MC, V. **Map** p411 U7.

Championing avant-garde interior design, the Future Perfect showcases international and local talent. Heather Dunbar's 'Graf' pillows ($175) employ folksy needlepoint to recreate Brooklyn graffiti, while Parsons graduate Sarah Cihat's 'rehabilitated' china is reglazed with appealing retro-vibe images (phonographs, astronauts, anchors). The innovative Williamsburg design store recently opened a Manhattan outpost.

Other locations 55 Great Jones Street, between Bowery & Lafayette Street, East Village (1-212 473 2500).

MUSIC & ENTERTAINMENT

CDs & records

Academy Annex

96 North 6th Street, between Berry Street & Wythe Avenue, Williamsburg, Brooklyn (1-718 218 8200, www.academyannex.com). Subway L to Bedford Avenue. **Open** noon-8pm Mon-Thur, Sun; noon-10pm Fri, Sat. **Credit** AmEx, Disc, MC, V. **Map** p411 U7.

Located just up the street from the Music Hall of Williamsburg, Academy Records' Brooklyn outpost finds its true niche in acts not yet sufficiently well-known to play at the largish neighbouring venue. The Annex actively stocks local music, proclaiming on its website, 'If you run a local label, or are in a band with material released on vinyl, we'd love to carry it.' From Woodsist to the Social Registry, the labels that make up the current New York scene are all well represented.

Future Perfect.

Colony Records

Brill Building, 1619 Broadway, at 49th Street, Theater District (1-212 265 2050, www.colonymusic.com). Subway N, R to 49th Street; 1 to 50th Street. **Open** 9am-1am Mon-Sat; 10am-midnight Sun. **Credit** AmEx, Disc, MC, V. **Map** p404 D23.

Push the musical-note door handles to enter a portal to Times Square's past; Colony, a longtime resident of the rockin' Brill Building, was founded in 1948. In addition to sheet music (the selection covers everything from an AC/DC songbook to hot Broadway musicals, such as *Billy Elliot* and *In the Heights*), CDs and vinyl, there are glass cases full of era-spanning ephemera. Get a whiff of the King with Elvis 'Teddy Bear' perfume from the '50s ($500) or pay tribute to the original superwaif in a pair of cream lace tights 'inspired by Twiggy' ($50).

Downtown Music Gallery

13 Monroe Street, between Catherine & Market Streets, Chinatown (1-212 473 0043, www.downtownmusicgallery.com). Subway J, M, Z to Chambers Street; 4, 5, 6 to Brooklyn Bridge-City Hall. **Open** noon-6pm Mon; noon-8pm Thur-Sun; also by appt. **Credit** ($100 min) AmEx, Disc, MC, V. **Map** p402 F31.

Many landmarks of the so-called Downtown music scene have shuttered, but as long as DMG persists, the community will have a sturdy anchor. The shop stocks the city's finest selection of avant-garde jazz, contemporary classical, progressive rock and related styles. An entire CD display devoted to John Zorn's Tzadik imprint illustrates the store's die-hard devotion.

★ Other Music

15 E 4th Street, between Broadway & Lafayette Street, East Village (1-212 477 8150). Subway B, D, F, M to Broadway-Lafayette Street; 6 to Bleecker Street. **Open** 11am-9pm Mon-Fri; noon-8pm Sat; noon-7pm Sun. **Credit** AmEx, DC, Disc, MC, V. **Map** p403 E29.

Other Music opened in the shadow of Tower Records in the mid '90s, a pocket of resistance to chain-store tedium. All these years later, the Goliath across the street is gone, but tiny Other Music carries on. Whereas the shop's mishmash of indie rock, experimental music and stray slabs of rock's past once seemed adventurous, the curatorial foundation has proved prescient, amid the emergence of mixed-genre venues in the city.

Musical instruments

Sam Ash Music

156 W 48th Street, between Sixth & Seventh Avenues, Theater District (1-212 719 2299, www.samashmusic.com). Subway B, D, F, M to 47th-50th Streets-Rockefeller Center; N, R to 49th Street. **Open** 10am-8pm Mon-Sat; noon-6pm Sun. **Credit** AmEx, DC, Disc, MC, V. **Map** p404 D23.

This octogenarian musical instrument emporium dominates its Midtown block with three contiguous shops. New, vintage and custom guitars of all varieties are available, along with amps, DJ equipment, drums, keyboards, recording equipment, turntables and an array of sheet music.

Other locations 2600 Flatbush Avenue, at Hendrickson Place, Flatlands, Brooklyn (1-718 951 3888); 113-25 Queens Boulevard, at 76th Road, Forest Hills, Queens (1-718 793 7983).

SPORTS & FITNESS

Blades, Board & Skate

659 Broadway, between Bleecker & Bond Streets, Greenwich Village (1-212 477 7350, www.blades.com). Subway B, D, F, M to Broadway-Lafayette Street; 6 to Bleecker Street. **Open** 10am-9pm Mon-Sat; 11am-7pm Sun. **Credit** AmEx, Disc, MC, V. **Map** p403 E29.

The requisite clothing and accessories are sold here, alongside in-line skates, skateboards and snowboards. The Upper West Side branch rents out in-line skates for a roll in Central Park (*see also p345*).

Other locations 156 W 72nd Street, between Broadway & Columbus Avenue (1-212 787 3911).

Paragon Sporting Goods

867 Broadway, at 18th Street, Flatiron District (1-212 255 8036, www.paragonsports.com). Subway L, N, Q, R, 4, 5, 6 to 14th Street-Union Square. **Open** 10am-8pm Mon-Sat; 11am-7pm Sun. **Credit** AmEx, DC, Disc, MC, V. **Map** p403 E27.

Three floors of equipment and clothing for almost every activity, from the everyday (a slew of gym gear, trainers and sunglasses) to the more niche (badminton, kayaking) make this the prime sports-gear spot in the city.

TICKETS

While it's cheaper to buy tickets for performances directly from the venue, many don't offer this option, especially for booking online. The main booking agencies for concerts and other events are **Ticketmaster** (1-800 745 3000, www.ticketmaster.com) and **TicketWeb** (1-866 468 7619, www.ticketweb.com), while **Telecharge** (1-212 239 6200, www.telecharge.com) focuses on Broadway and Off Broadway shows.

TRAVELLERS' NEEDS

Got carried away in the shops? **XS Baggage** (1-718 301 5803, www.xsbaggage.com) will ship a single suitcase or multiple boxes to almost anywhere in the world, by air or sea. **Flight 001** (*see p249*) sells all manner of travel aids and accessories. For mobile phone hire and computer repairs, *see p236*.

Arts & Entertainment

Radio City Music Hall. *See p327.*

Calendar

Mermaids, dragons, Santa Claus – they're all on parade here.

New Yorkers hardly struggle to find something to celebrate. The venerable city-wide traditions are well known, but don't miss the neighbourhood shindigs: you can soak up the local vibe at quirky annual events such as Brooklyn's **Mermaid Parade** or East Village beatnik bash **Howl!**, and take advantage of free summer concerts and outdoor films in the city's green spaces, such as Bryant, Central and Madison Square Parks.

For more festivals and events, check out the other chapters in the Arts & Entertainment section. Specific dates are given for 2011/12 where possible, but before you set out or plan a trip around an event, it's wise to call first as dates, times and locations are subject to change. For the latest listings, consult the Own This City section of *Time Out New York* magazine or visit www.timeoutnewyork.com.

MAY-JULY

Lower East Side Festival of the Arts

Theater for the New City, 155 First Avenue, between 9th & 10th Streets (1-212 254 1109, www.theaterforthenewcity.net/les). Subway L to First Avenue; 6 to Astor Place. **Date** 27-29 May. **Map** p403 F28.

This 15th annual celebration of artistic diversity features performances by dozens of theatrical troupes, poetry readings, films and family-friendly programming. It's run by the Theater for the New City company, which has been performing political and community-themed plays in New York since 1971.

Washington Square Outdoor Art Exhibit

Various streets surrounding Washington Square Park, Greenwich Village (1-212 982 6255, www.washingtonsquareoutdoorartexhibit.org). Subway A, B, C, D, E, F to W 4th Street; R to 8th Street-NYU. **Date** 28-30 May and 4, 5 June; 4-6, 10, 11 Sept.

Since 1931, this outdoor exhibit has filled the area around Washington Square with a fine mix of photography, sculpture, paintings and unique crafts. If you miss it in May and June, you'll have another chance to browse in September.

Red Hook Waterfront Arts Festival

Various locations in Red Hook, Brooklyn (1-718 596 2507, www.bwac.org). Subway A, C, F to Jay Street-Borough Hall, then B61 bus to Van Brunt Street; F, G to Smith-9th Streets, then B77 bus to Van Brunt Street. **Date** 4-5 June.

This rapidly evolving neighbourhood cultural bash includes dance, music and spoken word performances from local artists, and runs in tandem with the Brooklyn Waterfront Artists' Pier Show.

Central Park SummerStage

Rumsey Playfield, Central Park, entrance on Fifth Avenue, at 72nd Street (1-212 360 2777, www.summerstage.org). Subway 6 to 68th Street-Hunter College. **Date** June-Aug. **Map** p405 E20.

These free concerts embody summer for many New Yorkers, and break down the boundaries between artistic mediums. Rockers, orchestras, authors and dance companies take over the stage at this very popular, mostly free annual series. Show up early or plan to listen from outside the gates (not a bad option if you bring a blanket and snacks). Note that tickets are required for some of the benefit shows and other special events.

Shakespeare in the Park

Date June-Aug.

See p359.

★ River to River Festival

Various venues along the West Side & southern waterfronts of Manhattan (no phone, www.rivertorivernyc.org). **Date** June-mid Sept.

Lower Manhattan organisations present hundreds of free events – from walks to all manner of arts performances – at various waterside venues. Performers in 2010 included Burning Spear and Antibalas. For the past few years, bookings at South Street Seaport in particular have made this one of the coolest concert series in town.

Museum Mile Festival

Fifth Avenue, from 82nd to 105th Streets, Upper East Side (1-212 606 2296, www.museummile festival.org). **Date** 14 June.

Nine of the city's most prestigious art institutions – including the Guggenheim, the Met, Cooper-Hewitt National Design Museum and the Museum of the City of New York – open their doors to the public free of charge. Music, dance performances and children's activities have turned this into a much anticipated 23-block-long celebration.

National Puerto Rican Day Parade

Fifth Avenue, from 44th to 86th Streets (1-718 401 0404, www.nationalpuertoricanday parade.org). **Date** early June.

Salsa music blares, and scantily clad revellers dance along the route or ride colourful floats at this free-wheeling celebration of the city's largest Hispanic community. The party can spill into Central Park, so if you're there you might become part of it.

Egg Rolls & Egg Creams Festival and Block Party

Eldridge Street Synagogue, 12 Eldridge Street, between Canal & Division Streets, Lower East Side (1-212 219 0903, www.eldridgestreet.org). Subway B, D to Grand Street; F to East Broadway. **Date** 5 June. **Map** p402 F31.

This block party celebrating the convergence of Jewish and Chinese traditions on the Lower East Side turns ten this year, with acrobats, yarmulke makers, Torah scribes, language lessons and, of course, plenty of the titular treats.

★ Mermaid Parade

Coney Island, Brooklyn (1-718 372 5159, www.coneyisland.com/mermaid). Subway D, F, N, Q to Coney Island-Stillwell Avenue. **Date** 19 June.

Decked-out mermaids and mermen of all shapes, sizes and ages share the parade route with elaborate, kitschy floats, come rain or shine. It's the wackiest summer solstice event you'll see, and draws a suitably diverse crowd. Check the website for details; the parade location varies each year.

Broadway Bares

Roseland Ballroom, 239 W 52nd Street, between Broadway & Eighth Avenue, Theater District (1-212 840 0770, www.broadwaycares.org/ broadwaybares). Subway 1 to 50th Street. **Date** 19 June. **Map** p404 D23.

Equal parts ingenious and unusual, this annual fundraiser for Broadway Cares/Equity Fights AIDS is your chance to see some of the Great White Way's hottest bodies sans costumes. Broadway Cares also hosts an annual auction of autographed teddy bears ('Broadway Bears') in February, and a show-tune filled Easter Bonnet Competition in April, as well as theatre-themed events throughout the year.

★ NYC LGBT Pride March

From Fifth Avenue, at 52nd Street, to Christopher Street (1-212 807 7433, www.hopinc.org). **Date** 26 June.

NYC LGBT Pride March.

Radio City Christmas Spectacular. *See p266.*

Downtown Manhattan becomes a sea of rainbow flags as lesbian, gay, bisexual and transgendered people from the city and beyond parade down Fifth Avenue in commemoration of the 1969 Stonewall Riots. After the march, there's a massive street fair and a dance on the West Side piers.

Summer Restaurant Week

Various locations (no phone, www.nycvisit.com/restaurantweek). **Date** late June/early July.

Twice a year, for two weeks or more at a stretch, some of the city's finest restaurants dish out three-course prix-fixe lunches for around $24; some places also offer dinner for $35. For the full list of participating restaurants, visit the website. Unsurprisingly, the tradition is immensely popular so be sure to make reservations well in advance.

► *See also p268 Winter Restaurant Week.*

★ Midsummer Night Swing

Lincoln Center Plaza, Columbus Avenue, between 64th & 65th Streets, Upper West Side (1-212 875 5766, www.lincolncenter.org). Subway 1 to 66th Street-Lincoln Center. **Date** 28 June-16 July. **Map** p405 C21.

Lincoln Center's plaza is turned into a giant dancefloor as bands play salsa, Cajun, swing and other music. Each night's dance party (Tue-Sat) is devoted to a different dance style, and is preceded by lessons. Beginners are, of course, welcome.

Celebrate Brooklyn!

Prospect Park Bandshell, Prospect Park West, at 9th Street, Park Slope, Brooklyn (1-718 855 7882, www.bricartsmedia.org). Subway F to Seventh Avenue. **Date** mid June-late Aug. **Map** p410 T12.

Non-profit community arts organisation BRIC launched this series of outdoor performances to revitalise Prospect Park, and now the festival is Brooklyn's premier summer culture offering. It includes music, dance, film and spoken word acts, and has showcased the likes of Philip Glass, TV on the Radio and the Buena Vista Social Club. A $3 donation is requested and there's an admission charge for some shows.

New York Philharmonic Concerts in the Parks

Date July-Aug.

See p313 **Everything Under the Sun**.

P.S.1 Warm Up

Date July-Sept.

See p337.

Macy's Fourth of July Fireworks

Waterfront locations vary (1-212 494 4495). **Date** 4 July.

The city's star Independence Day attraction is also the nation's largest Fourth of July fireworks display. Usually launched from barges on the East River, in 2009 the fireworks moved to the Hudson for the first time since the 9/11 attacks, and they'll remain there for 2011's display. The pyrotechnics start at around 9pm, but you'll need to scope out your vantage point early. Keep in mind, however, that spectators are packed like sardines at prime public spots, so many choose to keep their distance.

Nathan's Famous Fourth of July International Hot Dog Eating Contest

Outside Nathan's Famous, corner of Surf & Stillwell Avenues, Coney Island, Brooklyn (1-718 946 2202, www.nathansfamous.com). Subway D, F, N, Q to Coney Island-Stillwell Avenue. **Date** 4 July.

Liable to amuse and appal in equal measure, this annual Fourth of July event, which is organised by the 95-year-old Coney Island hot-dog vendor, holds an undeniable fascination. Eaters gather from all over the world for the granddaddy of all pig-out contests. Maybe not palatable for the fastidious.

Harlem Week

Various Harlem locations (1-212 862 8477, www.harlemweek.com). Subway B, C, 2, 3 to 135th Street. **Date** mid July-Aug.

Get into the groove at this massive culture fest, which began in 1974 as a one-day event celebrating all things Harlem. Harlem Day is still the centrepiece of the event, but 'Week' is now a misnomer; besides the street fair serving up music, art and food along 135th Street (on 14 Aug), a wealth of concerts, films, dance performances, fashion and sports events are on tap for more than a month.

AUGUST-OCTOBER

Lincoln Center Out of Doors

For listings, *see p312* **Lincoln Center**.
Date Aug. **Map** p405 C21.

Free dance, music, theatre, opera and more make up the programme at this family-friendly and ambitious festival organised by the Upper West Side's premier performing-arts institution.

New York International Fringe Festival

Various locations (1-212 279 4488, www.fringenyc.org). **Date** 12-28 Aug.

Wacky and sometimes wonderful, Downtown's Fringe Festival – inspired by the Edinburgh original and celebrating its 15th anniversary in 2011 – shoehorns hundreds of arts performances into 16 theatre-crammed days. And *Time Out New York* magazine is committed to reviewing each and every one.

▶ *See p360 for more information on Off-Off Broadway shows.*

Howl!

Various East Village locations (1-212 505 2225, www.howlfestival.com). **Date** 9-11 Sept.

Taking its name from the poem by neighbourhood resident Allen Ginsberg, this three-day Beat and boho fest is a grab bag of art events, film screenings, poetry readings, performance art and much more.

West Indian-American Day Carnival

Eastern Parkway, from Utica Avenue to Grand Army Plaza, Brooklyn (1-718 467 1797, www.wiadca.org). Subway 2, 3 to Grand Army Plaza; 3, 4 to Crown Heights-Utica Avenue. **Date** 5 Sept.

The streets come alive with the jubilant clangour of steel-drum bands and the steady throb of calypso and soca music at this colourful cultural celebration. Mas bands – and costumed marchers – dance along the route and thousands move to the beat, while vendors sell Caribbean crafts, clothing and food.

Broadway on Broadway

43rd Street, at Broadway, Theater District (1-212 768 1560, www.broadwayonbroadway.com). Subway N, Q, R, S, 1, 2, 3, 7 to 42nd Street-Times Square. **Date** mid Sept. **Map** p404 D24.

At the start of each theatre season, Broadway's biggest stars convene in the middle of Times Square for one night to belt out show-stopping numbers. The mega-concert features appearances from nearly every Broadway play and musical, including sneak previews of the season's new productions.

Feast of San Gennaro

Mulberry Street, from Canal to Houston Streets, Little Italy (1-212 768 9320, www.sangennaro.org). Subway B, D, F to Broadway-Lafayette Street; J, M, N, Q, R, Z, 6 to Canal Street.
Date 15-25 Sept. **Map** p404 F30.

This massive 11-day street fair stretches along the main drag of what's left of Little Italy. Come after dark, when sparkling lights arch over Mulberry Street and the smells of frying *zeppole* (custard- or jam-filled fritters) and sausages hang in the sultry air. On the final Saturday in September, a statue of San Gennaro is carried in a Grand Procession outside the Most Precious Blood Church (109 Mulberry Street, between Canal & Hester Streets).

Dumbo Arts Festival

Various locations in Dumbo, Brooklyn (1-718 694 0831, www.dumboartsfestival.com). Subway A, C to High Street; F to York Street. **Date** 23-25 Sept.

Dumbo has been an artists' enclave for decades, and this weekend of art appreciation is hugely popular with the local community of creative types and their counterparts in other boroughs. The festival progamme features concerts, forums, a short-film series and studio visits.

Atlantic Antic

Atlantic Avenue, from Fourth Avenue to Hicks Street, Brooklyn (1-718 875 8993, www.atlanticave.org). Subway B, Q, 2, 3, 4, 5 to Atlantic Avenue; D, M, N, R to Pacific Street.
Date 25 Sept.

INSIDE TRACK
TIMES SQUARE TIPS

If you want to be at the epicentre of the New Year's Eve celebration at One Times Square, you'll have to head out early – Lori Raimondo of the Times Square Alliance estimates that the barricaded areas closest to the ball drop reach capacity between 2pm and 4pm. And forget toasting the new year with champagne – public drinking is illegal in NYC.

ING New York City Marathon

Entertainment, ethnic food, children's activities and the inimitable World Cheesecake-Eating Contest pack the avenue with wide-eyed punters at this monumental Brooklyn festival.

New York Film Festival
Date late Sept-mid Oct.
See p290.

★ Open House New York
Various locations (1-917 583 2398, www.ohny.org). **Date** 8-9 Oct.
Get an insider's view – literally – of the city that most locals haven't even seen. More than 100 sites of architectural interest that are normally off-limits to the public throw open their doors during a weekend of urban exploration. A wide range of lectures and an educational programme are also on offer all week.

Next Wave Festival
For listings, *see p311* **Brooklyn Academy of Music** (www.bam.org). **Date** early Oct-mid Dec.
The festival is among the most highly anticipated of the city's autumn culture offerings, as it showcases only the very best in avant-garde music, dance, theatre and opera. Legends like Ingmar Bergman, Meredith Monk and Steve Reich are among the many luminaries the fest has hosted.

CMJ Music Marathon & FilmFest
Various locations (1-917 606 1908, www.cmj.com). **Date** 15-19 Oct.
The annual *College Music Journal* schmooze-fest draws thousands of fans and music-industry types to one of the best showcases for new rock, indie rock, hip hop and electronica acts. The FilmFest, which runs in tandem with the music blowout, includes a wide range of feature and short films (many music-related) and pulls in a suitably hip crowd.

Village Halloween Parade
Sixth Avenue, from Spring to 21st Streets (no phone, www.halloween-nyc.com). **Date** 31 Oct.
The sidewalks at this iconic Village shindig are always packed beyond belief. For the best vantage point, don a costume and watch from inside the parade (the line-up starts at 6.30pm on Sixth Avenue, at Spring Street; the parade kicks off at 7pm).

NOVEMBER-JANUARY

New York Comedy Festival
Various venues (no phone, nycomedyfestival.com). **Date** 2-6 Nov.
Presented in association with Comedy Central, this five-day laugh fest features big-name talent (Tracy Morgan, Louis CK and Lewis Black were among the headliners in 2010) as well as up-and-comers.

ING New York City Marathon
Staten Island side of the Verrazano-Narrows Bridge, to Tavern on the Green, in Central Park (1-212 423 2249, www.ingnycmarathon.org). **Date** 6 Nov.
Catch sight of 35,000 marathoners as they hotfoot it (or, alternatively, puff, pant and stagger) through all five boroughs over a 26.2-mile course. Grab a spot to get a good view of the passing herd.

Radio City Christmas Spectacular
For listings, *see p327* **Radio City Music Hall.** **Date** Mid Nov-late Dec.
High-kicking precision dance troupe the Rockettes and an onstage nativity scene with live animals are the rather kitsch attractions at this (pricey) annual homage to the Yuletide season. *Photo p264.*

Macy's Thanksgiving Day Parade & Balloon Inflation
Central Park West, at 77th Street to Macy's, Broadway, at 34th Street (1-212 494 4495, www.macysparade.com). **Date** 23, 24 Nov.
At 9am on Thanksgiving Day, the stars of this nationally televised parade are the gigantic balloons, the elaborate floats and good ol' Santa Claus. The evening before, New Yorkers brave the cold night air to watch the rubbery colossi take shape at the inflation area (from 77th to 81st Streets, between Central Park West & Columbus Avenue).

Rockefeller Center Tree-Lighting Ceremony
Rockefeller Center, Fifth Avenue, between 49th & 50th Streets, Midtown (1-212 332 6868, www.rockefellercenter.com). Subway B, D, F to 47th-50th Streets-Rockefeller Center. **Date** early Dec. **Map** p404 E23.

Proceedings start at 7pm, but this festive celebration is always mobbed, so get there as early as you can. The actual lighting takes place at the end of the programme; most of the two-hour event is devoted to celebrity performances (Aretha Franklin and Alicia Keys have been among recent human luminaries). Then the 30,000 energy-efficient LEDs covering the massive evergreen are switched on to mass oohs and ahs. If you'd rather gouge out your eyeballs with the tree's nine-and-a-half-foot-diameter Swarovski-crystal star than brave the crush, there's plenty of time during the holiday season to view the illuminated spectacle at your leisure.

Unsilent Night

Washington Square Arch, Fifth Avenue, at Waverly Place, to Tompkins Square Park (no phone, www.unsilentnight.com). Subway A, B, C, E, D, F to W 4th Street. **Date** mid Dec.

Phil Kline's boom box chorale parade has become a bona fide holiday tradition: his luminous, shimmering wash of bell tones is one of the loveliest communal new music experiences you'll ever witness.

National Chorale Messiah Sing-In

Avery Fisher Hall, Lincoln Center, Columbus Avenue, at 65th Street, Upper West Side (1-212 333 5333, www.lincolncenter.org, www.messiahsingalong.com). Subway 1 to 66th Street-Lincoln Center. **Date** mid Dec. **Map** p405 C21.

Hallelujah! Chase those holiday blues away by joining the National Chorale and hundreds of your fellow audience members in a rehearsal and performance of Handel's *Messiah*. No previous singing experience is necessary to take part, and you can buy the score on site, though picking one up early for advance perusal would certainly help novices.

Emerald Nuts Midnight Run

Naumburg Bandshell, middle of Central Park, at 72nd Street (1-212 860 4455, www.nyrrc.org). Subway B, C to 72nd Street; 6 to 68th Street-Hunter College. **Date** 31 Dec. **Map** p405 E20.

If you have managed to stay sober, you can see in the new year with a four-mile jog through the park, organised by the New York Road Runners. There's also a masquerade parade, fireworks, prizes and a (booze-free) toast at the halfway mark.

► *For more about running in New York, see p346.*

New Year's Eve in Times Square

Times Square, Theater District (1-212 768 1560, www.timessquarenyc.org/nye/nye). Subway N, Q, R, S, 1, 2, 3, 7 to 42nd Street-Times Square. **Date** 31 Dec. **Map** p404 D24.

Get together with a million others and watch the giant illuminated Waterford Crystal ball – the new, 12-foot geodesic sphere, double the size of its predecessors, debuted in 2008 – descend amid a blizzard of confetti and cheering. There are DJs, celebrity guests and flashy entertainment, but also freezing temperatures, densely packed crowds, no public conveniences – and very tight security.

New Year's Day Marathon Benefit Reading

For listings, *see p271* **Poetry Project**. **Date** 1 Jan.

Some big-name Bohemians (Penny Arcade and

St Patrick's Day Parade. *See p268.*

Philip Glass were among the 2010 roll-call) step up to the mic during this all-day spoken-word spectacle, organised by the Poetry Project, at St Marks Church in the East Village.

Winter Restaurant Week

For listings, *see p264* **Summer Restaurant Week**. **Date** late Jan/early Feb.

The Winter Restaurant Week provides yet another opportunity to sample delicious gourmet food at highly palatable prices.

Chinese New Year

Around Mott Street, Chinatown (www.explorechinatown.com). Subway J, M, N, Q, R, Z, 6 to Canal Street. **Date** Feb 3.

Gung hay fat choy!, the greeting goes. Chinatown bustles with colour and is charged with energy during the two weeks of the Lunar New Year. Festivities include a staged fireworks display, a vivid dragon parade, various performances and a predictable wealth of delicious Chinese food.

FEBRUARY-APRIL

ADAA: The Art Show

Seventh Regiment Armory, 643 Park Avenue, between 66th & 67th Streets, Upper East Side (1-212 488 5550, www.artdealers.org/artshow). Subway 6 to 68th Street-Hunter College. **Date** late Feb/early Mar. **Map** p405 E21.

Whether you're a serious collector or a casual art fan, this vast fair, presented by the Art Dealers Association of America, offers the chance to peruse some of the world's most impressive, museum-quality pieces on the market. Seventy exhibitions feature paintings, drawings, photography, sculpture and multimedia works dating from the 17th century to the present.

Ringling Bros and Barnum & Bailey Circus Animal Walk

34th Street, from the Queens Midtown Tunnel to Madison Square Garden, Seventh Avenue, between 31st & 33rd Streets (1-212 307 7171, www.ringling.com). **Date** Mar.

Midnight parades open and close the Ringling Bros and Barnum & Bailey circus's NYC run; true circus freaks make the trek to see elephants, horses and zebras march through the tunnel and on to the streets of Manhattan in this surreal spectacle.

Armory Show

Piers 92 & 94, Twelfth Avenue, at 55th Street, Hell's Kitchen (1-212 645 6440, www.thearmoryshow.com). Subway C, E to 50th Street. **Date** 1-4 Mar. **Map** p405 B22.

This contemporary international art mart debuted in Gramercy Park's 69th Regiment Armory in 1999. Now held on the Hudson River, it has expanded to include older 20th-century work.

St Patrick's Day Parade

Fifth Avenue, from 44th to 86th Streets (www.saintpatricksdayparade.com). **Date** 17 Mar.

Dating from 1762, this massive march is one of the city's longest-running annual traditions. If you feel like braving huge crowds and potentially nasty weather, you'll see thousands of green-clad merrymakers strutting to the sounds of pipe bands. *Photo p267.*

Easter Parade

Fifth Avenue, from 49th to 57th Streets (1-212 484 1222). Subway E, M (M weekdays) to Fifth Avenue-53rd Street. **Date** 8 Apr 2012.

'Parade' is something of a misnomer for this little festival of creative-hat wearers. Starting at 11am on Easter Sunday, Fifth Avenue becomes a car-free promenade of gussied-up crowds milling around and showing off their extravagant bonnets. Be sure to arrive early to secure a prime viewing spot near St Patrick's Cathedral, at 50th Street.

SOFA New York

Seventh Regiment Armory, 643 Park Avenue, at 67th Street, Upper East Side (1-800 563 7632, www.sofaexpo.com). Subway 6 to 68th Street-Hunter College. **Date** mid-late Apr. **Map** p405 E21.

Browse this giant show of Sculptural Objects and Functional Art – including fine art, ceramics, sculpture and jewellery – and you might come home with a serious treasure.

Sakura Matsuri (Cherry Blossom Festival)

For listings, *see p133* **Brooklyn Botanic Garden**. **Date** late April-early May 2012.

The climax to the cherry blossom season, when the BBG's 220 trees are in flower, the annual *sakura matsuri* celebrates both the blooms and Japanese culture with concerts, traditional dance, sword demonstrations and tea ceremonies.

★ Tribeca Film Festival

Date late April-early May.
See p290.

Bike New York: Five Boro Bike Tour

Battery Park to Staten Island (1-212 932 2453, www.bikenewyork.org). Subway A, C, J, M, Z, 1, 2, 3 to Chambers Street; R, W to City Hall; 4, 5, 6 to Brooklyn Bridge-City Hall, then bike to Battery Park. **Date** 13 May. **Map** p402 E34.

Thousands of cyclists take over the city for a 42-mile Tour de New York. (Pedestrians and motorists should plan for extra getting-around time on this date.) Advance registration is required if you want to take part. Event organisers suggest using the trains listed above, as some subway exits below Chambers Street may be closed to bike-toting cyclists for safety reasons, and bikes are not allowed at the South Ferry (1 train), Whitehall Street (R, W) and Bowling Green (4, 5) stations.

Books & Poetry

NYC has a voracious appetite for words.

New York has long been the literary capital of the US, partly because the major publishers have their headquarters here, along with magazines such as the *New Yorker*, but also because the urban landscape has proved to be a bottomless source of inspiration to writers who've flocked to the city and made it their own. Can you imagine Edith Wharton without her dissection of high-society Manhattan? Or Jonathan Lethem without his imaginative grasp of urban eccentrics and sidewalk enthusiasm? For storytellers, New York's complexities still provide unbeatable material.

AUTHOR APPEARANCES

Almost every touring literary luminary stops in New York City to read, the places they read at being almost as varied as the city: bookshops, libraries and even bars. Small, independent stores that sometimes host events include feminist-progressive hangout **Bluestockings** (*see p303*) and cosy second-hand Brooklyn shop **Freebird** (123 Columbia Street, between Degraw & Kane Streets, Cobble Hill, Brooklyn, 1-718 643 8484, www.freebirdbooks.com, closed Mon-Wed). Reading series such as Mixer, held at music venue **Cake Shop** (*see p321*), pair writers – often with a pop-cultural bent – with musical guests. The venues that we've listed below hold regular readings.

Barnes & Noble Union Square

33 E 17th Street, between Broadway & Park Avenue South, Union Square (1-212 253 0810, www.barnesandnoble.com). Subway L, N, Q, R, 4, 5, 6 to 14th Street-Union Square. **Admission** free. **Map** p403 E27.

The chain's city-wide branches host a variety of consistently good author events, but the Union Square flagship offers the most vibrant and well-curated series, Upstairs at the Square, which pairs writers with musical performers. Where else can you see novelist and cultural critic Kurt Andersen along with singer-songwriter Regina Spektor? Or catch Barack Obama favourite Joseph O'Neill on the same bill as Aimee Mann?

► *Preface a visit here with a spin around the fabled '18 miles of books' at the nearby Strand Book Store (see p235).*

BookCourt

163 Court Street, between Dean & Pacific Streets, Cobble Hill, Brooklyn (1-718 875 3677, www.bookcourt.org). Subway F, G to Bergen Street; 2, 3, 4, 5 to Borough Hall. **Admission** free. **Map** p410 S10.

This small yet thoroughly wonderful local bookstore has helpful staff and an impressive reading series. There's often a bonus too if you go along, as the readings are sometimes followed by a party. Recent readers have included Don DeLillo, Stephen Elliott and Jennifer Egan.

★ Happy Ending Series

Happy Ending, Joe's Pub, 425 Lafayette Street, between Astor Place & E 4th Street, East Village (1-212 539 8770, www.joespub.com). Subway N, R to 8th Street-NYU; 6 to Astor Place). **Admission** $15. **Credit** AmEx, DC, MC, V. **Map** p403 F30.

Host Amanda Stern's convivial literary series is a great mix of authorial brilliance and endearing self-mockery. As well as the readings, the event, complete with its comic monologues and musical performances, requires participants to take some sort of onstage chance – which means you might get to witness your favourite authors playing the ukelele or tap-dancing. Readers have included Richard Price, Ed Park, Heidi Julavits and Samantha Hunt.

Housing Works Bookstore Café

For listings, *see p235*. **Admission** free.

The emerging and the illustrious mingle at the mic; at a recent evening of readings, 'Love: A Rebuke', *Harper's Magazine* invited Colson Whitehead, Heidi Julavits and Sam Lipsyte to dis Cupid.

★ KGB Bar

2nd Floor, 85 E 4th Street, between Second & Third Avenues, East Village (1-212 505 3360, www.kgbbar.com). Subway F to Lower East Side-Second Avenue; 6 to Astor Place. **Admission** free. **Map** p403 F29.

This dark and formerly smoky East Village hang-out, with an old-school communist theme, runs several top-notch weekly series featuring NYC writers, poets, fantasy authors, travel writers and others.

McNally Jackson Bookstore

For listings, *see p233.* **Admission** free.

This excellent Canadian import, which stocks a distinctly international selection, invites a wide range of non-fiction writers and novelists – including Keith Gessen, Garrison Keillor and Francine Prose, among others – to read in its comfortable café space.

New School

66 W 12th Street, between Fifth & Sixth Avenues, Greenwich Village (1-212 229 5353, 1-212 229 5488 tickets, www.newschool.edu). Subway F to 14th Street; L to Sixth Avenue. **Admission** free-$15. **Credit** AmEx, DC, MC, V. **Map** p403 E28.

A great place to hear award-winning authors; contributors to the *Best American Poetry* anthology and finalists for the National Book Award read here annually. The New School also hosts round tables, such as a Greil Marcus-led discussion of the intellectual reference book *A New Literary History of America.*

New York Public Library

Stephen A Schwarzman Building, Celeste Bartos Forum, 42nd Street, at Fifth Avenue, Midtown (1-212 930 0571, www.nypl.org/events). Subway B, D, F to 42nd Street; 7 to Fifth Avenue. **Admission** $25; $15 reductions. **No credit cards**. **Map** p404 E24.

The 'Live from the NYPL' series is ambitious and well-curated – a magnet for the smart set. All of the programming is superb, but the stand-out events are the Robert Silvers lectures, in which thinkers tackle complex intellectual issues. Oliver Sacks recently talked about the brain, music and how we process sensory experience.

► *For tours of the library itself, see p103.*

92nd Street Y

1395 Lexington Avenue, at 92nd Street, Upper East Side (1-212 415 5500, www.92y.org). Subway 6 to 96th Street. **Admission** $10-$40. **Credit** AmEx, DC, MC, V. **Map** p406 F17.

Big-name novelists, essayists, journalists and poets preside over some grand intellectual feasts here, with talks by critic James Wood, as well as a worthwhile reading series featuring the likes of Ian McEwan, Salman Rushdie, Toni Morrison and Jonathan Franzen. The Biographers/Critics and Brunch events are also popular, allowing participants to munch on bagels as such authors as Joyce Carol Oates chat about their work.

► *For the Y's classical music offerings, see p317.*

★ NYU's Lillian Vernon Creative Writers House

58 W 10th Street, between Fifth & Sixth Avenues, Greenwich Village (1-212 998 8816, cwp.fas.nyu/page/readingseries). Subways A, B, C, D, E, F to W 4th Street. **Admission** free. **Map** p403 E28.

A major destination for literary authors with devout followings, this space – part of NYU – has recently showcased Jonathan Safran Foer, Zadie Smith, Rick Moody and Jennifer Egan.

★ 192 Books

For listings, *see p233.* **Admission** free.

Essentially New York Writers

Who has the last word on NYC?

MICHAEL MILLER, FORMER BOOKS EDITOR, TIME OUT NEW YORK MAGAZINE: '**Joan Didion**'s non-fiction writing – her essay collections, her criticism in the *New York Review of Books* and the *Year of Magical Thinking* – is stylish, calmly fierce and insightful, whether she's analysing broad political issues or individual human beings. No other living New York writer has meant more to so many people I know.'

JOHN FREEMAN, EDITOR OF GRANTA: '**Edmund White**. His *Farewell Symphony* and his new one, *City Boy*. Like so many of the city's great observers, he came here from the Midwest. In his books you see the wonderful fantasia of the place from afar, the fury of its energy, and then as he becomes a New Yorker it deepens into a richer portrait.'

RICK MOODY, AUTHOR OF THE ICE STORM: 'My choice is **Ben Marcus**, because I want the English language to do things it hasn't done before, and I want American fiction to do things it hasn't done before, and I want to be in a state of arrest at the moment of gazing upon a page of text, and Ben is one of those very few writers who can do that for me.'

This lovely independent bookstore supplements its artsy selection of books with a phenomenal reading series, bringing in top authors such as Joan Acocella, Ben Ratliff, Joan Didion and Wayne Koestenbaum to read from their works.

Poetry Project

St Mark's Church in-the-Bowery, 131 E 10th Street, at Second Avenue, East Village (1-212 674 0910, www.poetryproject.org). Subway L to First Avenue; 6 to Astor Place. **Admission** $8; $7 reductions. **No credit cards. Map** p403 F28.

The Project, housed in a lovely old church, has hosted an amazing roster of poets since its inception in 1966.

Poets House

10 River Terrace, between Murray Street & Park Place West, Battery Park City (1-212 431 7920, www.poetshouse.org). Subway 1, 2, 3 to Chambers Street. **Open** 11am-7pm Tue-Fri; 11am-6pm Sat. **Admission** free-$10. **Credit** AmEx, DC, MC, V. **Map** p402 D32.

Founded in 1985 by poet Stanley Kunitz and arts administrator Elizabeth Kray, Poets House has long been a gathering place open to anyone who writes or reads verse. In 2009, it moved from its Soho location to its new 'green' space (Bill Murray famously read to its construction workers during one of their breaks) near the Hudson River, where it continues to offer classes, workshops and author events. You might hear a discussion with such award-winning authors as Rae Armantrout, Yusef Komunyakaa and John D'Agata; the library, open to all and free of charge, houses more than 50,000 volumes you can peruse at your leisure.

Powerhouse Arena

37 Main Street, between Front & Water Streets, Dumbo, Brooklyn (1-718 666 3049, www.powerhousearena.com). Subway A, C to High Street; F to York Street. **Admission** free. **Map** p411 S9.

Powerhouse publishes excellent photo books on everything from graffiti art to Darfur. Its cavernous, industrial-style space serves as a gallery and hosts some great literary events – readings by TC Boyle, Daniel Menaker and Paul Auster, to name a few.

St Mark's Bookshop Reading Series

Solas Bar, 232 E 9th Street, between Second & Third Avenues, East Village (1-212 260 7853, smartbooksblogspot.com). Subway N, R to 8th Street; 6 to Astor Place. **Admission** free. **Map** p403 F28.

This independent bookshop has a reading series with downtown spirit. Recent readers have included such novelists as Christopher Sorrentino, Brian Evenson and Percival Everett, as well as the avant-garde theatre legend Richard Foreman.

192 Books.

SPOKEN WORD

Most spoken word events begin with a featured poet or two, before moving on to an open mic. If you'd like to take part, show up a little early and ask for the sign-up sheet.

Bowery Poetry Club

308 Bowery, between Bleecker & Houston Streets, East Village (1-212 614 0505, www.bowerypoetry.com). Subway F to Lower East Side-Second Avenue; 6 to Bleecker Street. **Admission** free-$10. **No credit cards. Map** p403 F29.

The BPC features high-energy spoken word events, plus hip hop, burlesque, comedy, theatre and workshops. The Urbana Poetry Slam team (who've won the national poetry slam championship three times) leads an open mic on Tuesday nights.

Moth StorySLAM

Various venues (1-212 742 0551, www.themoth.org). **Admission** $7. **No credit cards.**

Known for its big-name monthly storytelling shows, the Moth also sponsors four open slams in various venues every month. Ten raconteurs get five minutes each to tell a story (no notes are allowed) to a panel of judges.

Nuyorican Poets Café

236 E 3rd Street, between Avenues B & C, East Village (1-212 505 8183, www.nuyorican.org). Subway F to Lower East Side-Second Avenue. **Admission** $7-$15. **Credit** AmEx, DC, Disc, MC, V. **Map** p403 G29.

This East Village arts centre is known for its raucous slams, jam sessions and anything-goes open mics.

Children

Kids love the Big Apple's crunch.

If you want to make your children fall in love with New York City in five minutes flat, head for Times Square after dark, when the electronic billboards are as dazzling as a fireworks display. They'll be enthralled. That was easy – but what next?

Happily, the city is experiencing a serious baby boom, and it's bursting with cultural, culinary and just plain fun destinations for families. The Statue of Liberty and Rockefeller Center's Top of the Rock are not to be missed, but they're just the beginning.

If you or your offspring start to feel overwhelmed by the constant activity, head to one of the city's green spaces or many playgrounds. And for the latest child-friendly events, pick up a copy of the monthly magazine *Time Out New York Kids*, or visit the website www.timeoutkids.com.

SIGHTSEEING & ENTERTAINMENT

Animals & nature

See also p106 **Central Park**.

★ Bronx Zoo

For listings, *see p147.*

Step aboard the Wild Asia Monorail (open Apr-Nov, admission $4), which tours 38 acres of exhibits housing elephants, Indo-Chinese tigers, antelope, Mongolian wild horses and more. Madagascar! is a permanent home to exotic animals from the lush island nation off the eastern coast of Africa. Among its residents are lemurs, giant crocodiles, lovebirds, radiated tortoises and, coolest (and grossest) of all, hissing cockroaches. Four lemurs and one sifaka were born in the exhibit in its first year.

▶ *For Central Park Zoo, see p108. There are also zoos in Brooklyn (see p133) and Queens (see p142).*

New York Aquarium

610 Surf Avenue, at West 8th Street, Coney Island, Brooklyn (1-718 265 3474, www.nyaquarium.com). Subway D, N to Coney Island-Stillwell Avenue; F, Q to W 8th Street-NY Aquarium. **Open** *1 Nov-1Apr* 10am-4.30pm daily; *2 Apr-27 May* 10am-5pm Mon-Fri, 10am-5.30pm Sat, Sun; *28 May-31 Oct* 10am-6pm Mon-Fri; 10am-7pm Sat, Sun. **Admission** $13; $9-$10 reductions; free under-3s. Pay what you wish from 3pm Fri. **Credit** AmEx, DC, Disc, MC, V.

Like the rest of Coney Island, this aquarium has seen better times, but it is sprucing itself up with new exhibits like Glovers Reef, a 150,000-gallon tank simulating the famed tropical ecosystem of Belize, and Alien Stingers, an impressive indoor display of some rather elegant jellyfish. Among the aquarium's most beloved inhabitants are its walruses and sea lions (make sure your kids catch the outdoor sea-lion show). Another highlight are the daily shark, penguin, walrus and sea-otter feedings (call for exact times and locations).

FREE Prospect Park Audubon Center

Prospect Park, enter from Ocean Avenue, at Lincoln Road, Brooklyn (1-718 287 3400, www.prospectpark.org/audubon). Subway B, Q to Prospect Park. **Open** *May-July, Sept, Oct* noon-5pm Thur-Sun. *Aug* noon-6pm Thur-Sun. *Apr, Nov* noon-5pm Sat, Sun. *Dec-Mar* noon-4pm Sat, Sun. **Admission** free. **Map** p410 U12.

INSIDE TRACK TALL TIPS

If you want to show your child a bird's-eye New York panorama, try the Rockefeller Center's **Top of the Rock** (*see p103*) rather than the **Empire State Building**. The ride up is like an amusement park adventure, and the tall, railing-less glass panels separating you from the city make the views all the more breathtaking.

Overlooking Prospect Lake, the Audubon Center is dedicated to nature education and wildlife preservation. Start at the visitor centre, and stick around for woodland tours, storytelling, bird-watching, pedal-boat rides and other activities.

FREE Queens County Farm Museum

73-50 Little Neck Parkway, Floral Park, Queens (1-718 347 3276, www.queensfarm.org). Subway E, F to Kew Gardens-Union Turnpike, then Q46 bus eastbound to Little Neck Parkway. **Open** 10am-5pm Mon-Fri (outdoors only); 10am-5pm Sat, Sun. **Admission** free (except special events).

Stroll through apple and pear orchards, take a hayride ($2) or a guided tour of an 18th-century farmhouse (both weekends only) and see sheep and goats at NYC's only working historical farm. On your way in, pick up some feed at the gift store so your little one can treat the animals to a nibble.

Museums

Defying the stuffy cliché, many of Manhattan's most venerable institutions are extremely child-friendly. The **Museum of Modern Art** (*see p102*), the **Metropolitan Museum of Art** (*see p114*) and the **Rubin Museum** (*see p91*) offer workshops for kids of all ages; check their websites for schedules. The Met, with its mummies and Temple of Dendur, a real ancient Egyptian temple, is a particular hit with kids, as long as you don't try to tackle too much of the massive collection.

Even very young children will love exploring the **American Museum of Natural History** (*see p118*). The museum's Fossil Halls are home to huge, reconstructed and beloved dinosaurs, plus the world's largest collection of vertebrate fossils (nearly a million specimens).

Elsewhere, children and adults will be fascinated by the amazing scale-model *Panorama of the City of New York* at the **Queens Museum of Art** (*see p142*). Youngsters can pretend to drive a real bus and board vintage subway cars at the **New York Transit Museum** (*see p130*), while the highlight at the aircraft carrier-turned-attraction **Intrepid Sea, Air and Space Museum** (*see p98*) is the new Exploreum, an indoor activity zone divided into areas with nautical aviation, cosmos and onboard life themes. Mischievous types will enjoy having their mugshots taken and hanging out behind bars in the **New York City Police Museum**'s (*see p72*) on-site jail cell.

★ Brooklyn Children's Museum

145 Brooklyn Avenue, at St Marks Avenue, Crown Heights, Brooklyn (1-718 735 4400, www.brooklynkids.org). Subway A, C to Nostrand Avenue; C to Kingston-Throop Avenue; 3 to Kingston Avenue. **Open** 11am-1pm (Totally Tots only), 1pm-5pm Wed-Fri; 10am-5pm Sat, Sun. **Admission** $7.50; free under-1s. **Credit** AmEx, DC, Disc, MC, V. **Map** p410 V11.

The city's oldest museum for kids is now one of its best after a recent renovation. The star attraction, 'World Brooklyn', is an interactive maze of small mom-and-pop shops based on real-world Brooklyn businesses. 'Neighborhood Nature' puts the spotlight on the borough's diverse ecosystems with a collection of pond critters in terrariums and a tide-pool touch tank. Under-fives will delight in 'Totally Tots', a sun-drenched play space with a water station, a sand zone, and a special hub for babies 18 months and under.

Children's Museum of Manhattan

212 W 83rd Street, between Amsterdam Avenue & Broadway, Upper West Side (1-212 721 1234, www.cmom.org). Subway B, C to 81st Street-Museum of Natural History; 1 to 86th Street. **Open** 10am-5pm Tue-Sun. **Admission** $10; $7 reductions; free under-1s. **Credit** AmEx, DC, MC, V. **Map** p405 C19.

This must-see children's museum, a mainstay in every Upper West Side child's social agenda, promotes literacy, multiculturalism and creativity through its permanent and temporary interactive exhibitions and programmes. 'PlayWorks', an imaginiative play environment, and 'Little West Side', a mini version of the neighbourhood, are for babies and toddlers up to the age of four; 'Adventures with Dora and Diego', a bilingual playspace that transports visitors to some of the Nickelodeon TV show's settings, is for ages two to six; and 'Gods Myths & Mortals' introduces kids six and up to the culture of ancient Greece.

Brooklyn Children's Museum.

ARTS & ENTERTAINMENT

Central Park Zoo. *See p272.*

Children's Museum of the Arts

182 Lafayette Street, between Broome & Grand Streets, Soho (1-212 274 0986, www.cmany.org). Subway 6 to Spring Street. **Open** noon-5pm Wed, Fri-Sun; noon-6pm Thur. **Admission** $10; free under-1s. Pay what you wish 4-6pm Thur. **Credit** AmEx, DC, Disc, MC, V. **Map** p403 E30.

The focus at this gallery space is on teaching, creating, collecting and exhibiting kids' artwork. The walls usually showcase an engaging temporary exhibit juxtaposed with works from the museum's collection of over 2,000 pieces of children's art.

New York Hall of Science

47-01 111th Street, at 47th Avenue, Flushing Meadows-Corona Park (1-718 699 0005, www.nysci.org). Subway 7 to 111th Street. **Open** *July, Aug* 9.30am-5pm Mon-Fri; 10am-6pm Sat, Sun. *Sept-Mar* 9.30am-2pm Tue-Thur; 9.30am-5pm Fri; 10am-6pm Sat, Sun. *Apr-June* 9.30am-2pm Mon-Thur; 9.30am-5pm Fri; 10am-6pm Sat, Sun. **Admission** $11; $8 reductions. *Sept-June* free 2-5pm Fri, 10-11am Sun. *Science playground* (open Mar-Dec) extra $4; Rocket Park Mini Golf extra $6; $5 reductions. **Credit** AmEx, DC, Disc, MC, V.

Known for the 1964 World's Fair pavilion in which it is housed and the rockets from the US space programme that flank it, this museum has always been worth a trek for its discovery-based interactive exhibits. Its massive expansion in 2005 added a new building that houses such permanent exhibits as 'Hidden Kingdoms', where kids get their hands on microscopes, and 'Search for Life Beyond Earth', which investigates the solar system and the different planetary environments. From March until December, the 30,000sq ft (2,800sq m) outdoor Science Playground teaches children the principles of balance, gravity and energy. Joining it is a new mini-golf course in Rocket Park, which is dotted with refurbished rockets from the 1960s space race.

INSIDE TRACK BROOKLYN BRIDGE CROSSING

No matter what age your child is, a trip across the **Brooklyn Bridge** is a thrill. Start in Manhattan and reward yourselves on the other side with house-made ice-cream from the **Brooklyn Ice Cream Factory** (Old Fulton & Water Streets), a romp in a park and breathtaking views.

Performing arts

The New York City Ballet's **Nutcracker** (*see p283* David H Koch Theater) is an annual Christmas family tradition. In spring, **Ringling Bros and Barnum & Bailey**'s three-ring circus comes to Madison Square Garden (*see p338*). In summer, **Madison Square Park** (*see p91*) hosts children's concerts; it also has an award-winning playground and a branch of the excellent Shake Shack (*see p202*) on-site.

Big Apple Circus

Damrosch Park, Lincoln Center, 62nd Street, between Columbus & Amsterdam Avenues, Upper West Side (1-212 268 2500,

www.bigapplecircus.org). Subway 1 to 66th Street-Lincoln Center. **Shows** *Oct-Jan* times vary. **Tickets** $15-$92. **Credit** AmEx, DC, Disc, MC, V. **Map** p405 C21.
New York's Big Apple is a travelling circus that was founded in 1977 as an intimate answer to the scale of the Ringling Bros operation. The clowns at this non-profit organisation are among the most creative to be found in the country. If you always wanted to run away to the circus, attend the special late show on New Year's Eve, at the end of which the entire audience joins the performers in the ring.

★ Bowery Kids

For listings, *see p271* **Bowery Poetry Club**. **Shows** *Sept-July* noon Sun. **Tickets** $10.
While you may happen upon a magic show or play at Bowery Kids, the children's line-up at this Lower East Side performance space is dominated by kiddie rock concerts. Children are free to jump up and down, sing along and munch on healthy snacks sold at an on-site café while the reverb gets to them.

Carnegie Hall Family Concerts

For listings, *see p312*. **Tickets** $9.
Even children who solemnly profess to hate classical music are usually impressed by a visit to Carnegie Hall. The Family Concert series builds on that, featuring first-rate classical, world music and jazz performers and runs from November to March (recommended for ages five to 12).

Just Kidding at Symphony Space

For listings, *see p317*. **Shows** *Oct-early May* Sat (times vary). **Tickets** $11-$25; $9-$15 reductions.
Tell your munchkins to forgo their weekly dose of cartoons. In Manhattan, kids can spend Saturday mornings grooving to live concerts or watching theatre, dance or a puppet show instead. Symphony Space's Just Kidding series features both local and nationally recognised talent, from kid rockers and bluegrass bands to hip hop storytellers and acts like local star Gustaver Yellowgold.

Manhattan Children's Theatre

52 White Street, between Broadway & Church Street, Tribeca (1-212 226 4085, www.manhattanchildrenstheatre.org). Subway N, Q, R, 4, 5, 6 to Canal Street; 1 to Franklin Street. **Shows** *Sept-May* noon, 2pm Sat, Sun. **Tickets** $20-$50. **No credit cards**. **Map** p402 E31.
At the company's 74-seat playhouse, kids climb onto rows of padded benches set up in descending stadium formation, which means everyone (even the tiniest tot in the back) enjoys an unobstructed view. The folks at MCT take their shows quite seriously, as their source material – either classic or contemporary children's literature – illustrates.

★ New Victory Theater

For listings, *see p357*.
As New York's only full-scale young people's theatre, the New Victory presents international theatre and dance companies at junior prices. Recent shows have included *Elephant*, a show of African songs and tribal dances by British and South African performers, and *The Butterfly Garden*, an interactive staging of a caterpillar's metamorphosis. Shows often sell out well in advance, so reserve seats early.

Puppetworks

338 Sixth Avenue, at 4th Street, Park Slope, Brooklyn (1-718 965 3391, www.puppetworks.org). Subway F to 7th Avenue. **Shows** 12.30pm, 2.30pm Sat, Sun. **Tickets** $8; $7 under-12s. **No credit cards. Map** p410 T11.

The Brooklyn company puts on musicals adapted from fairy tales and children's stories that feature a cast of marionettes operated by two puppeteers (the voice and music track is pre-recorded). The company also demonstrates how the puppets work at the beginning of each performance. The Wizard of Oz is the 2011 summer offering (until 21 Aug).

► *For the Swedish Cottage Marionette Theater, in Central Park, see p277.*

Teatro SEA Los Kabayitos Puppet & Children's Theatre

107 Suffolk Street, between Delancey & Rivington Streets, Lower East Side (1-212 529 1545, www.sea-ny.org). Subway F to Delancey Street; J, M, Z to Essex Street. **Shows** times vary. **Tickets** $15; $12.50 reductions. **Credit** AmEx, DC, MC, V. **Map** p403 G29.

Spanish and English feature prominently in every show at this cheery theatre, which adapts both Spanish and Latin American fairy tales for its puppet productions. Recent shows have included Los Titeres de Cachiporra, a comic tale written by Federico Garcia Lorca. Budding linguists get the chance to hone their skills – especially after curtain calls, when actors mingle with the audience.

FREE Theatreworks/NYC

Lucille Lortel Theatre, 121 Christopher Street, between Bleecker & Hudson Streets, West Village (1-212 647 1100, www.theatreworksusa.org). Subway 1 to Christopher Street. **Shows** *mid July-late Aug* times vary. **Admission** free. **Map** p403 D28.

The respected travelling company Theatreworks/USA has developed a reputation for producing dependable, mostly musical, adaptations of kid-lit classics; a New York branch was formed in 2005. Children's shows are on offer at this highly regarded Off Broadway theatre in the summer only. Come early, as seats are first come, first served.

PARKS & PLAY SPACES

Most New Yorkers don't have their own garden – instead, they let off steam in parks. The most popular of all is **Central Park** (*see p106*), which has places and programmes just for kids.

Battery Park City Parks

Hudson River, between Chambers Street & Battery Place, Battery Park City (1-212 267 9700, www.bpcparks.org). Subway A, C, 1, 2, 3 to Chambers Street; 1 to Rector Street. **Open** 6am-1am daily. **Admission** free. **Map** p402 D32.

Besides watching the boats along the Hudson, kids can enjoy Teardrop Park, one of New York's best playgrounds, an open field for ball games, Frisbee and lazing, and a park house that has balls, board

Exploring Life Underground

Art you can touch.

More than 150 works of art have been installed in more than 142 subway stations in the Manhattan Transit Authority's Arts for Transit program, but among New York's children, *Life Underground* is surely the most popular. Constructed by Tom Otterness in his Gowanus studio, the installation consists of some 100 bronze sculptures placed throughout the multi-level station at 14th Street and Eighth Avenue. They represent lore associated with New York below ground (witness the alligator emerging from beneath a manhole cover with a man clamped in its chompers) as well as the construction of the subway system and its daily use.

Yes, the figures are cute – their rounded proportions, money bag heads and clunky, outsize shoes evoke early cartoons – but they're also devious (the fare jumper), pushy (a fellow clutching a bag of loot claims a seat on a bench) and industrious (various figures sweep pennies, hoist a beam and haul a giant token). That insistent busyness, as much as the sculptures' whimsy, accounts for their vast appeal. This is art kids want to touch, and for once, they can. The Eighth Avenue 14th Street subway station is on the A, C, E and L lines.

games and toys. Kids' events are held from May to October; don't miss the picnic garden near the Chambers Street entrance, where children love to interpret (and climb on) sculptor Tom Otterness's *Real World* installation.

Chelsea Piers

For listings, *see p343.*
This vast and hugely bustling complex on the Hudson River features a bowling alley, roller rink, pool, toddler gym, ice-skating rink, batting cages and rock-climbing walls, as well as gym staples like basketball courts and weight rooms.

Central Park

For more information and a calendar of events, visit www.centralparknyc.org. Don't miss the antique **Friedsam Memorial Carousel** ($1 per ride). There are 21 playgrounds in the park; the large **Heckscher Playground**, in the southwest corner (between Seventh Avenue and Central Park South, from 61st to 63rd Streets), sprawls over more than three acres and has an up-to-date adventure area and handy restrooms.

Central Park Zoo

For listings, *see p108.*
The stars here are the penguins and the polar bear, which live in glass habitats so you can watch their underwater antics. A brand-new snow leopard environment opened in 2009, and its creation even changed the zoo's topography. The Zoo's annual Chillout! Weekend in early August offers penguin and polar-bear shows, ice-carvers, games and other frosty fun in the dog days of summer. The Tisch Children's Zoo, a stone's throw away, houses species that enjoy being petted – and fed.

Conservatory Water

Central Park, entrance on Fifth Avenue, at 72nd Street. Subway 6 to 68th Street-Hunter College. **Map** p405 E20.
Nicknamed Stuart Little Pond after EB White's story-book mouse, this is a mecca for model-yacht racers. When the boatmaster is around, you can rent a remote-controlled vessel (Apr-Oct 10am-7pm Mon-Fri, Sun, 2-7pm Sat, weather permitting, $10/30mins). Kids are drawn to two statues near the pond: the bronze rendering of Lewis Carroll's Alice, the Mad Hatter and the White Rabbit is an irresistible climbing spot, while the Hans Christian Andersen statue is a gathering point for free storytelling sessions (11am-noon Sat, early June-late Sept).

FREE Henry Luce Nature Observatory

Belvedere Castle, midpark, off the 79th Street Transverse Road (1-212 772 0210). Subway B, C to 81st Street-Museum of Natural History. **Open** 10am-4.30pm Tue-Sun. **Admission** free. **Map** p405 D19.
Inside Belvedere Castle, telescopes, microscopes and hands-on exhibits teach kids about the plants and animals living in the park. With a photo ID, you can borrow a Discovery Kit: binoculars, bird-watching guide and other cool tools to explore nature in all its glory.

★ Swedish Cottage Marionette Theater

Central Park West, at 81st Street (1-212 988 9093). Subway B, C to 81st Street-Museum of Natural History. **Shows** *Oct-June* 10.30am, noon Tue, Thur, Fri; 10.30, noon, 2.30pm Wed; 1pm Sat, Sun. *July, Aug* 10.30am, noon Mon-Fri. **Tickets** $8; $5 reductions. **No credit cards. Map** p405 D19.
Tucked just inside the western boundary of Central Park is a curiously incongruous old wooden structure. Designed as a schoolhouse, the building was Sweden's entry in the 1876 Centennial Exposition in Philadelphia (it was moved to NYC a year later). Inside is one of the best-kept secrets (and deals) in town: a tiny marionette theatre with regular shows. Reservations are recommended.

Trump Wollman Rink & Victorian Gardens

Trump Wollman Rink For listings, *see p345.* **Victorian Gardens** *1-212 982 2229, www.victoriangardensnyc.com. Subway N, R to Fifth Avenue-59th Street.* **Open** *mid May-mid Sept* 11am-7pm Mon-Thur; 11am-8pm Fri; 10am-9pm Sat; 10am-8pm Sun. **Admission** $6.50 Mon-Fri; $7.50 Sat, Sun. Free children under 36in tall. Games & rides cost extra. **Credit** AmEx, DC, Disc, MC, V. **Map** p405 D21.
Skating in Central Park amid snowy trees, with grand apartment buildings towering in the distance, is a New York tradition, and a classic image of the city that never seems to tarnish with passing years. This popular (read: crowded) rink offers lessons and skate rentals, plus a snack bar where you can warm up with hot chocolate. In summer, the site hosts the Victorian Gardens, a nostalgic amusement park geared towards younger children. It's hardly white-knuckle stuff, but the mini-teacup carousel and Rio Grande train are bound to thrill little kids.
► *For more skating rinks, see p345.*

RESTAURANTS & CAFÉS

★ Alice's Teacup

102 W 73rd Street, at Columbus Avenue, Upper West Side (1-212 799 3006, www.alicesteacup.com). Subway B, C to 72nd Street. **Open** 8am-8pm daily. **Credit** AmEx, DC, Disc, MC, V. **Map** p405 C20.
Beloved by Disney-adoring children, this magical spot offers much more than tea (though the three-tiered version, comprising an assortment of sandwiches, scones and desserts, truly is a treat). The brunch menu is fit for royalty, with Alice's Curious French Toast (it's drenched in fruit coulis, crème

anglaise and syrup) and scones in scrumptious flavours like blueberry and pumpkin. In the afternoon, the special after-school snack menu features own-made graham crackers and honey, and banana bread topped with jam. At a little shop in the front of the eaterie, you can outfit your fairy princess in training with a pair of glittery wings.
Other locations 156 E 64th Street, at Lexington Avenue, Upper East Side (1-212 486 9200); 220 E 81st Street, between Second & Third Avenues, Upper East Side (1-212 734 4832).

Bubby's

120 Hudson Street, at North Moore Street, Tribeca (1-212 219 0666, www.bubbys.com). Subway A, C, E to Canal Street; 1 to Franklin Street. **Open** 24hrs, from 6am Tue to 11pm Mon. **Credit** (no credit cards weekend brunch) AmEx, DC, MC, V. **Map** p402 E31.

On weekend mornings, a 'We love kids!' attitude and a no-reservations policy add up to pleasant, barely controlled chaos. Children and adults alike will enjoy savoury treats such as alphabet chicken soup, mac and cheese, and an array of salads, burgers and barbecue fare. If you're Brooklyn-bound, dine at the huge Dumbo location (cash only; closed Mon-Wed), which is directly across the street from a great playground with Manhattan skyline views.
Other locations 1 Main Street, between Plymouth & Water Streets, Dumbo, Brooklyn (1-718 222 0666).

Dylan's Candy Bar

1011 Third Avenue, at 60th Street, Upper East Side (1-646 735 0078, www.dylanscandybar.com). Subway N, R, 4, 5, 6 to Lexington Avenue-59th Street. **Open** 10am-10pm Mon-Thur; 9am-11pm Fri, Sat; 10am-9pm Sun. **Credit** AmEx, DC, MC, V. **Map** p405 F22.

Think of this sweet shop as Candyland's supply room. The colourful, three-floor emporium, with packaged candy in the basement, bulk selections at ground level, and a café/ice-cream parlour on the top floor, will satisfy your entire family's sugar cravings. After you've treated the kids to some bubblegum-flavoured ice-cream upstairs, pick up the shop's speciality, Clodhopper chocolate fudge-covered graham clusters, in a cool plastic 'paint can' to take home.
► *Would-be Charlie Buckets should also head to Jacques Torres Chocolate; see p250.*

Kitchenette

156 Chambers Street, between West Broadway & Greenwich Street, Tribeca (1-212 267 6740, www.kitchenetterestaurant.com). Subway A, C, 1, 2, 3 to Chambers Street. **Open** 7.30am-11pm Mon-Fri; 9am-11pm Sat, Sun. **Credit** AmEx, DC, MC, V. **Map** p402 E31.

On Sunday mornings, packs of parents and their kids head to this haven of home-style cooking, or its uptown sister, to partake of one of the top brunches in the city. There are many imaginative egg dishes, but your carb-loving tot can likely make a meal out of a fluffy, fist-size biscuit with a dollop of strawberry butter. Kitchenette's no disappointment at night, either: try the honey-fried chicken.
Other locations 1272 Amsterdam Avenue, between 122nd & 123rd Streets, Upper West Side (1-212 531 7600).

Perch Café

365 Fifth Avenue, between 5th & 6th Streets, Park Slope, Brooklyn (1-718 788 2830, www.theperchcafe.com). Subway D, F, G, M, N, R to Fourth Avenue-9th Street. **Open** 8am-9pm Mon-Thur, Sun; 8am-11pm Fri, Sat. **Credit** ($10 min) AmEx, DC, Disc, MC, V. **Map** p410 T11.

You don't get much more child-friendly than Perch Café. Built-in banquettes and sleek sofas are roomy enough for the whole family, and there's plenty of space for a pushchair both inside and in the back garden. Patrons love the classic egg, bacon and cheese sandwich, the baked rosemary chicken and the hunk of love that is the red-velvet cake. Your kids will also enjoy weekday on-site sing-along concerts ($5 per family) by adored local musicians.

S'MAC

345 E 12th Street, between First & Second Avenues, East Village (1-212 358 7912, www.smacnyc.com). Subway L to First Avenue. **Open** 11am-11pm Mon-Thur, Sun; 11am-1am Fri, Sat. **Credit** AmEx, DC, Disc, MC, V. **Map** p403 F28.

Twelve varieties of mac and cheese range from simple all-American (mild enough for picky types) to a more complex dish – with brie, roasted figs and shiitake mushrooms, or mac and manchego with fennel and shallots. There's a size for everyone: 'nosh' (great for kids), 'major munch' (a hearty adult serving), 'mongo' (if you want leftovers to take with you) and 'partay' (which serves 8-12). Children are offered a regular bowl in lieu of the sizzling skillet in which meals are typically served.

BABYSITTING

Baby Sitters' Guild

1-212 682 0227, www.babysittersguild.com.
Bookings 9am-9pm daily. **No credit cards** (except when paying through hotel).

Long- or short-term sitters cost from $25 per hour and up (four-hour minimum), plus transportation ($4.50, or $10 after midnight). Sitters are available around the clock, and speak 16 languages between them.

Pinch Sitters

1-212 260 6005, www.nypinchsitters.com.
Bookings 8am-5pm Mon-Fri. **No credit cards**.

Charges are $20 per hour (four-hour minimum), plus the babysitter's cab fare after 9pm ($10 maximum). A $35 fee is levied for cancellations with less than 24 hours' notice.

Comedy

Live from New York…

Since the 1960s, the history of New York comedy has been written on stage, night after night, by its definitive voices: the iconoclasts (Lenny Bruce, Andy Kaufman); the obsessives (Woody Allen, Jerry Seinfeld); the powerhouses (Richard Pryor, Chris Rock); the defamers and the self-deprecators (Joan Rivers, Rodney Dangerfield). Today, there are rooms to suit every comic disposition as touring professionals and first-timers alike aim to make their mark with audiences, equipped with little more than a stage and a microphone.

COMEDY VENUES

★ 92YTribeca

200 Hudson Street, at Canal Street, Tribeca (1-212 601 1000, www.92ytribeca.com). Subway A, C, E, 1 to Canal Street. **Shows** varies. **Admission** $10-$20. **Average drink** $5. **Credit** (tickets only) AmEx, Disc, MC, V. **Map** p403 D30.

As a venue responsible for all sorts of cultural programming, it's amazing that 92YTribeca has time to concoct such an energising slate of comedic events. With regular evenings of stand-up and conversations with comedy legends, plus storytelling and singalong musical film screenings, there's something for everyone. Keep an eye out for Comedy Below Canal, a series that often includes popular performers from HBO or Comedy Central.

Broadway Comedy Club

318 W 53rd Street, between Eighth & Ninth Avenues, Theater District (1-212 757 2323, www.broadwaycomedyclub.com). Subway C, E to 50th Street. **Shows** daily, times vary. **Admission** $15-$20 (2-drink min). **Average drink** $7. **Credit** AmEx, DC, Disc, MC, V. **Map** p404 D23.

BCC features TV faces and club circuit regulars. On Friday and Saturday, it's home to Chicago City Limits (1-212 888 5233, www.chicagocitylimits.com); the group's format of topical sketches, songs and audience-inspired improv is a little dated.

About the author

***Matthew Love** is a journalist, performer and comedy writer. He regularly contributes to* Time Out New York *magazine and the* Onion*'s* AV Club.

Carolines on Broadway

1626 Broadway, between 49th & 50th Streets, Theater District (1-212 757 4100, www.carolines.com). Subway N, R to 49th Street; 1 to 50th Street. **Shows** varies. **Admission** $20-$50 (2-drink min). **Average drink** $8. **Credit** AmEx, DC, MC, V. **Map** p404 D23.

Carolines on Broadway is a New York City institution. It's attained that status in part because of its long-term relationships with national headliners, sitcom stars and cable-special pros, which ensures that its stage always features marquee names. Although a majority of the bookings skew towards mainstream appetites, the club also makes time for undisputedly darker and edgier fare such as Paul Mooney and Louis CK.

Castlebraid Comedy

114 Troutman Street, between Central & Evergreen Avenues, Bushwick, Brooklyn (1-718 449 6554, www.castlebraid.com). Subway M to Central Avenue; J, M, Z to Myrtle-Broadway. **Shows** 9pm Thur. **Admission** free. **Average drink** $2. **No credit cards. Map** p411 W9.

INSIDE TRACK FREE LAUGHS

Some of the city's most consistently worthwhile shows are also free: line up outside the **Upright Citizens Brigade Theatre** early Sunday evening to nab tickets for the 9.30pm session of big-name improv jam **ASSSSCAT 3000**, or reserve your seats online for the theatre's free, weekly stand-up showcase **Whiplash** late on Monday night.

When comedian Scott Moran launched the first Castle Braid Comedy Festival in September 2010, he enticed a great number of New York's rising comic stars – and their fans – to converge over the course of six days. Since then, he's continued to prove his skill for booking talent and bringing audiences to this quirky apartment complex turned artist commune by hosting a weekly show there. Guests should feel right at home, especially when some of the venue's residents come dressed in their pyjamas.

Comedy Cellar

117 MacDougal Street, between Bleecker & W 3rd Streets, Greenwich Village (1-212 254 3480, www.comedycellar.com). Subway A, B, C, D, E, F, M to W 4th Street. **Shows** 9pm, 11pm Mon-Thur, Sun; 8pm, 9.45pm, 11.30pm Fri; 7.30pm, 9.15pm, 11pm, 12.45am Sat. **Admission** $12-$18 (2-drink min). **Average drink** $7. **Credit** AmEx, DC, MC, V. **Map** p403 E29.

Despite being dubbed one of the best stand-up clubs in the city year after year, the Comedy Cellar has maintained a hip, underground feel. It gets incredibly crowded, but the bookings, which typically include no-nonsense comics Dave Chapelle, Jim Norton and Marina Franklin, are enough to distract you from your bachelorette party neighbours.

Essentially New York Stand-ups

Funny people name their favourites.

RICKY GERVAIS, COMEDIAN: 'Louis CK is not just New York's finest comedian, but probably America's. We have become friends and send more insulting emails to each other than you can ever imagine. He is original, brave and honest. But he is fat, bald and ginger.'

HARLAN HARPER, CO-FOUNDER OF COMIX: 'Jim Norton, [the late] **Greg Giraldo**, **Jim Gaffigan** and **Dave Attell** have come up through the ranks of comedy. They epitomise what New York comedy is, as, say, compared to LA. It's thinking person's comedy.'

DL HUGHLEY, COMEDIAN AND 98.7 KISS-FM HOST: 'Essential pick – I would say **Paul Mooney**. He's always fresh and relevant, even into his sixties. He not only embodies New York: he's a huge part of a counterculture that's cool for me to watch. He's also one of the few comedians that can sell out a show in the city at 1.30am.'

Comic Strip Live

1568 Second Avenue, between 81st & 82nd Streets, Upper East Side (1-212 861 9386, www.comicstriplive.com). Subway 4, 5, 6 to 86th Street. **Shows** 8.30pm Mon-Thur; 8.30pm, 10.30pm, 12.30am Fri; 8pm, 10.30pm, 12.30am Sat; 8pm Sun. **Admission** $20-$25 (2-drink min). **Average drink** $10. **Credit** AmEx, DC, Disc, MC, V. **Map** p405 F19.

The Upper East Side isn't exactly a breeding ground for edgy entertainment, so you'll be grateful to find this fabled, long-running showcase. Established in 1975, CSL launched the careers of Eddie Murphy and Chris Rock. The fare is more standard these days, but the club does attract a lot of stand-ups from the late-night talk-show circuit.

★ Comix

353 W 14th Street, between Eighth & Ninth Avenues, Meatpacking District (1-212 524 2500, www.comixny.com). Subway A, C, E to 14th Street. **Shows** 8pm Mon-Thur; 8pm, 10.30pm Fri, Sat. **Admission** $5-$35 (2-drink min). **Average drink** $8. **Credit** AmEx, DC, Disc, MC, V. **Map** p403 C27.

Over the past few years, Comix has emerged as the club bridging the gap between the alternative and mainstream comedy worlds; its programming hovers somewhere between blockbuster spots like Carolines and the city's smaller, scrappier venues. The result is a mix of big names at the weekend and impressive up-and-comers during the week.

► *Downstairs is the cover-free Ochi's Lounge, home to emerging acts and experimental shows.*

Dangerfield's

1118 First Avenue, between 61st & 62nd Streets, Upper East Side (1-212 593 1650, www.dangerfields.com). Subway N, R to Lexington Avenue-59th Street; 4, 5, 6 to 59th Street. **Shows** 8.45pm Mon-Thur, Sun; 8.30pm, 10.30pm, 12.30am Fri; 8pm, 10.30pm, 12.30am Sat. **Admission** $15-$20 (2-drink min). **Average drink** $9. **Credit** AmEx, DC, Disc, MC, V. **Map** p405 F22.

The decor and gentility of New York City's oldest comedy club are throwbacks to the era of its namesake Rodney, who founded it as a cabaret in 1969. And instead of putting eight to ten comics in a showcase, Dangerfield's gives three or four stand-ups the opportunity to settle into longer acts. With any luck, one of the comics will goad Chario – the old guy who's been a waiter here for 41 of the club's 42 years – into barking out some of the comedic chestnuts he's picked up through the years as he circulates through the room.

Eastville Comedy Club

85 E 4th Street, between Bowery & Second Avenue, East Village (1-212 260 2445, www.eastvillecomedy.com). Subway F to Lower East Side-Second Avenue. **Shows** 9pm Mon-Thur;

Upright Citizens Brigade Theatre.

7pm, 9pm, 11pm Fri, Sat. **Admission** $10-$20 (2-drink min). **Average drink** $7. **Credit** AmEx, DC, MC, V. **Map** p403 F29.
The first dedicated stand-up club in this patch, Eastville puts up much of the same club-circuit talent that populates the city's other rooms, plus a fresh crop of comics from the downtown alt scene.

Gotham Comedy Club

208 W 23rd Street, between Seventh & Eighth Avenues, Chelsea (1-212 367 9000, www.gothamcomedyclub.com). Subway F, N, R, M to 23rd Street. **Shows** varies Mon-Thur; 8.30pm, 10.30pm Fri; 8pm, 10pm, 11.45pm Sat; 8.30pm Sun. **Admission** $15-$30 (2-drink min). **Average drink** $10. **Credit** AmEx, DC, MC, V. **Map** p404 D26.
Chris Mazzilli's vision for his club involves elegant surroundings, professional behaviour and mutual respect. That's why the talents he fosters, such as Jim Gaffigan, Tom Papa and Ted Alexandro, keep coming back here after they've found national fame.

Magnet Theater

254 W 29th Street, between Seventh & Eighth Avenues, Chelsea (1-212 244 8824, www.magnettheater.com). Subway A, C, E to 34th Street-Penn Station; 1 to 28th Street. **Shows** varies. **Admission** free-$7. **Average drink** $5. **No credit cards. Map** p404 D25.
The house teams and solo performers at Armando Diaz's upstart black box has grown strong, making Magnet one of the best places to watch improvisation in the city. You won't see too many famous faces onstage, but you will see thoughtful improv.

Peoples Improv Theater

2nd Floor, 154 W 29th Street, between Sixth & Seventh Avenues, Chelsea (1-212 563 7488, www.thepit-nyc.com). Subway 1 to 28th Street. **Shows** varies. **Admission** $free-$10. **Average drink** $4. **Credit** (online purchases only) Disc, MC, V. **Map** p404 D25.
While talented sketch groups perform on the weekends and improv teams pack them in on Wednesday nights, it's the teaching programme that put the PIT on the creative map. Teachers from *Saturday Night Live* and the *Daily Show,* as well as other accomplished stand-ups and writers, offer a rolling roster of classes.

Stand-Up New York

236 W 78th Street, at Broadway, Upper West Side (1-212 595 0850, www.standupny.com). Subway 1 to 79th Street. **Shows** 8.30pm Mon-Thur; 8pm, 10.15pm Fri, Sat; 8pm Sun. **Admission** $15-$20 (2-drink min). **Average drink** $9. **Credit** AmEx, DC, MC, V. **Map** p405 C19.
After some managerial shifts, this musty Uptown spot began to garner attention again. Though the line-ups, which include stalwart club denizens such as Jay Oakerson and Godfrey, keep things pretty simple, there's almost always one performer worth the trip.

★ Upright Citizens Brigade Theatre

307 W 26th Street, at Eighth Avenue, Chelsea (1-212 366 9176, www.ucbtheatre.com). Subway C, E to 23rd Street; 1 to 28th Street. **Shows** varies. **Admission** free-$10. **Average drink** $3. **No credit cards. Map** p404 D26.
The UCB has been the most visible catalyst in New York's current alternative comedy boom. The improv troupes and sketch groups anchored here are the best in the city. Stars of *Saturday Night Live* and writers for late-night talk shows gather on Sunday nights to wow crowds in the long-running ASSSSCAT 3000. Other premier teams include the Stepfathers (Fridays) and Death by Roo Roo (Saturdays). Get here early and choose a good seat – the venue has challenging sightlines.

Dance

From traditional ballet to avant-garde movement, it's in New York.

The New York dance scene still operates on an uptown (ballet) to downtown (contemporary dance) scale. **Lincoln Center** remains the hotspot for sophisticated offerings, with American Ballet Theatre and New York City Ballet crowding the plaza with balletomanes much of the year; the further downtown you travel, the more subversive it gets. Theatres that offer an abundance of experimental dance dot Chelsea and the East Village, but there is also good reason to cross the river and venture to Brooklyn, where Williamsburg, Bushwick and, now, Bedford-Stuyvesant, have sparked a new generation of dancers and choreographers.

NOTABLE NAMES & EVENTS

The companies of modern-dance icons such as Martha Graham, Alvin Ailey, Trisha Brown, Merce Cunningham, Paul Taylor and Mark Morris are still based in the city, alongside a wealth of contemporary choreographers who create works outside the traditional company structure. Even in financially perilous times, the downtown performance world is full of singular voices, including Sarah Michelson, John Jasperse, Trajal Harrell, Yasuko Yokoshi, Dean Moss and Ann Liv Young, as well as collectives such as AUNTS, a group of young artists who present performances in unlikely places. Dance isn't only relegated to devoted spaces – the intimate basement theatre at the **New Museum of Contemporary Art** (*see p81*) has provided a stage for work by Trajal Harrell and Jonah Bokaer, for example.

The scene is especially vibrant in autumn and spring. It's relatively quiet in summer, apart from outdoor performances at **Central Park SummerStage** (*see p262*), **Lincoln Center Out of Doors** (*see p265*), and the **River to River Festival** (*see p262*) throughout lower Manhattan.

In the early autumn, three dance festivals – **DanceNow/NYC**, held mainly at New York Live Arts (formerly the Dance Theater Workshop), **Fall for Dance**, at City Center and, best of all, the multidisciplinary, multi-venue **Crossing the Line**, presented by the French Institute Alliance Française (22 E 60th Street, between Madison & Park Avenues, 1-212 355 6160, www.fiaf.org) – herald the return of the season. See *Time Out New York* magazine for current listings.

About the author

Gia Kourlas *is the Dance editor of* Time Out New York *magazine and a regular contributor to the* New York Times.

MAJOR VENUES

★ Baryshnikov Arts Center

450 W 37th Street, between Ninth & Tenth Avenues, Hell's Kitchen (1-646 731 3200, www.bacnyc.org). Subway A, C, E to 34th Street-Penn Station. **Tickets** free-$25. **Credit** AmEx, DC, MC, V. **Map** p404 C25.

Former artistic director of the American Ballet Theatre, Mikhail Baryshnikov is something of an impresario. His home base, on a stark overpass near the Lincoln Tunnel, includes several inviting studios, the Howard Gilman Performance Space – a 192-seat theatre – and superb facilities for rehearsals and workshops. Last year saw the unveiling of the newly renovated Jerome Robbins Theatre: at 238 seats, it's both intimate and refined. The multidisciplinary Wooster Group is the resident company.

Brooklyn Academy of Music

For listings, *see p311.*

Showcasing local and visiting companies, the Brooklyn Academy of Music (or BAM) is one of New York's most prominent cultural institutions. The 2,100-seat Howard Gilman Opera House, with its

Federal-style columns and carved marble, is a regal dance venue, where the Mark Morris Dance Group regularly performs (along with out-of-towners such as Ohad Naharin and William Forsythe). The 1904 Harvey Theater hosts contemporary choreographers – past artists have included Wally Cardona, John Jasperse and Sarah Michelson. Annual events include the Dance Africa Festival, held each Memorial Day weekend (late May), and the Next Wave Festival, which showcases established groups from New York and abroad. *Photos p285.*

Danspace Project

St Mark's Church in-the-Bowery, 131 E 10th Street, at Second Avenue, East Village (1-212 674 8112 information, 1-866 811 4111 reservations, www.danspaceproject.org). Subway L to Third Avenue; 6 to Astor Place. **Tickets** $18-$22. **No credit cards**. **Map** p403 F28.

A space is only as good as its producer, and executive director Judy Hussie-Taylor has injected new life into Danspace's programming. Moreover, the space itself – a high-ceilinged sanctuary – is very handsome. Ticket prices are reasonable, making it easy to take a chance. Look for 'Stella, Mother', a dance novella premiering in late spring 2011.

★ David H Koch Theater

Lincoln Center, 64th Street, at Columbus Avenue, Upper West Side (1-212 870 5570, www.nycballet.com). Subway 1 to 66th Street-Lincoln Center. **Tickets** $20-$125. **Credit** AmEx, DC, Disc, MC, V. **Map** p405 C21.

The neoclassical New York City Ballet headlines at this opulent, just-renovated theatre, which Philip Johnson designed to resemble a jewellery box. The company offers up its popular *The Nutcracker* at the very end of November, carrying just into the New Year; the spring season usually begins in April. Ballets by George Balanchine are performed by a wonderful crop of young dancers; there are also plenty by Jerome Robbins, Peter Martins (the company's ballet master in chief) and former resident choreographer Christopher Wheeldon.

Joyce Theater

175 Eighth Avenue, at 19th Street, Chelsea (1-212 242 0800, www.joyce.org). Subway A, C, E to 14th Street; 1 to 18th Street; L to Eighth Avenue. **Tickets** $10-$59. **Credit** AmEx, DC, Disc, MC, V. **Map** p403 D27.

This intimate space houses one of the finest theatres – we're talking about sightlines – in town. Companies and choreographers that present work here, among them Ballet Hispanico, Pilobolus Dance Theater and Doug Varone, tend to be somewhat traditional. The Joyce also hosts dance throughout much of the year – Pilobolus is a summer staple. At the Joyce Soho, emerging companies present work most weekends. **Other locations** 155 Mercer Street, between Houston & Prince Streets, Soho (1-212 334 7479).

★ Kitchen

512 W 19th Street, between Tenth & Eleventh Avenues, Chelsea (1-212 255 5793, www.thekitchen.org). Subway A, C, E to 14th Street; L to Eighth Avenue. **Tickets** free-$15. **Credit** AmEx, DC, MC, V. **Map** p403 C27.

The Kitchen, led by Debra Singer, offers some of the best experimental dance around – inventive, provocative and rigorous. Some of the artists who have presented work here are the finest in New York: Sarah Michelson, who also curates artists, Bill T Jones, Jon Kinzel, Ann Liv Young and Jodi Melnick.

Metropolitan Opera House

For listings, *see p315.*

A range of international companies, from the Paris Opera Ballet to the Kirov, performs at the Met. In spring, the majestic space is home to American Ballet Theatre, which presents full-length traditional story ballets, contemporary classics by Frederick Ashton and Antony Tudor, and the occasional world première by the likes of Twyla Tharp. The acoustics are wonderful, but the theatre is immense: get as close to the stage as you can afford.

New York City Center

131 W 55th Street, between Sixth & Seventh Avenues, Midtown (1-212 581 7907, www.nycitycenter.org). Subway B, D, E to Seventh Avenue; F, N, Q, R to 57th Street. **Tickets** $15-$150. **Credit** AmEx, DC, MC, V. **Map** p405 D22.

Before the Lincoln Center changed the city's cultural geography, this was the home of the American Ballet Theatre, the Joffrey Ballet and the New York City Ballet. City Center's lavish decor is golden – as are the companies that pass through here. The regulars are Alvin Ailey American Dance Theater, the Paul Taylor Dance Company and Morphoses/the Wheeldon Company. In autumn, the popular Fall for Dance Festival has tickets to mixed bills for just $10.

New York Live Arts

BessieSchönberg Theater, 219 W 19th Street, between Seventh & Eighth Avenues, Chelsea (1-212924 0077, www.newyorklivearts.org). Subway 1 to 18thStreet. **Tickets** $20-$25. **Credit** AmEx, DC, MC, V. **Map** p403 D27.

In December 2010, the Dance Theater Workshop and the Bill T Jones/Arnie ZaneDance Company merged to form New York Live Arts, which is dedicated to contemporary dance under Mr Jones and the workshop's director Carla Peterson.

OTHER VENUES

Abrons Arts Center

466 Grand Street, at Pitt Street, Lower East Side (1-212 598 0400, www.henrystreet.org/arts). Subway F to Delancey-Essex; B, D to Grand Street. **Tickets** $15-$20. **Credit** AmEx, DC, MC, V. **Map** p403 G30.

Once the headquarters of the Alwin Nikolais Dance Theater, this proscenium theatre now focuses on contemporary dance (plus music and other performances); past artists have included Miguel Gutierrez, Jonah Bokaer and Lawrence Goldhuber.

Ailey Citigroup Theater

Joan Weill Center for Dance, 405 W 55th Street, at Ninth Avenue, Hell's Kitchen (1-212 405 9000, www.alvinailey.org). Subway A, B, C, D, 1 to 59th Street-Columbus Circle; N, Q, R to 57th Street. **Tickets** $10-$50. **Credit** AmEx, DC, Disc, MC, V. **Map** p405 C22.

The elegant home of Alvin Ailey American Theater contains this flexible downstairs venue; when not in use as rehearsal space by the company or for the home seasons of Ailey II, its terrific junior ensemble, it is rented to a range of groups of varying quality.

★ Center for Performance Research

Greenbelt, Unit 1, 361 Manhattan Avenue, at Jackson Street, Williamsburg, Brooklyn (1-718 349 1210, www.cprnyc.org). Subway L to Graham Avenue. **Tickets** $12-$15. **Credit** DC, MC, V. **Map p**411 V8.

Based in a new LEED-certified green building with a 45ft by 45ft (14m by 14m) performing space, CPR, founded and curated by choreographers Jonah Bokaer and John Jasperse, represents a new trend of artists taking control of the means of production. Presentations are sporadic, so check the website.

Dance New Amsterdam (DNA)

280 Broadway, at Chambers Street, Financial District (1-212 625 8369, www.dnadance.org). Subway J, M, R, Z, 4, 5, 6 to City Hall. **Tickets** $8-$25. **Credit** AmEx, DC, Disc, MC, V. **Map** p402 E31.

Housed in the historic Sun Building, DNA has a 135-seat theatre that hosts about 50 performances a year. Past performers have included Urban Bush Women, Julie Bour and Foofwa d'Imobilité.

Dixon Place

161 Chrystie Street, at Delancey Street, Lower East Side (1-212 219 0736, www.dixonplace.org). Subway F to Lower East Side-Second Avenue; J, M, Z to Bowery-Delancey Streets. **Tickets** $6-$15. **Credit** AmEx, DC, Disc, MC, V. **Map** p403 F30.

Over two decades after Ellie Covan started hosting experimental performances in her living room, this plucky organisation finally opened a state-of-the-art space on the Lower East Side. Along with a main-stage theatre, there is a pub – perfect for post-show discussions. Dixon Place supports emerging artists and works in progress; summer events include the annual Hot! festival of lesbian and gay arts.

Flea

41 White Street, between Church Street & Broadway, Tribeca (1-212 352 3101, www.theflea.org). Subway A, C, E, N, Q, R, 6 to Canal Street; 1 to Franklin Street. **Tickets** free-$40. **Credit** AmEx, DC, Disc, MC, V. **Map** p402 E31.

Two stages here host a variety of offerings including the well-attended free monthly series, Dance Conversations at the Flea, curated by Nina Winthrop and Tami Stronach.

Harlem Stage at the Gatehouse

150 Convent Avenue, at W 135th Street, Harlem (1-212 281 9240, www.harlemstage.org). Subway 1 to 137th Street-City College. **Tickets** free-$45. **Credit** AmEx, DC, MC, V. **Map** p407 C12.

Performances at this theatre, formerly an operations centre for the Croton Aqueduct water system, celebrate African-American life and culture. Troupes that have graced this flexible space, designed by Frederick S Cook and now designated a New York City landmark, include the Bill T Jones/Arnie Zane Dance Company. Each spring, the space hosts the E-Moves Festival.

La MaMa ETC

74A E 4th Street, between Bowery & Second Avenue, East Village (1-212 475 7710, www.lamama.org). Subway F to Lower East Side-Second Avenue; 6 to Astor Place. **Tickets** $10-$25. **Credit** AmEx, DC, MC, V. **Map** p403 F29.

This experimental theatre – an East Village landmark – hosts the La MaMa Moves dance festival every year, featuring a variety of up-and-coming artists, and presents international troupes throughout the year. While shows here can be worthwhile, some programming is marginal.

Merce Cunningham Studio

11th Floor, 55 Bethune Street, between Washington & West Streets, West Village (1-212 255 8240, www.merce.org). Subway A, C, E to 14th Street; L to Eighth Avenue. **Tickets** $10-$50. **Credit** AmEx, DC, Disc, MC, V. **Map** p403 C28.

Located in the Westbeth complex on the far edge of the West Village, this beautiful studio is rented to independent choreographers, so the quality does vary. However, if you need an extra incentive, this is where Merce Cunningham choreographed for many years until his death in 2009. The stage and seating area are in a large dance studio, so be prepared to take off your shoes.

★ Movement Research at the Judson Church

55 Washington Square South, at Thompson Street, Greenwich Village (1-212 598 0551, www.movementresearch.org). Subway A, B, C, D, E, F, M to W 4th Street. **Tickets** free. **Map** p403 E28.

This free performance series, staged in a historic religious building, is a great place to check out experimental works and up-and-coming artists. Performances are held every Monday evening, from

Brooklyn Academy of Music. See p282.

September to July. The group's autumn and spring festivals, which take place roughly in December and June, feature a week-long series of performances and are held in venues throughout the city.

Performance Space 122

For listings, *see p360.*

Emerging choreographers present new works in the auditorium of this former public school. Ronald K Brown and Doug Varone started out here, while more recent artists have included Maria Hassabi and Megan Sprenger.

Symphony Space

2537 Broadway, at 95th Street, Upper West Side (1-212 864 5400, www.symphonyspace.org). Subway 1, 2, 3 to 96th Street. **Box office** 3-6pm Mon (show days only); 1-6pm Tue-Sun. **Tickets** vary. **Credit** AmEx, MC, V. **Map** p406 C17.

The World Music Institute hosts traditional dancers from around the globe at this multidisciplinary performing arts centre, but Symphony Space also stages works by contemporary choreographers, especially with its spring Thalia dance season.

► *See p288 for details of the Thalia cinema.*

Film & TV

Get in the shot.

Woody, Marty, Spike: by now the whole world is on first-name terms with New York's canonical legends. Even if this is your first visit to NYC, the cityscape will feel familiar; every corner – even the subway – has been immortalised on celluloid. It's easy to feel as if you've walked on to a massive movie set, especially when photogenic landmarks such as the Empire State Building pan into view. And you might even stumble upon an actual shoot – the thriving local film industry is based in Queens. Many high-profile TV shows are also produced here and, if you're organised (and lucky), you could snag tickets to a studio taping.

FILM

Few cities offer the film lover as many options as New York. If you insist, you can check out the blockbusters at the multiplexes on 42nd Street. But Gotham's gems are its arthouses, museums and rep and cutting-edge cinemas. For listings, see *Time Out New York* magazine.

Art & revival houses

Angelika Film Center
18 W Houston Street, at Mercer Street, Soho (1-212 995 2000, www.angelikafilmcenter.com). Subway B, D, F, M to Broadway-Lafayette Street; N, R to Prince Street; 6 to Bleecker Street. **Tickets** $13; $9 reductions. **Credit** AmEx, DC, MC, V. **Map** p403 E29.
When it opened in 1989, the Angelika immediately became a player in the then-booming Amerindie scene, and the six-screen cinema still puts the emphasis on edgier fare, both domestic and foreign. The complex is packed at weekends, so come extra early or visit the website to buy advance tickets.

Anthology Film Archives
32 Second Avenue, at 2nd Street, East Village (1-212 505 5181, www.anthologyfilmarchives.org). Subway F to Lower East Side-Second Avenue; 6 to Bleecker Street. **Tickets** $9; $7 reductions. **No credit cards**. **Map** p403 F29.
This red-brick building feels a bit like a fortress – and, in a sense, it is one, protecting the legacy of NYC's fiercest experimenters. Anthology is committed to screening the world's most adventurous films, from 16mm found-footage works to digital video dreams. Dedicated to the preservation, study and exhibition of independent and avant-garde film, it houses a gallery and film museum as well as two cinema screens.

★ BAM Rose Cinemas
Brooklyn Academy of Music, 30 Lafayette Avenue, between Ashland Place & St Felix Street, Fort Greene, Brooklyn (1-718 636 4100, www.bam.org). Subway B, Q, 2, 3, 4, 5 to Atlantic Avenue; C to Lafayette Street; D, M, N, R to Pacific Street; G to Fulton Street. **Tickets** $12; $9 reductions. **Credit** AmEx, DC, MC, V. **Map** p410 T10.
Brooklyn's premier art-film venue does double duty as a rep house for well-programmed classics on 35mm and as a first-run multiplex for indie films. It's recently started to host an annual best-of-Sundance programme – far more convenient than going to Utah.

Cinema Village
22 E 12th Street, between Fifth Avenue & University Place, Greenwich Village (1-212 924 3363, www.cinemavillage.com). Subway L, N, Q, R, 4, 5, 6 to 14th Street-Union Square. **Tickets** $11; $6-$8 reductions. **Credit** DC, MC, V. **Map** p403 E28.

About the author
Joshua Rothkopf *is the senior film critic at Time Out New York magazine. His writing has also appeared in* Penthouse, Details *and the* Village Voice.

A classic marquee that charmed Noah Baumbach long before he made *The Squid and the Whale,* this three-screener specialises in indie flicks, cutting-edge documentaries and foreign films. Check out the subway turnstile that admits ticket holders to the lobby.

★ Film Forum

209 W Houston Street, between Sixth Avenue & Varick Street, West Village (1-212 727 8110, www.filmforum.org). Subway 1 to Houston Street. **Tickets** $12; $6 reductions. **Credit** (online purchases only) MC, V. **Map** p403 D29.

The city's leading tastemaking venue, Film Forum is programmed by a fest-scouring staff that takes its duties as seriously as a Kurosawa samurai. A recent renovation included new seats. *Photo p289.*

★ IFC Center

323 Sixth Avenue, at W 3rd Street, Greenwich Village (1-212 924 7771, www.ifccenter.com).

How Movies Get Made in NYC

The blood, sweat and tears behind the lights, camera, action.

How do film crews actually do their jobs at public sites like bridges, the subway, streets and buildings? 'You're always going to affect something,' says location manager Mike Kriaris. 'I always equate it to dealing with a body of water: It's easier to redirect it around you than it is to dam it up.'

On the subway

The Hoyt–Schermerhorn station in Downtown Brooklyn houses an abandoned platform and a quarter mile of unused track, which is great for filming (Martin Scorsese shot the video for Michael Jackson's *Bad* here). For *Salt*, Kriaris got permission from the MTA to use the station and one of its newer trains; he also requested a cleanup crew, who removed trash and dust from the tracks and platform. Each day during filming, they'd spend two hours setting up. Luckily for commuters, even Angelina Jolie couldn't affect subway travel: normal operations continued unaware on the functional tracks.

Inside buildings

In the comedy *The Other Guys*, Steve Coogan plays an evil financier. To create his office, Kriaris worked with Rockefeller Center owner Tishman Speyer to take over part of the Top of the Rock observation deck. Contending with tourists, however, proved challenging. Kriaris and his team would start setting up at 12:01am, when Rockefeller Center closed to the public, but civilians were in the building by 8am, while filming was still taking place. 'We'd be carrying equipment out and there'd be tourists coming and going,' Kriaris recalls.

In the street

Before shooting anywhere, location managers must collaborate with city agencies, including the Mayor's Office of Film, Theatre & Broadcasting (MOFTB). Then, it's a matter of crowd control. To film the scene in *Sex and the City* in which a jilted Carrie Bradshaw confronts Mr Big outside the New York Public Library, Kriaris hired 15 production assistants and two police officers to prevent the paparazzi and 1,500 excited onlookers from swarming Sarah Jessica Parker. While six traffic cops stopped cars from turning on to the street, security guards kept an eye on overzealous fans.

Sex and the City.

Atop bridges

The Queensboro Bridge has hosted many an action sequence (the climactic scene of *Spider-Man* was shot there), but a *Salt* scene involved some serious coordination. Jolie hijacks a police car and sends it plummeting over an exit ramp on to vehicles parked on the street below. Kriaris needed permission from the MOFTB as well as the Department of Transportation's Division of Bridges, which let him shut down an entrance ramp on the Queens side of the bridge. Then, he hired six traffic officers and two police cars to keep bridge traffic moving 100 yards behind the camera as it travelled across the bridge.

Subway A, B, C, D, E, F, M to W 4th Street. **Tickets** $13; $9 reductions. **Credit** AmEx, DC, MC, V. **Map** p403 D29.
The long-darkened 1930s Waverly was once again illuminated in 2005 when it was reborn as a modern three-screen arthouse, showing the latest indie hits, choice midnight cult items and occasional foreign classics. You may rub elbows with the actors on the screen, as many introduce their work on opening night. A high-toned café provides sweets, lattes and substantials.

★ Landmark Sunshine Cinema

141-143 E Houston Street, between First & Second Avenues, East Village (1-212 330 8182). Subway F to Lower East Side-Second Avenue. **Tickets** $12.50; $9 reductions. **Credit** AmEx, DC, Disc, MC, V. **Map** p403 F29.
Once a renowned Yiddish theatre, this comfortable, date-friendly venue has snazz and chutzpah to spare. Intimate cinemas and excellent sound are a beautiful complement to the indie films; here, too, is New York's most consistently excellent midnight series.

Leonard Nimoy Thalia

Symphony Space, 2537 Broadway, at 95th Street, entrance on 95th Street, Upper West Side (1-212 864 5400, www.symphonyspace.org). Subway 1, 2, 3 to 96th Street. **Tickets** $12; $10 reductions. **Credit** AmEx, DC, MC, V. **Map** p406 C17.

Essentially New York Film

Above-the-credits names weigh in.

Sweet Smell of Success.

DAVID FEAR, FILM EDITOR, TIME OUT NEW YORK: 'We named Spike Lee's **Do the Right Thing** the best NYC movie a few years back, and we stand by what we wrote then: "Made as a direct response to the Howard Beach incident, Spike's story about New York's racial melting pot coming to a boil encompasses Brooklyn in full: the mix of ethnicity and classes, stoop culture and gentrification, pride and anger... in short, the overall volatility of the modern urban experience. All this, and Rosie Perez dancing to Public Enemy's 'Fight the Power'."'

MARTIN SCORSESE, DIRECTOR: 'Ah! See, now, the interesting thing is – which time period? You know? For me, I guess, my early teens, it would probably be **Sweet Smell of Success**. I'm sure a number of people have already said the same thing. A truly great film.'

JIM JARMUSCH, DIRECTOR: 'I have [on my list] movies like **The Cameraman** by Buster Keaton, which was all shot in the streets of New York; **The Cool World** by Shirley Clarke, which is an unheralded masterpiece in my opinion. I also love **Shadows**, [John] Cassavetes's first film, which was almost all shot in New York, and **Pull My Daisy**. And of course, Charlie Ahearn's film **Wild Style**. What about **Midnight Cowboy** and **Shaft** and **Black Caesar** and **Mean Streets** and **Gloria** and **The King of Comedy** and Abel Ferrara's films? And **The Thin Man**, **My Man Godfrey**, **Scarlet Street**, **The Big Clock**, **The Naked City**... I'm not very helpful.'

BRUCE GOLDSTEIN, DIRECTOR OF REPERTORY PROGRAMMING, FILM FORUM: 'The ones that have extensive location work are the ones I love: a film like Jules Dassin's **The Naked City**, which is one of the first Hollywood sound films to go out on location. I think the greatest thriller ever made in New York is **The Taking of Pelham One Two Three**. The other one that I'm nuts about is **Sweet Smell of Success**. As far as cinematography and capturing the end of the heyday of Times Square, it's an amazing movie.'

SPIKE LEE, DIRECTOR: 'Well, I have a list of them. **Mean Streets**, **Raging Bull**, **West Side Story**, **Dog Day Afternoon**, **Serpico**, **Shaft**. I'll include **On the Waterfront** even though it's Hoboken. **The Godfather**. Those films are definitely New York films. And you can include Woody Allen films there too. But those Woody Allen films – and this is no disrespect to the master, which he is – they're not really the diversity that one sees in New York City.'

Film Forum. *See p287.*

The famed Thalia arthouse, featured in *Annie Hall* (when it was screening *The Sorrow and the Pity*), was recently upgraded, but it's still trying to find its identity. The fare is eclectic, but the classics are reliable: a month of Hepburn and Tracy, for instance.

Maysles Cinema

343 Malcolm X Boulevard (Lenox Avenue), between 127th & 128th Streets, Harlem (1-212 582 6050, ext 207, www.mayslesinstitute.org). Subway A, B, C, D, 2, 3 to 125th Street. **Tickets** *Suggested donation* $10. **No credit cards**. **Map** p407 D13.

Hidden behind a storefront, this 55-seat newcomer serves up an eclectic stew. You might catch rousing hip hop and reggae films, a panel discussion about Times Square starring a zonked-out sex performer from Gotham's sleazy days, or rarities such as *Demon Lover Diary* and *The Police Tapes*.

Paris Theatre

4 West 58th Street, between Fifth & Sixth Avenues, Midtown (1-212 688 3800, www.paristheatre.com). Subway N, R to Fifth Avenue-59th Street. **Tickets** $13; $9 reductions. **Credit** AmEx, MC, V. **Map** p405 E22.

The elegant, single-screen Paris is one of the oldest continually operating movie houses in the country (it was founded in 1948). Its plush carpets and seats, tiny lobby and lack of any on-screen advertising set it apart even from the city's indie houses. It screens new and revival French films whenever possible.

Quad Cinema

34 W 13th Street, between Fifth & Sixth Avenues, Greenwich Village (1-212 255 8800, www.quadcinema.com). Subway F 14th Street; L to Sixth Avenue. **Tickets** $11; $8 reductions. **Credit** AmEx, DC, Disc, MC, V. **Map** p403 E28.

The Quad Cinema's four small screens show a wide range of foreign and American indie films. However, the real standouts at this Greenwich Village operation are the latest offerings related to gay sexuality and politics.

▶ *For camper, gay-oriented cinema, check out the Chelsea Classics film series, held at the Clearview Cinemas in Chelsea; see p310.*

Museums & societies

★ Film Society of Lincoln Center

Walter Reade Theater, 70 Lincoln Center Plaza, between Broadway & Amsterdam Avenue, Upper West Side (1-212 875 5601, www.filmlinc.com). Subway 1 to 66th Street-Lincoln Center. **Tickets** $12; $8-$9 reductions. **Credit** (online purchases only) MC, V. **Map** p405 C21.

Founded in 1969 to promote contemporary film, the FSLC now also hosts the prestigious New York Film Festival. Programmes are usually thematic, with an international perspective. Until 2011, when Lincoln Center's state-of-the-art Elinor Bunin-Munroe Film Center opens on the south side of 65th Street with two screens, a gallery and a café, your film-going needs will be met here.

★ Museum of Modern Art

For listings, *see p102.* **Tickets** free with museum admission, or $10; $6-$8 reductions; free under-16s. **Credit** AmEx, DC, MC, V.

Renowned for its superb programming of art films and experimental work, MoMA draws from a vast vault. You have to buy tickets in person at the museum at the lobby desk or the film desk (see www.moma.org or phone 1-212 708 9480 for more information), but you can take in some paintings or sculptures while you're there.

Museum of the Moving Image
For listings, *see p141.* **Tickets** vary. **Credit** AmEx, DC, MC, V.
Like the rest of the museum, MMI's theatre has received a magnificent renovation, resulting in a state-of-the-art 264-seat cinema. Expect excellent prints and screenings of the classics as well as inspired selections.

Foreign-language specialists

You can catch the latest foreign-language flicks at art and revival houses, but there is a wealth of specialist venues as well, including the **French Institute Alliance Française** (22 E 60th Street, 1-212 355 6100, www.fiaf.org), the **Japan Society** (*see p105*) and **Scandinavia House** (*see p93*). The **Asia Society & Museum** (*see p110*) screens works from Asian countries plus Asian-American productions.

Film festivals

From late September to early October, the Film Society of Lincoln Center hosts the **New York Film Festival** (1-212 875 5050, www.filmlinc.com), a showcase packed with premières, features and short flicks from around the globe. Together with Lincoln Center's *Film Comment* magazine, the FSLC also offers the popular **Film Comment Selects**, showcasing films that have yet to be distributed in the US.

January brings the annual **New York Jewish Film Festival** (1-212 875 5600, www.thejewishmuseum.org) to Lincoln Center's Walter Reade Theater. At the end of February, the **New York International Children's Film Festival** kicks off two weeks of anime, shorts and features made for kids and teens (www.gkids.com).

Each spring, the Museum of Modern Art and the Film Society of Lincoln Center sponsor the highly regarded New Directors/New Films series, presenting works by on-the-cusp filmmakers. And in late April/early May, Robert De Niro's **Tribeca Film Festival** (1-212 941 2400, www.tribecafilmfestival.org) draws around 400,000 fans to screenings of independent movies. It's followed by the **New York Lesbian & Gay Film Festival** (1-212 571 2170, www.newfest.org), which takes place in June, while summer sees several outdoor film festivals (*see below* **Inside Track**).

INSIDE TRACK OUTDOOR MOVIES

With summer arrives the wonderful New York tradition of free outdoor movie festivals. Look out for the **Bryant Park Summer Film Festival** in Midtown (1-212 512 5700, www.bryantpark.org); **Movies with a View** in Brooklyn Bridge Park (1-718 802 0603, www.brooklynbridgepark.org); the **River to River Festival** across Lower Manhattan (*see p262*); and **Summer on the Hudson** in Riverside Park South (1-212 408 0219).

TV STUDIO TAPINGS

Colbert Report
513 W 54th Street, between Tenth & Eleventh Avenues, Hell's Kitchen (www.colbertnation.com/tickets). Subway C, E to 50th Street. **Tapings** 6pm Mon-Thur. **Map** p405 C22.
Sarcastic correspondent Stephen Colbert's parody of Bill O'Reilly's right-wing political talk show tells viewers why everyone else's opinions are 'just plain wrong'. Reserve tickets online at least six months ahead, or try your luck getting standby tickets on the day at 4pm. You must be 18 and have photo ID.

Daily Show with Jon Stewart
513 W 54th Street, between Tenth & Eleventh Avenues, Hell's Kitchen (www.thedailyshow.com/tickets). Subway C, E to 50th Street. **Tapings** 5.45pm Mon-Thur. **Map** p405 C22.
Many viewers believe they get a fairer view of current affairs from Stewart's irreverent take than they do from the network news. Reserve tickets at least three months ahead online; as ticket distribution may be in excess of studio capacity, admission is not guaranteed. You must be over 18 and have photo ID.

Late Show with David Letterman
1697 Broadway, between 53rd & 54th Streets, Midtown (1-212 975 1003, www.cbs.com/late_night/late_show/tickets). Subway B, D, E to Seventh Avenue. **Tapings** 4.30pm, 7pm Mon; 4.30pm Tue-Thur. **Map** p405 D22.
Letterman's sardonic humour has been a defining feature of the late-night landscape for decades. Seats are hard to get: fill out a request form online, or try to get a standby ticket by calling 1-212 247 6497 at 11am on the day. You must be 18 with photo ID.

Saturday Night Live
30 Rockefeller Plaza, Sixth Avenue, between 49th & 50th Streets, Midtown (1-212 664 3056, www.nbc.com/snl). Subway B, D, F, M to 47th-50th Streets-Rockefeller Center. **Tapings** *Dress rehearsal* 8pm. *Live show* 11.30pm. **Map** p405 D22.
Tickets to this long-running comedy sketch show are assigned by lottery every autumn. Send an email to snltickets@nbcuni.com in August, or try the standby lottery on the day. Line up by 7am (but get there much earlier) under the NBC Studio marquee (49th Street side of 30 Rockefeller Plaza). You must be over 16 with photo ID.

Galleries

Seeking cheaper spaces, the art scene is forever on the move.

The worldwide financial meltdown has cut deep into the art world: the prices at auction for some of the biggest names in contemporary art have been nearly halved in the past two years. Remarkably, however, New York's gallery scene has largely managed to persevere.

Granted, an estimated 25 to 30 galleries have shut since autumn 2008, especially in Chelsea, the city's most concentrated gallery district, where in recent years rents had skyrocketed along with the art market. But the damage was not nearly as widespread as in the period following the stock market crash of 1987, when an entire art neighbourhood – the East Village – disappeared. The dealers who experienced that era first-hand had learned their lesson – many own their spaces outright. Meanwhile, some landlords have been flexible, figuring that a gallery behind on its rent is better than an empty space.

FINE ART

In **Chelsea**'s converted industrial spaces, you'll find group shows by up-and-comers, blockbuster exhibitions from art-world celebrities and a slew of provocative work. However, in the past few years, the **Lower East Side** has seen a steady migration of dealers, and the area's growth has accelerated with the crash of the real-estate market. LES galleries are, as a rule, much smaller than those in Chelsea, but the lower rents have allowed young dealers to open shop, bringing a whole new generation of artists to public attention. The New Museum of Contemporary Art (*see p81*), which relocated to the Bowery in late 2007, also serves as a magnet, drawing gallerists, artists and art-lovers to the neighbourhood. This reinvigoration seems to have rebounded on New York's entire gallery scene, including once-booming **Soho**, which has seen a scattering of new spaces open.

Uptown, the Museum Mile galleries cater to more traditional tastes and show the work of mid-career and established artists alongside the old masters, while the old-guard 57th Street crew turns out a continuous series of blue-chip shows.

In Brooklyn, **Williamsburg** has a number of top-quality galleries around Bedford Avenue – you'll find more experimental and street-art influenced fare in nearby **Bushwick**. Queens' artistic hotbed lies in **Long Island City**, where MoMA's scrappier sibling, P.S.1 Contemporary Art Center (*see p138*), never fails to satisfy the art pilgrims who venture there. For events in the area, check www.licartists.org.

Note that galleries are generally closed on Mondays, and many are open only on weekdays from May or June to early September (and some close for part or all of August). We've given summer hours for most venues, but it's always wise to call before heading out. *Time Out New York* magazine has the latest listings and reviews; the website **ArtCat** (www.artcat.com) lists citywide shows and opening receptions.

Tribeca & Soho

Subway A, C, E, J, M, N, Q, R, Z, 1, 6 to Canal Street; B, D, F, M to Broadway-Lafayette Street; N, R to Prince Street; 6 to Spring Street.

★ Drawing Center

35 Wooster Street, between Broome & Grand Streets (1-212 219 2166, www.drawingcenter.org). **Open** *Sept-July* noon-6pm Wed, Fri-Sun; noon-8pm Thur. **Map** p403 E30.

Established in 1977 as a stronghold of works on paper, this non-profit Soho standout assembles critically acclaimed programmes – including shows of museum-calibre legends like Philip Guston, James Ensor, Willem de Kooning and Odilon Redon – but also 'Selections' surveys of newcomers drawn entirely from its flat files open to submission by all. Current art stars such as Kara Walker, Turner Prize winner Chris Ofili and Julie Mehretu received some of their earliest NYC exposure here.

Harris Lieberman

89 Vandam Street, between Greenwich & Hudson Streets (1-212 206 1290, www.harrislieberman.com). **Open** *Sept-June* 11am-6pm Tue-Sat. *July, Aug* 11am-6pm Tue-Fri. **Map** p403 D30.
This outpost near the Hudson was launched in 2005 by a husband-and-wife team, both long-time directors on the Chelsea scene. Their wide range of experience, coupled with a keen eye, translates to a young international stable that includes, among others, painter Matthias Dornfeld (who limns darkly colourful primitivistic portraits and still lifes) and Alexandre Singh (whose rebus-like, flow-chart installations of images are composed of photocopies taken from found sources).

★ Peter Blum

99 Wooster Street, between Prince & Spring Streets (1-212 343 0441, www.peterblumgallery.com). **Open** *Sept-July* 10am-6pm Tue-Fri; 11am-6pm Sat. **Map** p403 E30.
This elegant gallery space is manned by a dealer with an impeccable eye and wide-ranging tastes. Exhibitions have run the gamut from drawings by Robert Ryman and Alex Katz to terracotta funerary figures from West Africa and colourful quilts from the hands of noted African-American folk artist Rosie Lee Tompkins.
Other locations 526 W 29th Street, between Tenth & Eleventh Avenues, Chelsea (1-212 244 6055).

Ronald Feldman Fine Arts

31 Mercer Street, between Canal & Grand Streets (1-212 226 3232, www.feldmangallery.com). **Open** *Sept-June* by appt Mon; 10am-6pm Tue-Sat. *July, Aug* 10am-6pm Mon-Thur; 10am-3pm Fri. **Map** p403 E30.
This Soho pioneer brought landmark shows of such legendary avant-gardists as Eleanor Antin and Leon Golub to the New York scene, and regularly takes chances on newer talents.

> **INSIDE TRACK**
> **ART AND COMMERCE WALK**
>
> Slender park-promenade the **High Line** (*see p96* **Profile**) connects the shops, bars and restaurants of the Meatpacking District with the galleries of Chelsea, combining all these pleasures with a scenic walk in the middle.

★ Team Gallery

83 Grand Street, between Greene & Wooster Streets (1-212 279 9219, www.teamgal.com). **Open** *Oct-May* 10am-6pm Tue-Sat. *June-Sept* 10am-6pm Mon-Fri. **Map** p403 E30.
José Freire relocated his gallery from a hip Chelsea address to this high-ceilinged space in 2006, confirming that Downtown is once again the place to be. The gallery showcases such bright young hotshots as photographer Ryan McGinley and web-artist Cory Arcangel, and also represents more established artists, including minimalist assemblagist and installation artist Ross Knight.

Lower East Side

Subway F to East Broadway or Delancey Street; F to Lower East Side-Second Avenue; J, M, Z to Delancey-Essex Streets.

Canada

55 Chrystie Street, between Canal & Hester Streets (1-212 925 4631, www.canadanewyork.com). **Open** *Sept-mid Aug* noon-6pm Wed-Sun. **Map** p403 F30.
A trailblazer of the Chinatown/Lower East Side gallery phenomenon, Canada opened its doors at the foot of the Manhattan Bridge in 2000. Its directors, three of them artists, strive to support a wide range of work – from paintings and mixed-media installations to performance – by artists such as Devendra Banhart, Michael Mahalchick and Carrie Moyer.

DCKT Contemporary

195 Bowery, between Rivington & Delancey Streets (1-212 741 9955, www.dcktcontemporary.com). **Open** *Sept-mid Aug* 11am-6pm Tue-Fri; noon-6pm Sat; noon-5pm Sun. **Map** p403 F30.
DCKT are the initials of Dennis Christie and Ken Tyburski, who first founded their space in Chelsea in 2003 before moving five years later to the ground zero of the LES artquake: the stretch along Bowery near the New Museum. DCKT's programme ranges from painting and sculpture to video and photography, and its stable includes such interesting names as Exene Cervenka, former vocalist for legendary LA punk band X, and Cordy Ryman, son of minimalist painting pioneer Robert Ryman.
► *For details of the nearby New Museum of Contemporary Art, see p81.*

★ Eleven Rivington

11 Rivington Street, between Bowery & Chrystie Street (1-212 982 1930, www.elevenrivington.com). **Open** *Sept-mid Aug* noon-6pm Wed-Sun. **Map** p403 F30.
Established in September 2007, and located in the lobby of the Off Soho Suites hotel, this offshoot of 57th Street's Greenberg Van Doren gallery offers an impeccable Midtown atmosphere in small-storefront form. The artworks on display are just as classy,

Team Gallery.

ranging from Volker Hueller's evocations of classical modernism via hand-coloured etchings to Jacob Kassay's silver-plated abstract canvases.
Other locations Greenberg Van Doren Gallery, 7th Floor, 730 Fifth Avenue, at 57th Street (1-212 445 0444, www.gvdgallery.com).

Invisible-Exports

14A Orchard Street, between Canal & Hester Streets (1-212 226 5447, www.invisible-exports.com). **Open** *Sept-mid Aug* 11am-6.30pm Wed-Sun, or by appt. **Map** p403 G30.

Risa Needleman and Benjamin Tischer describe their venue as being dedicated to 'superior conceptual work'. And, if by that, they mean art with a certain outré, countercultural edge, they'll get no argument here. Invisible-Exports has presented collages by transgenderist and multimedia visionary Genesis Breyer P-Orridge, elided images of vintage gay porn by Stephen Irwin, and Lisa Kirk's installational homages to revolutionary violence.

Lisa Cooley

34 Orchard Street, between Canal & Hester Streets (1-212 680 0564, www.lisa-cooley.com). **Open** *Sept-mid Aug* noon-6pm Wed-Sun. **Map** p403 G30.

Formerly director of Houston's Mixture Gallery and Nicole Klagsbrun in New York, Lisa Cooley opened her shop in 2008, and quickly established herself as one of the neighbourhood's sought-after gallerists. Her roster of artists seems to share a penchant for conceptualist sleight-of-hand mixed with unexpected materials – most notably Erin Shirreff's 'moon rock' photos (actually images of hand-fashioned clay blobs) and Josh Faught's fibre-art sculptures made from woven afghans, garden trellises and nail polish.

★ Miguel Abreu Gallery

36 Orchard Street, between Canal & Hester Streets (1-212 995 1774, www.miguelabreu gallery.com). **Open** *Sept-mid June* 11am-6.30pm Wed-Sun. *Mid June-mid Aug* 11am-6.30pm Tue-Sat. **Map** p403 G30.

A filmmaker as well as founding member of the legendary Threadwaxing alternative space in Soho (now closed), Miguel Abreu ventured into dealing in 2006. Hosting a highly intellectual series of performances, art-theory seminars and film screenings, as well as exhibitions, the gallery represents conceptually inspired artists. The list includes RH Quaytman, who creates hauntingly enigmatic images silk-screened on to wood panels; Eileen Quinlan, whose abstract photos have a similarly evasive quality; and Blake Rayne, whose heavily coded paintings and objects delve deep into the philosophical foundations of art and representation.

► *See p80 for more on the Orchard Street area.*

On Stellar Rays

133 Orchard Street, between Delancey & Rivington Streets (1-212 598 3012, www.onstellarrays.com). **Open** 11am-6pm Wed-Sat; noon-6pm Sun. **Map** p403 F30.

The name originates from a ninth-century text by the Arab philosopher and polymath, Abu Yusuf Yaqub ibn Ishaq al-Kindi. The book, entitled *De Radiis* (*On Rays*) posits the effect of astral rays on perception in the material world. Aptly, the venue's slate of group exhibitions, solo shows and performances appears to express some idea of art as cultural physics – notably Tommy Hartung's video adaptation of the BBC's *Ascent of Man* series and Debo Eilers' Day-Glo assemblages of everyday flotsam paired with screen-grabs of cluttered computer desktops.

Participant Inc

253 E Houston Street, between Norfolk & Suffolk Streets (1-212 254 4334, www.participantinc.org). **Open** noon-7pm Wed-Sun. **Map** p403 G29.

Non-profit, alternative gallery Participant Inc opened at a time (2002) when there was no LES art scene to speak of, and Chelsea ruled as the hub for contemporary art. Since then, the bi-level, industrial space has become an art mainstay of the area, offering thoughtfully curated group exhibitions, and edgy solo projects such as Laura Parnes's sleekly cinematic video based on *Blood and Guts in High School* by punk-feminist author Kathy Acker.

Rachel Uffner Gallery

47 Orchard Street, between Grand & Hester Sreets (1-212 274 0064, www.racheluffner.com). **Open** *Sept-mid Aug* 11am-6pm Wed-Sun, or by appt. **Map** p403 G30.

After cutting her teeth working at Christie's and as director for Chelsea's D'Amelio Terras gallery, Rachel Uffner opened her own space in 2008. Her small stable of artists is eclectic, but they share a sensibility that could be called painterly – although not all of them paint. For example, Roger White's understated watercolours cross back and forth between patterny abstraction and recognisable subjects, while Sara Greenberger Rafferty makes C-prints of found magazine images that allude to the function of memory.

★ Salon 94 Freemans

1 Freeman Alley, between Rivington & Stanton Streets (1-212 529 7400, www.salon94.com). **Open** *Sept-mid Aug* 1-6 pm Tue; 11am-6pm Wed-Sat; 2-6pm Sun. **Map** p403 F29.

Salon 94 Freemans is the Downtown outpost of the project space created within the Upper East Side townhouse shared by dealer Jeanne Greenberg Rohatyn and her husband Nicolas Rohatyn. In contrast to the Uptown spot's light, airy environs, this branch has a darker, tougher feel, with its concrete flooring and old timber columns. Works by the couple's stable of artists – paintings by veteran photorealist and glamour deconstructionist Marilyn Minter, totemic sculptures by Huma Bhabha – look at home in either place.

Other locations 12 E 94th Street, between Fifth & Park Avenues (1-646 672 9212).

► *Freeman Alley is also home to the enduringly popular restaurant Freemans; see p191.*

Sue Scott Gallery

1 Rivington Street, at Bowery (1-212 358 8767, www.suescottgallery.com). **Open** *Sept-mid Aug* 11am-6pm Tue-Sat; noon-6pm Sun. **Map** p403 F30.

The adjunct curator of contemporary art at the Orlando Museum of Art for 19 years, Sue Scott brings a practised eye to her second-floor gallery, stocking it with a small, tight line-up of artists that tips predominantly, though not entirely, towards painters. Look out for Suzanne McClelland's gestural, quasi-abstract canvases, Franklin Evans's softly geometric watercolours and Tom McGrath's vaguely unsettling suburban landscapes.

Chelsea

Subway A, C, E to 14th Street; C, E to 23rd Street; L to Eighth Avenue.

Chelsea's main gallery district is on the far West Side, between Tenth and Eleventh Avenues, from 19th to 29th Streets. The subway takes you only as far as Eighth Avenue, so you'll have to walk west or take the M23 crosstown bus.

Andrea Rosen Gallery

525 W 24th Street, between Tenth & Eleventh Avenues (1-212 627 6000, www.andrearosengallery.com). **Open** *Sept-June* 10am-6pm Tue-Sat. *July, Aug* 10am-6pm Mon-Fri. **Map** p404 C26.

During the past 20 years, Andrea Rosen has established several major careers: the late Felix Gonzalez-Torres got his start here (the gallery handles his estate), as did Wolfgang Tillmans, Andrea Zittel and John Currin (who left for Gagosian in 2003). It also represents much-touted young sculptor David Altmejd. *Photo p296.*

Andrew Kreps Gallery

525 W 22nd Street, between Tenth & Eleventh Avenues (1-212 741 8849, www.andrewkreps.com). **Open** *Sept-June* 10am-6pm Tue-Sat. *July, Aug* varies. **Map** p404 C26.

The radicals in Andrew Kreps's adventurous stable of artists include Ricci Albenda, Roe Ethridge, Robert Melee and Ruth Root.

★ Anton Kern Gallery

532 W 20th Street, between Tenth & Eleventh Avenues (1-212 367 9663, www.antonkerngallery.com). **Open** *Sept-June* 10am-6pm Tue-Sat. *July, Aug* 10am-6pm Mon-Fri. **Map** p403 C27.

The son of artist Georg Baselitz, Kern presents young American and European artists whose installations have provided the New York art scene with some of its most visionary shows. Kai Althoff, Sarah Jones and Jim Lambie have all been featured here.

D'Amelio Terras

525 W 22nd Street, between Tenth & Eleventh Avenues (1-212 352 9460, www.damelioterras.com). **Open** *Sept-May* 10am-6pm Tue-Sat. *June-Aug* 10am-6pm Mon-Fri. **Map** p404 B26.

D'Amelio Terras was one of the first spaces to set up shop in Chelsea, back in the 1990s. The gallery devotes the month of January to specially curated examinations of post-war art in an effort to set the stage for – and educate the public about – the rest of its programme, which features museum-calibre artists such as Joanne Greenbaum, Matt Keegan and Cornelia Parker.

Mary Boone Gallery. *See p297*.

Andrea Rosen Gallery. See p294.

★ David Zwirner

519, 525 & 533 W 19th Street, between Tenth & Eleventh Avenues (1-212 727 2070, www.davidzwirner.com). **Open** *Sept-June* 10am-6pm Tue-Sat. *July, Aug* 10am-6pm Mon-Fri. **Map** p403 C27.

David Zwirner mixes museum-quality shows of historical figures and movements (Dan Flavin, West Coast Minimalism) with a head-turning array of international contemporary artists that includes such luminaries as Marcel Dzama, Luc Tuymans, Chris Ofili, Neo Rauch and Lisa Yuskavage.

Friedrich Petzel Gallery

535 & 537 W 22nd Street, between Tenth & Eleventh Avenues (1-212 680 9467, www.petzel.com). **Open** *Sept-June* 10am-6pm Tue-Sat. *July, Aug* 10am-6pm Mon-Fri. **Map** p404 C26.

The Friedrich Petzel Gallery represents some of the brightest young stars on the international scene, so you can count on some intriguing shows. Sculptor Keith Edmier, photographer Dana Hoey, painter and filmmaker Sarah Morris, and installation artists Jorge Pardo and Philippe Parreno all show here.

Gagosian Gallery

555 W 24th Street, between Tenth & Eleventh Avenues (1-212 741 1111, www.gagosian.com). **Open** *Sept-June* 10am-6pm Tue-Sat. *July, Aug* 10am-6pm Mon-Fri. **Map** p404 C26.

A massive figure on the international art scene, Larry Gagosian has hugely successful outposts in Los Angeles, London and Rome, in addition to three spaces in NYC. His mammoth contribution to 24th Street's top-level galleries showcases work by prominent art-world names, including Richard Serra, Ellen Gallagher, Damien Hirst, Julian Schnabel, Georg Baselitz and Richard Artschwager.

Other locations 522 W 21st Street, between Tenth & Eleventh Avenues, Chelsea (1-212 741 1717); 980 Madison Avenue, at 76th Street, Upper East Side (1-212 744 2313).

Gladstone Gallery

515 W 24th Street, between Tenth & Eleventh Avenues (1-212 206 9300, www.gladstonegallery.com). **Open** *Sept-June* 10am-6pm Tue-Sat. *July, Aug* 10am-6pm Mon-Fri. **Map** p404 C26.

Gladstone is strictly blue-chip, focusing on such conceptualist and daring talents as Matthew Barney, Sarah Lucas and Anish Kapoor.

★ Greene Naftali

8th Floor, 508 W 26th Street, between Tenth & Eleventh Avenues (1-212 463 7770, www.greenenaftaligallery.com). **Open** *Sept-June* 10am-6pm Tue-Sat. *July* 10am-6pm Mon-Fri. **Map** p404 C26.

Even non-art lovers will enjoy a visit to Greene Naftali, a gallery that's worth checking out purely for its wonderful light and spectacular panorama. But the always-keen vision of Carol Greene outdoes even the gallery's eighth-floor view. Mavericks such as sculptor Rachel Harrison and video artist Paul Chan please critics and casual browsers.

John Connelly Presents

625 W 27th Street, between Eleventh & Twelfth Avenues (1-212 337 9563, www.johnconnellypresents.com). **Open** *Sept-June* 11am-6pm Tue-Sat. *July, Aug* 11am-6pm Mon-Fri. **Map** p404 B26.

Connelly, a long-time director of the Andrea Rosen Gallery, quickly earned a reputation as one of New York's most exciting young dealers after he struck out on his own. Expect provocative shows with an emphasis on cheeky installation art on the order of the *Coat Check Chimes* created for the 2008 Whitney Biennial by gallery regular and self-styled 'polymorphous bastard conceptualist' Mungo Thomson.

► *Aperture Gallery, specialising in photography, is a block east of here; see p300.*

Lehmann Maupin

540 W 26th Street, between Tenth & Eleventh Avenues (1-212 255 2923, www.lehmannmaupin.com). **Open** *Sept-June* 10am-6pm Tue-Sat. *July, Aug* 10am-6pm Mon-Fri. **Map** p404 C26.

Epic exhibitions in this Rem Koolhaas-designed former garage feature hip international artists – think Tracey Emin, Gilbert & George, Teresita Fernandez, Do-Ho Suh and Juergen Teller. Lehmann Maupin also recently opened an outpost in the Lower East Side.

Other locations 201 Chrystie Street, between Rivington & Stanton Streets, Lower East Side (1-212 254 0054).

Leo Koenig Inc

545 W 23rd Street, between Tenth & Eleventh Avenues (1-212 334 9255, www.leokoenig.com). **Open** *Sept-July* 10am-6pm Tue-Sat. **Map** p404 C26.

The son of Kasper Koenig, the internationally renowned curator and museum director, Leo has been making a name for himself by putting on shows by cutting-edge talents including Torben Giehler, Christian Schumann and Wendy White.

Luhring Augustine

531 W 24th Street, between Tenth & Eleventh Avenues (1-212 206 9100, www.luhringaugustine.com). **Open** *Sept-June* 10am-6pm Tue-Sat. *July, Aug* 10am-5.30pm Mon-Fri. **Map** p404 C26.

Designed by Richard Gluckman, the area's architect of choice, this gallery features work from an impressive assemblage of contemporary artists, such as British sculptor Rachel Whiteread, Swiss video star Pipilotti Rist, and Americans Janine Antoni, Larry Clark and Gregory Crewdson.

Mary Boone Gallery

541 W 24th Street, between Tenth & Eleventh Avenues (1-212 752 2929, www.maryboonegallery.com). **Open** *Sept-June* 10am-6pm Tue-Sat. *July, Aug* by appt. **Map** p404 C26.

Art dealer Mary Boone made her name in the 1980s representing Julian Schnabel, Jean-Michel Basquiat and Francesco Clemente at her renowned Soho gallery. She later moved to Midtown and then, in 2000, added this sweeping space inside a former garage, showing established artists including David Salle, Barbara Kruger and Eric Fischl alongside up-and-comers such as Brian Alfred and Hilary Harkness. *Photo p295.*

Other locations 745 Fifth Avenue, between 57th & 58th Streets, Midtown (1-212 752 2929).

Matthew Marks Gallery

523 W 24th Street, between Tenth & Eleventh Avenues (1-212 243 0200, www.matthewmarks.com). **Open** *Sept-June* 11am-6pm Tue-Sat. *July-mid Aug* 11am-6pm Mon-Fri. **Map** p404 C26.

With its arrival in 1994, the Matthew Marks Gallery became a driving force behind Chelsea's transformation into one of the city's top art destinations and, with four outposts to its name, it remains one of the neighbourhood's powerhouses. The gallery showcases internationally renowned talent, including Robert Gober, Nan Goldin, Andreas Gursky, Ellsworth Kelly and Brice Marden.

Other locations 521 W 21st Street, 522 W 22nd Street & 526 W 22nd Street, all between Tenth & Eleventh Avenues, Chelsea.

Metro Pictures

519 W 24th Street, between Tenth & Eleventh Avenues (1-212 206 7100, www.metropicturesgallery.com). **Open** *Sept-June* 10am-6pm Tue-Sat. *July* 10am-6pm Mon-Fri. **Map** p404 C26.

Metro Pictures is best known for representing art-world superstar Cindy Sherman, along with such big contemporary names as multimedia artist Mike Kelley, Robert Longo – famous for his works produced using photography and charcoal – and the late German artist Martin Kippenberger.

Paula Cooper Gallery

534 W 21st Street, between Tenth & Eleventh Avenues (1-212 255 1105, www.paulacoopergallery.com). **Open** *Sept-June* 10am-6pm Tue-Sat. *July, Aug* 10am-5pm Mon-Fri. **Map** p404 C26.

INSIDE TRACK
BEYOND WILLIAMSBURG

Bushwick's wealth of industrial buildings has attracted artists priced out of nearby Williamsburg. The majority of galleries here are artist run, near the Morgan Avenue stop on the L train and open weekends only. Reflecting its abundance in the neighbourhood, street art is the focus of many galleries, including **Factory Fresh** (1053 Flushing Avenue, between Knickerbocker & Morgan Avenues, 1-917 682 6753, www.factoryfresh.net) and **Ad Hoc Art** (49 Bogart Street, between Moore & Seigel Streets, 1-917 602 2153, www.adhocart.org).

Cooper has created an impressive art temple for worshippers of contemporary work, building its reputation on minimalist and conceptualist work (Andres Serrano, Carl Andre, et al). You'll also see shows featuring younger artists such as Kelley Walker and John Tremblay.
Other locations 521 W 21st Street, between Tenth & Eleventh Avenues, Chelsea (1-212 255 5247); 465 W 23rd Street, between Ninth & Tenth Avenues, Chelsea (1-212 255 1105).

Postmasters

459 W 19th Street, between Ninth & Tenth Avenues (1-212 727 3323, www.postmastersart.com). **Open** *Sept-July* 11am-6pm Tue-Sat. *Aug* by appt. **Map** p403 C27.
Run by the savvy duo of Magdalena Sawon and Tamas Banovich, Postmasters occupies a vast converted garage. The emphasis here is on technologically inflected art, most of which leans towards the conceptual, in the form of sculpture by David Herbert and Jack Risley, painting by Steve Mumford and David Diao, and new media by Katarzyna Kozyra, Anthony Goicolea and Natalie Jeremijenko, among others.

303 Gallery

547 W 21st Street, between Tenth & Eleventh Avenues (1-212 255 1121, www.303gallery.com). **Open** *Sept-June* 10am-6pm Tue-Sat. *July, Aug* 10am-6pm Mon-Fri. **Map** p404 C26.
A mainstay of Chelsea (and before that the Soho and East Village scenes of the late 1980s and early '90s), the gallery got its start in an offbeat location: the Park Avenue South apartment of principal Lisa Spellman (hence the name: it's her old address). Over the years, 303 has fostered the careers of critically acclaimed artists working in a variety of media, among them photographers Thomas Demand, Florian Maier-Aichen and Stephen Shore, and painters Inka Essenhigh, Maureen Gallace, Mary Heilmann and Karen Kilimnik.

★ Zach Feuer/LFL

530 W 24th Street, between Tenth & Eleventh Avenues (1-212 989 7700, www.zachfeuer.com). **Open** *Sept-June* 10am-6pm Tue-Sat. *July, Aug* 10am-6pm Tue-Fri. **Map** p404 B26.
Feuer opened his first Chelsea space in 2000, when he was still only in his early twenties. Now in a new, larger location, with an emphasis on formal painting and sculpture, the gallery has amassed a roster of artists whose work is regularly exhibited in museums around the world. Look out for Phoebe Washburn's large-scale wood installations and works by hot painters Tal R and Dana Schutz.

57th Street & around

Subway E, M to Fifth Avenue-53rd Street; F to 57th Street; N, R to Fifth Avenue-59th Street.

Marian Goodman Gallery

4th Floor, 24 W 57th Street, between Fifth & Sixth Avenues (1-212 977 7160, www.mariangoodman.com). **Open** *Sept-June* 10am-6pm Mon-Sat. *July, Aug* 10am-6pm Mon-Fri. **Map** p405 E22.
This highly regarded space has a host of renowned art-world names on its books. In particular, look out for John Baldessari, Christian Boltanski, Maurizio Cattelan, Gabriel Orozco, Gerhard Richter, Thomas Struth and Jeff Wall, among many others.

Pace Wildenstein

2nd Floor, 32 E 57th Street, between Madison & Park Avenues (1-212 421 3292, www.pacewildenstein.com). **Open** *Sept-May* 9.30am-6pm Tue-Fri; 10am-6pm Sat. *June-Aug* 9.30am-6pm Mon-Thur; 9.30am-4pm Fri. **Map** p405 E22.
To view shows by a few of the 20th century's most significant artists, head to this NYC institution, where you'll find pieces by Chuck Close, Agnes Martin, Pablo Picasso, Elizabeth Murray and Kiki Smith. The Pace Prints division at this location exhibits works on paper by everyone from old masters to notable contemporaries (in addition, there's now a stand-alone contemporary-only print outpost in Chelsea). The gallery also deals in fine ethnic and world art.
Other locations 545 W 22nd Street (1-212 989 4258), 534 W 25th Street (1-212 929 7000), 521 W 26th Street (1-212 629 6100); all between Tenth & Eleventh Avenues, Chelsea.
► *Pace/MacGill, which specialises in photography, occupies the same 57th Street building; see p300.*

Tibor de Nagy

12th Floor, 724 Fifth Avenue, between 56th & 57th Streets (1-212 262 5050, www.tibordenagy.com). **Open** *Sept-May* 10am-5.30pm Tue-Sat. *June-Aug* 10am-5.30pm Mon-Fri. **Map** p405 E22.
While this long-standing gallery presents contemporary work in several media, the real speciality here is painting, particularly landscapes, although there are a couple of worthwhile collagists among the coterie. Stand-outs include Tom Burckhardt and Jess and Sarah McEneaney.

Upper East Side

★ Hauser & Wirth

32 E 69th Street, between Madison & Park Avenues (1-212 794 4970, www.hauserwirth.com). Subway 6 to 68th Street-Hunter College. **Open** *mid Aug-July* 10am-6pm Tue-Sat. **Map** p405 E20.
Located in a stylishly renovated townhouse, this space is the newly opened New York branch of the notable gallery based in London and Zurich. The exhibitions focus on well-established contemporary artists whose careers have stretched over decades – figures such as Paul McCarthy and Ida Applebroog. Hauser & Wirth has also mounted imaginative historical projects, such as its recreation of Allan

Kaprow's seminal early-'60s installation, *Yard*, reinterpreted by artists William Pope.L, Joshiah McElheny and Sharon Hayes.

Mitchell-Innes & Nash

5th Floor, 1018 Madison Avenue, between 78th & 79th Streets (1-212 744 7400, www.miandn.com). Subway 6 to 77th Street. **Open** *Sept-July* 10am-5pm Mon-Fri. **Map** p405 E19.

Husband-and-wife team David Nash and Lucy Mitchell-Innes, both former Sotheby's specialists, opened this gallery more than a decade ago with an ambitious programme of Impressionist, modern and contemporary works.

Other locations 534 W 26th Street, between Tenth & Eleventh Avenues, Chelsea (1-212 744 7400).

Brooklyn

Black & White Project Space

483 Driggs Avenue, between North 9th & North 10th Streets, Williamsburg (1-718 599 8775, www.blackandwhiteprojectspace.org). Subway L to Bedford Avenue. **Open** noon-6pm Fri-Sun. **Map** p411 U7.

Founder Tatyana Okshteyn is good at finding fresh new talent. At a typical show opening, you can expect to see large-scale installations in the outdoor courtyard, and enthusiastic gallerygoers spilling out on to the sidewalk.

Other locations 636 W 28th Street, between Eleventh & Twelfth Avenues, Chelsea (1-212 244 3007).

Brooklynite Gallery

334 Malcolm X Boulevard, between Bainbridge & Decatur Streets, Bedford-Stuyvesant (1-347 405 5976, www.brooklynitegallery.com). Subway A, C to Utica Avenue. **Open** (during shows) 1-7pm Thur-Sat. **Map** p410 W10.

This pioneer in Bedford-Stuyvesant has a façade made entirely of recycled fridge doors, a rad LED display above the entrance and a beautiful backyard. The Brooklynite Gallery's programme, which concentrates on pop and street art from around the world, is equally compelling.

▶ *For more Brooklyn street-art specialists, see p127, Inside Track.*

Pierogi

177 North 9th Street, between Bedford & Driggs Avenues, Williamsburg (1-718 599 2144, www.pierogi2000.com). Subway L to Bedford Avenue. **Open** *Sept-July* 11am-6pm Tue-Sun, or by appt. **Map** p411 U7.

Pierogi, one of Williamsburg's established galleries, presents the Flat Files, a series of drawers containing works on paper by some 800 artists. Don't pass up the chance to don the special white gloves and handle the archived artwork yourself.

Other locations The Boiler, 191 North 14th Street, between Berry Street & Wythe Avenue (1-718 599 2144).

Elsewhere

Gavin Brown's Enterprise

620 Greenwich Street, at Leroy Street, West Village (1-212 627 5258, www.gavinbrown.biz). Subway 1 to Houston Street. **Open** *Sept-June* 10am-6pm Tue-Sat. *July-mid Aug* 10am-6pm Mon-Fri. **Map** p403 D29.

Brown always has his finger on the pulse. The London native has given starts to such contempo-

Paula Cooper Gallery. *See p297.*

rary art stars as Elizabeth Peyton. This informal gallery also showcases the creative output of Rob Pruitt and Peter Doig, among others.

Haunch of Venison

20th Floor, 1230 Sixth Avenue (Avenue of the Americas), between 48th & 49th Streets, Midtown (1-212 259 0000, www.haunchofvenison.com). Subway B, D, F, M to 47-50th Streets-Rockefeller Center. **Open** 10am-6pm Tue-Sat, or by appt. **Map** p404 D23.

After Christie's auction house acquired the London-born mega-gallery in a buyout that set art-world eyebrows soaring, it opened this New York branch. The five-room penthouse space designed by Steven Learner Studio (which received the American Architecture Award in 2009) accommodates museum-quality, bluest-of-blue-chip shows – for example, its themed group exhibitions such as 'The Figure and Dr Freud', which featured interpretations of the nude by artists as diverse as Picasso, Mel Ramos and Cecily Brown.

Maccarone

630 Greenwich Street, at Morton Street, West Village (1-212 431 4977, www.maccarone.net). Subway 1 to Houston Street. **Open** *Sept-June* 10am-6pm Tue-Sat. *July, Aug* 10am-6pm Mon-Fri. **Map** p403 D29.

The former Luhring Augustine director Michele Maccarone, an outspoken dealer and activist for artists, holds court in this large space, where she dedicates herself to representing artists such as Nate Lowman, Corey McCorkle and Christian Jankowski.

★ SculptureCenter

44-19 Purves Street, at Jackson Avenue, Long Island City, Queens (1-718 361 1750, www.sculpture-center.org). Subway E, M to 23rd Street-Ely Avenue; G to Long Island City-Court Square; 7 to 45th Road-Court House Square. **Open** 11am-6pm Mon, Thur-Sun. $5 suggested donation. **Map** p412 V5.

One of the best places in New York City to see work by blossoming and mid-career artists, this non-profit space – housed inside an impressive former trolley-repair shop that was redesigned by acclaimed architect Maya Lin in 2002 – is known for its very broad definition of sculpture.

White Columns

320 W 13th Street (entrance on Horatio Street), between Hudson & 4th Streets, Meatpacking District (1-212 924 4212, www.whitecolumns.org). Subway A, C, E, 1, 2, 3 to 14th Street; L to Eighth Avenue. **Open** noon-6pm Tue-Sat. **Map** p403 D28.

British-born Matthew Higgs – artist, writer, former Turner Prize judge and now director and chief curator here at New York's oldest alternative art space – has been getting high marks for shaking things up. He has kept White Columns committed to under-represented artists, while also expanding the curatorial focus far beyond New York.

PHOTOGRAPHY

For an overview of photography exhibitions, keep an eye out for the bimonthly directory *Photograph* ($8 at galleries, select bookstores or online at www.photographmag.com).

Aperture Gallery

4th Floor, 547 W 27th Street, between Tenth & Eleventh Avenues, Chelsea (1-212 505 5555, www.aperture.org). Subway C, E to 23rd Street; 1 to 28th Street. **Open** 10am-6pm Mon-Sat. **Map** p404 B26.

This gallery is located in the headquarters of the Aperture Foundation, a non-profit organisation established in 1952 by a group that included legendary photographers Ansel Adams, Dorothea Lange and Minor White. As well as exhibitions, the space hosts free artists' lectures, discussions and other events.

Howard Greenberg Gallery

41 E 57th Street, at Madison Avenue, Midtown East (1-212 334 0010, www.howardgreenberg.com). Subway N, R to Fifth Avenue-59th Street. **Open** *Sept-June* 10am-6pm Tue-Sat. *July, Aug* 10am-6pm Mon-Thur; 10am-5pm Fri. **Map** p405 E22.

Founded in 1981 and originally called Photofind, the Howard Greenberg Gallery was one of the first spaces to exhibit photojournalism and street photography. The gallery's collection includes images by Berenice Abbott, Edward Steichen and Henri Cartier-Bresson.

Pace/MacGill

9th Floor, 32 E 57th Street, between Madison & Park Avenues, Midtown East (1-212 759 7999, www.pacemacgill.com). Subway N, R to Lexington Avenue-59th Street; 4, 5, 6 to 59th Street. **Open** *Sept-late June* 9.30am-5.30pm Tue-Fri; 10am-6pm Sat. *Late June-Aug* 9.30am-5.30pm Mon-Thur; 9.30am-4pm Fri. **Map** p405 E22.

Pace/MacGill shows work by such established names as Walker Evans, Robert Frank and Irving Penn, in addition to groundbreaking contemporaries such as Chuck Close and Kiki Smith.

Yossi Milo

525 W 25th Street, between Tenth & Eleventh Avenues, Chelsea (1-212 414 0370, www.yossimilo.com). Subway C, E to 23rd Street; L to Eighth Avenue. **Open** *Sept-June* 10am-6pm Tue-Sat. *July, Aug* 10am-6pm Mon-Fri. **Map** p404 B26.

Yossi Milo's impressive roster of international camera talent encompasses artists who are beginning to build up a following, as well as more established photographers. Look out for innovative work by Tierney Gearon, Philippe Gronon and Pieter Hugo.

Gay & Lesbian

The true gay capital of America.

San Francisco often claims the title of America's queerest city, but Gotham, even though it can be rough, tough and expensive, remains a beacon for gay men and lesbians who want to be a part of the action.

From the Great White Way to bohemian Brooklyn, New York's famed arts scene is awash with queers, as are the worlds of media, fashion and design. The LGBT community also wields considerable political clout, and several local politicians are out and proud (including City Council President Christine Quinn). However, the city has a way to go before it's a gay paradise; while the New York State Assembly passed a motion to legalise same-sex marriages in December 2009, the New York State Senate voted it down.

GAY NEIGHBOURHOODS

From a historical point of view, the gayest spot in New York City just might be Sheridan Square, in the heart of the charming **West Village**. The tiny triangular park served as a battlefield in June 1969, when fed-up patrons of the Stonewall Bar across the street rose up against the police, who used to routinely raid homosexual establishments and arrest their customers. The Stonewall riots sparked the modern gay-rights movement, and Sheridan Square became the epicentre of a neighbourhood 'liberated' by gay activists, with **Christopher Street** as its main drag.

Christopher Street still offers a hotchpotch of gay bars, stores selling rainbow-theme knick-knacks, and vogueing teenagers who are heading for their Pier 45 hangout, but the West Village no longer reigns as queen of gaydom (except during Gay Pride; *see right* **The Queer Calendar**).

Beginning in the mid-1990s, much of the scene shifted north to **Chelsea**, with Eighth Avenue between 14th and 23rd Streets serving as a runway for buffed Chelsea boys eager to show off their biceps, triceps and pecs.

Some would argue that Chelsea is still the hub of gay life in New York; however, for the past decade, the buzz has been all about New York's 'new' gay neighbourhood, **Hell's Kitchen**. The area's residents include many dancers and actors employed in the nearby Theater District, and there's a lively restaurant and bar scene, with most of the drinking, dining and strutting taking place on Ninth Avenue in the 40s and 50s.

But for many queer folks, especially young people, even the idea of a gay ghetto is squaresville. Why limit yourself to a few blocks when virtually all of Manhattan can be classified as gay friendly? That includes the **East Village** with its steadfast network of nightspots that cater to dykes and gays on the creative, alternative side.

You'll also find plenty of queer stomping grounds in the outer boroughs. In Brooklyn, leafy **Park Slope** is a long-time enclave for lesbians and gay men of all types. Hip **Williamsburg** is also home to a large gay population. And over in Queens, the diverse locale of **Jackson Heights** has several LGBT bars and clubs, and a large Latin queer population.

(For more views on hot 'gaybourhoods', *see p302* **Essentially New York**.)

THE QUEER CALENDAR

NYC Pride, New York's biggest queer event, takes place in June (18-26 June in 2011), bringing with it a glittering swirl of parties and

About the author

Les Simpson is a contributing writer to Time Out New York magazine and – as his drag alter ego Linda – a frequent performer on the gay circuit.

performances. Although some jaded New Yorkers find the celebration a little passé, there are still a half-million or so participants and spectators at the **NYC LGBT Pride March** (*see p263*), which takes five hours to wind down Fifth Avenue from Midtown to the West Village. During the summer, New York's gay social scene extends to scenic Fire Island, home to the neighbouring beach resorts of Cherry Grove and The Pines, which are about a 90-minute train and ferry ride from Manhattan. In the autumn, Hallowe'en is a major to-do, with bars and clubs packed with costumed revellers.

INFORMATION & MEDIA

In what is something of a sign of the times, there are no specifically gay bookstores left in New York. The last one in existence, Oscar Wilde, closed in 2009 after 41 years in business.

Essentially New York Gaybourhoods

Which is the queerest of them all?

BETH GREENFIELD, GAY & LESBIAN EDITOR, TIME OUT NEW YORK: '**Hell's Kitchen** is like a throwback to a nascent gay Chelsea – cute young boys everywhere, bringing a happy buzz to slick new lounges and eateries – but with the added benefit of being on the edge of the Theater District. What could be gayer?'

RUFUS WAINWRIGHT, DIVO, MUSICIAN: 'I live at 23rd and Ninth – the border of Gay Oz [Chelsea]. But I find myself more interested in **Hell's Kitchen** these days: it's where all the Midwestern boys go when they want to be on Broadway. Very gay.'

Hell's Kitchen.

JOSH WOOD, PROMOTER-PRODUCER: 'Hell's Kitchen, Hell's Smitchen. I think it's great that there's a new gay neighbourhood, but it lacks history and depth. The **West Village** is not only the most important gay neighbourhood in New York, it's one of the most important in the US.'

DANIEL O'DONNELL, NEW YORK STATE ASSEMBLY MEMBER: 'Culturally, **Hell's Kitchen** is the essential NYC gay vvneighbourhood. It has a thriving nightlife, including fun, accessible gay bars, and is home to some of the best theatre in the world.'

MICHAEL MUSTO, COLUMNIST, AUTHOR OF FORK ON THE LEFT, KNIFE IN THE BACK: 'Hell's Kitchen has risen as a gay hub because of the slightly cheaper rents and the bars that have popped up, like Therapy and the Ritz. But there's not a lot of lesbian action there, and the neighbourhood has a transient feel, without much substance or history. I'd have to say the **West Village** is actually the most essential gay neighbourhood. It's rich with history, since it was the 1969 rebellion at the Stonewall tavern on Christopher Street that spearheaded the LGBT community's fight for visibility and acceptance. And Stonewall is still there and open! And usually teeming with lesbians!'

GLENNDA TESTONE, EXECUTIVE DIRECTOR OF THE LGBT COMMUNITY CENTER: '[The essential gay neighbourhood] is **the Village**, in my opinion. First, obviously, because the Center is there, which draws LGBT people from all over the country. There is also the historical significance. Finally, the number one question at the front desk of the Center is "How do I get to Christopher Street?"'

For queer titles, check out the LGBT sections of the bookstore chains; **Bluestockings** has a good selection.

For weekly activities, *Time Out New York*'s Gay & Lesbian section provides information on happenings all around the city. Also popular is the gay entertainment magazine *Next* (www.nextmagazine.com), which recently bought out its longtime rival *HX* and offers extensive boy-centric information on bars, clubs, restaurants and events. The monthly *Go!* (www.gomag.com), 'a cultural road map for the city girl,' gives the lowdown on the lesbian nightlife and travel scene. *Gay City News* (www.gaycitynews.com) provides feisty political coverage with an activist slant. All are free and widely available in street boxes, at gay and lesbian bars, and in bookstores. *MetroSource* (www.metrosource.com) is a bi-monthly glossy with a fashion victim angle and tons of listings.

Bluestockings

172 Allen Street, between Rivington & Stanton Streets, Lower East Side (1-212 777 6028, http://bluestockings.com). Subway F to Lower East Side-Second Avenue. **Open** 11am-11pm daily. **Credit** AmEx, DC, MC, V. **Map** p403 F29.

This radical bookstore, Fairtrade café and activist resource centre stocks LGBT literature and regularly hosts queer events (often with a feminist slant), including dyke knitting circles, trans-politics forums and women's open-mic nights.

★ Lesbian, Gay, Bisexual & Transgender Community Center

208 W 13th Street, between Seventh & Eighth Avenues, West Village (1-212 620 7310, www.gaycenter.org). Subway A, C, E, 1, 2, 3 to 14th Street; L to Eighth Avenue. **Open** 9am-10pm Mon-Fri; 11am-11pm Sat; 11am-9pm Sun. **Map** p403 D27.

Founded in 1983, the Center provides information and a gay support network. As well as being a friendly resource that offers guidance to gay tourists, it is used as a venue for 300-plus groups. The National Museum & Archive of Lesbian & Gay History (open to the public 6-8pm Thur) and the Pat Parker/Vito Russo Library are housed here, as is an art gallery and small internet room (11am-9pm Mon-Fri, noon-6pm Sat, Sun, $3/hr).

★ Lesbian Herstory Archives

484 14th Street, between Eighth Avenue & Prospect Park West, Park Slope, Brooklyn (1-718 768 3953, www.lesbianherstoryarchives.org). Subway F to 15th Street-Prospect Park. **Open** varies. **Map** p410 T12.

The Herstory Archives contain more than 20,000 books (cultural theory, fiction, poetry, plays), 1,600 periodicals and assorted memorabilia. The cosy brownstone also hosts occasional screenings, readings and social gatherings, plus an annual open house in June to coincide with Brooklyn Pride.

WHERE TO STAY

Chelsea Mews Guest House

344 W 15th Street, between Eighth & Ninth Avenues, Chelsea (1-212 255 9174, www.chelseamewsguesthouse.com). Subway A, C, E to 14th Street; L to Eighth Avenue. **Rates** $175-$200 double. **Rooms** 8. **No credit cards**. **Map** p403 C27.

Built in 1840, this guesthouse caters to gay men. The rooms are comfortable and well furnished and, in most cases, share a bathroom with only one neighbour. Bikes and a laundry service are complimentary. The charming Anne Frank Suite (room 110) has two twin beds and a private bathroom. It's a good choice for dapper types: the room prices include washing and pressing of your clothing.

Internet (wireless, free). No smoking. Room service.

Chelsea Pines Inn

317 W 14th Street, between Eighth & Ninth Avenues, Chelsea (1-212 929 1023, 1-888 546 2700, www.chelseapinesinn.com). Subway A, C, E to 14th Street; L to Eighth Avenue. **Rates** (incl breakfast) $139-$289 double. **Rooms** 22. **Credit** AmEx, DC, Disc, MC, V. **Map** p403 C27.

On the border of Chelsea and the West Village, Chelsea Pines welcomes gay guests of all persuasions. The 25 rooms here are clean and comfortable, with classic-film themes; all have private bathrooms, and are equipped with a radio, a TV, a refrigerator and free Wi-Fi.

Concierge. Internet (wireless, free). No smoking. TV: DVD.

★ Colonial House Inn

318 W 22nd Street, between Eighth & Ninth Avenues, Chelsea (1-212 243 9669, 1-800 689 3779, www.colonialhouseinn.com). Subway C, E to 23rd Street. **Rates** (incl breakfast) $130-$180 double. **Rooms** 22. **Credit** DC, MC, V. **Map** p404 C26.

This beautifully renovated 1850s townhouse sits on a quiet street in Chelsea. Run by (and primarily for) gay men, it's a great place to stay, even if some of the cheaper rooms are a bit snug. Bonuses include a fireplace in three of the deluxe rooms, two new suites, a rooftop deck for all (nude sunbathing is allowed) and an owner, Mel Cheren, who's famous in the music world as the CEO of West End Records.

Internet (wireless, $3/hr; use of computer, $12/hr). No smoking.

East Village B&B

244 E 7th Street, between Avenues C & D, East Village (no phone, evbandb@juno.com). Subway F to Lower East Side-Second Avenue; L to First

Avenue. **Rates** (incl breakfast) $120-$175 double. **Rooms** 2. **Credit** AmEx, DC, Disc, MC, V. **Map** p403 G28.

This lesbian-owned gem is tucked neatly inside a turn-of-the-20th-century apartment building on a quiet East Village block. The space has gleaming wood floors, exposed brick walls and slick retro (1970s) furniture, as well as an eclectic art collection. The bedrooms are done up in bold colours against white walls; one of the bathrooms includes a small tub, while the living room has a TV and a CD player.

Internet (wireless, free). No smoking.

Incentra Village House

32 Eighth Avenue, between Jane & W 12th Streets, West Village (1-212 206 0007, www.incentravillage.com). Subway A, C, E to 14th Street; L to Eighth Avenue. **Rates** $219-$249 double. **Rooms** 13. **Credit** AmEx, DC, MC, V. **Map** p403 D28.

Two cute 1841 townhouses in the Meatpacking District make up this nicely restored and gay-run guesthouse. The spacious rooms have private bathrooms and kitchenettes; some also have fireplaces. A 1939 Steinway baby grand graces the parlour and sets a tone of easy sophistication.

Disabled-adapted rooms. Internet (wireless, free). No smoking. TV: DVD.

Ivy Terrace

230 E 58th Street, between Second & Third Avenues, Midtown East (1-516 662 6862, www.ivyterrace.com). Subway N, R to Lexington Avenue-59th Street; 4, 5, 6 to 59th Street. **Rates** (incl breakfast) $255-$300 double. **Rooms** 6. **Credit** AmEx, DC, Disc, MC, V. **Map** p405 F22.

This lovely lesbian-run B&B has six cosy rooms with high ceilings and wooden floors. Some have old-fashioned sleigh beds; the Zen room is more modern. The owners serve breakfast each morning, but you're also free to make your own meals: each room has a gas stove and a full-size fridge for those essential midnight feasts.

Internet (wireless, free). No smoking.

RESTAURANTS & CAFES

The sight of same-sex couples holding hands across a candlelit table is pretty commonplace in New York. But if you want to increase the chances of being part of the majority when you dine, check out the following gay-friendly places.

★ Counter

105 First Avenue, between 6th & 7th Streets, East Village (1-212 982 5870, www.counternyc.com). Subway F to Lower East Side-Second Avenue. **Open** 5pm-midnight Mon-Thur; 5pm-1am Fri; 11am-1am Sat; 11am-midnight Sun. **Main courses** $17. **Credit** DC, Disc, MC, V. **Map** p403 F28.

This hip, lesbian-owned vegetarian bistro has a wine bar with more than 200 organic and bio-dynamic offerings; the organic martinis are also a big draw. Locally grown produce is used whenever possible; the kitchen even caters to purists, with

Lips.

ARTS & ENTERTAINMENT

raw dishes on the menu alongside healthy cooked fare such as the East Side Burger made of mushroom pâté, seitan and herbs. There's a popular brunch at weekends.

★ Elmo

156 Seventh Avenue, between 19th & 20th Streets, Chelsea (1-212 337 8000, www.elmorestaurant.com). Subway 1 to 18th Street. **Open** 11am-midnight Mon-Thur; 11am-1am Fri, Sat; 10am-midnight Sun. **Main courses** $15. **Credit** AmEx, DC, MC, V. **Map** p403 D27.

The attraction at this spacious, brightly decorated eaterie is the good, reasonably priced food. Then there's the bar, which provides a view of the dining room that's jammed with guys in clingy tank tops. And that's before you come to the basement venue, which holds readings, comedy and drag shows, plus the occasional chic lesbian soirée.

44 & X Hell's Kitchen

622 Tenth Avenue, at 44th Street, Hell's Kitchen (1-212 977 1170, www.44andx.com). Subway A, C, E to 42nd Street-Port Authority. **Open** 11.30am-2.30pm, 5.30-11.45pm Mon-Wed; 11.30am-2.30pm, 5.30pm-12.15am Thur-Sat; 11.30am-2.45pm, 5.30-10.45pm Sun. **Main courses** $26. **Credit** AmEx, DC, MC, V. **Map** p404 C24.

Fabulous queens pack out this sleek dining space, one of the first bright spots on quickly gentrifying Tenth Avenue. It's situated alongside the Theater District and the Manhattan Plaza high-rises, so it tends to attract actors (and those seeking them). The mostly American cuisine is great too – from classics such as creamy mac 'n' cheese to filet mignon.

Lips

227 E 56th Street, between Second and Third Avenues (1-212 675 7710, www.lipsnyc.com). Subway N, Q, R, 4, 5, 6 to Lexington Avenue-59th Street. **Open** 5.30pm-midnight Tue-Thur; 5.30pm-1am Fri, Sat; noon-4pm, 5.30-11pm Sun. **Main courses** $13. **Credit** AmEx, Disc, MC, V. **Map** p403 C28.

Like a little camp with your continental cuisine? Frankie Coctktail and All-Beef Patty are just a couple of the illustrious staff members at this drag-themed eaterie, which recently moved uptown. The waitresses dazzle the patrons with spirited lip-synching numbers, but it's best to avoid the weekends when the place is invaded by screeching bachelorette parties.

Manatus

340 Bleecker Street, between Christopher & W 10th Streets (1-212 989 7042, www.manatusnyc.com). Subway 1 to Christopher Street-Sheridan Square. **Open** 24hrs daily. **Main courses** $12. **Credit** AmEx, DC, MC, V. **Map** p403 D28.

Manatus both is and isn't your typical greasy-spoon diner. There are the standard plastic-coated menus listing dozens of fried food items but distinguishing the place is a full bar, flattering lighting and a flaming gay clientele, especially late at night when tipsy bar-goers pile in.

★ Rocking Horse Café

182 Eighth Avenue, between 19th & 20th Streets, Chelsea (1-212 463 9511, www.rockinghorsecafe.com). Subway C, E to 23rd Street. **Open** 11am-midnight Mon-Thur, Sun; noon-midnight Fri; 11am-midnight Sat. **Main courses** $16. **Credit** AmEx, DC, MC, V. **Map** p403 D27.

Eclectic Mexican cuisine is what originally established the Rocking Horse Café as a unique eating place in Chelsea, but the bar now holds a distinguished reputation for the tongue-numbingly stiff frozen margaritas it serves. Decked out in bright colours, it's also still good for ogling beautiful boys doing the Eighth Avenue strut.

Superfine

126 Front Street, between Jay & Pearl Streets, Dumbo, Brooklyn (1-718 243 9005). Subway F to York Street. **Open** 11.30am-3pm, 6-11pm Tue-Fri; 6-11pm Sat; 11.30am-3pm, 6-10pm Sun. **Main courses** $18. **Credit** AmEx, DC, Disc, MC, V. **Map** p411 T9.

Owned by a couple of super-cool lesbians, this eaterie, bar and gallery serves Mediterranean cuisine in its massive, hip space. The mellow vibe and pool table draw a mixed, local crowd. The South-western themed Sunday brunches are delicious – and justifiably popular.

Vynl

754 Ninth Avenue, between 50th & 51st Streets (1-212 974 2003, vynl-nyc.com). Subway C, E to 50th Street. **Open** 11am-11pm Mon; 11am-midnight Tue-Thur; 11am-1am Fri; 9.30am-1am Sat; 9.30am-11pm Sun. **Main courses** $14. **Credit** AmEx, DC, MC, V. **Map** p404 C23.

The boys seem to love this record-themed eaterie, where old albums adorn the walls above the cosy booths, and menu items are an odd mishmash of

INSIDE TRACK ETHNIC AFFAIRS

Not all of New York's myriad ethnic groups have bustling queer contingents (where are the gay Finns?), but for same-sex-loving Arabs, the action, including male belly dancers, revolves around the long-running dance party **Habibi** (www.izmix.com). Bollywood tunes rule at **Desilicious** (www.sholayevents.com), which attracts hundreds of South Asian partygoers. Latin-Americans of all ethnicities flock to **Escuelita** (*see p309*).

ARTS & ENTERTAINMENT

Henrietta Hudson.

comfort food (burgers, turkey meatloaf, fried chicken, spaghetti and meatballs) and Asian cuisine (massaman curry, veggie-basil stir-fry, sesame chicken). Cocktails are themed – Fiona Apple-tini, Peaches & Herb – and the vibe is all-around fun.
► *There's another Vynl in Chelsea (102 Eighth Avenue, at 15th Street, 1-212 400 2118).*

BARS & CLUBS

'It ain't what it used to be,' grumble veterans of New York's gay nightlife. And they're right. The after-hours scene is continually morphing – sometimes for the better, sometimes not.

For dancefloor fanatics, the news is not good. As Manhattan has gentrified, many of its gay dance clubs have bitten the dust, and there are now a limited number of venues where you can shake your booty. Taking up the slack are a wide variety of bars and lounges, with the action often shifting from one venue to another depending on the night of the week. During the week, you're more likely to find the hardcore party crowd, who cede the bars at weekends to the 'amateurs'. It's a fickle scene and the best way to find out what's hot is to simply ask around – New Yorkers love sharing their insider knowledge.

Whatever your nightlife pleasure – sleek martini lounge or kinky leather cave, dive bar or kitschy neighbourhood hangout – you are sure to find a queer watering hole that suits in New York. Many offer happy hours, drink specials, live shows, go-go dancers and rotating theme nights, such as bingo parties or 'talent' contests. All bars, gay or straight, enforce the state-wide drinking age of 21; always carry picture ID as you might be asked to show it, even if your 21st birthday is a distant memory.

Lower East Side & the East Village

★ B Bar

40 E 4th Street, at Bowery (1-212 475 2220, www.bbarandgrill.com). Subway F to Second Avenue-Lower East Side; 6 to Astor Place. **Open** 10pm-4am Tue. **Average drink** $9. **Credit** AmEx, DC, Disc, MC, V. **Map** p403 F29.

On Tuesdays, this sprawling bar-restaurant is the setting for Beige, a long-running see-and-be-seen party that packs in hundreds of urbane young men and the occasional celebrity, such as party-hearty actor Alan Cummings. A spacious patio area serves as a smoking lounge. (The rest of the week, the place is hetero territory.)

Cock

29 Second Avenue, between 2nd & 3rd Streets (no phone, www.thecockbar.com). Subway F to Lower East Side-Second Avenue. **Open** 11pm-4am daily. **Admission** $5-$10. **Average drink** $5. **No credit cards. Map** p403 F29.

This grungy hole-in-the-wall still holds the title of New York's sleaziest gay hangout, but nowadays it's hit-and-miss. At weekends, it's a packed grind-fest, but on other nights the place is often depressingly under-populated. It's best to go very late when the cruising is at its peak.

★ Eastern Bloc

505 E 6th Street, between Avenues A & B (1-212 777 2555, www.easternblocnyc.com). Subway F to Lower East Side-Second Avenue. **Open** 7pm-4am daily. **Average drink** $7. **No credit cards**. **Map** p403 G28.

This cool little space has mostly shed its commie revolutionary decor for a funky living-room feel, including an ancient TV that plays videos of *Soul Train*. The bartenders are cuties, and there are nightly themes, DJs and happy hours to get the ball rolling.

Nowhere

322 E 14th Street, at First Avenue (1-212 477 4744). Subway L to First Avenue. **Open** 3pm-4am daily. **Average drink** $6. **No credit cards**. **Map** p403 F27.

Low ceilings and dim lighting help to create a speakeasy vibe at this subterranean bar. The place attracts everyone from cross-dressers to bears, thanks to a fun line-up of theme nights. The pool table is also a big draw.

► *The same folks run the nearby Phoenix (447 E 13th Street, between First Avenue & Avenue A, 1-212 477 9979).*

West Village

Chi Chiz

135 Christopher Street, at Hudson Street (1-212 462 0027, www.chichiz.com). Subway 1 to Christopher Street-Sheridan Square. **Open** 2pm-4am daily. **Average drink** $6. **No credit cards**. **Map** p403 D29.

One of a string of neighbourhood gay pubs along Christopher Street, this cruisey spot is an African-American stronghold. Many of the patrons are regulars, but a steady stream of newcomers keep the sexual energy flowing. The decor is blah, but the music is good and the drinks pack a wallop.

★ Cubbyhole

281 W 12th Street, between 4th Street & Greenwich Avenue (1-212 243 9041, www.cubbyholebar.com). Subway A, C, E to 14th Street; L to Eighth Avenue. **Open** 4pm-4am Mon-Fri; 2pm-4am Sat, Sun. **Average drink** $7. **No credit cards**. **Map** p403 E28.

This minuscule lesbian spot is always filled with flirtatious girls (and their dyke-friendly boy pals), with the standard set of Melissa Etheridge or KD Lang blaring in the background. Chinese lanterns, tissue paper fish and old holiday decorations emphasise the festive, homespun charm.

Henrietta Hudson

438 Hudson Street, between Morton Street & Hudson Street (1-212 924 3347, http://henriettahudson.com). Subway 1 to Christopher Street-Sheridan Square. **Open** 5pm-2am Mon, Tue; 4pm-4am Wed-Fri; 2pm-4am Sat, Sun. **Average drink** $7. **Credit** AmEx, DC, MC, V. **Map** p409 D29.

A much-loved lesbian bar, this glam lounge attracts hottie girls from all over the area, especially the nearby 'burbs. Every night is a different party, with hip hop, pop, rock and live shows among the musical pulls. Super-cool Lisa Cannistraci is in charge.

Monster

80 Grove Street, at Sheridan Square (1-212 924 3558, www.manhattan-monster.com). Subway 1 to Christopher Street-Sheridan Square. **Open** 4pm-4am Mon-Fri; 2pm-4am Sat, Sun. **Admission** $4-$8. **Average drink** $6. **No credit cards**. **Map** p403 D28.

Upstairs, locals gather to sing showtunes in the piano lounge, adorned with strings of lights and rainbow paraphernalia. And, honey, you haven't lived till you've witnessed a bunch of tipsy queers belting out the best of Broadway. The downstairs disco caters to a young, fun outer-borough crowd.

Stonewall Inn

53 Christopher Street, at Waverly Place (1-212 488 2705, www.thestonewallinnnyc.com). Subway 1 to Christopher Street-Sheridan Square. **Open** 2pm-4am daily. **Average drink** $9. **Credit** AmEx, DC, MC, V. **Map** p403 D28.

This gay landmark is located next door to the famous original, the site of the 1969 gay rebellion against police harassment. Is it hip? No. But you have to give the Stonewall credit for being one of the few queer bars that caters equally to males and females. Special nights range from dance soirées (upstairs) to bingo gatherings.

► *While you're here, check out George Segal's sculptures in nearby Christopher Park;* *see p87.*

Chelsea & Flatiron District

★ Barracuda

275 W 22nd Street, between Seventh & Eighth Avenues (1-212 645 8613). Subway C, E to 23rd Street. **Open** 4pm-4am daily. **Average drink** $7. **No credit cards**. **Map** p404 D26.

This long-time staple has a lot less attitude than most of the competition. Guys from the neighbourhood converse in the low-lit bar up front or relax in the lounge in the back. Drag queens perform during the week and there's never a cover charge.

★ Eagle

554 W 28th Street, at Eleventh Avenue (1-646 473 1866, www.eaglenyc.com). Subway C, E to 23rd Street. **Open** 10pm-4am Tue-Sat; 5pm-4am Sun. **Average drink** $6. **No credit cards**. **Map** p404 C26.

You don't have to be a kinky leather daddy to enjoy this manly outpost, but it definitely doesn't hurt. Surprisingly spic-and-span, this fetish bar is home to an array of beer blasts, foot-worship fêtes and leather soirées, plus simple pool playing and cruising nights. In summer, it hosts rooftop barbecues.

G Lounge

225 W 19th Street, at Seventh Avenue (1-212 929 1085, http://glounge.com). Subway 1 to 18th Street. **Open** 4pm-4am daily. **Average drink** $9. **No credit cards**. **Map** p403 D27.

The neighbourhood's original slick boy lounge – a rather moodily lit cave with a cool brick-and-glass arched entrance – wouldn't look out of place in an upscale boutique hotel. It's a favourite after-work cocktail spot, where an excellent roster of DJs stays on top of the mood.

Gym Sports Bar

167 Eighth Avenue, between W 18th Street & W 19th Street (1-212 337 2439, www.gymsportsbar.com). Subway A, C, E to 14th Street; L to Eighth Avenue. **Open** 4pm-2am Mon-Thur; 4pm-4am Fri; 1pm-4am Sat; 1pm-2am Sun. **Average drink** $8. **Credit** AmEx, DC, Disc, MC, V. **Map** p403 D27.

This popular spot is all about games – of the actual sporting variety, that is. Catch theme parties that revolve around gay sports leagues, play at the pool tables and video games, or watch the pro events from rodeo competitions to figure skating (everyone's favourite) shown on big-screen TVs.

Splash

50 W 17th Street, between Fifth & Sixth Avenues (1-212 691 0073, www.splashbar.com). Subway F, M to 14th Street; L to Sixth Avenue. **Open** 4pm-4am daily. **Admission** $5-$25. **Average drink** $9. **No credit cards**. **Map** p403 E27.

This NYC queer institution offers 10,000sq ft of dance and lounge space, staffed by super-muscular (and shirtless) bartenders. Nationally known DJs still rock the house, while local drag celebs give good face, and in-house VJs flash hypnotic snippets of classic musicals spliced with video visuals.

Hell's Kitchen & Theater District

Bartini

642 Tenth Avenue, between 45th & 46th Streets, Hell's Kitchen (1-917 388 2897, http://bartiniultralounge.com). Subway A, C, E to 42nd

INSIDE TRACK PARTY PEOPLE

To keep up with NYC's after-dark scene, just follow its top promoters. Upscale pretty boys tag along with **Josh Wood** (www.joshwoodproductions.com), the circuit crowd flocks to the legendary **Saint** parties (www.saintatlarge.com) and the art-boy scene is loyal to **Spank** dance parties (www.spankzine.wordpress.com). Lipstick lesbians should check out **Shescape** (www.shescape.com), queer cool girls like **Snapshot** (www.snapshotnyc.com) and homos of all stripes can be found at impresario **Murray Hill**'s gender-bending variety shows (www.mistershowbiz.com).

Street-Port Authority. **Open** 4pm-4am daily. **Average drink** $9. **Credit** AmEx, DC, Disc, MC, V. **Map** p404 C23.
The newest spot in the neighbourhood, located in the former Tenth Ave Lounge space, is a study in white – white bar, white bar stools, white trim on gray walls. It's all rather lovely and clean, until you down one too many pretty cocktails, which is a cinch to do here. (Try the vitamin-infused vodka for help with your hangover.)

Escuelita

301 W 39th Street, at Eighth Avenue (1-212 631 0588, www.enyclub.com). Subway A, C, E to 42nd Street-Port Authority. **Open** 10pm-4am Mon, Tue, Thur-Sat; 8pm-4am Sun. **Admission** $5-$20. **Average drink** $8. **Credit** DC, MC, V. **Map** p404 D24.
This basement dance club is a hub for New York's vast and varied gay Latin community (embracing Puerto Ricans, Dominicans and Colombians, among others). The main attraction on Fridays and Saturdays is an extravagant and dramatic drag show (in English and Spanish) at 2am. Throughout the week there's also karaoke, go-go boy contests and DJs spinning house, hip hop and salsa.

GirlNation

Nation, 12 W 45th Street, between Fifth & Sixth Avenues (1-212 391 8053, girlnationnyc.com). Subway B, D, F, M to 47-50 Street-Rockefeller Center. **Open** 10pm-4am Sat. **Admission** $5-$11. **Average drink** $7. **Credit** AmEx, DC, MC, V. **Map** p404 E24.
This lesbian bash is the place to be on Saturday nights. The two-level space, on a quiet, business-minded block of Midtown, gets rowdy and super-fun with its diverse and very cute crowd of girls, who flock here from all over the city to dance, drink and flirt themselves senseless.

Ritz

369 W 46th Street, between Eighth & Ninth Avenues (1-212 333 4177). Subway A, C, E to 42nd Street-Port Authority. **Open** 4pm-4am daily. **Average drink** $7. **Credit** AmEx, DC, MC, V. **Map** p404 C23.
Not at all ritzy but located among the upscale eateries of Restaurant Row, this is the ideal spot for a pre- or post-theatre cocktail. Or skip Broadway altogether and just belly up to the always-mobbed (especially at happy hour) front bar, where the drinks are stiff and the regulars chatty. The back of the lounge is host to regular performances and dance parties.

★ Therapy

348 W 52nd Street, between Eighth & Ninth Avenues (1-212 397 1700, www.therapy-nyc.com). Subway C, E to 50th Street. **Open** 5pm-2am Mon-Wed, Sun; 5pm-4am Thur-Sat. **Average drink** $8. **Credit** AmEx, DC, MC, V. **Map** p404 C23.
Therapy is just what your analyst ordered. The minimalist, dramatic two-level space offers up comedy and musical performances, some clever cocktails (including the Freudian Sip) and a crowd of well-scrubbed boys. You'll also find good food and a cosy fireplace to boot.

Townhouse

236 E 58th Street, between Second & Third Avenues (1-212 754 4649, www.townhouseny.com). Subway N, R to Lexington Avenue-59th Street; 4, 5, 6 to 59th Street. **Open** 4pm-3am Mon-Wed, Sun; 4pm-4am Thur-Sat. **Average drink** $8. **No credit cards**. **Map** p405 F22.
This popular gentlemen's bar is a throwback to more formal times (a dress code forbids sneakers and jeans and many patrons wear smart jackets), with a pianist providing tunes in the carpeted lounge. Men of a certain age dominate (50-year-olds are considered spring chickens), but you'll also find plenty of young fogies in their 20s and 30s.

Uptown

★ No Parking

4168 Broadway, between 176th & 177th Streets (1-212 923 8700). Subway A, C, 1 to 168th Street. **Open** 5pm-3am Mon-Thur, Sun; 5pm-4am Fri, Sat. **Average drink** $6. **No credit cards**. **Map** p409 B6.
If you're feeling frisky, head straight to No Parking in Washington Heights, where a beefy doorman frisks you before entering. Don't be scared, though: the only pistols these cute locals are packing are the fun kind. The bar also boasts a crew of awesome R&B, disco and hip hop video DJs.

Suite

992 Amsterdam Avenue, at 109th Street (1-212 222 4600, www.suitenyc.com). Subway 1, 2, 3 to 110th Street. **Open** 5pm-4am daily. **Average drink** $7. **Credit** ($15 min) AmEx, DC, Disc, MC, V. **Map** p406 C15.
You can't miss Suite – the exterior walls are covered in a tacky brown siding. But inside, the atmosphere is cosy. The crowd is a mix of local residents and students from nearby Columbia University, who cheer on the bar's stable of drag performers as they strut their stuff on the dinky stage.

Brooklyn

Excelsior

390 Fifth Avenue, between 6th & 7th Streets, Park Slope (1-718 832 1599, http://excelsiorbrooklyn.com). Subway F, M, R to Fourth Avenue-9th Street. **Open** 6pm-4am Mon-Fri; 2pm-4am Sat, Sun. **Average drink** $6. **No credit cards**. **Map** p410 T11.
Homey Excelsior has a spacious deck and garden, and, inside, an eclectic jukebox and excellent choice

of beers on tap. This straight-friendly spot attracts gay men, lesbians and their hetero pals looking to catch up without the fuss found in trendy lounge bars.

Ginger's Bar

363 Fifth Avenue, between 5th & 6th Streets, Park Slope (1-718 788 0924, www.gingersbar brooklyn.com). Subway F, M, R to Fourth Avenue-9th Street. **Open** 5pm-4am Mon-Fri; 2pm-4am Sat, Sun. **Average drink** $6. **No credit cards. Map** p410 T11.

The front room of Ginger's, with its dark-wood bar, looks out on to a bustling street. The back, which has an always-busy pool table, evokes a rec room, while the patio feels like a friend's yard. This local hangout is full of all sorts of dykes, many with their dogs – or favourite gay boys – in tow.

★ Metropolitan

559 Lorimer Street, at Metropolitan Avenue, Williamsburg (1-718 599 4444). Subway G to Metropolitan Avenue; L to Lorimer Street. **Open** 3pm-4am daily. **Average drink** $6. **No credit cards. Map** p411 V8.

Some Williamsburg spots are a little pretentious, but not this refreshingly unfancy bar, which resembles a 1960s ski lodge, complete with a brick fireplace. Guys dominate most nights (except for Wednesday's lesbian party), but there's always a female contingent, and even some straight folks join the crowd. The place to be in summer is the bar's fantastic patio, which features weekend barbecues.

Sugarland

221 North 9th Street, between Driggs & Roebling Streets (no phone). Subway L to Lorimer Street. **Open** 5pm-4am daily. **Admission** $5. **Average drink** $6. **No credit cards.**

Located smack dab in the middle of hipster central, Metropolitan's lesbian sister venue is more like a huge bar than a nightclub, and is a dancing destination at the weekends for hordes of young, cute and enthusiastic partygoers – pop music rules. Week nights, when the attractions include karaoke and open-mic shows, are more hit or miss.

CULTURE CLUBS

Looking for a social scene that stretches beyond the usual round of bars and clubs? Join these queer-centric activities.

Big Apple Ranch

Fifth floor, 39 W 19th Street, between Fifth & Sixth Avenues, Flatiron District (1-212 358 5752, www.bigappleranch.com). Subway N, R to 23rd Street; 1 to 18th Street. **Open** 8pm-1am Sat. **Admission** $10. **Average drink** $6. **No credit cards. Map** p403 E27.

If throbbing house music isn't your style, a lively alternative is this gay and lesbian country and western bash – a chance to don your chaps and do-si-do. The dance venue offers lessons at 8pm, followed by the party at 9pm every Saturday.

Chelsea Classics

Clearview Chelsea, 260 W 23rd Street, between Seventh & Eighth Avenues, Chelsea (1-212 691 5519, www.clearviewcinema.com/classics). Subway C, E, 1 to 23rd Street. **Shows** 7pm, 9.30pm Thur. **Admission** $7.50. **Credit** AmEx, Disc, MC, V. **Map** p404 D26

Green-haired drag goddess Hedda Lettuce hosts weekly screenings of camp masterpieces, from *Mildred Pierce* to *Mommy Dearest.*

Dixon Place

161A Chrystie Street, between Rivington & Delancey Streets, Lower East Side (1-212 219 0736, www.dixonplace.org). Subway F to Second Avenue-Lower East Side. **Admission** $5-$25. **Credit** AmEx, MC, V. **Map** p403 F30.

For years, Dixon Place operated out of a ratty walk-up on the Bowery, outfitted with a motley crew of couches and armchairs that seated a small but dedicated audience. Now, in its new Lower East Side home, a steady flow of quirky queer shows – including dance, theatre, music and spoken word – attract both old and new fans to its slick, matching seats.

New York Gallery Tours

1-212 946 1548, www.nygallerytours.com

Former gay-studies professor and art critic Rafael Risemberg conducts monthly tours (Sept-June) of Chelsea's gallery district, visiting shows by LGBT artists and 'others of interest to a queer sensibility'.

SEEKING SEX

You will find many of New York's private man-on-man parties listed at www.cruisingforsex.com (which also reveals public cruising areas). Venues open to one and all include the hit-and-miss **East Side Club** (227 E 56th Street, between Second & Third Avenues, 1-212 753 2222), the frisky and sometimes not very clean **West Side Club** (27 W 20th Street, second floor, between Fifth & Sixth Avenues, 1-212 691 2700), and the underground (and frequently shuttered) **Bijou** (82 E 4th Street, at Second Avenue, behind the red door, no phone), where porn on a big screen is just a warm-up for the private-play booths.

Annual sex-themed events include the **Folsom Street East festival** (www.folsomstreeteast.org), an S&M spectacle held in June in Chelsea, and the **HustlaBall** (www.hustlaball.com), sponsored by Rentboy.com and starring many of its stud escorts. Libidinous lesbians should head to the wild monthly women's sex party **Submit** (1-718 789 4053, www.submitparty.com) and its adventurous punters.

Music

From the classical cream to brave new sounds, NYC makes a big noise.

What's your preferred New York soundtrack? The Harlem jazz of Duke Ellington or Thelonious Monk? The infectious punk of the Ramones or the hipster stylings of the Strokes? Or the street-savvy rhymes of Run-DMC or Jay-Z? From the emergence of the Gershwin brothers through the bebop revolution to the punk scene at (now defunct) CBGB and the birth of hip hop, the city holds a stellar place in musical history.

You can experience some of that history in iconic theatres and clubs such as Carnegie Hall, Radio City Music Hall – and the Village Vanguard. But don't let New York's past overshadow its present – new experiments playing out in small clubs could create the next breakthrough.

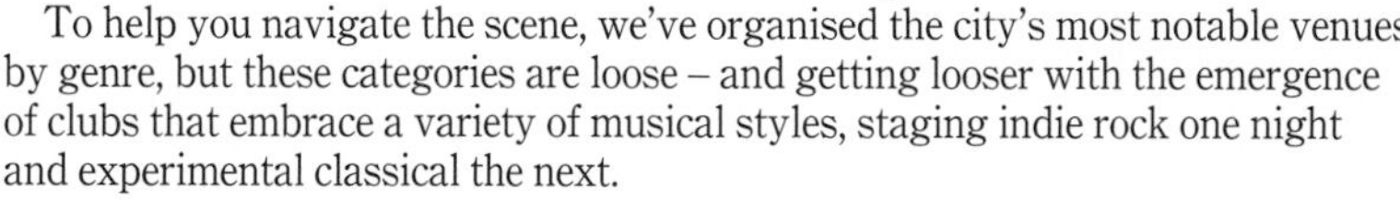

To help you navigate the scene, we've organised the city's most notable venues by genre, but these categories are loose – and getting looser with the emergence of clubs that embrace a variety of musical styles, staging indie rock one night and experimental classical the next.

Classical & Opera

The New York classical music scene has been largely unaffected by the economic downturn that has had such an impact on the rest of the country. The New York City Opera (*see p315* **David H Koch Theater**) rebounded from its staffing crisis – general manager-designate Gerard Mortier left suddenly due to budget cuts – with the arrival of former Miller Theatre executive director George Steel. Steel has managed to steer the 'people's opera' into a new, and increasingly financially sound, era.

Alan Gilbert has also made (sound) waves as the new music director of the **New York Philharmonic** (*see p315* **Avery Fisher Hall**), bringing in a new rush of modern composers to mix with the old school.

Meanwhile, some of the most exciting work is happening outside of Lincoln Center and Carnegie Hall. **(Le) Poisson Rouge** (*see p324*), which reinvigorated the Village's music scene in 2008, continues its tradition of booking without boundaries, featuring some of the 20th and 21st centuries' most acclaimed composers and singers, many of whom are also seen on the stage of the Metropolitan Opera House. Experimental and rock venues such as **Galapagos Art Space** (*see p322*) and the **Stone** (*see p332)* have joined the groundswell, paving the way for younger venues with a more intimate approach to music.

The standard New York concert season lasts from September to June, but there are plenty of summer events and performances (*see p313* **Everything Under the Sun**). Box office hours may change in summer, so phone ahead or check websites for times.

Information & tickets

You can buy tickets directly from most venues, whether by phone, online or at the box office. However, a surcharge is generally added to tickets not bought in person. For more on tickets, *see p260.*

MAJOR CONCERT HALLS

Brooklyn Academy of Music

Peter Jay Sharp Building *30 Lafayette Avenue, between Ashland Place & St Felix Street, Fort Greene, Brooklyn. Subway B, Q, 2, 3, 4, 5 to Atlantic Avenue; C to Lafayette Avenue; D, M, N, R to Pacific Street; G to Fulton Street.*
BAM Harvey Theater *651 Fulton Street at Rockwell Place, Fort Greene, Brooklyn. Subway 2, 3, 4, 5 to Nevins Street; B, M, Q, R to DeKalb*

Avenue; C to Lafayette Avenue; G to Fulton Street. **Both** *1-718 636 4100, www.bam.org.* **Box office** noon-6pm Mon-Sat. *Phone bookings* 10am-6pm Mon-Fri; noon-6pm Sat; noon-4pm Sun (show days). **Tickets** vary. **Credit** AmEx, MC, V. **Map** p410 T10.

America's oldest performing arts academy continues to present some of the freshest programming in the city. Every year in autumn and winter, the Next Wave Festival provides avant-garde music, dance and theatre, while 2010 heralded the inaugural BAM Opera Festival, with conductor and Baroque guru William Christie. The nearby BAM Harvey Theater offers a smaller and more atmospheric setting for new creations by composers such as Tan Dun, So Percussion and Meredith Monk, as well as innovative stagings of Baroque opera. March saw the US premiere of the Canadian Opera Company's memorable *The Nightingale and Other Short Fables* by Igor Stravinsky.

★ Carnegie Hall

154 W 57th Street, at Seventh Avenue, Midtown (1-212 247 7800, www.carnegiehall.org). Subway N, Q, R to 57th Street. **Box office** 11am-6pm Mon-Sat; noon-6pm Sun. *Phone bookings* 8am-8pm daily. **Tickets** $20-$220. **Credit** AmEx, Disc, MC, V. **Map** p405 D22.

Artistic director Clive Gillinson continues to put his stamp on Carnegie Hall. The stars – both soloists and orchestras – still shine brightly inside this renowned concert hall in the Isaac Stern Auditorium. But it's the spunky upstart Zankel Hall that has generated the most buzz, offering an eclectic mix of classical, contemporary, jazz, pop and world music. Next door, the Weill Recital Hall hosts intimate concerts and chamber music programmes. During the 2011-12 season, look out for the continuation of Ensemble ACJW, which comprises some of the city's most exciting young musicians and also performs at the Juilliard School of music.

INSIDE TRACK
BACKSTAGE PASSES

It's possible to go behind the scenes at several of the city's major concert venues. **Backstage at the Met** (1-212 769 7020, $16, $10 reductions) shows you around the famous house during opera season, which runs from September to May. A tour of **Carnegie Hall** (1-212 903 9765, $10, $3-$7 reductions) ushers you through what is perhaps the world's most famous concert hall. For $18, you may also sit in on an open rehearsal of the **New York Philharmonic** (1-212 875 5656), held before a concert series (usually twice a month).

Lincoln Center

Columbus Avenue, between 62nd & 65th Streets, Upper West Side (1-212 546 2656, www.lincolncenter.org). Subway 1 to 66th Street-Lincoln Center. **Map** p405 C21.

Built in the early 1960s, this massive complex is the nexus of Manhattan's – in fact, probably the whole country's – performing arts scene. Visitors can now benefit from its recently completed major revamp. The Lincoln Center hosts lectures and symposia in the **Rose Building**, Sunday recitals and Rob Kapilow's 'What Makes it Great?' series at the **Walter Reade Theater** (*see p289*) and events in its main concert halls (*see below*), and its **Vivian Beaumont Theater** and **Mitzi E Newhouse Theater** (for both, *see p355*). Also at the Lincoln Center are the **Juilliard School** (*see p318*) and the **Fiorello H La Guardia High School of Music & Art and Performing Arts** (108 Amsterdam Avenue, between 64th & 65th Streets, www.laguardiahs.org), which frequently hosts performances by professional ensembles as well as students who may go on to be the stars of tomorrow.

Big stars such as Valery Gergiev, Riccardo Muti and Leif Ove Andsnes are Lincoln Center's meat and potatoes. Lately, though, the divide between the flagship Great Performers season and the more audacious, multidisciplinary **Lincoln Center Out of Doors Festival** (*see p265*) continues to narrow. The **Mostly Mozart Festival** (late July-Aug), a formerly moribund four-week summer staple, has been thoroughly reinvented with progressive bookings and innovative juxtapositions, featuring recent works by Mark Morris and John Adams.

The main entry point for Lincoln Center is from Columbus Avenue, at 65th Street, but the venues that follow are spread out across the square of blocks from 62nd to 66th Streets, between Amsterdam and Columbus Avenues. Tickets to most performances at Lincoln Center are sold through **Centercharge** (1-212 721 6500). There is now a central box office selling discounted tickets to same-day performances, at the new **David Rubenstein Atrium** (*see p98* **Not Just the Ticket**).

Alice Tully Hall

1-212 875 5050. **Box office** 10am-6pm Mon-Sat; noon-6pm Sun. **Tickets** vary. **Credit** AmEx, DC, Disc, MC, V.

Alice lives here again after an 18-month renovation that turned the cosy home of the Chamber Music Society of Lincoln Center (1-212 875 5788) into a world-class, 1,096-seat theatre. A new contemporary foyer with an elegant (if a bit pricey) café is immediately striking, but, more importantly, the revamp also brought dramatic acoustical improvements.

Everything Under the Sun

When summer arrives, New York's music scene goes outside to soak it up.

New York Philharmonic Concert in the Park.

The main fixture on the summer calendar is **Central Park SummerStage** (*see p262*), a New York institution that has an ear for every sound under the sun. The series has brought great world music to the city for decades. Many of the shows are free, with a handful of rock-centred benefits (TV on the Radio, the reunited Pavement) covering for them.

Not far from Central Park is **Lincoln Center** (*see p312*), where the multi-tiered floor plan allows for several outdoor stages. The most popular venues are the North Plaza, which houses the **Midsummer Night Swing** concerts (*see p264*), and the Damrosch Park Bandshell, which rolls out the red carpet for the likes of Sonny Rollins.

There's also plenty of action taking place Downtown. The South Street Seaport has been booking hip shows (the Pains of Being Pure at Heart, Here We Go Magic) as part of the **River to River Festival** (1-212 732 7678, www.seaportmusicfestival.com; *see also p262*), while the historic fort of Castle Clinton in Battery Park welcomes roots artists where the US Army once set up shop. (Tickets must be picked up in person on the day of a show, and they always go fast.)

If your tastes are more classical, the **Metropolitan Opera** (www.metopera.org) and the **New York Philharmonic** (www.nyphil.org) both stage free concerts in Central Park and other large green spaces during the summer months.

Avery Fisher Hall

1-212 875 5030. **Box office** 10am-6pm Mon-Sat; noon-6pm Sun. **Tickets** vary. **Credit** AmEx, DC, Disc, MC, V.

This handsome, comfortable 2,700-seat hall is the headquarters of the New York Philharmonic (1-212 875 5656, www.nyphil.org), the country's oldest symphony orchestra (founded in 1842) – and one of its finest. Depending on who you ask, the sound ranges from good to atrocious. Inexpensive, early-evening 'rush hour' concerts and open rehearsals are presented on a regular basis. The ongoing Great Performers series features top international soloists and ensembles.

David H Koch Theater

1-212 870 5570. **Box office** 10am-7.30pm Mon; 10am-8.30pm Tue-Sat; 11.30am-7.30pm Sun. **Tickets** $10-$140. **Credit** AmEx, DC, Disc, MC, V.

As well as the New York City Ballet (*see p283*), the recently renovated and rechristened David H Koch Theater is home to the New York City Opera (www.nycopera.com). The company has long tried to overcome its second-best reputation by being ambitious, innovative and defiantly populist: rising American singers often take their first bows here and productions are consistently young and sexy under new director George Steel. Following a lengthy closure for the revamp in 2009, the NYCO has returned to the space with its vastly improved acoustics. The 2011-12 season runs from October to April.

Metropolitan Opera House

1-212 362 6000, www.metopera.org. **Box office** 10am-8pm Mon-Sat; noon-6pm Sun. **Tickets** $25-$310. **Credit** AmEx, DC, Disc, MC, V.

The grandest of the Lincoln Center buildings, the Met is a spectacular place to see and hear opera. It hosts the Metropolitan Opera from September to May, with major visiting companies appearing in summer. Audiences are knowledgeable and fiercely devoted, with subscriptions remaining in families for generations. Opera's biggest stars appear here regularly, and artistic director James Levine, who celebrated his fortieth illustrious year at the Met during the 2010-11 season, has turned the orchestra into a true symphonic force. Among the season's highlights were the first two instalments of a new production of Wagner's Ring, *Das Rheingold* and *Die Walküre*, directed by the innovative Robert Lepage. The Ring cycle will be completed during 2011-12.

The Met had already started becoming more inclusive before current impresario Peter Gelb took the reins in 2006. Now, the company is placing a priority on creating novel theatrical experiences with visionary directors (Lepage, Bartlett Sher, Richard Eyre, Patrice Chéreau) and assembling a new company of physically graceful, telegenic stars (Anna Netrebko, Danielle de Niese, Jonas Kaufmann, Erwin Schrott). Its high-definition movie-theatre broadcasts continue to reign supreme outside the opera house. Although most tickets are expensive, 200 prime seats (50 of which are reserved for over-65s) for all performances from Monday to Thursday are sold for a mere $20 apiece two hours before the curtain.

INSIDE TRACK
LUNCH WITH THE ORCHESTRA

A variety of cheap or free lunchtime concerts are held around New York by some of the city's brightest up-and-comers. The weekly early music series **Midtown Concerts** presides over St Bartholomew's Church (*see p318*) every Wednesday at 1.15pm. Downtown, **Juilliard artists** are regulars in the lobby of 180 Maiden Lane, an office building near South Street Seaport; meanwhile, stately sanctuary Trinity Church (*see p72*) offers Thursday-afternoon recitals for a suggested donation of $5 in its **Concerts at One** series.

OTHER VENUES

★ Bargemusic

Fulton Ferry Landing, between Old Fulton & Water Streets, Dumbo, Brooklyn (1-718 624 2083, www.bargemusic.org). Subway A, C to High Street; F to York Street; 2, 3 to Clark Street. **Tickets** $15-$35. **Credit** (advance purchases only) MC, V. **Map** p411 S9.

This former coffee bean barge usually presents four chamber concerts a week (plus one jazz programme), set against a panoramic view of lower Manhattan. It's a magical experience (and the programming has recently grown more ambitious), but wrap up in the winter. When the weather warms, enjoy a drink on the upper deck during the interval.

Frick Collection

For listings, *see p111.* **Tickets** $30.

Concerts in the Frick Collection's elegantly appointed concert hall are a rare treat, generally featuring both promising debutants and lesser-known but world-class performers. Concerts are broadcast live in the Garden Court, where tickets aren't required.

Gilder Lehrman Hall

Morgan Library & Museum, 225 Madison Avenue, at 36th Street, Murray Hill (1-212 685 0008, www.themorgan.org). Subway 6 to 33rd Street. **Tickets** vary. **Credit** AmEx, MC, V. **Map** p404 E25.

This elegant, 280-seat gem of a concert hall is a perfect venue for song recitals and chamber groups. The St Luke's Chamber Ensemble and Glimmerglass Opera were quick to establish a presence here.

Apollo Theatre. *See p321.*

Merkin Concert Hall

Kaufman Center, 129 W 67th Street, between Broadway & Amsterdam Avenue, Upper West Side (1-212 501 3330, www.kaufman-center.org). Subway 1 to 66th Street-Lincoln Center. **Box office** *Sept-June* noon-7pm Mon-Thur, Sun; noon-4pm (until 3pm Nov-Jan) Fri. *July-Aug* noon-4pm Mon-Fri. **Tickets** usually $10-$50. **Credit** AmEx, MC, V. **Map** p405 C21.

On a side street in the shadow of Lincoln Center, this renovated 449-seat gem offers a robust mix of early music and avant-garde programming, plus a healthy amount of jazz, folk and some more eclectic fare. A number of singers making a splash in Europe (including Dina Kuznetsova and Magali Léger) have begun to up the hall's operatic reputation as well.

★ Metropolitan Museum of Art

For listings, *see p114.* **Tickets** $25-$75.

When it comes to established virtuosos and revered chamber ensembles, the Met's year-round programming is rich and full (and ticket prices can be correspondingly high). The museum has established a youthful resident ensemble: the Metropolitan Museum Artists in Concert.

▶ *At Christmas, early music concerts are held in the Fuentidueña Chapel at the Cloisters; see p124.*

★ Miller Theatre at Columbia University

2960 Broadway, at 116th Street, Morningside Heights (1-212 854 7799, www.millertheatre.com). Subway 1 to 116th Street-Columbia University. **Box office** noon-6pm Mon-Fri (plus 2hrs before performance on show days). **Tickets** $7-$35. **Credit** AmEx, MC, V. **Map** p407 C14.

The Miller Theatre is at the forefront of making contemporary classical music sexy in NYC. The credit belongs to former executive director George Steel, who proved that presenting challenging fare in a casual, unaffected setting could attract young audiences – and hang on to them. With Steel now at City Opera, director Melissa Smey seems to be continuing the tradition with programmes ranging from early music to contemporary, highlighted by musical upstarts such as the American Contemporary Music Ensemble and pianist Simone Dinnerstein.

92nd Street Y

1395 Lexington Avenue, at 92nd Street, Upper East Side (1-212 415 5500, www.92y.org). Subway 6 to 92nd Street. **Box office** 9am-7pm Mon-Thur; 9am-5pm Fri. **Tickets** from $20. **Credit** AmEx, DC, MC, V. **Map** p406 F17.

The Y has always stood for solidly traditional orchestral, solo and chamber masterpieces. But the organisation also fosters the careers of young musicians and explores European and Jewish-American music traditions, with innovative results. In addition to showcasing several master classes (such as clarinettist David Krakauer), recent performers have included violinist Joshua Bell.

Symphony Space

2537 Broadway, between 94th & 95th Streets, Upper West Side (1-212 864 5400, www.symphonyspace.org). Subway 1, 2, 3 to 96th Street. **Box office** 3-6pm Mon (show days only); 1-6pm Tue-Sun. **Tickets** vary. **Credit** AmEx, MC, V. **Map** p406 C17.

Despite the name, programming at Symphony Space is anything but orchestra-centric: recent seasons have featured sax quartets, Indian classical music, a capella ensembles and HD opera simulcasts from Europe. The annual Wall to Wall marathons (usually held in the spring) serve up a full day of music free of charge, all focused on a particular composer. Members of the New York Philharmonic are regular guests here in more intimate chamber concerts.

Tenri Cultural Institute

43A W 13th Street, between Fifth & Sixth Avenues, Greenwich Village (1-212 645 2800, www.tenri.org). Subway F, M to 14th Street; L to Sixth Avenue; L, N, Q, R, 4, 5, 6 to 14th Street-Union Square. **Tickets** vary. **Credit** AmEx, MC, V. **Map** p403 E27.

A non-profit organisation devoted to promoting the Japanese language and appreciation of international art, Tenri also regularly hosts concerts by New York's leading contemporary music ensembles, such as the American Modern Ensemble, in its clean gallery space.

Churches

From sacred to secular, a thrilling variety of music is performed in New York's churches. Superb acoustics, out-of-this-world choirs and serene surroundings make these houses of worship particularly attractive venues. A bonus is that some concerts are free or very cheap.

Church of the Ascension

12 W 11th Street, between Fifth & Sixth Avenues, Greenwich Village (1-212 358 1469, www.voicesofascension.org). Subway N, R to 8th Street-NYU. **Tickets** $10-$50. **Credit** (advance purchases only) MC, V. **Map** p403 E28.

There's a first-rate professional choir, the Voices of Ascension, at this little Village church. You can catch the choir at Lincoln Center on occasion, but home turf is the best place to hear it.

Church of St Ignatius Loyola

980 Park Avenue, between 83rd & 84th Streets, Upper East Side (1-212 288 2520, www.saintignatiusloyola.org). Subway, 4, 5, 6 to 86th Street. **Tickets** $5-$60. **Credit** AmEx, Disc, MC, V. **Map** p406 E18.

The 'Sacred Music in a Sacred Space' series is a high point of Upper East Side music culture. Lincoln Center also holds concerts here, capitalising on the church's fine acoustics and prime location.

Corpus Christi Church

529 W 121st Street, between Amsterdam Avenue & Broadway, Morningside Heights (1-212 666 9266, www.mb1800.org). Subway 1 to 116th Street-Columbia Unversity. **Tickets** $15-$40. **Credit** MC, V. **Map** p407 C14.

Fans of early music can get their fix from 'Music Before 1800', a series that regularly imports the world's leading antiquarian artists and ensembles.

St Bartholomew's Church

325 Park Avenue, at 51st Street, Midtown East (1-212 378 0248, www.stbarts.org). Subway E, M to Lexington Avenue-53rd Street; 6 to 51st Street. **Tickets** vary. **Credit** AmEx, MC, V. **Map** p403 E23.

This magnificent church hosts the Summer Festival of Sacred Music, one of the city's most ambitious choral music series. It fills the rest of the year with performances by resident ensembles and guests.

St Thomas Church Fifth Avenue

1 W 53rd Street, at Fifth Avenue, Midtown East (1-212 757 7013, www.saintthomaschurch.org). Subway E, M to Fifth Avenue-53rd Street. **Tickets** free-$90. **Credit** AmEx, Disc, MC, V. **Map** p405 E22.

The country's only fully accredited choir school for boys keeps the great Anglican choral tradition alive in Gotham. St Thomas's annual performance of Handel's *Messiah* is a must-hear that's worth the rather steep ticket price.

Schools

The **Juilliard School** and the **Manhattan School of Music** are renowned for their talented students, faculty and artists in residence, all of whom regularly perform for free or at low cost. Lately, **Mannes College of Music** has made great strides.

Juilliard School

60 Lincoln Center Plaza, Broadway, at 65th Street, Upper West Side (1-212 769 7406, www.juilliard.edu). Subway 1 to 66th Street-Lincoln Center. **Tickets** usually free. **Map** p405 C21.

New York City's premier conservatory stages weekly concerts by student soloists, orchestras and chamber ensembles, as well as elaborate opera productions that can often rival many professional productions. It's likely the singers you see here will be making their Met or City Opera debuts within the next few years.

Manhattan School of Music

120 Claremont Avenue, at 122nd Street, Morningside Heights (1-212 749 2802, ext 4428, www.msmnyc.edu). Subway 1 to 125th Street. **Tickets** usually free. **Map** p407 B14.

The Manhattan School offers master classes, recitals and off-site concerts by its students and faculty as well as visiting professionals. The American String Quartet has been in residence here since 1984 and gives concerts regularly, while the Augustine Guitar Series includes recitals by top soloists. Recently, MSM has also become known for performing opera rarities, such as Fauré's *Penelope*.

Mannes College of Music

150 W 85th Street, between Columbus & Amsterdam Avenues, Upper West Side (1-212 580 0210, www.mannes.edu). Subway B, C, 1 to 86th Street. **Tickets** usually free. **Map** p406 C18.

In addition to student concerts and faculty recitals, Mannes also mounts its own ambitious, historically themed concert series; the summer is given over to festivals and workshops for instrumentalists. Productions by the Mannes Opera, whose fresh-faced members are drilled by seasoned opera professionals, are a perennial treat.

Opera companies

The **Metropolitan Opera** (*see p315*) and the **New York City Opera** (*see p315* **David H Koch Theater**) may be the leaders of the pack, but they're hardly the only game in town. Call the organisations or check online for information and prices, schedules and venues.

American Opera Projects

South Oxford Space, 138 S Oxford Street, between Atlantic Avenue & Hanson Place, Fort Greene, Brooklyn (1-718 398 4024, www.operaprojects.org). Subway B, Q, 2, 3, 4, 5 to Atlantic Avenue; C to Lafayette Avenue; D, M, N, R to Pacific Street; G to Fulton Street. **Tickets** vary (average $20). **Credit** AmEx, Disc, MC, V. **Map** p410 T10.

AOP is not so much an opera company as a living, breathing workshop that allows you the opportunity to follow a new work from gestation to completion. Shows can be anything from a table reading of a libretto to a complete orchestral production.

INSIDE TRACK
BANG ON A CAN

Now in its 23rd year, **Bang on a Can** (www.bangonacan.org) kicks off its summer season with the Bang on a Can Marathon, 12 straight hours of non-stop free music in a convivial, kid-friendly atmosphere (26 June 2011, World Financial Center Winter Garden; *see p69*). Recent composers and musicians have included Ryuichi Sakamoto, Pulitzer Prize winner (and BoaC co-founder) David Lang and Sonic Youth's Thurston Moore.

Cake Shop. See p321.

Amore Opera Company

Connelly Theatre, 220 E 4th Street, between Avenues A & B, Lower East Side (no phone, www.amoreopera.org). Subway F to Lower East Side-Second Avenue. **Tickets** $15-$35. **Credit** (advance purchases only) AmEx, Disc, MC, V. **Map** p403 G29.

One of two successors to the late, great Amato Opera Company, the Amore has literally inherited the beloved former company's sets and costumes. Many of the cast members have migrated as well to keep the feisty Amato spirit alive. In 2011, they've made their base at the Connelly Theatre, with productions in May of *Carmen.*

Dicapo Opera Theatre

184 E 76th Street, between Lexington & Third Avenues, Upper East Side (1-212 288 9438, www.dicapo.com). Subway 6 to 77th Street. **Tickets** $50. **Credit** AmEx, MC, V. **Map** p405 F20.

This top-notch chamber-opera troupe benefits from City Opera-quality singers performing in a delightfully intimate setting in the basement of St Jean Baptiste Church. Dicapo has recently augmented its diet of standard classics with a healthy dose of offbeat works and even premières, thanks in part to composer Tobias Picker's arrival as artistic adviser.

★ Gotham Chamber Opera

Harry de Jur Playhouse, 466 Grand Street, at Pitt Street, Lower East Side (1-212 598 0400, www.gothamchamberopera.com). Subway B, D to Grand Street; F to East Broadway; F, J, M, Z to Delancey-Essex Streets. **Tickets** $30-$125. **Credit** AmEx, MC, V. **Map** p403 G30.

Though they've recently expanded to other venues in the city – such as the Hayden Planetarium for a highly imaginative production of Haydn's *Il Mondo della Luna* – this fine young company specialising in chamber opera is still for the most part a Lower East Side staple. Expect a treasure trove of rarely staged shows (directed by the likes of Mark Morris and Tony-winner Diane Paulus) specifically designed for smaller forces in intimate settings. If you're here in November 2011, be sure to catch the world premiere of *Dark Sisters* by Nico Muhly, a protégé of Philip Glass.

Rock, Pop & Soul

Even as the recording industry crumbles, Manhattan and Brooklyn remain packed with music venues, from hole-in-the-wall dives to resplendent Midtown theatres. Plan accordingly and you can catch more than one world-class show on any given night. For smaller gigs, the best bets lie across Downtown Manhattan and parts of Brooklyn. Rock music dominates the Lower East Side and Williamsburg, which is the new epicentre of the young music scene.

As well as increasingly eclectic fare within venues, gigs are busting out of their usual club and concert hall confines: two of the most interesting new venues are mixed use. The **City Winery** crushes and ferments grapes as well as staging shows, while **Brooklyn Bowl** (*see p344*) has a 600-capacity music space that features small acts for tiny cover charges as well as a smattering of larger concerts (Art Brut, Sharon Jones & the Dap-Kings).

Playing Away

Classical breaks free from its stuffy image – and the concert hall.

Galapagos Art Space.

Downtown is looking like Uptown is looking like Downtown these days in the classical music world. Attend a concert at Lincoln Center and you'll likely see a number of twenty- and thirtysomethings in the audience, clad in vintage suits with matching Chuck Taylors, or leggings peeping out under a thrift-store Donna Karan find. A new breed of musical omnivore, the 'opster' (opera hipster) is becoming ubiquitous in both the traditional houses and upstart clubs scattered around the Village and Brooklyn.

While New York has always been a nexus for myriad music scenes, the recent increase in casual, intimate clubs serving up programmes with a healthy dose of classical – both traditional and modern – has allowed the genre, often perceived as stuffy, to let its hair down.

'The culture that comes with classical music and the culture that people expect is this formal behaviour,' explains Gabriel Prokofiev (grandson of Sergei Prokofiev), head of the Nonclassical label in London and a composer/performer in his own right. 'But it isn't how classical used to be. If you go back to the time of Mozart, for example, all his stuff was performed in quite informal settings.'

Prokofiev is one of many in the brave new musical world – which goes under a variety of names, including alt-, indie or new classical – performing in casual settings and encouraging audiences to talk, move around or grab a drink in the middle of a piece. In other words: they're being encouraged to react to and engage with the music.

Far from being a flash in the pan, genre-mixing Village venue **(Le) Poisson Rouge** (*see p324*) plays host to the likes of Prokofiev and Metropolitan Opera soprano Danielle de Niese; non-profit performing arts space the **Tank** (354 W 45th Street, between Eighth & Ninth Avenues, Midtown, 1-212 563 6269, www.thetanknyc.org) is a favourite of the American Contemporary Music Ensemble; experimental music space the **Stone** (*see p332*) is a mainstay for post-rock, post-classical quintet Victoire; and Brooklyn's **Galapagos Art Space** (*see p322*) tempers its burlesque shows with New Amsterdam Records' monthly new-music series Archipelago.

'We see this as something that people can embrace from lots of different directions,' says New Amsterdam's co-director and composer Judd Greenstein. 'It's chamber music… but it's also chamber music that reaches out in many musical directions and has deep connections to non-classical music in a lot of ways… The idea was to create a regular outlet for the music that normally doesn't have a home in a normal classical music or rock setting.'

It certainly seems to have found a home – and receptive audience – in NYC.

Information & tickets

Tickets are usually available from clubs in advance and at the door, though a few small and medium-size venues also sell tickets through local record stores. For larger events, buy online through the venue's website or through **Ticketmaster** or **Ticket Web** (for both, *see p260*). Remember to phone ahead for information and show times, which often change without notice.

MAJOR ARENAS & STADIUMS

Izod Center

For listings, *see p338* **Meadowlands Sports Complex**.

New Jersey's answer to Madison Square Garden has played host to the likes of Beyoncé, the Jonas Brothers and, of course, Bruce Springsteen and the E-Street Band. Sometimes, shows that sell out at the Garden may be available here, just a bus ride away.

★ Madison Square Garden

For listings, *see p338*.

Some of music's biggest acts – Jay-Z, Neil Young, Britney Spears – come out to play at the world's most famous basketball arena. Whether you'll actually be able to get a look at them depends on your seat number or the quality of your binoculars. The arena is far too vast for a rich concert experience, ugly and a little bit musty, but it remains part of the fabric of New York and begrudgingly beloved. There's also a smaller theatre within the complex.

Nassau Veterans Memorial Coliseum

For listings, *see p338*.

Long Island's arena hosts mainstream acts such as Lil Wayne and Metallica, punctuated by teen shows (Miley Cyrus, the Jonas Brothers) and, best of all, over-the-top Bollywood showcases.

VENUES

★ Apollo Theater

253 W 125th Street, between Adam Clayton Powell Jr Boulevard (Seventh Avenue) & Frederick Douglass Boulevard (Eighth Avenue), Harlem (1-212 531 5300, www.apollotheater.org). Subway A, B, C, D, 1 to 125th Street. **Box office** 10am-6pm Mon-Fri; noon-5pm Sat. **Tickets** $17-$100. **Credit** AmEx, DC, Disc, MC, V. **Map** p407 D13.

Visitors may think they know this venerable theatre from TV's *Showtime at the Apollo*. But as the saying goes, the small screen adds about ten pounds: the city's home of R&B and soul music is actually quite cosy. Known for launching the careers of Ella Fitzgerald and D'Angelo, among many others, the Apollo continues to mix veteran talents such as Dianne Reeves with younger artists such as John Legend.

Barbès

376 9th Street, between Sixth & Seventh Avenues, Park Slope, Brooklyn (1-347 422 0248, www.barbesbrooklyn.com). Subway F to Seventh Avenue. **Open** 5pm-2am Mon-Thur; noon-4am Fri, Sat; noon-2am Sun. **Tickets** free-$10. **Credit** (bar only) DC, Disc, MC, V. **Map** p410 T11.

Show up early if you want to get into Park Slope's global-bohemian club – it's tiny. Run by musically inclined French expats, this boîte brings in traditional swing and jazz of more daring stripes – depending on the night, you could catch African, French, Brazilian or Colombian music or acts that often defy categorisation (One Ring Zero). Chicha Libre, a Brooklyn band reviving psychedelic Peruvian music, holds down Mondays.

Beacon Theatre

2124 Broadway, between 74th & 75th Streets, Upper West Side (1-212 465 6500, www.beacontheatrenyc.com). Subway 1, 2, 3 to 72nd Street. **Box office** 11am-7pm Mon-Sat. **Tickets** $15-$175. **Credit** AmEx, DC, MC, V. **Map** p405 C20.

This spacious former vaudeville theatre, resplendent after a recent renovation, hosts a variety of popular acts, from 'Weird Al' Yankovic to ZZ Top; once a year, the Allman Brothers take over for a lengthy residency. While the vastness can be daunting to performers and audience alike, the gaudy interior and Uptown location make you feel as though you're having a real night out on the town.

★ Bowery Ballroom

6 Delancey Street, between Bowery & Chrystie Street, Lower East Side (1-212 533 2111, www.boweryballroom.com). Subway B, D to Grand Street; J, M, Z to Bowery; 6 to Spring Street. **Box office** at Mercury Lounge (*see p327*). **Tickets** $12-$35. **Credit** (bar only) AmEx, DC, MC, V. **Map** p403 F30.

The Bowery Ballroom is probably the best venue in the city for seeing indie bands, either on the way up or holding their own. Still, the Bowery also manages to bring in a diverse range of artists from home and abroad. You can expect a clear view and bright sound from any spot in the venue. The spacious downstairs lounge is a great place to relax and socialise between (or during) sets.

Bowery Poetry Club

For listings, *see p271*.

The name of this colourful joint reveals its roots, but it's also the truest current iteration of the East Village's arts scene: all kinds of jazz, folk, hip hop and improv theatre acts can be found here.

★ Cake Shop

152 Ludlow Street, between Rivington & Stanton Streets, Lower East Side (1-212 253 0036, www.cake-shop.com). Subway F to Lower East

Highline Ballroom.

Side-Second Avenue. **Open** 5pm-2am Mon-Thur, Sun; 5pm-4am Fri, Sat. **Tickets** $6-$12. **Credit** DC, Disc, MC, V. **Map** p403 G29.
It can be difficult to see the stage in this narrow, stuffy basement space, but the Cake Shop gets big points for its keen indie and underground-rock bookings, among the best and most adventurous in town. The venue lives up to its name, selling vegan pastries and coffee upstairs, while the back room at street level sells record-store ephemera. *Photo p319.*
► *The owners recently opened a Williamsburg outpost, Bruar Falls (245 Grand Street, between Driggs Avenue & Roebling Street, www.bruarfalls.com), with a similar vibe but fewer shows.*

City Winery
155 Varick Street, at Vandam Street, Tribeca (1-212 608 0555, www.citywinery.com). Subway 1 to Houston Street. **Open** 11.30am-3pm, 5.30pm-midnight daily. **Tickets** (online only) $10-$20. **Credit** AmEx, DC, Disc, MC, V. **Map** p403 D30.
Unabashedly grown-up and yuppie-friendly, this slick new club launched by oenophile Michael Dorf is New York's only fully functioning winery – as well as a 350-seat concert space. Acts tend to be on the quiet side – this is, after all, a wine bar – but that doesn't mean the shows lack bite. Younger singer-songwriters such as Keren Ann and Diane Birch have appeared, but the place is dominated by older artists (David Johansen, Los Lobos).
► *Michael Dorf was also the founder of the Knitting Factory; see p324.*

Fillmore New York at Irving Plaza
17 Irving Place, at 15th Street, Gramercy Park (1-212 777 6800, www.livenation.com). Subway L, N, Q, R, 4, 5, 6 to 14th Street-Union Square. **Box office** noon-6.30pm Mon-Fri; 1-4pm Sat. **Tickets** $10-$65. **Credit** AmEx, DC, MC, V. **Map** p403 E27.
Lying just east of Union Square, this mid-sized rock venue has served as a Democratic Party lecture hall (in the 19th century), a Yiddish theatre and a burlesque house (Gypsy Rose Lee made an appearance). New York rock fans still know it as simply 'Irving Plaza'; it received the 'Fillmore' addition in 2007 and was inaugurated with a Lily Allen show. Regardless, it's a great place to see big stars keeping a low profile (Jeff Beck, Devo and Lenny Kravitz) and medium heavies on their way up.

Galapagos Art Space
16 Main Street, at Water Street, Dumbo, Brooklyn (1-718 222 8500, www.galapagosartspace.com). Subway A, C to High Street; F to York Street. **Shows** vary. **Admission** free-$20. **Credit** (bar only) AmEx, DC, MC, V. **Map** p411 S9.
The Galapagos Art Space established itself in Williamsburg years before the neighbourhood's renaissance – and, like all colonisers, eventually got

squeezed out of the scene it helped to create. The new, much larger space in Dumbo offers a grander mix of the cultural offerings for which Galapagos is known and loved: music, performance art, burlesque, drag queens and other weird stuff. Just be careful not to fall into the pools of water strategically placed through the club.

Glasslands Gallery

289 Kent Avenue, between South 1st & 2nd Streets, Williamsburg, Brooklyn (1-718 599 1450, htttp://glasslands.blogspot.com). Subway L to Bedford Avenue. **Shows** vary. **Admission** free-$10. **No credit cards. Map** p411 U8.

If you're looking to catch a Brooklyn buzz band before it breaks, look here. Marvel at the cool DIY decor (we're partial to the cloudlike creations adorning the ceiling above the stage) while nodding to sets from local indie faves like Ducktails and Cults. The music/burlesque/party destination spotlights less-hyped acts; metal band Liturgy has rocked the house, and Canadian electro-rock crew Suuns have played here.

Goodbye Blue Monday

1087 Broadway, at Dodworth Street, Bushwick, Brooklyn (1-718 453 6343, www.goodbye-blue-monday.com). Subway J to Kosciuszko Street. **Open** 11am-2am Mon-Thur, Sun; 11am-3am. Fri, Sat. **Shows** vary. **No credit cards. Map** p411 W9.

Relax while taking in this cult Bushwick drinkery's distinct junkyard aesthetic (the walls are lined with old books, random lamps and retro radios). The acts that play here are pretty eclectic, ranging from anti-folk to experimental jazz, and, best of all, gigs are always free. If you can, check out the popular Bushwick Book Club series, where bands play new tunes based on that month's reading assignment.

Gramercy Theatre

127 E 23rd Street, between Park & Lexington Avenues, Gramercy Park (1-212 777 6800, www.livenation.com). Subway N, R, 6 to 23rd Street. **Box office** at Fillmore New York at Irving Plaza (*see p323*). **Tickets** $10-$100. **Credit** AmEx, DC, MC, V. **Map** p404 E26.

The Gramercy Theatre looks exactly like what it is, a run-down former movie theatre; yet it has a decent sound system and good sightlines. Concertgoers can lounge in raised seats on the top level or get closer to the stage. Bookings have included such Baby Boom underdogs as Loudon Wainwright III and Todd Rundgren, and the occasional hip hop show (Kool Keith, Asher Roth), but tilt towards musty, 1990s-flavoured rock bands.

Hammerstein Ballroom

Manhattan Center, 311 W 34th Street, between Eighth & Ninth Avenues, Garment District (1-212 279 7740, www.mcstudios.com). Subway A, C, E to 34th Street-Penn Station. **Tickets** $10-$150 (through Ticketmaster 1-212 307 7171). **Credit** AmEx, DC, MC, V. **Map** p404 C25.

Queues can wind across the block, drinks prices are high, and those seated in the balcony should bring binoculars if they want a clear view of the band. Still, this cavernous space regularly draws big performers in the limbo between club and arena shows. The once-poor sound quality has been rectified, but unless you land tickets on the floor, it takes an amazing act to make a night special.

Highline Ballroom

431 W 16th Street, between Ninth & Tenth Avenues, Chelsea (1-212 414 5994, www.highlineballroom.com). Subway A, C, E to 14th Street; L to Eighth Avenue. **Box office** 11am-10pm daily. **Admission** free-$80 ($10 food/drink min). **Credit** AmEx, DC, Disc, MC, V. **Map** p403 C27.

This West Side club, which is situated next to a Western Beef grocer, is LA-slick and bland, in a corporate sense. But despite this, it has a lot to recommend it: the sound is top-of-the-heap and sightlines are pretty good. The bookings are also impressive, whether a club appearance from the Arctic Monkeys or the great drag performer Justin Bond. Perhaps coolest of all is a weekly late-night residency by the Roots, who swing by after *Late Night with Jimmy Fallon* tapings in the mood to jam – and more often than not they are accompanied by big-name surprise guests.

★ Joe's Pub

Public Theater, 425 Lafayette Street, between Astor Place & E 4th Street, East Village (1-212 539 8770, www.joespub.com). Subway N, R to 8th Street-NYU; 6 to Astor Place. **Box office** 1-6pm Mon, Sun; 1-7pm Tue-Sat. **Tickets** $12-$30. **Credit** AmEx, DC, MC, V. **Map** p403 E28.

One of the city's premier small spots for sit-down audiences, Joe's Pub brings in impeccable talent of all genres and origins. While some well-established names play here (Pete Townshend's 'From the Attic' show, to give an example), Joe's also lends its stage for up-and-comers (this is where Amy Winehouse made her debut in the United States), drag acts and cabaret performers. A small but solid menu and deep bar selections seal the deal – just be sure to keep an eye on the drinks prices. *Photos p325.*

INSIDE TRACK
LOCAL (GUITAR) HEROES

Hometown band the **Strokes** began their fantastically quick rise with a residency at the modest Lower East Side rock club **Mercury Lounge** (*see p327*) in 2000 (the Moldy Peaches opened).

Knitting Factory Brooklyn

361 Metropolitan Avenue, at Havemeyer Street, Williamsburg, Brooklyn (1-347 529 6696, www.knittingfactory.com). Subway L to Lorimer Street; G to Metropolitan Avenue. **Open** varies. **Tickets** free-$25. **Map** p411 U8.

Once a downtown Manhattan incubator of experimental music – both of the jazz and indie-rock variety – Knitting Factory is now a straightforward rock venue with outposts across the country (but not, curiously, Manhattan). The newly opened Brooklyn location pales in comparison to the original club, with largely rote bookings comparable to any other mid-size venue. But it remains a professional, well-managed club, with a happening front-room bar.

▶ *For Knitting Factory founder Michael Dorf's latest venture, see p322 City Winery.*

Lakeside Lounge

162 Avenue B, between 10th & 11th Streets, East Village (1-212 529 8463, www.lakesidelounge.com). Subway L to First Avenue; N, Q, R, 4, 5, 6 to 14th Street-Union Square. **Shows** 9pm Mon-Thur, Sun; 11pm Fri, Sat. **Admission** free. **Credit** AmEx, DC, MC, V. **Map** p403 G28.

Because this easy-going joint is co-owned by guitarist and producer Eric Ambel, the roadhouse and roots acts that play tend to be fun. Local country-tinged talents often appear, and bigger names such as Amy Rigby stop by occasionally. The bar, the jukebox and the photo booth are all attractions in their own right – and there's never a cover charge.

★ (Le) Poisson Rouge

158 Bleecker Street, at Thompson Street, Greenwich Village (1-212 505 3474, www.lepoissonrouge.com). Subway A, B, C, D, E, F, M to W 4th Street. **Open** 5pm-2am Mon-Wed, Sun; 5pm-4am Thur-Sat. **Box office** 5-10pm daily. **Tickets** free-$30. **Credit** AmEx (bar only), DC, Disc, MC, V. **Map** p403 E29.

Tucked into the basement of the long-gone Village Gate – a legendary performance space that hosted everyone from Miles Davis to Jimi Hendrix – (Le) Poisson Rouge was opened in 2008 by a group of young music enthusiasts with ties to both the classical and indie-rock worlds. The cabaret space's booking policy reflects both camps, often on a single bill. No other joint in town books such a wide range of great music, whether from a feverish Malian band (Toumani Diabaté's Symmetric Orchestra), moody Birmingham indie favourites (Broadcast), young classical stars (pianist Simone Dinnerstein) or even a children's pop crooner (Ralph's World).

Essentially New York Albums

Music makers, and lovers, select the sounds of the city.

STEVE SMITH, MUSIC EDITOR, TIME OUT NEW YORK: 'Along with fellow Def Jam trio Beastie Boys, Queens' **Run-DMC** successfully smuggled hip hop into suburbia in the mid-1980s, most prominently with their third album, *Raising Hell*. While the Aerosmith collaboration 'Walk This Way' captured a million classic-rock hearts, it's the full LP – with its spare beats, tag-team vocals, and shout-outs to DJs and sneakers – that was an outer-borough masterpiece.'

SCOTT IAN, GUITARIST, ANTHRAX: 'My No.1 choice is the **Ramones**' *Rocket to Russia*. As a kid from Queens that used to sit in his room and play along to 'Teenage Lobotomy', the Ramones gave me hope. I looked like them: long hair, leather jacket and Levi's. I know they invented punk rock, but for me it was more personal. They were the door to another world.'

CHUCK D, RAPPER AND PRODUCER, PUBLIC ENEMY: '[**Run-DMC**'s] *Raising Hell*, oh yeah! That's my all-time favourite. It was just this clash of rock, rap and everything that was going on in New York at the time. [Beastie Boys'] *Licensed to Ill* did that too. Also, Anthrax was so important. Everything after them was thrash.'

LYDIA LUNCH, SINGER AND ACTOR: '**Suicide**'s self-titled album from 1977 perfectly sums up the insanity, desperation and horrific beauty of the ghost of New York City at its most urgent.'

JULIAN CASABLANCAS, SINGER, THE STROKES: 'This ridiculously rad bootleg I have of **Bob Marley and the Wailers** live at the Apollo. I think it's from 1978.'

SHARON VAN ETTEN, FOLK SINGER: 'My essential New York album would have to be **Antony and the Johnsons**' *I Am a Bird Now*. There is not one song on the album that does not make every hair on the back of my neck stand on end. One can tell by the calibre of contributors to the album that Antony is held in high regard by some of the best writers of my lifetime: Lou Reed, Rufus Wainwright, Boy George, Devendra Banhart...

Joe's Pub. See p323.

Living Room

154 Ludlow Street, between Rivington & Stanton Streets, Lower East Side (1-212 533 7235, www.livingroomny.com). Subway F to Lower East Side-Second Avenue; J, M, Z to Delancey-Essex Streets. **Open** 6.30pm-2am Mon-Thur, Sun; 6.30pm-4am Fri, Sat. **Admission** free-$15 (1-drink min). **No credit cards. Map** p403 G29.

Many local clubs claim to be the place where Norah Jones got her start, but the Living Room is the real McCoy – she even donated a piano as a way of saying thanks to the place. Mind you, that was in the venue's older (and rather drabber) location of a former fried-chicken establishment; since moving to the Lower East Side's version of Main Street, the stream of singer-songwriters has taken on a bit more gleam, and the warmly lit environs always seem to be bustling. Upstairs is Googie's Lounge, an even more intimate space. Owners Steve Rosenthal and Jennifer Gilson continue to unearth new talent.

Southpaw. *See p328.*

★ Maxwell's

1039 Washington Street, at 11th Street, Hoboken, NJ (1-201 798 0406, www.maxwellsnj.com). PATH train to Hoboken, then taxi, Red Apple bus or NJ Transit 126 bus to 11th Street. **Open** 5pm-2am Mon-Thur; 5pm-3am Fri, Sat; 11am-midnight Sun. **Tickets** $7-$25. **Credit** AmEx, DC, Disc, MC, V.

The trip to Maxwell's can be a hassle, but the 15-minute walk once you're finally off the PATH train can make you feel like you're in small-town America. The restaurant in front is big and friendly; for dessert you can feast on musical fare from popular indie-rock acts (the Fiery Furnaces, Big Pink) and garage favourites (King Khan & BBQ Show). Hometown heroes Yo La Tengo stage their more or less annual Hanukkah shows here.

Mercury Lounge

217 E Houston Street, between Essex & Ludlow Streets, Lower East Side (1-212 260 4700, www.mercuryloungenyc.com). Subway F to Lower East Side-Second Avenue. **Box office** noon-7pm Mon-Sat. **Tickets** $8-$20. **Credit** (bar only) AmEx, DC, Disc, MC, V. **Map** p403 G29.

The unassuming, boxy Mercury Lounge is an old standby, with solid sound and sightlines (and a cramped bar in the front room). There are four-band bills most nights, although they can seem stylistically haphazard and set times are often later than advertised. (It's a good rule of thumb to show up half an hour later than you think you should.) Some of the bigger shows sell out in advance.

Music Hall of Williamsburg

66 North 6th Street, between Kent & Wythe Avenues, Williamsburg, Brooklyn (1-718 486 5400, www.williamsburgmusichall.com). Subway L to Bedford Avenue. **Box office** 11am-6pm Sat. **Tickets** $12-$35. **Credit** (online purchases only) AmEx, DC, Disc, MC, V. **Map** p411 U7.

When, in 2007, the local promoter Bowery Presents found itself in need of a Williamsburg outpost, it gave the former Northsix a facelift and took over the bookings. It's basically a Bowery Ballroom in Brooklyn – and bands such as Sonic Youth, Woods and Wolfmother headline, often on the day after they've played Bowery Ballroom or Terminal 5.

92YTribeca

200 Hudson Street, between Canal & Desbrosses Streets, Tribeca (1-212 601 1000, www.92ytribeca.com). Subway A, C, E, 1 to Canal Street. **Box office** 9am-3pm Mon, Tue; 9am-10pm Wed; 9am-midnight Thur, Fri; 5pm-midnight Sat; 10am-3pm Sun. **Tickets** free-$35. **Credit** AmEx, DC, MC, V. **Map** p402 D30.

The downtown outpost of the 92nd Street Y, 92YTribeca is ostensibly a cultural centre for hip young Jews. Yet the recently hatched club – which houses a performance space, screening room, art gallery and café – is by no means restricted to Jewish events or artists. In fact, it has quickly become one of the most daring venues in Manhattan. The club's breadth is impressive, featuring obscure indie-rock, world music, country and mixed-media shows.

Best Buy Theater

1515 Broadway, at 44th Street, Theater District (1-212 930 1950, www.bestbuytheater.com). Subway N, Q, R, S, 1, 2, 3, 7 to 42nd Street-Times Square. **Box office** noon-6pm Mon-Sat. **Tickets** $20-$80. **Credit** AmEx, DC, MC, V. **Map** p404 D24.

This large, corporate club begs for character but finds redemption in its creature comforts. The sound and sightlines are both good, and there's even edible food. Those who wish to look into a musician's eyes can stand in the ample front section; foot-weary fans can sit in the cinema-like section at the back. It's a comfortable place to see a well-known band that hasn't (yet) reached stadium-filling fame.

Pete's Candy Store

709 Lorimer Street, between Frost & Richardson Streets, Williamsburg, Brooklyn (1-718 302 3770, www.petescandystore.com). Subway L to Lorimer Street. **Open** 5pm-2am Mon-Wed; 5pm-4am Thur, Sat; 4pm-4am Fri; 4pm-2am Sun. **Admission** free. **Credit** AmEx, DC, MC, V. **Map** p411 V7.

An overlooked gem tucked away in an old candy shop, Pete's is beautifully ramshackle, tiny and always free. The performers are generally unknown and crowds can be thin, but it can be a charming place to catch a singer-songwriter. Worthy underdogs may stop by for casual sets. If worse comes to worst, you can hang out at the bar up front.

Pianos

158 Ludlow Street, between Rivington & Stanton Streets, Lower East Side (1-212 505 3733, www.pianosnyc.com). Subway F to Delancey Street; J, M, Z to Delancey-Essex Streets. **Open** 3pm-4am daily. **Admission** free-$12. **Credit** AmEx, DC, MC, V. **Map** p403 G29.

In recent years, a lot of the cooler bookings have moved down the block to venues such as Cake Shop or to Brooklyn. Still, while sound is often lousy and the room can get uncomfortably mobbed, there are always good reasons to go back to Pianos – very often the under-the-radar, emerging rock bands that make local music scenes tick.

★ Radio City Music Hall

1260 Sixth Avenue, at 50th Street, Midtown (1-212 247 4777, www.radiocity.com). Subway B, D, F, M to 47th-50th Streets-Rockefeller Center. **Box office** 11.30am-6pm Mon-Sat. **Tickets** $25-$150. **Credit** AmEx, DC, MC, V. **Map** p404 D23.

Few rooms scream 'New York City!' more than this gilded hall, which has recently drawn Ne-Yo, Leonard Cohen and Yeah Yeah Yeahs as headliners.

The greatest challenge for any performer is not to be upstaged by the awe-inspiring art deco surroundings. On the other hand, those same surroundings lend historic heft to even the flimsiest showing. Bookings are all over the map; expect everything from seasonal staples like the Rockettes to druggy Brit-rock outfit Spiritualized.

Roseland

239 W 52nd Street, between Broadway & Eighth Avenue, Theater District (1-212 247 0200, www.roselandballroom.com). Subway B, D, E to Seventh Avenue; C to 50th Street. **Box office** at Fillmore New York at Irving Plaza (*see p323*). **Tickets** $17-$75. **Credit** (advance purchases only) AmEx, DC, MC, V. **Map** p404 D23.

This dreary Times Square club is bigger than Irving Plaza and smaller than the Hammerstein Ballroom. As such, it draws big talent (Yo La Tengo, Them Crooked Vultures) but remains a vaguely depressing place to spend a night, recalling a dank, slightly neglected rec room.

Sidewalk Café

94 Avenue A, at 6th Street, East Village (1-212 473 7373). Subway 6 to Astor Place. **Open** 9am-3am Mon-Thur, Sun; 24hrs Fri, Sat. **Admission** free (2-drink min). **Credit** AmEx, DC, Disc, MC, V. **Map** p403 G28.

Despite its cramped, awkward layout, the Sidewalk Café is the focal point of the city's anti-folk scene – although that category means just about anything from piano pop to wry folk. Nellie McKay, Regina Spektor and the Moldy Peaches all started here.

SOB's

204 Varick Street, at Houston Street, Tribeca (1-212 243 4940, www.sobs.com). Subway 1 to Houston Street. **Box office** 11am-6pm Mon-Sat. **Tickets** $5-$40. **Credit** (food & bar only) DC, Disc, MC, V. **Map** p403 D29.

The titular Sounds of Brazil (SOB, geddit?) are just some of the many global genres that keep this venue hopping. Hip hop, soul, reggae and Latin beats figure in the mix, with BLK JKS, Gil Scott-Heron and Eddie Palmieri each appearing of late. The drinks are expensive, but the sharp-looking clientele doesn't seem to mind.

Southpaw

125 Fifth Avenue, between Sterling & St Johns Places, Park Slope, Brooklyn (1-718 230 0236, www.spsounds.com). Subway B, Q, 2, 3, 4, 5 to Atlantic Avenue; D, M, N, R to Pacific Street. **Open** 8pm-2am Tue-Thur, Sun; pam-4am Fri, Sat. **Tickets** free-$20. **No credit cards.** **Map** p410 T11.

This cool space welcomes prime outfits (the Feelies, Dean & Britta) that would otherwise play in slightly larger Manhattan rooms, and also hosts the Rub, a monthly Saturday night funk and hip hop party. Increasingly, it is one of the city's more welcoming clubs for hip hop, especially of the non-billionaire variety (Tanya Morgan, Jean Grae). Like its Park Slope neighbourhood, Southpaw tends to draw cool, mellow audiences; with all the elbow room, getting to the (huge) bar is no problem. *Photos p326.*

Terminal 5

610 W 56th Street, between 11th & 12th Avenues, Hell's Kitchen (1-212 260 4700, www.terminal5nyc.com). Subway A, B, C, D, 1 to 59th Street-Columbus Circle. **Box office** at Mercury Lounge (*see p327*). **Tickets** $15-$90. **Credit** (online purchases & bar only) AmEx, Disc, MC, V. **Map** p405 C22.

Opened by Bowery Presents, this three-floor, 3,000-capacity place is the largest Midtown venue to set up shop in more than a decade. Bookings include bands that only a short time ago were playing in the smaller Bowery confines (Passion Pit), plus bigger stars (Gossip, The Dead Weather) and scruffy veterans with their loyal fan bases (Robert Earl Keen, Levon Helm).

★ Town Hall

123 W 43rd Street, between Sixth Avenue & Broadway, Theater District (1-212 840 2824, www.the-townhall-nyc.org). Subway B, D, F, M to 42nd Street-Bryant Park; N, Q, R, S, 1, 2, 3, 7 to 42nd Street-Times Square. **Box office** noon-6pm Mon-Sat. **Tickets** $10-$120. **Credit** AmEx, DC, MC, V. **Map** p404 D24.

Acoustics at the 1921 'people's auditorium' are superb, and there's no doubting the gravitas of Town Hall's surroundings – the building was designed by illustrious architects McKim, Mead & White as a meeting house for a suffragist organisation. Ornette Coleman, Grizzly Bear and Ray Davies have performed here in recent times, and smart indie songwriters such as the Magnetic Fields have set up shop for a number of nights.

Union Hall

702 Union Street, between Fifth & Sixth Avenues, Park Slope, Brooklyn (1-718 638 4400, www.unionhallny.com). Subway M, R to Union Street. **Open** 4pm-4am Mon-Fri; noon-4am Sat, Sun. **Tickets** $5-$20. **Credit** AmEx, DC, MC, V. **Map** p410 T11.

The spacious main floor of this Brooklyn bar has a garden, food service and a *bocce* ball court. Tucked in the basement is a comfortable space dominated by the more delicate side of indie rock, with infrequent sets by indie comics such as Daniel Kitson and Eugene Mirman.

Union Pool

484 Union Avenue, at Meeker Avenue, Williamsburg, Brooklyn (1-718 609 0484, www.myspace.com/unionpool). Subway L to Lorimer Street; G to Metropolitan Avenue.

Open 5pm-4am Mon-Fri; 1pm-4am Sat, Sun. **Tickets** $5-$12. **Credit** (bar only) AmEx, DC, MC, V. **Map** p411 V8.

Wind through the kitschy backyard space of this modest Williamsburg bar and you'll find yourself back indoors, facing a modest stage in a small room. Local stars check in from time to time (members of TV on the Radio and Yeah Yeah Yeahs have showed off their side-projects here), but it's dominated by well-plucked smaller indie acts such as the Larkin Grimm and Sharon Van Etten.

United Palace Theatre

4140 Broadway, at 175th Street, Washington Heights (1-212 568 5260, www.ticketmaster.com). Subway A to 175th Street. **Box office** noon-6pm Mon-Sat. **Tickets** $50-$150. **No credit cards**. **Map** p409 B7.

This renovated movie house, which was once a vaudeville theatre, dates from the 1930s. And it really does feel as if you've entered a palace here, with its shimmering chandeliers, ornate detailed ceiling and gold-drenched corridors. The venue's solid booking has ranged, over the past few years, from popular young acts such as Vampire Weekend, Interpol and Arcade Fire to stalwarts of the music world like Bob Dylan and the Allman Brothers Band. At the top end of Manhattan, far beyond the traditional nightlife or tourist zone, the theatre is nevertheless easily accessible by subway.

Webster Hall

125 E 11th Street, between Third & Fourth Avenues, East Village (1-212 353 1600, www.websterhall.com). Subway L to Third Avenue; N, Q, R, 4, 5, 6 to 14th Street-Union Square. **Box office** at Mercury Lounge (*see p327*). **Tickets** $15-$50. **Credit** AmEx, DC, MC, V. **Map** p403 F28.

A great-sounding alternative for bands (and fans) who've had their fill of the comparably sized Irving Plaza, Webster Hall is booked by Bowery Presents, the folks who run Bowery Ballroom and Mercury Lounge. Expect to find high-calibre indie acts (Animal Collective, Battles, Gossip), but be sure to show up early if you want a decent view. A smaller space downstairs, the Studio at Webster Hall, hosts cheaper shows, mainly by local bands.

Jazz, Blues & Experimental

Ever since Duke Ellington urged folks to take the A train up to Harlem, New York has been a hotbed of improvisational talent. The ghosts of the Duke, Billie Holiday and Louis Armstrong haunt the classic venues uptown, while in the Village, you can soak up the vibe at clubs that once provided a platform for the virtuoso experimentations of Miles Davis, John Coltrane and Thelonious Monk. Boundaries are still being pushed in small bare-bones spaces such as **Zebulon** and the **Stone**.

For well-known jazz joints such as the **Village Vanguard** and **Birdland**, booking ahead is recommended.

BB King Blues Club & Grill

237 W 42nd Street, between Seventh & Eighth Avenues, Theater District (1-212 997 4144, www.bbkingblues.com). Subway A, C, E to 42nd Street-Port Authority; N, Q, R, S, 1, 2, 3, 7 to 42nd Street-Times Square. **Box office** 10.30am-midnight daily. **Tickets** $12-$150. **Credit** AmEx, DC, Disc, MC, V. **Map** p404 D24.

BB's Times Square joint stages one of the most varied music schedules in town. Cover bands and tributes fill the gaps between big-name bookings such as Ralph Stanley and Little Richard, but the venue has also hosted metal (Napalm Death, Obituary) and hip hop (various Wu-Tang associates). For many shows, the best seats are at the dinner tables at the front, but the menu prices are steep (and watch out for drink minimums). On Sundays, the Harlem Gospel Choir's buffet brunch ($42) raises the roof.

Birdland

315 W 44th Street, between Eighth & Ninth Avenues, Theater District (1-212 581 3080, www.birdlandjazz.com). Subway A, C, E to 42nd Street-Port Authority. **Open** 5pm-1am daily. **Tickets** $20-$50 ($10 food/drink min). **Credit** AmEx, DC, Disc, MC, V. **Map** p404 C24.

Its name is synonymous with jazz (Kurt Elling, Pharoah Sanders), but Birdland is also a prime cabaret destination (Christine Andreas, Christine Ebersole) and the bookings in both fields are great. The Chico O'Farrill Afro-Cuban Jazz Orchestra owns Sundays, and David Ostwald's Louis Armstrong Centennial Band hits on Wednesdays; Mondays see cabaret's waggish Jim Caruso and his Cast Party.

Blue Note

131 W 3rd Street, between MacDougal Street & Sixth Avenue, Greenwich Village (1-212 475 8592, www.bluenote.net). Subway A, B, C, D, E, F, M to W 4th Street. **Shows** 8pm, 10.30pm Mon-Thur; 8pm, 10.30pm, 12.30am Fri, Sat; 12.30pm, 2.30pm, 8pm, 10.30pm Sun. **Tickets** $10-$75 ($5 food/drink min). **Credit** AmEx, DC, MC, V. **Map** p403 E29.

The Blue Note prides itself on being 'the jazz capital of the world'. Bona fide musical titans (Cecil Taylor, Charlie Haden) rub against hot young talents (the Bad Plus), while the close-set tables in the club get patrons rubbing up against each other. The Late Night Groove series and the Sunday brunches are the best bargain bets.

Carnegie Hall

For listings, *see p312*.

Carnegie Hall means the big time. In recent years, though, the 599-seat, state-of-the-art Zankel Hall has greatly augmented the venue's pop, jazz and world music offerings. Between both halls, the complex has welcomed Dave Brubeck, Bobby McFerrin and Fred Hersch, among other high-wattage names.

Cornelia Street Café

29 Cornelia Street, between Bleecker & W 4th Streets, Greenwich Village (1-212 989 9319, www.corneliastreetcafe.com). Subway A, B, C, D, E, F, M to W 4th Street. **Open** 10am-midnight daily. **Tickets** $8-$12 ($7 drink min). **Credit** (food & bar only) AmEx, DC, Disc, MC, V. **Map** p403 D29.

Upstairs at the Cornelia Street Café is a cosy little eaterie. Downstairs is an even cosier music space hosting adventurous jazz, poetry, world music and folk. Regular mini-festivals spotlight blues, songwriters and new concert-theatre works.

55 Bar

55 Christopher Street, between Seventh Avenue South & Waverly Place, West Village (1-212 929 9883, www.55bar.com). Subway 1 to Christopher Street-Sheridan Square. **Open** 3pm-4am daily. **Tickets** free-$20. **No credit cards. Map** p403 D28.

This tiny Prohibition-era dive is one of New York's most artist-friendly rooms, thanks to its knowledgeable, appreciative audience. You can catch emerging talent almost every night at the free-of-charge early shows; late sets regularly feature established artists such as Chris Potter and Mike Stern.

★ Iridium

1650 Broadway, at 51st Street, Theater District (1-212 582 2121, www.iridiumjazzclub.com). Subway 1 to 50th Street; N, R to 49th Street. **Shows** 8pm, 10pm Mon; 8.30pm, 10.30pm Tue-Sun. **Tickets** $25-$50 ($10-$25 food/drink min). **Credit** AmEx, DC, Disc, MC, V. **Map** p404 D23.

One of the nicer places to dine while being hit with top-shelf jazz, Iridium is located bang in the middle of Broadway's bright lights. Recent guests have included the Cyrus Chestnut Trio and David Sánchez Quartet. Occasionally, the club strays from traditional jazz bookings, featuring sets by roots singer John Hammond and a capella group the Bobs.

★ Jazz at Lincoln Center

Frederick P Rose Hall, Broadway at 60th Street, Upper West Side (1-212 258 9800, www.jalc.org). Subway A, B, C, D, 1 to 59th Street-Columbus Circle. **Shows** *Rose Theater & Allen Room* vary. *Dizzy's Club Coca-Cola* 7.30pm, 9.30pm Mon-Thur, Sun; 7.30pm, 9.30pm, 11.30pm Fri, Sat. **Box office** 10am-6pm Mon-Sat; noon-6pm Sun. **Tickets** *Rose Theater* $30-$120. *Allen Room* $55-$65. *Dizzy's Club Coca-Cola* $10-$35 ($5-$10 food/drink min). **Credit** AmEx, DC, MC, V. **Map** p405 D22.

The jazz arm of Lincoln Center is actually several blocks away from the main campus, high atop the Time Warner Center. It includes three rooms: the Rose Theater is a traditional mid-size space, but the crown jewels are the Allen Room and the smaller Dizzy's Club Coca-Cola, with stages that are framed by enormous windows looking on to Columbus Circle and Central Park. The venues feel like a Hollywood cinematographer's vision of a Manhattan jazz club. Some of the best players in the business regularly grace the spot; among them is Wynton Marsalis, Jazz at Lincoln Center's famed artistic director.

Jazz Gallery

290 Hudson Street, between Dominick & Spring Streets, Soho (1-212 242 1063, www.jazzgallery.org). Subway A, C, E to Spring Street. **Shows** vary. **Tickets** $10-$35. **Credit** (online purchases only) AmEx, Disc, MC, V. **Map** p403 D30.

The fact that there's no bar here should be a tip-off: the Jazz Gallery is a place to witness true works of art, from the sometimes obscure but always interesting jazzers who play the club (Lee Konitz and Steve Coleman, to name a couple) to the photos and artefacts displayed on the walls. The diminutive room's acoustics are sublime.

Jazz Standard

116 E 27th Street, between Park Avenue South & Lexington Avenue, Flatiron District (1-212 576 2232, www.jazzstandard.com). Subway 6 to 28th Street. **Shows** 7.30pm, 9.30pm Mon-Thur; 7.30pm, 9.30pm, 11.30pm Fri, Sat. **Tickets** $20-$35. **Credit** AmEx, DC, Disc, MC, V. **Map** p404 E26.

Jazz Standard's airy, multi-tiered floor plan makes for splendid sightlines to match the sterling sound. In keeping with the rib-sticking chow upstairs at Danny Meyer's Blue Smoke barbecue joint, the jazz is often of the groovy, hard-swinging variety, with musicians such as trumpeter Dave Douglas and pianist Gonzalo Rubalcaba. The mighty Mingus Big Band, long-time local favourites, hold down Monday nights.

Lenox Lounge

288 Malcolm X Boulevard (Lenox Avenue), between 124th & 125th Streets, Harlem (1-212 427 0253, www.lenoxlounge.com). Subway 2, 3 to 125th Street. **Open** noon-4am daily. **Admission** free-$20 ($16 drink min). **Credit** AmEx, DC, Disc, MC, V. **Map** p407 D13.

This classy art deco lounge once hosted Billie Holiday and has drawn stars since the late 1930s. Saxist Patience Higgins's Sugar Hill Jazz Quartet jams into the wee hours on Monday nights.

► *For further details about the bar, see p225.*

Merkin Concert Hall

For listings, *see p317.*

Just north of Lincoln Center, the recently refurbished Merkin provides a polished platform for classical

Jazz Gallery.

and jazz composers. Chamber music, jazz, folk, cabaret and experimental performers take the stage at this intimate venue. Popular annual series include the New York Festival of Song, WNYC's New Sounds Live and Broadway Close Up.

92nd Street Y

For listings, *see p317.*
Best known for the series Jazz in July and spring's Lyrics & Lyricists, this multi-disciplinary cultural centre also offers gospel, mainstream jazz and singer-songwriters. The small, handsome theatre provides a fine setting for the sophisticated fare.

St Nick's Pub

773 St Nicholas Avenue, at 149th Street (1-212 283 7132, www.stnicksjazzpub.net). Subway A, B, C, D, 1 to 145th St. **Shows** vary. **Admission** free (2-drink min). **No credit cards**. **Map** p408 C10.
When Duke Ellington urged taking the A train to Sugar Hill, subterranean St Nick's Pub was probably the type of place he had in mind. Saturday's Africa Night kicks off at 10pm and is alive with the pulsating rhythms and infectious call-and-response exchanges of an informal French West African collective. And Mondays, when the joint is enveloped by its legendary jam session, you'll be glad you heeded the Duke's advice.

★ Smalls

183 W 10th Street, between Seventh Avenue South & W 4th Street, West Village (1-212 252 5091, www.smallsjazzclub.com). Subway 1 to Christopher Street-Sheridan Square. **Open** 7.30pm-4am daily. **Admission** $10-20. **No credit cards**. **Map** p403 D28.
Sometimes you want old-school jazz sans the shtick you've come to expect at a dinner-club gig. Luckily, this cosy basement venue is still kicking. Inside, it feels like one of those hole-in-the-wall NYC jazz haunts of yore over which fans routinely obsess. The line-up is really solid, with a fun late-night jam session starting after midnight each evening. Smalls also offers a big concession for the grown-ups: a liquor licence and a fully stocked bar. It's still a place to catch the best and brightest up-and-comers as well as the occasional moonlighting star.

Smoke

2751 Broadway, between 105th & 106th Streets, Upper West Side (1-212 864 6662, www.smokejazz.com). Subway 1 to 103rd Street. **Shows** 8pm, 9.30pm, 11pm (jam session) Mon; 8pm, 10pm, 11.30pm Tue-Sun. **Admission** $9 ($20 food/drink min per set) Mon-Thur, Sun; $30 ($10 food/drink min) Fri, Sat. **Credit** AmEx, DC, Disc, MC, V. **Map** p406 C16.
Not unlike a swanky living room, Smoke is a classy little joint that acts as a haven for local jazz legends and touring artists looking to play an intimate space. Early in the week, evenings are themed: on Sunday, it's Latin jazz; Tuesday, organ jazz. At weekends, renowned jazzers hit the stage, relishing the opportunity to play informal gigs uptown.

★ Stone

Avenue C, at 2nd Street, East Village (no phone, www.thestonenyc.com). Subway F to Lower East Side-Second Avenue. **Shows** 8pm, 10pm Tue-Sun. **Admission** $10. **No credit cards**. **Map** p403 G29.
Don't call sax star John Zorn's not-for-profit venture a 'club'. You'll find no food or drinks here, and no nonsense, either: the Stone is an art space dedicated to 'the experimental and the avant-garde'. If you're down for some rigorously adventurous sounds (Anthony Coleman, Okkyung Lee, Tony Conrad), Zorn has made it easy: no advance sales, and all ages admitted (under-19s get discounts). The bookings are left to a different artist-cum-curator each month. Increasingly, the space welcomes adventurous rock acts (Danielson, Tune-Yards).

★ Village Vanguard

178 Seventh Avenue South, at Perry Street, West Village (1-212 255 4037, www.village vanguard.com). Subway A, C, E, 1, 2, 3 to 14th Street; L to Eighth Avenue. **Shows** 9pm, 11pm daily. **Tickets** (incl $10 of drinks) $30 Mon; $35 Tue-Sun. **Credit** (online purchases only) AmEx, MC, V. **Map** p403 D28.
Having celebrated its 75th birthday in 2010 and still going strong, the Village Vanguard is one of New York's legendary jazz centres. History surrounds you: John Coltrane, Miles Davis and Bill Evans have all grooved in this hallowed hall. Big names both old and new continue to fill the schedules; the 2009 Grammy Award-winning 16-piece Vanguard Jazz Orchestra has been the Monday-night regular for more than 40 years. Reservations are recommended.

Zebulon

258 Wythe Avenue, between Metropolitan Avenue & North 3rd Street, Williamsburg, Brooklyn (1-718 218 6934, www.zebuloncafeconcert.com). Subway L to Bedford Avenue. **Open** 5.30pm-4am Mon-Thur; 4pm-4am Sat, Sun. **Admission** free. **Credit** AmEx. **Map** p411 U7.

INSIDE TRACK SINGING ALONG

All of the non-hotel cabaret rooms have open-mic nights where show-tune lovers can briefly seize the spotlight. However, those who prefer to sing communally should head to the venerable West Village piano bar **Marie's Crisis** (59 Grove Street, between Seventh Avenue South & Bleecker Street, no phone).

While emphasising young firebrands (Gold Sparkle Band, Tyshawn Sorey) over the establishment, this killer jazz spot also welcomes the daring wing of the local rock scene (such as great singer-songwriter Hannah Marcus). While the café opens in the afternoon, don't expect live music until closer to 10pm.

Cabaret

Bob Fosse's classic 1972 movie musical *Cabaret* depicts a world of fleshy burlesque decadence. But at most cabaret shows today, it's just the music that gets stripped down: reduced to its bare essence by a vocalist in a cosy club. The intense intimacy of the experience can make it transformative if you're lucky, or mortifying if you're not. Manhattan's fanciest cabarets are in three fashionable hotels: the **Oak Room** (at the Algonquin), **Feinstein's** (at the Loews Regency) and **Café Carlyle** (at, yes, the Carlyle). Local clubs such as **Don't Tell Mama** and the **Duplex** are cheaper and more casual, but the talent is often entry-level. The **Laurie Beechman Theater** and the **Metropolitan Room** fall between these two poles.

Classic nightspots

Café Carlyle

Carlyle, 35 E 76th Street, at Madison Avenue, Upper East Side (1-212 744 1600, 1-800 227 5737 reservations, www.thecarlyle.com). Subway 6 to 77th Street. **Shows** *Sept-May* 8.45pm Mon-Thur; 8.45pm, 10.45pm Fri, Sat. *June* reduced schedule. **Admission** $65-$125 (sometimes with compulsory dinner). **Credit** AmEx, DC, Disc, MC, V. **Map** p405 E20.

With its airy murals by Marcel Vertes, this elegant boîte in the Carlyle hotel is the epitome of New York class, attracting such top-level singers as Elaine Stritch, Judy Collins, Christine Ebersole and Ute Lemper. Woody Allen often plays clarinet with Eddie Davis and his New Orleans Jazz Band on Mondays.

▶ *Bemelmans Bar, across the hall, has an excellent pianist for those who want to drink in the atmosphere at a lower price; see p225.*

Feinstein's at the Loews Regency

Loews Regency Hotel, 540 Park Avenue, at 61st Street, Upper East Side (1-212 339 4095, www.feinsteinsattheregency.com). Subway N, R to Lexington Avenue-59th Street; 4, 5, 6 to 59th Street. **Shows** 8.30pm Tue-Thur, Sun; 8pm, 10.30pm Fri, Sat. **Admission** $40-$95 ($40 food/drink min). **Credit** AmEx, DC, Disc, MC, V. **Map** p405 E22.

Michael Feinstein, cabaret's crown prince, draws A-list talent to this swanky room in the Regency hotel. The shows and the drinks are pricey, but you usually get what you pay for. Recent star performers have included Chita Rivera, Betty Buckley and Rita Moreno, as well as Hollywood types (Lynda Carter, Tony Danza) dabbling in music.

★ Oak Room

Algonquin Hotel, 59 W 44th Street, between Fifth & Sixth Avenues, Midtown (1-212 840 6800, 1-212 419 9331 reservations,

Rodeo Bar & Grill. *See p334.*

www.algonquinhotel.com). Subway B, D, F, M to 42nd Street-Bryant Park; 7 to Fifth Avenue. **Shows** 8.30pm Tue-Thur; 8.30pm, 11pm Fri, Sat. **Admission** $50-$75 ($30 drink min; $60 dinner compulsory for 8.30pm Fri & Sat shows). **Credit** AmEx, DC, Disc, MC, V. **Map** p404 E24.
This banquette-lined room is the perfect place in which to enjoy cabaret eminences such as Karen Akers, Jack Jones and Andrea Marcovicci, plus rising stars such as the ethereal Maude Maggart and the formidable jazz singer Paula West. The pianist and bebop icon Barbara Carroll plays a luminous brunch show on many Sundays.
► *For staying at the Algonquin Hotel, see p174.*

Standards

Don't Tell Mama

343 W 46th Street, between Eighth & Ninth Avenues, Theater District (1-212 757 0788, www.donttellmamanyc.com). Subway A, C, E to 42nd Street-Port Authority. **Open** *Piano bar* 9pm-4am daily. **Shows** vary; 2-4 shows per night. **Admission** $5-$20 (2-drink min). *Piano bar* free (2-drink min). **Average drink** $8. **Credit** AmEx, DC, Disc, MC, V. **Map** p404 C23.
Showbiz pros and piano-bar buffs adore this dank but homey Theater District stalwart, where acts range from the strictly amateur to potential stars of tomorrow. The line-up may include pop, jazz and musical-theatre singers, as well as comedians and drag artists (including the fabulous Judy Garland impersonator Tommy Femia).

Duplex

61 Christopher Street, at Seventh Avenue South, West Village (1-212 255 5438, www.theduplex.com). Subway 1 to Christopher Street-Sheridan Square. **Open** *Piano bar* 9.30pm-4am daily. **Shows** 7pm, 9pm daily. **Admission** $5-$15 (2-drink min). **Average drink** $7. **Credit** AmEx, DC, MC, V. **Map** p403 D28.
This cosy, brick-lined room, located upstairs from a piano bar in the heart of the West Village, is a good-natured testing ground for new talent. The eclectic offerings often come served with a generous dollop of good, old-fashioned camp; regular acts include the amusing neo-lounge duo known as Gashole.

Laurie Beechman Theater

407 W 42nd Street, at Ninth Avenue, Theater District (1-212 695 6909, www.westbankcafe.com). Subway A, C, E to 42nd Street-Port Authority. **Shows** vary; 1-2 shows per night. *Open mic* 10.30pm-2am Fri. **Admission** $15-$25 ($15 food/drink min). **Average drink** $12. **Credit** AmEx, DC, MC, V. **Map** p404 C24.
Tucked away beneath the West Bank Café on 42nd Street, the Beechman provides a popular space for comedy shows (Joan Rivers has made it her testing ground for new material) as well as singers from the worlds of musical theatre and cabaret. The irrepressible Brandon Cutrell hosts the After Party, a racy open-mic show-tune showcase that pulls in the crowds on Friday nights.

★ Metropolitan Room

34 W 22nd Street, between Fifth & Sixth Avenues, Flatiron District (1-212 206 0440, www.metropolitanroom.com). Subway F, N, R to 23rd Street. **Shows** vary. **Admission** $15-$35 (2-drink min). **Average drink** $12. **Credit** AmEx, MC, V. **Map** p404 E26.
The Met Room has established itself as the must-go venue for high-level nightclub singing that won't bust your wallet. Regular performers range from rising musical-theatre stars to established cabaret acts (including Baby Jane Dexter and English songstress Barb Jungr), plus legends such as Tammy Grimes, Julie Wilson and Annie Ross.

World, Country & Roots

Among the cornucopia of live entertainment programmes at the **Brooklyn Academy of Music** (*see p311*) is that of the **BAMcafé** above the lobby, which comes to life on weekend nights with country, world music and other genres. (*See also p328* **SOB's**, *p321* **Barbès** and *p329* **BB King Blues Club & Grill**.)

Nublu

62 Avenue C, between 4th & 5th Streets, East Village (1-646 546 5206, www.nublu.net). Subway F to Lower East Side-Second Avenue. **Open** 8pm-4am daily. **Admission** $5-$10. **No credit cards**. **Map** p403 G29.
Nublu's prominence on the local globalist club scene has been inversely proportional to its size. A pressure-cooker of creativity, the venue gave rise to the Brazilian Girls, who started jamming at one late-night session and haven't stopped yet, and started NYC's romance with the northern Brazilian style *forró*. Even on weeknights, events usually start no earlier than 10pm – but if you show up early (and find the unmarked door), the bar is well stocked.

Rodeo Bar & Grill

375 Third Avenue, at 27th Street, Gramercy Park (1-212 683 6500, www.rodeobar.com). Subway 6 to 28th Street. **Shows** 9pm Mon, Tue, Sun; 10pm Wed, Thur; 11pm Fri, Sat. **Admission** free. **Credit** AmEx, DC, Disc, MC, V. **Map** p404 F26.
The unpretentious, if sometimes raucous crowd, roadhouse atmosphere and absence of a cover charge help make the Rodeo the city's best roots club, with a steady stream of rockabilly, country and related sounds. Kick back with a beer from the bar – a hollowed-out bus in the middle of the room. *Photo p333.*

Nightlife

The beat goes on in the great metropolis.

Ever wonder how New York earned the right to be called the 'city that never sleeps'? Hint: it's not because of the late-night rubbish collections, chorus of car alarms or even the vats of coffee that Gothamites guzzle daily. No, the town was given that sobriquet for one thing only – its nightlife legacy. This is where David Mancuso transformed DJing into storytelling at the Loft, where Area turned clubbing into an art experience in the 1980s, and where Jackie 60 rode that experience into a freaky-deaky sunset. And we're happy to report that it's still easy to slip into a sleep-deprived stupor carousing NYC's clubs – despite a long list of potential party-killers, including club-loathing mayors and a major-league recession.

THE LOCAL SCENE

Even clubland's old-timers – those who like to begin sentences with 'Back when I was a kid' – agree: the current state of NYC nightlife is strong. Granted, there haven't been any essential new clubs opening their doors lately, but, given the current economic situation, it would be more shocking if there had been. A bad economy can be good for clubland, fostering a more vibrant, underground (and, frankly, cheaper) side of the scene, rather than spots that serve pedestrian beats and $400 bottles.

To that end, there's been a burst of 'secret-location' shindigs in the past few years, which are generally held in out-of-the-way warehouses and lofts. By the nature of the event, these parties can be a bitch to find out about for those not in the loop, but if you keep your eye on underground-clubbing websites, such as www.rhythmism.com and www.residentadvisor.net – and, of course, your indispensable *Time Out New York* weekly clubs listings – you'll be led in the right direction.

Even the old-guard dance clubs, such as **Sullivan Room** and **Cielo**, have stepped up their games, attracting the world's top DJs to spin everything from hip hop and electro to cutting-edge dubstep and techno. Dinosaur venues such as **Webster Hall** and glammed-up superclubs such as **Pacha** have got in on the act, with the former hosting the happening Girls & Boys gala every Friday, and the latter digging deeper for its DJs than ever.

CLUBS

★ Bunker

Public Assembly (back room), 70 N 6th Street, between Kent & Wythe Avenues, Williamsburg, Brooklyn (1-718 782 5188, www.beyondbooking.com/thebunker). Subway L to Bedford Avenue. **Open** 10pm-6am various Fridays. **Admission** $10-$20. **Average drink** $6. **Credit** (bar only) AmEx, DC, MC, V. **Map** p411 U7.

Gotham's electronic music fans were in a tizzy when Tonic, the longtime home of the Bunker, closed in 2007, but the shindig is now happily ensconced in Williamsburg's Public Assembly. And, as befits the party that helped to kick off the current craze for all things techno in NYC, residents DJ Spinoza, Derek Plaslaiko and Eric Cloutier are still scoring at their (usually) monthly Friday-night get-together – big guns from labels such as Spectral Sound and Kompakt regularly pack the bunker-like space.

INSIDE TRACK WALLET ESSENTIALS

Most clubs operate an over-21 policy, and even if you're in the running for the World's Oldest Clubber award, you'll need a government-issued ID (such as a passport or driving licence) to gain admission. It's also worth carrying cash as most clubs won't accept credit cards at the door.

★ Cielo

18 Little W 12th Street, at Ninth Avenue, Meatpacking District (1-212 645 5700, www.cieloclub.com). Subway A, C, E to 14th Street; L to Eighth Avenue. **Open** 10pm-4am Mon, Wed-Sat. **Admission** $12-$25. **Average drink** $10. **Credit** AmEx, DC, MC, V. **Map** p403 C28.

You'd never guess from the Heidi Montag wannabes hanging out in the neighbourhood that the attitude at this club is close to zero – at least once you get past the bouncers guarding the door. On the sunken dance-floor, hip-to-hip crowds gyrate to deep beats from top DJs, including NYC old-schoolers François K, Tedd Patterson and Louie Vega. Cielo, which features a crystal-clear sound system (by the legendary Funktion One), has won a bevy of 'best club' awards in its half decade of existence.

Love Club

179 MacDougal Street, at 8th Street, Greenwich Village (1-212 477 5683, www.musicislove.net). Subway A, B, C, D, E, F, M to W 4th Street; N, R to 8th Street-NYU. **Open** 9pm-4am Mon, Wed, Sun; 10pm-4am Thur, Fri, Sat. **Admission** $10-$30. **Average drink** $8. **Credit** AmEx, MC, V. **Map** p403 E28.

The focus here is squarely on the music, ranging from techno and electro to deep house and hip hop. It's hardly a revolutionary concept, but in today's nightlife world of going for the quick buck, Love stands out from the crowd. The main room is a sparsely furnished box, but the DJ line-up is pretty impressive – the likes of the seminal Chicago house DJ Derrick Carter have graced the decks – and the sound system, from the famed Gary Stewart Audio, is one of the best.

Marquee

289 Tenth Avenue, between 26th & 27th Streets, Chelsea (1-646 473 0202, www.marqueeny.com). Subway C, E to 23rd Street. **Open** 11pm-4am Mon-Sat. **Admission** $20. **Average drink** $10. **Credit** AmEx, DC, Disc, MC, V. **Map** p404 C26.

The owners tore the roof off a former garage and custom-made everything here: the vaulted ceiling, the glass-beaded chandelier, even the champagne buckets. The centrepiece is a spectacular double-sided staircase that leads to a mezzanine overlooking the action below. Don't expect much musically, though: as with many venues where the scene trumps the tunes, it's largely middle-of-the-road fare (Christina Aguilera and Paris Hilton both had their album-release parties here).

Pacha

618 W 46th Street, between Eleventh & Twelfth Avenues, Hell's Kitchen (1-212 209 7500, www.pachanyc.com). Subway C, E to 50th Street. **Open** 10pm-8am Fri, Sat. **Admission** $20-$40. **Average drink** $9. **Credit** (bar only) AmEx, MC, V. **Map** p404 B23.

The worldwide glam-club chain Pacha, with out-posts in nightlife capitals such as Ibiza, London and Buenos Aires, hit the US market in 2005 with this swanky joint helmed by superstar spinner Erick Morillo. The spot attracts heavyweights ranging from local hero Danny Tenaglia to international crowd-pleasers such as Fedde Le Grande and Benny Benassi. Like most big clubs, it pays to check the line-up in advance if you're into underground (as opposed to lowest-common-denominator) beats.

★ Santos Party House

96 Lafayette Street, at Walker Street, Tribeca (1-212 584 5492, www.santospartyhouse.com). Subway J, M, N, Q, R, Z, 6 to Canal Street. **Open** varies; usually 7pm-4am daily. **Admission** $10-$16. **Average drink** $9. **Credit** AmEx, Disc, MC, V. **Map** p402 E31.

Launched by a team that includes rocker Andrew WK, Santos Party House – two black, square rooms done out in a bare-bones, generic club style – was initially hailed as a scene game-changer. While those too-high expectations didn't exactly pan out, it's still a rock-solid choice, with nights featuring everything from top-shelf hip hop to underground house.

Santos Pary House.

P.S.1 Warm Up.

Sapphire

249 Eldridge Street, between Houston & Stanton Streets, Lower East Side (1-212 777 5153, www.sapphirenyc.com). Subway F to Lower East Side-Second Avenue. **Open** 7pm-4am daily. **Admission** free-$5. **Average drink** $7. **Credit** (bar only) AmEx, Disc, MC, V. **Map** p403 F29.

Sapphire's bare walls and minimal decor are as raw as it gets, yet the energetic, unpretentious clientele is oblivious to the (lack of) aesthetic. A dance crowd packs the place all week – various nights feature house, hip hop, reggae and disco.

Sullivan Room

218 Sullivan Street, between Bleecker & W 3rd Streets, Greenwich Village (1-212 252 2151, www.sullivanroom.com). Subway A, B, C, D, E, F, M to W 4th Street. **Open** 10pm-5am Tue, Thur-Sat. **Admission** $5-$20. **Average drink** $8. **Credit** (bar only) AmEx, Disc, DC, MC, V. **Map** p403 E29.

Where's the party? It's right here in this unmarked subterranean space, which hosts some of the best deep-house, tech-house and breaks bashes the city has to offer. It's an unpretentious place, but hell, all you really need are thumpin' beats and a place to move your feet? Keep a lookout for the nights hosted by local stalwarts Sleepy & Boo, featuring top house music stars like Derrick Carter and Mark Farina.

Webster Hall

125 E 11th Street, at Third Avenue, East Village (1-212 353 1600, www.websterhall.com). Subway L to Third Avenue; N, Q, R, 4, 5, 6 to 14th Street-Union Square. **Open** 10pm-3am Thur-Sat. **Admission** free-$30. **Average drink** $8. **Credit** AmEx, DC, MC, V. **Map** p403 F28.

The grand Webster Hall isn't exactly on clubland's A-list, due to a populist DJ policy and a crowd that favours muscle shirts and gelled hair. But hey, it's been open, on and off, since 1866, so it must be doing something right.

ROVING & SEASONAL PARTIES

New York has a number of peripatetic and season-specific parties. Nights, locations and prices vary, so call or check the websites listed.

Blkmarket Membership

www.blkmarketmembership.com.

Competing with the Bunker (*see p335*) for the unofficial title of NYC's best techno party, the Blkmarket crew hosts bashes in the city's established clubs as well as out-of-the-way warehouse spaces.

★ Body & Soul

www.bodyandsoul-nyc.com.

Some people call the long-running spiritual-house hoedown Body & Soul the best party ever to fill a dancefloor in NYC. The Sunday-night tea dance, helmed by the holy DJ trinity of Danny Krivit, Joe Claussell and François K, is certainly in the top ten. It's no longer a weekly affair – nowadays, three editions a year will have to do – but it's still a spectacle, with a few thousand sweaty revellers dancing their hearts out.

★ P.S.1 Warm Up

P.S.1 Contemporary Art Center (for listings, *see p138*). **Open** July, Aug 2-9pm Sat. **Admission** (incl museum admission) $15. **Average drink** $6. **No credit cards**. **Map** p412 V5.

Since 1997, P.S.1's courtyard has played host to one of the most anticipated, resolutely underground clubbing events in the city. Thousands of dance music fanatics make the pilgrimage to Long Island City on summer Saturdays to drink and dance.

▶ *For details of the exhibition space, see p138.*

Turntables on the Hudson

www.turntablesonthehudson.com.

This ultra-funky affair lost its longtime home at the Lightship Frying Pan when the city put the kibosh on the vessel's parties, but they still pop up.

INSIDE TRACK GIANT STEP

Music-marketing company Giant Step's parties have been among the best of the nu-soul scene since the early 1990s. Sadly, the gang doesn't throw as many fêtes as they used to, but keep an eye on their website (www.giantstep.net) – on the rare occasion they decide to pack a dancefloor, you'd be a fool to miss it.

Sport & Fitness

Take in a Yankee game or take to the ice at Rockefeller Center.

As anyone who's ever witnessed one of the Yankees' many World Series victory parades down the 'Canyon of Heroes' (a spot reserved for ticker-tape parades on Broadway) can attest, New Yorkers are wild about their professional sports teams. Even basketball's lowly Knicks command rapt attention from locals, though it generally turns to scorn as each succeeding dismal year takes them further from their heyday.

Following baseball's Yankees' and Mets' moves into flashy new stadiums in 2009, football's Giants and Jets debuted their new home – the New Meadowlands Stadium (on the same site as the old one) – in 2010. But even if you loathe everything New York teams represent (big payrolls, bigger egos), there are plenty of worthwhile off-field activities.

SPECTATOR SPORTS

Major venues

All advance tickets for events at the major venues listed below are sold through **Ticketmaster** (*see p260*).

Madison Square Garden

Seventh Avenue, between 31st & 33rd Streets, Garment District (1-212 465 6741, www.thegarden.com). Subway A, C, E, 1, 2, 3 to 34th Street-Penn Station. **Box office** 9am-6pm Mon-Fri; 10am-6pm Sat; noon-2hr before event begins Sun. **Tickets** vary. **Credit** AmEx, DC, Disc, MC, V. **Map** p404 D25.

The New York Rangers (hockey; *see p340*) and New York Knicks and New York Liberty (basketball; *see p339*) call this home.

▶ *For more on the arena's history, see p94.*

Meadowlands Sports Complex

East Rutherford, NJ (1-201 935 3900, www.meadowlands.com). NJ Transit train from Penn Station to Secaucus Junction, then Meadowlands Line to Meadowlands Station. **Box office** 11am-6pm Mon-Fri; varies Sat, Sun depending on event. **Tickets** vary. **No credit cards.**

The Izod Center (which is now used only for mega concerts), the Meadowlands Racetrack (*see p341*) and New Meadowlands Stadium are all part of this massive multi-venue complex that is situated across the Hudson River. *Photo p340.*

Nassau Veterans Memorial Coliseum

1255 Hempstead Turnpike, Uniondale, Long Island (1-516 794 9303, www.nassaucoliseum.com). LIRR train from Penn Station to Hempstead, then N70, N71 or N72 bus. **Box office** 9.30am-4.45 Mon-Fri. **Tickets** vary. **Credit** AmEx, Disc, MC, V.

Where the New York Islanders hockey team (*see p340*) keeps sports in Long Island alive, and where you can also catch the occasional monster truck rally alongside the usual cavalcade of sell-out concerts.

Prudential Center

165 Mulberry Street, between Edison Place & Lafayette Street, Newark, NJ (1-973 757 6000, 1-800 745 3000 Ticketmaster, www.prucenter.com). PATH train to Newark. **Box office** 11am-6pm Mon-Fri. **Tickets** vary. **Credit** AmEx, MC, V.

The home of the New Jersey Devils hockey team (*see p340*) and – for now – the Nets basketball team (*see p339*) is one of the fanciest buildings in Newark.

Baseball

New York lays claim to the most storied baseball history of any city. The **New York Yankees** have won 27 World Series championships in its 100-plus year history, including an impressive romp through the 2009 play-offs, culminating in a World Series victory; they are perennial contenders. The **New York Mets**, who have not won the Series since 1986, are in less awesome shape; among their most recent campaign's lowlights was star pitcher Francisco Rodriguez sustaining a season-ending broken hand while punching his girlfriend's father.

Their new stadiums have received middling reviews. The pulled pork sandwiches at Citi Field's Blue Smoke restaurant are aces for the Mets, but the increased ticket prices and mall-ish feeling of the new Yankee Stadium are strikes against it. The Major League Baseball season runs from April to September, with play-offs in October.

NYC also has two minor-league clubs: the **Brooklyn Cyclones**, in Coney Island, and the **Staten Island Yankees**. While both may lack the star power of the big leagues, the price and surrounding stadium scenery can't be beat.

Brooklyn Cyclones *MCU Park, 1904 Surf Avenue, between W 17th & 19th Streets, Coney Island, Brooklyn (1-718 449 8497, www.brooklyncyclones.com). Subway D, F, N, Q to Coney Island-Stillwell Avenue.* **Box office** 10am-5pm Mon-Fri; 10am-4pm Sat. **Tickets** $4-$16. **Credit** AmEx, DC, Disc, MC, V.

★ **New York Mets** *Citi Field, Roosevelt Avenue, near 126th Street, Flushing, Queens (1-718 507 8499, newyork.mets.mlb.com). Subway 7 to Mets-Willets Point.* **Box office** 9am-6pm Mon-Fri; 9am-5pm Sat, Sun. **Tickets** $12-$440. **Credit** AmEx, DC, Disc, MC, V.

★ **New York Yankees** *Yankee Stadium, River Avenue, at 161st Street, Bronx (1-718 293 6000, newyork.yankees.mlb.com). Subway B, D, 4 to 161st Street-Yankee Stadium.* **Box office** 9am-5pm Mon-Sat; 10am-4pm Sun; also during games. **Tickets** $5-$300. **Credit** AmEx, DC, Disc, MC, V.

Staten Island Yankees *Richmond County Bank Ballpark, 75 Richmond Terrace, at Bay Street, Staten Island (1-718 720 9265, www.siyanks.com). Staten Island Ferry to St George Terminal.* **Box office** 10am-5pm Mon-Fri; also during games. **Tickets** $5-$13. **Credit** AmEx, DC, Disc, MC, V.

Basketball

After being an NBA force in the 1990s, the **New York Knicks** have spent the last decade in the wilderness, but they invariably inspire optimism at the beginning of each year. Many of this year's hopes centre on the acquisition of superstar Amar'e Soudemire in 2010. Now that the stalled Atlantic Yards development project is forging ahead, work has begun on the **New Jersey Nets**' future Brooklyn home, the Barclays Center, which is expected to be ready for the 2012-2013 season.

The NBA season begins at the tail end of October and runs into the middle of April (the play-offs last for quite a while), and it is then followed by the WNBA season in May, featuring the **New York Liberty** women's basketball team.

New York Knicks *Madison Square Garden* (for listings, *see p338*). *www.nba.com/knicks.com.* **Tickets** $35-$3,000.

New York Liberty *Madison Square Garden* (for listings, *see p338*). *www.wnba.com/liberty.com.* **Tickets** $10-$260.

New Jersey Nets *Prudential Center, Newark, NJ* (for listings, *see p338*). *1-800 765 6387, www.nba.com/nets.com.* **Tickets** $10-$1,950.

New Meadowlands Stadium.

Meadowlands Sports Complex. See p338.

Boxing

★ Church Street Boxing Gym

25 Park Place, between Broadway & Church Street, Financial District (1-212 571 1333, www.nyboxinggym.com). Subway 2, 3 to Park Place; 4, 5, 6 to Brooklyn Bridge-City Hall. **Open** varies. **Tickets** $30-$75. **Credit** (online purchases only) AmEx, MC, V. **Map** p402 E32.

Thanks to pound-for-pound superstars Floyd Mayweather and Manny Pacquiao, boxing has been enjoying a bit of a resurgence of late. This workout gym and amateur boxing venue has seen the likes of Mike Tyson and Roy Jones Jr since it opened in 1997.

Gleason's Gym

77 Front Street, 2nd floor, between Main & Washington Streets, Dumbo, Brooklyn (1-718 797 2872, www.gleasonsgym.net). Subway F to York Street. **Open** varies. **Tickets** $20. **Credit** AmEx, Disc, MC, V. **Map** p411 T11.

Gleason's is one of the legendary names in boxing history. Founded in 1937, when New York was the centre of the boxing universe, the gym was the sweat-stained home-from-home to fighters such as middleweights Jake La Motta, Thomas 'Hitman' Hearns and Marvin Hagler. Even though heavyweight boxers Muhammad Ali and Joe Frazier were rivals in the ring, they too both trained here.

Madison Square Garden

For listings, *see p338*. **Tickets** $25-$1,200.

The Garden still hosts some great pro fights, plus the annual Golden Gloves amateur championships.

Football

The **New York Jets** haven't been to the Super Bowl since 1969, but after years of mediocrity they have suddenly blossomed into one of the NFL's elite teams behind young quarterback Mark Sanchez. The **New York Giants** have been a disappointment since winning the title in 2008, yet remain one of the better teams, with a star quarterback of their own, Eli Manning. Tickets can be almost impossible to get (games sell out well ahead), but there are usually stray tickets floating around the internet in the lead-up to a gridiron clash. The season starts in September; play-offs are in January.

New York Giants *New Meadowlands Stadium* (for listings, *see p338*). *1-201 935 8222, www.giants.com.* **Tickets** $30-$300.

New York Jets *New Meadowlands Stadium* (for listings, *see p338*). *1-800 469 5387, www.newyorkjets.com.* **Tickets** $95-$150.

Hockey

Hockey doesn't have quite the following it used to in New York, but some of the young talents in the league (Alex Ovechkin, Sidney Crosby) ensure that there are reasons to tune in. The **New Jersey Devils** continue to play at a consistently high level at their digs in Newark; the **New York Rangers** and debonair Swedish goalie Henrik Lundqvist are still a draw; and the **New York Islanders**... are still the Isles. The season starts in late September or early October, and runs until April.

New Jersey Devils *Prudential Center* (for listings, *see p338*). *devils.nhl.com*. **Tickets** $7-$249.
New York Islanders *Nassau Veterans Memorial Coliseum* (for listings, *see p338*). *islanders.nhl.com*. **Tickets** $35-$195.
New York Rangers *Madison Square Garden* (for listings, *see p338*). *rangers.nhl.com*. **Tickets** $57-$288.

Horse racing

Thoroughbreds run at all three major racetracks near Manhattan, but the racing industry has taken a hit from declining interest in the sport coupled with the recession. High-profile events could be cancelled in 2011.

Aqueduct Racetrack

110-00 Rockaway Boulevard, at 110th Street, Jamaica, Queens (1-718 641 4700, www.nyra.com). Subway A to Aqueduct Racetrack. **Races** *Thoroughbred* Oct-Apr Wed-Sun. **Admission** free.
The Wood Memorial, New York's most important Kentucky Derby prep race, is usually held in April.

Belmont Park

2150 Hempstead Turnpike, Elmont, Long Island (1-516 488 6000, www.nyra.com). LIRR train from Penn Station to Belmont Park. **Races** *Thoroughbred* late Apr-Oct Wed-Sun. **Admission** $3. **No credit cards**.
This big beauty of an oval is home to the third and longest leg of US horse racing's Triple Crown, the mile-and-a-half Belmont Stakes in June.

Gleason's Gym.

INSIDE TRACK
PLAY WITH THE PROS

The **USTA Billie Jean King National Tennis Center** (1-718 760 6200, www.ntc.usta.com) may host the US Open (*see below*), but scrubs looking to experience the high life are welcome at its 46 courts the rest of the year (reservations are required two days in advance, $20-$62/hr). You might even spot a Williams sister or Roger Federer if you time it right.

Meadowlands Racetrack

Meadowlands Sports Complex (for listings, *see p338. 1-201 843 2446, www.thebigm.com).* **Races** *Thoroughbred* Sept-Nov. *Harness* Nov-Aug. **Admission** $1. **No credit cards**.
Meadowlands Racetrack offers an established programme of harness (trotting) and thoroughbred racing. In August, the prestigious Hambletonian Triple Crown harness race gets underway. *Photo p343.*

Soccer

In 2010, the **New York RedBulls** moved into a brand new home – the 25,000 seat RedBull Arena, about 45 minutes outside the city in Harrison, New Jersey – and acquired their first true superstar: Thierry Henry. They remain one of the more successful teams in the MLS, though not yet among the elite.
RedBulls *Red Bull Arena, 600 Cape May Street, Harrison, NJ (1-201 583 7000, www.newyork redbulls.com, www.redbullarena.us). PATH train from World Trade Center to Harrison Station.* **Tickets** $22-$45. **Credit** AmEx, Disc, MC, V.

Tennis

★ US Open

USTA Billie Jean King National Tennis Center, Flushing Meadows-Corona Park, Queens (1-866 673 6849, www.usopen.org). Subway 7 to Mets-Willets Point. **Tickets** $22-$120. **Credit** AmEx, DC, MC, V.
For two weeks in August and September every year, hordes of fans descend on Queens to watch the world's finest players compete for the US Open Championship in this Grand Slam tournament. Tickets go on sale in the spring.

Life in the Gutter

A louche new breed of bowling alley has more than balls.

Blame it on *The Big Lebowski*, the Coens' 1998 cult film that spawned a nationwide (and UK) screening-and-bowling festival, but the preserve of ageing, chain-smoking, overweight white dudes has experienced a serious shift in demographic.

Located inside Port Authority, **Leisure Time Bowl** (*see p344*) used to be your typically run-down, nicotine-stained alley. But after a slick revamp that includes a 'fast-food bistro' and lounge, it now enforces a dress code: guys aren't allowed to wear hats or baggy jeans (what would the Dude say?).

But it's not just about style; the latest spots go beyond the Bud-and-burger formula. Sweeping in on the ironically retro tide, the **Gutter** (200 North 14th Street, between Wythe Avenue & Berry Street, Williamsburg, Brooklyn, 1-718 387 3585, www.thegutterbrooklyn.com) opened in 2007. The eight-lane bowling alley looks straight out of early-1980s Milwaukee. Locals toss frames, then retreat to the lounge decorated with trophies and ancient beer signs, to drown their seven-ten-split sorrows. A dozen killer microbrews on tap include such local suds as Chelsea Checker Cab and Six Point Brownstone.

Hot on its rubber-soled heels, the much larger **Brooklyn Bowl** (*see p344*), which opened in summer 2009, ups the ante with a menu from favourite local eaterie Blue Ribbon (crispy pork rinds doused in cilantro and peppers, fatty brisket) and a full-size concert venue.

The block-long former 19th-century ironworks foundry takes its design cues from the Coney Island of the 1930s and '40s, with reproductions of old freak-show posters and carnival-game relics, and retro 'carny cocktails' (the potent Mind Reader features ginger liqueur, rye, honey and lemon). All of the beer – by Sixpoint, Kelso and next-door Brooklyn Brewery – is made in the borough.

Not to be outdone, Greenwich Village's **Bowlmor Lanes** (*see p343*) recently opened a carnival-style nightclub (www.carnivalnyc.com) on its top floor, mixing innocent amusements and debauchery.

The 16,000sq ft (1,500sq m) space has plenty of room for wandering stilt walkers, sword swallowers and jugglers, and you can try your hand at old-school shooting games or a dunk tank. If that all sounds a little tame, order the Dunk Tank: a two-gallon concoction of vodka, malibu, gin and juice.

Brooklyn Bowl.

Meadowlands Racetrack. *See p341.*

ACTIVE SPORTS

Gyms & sports centres

The fitness centres below offer single-day memberships. If you can schedule a workout during off-peak hours, there'll probably be less competition for machines. Call for class details.

★ Chelsea Piers

Piers 59-62, W 17th to W 23rd Streets, at Eleventh Avenue, Chelsea (1-212 336 6666, www.chelseapiers.com). Subway C, E to 23rd Street. **Open** varies. **Map** p403 C27.

Chelsea Piers is still the most impressive all-in-one athletic facility in New York. Between the Sky Rink (Pier 61, 1-212 336 6100), the bowling alley (between Piers 59 & 60, 1-212 835 2695) and the driving range (Pier 59, 1-212 336 6400) and scads of other choices, there's definitely something for everyone here. But wait, there's more! The Field House (Pier 62, 1-212 336 6500) has a climbing wall, a gymnastics training centre, batting cages and basketball courts. At the Sports Center Health Club (Pier 60, 1-212 336 6000), you'll find an expansive gym, complete with comprehensive weight deck and 100 cardiovascular machines plus classes covering everything from boxing to triathlon training in the 25-yard pool.

Crunch

404 Lafayette Street, between Astor Place & 4th Street, East Village (1-212 614 0120, www.crunch.com). Subway N, R to 8th Street-NYU; 6 to Astor Place. **Open** 24hrs from 5am Mon-9pm Sat; 8am-9pm Sun. **Admission** $35 day pass. **Credit** AmEx, Disc, MC, V. **Map** p403 F28.

With eight branches in Manhattan and two in Brooklyn, Crunch works hard to take the tedium out of a gym session; this East Village location features a boxing ring, Pilates sessions and a weekly evening DJ spot to amp up your workout.

Crunch is known for its roster of imaginative classes – for example, 'surfboarding' using a BOSU Balance Trainer and Gliding Discs; 'celebrity body' modelled on stars' workouts; and dance based on choreography in current Broadway shows.

Other locations throughout Manhattan and Brooklyn.

New York Sports Club

151 E 86th Street, between Lexington & Third Avenues, Upper East Side (1-800 301 1231, www.mysportsclub.com). Subway 4, 5, 6 to 86th Street. **Open** 5.30am-11pm Mon-Thur; 5am-10pm Fri; 7am-9pm Sat, Sun. **Admission** $25 day pass. **Credit** AmEx, Disc, MC, V. **Map** p406 F18.

A day membership at New York Sports Club includes aerobics classes and access to the weights room, cardio machines, steam room and sauna. The 62nd and 86th Street branches feature squash courts, and several locations have pools (the website allows you to search for specific features).

Other locations throughout the city.

Bowling

See also p342 **Life in the Gutter**.

Bowlmor Lanes

110 University Place, between 12th & 13th Streets, Greenwich Village (1-212 255 8188, www.bowlmor.com). Subway L, N, Q, R, 4, 5, 6 to

14th Street-Union Square. **Open** 4pm-1am Mon, Tue; 4pm-2am Wed, Thur; 11am-3am (under-21s not admitted after 7pm) Fri, Sat; 11am-1am Sun. **Cost** $12-$13 per person per game; $6 shoe hire. **Credit** AmEx, MC, V. **Map** p403 E28.
With 42 lanes, Bowlmor is the fanciest of New York City's bowling alleys. You can request drink service, and there's a new carnival-style nightclub on its top floor. For the budget conscious, every Monday is 'Night Strike': unlimited bowling after 9pm for $24.

★ Brooklyn Bowl

61 Wythe Avenue, between North 11th & North 12th Streets, Brooklyn (1-718 963 3369, www.brooklynbowl.com). Subway L to Bedford Avenue. **Open** (over-21s except noon-6pm Sat) 6pm-2am Mon-Thur; 6pm-4am Fri; noon-4am Sat; noon-2am Sun. **Cost** $20 per lane per 30mins Mon-Fri; $25 per lane per half hour Sat, Sun; $4 shoe hire. **Credit** AmEx, DC, MC, V. **Map** p411 U7.
Brooklyn's newest bowling alley is a sprawling homage to good food, local beer and casual bowlers. We say 'casual' because the pins seem to be strung together with fishing wire for easy resetting. It slightly affects the game, although not the fun.

Leisure Time Bowl

550 Ninth Avenue, between 40th & 41st Streets, Hell's Kitchen (1-212 268 6909, www.leisuretimebowl.com). Subway A, C, E to 42nd Street-Port Authority. **Open** 10am-midnight Mon-Wed; 10am-1am Thur; 10am-3am Fri; 11am-3am Sat; 11am-11pm Sun. **Cost** from $7 per game. **Credit** AmEx, Disc, MC, V. **Map** p404 C24.
This 26-lane alley in the Port Authority has eschewed bare-bones bowling for a more clubby atmosphere (there's even a dress code for the boys); it recently opened a 'fast-food bistro' and an arcade area.

Cycling

Cycling is a divisive topic in New York. The cyclists hate the motorists for driving in their bike lanes and often running them off the road, but the pedestrians hate the bikers for much the same reasons. Still, cycling is a great way to see the city – on two wheels you can cover more distance than by walking, without going underground or boarding a bus. The **Manhattan Waterfront Greenway**, a 32-mile (52-kilometre) route that circumnavigates the island of Manhattan, is a fantastic asset: you can now ride, uninterrupted, along the Hudson River from Battery Park up to the George Washington Bridge, at 178th Street. The free *NYC Cycling Map*, covering cycle lanes in all five boroughs, is available from the **Department of City Planning Bookstore** (22 Reade Street, between Broadway & Elk Street, Civic Center, open noon-4pm Mon, 10am-1pm Tue-Fri, 1-212 720 3667), or you can download it from www.nyc.gov/planning. You can also get free maps at **Transportation Alternatives** (Suite 1002, 10th Floor, 127 W 26th Street, between Sixth & Seventh Avenues, Chelsea, 1-212 629 8080, www.transalt.org, closed Sat & Sun), a non-profit group that lobbies for more bike-friendly streets, or download them from its website.

Organised bike rides are available from a number of outfits. The 'queer and queer-friendly' group **Fast & Fabulous** (1-212 567 7160, www.fastnfab.org) leads tours that usually meet in Central Park and head out of the city. **Five Borough Bicycle Club** (www.5bbc.org) offers a full slate of leisurely rides around the city, as well as jaunts that head further afield. Best of all, most trips are free. **Time's Up!** (1-212 802 8222, www.times-up.org), an alternative-transportation advocacy group, organises many of the city's most innovative cycling events, including the monthly Critical Mass and rides along the riverside. For other bike tours, *see p56*; for the annual **Bike New York: The Great Five Boro Bike Tour**, *see p268*.

Cycle hire is available from the following:

Bike and Roll *Pier 84, 557 Twelfth Avenue, at 43rd Street, Midtown (1-212 260 0400, www.bikeandroll.com/newyork). Subway A, C, E to 42nd Street-Port Authority.* **Open** (weather permitting) *mid Mar-mid May, Sept-mid Nov* 9am-7pm daily. *Mid May-Aug* 8am-8pm daily. **Rates** (incl helmet) $12-$20/hr; $39-$69/day. Rent at one branch and drop off at another for an extra $5. **Credit** AmEx, MC, V (credit card & ID required for rental). **Map** p404 B24.
Other locations throughout the city.

Gotham Bike Shop *112 W Broadway, between Duane & Reade Streets, Tribeca (1-212 732 2453, www.gothambikes.com). Subway A, C, 1, 2, 3 to Chambers Street.* **Open** 10am-6.30pm Mon, Wed, Fri, Sat; 10am-7.30pm Thur; 10.30am-5pm Sun. **Rates** (incl helmet) $10/hr; $30/24hrs. **Credit** AmEx, Disc, MC, V (credit card & ID required for rental). **Map** p402 E31.

Loeb Boathouse *Central Park, entrance on Fifth Avenue, at 72nd Street (1-212 517 2233, www.centralparknyc.org). Subway 6 to 68th Street-*

THE BEST RESERVOIR JOGS

Follow in the fitness footsteps of Jackie Kennedy Onassis, who used to jog around the Central Park reservoir that carries her name. The path commands spectacular views of the skyscrapers surrounding the park, especially when you reach the northern bank and look southwards.

Hunter College. **Open** 10am-6pm daily, weather permitting. **Rates** (incl helmet) $9-$15/hr. **No credit cards** (but required as ID for rental). **Map** p405 E20.

Metro Bicycles *1311 Lexington Avenue, at 88th Street, Upper East Side (1-212 427 4450, www.metrobicycles.com). Subway 4, 5, 6 to 86th Street*. **Open** usually 10am-6pm daily (call to check). **Rates** $9/hr; $45/day. **Credit** AmEx, Disc, MC, V. **Map** p406 E18.

Other locations throughout the city.

Horse riding

Kensington Stables

51 Caton Place, between Coney Island Avenue & E 8th Street, Kensington, Brooklyn (1-718 972 4588, www.kensingtonstables.com). Subway F to Fort Hamilton Parkway. **Open** 10am-dusk daily. **Rates** *Guided trail ride* $37/hr. *Private lessons* (reservations required) $57/hr. **Credit** AmEx, Disc, MC, V. **Map** p410 U13.

Designed in the pre-automotive age, Brooklyn's beautiful Prospect Park was meant to be explored by horseback. Guided rides can be tailored based on rider experience, but none is really necessary.

Ice skating

Pond at Bryant Park

Bryant Park, Sixth Avenue, between 40th & 42nd Streets, Midtown (1-212 768 4242, www.thepond atbryantpark.com). Subway B, D, F, M to 42nd Street-Bryant Park; 7 to Fifth Avenue. **Open** early Nov-mid Jan. **Rates** free. *Skate rental* $13. **No credit cards**. **Map** p404 E24.

Access to Bryant Park's seasonal 17,000sq ft rink is free if you have your own skates. From early November until Christmas the surrounding holiday crafts fair adds to the festive atmosphere.

Ice Rink at Rockefeller Center

1 Rockefeller Plaza, from 49th to 50th Streets, between Fifth & Sixth Avenues, Midtown (1-212 332 7654, www.patinagroup.com). Subway B, D, F, M to 47-50th Streets-Rockefeller Center. **Open** Oct-Mar. **Rates** $12-$16; $7.50-$8.50 reductions. *Skate rental* $8. **Credit** AmEx, DC, Disc, MC, V. **Map** p404 E23.

The most famous New York rink returns for its 75th season in 2011 – and it's bound to be as cramped as ever. Go early in the morning; otherwise, you can expect a one- to two-hour wait.

Trump Wollman Rink

Central Park, midpark at 62nd Street (1-212 439 6900, www.wollmanskatingrink.com). Subway N, R to Fifth Avenue-59th Street. **Open** *late Oct-Apr* 10am-2.30pm Mon, Tue; 10am-10pm Wed, Thur; 10am-11pm Fri, Sat; 10am-9pm Sun. **Rates** $10.50-$15; $4.75-$8.25 reductions. *Skate rental* $6.25. **No credit cards. Map** p405 E21.

Glide along beneath the trees of Central Park at this picturesque rink, which tends to be less crowded than Rockefeller Center's.

In-line skating

Many skaters congregate in Central Park, in and around the Mall (east of the Sheep Meadow, between 66th & 72nd Streets). The gear shop **Blades, Board & Skate** (156 W

Running in **Central Park**. *See p346.*

72nd Street, between Broadway & Columbus Avenue, 1-212 787 3911), convenient for the park, rents by the day ($20, incl helmet and other accoutrements).

Empire Skate Club of New York

1-212 774 1774, www.empireskate.org.
This club organises in-line and roller skating events, including island-hopping tours and the Tuesday Night Skate (weather permitting): meet outside Blades, Board & Skate (*see above*) at 8pm.

Kayaking

New York's waterways are an underappreciated part of the visitor's experience. Don't be afraid to see them up close in a one-person craft, but, for safety's sake, join an organised expedition.

Downtown Boathouse

Pier 96, Clinton Cove Park, 56th Street & West Side Highway, Hell's Kitchen (no phone, www.downtownboathouse.org). Subway A, C, E, 1 to Columbus Circle. **Open** *mid May-mid Oct* 9am-6pm Sat, Sun. *Classes* 6-8pm Wed (check website calendar for topics). **Rates** free. **Map** p405 B22.
Weather permitting, this volunteer-run organisation offers free, no-reservations kayaking in front of the boathouses, at three locations. Twenty-minute paddles are offered on a first-come, first-served basis. You must be able to swim.
Other locations Pier 40, West Side Highway, at W Houston Street; Riverside Park promenade, at 72nd Street.

Manhattan Kayak Company

Pier 66, Twelfth Avenue, at 26th Street, Chelsea (1-212 924 1788, www.manhattankayak.com). Subway C, E to 23rd Street. **Open** varies. **Rates** vary. **Credit** AmEx, DC, Disc, MC, V. **Map** p404 B26.
Run by veteran kayaker Eric Stiller, Manhattan Kayak offers a range of classes from beginners' to advanced, as well as tours. Adventures include an easy 90-minute Paddle & Pub Tour ($65) that ends at a bar, and a 3.5-hour circumnavigation of the Statue of Liberty ($125).

Running

Battery Park City's promenade, Riverside Park, rambling Central Park and Brooklyn's Prospect Park are all excellent running terrain.

New York Road Runners

9 E 89th Street, between Fifth & Madison Avenues, Upper East Side (1-212 860 4455, www.nyrrc.org). Subway 4, 5, 6 to 86th Street. **Open** 10am-8pm Mon-Fri; 10am-5pm Sat; 10am-3pm Sun. **Rates** vary. **Credit** AmEx, DC, MC, V. **Map** p406 E18.
Hardly a weekend passes without some sort of run or race sponsored by the NYRR, which is responsible for the New York City Marathon (*see p266*). Most races take place in Central Park and are open to the public. The club also offers classes and clinics.

NYC Hash House Harriers

1-212 427 4692, www.hashnyc.com. **Rates** $15 (covers food & beer after the run).
Hashing is a fantastic mix of exercise and debauchery. This group has been running around New York for over two decades. Their sport of choice consists of a 'hare' who plots a trail, which is deciphered and followed by the group. Afterwards, beer and bawdy songs are an integral part of the whole experience.

Swimming

The Harlem, Vanderbilt and West Side **YMCA**s (www.ymcanyc.org) have pools, as do some private gyms and many hotels. The city of New York also maintains several facilities. Its outdoor pools are free and open from late June to Labor Day (the first Monday in September): **Hamilton Fish** (Pitt Street, between Houston & Stanton Streets, 1-212 387 7687); **Asser Levy Pool** (23rd Street, between First Avenue & FDR Drive, 1-212 447 2020); **Tony Dapolito Recreation Center** (Clarkson Street, at Seventh Avenue South, 1-212 242 5228); **Recreation Center 54** (348 54th Street, between First & Second Avenues, 1-212 754 5411), which has an indoor pool; and, finally, the **Floating Pool Lady** (Barretto Point Park, 1-718 430 4601) – a seven-lane pool facility set on a barge in Hunts Point, Bronx. For a complete list, visit www.nycgovparks.org/facilities/pools.

Table tennis

New York Table Tennis Foundation

384 Broadway, between Walker & White Streets, Chinatown (1-646 772 2922, www.nyttf.com). Subway J, M, N, Q, R, Z, 6 to Canal Street. **Open** 1-10.30pm Mon-Thur; 2.30-11pm Fri; 11am-11pm Sat; 11am-6.30pm Sun. **Rates** $10 per person per hr. **Credit** AmEx, MC, V. **Map** p403 E27.
You'd better bring your A game and your best paddle to this underground table-tennis training facility. Casual players are welcome, but serious (very serious!) players are the majority of the clientele. Private lessons and workshops are offered at weekends.

Tennis

From April to November, the city maintains excellent municipal courts throughout the five boroughs. Single-play (one-hour) tickets cost $7. For a list of courts, visit www.nycgovparks.org/facilities/tennis.

Theatre

The curtain never falls.

In the shorthand of mass culture, the term 'Broadway' represents the highest echelon of theatrical achievement. In reality, things are somewhat different. The Great White Way is still the place to go for big musicals: the heart of mainstream New York theatre is pumping with fresh vigour in the 21st century, with the steady beat of blockbusters such as *Wicked* and *Jersey Boys*, as well as fresh infusions from smaller hits such as *Next to Normal*. But many of the best new plays, and the most original voices, can be found on the more intimate stages known as Off Broadway and Off-Off Broadway.

STAGE NOTES

The dazzling marquees of Broadway are increasingly powered by star wattage. Hugh Jackman, Denzel Washington, Scarlett Johansson, Daniel Craig, James Gandolfini and Catherine Zeta-Jones are just a few of the Hollywood draws that have recently boosted the box office. Musicals rely much less on star casting, but because shows are so expensive to stage, producers tend to favour the familiar: adaptations of hit movies (such as *Billy Elliot* and *The Addams Family*) have become common. At the time of writing, Broadway is steeling itself for the $60 million adaptation of *Spider-Man: Turn Off the Dark*, due to open in early 2011 with a score by U2's Bono and The Edge. A revival of *How to Succeed in Business without Really Trying*, starring Daniel Radcliffe, opened in April 2011.

TICKETS & INFORMATION

Nearly all Broadway and Off Broadway shows are served by one of the city's 24-hour ticketing agencies (we've provided them in our listings where relevant). For cheap seats, your best bet is one of the Theatre Development Fund's **TKTS** discount booths (*see p260*). If you're interested in seeing more than one Off-Off Broadway show or dance event, you might consider purchasing a set of four vouchers ($36) from the TDF, either online or at their offices (*see below* **TKTS**). For more ticket tips, *see p349, p357 and p360* **Inside Track**.

TKTS

Father Duffy Square, Broadway & 47th Street, Theater District (www.tdf.org). Subway N, Q, R, S, 1, 2, 3, 7 to 42nd Street-Times Square. **Open** *For evening tickets* 3-8pm Mon, Wed-Sat; 2-8pm Tue; 3-7pm Sun. *For same-day matinée tickets* 10am-2pm Wed, Sat; 11am-3pm Sun. **Credit** AmEx, DC, Disc, MC. **Map** p404 D24.

At this architecturally striking new base (*see p98* **Not Just the Ticket**), you can get tickets on the day of the performance for as much as 50% off face value. Although there is often a queue when it opens for business, this has usually dispersed one to two hours later, so it's worth trying your luck an hour or two before the show. The Downtown and Brooklyn branches, which are much less busy and open earlier (so you can secure your tickets on the morning of the show), also sell matinée tickets the day before a show (see website for hours). Never buy tickets from anyone who approaches you in the queue as they may have been obtained illegally.

Other locations Corner of Front & John Streets, South Street Seaport; 1 Metrotech Center, corner of Jay Street & Myrtle Avenue Promenade, Downtown Brooklyn.

BROADWAY

Technically speaking, 'Broadway' is the theatre district that surrounds Times Square on either side of Broadway (the actual avenue), mainly between 41st and 53rd Streets. This is where you'll find the grandest theatres in town: wood-panelled, frescoed jewel boxes, mostly built between 1900 and 1930. Officially, 39 of

them – those with more than 500 seats – are designated as being part of Broadway (plus the Vivian Beaumont Theater, uptown at Lincoln Center). Full-price tickets can set you back more than $100; the very best (so-called 'premium') seats may go up to $350.

The big shows are still there, and hard to miss. At any given point, however, there are also a handful of new plays, as well as serious revivals of classic dramas by the likes of Arthur Miller, Tennessee Williams and August Wilson. Each season also usually includes several small, artistically adventurous musicals to balance out the rafter-rattlers.

Long-running shows

Straight plays can provide some of Broadway's most stirring experiences, but they're less likely than musicals to enjoy long runs. Check *Time Out New York* magazine for current listings and reviews. (The playing schedules listed below are subject to change.)

The Addams Family

Lunt-Fontanne Theater, 205 W 46th Street, between Broadway and Eighth Avenue (1-800 982 2787, http://theaddamsfamilymusical.com). Subway A, C, E to 42nd St–Port Authority; N, Q, R to 42nd St S, 1, 2, 3, 7 to 42nd St–Times Square. **Box office** 10am-8pm Mon, Tue; 10am-8.30pm Wed-Sat; noon-6pm Sun. **Shows** 7pm Tue; 2pm, 8pm Wed; 8pm Thur, Fri; 2pm, 8pm Sat; 3pm Sun. **Length** 2hrs 30min; 1 intermission. **Tickets** $99-$134. **Credit** AmEx, Disc, MC, V. **Map** p404 D23.

Inspired by Charles Addams's macabre cartoons, this musical features pleasant, clever songs (by Andrew Lippa), sly jokes (by book writers Marshall Brickman and Rick Elice) and swoony visuals – yet the whole never soars to the heights we expect of a bona fide hit. But although the production could be edgier and more grotesque, it's not the crass theme-park disaster that some say it is. Nathan Lane, Bebe Neuwirth and a generally strong ensemble land their jokes and numbers with aplomb.

★ American Idiot

St James Theatre, 246 W 44th Street, between Broadway and Eighth Avenue (1-212 239 6200, http://americanidiotonbroadway.com). Subway A, C, E to 42nd Street–Port Authority; N, Q, R, S, 1, 2, 3, 7 to 42nd Street–Times Square. **Box office** 10am-8pm Mon-Sat; noon-6pm Sun. **Shows** 7pm Tue; 8pm Mon, Wed-Fri; 2pm, 8pm Sat; 3pm, 7.30pm Sun. **Length** 95min; no intermission. **Tickets** $32-$252. **Credit** AmEx, Disc, MC, V. **Map** p404 D24.

For the 95 minutes that this Green Day-scored rock musical has you in its white-knuckle grasp, it will electrify and overwhelm your senses. Michael Mayer pulls out all the directorial stops in this orgy of floor-pounding dance, video washes, concert lighting and constant movement. Suburban anomie, urban ennui and wartime tragedy: *American Idiot* is *Hair*'s sullen, cynical grandchild.

★ Billy Elliot

Imperial Theatre, 249 W 45th Street, between Broadway & Eighth Avenue, Theater District (Telecharge 1-212 239 6200, www.billyelliot broadway.com). Subway A, C, E to 42nd Street-Port Authority. **Box office** 10am-8.30pm Mon-Sat; noon-6pm Sun. **Shows** 7pm Tue; 2pm, 7.30pm Wed, Sat; 7.30pm Thur, Fri; 3pm Sun. **Length** 2hrs 50mins; 1 intermission. **Tickets** $41.50-$301.50. **Credit** AmEx, DC, Disc, MC, V. **Map** p404 D24.

Heart, grit and spectacular dancing make this London import – based on the beloved 2000 movie about an English mining-town boy who dreams of being a ballet dancer – one of the most passionate and exhilarating shows to land on Broadway in years. Stephen Daldry's superb direction pulls together dance, working-class drama and domestic tear-jerking into an electrifying whole.

Chicago

Ambassador Theatre, 219 W 49th Street, between Broadway and Eighth Avenue (1-212 239 6200, http://chicagothemusical.com). Subway C, E to 50th Street; N, R to 49th Street; 1 to 50th Street. **Box office** 10am-8pm Mon-Sat. **Shows** 8pm Mon, Tue, Thur, Fri; 2.30pm, 8pm Sat; 2.30pm, 7pm Sun. **Length** 2hrs 30mins; 1 intermission. **Tickets** $118-$289. **Credit** AmEx, Disc, MC, V. **Map** p404 D23.

This John Kander-Fred Ebb-Bob Fosse favourite – revived by director Walter Bobbie and choreographer Ann Reinking – tells the saga of chorus girl Roxie Hart, who murders her lover and, with the help of a huckster lawyer, becomes a vaudeville star.

Jersey Boys

August Wilson Theatre, 245 W 52nd Street, between Broadway & Eighth Avenue, Theater District (Telecharge 1-212 239 6200, www.jerseyboysinfo.com/broadway). Subway C, E, 1 to 50th Street. **Box office** 10am-8pm Mon-Sat;

INSIDE TRACK RUSH TICKETS

Some of the cheapest tickets on Broadway are 'rush' tickets, purchased on the day of a show at a theatre's box office (not all theatres have them). On average, they cost $25. Some venues reserve them for students, while others use a lottery system that's held two hours before the performance.

Lincoln Center Theater. *See p355.*

noon-6pm Sun. **Shows** 7pm Tue; 2pm, 8pm Wed, Sat; 8pm Thur, Fri; 3pm Sun. **Length** 2hrs 15mins; 1 intermission. **Tickets** $96.50-$351.50. **Credit** AmEx, DC, Disc, MC, V. **Map** p404 D23.
The Broadway musical finally does right by the jukebox with this nostalgic behind-the-music tale, presenting the Four Seasons' infectiously energetic 1960s tunes (including 'Walk Like a Man' and 'Big Girls Don't Cry') as they were intended to be performed. A dynamic cast under the sleek direction of Des McAnuff ensures that Marshall Brickman and Rick Elice's script feels canny instead of canned.

Wicked

Gershwin Theatre, 222 W 51st Street, between Broadway & Eighth Avenue, Theater District (Ticketmaster 1-800 982 2787, www.wicked themusical.com). Subway C, E, 1 to 50th Street.
Box office 10am-8pm Mon-Sat; noon-6pm Sun. **Shows** 7pm Tue; 2pm, 8pm Wed, Sat; 8pm Thur, Fri; 3pm Sun. **Length** 2hrs 45mins; 1 intermission. **Tickets** $51.25-$301.25. **Credit** AmEx, Disc, MC, V. **Map** p404 D23.
Based on novelist Gregory Maguire's 1995 riff on *The Wizard of Oz* mythology, *Wicked* is a witty prequel to the classic children's book and legendary movie. The show's combination of pop dynamism and sumptuous spectacle has made it the most popular show on Broadway. Teenage girls, especially, have responded in force to the story of how a green girl named Elphaba comes to be known as the Wicked Witch of the West. *Photos p353.*

OFF BROADWAY

As the cost of mounting a show on Broadway continues to soar, many serious playwrights are opening their shows in the less financially demanding environment of the Off Broadway houses. The theatres here have between 100 and 499 seats; tickets usually run from $35 to $75. Here, we've listed some reliable long-running shows, plus some of the best theatres and repertory companies.

Long-running shows

Avenue Q

New World Stages, 340 W 50th Street, between Eighth & Ninth Avenues, Theater District (Telecharge 1-212 239 6200, www.avenueq.com). Subway C, E, 1 to 50th Street.
Box office 1-6pm Mon, Sun; 1-7.30pm Tue-Sat. **Shows** 8pm Mon, Wed-Fri; 2pm, 8pm Sat; 3pm Sun. **Length** 2hrs 15mins; 1 intermission. **Tickets** $69.50-$126.50. **Credit** AmEx, DC, Disc, MC, V. **Map** p404 D23.
After seven years – that include a Broadway run and then a return to its Off Broadway roots – the sassy and clever puppet musical doesn't show its age. The current cast is perfectly capable and likable, and Robert Lopez and Jeff Marx's deft *Sesame Street*-esque novelty tunes about porn and racism still earn their laughs. *Avenue Q* remains a sly and winning piece of metamusical tomfoolery.

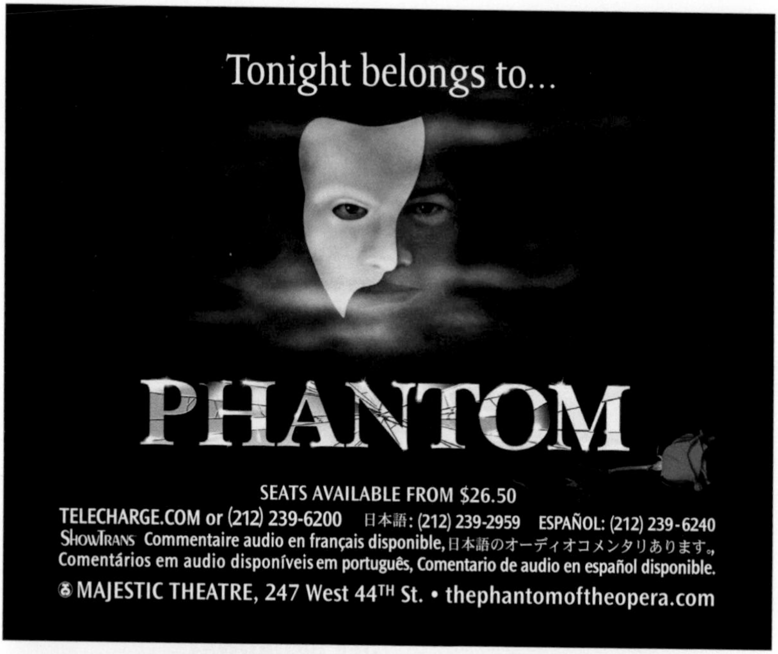
Tonight belongs to...
PHANTOM
SEATS AVAILABLE FROM $26.50
TELECHARGE.COM or (212) 239-6200 日本語: (212) 239-2959 ESPAÑOL: (212) 239-6240
ShowTrans Commentaire audio en français disponible, 日本語のオーディオコメンタリあります。,
Comentários em audio disponíveis em português, Comentario de audio en español disponible.
MAJESTIC THEATRE, 247 West 44TH St. • thephantomoftheopera.com

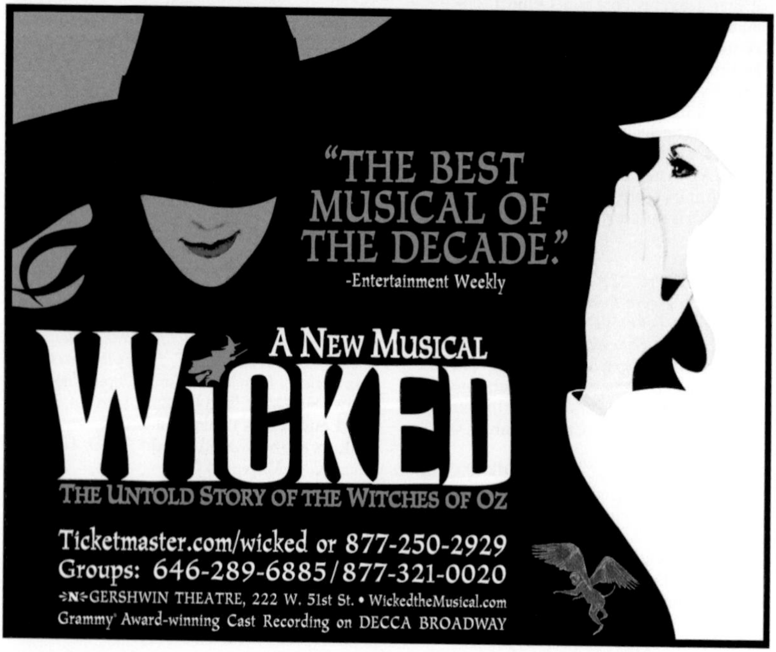
"THE BEST MUSICAL OF THE DECADE."
-Entertainment Weekly
A NEW MUSICAL
WICKED
THE UNTOLD STORY OF THE WITCHES OF OZ
Ticketmaster.com/wicked or 877-250-2929
Groups: 646-289-6885/877-321-0020
GERSHWIN THEATRE, 222 W. 51st St. • WickedtheMusical.com
Grammy Award-winning Cast Recording on DECCA BROADWAY

Blue Man Group

Astor Place Theatre, 434 Lafayette Street, between Astor Place & E 4th Street, East Village (1-212 254 4370, www.blueman.com). Subway N, R to 8th Street-NYU; 6 to Astor Place. **Box office** noon-7.45pm daily. **Shows** 8pm Mon-Thur; 7pm, 10pm Fri; 2pm, 5pm, 8pm Sat, Sun. **Length** 2hrs; no intermission. **Tickets** $69-$79. **Credit** AmEx, DC, Disc, MC, V. **Map** p403 F28.

Three deadpan men with extraterrestrial imaginations (and head-to-toe blue body paint) carry this long-time favourite, which may be the world's most accessible piece of multimedia performance art. A weird, exuberant trip through the trappings of modern culture, the show is as smart as it is ridiculous.

Fuerza Bruta: Look Up

Daryl Roth Theatre, 101 E 15th Street, at Union Square East (1-212 239 6200). Subway L, N, Q, R, 4, 5, 6 to 14th Street–Union Square. **Box office** 1pm-showtime Tue-Sun. **Shows** 8pm Tue-Fri; 7pm, 10pm Sat; 7pm Sun. **Length** 65mins; no intermission. **Tickets** $79. **Credit** AmEx, Disc, MC, V. **Map** p403 D27.

This visually impressive dance-rave thrill ride from Buenos Aires – half techno party, half avant-garde mood piece – includes a glum urban everyman on a treadmill, wet girls flopping on to a plastic ceiling and lots of angry stomp-dancing. Neither director Diqui James nor his energetic ensemble seems to care much about what it all means.

Repertory companies & venues

Atlantic Theater Company

336 W 20th Street, between Eighth & Ninth Avenues, Chelsea (Telecharge 1-212 239 6200, www.atlantictheater.org). Subway C, E to 23rd Street. **Box office** 6-8pm Tue-Fri; noon-2pm, 6-8pm Sat; 1-3pm Sun. **Tickets** $35-$65. **Credit** AmEx, DC, Disc, MC, V. **Map** p403 D27.

Created in 1985 as an offshoot of acting workshops led by playwright David Mamet and actor William H Macy, the dynamic Atlantic Theater Company has presented dozens of new plays, including Martin McDonagh's *The Lieutenant of Inishmore* and Duncan Sheik and Steven Sater's *Spring Awakening*. Both productions transferred to Broadway. Its 25th anniversary season was celebrated with a production of Harold Pinter's *The Collection* and *A Kind of Alaska*.

★ Brooklyn Academy of Music

Harvey Theater, 651 Fulton Street, between Ashland & Rockwell Places, Fort Greene, Brooklyn (1-718 636 4100, www.bam.org). Subway B, Q, 2, 3, 4, 5 to Atlantic Avenue; D, M, N, R to Pacific Street; G to Fulton Street. **Box office** noon-6pm Mon-Fri; noon-4pm Sat, Sun. **Tickets** $30-$90. **Credit** AmEx, DC, Disc, MC, V. **Map** p410 T10.

Wicked. *See p351.*

BAM's beautifully distressed Harvey Theater – along with its grand old opera house (two blocks away on Lafayette Avenue) – is the site of the annual multidisciplinary Next Wave Festival (*see p266*), as well as other international offerings. Recent headliners include a Cheek by Jowl staging of *Macbeth* and a *King Lear* starring Sir Derek Jacobi that closes in June 2011.

Classic Stage Company

136 E 13th Street, between Third & Fourth Avenues, East Village (1-212 677 4210, www.classicstage.org). Subway L, N, Q, R, 4, 5, 6 to 14th Street-Union Square. **Box office** noon-5pm Mon-Fri. **Tickets** $55-$75. **Credit** AmEx, DC, MC, V. **Map** p403 F27.

With a purview that includes Chekhov drama, medieval mystery plays and Elizabethan standards, Classic Stage Company (under artistic director Brian Kulick) makes the old new again with performances including open rehearsals, staged readings and full-blown productions. The company has a knack for attracting major stars, as a recent production of *Three Sisters* with Maggie Gyllenhaal and Peter Sarsgaard attests.

59E59

59 E 59th Street, between Madison & Park Avenues, Upper East Side (Ticket Central 1-212 279 4200, www.59e59.org). Subway N, R to Lexington Avenue-59th Street; 4, 5, 6 to 59th Street. **Box office** noon-7pm daily. **Tickets** $15-$60. **Credit** AmEx, DC, MC, V. **Map** p405 E22.

This chic, state-of-the-art venue, which comprises an Off Broadway space and two smaller theatres, is home to the Primary Stages company. It's also where you'll find the annual Brits Off Broadway festival, which imports some of the UK's best work for brief summer runs.

Flea Theater

41 White Street, between Broadway & Church Street, Tribeca (1-212 226 2407, www.theflea.org). Subway A, C, E, J, M, N, Q, R, Z, 1, 6 to Canal Street. **Box office** noon-6pm Mon-Sat. **Tickets** $15-$60. **Credit** AmEx, DC, MC, V. **Map** p402 E31.

Founded in 1997, Jim Simpson's cosy and well-appointed venue has presented avant-garde experimentation (such as the work of Mac Wellman) and politically provocative satires (by the likes of AR Gurney and Jonathan Reynolds). A second, basement theatre is home to the Flea's resident young acting company, the Bats.

Irish Repertory Theatre

132 W 22nd Street, between Sixth & Seventh Avenues, Chelsea (1-212 727 2737, www.irishrepertorytheatre.org). Subway F, M, 1 to 23rd Street. **Box office** 10am-6pm Mon-Fri; 11am-6pm Sat, Sun. **Tickets** $55-$60. **Credit** AmEx, DC, MC, V. **Map** p404 D26.

This company puts on compelling shows by Irish and Irish-American playwrights. Fine revivals of classics by the likes of Oscar Wilde and George Bernard Shaw alternate with plays by lesser-known modern authors. Its world premiere of Kelly Younger's *Banished Children of Eve* was very warmly received during the 2010-11 season.

Lincoln Center Theater

Lincoln Center, 150 W 65th Street, at Broadway, Upper West Side (Telecharge 1-212 239 6200, www.lct.org). Subway 1 to 66th Street-Lincoln Center. **Box office** 10am-8pm Mon-Sat; noon-6pm Sun. **Tickets** $35-$125. **Credit** AmEx, DC, Disc, MC, V. **Map** p405 C21.

The majestic and prestigious Lincoln Center Theater complex has a pair of amphitheatre-style drama venues. The Broadway house, the 1,138-seat Vivian Beaumont Theater is home to star-studded and elegant major productions. (When the Beaumont is tied up in long runs, such as the recent *South Pacific*, LCT presents its larger works at available Times Square theatres.) Downstairs from the Beaumont is the 338-seat Mitzi E Newhouse Theater, an Off Broadway space devoted to new work by the upper layer of American playwrights. In an effort to shake off its reputation for stodginess, in 2008, Lincoln Center launched LCT3, which presents the work of emerging playwrights and directors at the Duke (229 W 42nd Street, between Seventh and Eighth Avenues). All tickets are $20; see LCT website for details. *Photo p351.*

► *For music and festivals at Lincoln Center, see p312, and p264 and p265, respecitvely.*

Manhattan Theatre Club

Samuel J Friedman Theatre, 261 W 47th Street, between Broadway & Eighth Avenue, Theater

The Player's Club

Hobnob with the ghosts of Edwin Booth et al.

Granted, the **Player's Club** (16 Gramercy Park South, between Park Avenue South and Irving Place, 1-212 475 6116) is a little creaky, dim and desperately in need of a millionaire patron to shower some money upon it, but this club for theatrical folk is soaked in the history of the stage (more than 120 years of it). We love the second-floor library full of obscure plays from the early 20th century, and have enjoyed numerous readings at the monthly Project Shaw events. So, grab a martini and dust off your choicest bon mots. Who knows when the curtain will go down for the last time...?

Billy Elliot. *See p349.*

District (Telecharge 1-212 239 6200, www.manhattantheatreclub.com). Subway N, Q, R, S, 1, 2, 3, 7 to 42nd Street-Times Square. **Box office** noon-6pm Tue-Sun. **Tickets** $52-$111. **Credit** AmEx, DC, MC, V. **Map** p404 D24.
One of the city's most important non-profit companies, Manhattan Theatre Club spent decades as an Off Broadway outfit before moving into the 622-seat Friedman theatre in 2003. But it still maintains a 299-seat pied-à-terre at New York City Center (131 W 55th Street, between Sixth & Seventh Avenues), where it presents some of its best material – such as Lynn Nottage's 2009 Pulitzer Prize winner, *Ruined*. Twentysomethings (and indeed those under 20) can sign up for the 30 Under 30 Club to get tickets at both theatres for $30.

Mint Theater Company

3rd Floor, 311 W 43rd Street, between Eighth & Ninth Avenues, Theater District (1-212 315 0231, www.minttheater.org). Subway A, C, E to 42nd Street-Port Authority. **Box office** noon-6pm Mon-Sat; 11am-3pm Sun. **Tickets** $45-$55. **Credit** AmEx, DC, MC, V. **Map** p404 D24.
The Mint specialises in theatrical archaeology, unearthing obscure but worthy plays for a full airing. Recent productions have included rarities by AA Milne, DH Lawrence and JB Priestley.

New Victory Theater

209 W 42nd Street, between Seventh & Eighth Avenues, Theater District (1-646 223 3020, Telecharge 1-212 239 6200, www.newvictory.org). Subway N, Q, R, S, 1, 2, 3, 7 to 42nd Street-Times Square. **Box office** 11am-5pm Mon, Sun; noon-7pm Tue-Sat. **Tickets** $12.50-$35. **Credit** AmEx, DC, MC, V. **Map** p404 D24.
The New Victory Theater is a perfect symbol of the transformation that has occurred in Times Square. Built in 1900, Manhattan's oldest surviving theatre became a strip club and adult cinema in the sleazy days of the 1970s and '80s. Renovated by the city in 1995, the building now functions as a kind of kiddie Brooklyn Academy of Music, offering a full season of smart, adventurous, reasonably priced and family-friendly plays (including many international productions).

New World Stages

340 W 50th Street, between Eighth & Ninth Avenues, Theater District (Telecharge 1-239 6200, www.newworldstages.com). Subway C, E, 1 to 50th Street. **Box office** 1-6pm Mon, Sun; 1-7.30pm Tue-Sat. **Tickets** $25-$75. **Credit** AmEx, DC, MC, V. **Map** p404 C23.
Formerly a movie multiplex, this centre – one of the last bastions of commercial Off Broadway in New York – boasts a shiny, space-age interior and five stages, presenting everything from campy revues such as *Naked Boys Singing* to, more recently, the Broadway transfers *Avenue Q* and *The 39 Steps*.

★ New York Theatre Workshop

79 E 4th Street, between Bowery & Second Avenue, East Village (1-212 460 5475, www.nytw.org). Subway F to Lower East Side-Second Avenue; 6 to Astor Place. **Box office** 1-6pm Tue-Sun. **Tickets** $45-$65. **Credit** AmEx, DC, MC, V. **Map** p403 F29.
Founded in 1979, the New York Theatre Workshop works with emerging directors eager to take on challenging pieces. Besides plays by world-class artists like Caryl Churchill (*Far Away, A Number*) and Tony Kushner (*Homebody/Kabul*), this company also premièred *Rent*, Jonathan Larson's Pulitzer Prize-winning musical. The iconoclastic Flemish director Ivo van Hove has made the NYTW his New York pied-à-terre.

★ Playwrights Horizons

416 W 42nd Street, between Ninth & Tenth Avenues, Theater District (Ticket Central 1-212 279 4200, www.playwrightshorizons.org). Subway A, C, E to 42nd Street-Port Authority. **Box office** noon-8pm daily. **Tickets** $50-$75. **Credit** AmEx, DC, MC, V. **Map** p404 C24.
More than 300 important contemporary plays have premièred here, among them dramas such as *Driving Miss Daisy* and *The Heidi Chronicles* and musicals such as Stephen Sondheim's *Assassins* and *Sunday in the Park with George*. Recent seasons have included works by Craig Lucas and an acclaimed musical version of the cult film *Grey Gardens*.

★ Public Theater

425 Lafayette Street, between Astor Place & E 4th Street, East Village (1-212 539 8500, Telecharge 1-212 239 6200, www.publictheater.org). Subway N, R to 8th Street-NYU; 6 to Astor Place. **Box office** 1-6pm Mon, Sun; 1-7.30pm Tue-Sat. **Tickets** $50-$70. **Credit** AmEx, DC, MC, V. **Map** p403 F28.
The civic-minded Oskar Eustis is artistic director of this local institution dedicated to producing the work of new American playwrights but also known for its Shakespeare productions (Shakespeare in the Park). The building, an Astor Place landmark, has five stages, and is home to one of the city's most dynamic

INSIDE TRACK UNDERSTUDY REFUNDS

If you've come to see a particular performer on Broadway, you may be able to cash in your ticket if that star doesn't show up. As a general rule, you are entitled to a refund if the star's name appears above the title of the show. A card on the wall of the lobby will announce any absences that day – go to the box office if you want your money back.

Fuerza Bruta: Look Up. *See p353.*

troupes: the Labyrinth Theater Company, co-founded by actor Philip Seymour Hoffman.
▶ *The building is also home to Joe's Pub; see p323.*

Roundabout Theatre Company

American Airlines Theatre, 227 W 42rd Street between Seventh & Eighth Avenues, Theater District (1-212 719 1300, www.roundabout theatre.org). Subway N, Q, R, S, 1, 2, 3, 7 to 42nd Street-Times Square. **Box office** noon-6pm Tue-Sun. **Tickets** $63.75-$111.50. **Credit** AmEx, DC, MC, V. **Map** p404 D24.

Devoted entirely to revivals, the Roundabout pairs beloved old chestnuts with celebrity casts; it was the force behind recent stagings of *Sunday in the Park with George* by Stephen Sondheim and James Lapine, and Shaw's *Pygmalion*. In addition to its Broadway flagship, the company also mounts shows at Studio 54 (254 W 54th Street, between Broadway & Eighth Avenue) and Off Broadway's Laura Pels Theatre (111 W 46th Street, between Sixth & Seventh Avenues).

St Ann's Warehouse

38 Water Street, between Dock & Main Streets, Dumbo, Brooklyn (1-718 254 8779, www.stanns warehouse.org). Subway A, C to High Street; F to York Street. **Box office** 1-7pm Tue-Sat. **Tickets** $25-$75. **Credit** AmEx, DC, Disc, MC, V. **Map** p411 S9.

The adventurous theatergoer's alternative to BAM (*see p353*), St Ann's Warehouse offers an eclectic line-up of theatre and music. Recent shows have included high-level work by the Wooster Group and National Theatre of Scotland.

Second Stage Theatre

307 W 43rd Street, at Eighth Avenue, Theater District (1-212 246 4422, www.2st.com). Subway A, C, E to 42nd Street-Port Authority. **Box office** 10am-7pm Mon; 10am-8pm Tue-Sat; 10am-3pm Sun. **Tickets** $56-$70. **Credit** AmEx, DC, Disc, MC, V. **Map** p404 D24.

Occupying a beautiful Rem Koolhaas-designed space near Times Square, Second Stage Theatre specialises in American playwrights, and it hosted the New York première of Edward Albee's *Peter and Jerry*. Following in the footsteps of the Roundabout and the Manhattan Theatre Club, the company has announced plans to expand into Broadway's Helen Hayes Theatre.

Shakespeare in the Park at the Delacorte Theater

Park entrance on Central Park West, at 81st Street, then follow the signs (1-212 539 8750, www.publictheater.org). Subway B, C to 81st Street-Museum of Natural History. **Tickets** free. **Map** p405 D19.

The Delacorte Theater in Central Park is the fair-weather sister of the Public Theater (*see p357*). When

Starshine Burlesque. *See p360.*

not producing Shakespeare in the East Village, the Public offers the best of the Bard outdoors during the New York Shakespeare Festival (June-Sept). Free tickets (two per person) are distributed at the Delacorte at 1pm on the day of the performance. Around 9am is usually a good time to begin waiting, although the queue can start forming as early as 6am when big-name stars are on the bill. You can also enter an online lottery for tickets.
▶ *See p106 for other Central Park attractions.*

Signature Theatre Company

555 W 42nd Street, between Tenth & Eleventh Avenues, Midtown (1-212 244 7529, www.signaturetheatre.org). Subway A, C, E to 42nd Street-Port Authority. **Box office** 1-7pm Tue-Sat; noon-6pm Sun. **Tickets** $20-$65. **Credit** AmEx, DC, MC, V. **Map** p404 C24.

This award-winning company focuses on the works of a single playwright each season. Signature has delved into the oeuvres of Edward Albee, August Wilson, John Guare and Paula Vogel. Tony Kushner's *The Intelligent Homosexual's Guide to Capitalism and Socialism with a Key to the Scriptures* will be on stage until June 2011, as will the playwright's adaptation of Corneille's *L'Ilusion Comique* (titled *The Ilusion*)

★ Soho Rep

46 Walker Street, between Broadway & Church Street, Tribeca (Smarttix 1-212 868 4444, www.sohorep.org). Subway A, C, E, N, R, 6 to Canal Street; 1 to Franklin Street. **Box office**

9am-8pm Mon-Fri; 10am-8pm Sat; 10am-6pm Sun. **Tickets** 99¢-$30. **Credit** AmEx, DC, MC, V. **Map** p402 E31.
A couple of years ago, this Off-Off mainstay moved to an Off-Broadway contract, but tickets for most shows have remained cheap for Off Broadway. Artistic director Sarah Benson's programming is diverse and adventurous: recent productions include works by Young Jean Lee, Sarah Kane and the Nature Theater of Oklahoma.

Theatre Row

410 W 42nd Street, between Ninth & Tenth Avenues, Theater District (Ticket Central 1-212 279 4200, www.theatrerow.org). Subway A, C, E to 42nd Street-Port Authority. **Box office** 9am-8pm Mon-Fri; 10am-8pm Sat; 10am-6pm Sun. **Tickets** $18-$60. **Credit** AmEx, DC, MC, V. **Map** p404 C24.
A complex of five venues, Theatre Row hosts new plays and revivals by the trendy and celebrity-friendly New Group (*Aunt Dan and Lemon, Hurlyburly*), as well as scores of other productions by assorted theatre companies.

Vineyard Theatre

108 E 15th Street, at Union Square East, Union Square (1-212 353 0303, www.vineyardtheatre.org). Subway L, N, Q, R, 4, 5, 6 to 14th Street-Union Square. **Box office** 10am-6pm Mon-Fri. **Tickets** $45-$60. **Credit** AmEx, DC, MC, V. **Map** p403 E27.
This theatre produces excellent new plays and musicals, including the downtown cult hit and Tony Award-winning *Avenue Q* (*see p351*), both of which transferred to Broadway.

OFF-OFF BROADWAY

Technically, 'Off-Off Broadway' denotes a show that is presented at a theatre with fewer than 100 seats, usually for less than $25. It's where some of the most daring writers and performers – who aren't necessarily card-carrying union professionals – create their edgiest work: **Radiohole** (www.radiohole.com), the **International WOW Company** (www.internationalwow.org) and the cheekily named **National Theater of the United States of America** (www.ntusa.org) are among many troupes that offer inspired theatre. The **New York International Fringe Festival** (1-212 279 4488, www.fringenyc.org), held every August, provides a great opportunity to see the wacky side of the stage.

New York's burgeoning burlesque scene is a winking throwback to the days when the tease was as important as the strip. One reliable purveyor of retro smut is **Le Scandal** at the Laurie Beechman Theatre *(see p334)*. Also, keep an eye out for **Pinchbottom** (www.pinchbottom.com) and **Starshine Burlesque** (www.starshineburlesque.com).

INSIDE TRACK HOT TICKETS

Buzzed-about shows, especially those with big stars on the bill, sell out fast. Keep on top of openings by checking sites such as www.playbill.com and www.theatermania.com, as well as *Time Out New York*'s theatre blog, Upstaged. All feature the latest news and interviews; Theatermania also has an online booking service and discounted tickets for some shows.

Repertory companies & venues

For the multi-discipline **Dixon Place**, *see p284.*

The Brick

575 Metropolitan Avenue, between Lorimer Street & Union Avenue, Williamsburg, Brooklyn (1-718 907 3457, www.bricktheater.com). Subway G to Metropolitan Avenue; L to Lorimer Street. **Box office** opens 15mins before curtain. **Tickets** $15-$20. **No credit cards. Map** p411 V8.
This spunky, brick-lined venue presents a variety of experimental work. Its tongue-in-cheek themed summer series have included Moral Values, Pretentious and, most recently, Antidepressant Festivals.

HERE

145 Sixth Avenue, between Broome & Spring Streets, Soho (1-212 647 0202, Smarttix 1-212 868 4444, http://here.org). Subway C, E to Spring Street. **Box office** 4-10pm daily. **Tickets** $20-$35. **Credit** AmEx, DC, MC, V. **Map** p403 E30.
This recently renovated Soho arts complex, dedicated to non-profit arts enterprises, has been the launching pad for such shows as Eve Ensler's *The Vagina Monologues*. More recently, HERE has showcased the talents of puppeteer Basil Twist, singer Joey Arias and playwright-performer Taylor Mac.

★ Performance Space 122

150 First Avenue, at 9th Street, East Village (1-212 477 5288, www.ps122.org). Subway L to First Avenue; 6 to Astor Place. **Box office** 11am-6pm daily. **Tickets** $18-$25. **Credit** AmEx, DC, MC, V. **Map** p403 F28.
One of New York's most interesting venues, this non-profit arts centre just celebrated its 30th anniversary of presenting experimental theatre, performance art, music, film and video. Whoopi Goldberg, Eric Bogosian and John Leguizamo have all developed projects here. Australian trendsetter Vallejo Gantner is artistic director, and has been working to give the venue an international scope. The dance programming is noteworthy; *see p285.*

Escapes & Excursions

City Island. *See p367.*

Escapes & Excursions

Get outdoors.

Need a break from the city? You're in luck. New York is well situated for both coastal and countryside getaways, and there are plenty of worthwhile destinations within reach of the five boroughs. Bucolic areas such as New York State's Hudson Valley, north of Manhattan, are little more than an hour away; and although New Jersey is the butt of some unkind jokes, even hardened urbanites concede it has some lovely beaches that can be accessed in little more time than it takes to get across town on a bus. What's more, many getaway spots are accessible by public transport, allowing you to avoid the often exorbitant car-rental rates and the heavy summer traffic in and out of town.

Hit the Trails

The city's parks are great for a little casual relaxation. But if you're hankering after a real fresh-air escape, set off on one of these day hikes, between one and three hours away. Bring water and snacks: refuelling options are scarce.

BREAKNECK RIDGE

The trek at Breakneck Ridge is a favourite of hikers for its accessibility, its variety of trails and its views of the Hudson Valley and the Catskill Mountains. The trail head is a half mile walk along the highway from the Cold Spring stop on Metro-North's Hudson line (at weekends, the train stops closer to the trail, at the Breakneck Ridge stop). You can spend anywhere from two hours to a full day hiking Breakneck, so make sure you plan your route in advance.

You'll find the start of the trail on the river's eastern bank, atop a tunnel that was drilled out for Route 9D: it's marked with small white paint splotches (called 'blazes' in hiking parlance) on nearby trees. Be warned, though, that Breakneck got its name for a reason. The initial trail ascends 500 feet (150 metres) in just a mile and a half, and gains another 500 feet by a series of dips and rises over the next few miles. If you're not in good shape, you might want to think about an alternative hike. But if you do choose this path, there are plenty of dramatic overlooks where you can stretch out on a rock and take in the majestic Hudson River below.

After the difficult initial climb, Breakneck Ridge offers options for all levels of hikers, and several crossings in the first few miles provide alternative routes back down the slope. Trail information and maps of all the paths, which are clearly marked with differently coloured blazes along the way, are available from the New York-New Jersey Trail Conference; it's strongly recommended that you carry them with you.

Tourist information

New York-New Jersey Trail Conference
1-201 512 9348, www.nynjtc.org.

Getting there

By train Take the Metro-North Hudson train from Grand Central to the Cold Spring stop, or catch the line's early train to the Breakneck Ridge stop (Sat & Sun only). Journey time 1hr 15 mins; round-trip ticket $22.50-$30 ($11.50-$15 reductions). Contact the MTA (www.mta.info/mnr) for schedules.

HARRIMAN STATE PARK

Harriman State Park is just across the Hudson River and situated to the south-west of the sprawling campus of West Point. You can access its more than 200 miles of trails and 31 lakes from stops on the Metro-North Port Jervis line. Of the various trail options, our favourite is the **Triangle Trail**.This is an eight-mile jaunt that begins just past the parking lot at Tuxedo station (which is about an hour's journey from Penn Station). Triangle leads up steadily more than 1,000 feet towards the summit of Parker Cabin Mountain before turning south to offer lovely views of two lakes, Skenonto and Sebago. From there, it heads down steadily, although steeply at times, before ending after roughly five miles at a path marked with red dashes on white. It's a long distance to cover, but the terrain is varied and there are shortcuts. On a hot day, however, the best detour is to take a dip in one of the lakes followed by a nap in the sun.

Tourist information

Harriman State Park *1-845 786 2701, www.nysparks.state.ny.us.*
New York-New Jersey Trail Conference *1-201 512 9348, www.nynjtc.org.*

Getting there

By train Take the Metro-North/NJ Transit Port Jervis train, Penn Station to Tuxedo line (with a train switch in Secaucus, NJ). The journey takes 1hr 15mins, and a round-trip ticket costs $18.75 ($5.50 reductions). Contact the MTA (www.mta.info/mnr) for schedules.

INSIDE TRACK SLEEPY HOLLOW

South of Cold Spring is the small town of **Sleepy Hollow**. It's most famous as the putative location for Washington Irving's short story *The Legend of Sleepy Hollow*, later adapted into a movie by Tim Burton. Irving is buried in the village cemetery.

OTIS PIKE WILDERNESS

If you're looking for ocean views and a less aggressive hike, consider Fire Island's Otis Pike Wilderness Area. The journey takes 90 minutes on the LIRR from Penn Station to Patchogue, on Long Island, followed by a 45-minute ferry ride south to the Watch Hill Visitor Center, but the pristine beaches and wildlife are worth the effort. The stretch of preserved wilderness from Watch Hill to Smith Point is home to deer, rabbits, foxes and numerous types of seabirds, including the piping plover, which nests during the summer. Just be sure you stay out of the plovers' nesting grounds, which are marked with signs, and don't feed any wildlife you see along the way.

Apart from a few sand dunes, Fire Island is completely flat, although walking on the beaches and sandy paths can be slow going.

Breakneck Ridge.

After traversing the boardwalk leading from the Watch Hill Center, hike along Burma Road, a path that runs across the entire island, and in seven miles you'll arrive at the Wilderness Visitor Center at Smith Point.

Tourist information

Fire Island National Seashore
1-631 687 4750, www.nps.gov/fiis.

Getting there

By train/ferry Take the LIRR Montauk Line, Penn Station to Patchogue. Call 1-718 217 5477 for fares and schedules. For the Davis Park Ferry from Patchogue to Watch Hill, call 1-631 475 1665. The journey should take around 2hrs 30mins in total.

Head for the Ocean

BRIDGEHAMPTON

Celebrity-filled parties, polo matches and mansions may be the first image of the Hamptons that jumps to New Yorkers' minds, but the real reason folks started coming – and still come – here is the miles of shoreline along the ocean and bays. Southampton Town, which governs beaches from Westhampton through Sagaponack, allows for public access to the dunes at several points, and the waves are a draw even for surfers.

Still, the famed polo matches in Bridgehampton – which take place over six Saturdays in July and August, culminating in the **Mercedes-Benz Polo Challenge** (Bridgehampton Polo Club, Two Trees Farm, 849 Hayground Road, 1-631 537 8450, www.bhpolo.com) – have their allure. Find a spot on the side of the field opposite the VIP tent, where the real fans and polo players' families sit. Matches last about an hour and a half, with six seven-minute chukkers (periods of play), so bring a blanket or lawn chairs and pack a picnic – gather provisions from gourmet grocer **Citarella** (2209 Montauk Highway, 1-631 537 5990, www.citarella.com) or several farm stands that line Montauk Highway.

If you happen to be in town over the Labor Day weekend (3-4 September in 2011), visit the **Westhampton Festival of the Arts** show (Great Meadow, Main Street, Westhampton Beach, 1-631 421 1590, www.paragonartevents.com). This the juried event is held on the neighbouring town's Great Meadow; its paintings, photography, and other works are all for sale.

While most of the Long Island wine industry is concentrated on the North Fork, the South Fork has been making inroads over the past two decades. At the 125-acre winery **Channing Daughters** (1927 Scuttlehole Rd, 1-631-537 7224, www.channingdaughters.com), you can taste seven wines for $6.

In the event that your plans are thwarted by the heavens opening, hoof it to the Sag Harbor cinema (90 Main Street, Sag Harbor, NY, 1-631 725 0010, www.sagharborcinema.com, closed Tue & Wed), ten minutes from Bridgehampton, which shows independent films in an old movie-house setting.

INSIDE TRACK
LICENCE TO PARK

While there may be easy beach access in the Hamptons, the same cannot be said for the parking lots – visitors renting a car or motorbike will need a Hand-Held Permit application to enter. Download the application at www.town.southampton.ny.us, or call 1-631 728 8585 for more information.

Eating & drinking

Townline BBQ (3593 Montauk Highway, Sagaponack, NY, 1-631 537 2271, www.townlinebbq.com, closed Tue & Wed), a Southern comfort-food joint, has a solid following among locals. The small, hidden **Yama-Q** (2393 Main Street, Bridgehampton, NY, 1-631 537 0225) lies pretty well at the other end of the culinary spectrum, serving sushi and Japanese small plates. And if you're looking to dine like you came from that VIP tent, French bistro **Almond** (1970 Montauk Highway, Bridgehampton, NY, 1-631 537 8885, www.almondrestaurant.com, closed Tue & Wed from Labor Day to Memorial Day) has the requisite escargots, *frisée aux lardons* and roasted chicken.

Hotels

Affordable options include the **Enclave Inn** chainlet (1-631 537 2900, www.enclaveinn.com), with roadside locations in Wainscott, Bridgehampton and Southampton (summer $229-$279 double, two-night minimum; off-season $99-$149 double), and the **Inn at Quogue**, Westhampton's ritzier neighbour (47 Quogue Street, 1-631 653 6560, www.innatquogue.com; summer $325-$450 double, half-price Mon-Wed in July & Aug; spring and autumn $215-$275 double; winter $125-$190 double).

Sandy Hook.

Getting there

By bus Take the Hampton Jitney (1-212 362 8400, www.hamptonjitney.com) from one of many points in the city to Bridgehampton. The journey takes 2hrs 45 minutes, and the round-trip fare is $53 (reductions $49).

SANDY HOOK

The first thing you should know about Sandy Hook, New Jersey, is that there's a nude beach at its north end (Gunnison Beach, at parking lot G). The sights it affords compel boaters with binoculars to anchor close to shore, and there's also a cruisy gay scene – but there's much more to this 1,665-acre natural wonderland than sunbathers in the buff. With all that the expansive Hook has to offer, it's a little like an island getaway on the city's doorstep.

Along with seven miles of dune-backed ocean beach, the **Gateway National Recreation Area** is home to the nation's oldest lighthouse (which you can tour), as well as extensive fortifications from the days when Sandy Hook formed the outer line of defence for New York Harbor. You can explore the area's past at the **Fort Hancock Museum**, in the old post guardhouse, and at **History House**, located in one of the elegant century-old officer's houses that form an arc facing Sandy Hook Bay. The abandoned forts are worth a look as well.

Elsewhere, natural areas such as the **Maritime Holly Forest** attract an astounding variety of birds. In fact, large stretches of beach are closed in summer to allow the endangered piping plover a quiet place to mate. In winter the Audubon Society offers bird walks through the forest. You can also spot surfers catching waves within sight of the Manhattan skyline.

There's even a cool way to get there. Rather than braving awful traffic only to find that the beachfront parking lots are full, hop on the ferry from Manhattan and turn an excursion to the beach into a scenic mini-cruise. Once you dock at Fort Hancock, it's a short walk to most of the beaches; and if you've still got energy for more, shuttle buses will transport you to any one of the other six strands along the peninsula.

Eating & drinking

Hot dogs and other typical waterside snacks are available from concession stands at the beach areas. But for more ambitious grub – caesar salad with grilled tuna, for instance – head to the **Sea Gull's Nest** (1-732 872 0025), the park's sole restaurant; it's located at Area D, about three miles south of the ferry dock.

Alternatively, blanket picnics are permitted on the beach, so you can bring along goodies for dining alfresco. Guardian Park, at the south end of Fort Hancock, has tables and barbecue grills.

Tourist information

Sandy Hook Gateway National Recreation Area *1-732 872 5970, www.nps.gov/gate.*

Getting there

By boat Board the ferry weekdays and weekends (June-Sept) from E 35th Street at the East River or at Pier 11 in the Financial District (at the eastern end of Wall Street). Contact Sea Streak (1-800 262 8743, www.seastreak.com) for reservations, fares and departure times. The ride takes 45 minutes.

CITY ISLAND

It may look like a New England fishing village, but City Island, on the north-west edge of Long Island Sound, is part of the Bronx and accessible from anywhere in the city by public transport. With a population of fewer than 5,000, it formed the slightly gritty backdrop for films such as *Margot at the Wedding* and *A Bronx Tale*. Yet in its heyday, around World War II, it was home to no fewer than 17 shipyards. Seven America's Cup-winning yachts were built on the island – and, residents add, the Cup was lost in 1983, the very same year they stopped building the boats here.

City Island. See 367.

You'll find a room devoted to the island's past as a centre of maritime history at the free **City Island Historical Society and Nautical Museum** (190 Fordham Street, between Minnieford & King Avenues, 1-718 885 0008, open 1-5pm Sat, Sun). Housed in a quaint former schoolhouse, it's stocked with model ships, Revolutionary War artefacts and tributes to such local heroes as Ruby Price Dill, the island's first kindergarten teacher.

The island is also worth a summer evening trip. With crab shanties on every corner and boats bobbing in the background, the small community exudes maritime charm. There are still a handful of yacht clubs in operation on these shores and a few sailmakers in the phone book, but City Islanders are far more likely to head into Manhattan for work nowadays.

If you're here late at night, don't miss the eerie midnight views of nearby Hart Island. The former site of an insane asylum, a missile base and a narcotics rehab center, Hart is also home to NYC's public cemetery, where you can sometimes spot Rikers Island inmates burying the unnamed dead. How's that for a fishy tale?

Eating & drinking

Over on Belden Point are **Johnny's Reef** (2 City Island Avenue, 1-718 885 2086) and **Tony's Pier Restaurant** (1 City Island Avenue, 1-718 885 1424); both have outdoor seating. Grab a couple of beers and a basket of fried clams, sit at one of the picnic benches and watch the boats sail by.

Getting there

By train/bus Take the 6 train to Pelham Bay Park and transfer to the Bx29 bus east to City Island.

Museum Escapes

DIA:BEACON

Take a model example of early 20th-century industrial architecture. Combine it with some of the most ambitious and uncompromising art of the past 50 years. What do you get? One of the finest, most luxuriant aesthetic experiences on earth. Indeed, for the 24 artists whose work is on view, and for the visiting public, Dia Art Foundation's outpost in the Hudson Valley is truly a blessing.

The Dia Art Foundation's founders, Heiner Friedrich and his wife Philippa de Menil (an heir to the Schlumberger oil fortune), acquired many of their holdings in the 1960s and '70s. The pair had a taste for the minimal, the conceptual and the monumental, and supported artists with radical ideas about what art was, what it could do and where it should happen. Together with others of their generation, the Dia circle (Robert Smithson, Michael Heizer, Walter De Maria, Donald Judd and Dan Flavin) made it difficult to consider a work of art apart from its context – be it visual, philosophical or historical – ever again. Since 2003, that context has been the Riggio Galleries, a massive museum on a 31-acre tract of land overlooking the Hudson River, as Dia's hugely scaled collection had outgrown even its cavernous former galleries in Chelsea.

An 80-minute train ride from Grand Central Station, the 300,000-square-foot (27,000-square-metre) complex of three brick buildings was erected in 1929 as a box-printing factory for snack-manufacturing giant Nabisco (short for the National Biscuit Company). No less than 34,000 square feet (3,000 square metres) of north-facing skylights provide almost all of the illumination within. Nowhere does that light serve the art here better than in the immense gallery where 72 of the 102 canvases that make up Andy Warhol's rarely exhibited *Shadows*

(1978-79) hang end to end, like a mesmerising series of violet solar flares.

But what really sets Dia:Beacon apart from other museums is its confounding intimacy. The design of the galleries and gardens by California light-and-space artist Robert Irwin, in collaboration with the Manhattan architectural collective OpenOffice, seems close to genius. Not only does it make this enormous museum feel more like a private house, it also allows the gallery's curators to draw correspondences between artworks into an elegant and intriguing narrative of connoisseurship.

If you're travelling by car, consider stopping at **Storm King Art Center**, about 14 miles south-west of Beacon on the other side of the Hudson. The gorgeous, at times surreal sculpture park, open April through mid November, features monumental works by Maya Lin, Alexander Calder and Richard Serra, among others.

Further information

Dia:Beacon Riggio Galleries *3 Beekman Street, Beacon, NY (1-845 440 0100, www.diabeacon.org).* **Open** *Mid Apr-mid Oct* 11am-6pm Mon, Thur-Sun. *Mid Oct-mid Apr* 11am-4pm Mon, Fri-Sun. **Admission** $10; $7 reductions; free under-12s. **Credit** AmEx, MC, V.

The Boardwalk Goes Boutique

The formerly faded seaside belle of Atlantic City is back in fashion.

The New Jersey coastal town of Atlantic City is, to some nostalgics, synonymous with a kind of 1940s-vintage dinner-jacket-and-cigarettes glamour. But that's probably because they haven't been here in decades. In reality, it's a struggling gambling resort that long ago fell from its heyday perch. So why would anyone who doesn't have a craps addiction choose to visit? Because after a desperate, decade-long revitalisation, two ambitious, non-gaming hotels have opened, hoping to attract a clientele that would rather spend money than simply lose it.

The **Chelsea** (111 S Chelsea Avenue, at Pacific Avenue, 1-800 548 3030, www.thechelsea-ac.com; $89-$450 doubles) claims to be the first casino-free boutique hotel to arrive on the Boardwalk since the 1960s. The developer, Curtis Bashaw, converted two chain lodgings (a Howard Johnson and a Holiday Inn) into one destination. The 331 rooms, decorated in a campy retro style that recalls Mrs Robinson's lair, are joined by a spa, with two restaurants on opposite ends of the hotel from Philly restaurateur Stephen Starr: the Chelsea Prime steakhouse and upscale diner Teplitzky's, which overlooks a saltwater pool on the ground floor.

Perhaps the real coup of Bashaw's vision was his wooing of Beatrice Inn impresarios Paul Sevigny and Matt Abramcyk to design the hotel's nightlife programme, dubbed the Fifth. This is home to nightclub C5, a set of intimate bars-cum-performance-venues, and, in summer, the Cabana Club, an open-air, poolside boîte that might make Soho House members envious.

An even more luxurious option is the **Water Club** (1 Renaissance Way, 1-800 800 8817, www.thewaterclubhotel.com, $149-$800 double), a 43-floor tower operated by hotel/casino the **Borgata** (1 Borgata Way, 1-609 317 1000, www.theborgata.com). The opulence here is of the exotic-orchids, earth-toned-decor, designer spa variety. Sipping a cocktail and munching on consulting chef Geoffrey Zakarian's farm-fresh crudités in one of the outdoor poolside cabanas, you might even forget where you are. Miami? Mexico? It's a far cry from the image most of us have of the New Jersey resort.

For players, the poker tables aren't far away. The Borgata, connected to the Water Club physically, is the most Vegas-style of Atlantic City's casinos. Besides gambling, on any given night you can catch a concert or comedy show (Jay-Z, Rufus Wainwright and Jon Stewart have all recently appeared) and dine at a wealth of restaurants: Wolfgang Puck American Grille and Bobby Flay Steak, to name a couple.

But if all the decadence makes you want to get out for some local flavour, ask the concierge to get you a table at **Chef Vola's** (111 S Albion Place, between Pacific Avenue and the Boardwalk, 1-609 345 2022, www.chefvolas.com). At this family-run Italian restaurant, hidden in a basement close to the hotels, customers must be personally recommended.

To reach Atlantic City, take the Greyhound bus (1-800 231 2222, www.greyhound.com) from Port Authority (*see p372*). The journey takes 2hrs 40mins, and a round-trip ticket is $35.

Storm King Art Center *Old Pleasant Hill Road, Mountainville, NY (1-845 534 3115, www.stormking.org).* **Open** *Apr-Oct* 10am-5.30pm Wed-Sun. *Early-mid Nov* 10am-5pm Wed-Sun. **Admission** $12; $8-$10 reductions; free under-5s.

Getting there

By train Take the Metro-North train from Grand Central Terminal to Beacon station. The journey takes 1hr 20 minutes, and the round-trip fare is $26-$34.50 (reductions $13-$17). Discount rail and admission packages are available; for details, see www.mta.info/mnr.

COOPERSTOWN

A mecca for baseball devotees, Cooperstown, north of Manhattan, isn't known for much besides its famous hall of rawhide ephemera, old pine tar-stained lumber and October memories. For the large number of folks who don't care a lick about America's national pastime but are forced along for the ride, a weekend focused on baseball minutiae sounds about as thrilling a prospect as a DIY colonoscopy. Happily, though, there's more than Major League history to be found at this single-stop-light village (population 2,000) on the shores of Lake Otsego. The area's wooded hills are a welcome respite for those who would like nothing better than to take a Louisville Slugger to the heads of their baseball-obsessed companions.

The **National Baseball Hall of Fame & Museum** draws around 300,000 visitors a year. The actual hall is exactly what it claims to be: a corridor full of plaques. And as such, it's the museum that's the real diamond here. You'll see everything from Babe Ruth's locker to racist hate mail sent to Jackie Robinson and the glove worn by Willie Mays when he made his over-the-shoulder catch in the 1954 World Series.

Local shopping is devoted primarily to baseball, so if you're looking for vintage memorabilia or limited-edition collectibles, the **Cooperstown Bat Company** (118 Main Street, at Chestnut Street, 1-607 547 2415) is worth checking out. For a dose of non-sport history, take a walk through the **Christ Episcopal Churchyard Cemetery** (46 River Street, at Church Street, 1-607 547 9555), where the Cooper family is buried.

This may be the land of baseball, but it's brew country as well. The nearby **Brewery Ommegang** (656 County Highway 33, 1-800 544 1809, www.ommegang.com), set in a farmhouse, brews five award-winning ales, from the light Witte Ale to the strong Three Philosophers. You can see how the whole brewing process works at the 136-acre farmstead. The **Cooperstown Brewing Co** (110 River Street, at E Main Street, Milford, NY; 1-607 286 9330, www.cooperstownbrewing.com) offers daily tours ($3) on the hour from 11am to 5pm and informal tastings of its ales, porters and stouts.

On your way out of town, stop at **Howe Caverns** (255 Discovery Drive, Howes Cave, 1-518 296 8900, www.howecaverns.com; admission $21, $11-$18 reductions), located between Cooperstown and Albany. Don't get lost in this vast complex of underground caves made from limestone deposited hundreds of millions of years ago. The highlight is Lake Venus, hidden 156 feet below the ground and open for boat rides.

Eating & drinking

In town, the **Doubleday Café** (93 Main Street, at Pioneer Street, 1-607 547 5468) provides good American grub. At **Alex & Ika** (149 Main Street, at Chestnut Street, www.alexandika.com, 1-607 547 4070), hostess Ika Fognell and chef Alex Webster serve creative dishes such as spicy habanero shrimp cake and sake-seared salmon. The local dive, **Cooley's Stone House Tavern** (49 Pioneer Street, at Main Street, 1-607 544 1311), is a beautifully restored tavern that dates from before the Civil War, and is a good spot for a nightcap. For brewpubs in the area, *see above*.

Hotels

Check in at the **Inn at Cooperstown** (16 Chestnut Street, at Main Street, 1-607 547 5756, www.innatcooperstown.com, $108-$490). Four-poster beds, afternoon tea and a fireplace provide a cosy backdrop for the board games.

If you're looking for something a little more swanky, stay at the grand lakeside **Otesaga Hotel** (60 Lake Street, at Pine Boulevard, 1-800 348 6222, www.otesaga.com, $410-$650) and play a round on the par-72 golf course.

Further information

Cooperstown/Otsego County Tourism
1-607 643 0059/www.thisiscooperstown.com.
National Baseball Hall of Fame & Museum
25 Main Street, at Fair Street (1-888 425 5633, www.baseballhalloffame.org). **Open** *June-Aug* 9am-9pm daily. *Sept-May* 9am-5pm daily. **Admission** $16.50; $6-$11 reductions.

Getting there

By car Take I-87N to I90 to exit 25A. Take I-88W to exit 24. Follow Route 7 to Route 20W to Route 80S to Cooperstown. The journey takes 4hrs.

ESCAPES & EXCURSIONS

Directory

Brooklyn Bridge. *See p130.*

Getting Around

ARRIVING & LEAVING

By air

Three major airports serve the New York City area (along with smaller MacArthur Airport on Long Island). For a list of transport services between New York City and its major airports, call 1-800 247 7433. **Public transport** is the cheapest method of travelling between city and airport, but it can be frustrating and time-consuming – none of the local airports is particularly close or convenient – especially during rush hour.

Private bus or van services are usually the best bargains, but you need to allow extra time as vans will be picking up other passengers. As well as the choices for each airport, blue SuperShuttle (1-212 209 7000, 1-800 258 3826, www.supershuttle.com) vans offer door-to-door service between NYC and the major airports.

Yellow cabs can be flagged on the street or picked up from designated locations in airports. You may also reserve a car service in advance to pick you up or drop you off (*see p374*). Avoid car-service drivers and unlicensed 'gypsy cabs' at the baggage-claim areas or outside the terminal – it's illegal to solicit customers.

Airports

John F Kennedy International Airport *1-718 244 4444, www.panynj.gov/airports/jfk*

The **subway** is the cheapest option, but depending on your destination, it can be time-consuming. The **AirTrain** ($5) from JFK links to the A train at Howard Beach or the E, J and Z trains at Sutphin Boulevard-Archer Avenue ($2.25). For further information, visit www.panynj.gov/airports/jfk-airtrain. **Private bus and van services** are a good compromise between value and convenience. New York Airport Service (1-212 875 8200, www.nyairportservice.com) runs frequently between Manhattan and JFK (one way $15, round trip $27) from early morning to late night, with stops near Grand Central Terminal (Park Avenue, between 41st & 42nd Streets), near Penn Station (33rd Street, at Seventh Avenue), inside the Port Authority Bus Terminal (*see below*) and outside a number of Midtown hotels (for an extra charge). Buses also run from JFK to La Guardia (one way $13). A **yellow cab** from JFK to Manhattan will charge a flat $45.50 fare, plus toll (usually $5) and tip (if service is fine, give at least $7). The fare to JFK from Manhattan is not a set rate, but it is usually a little more. Check www.nyc.gov/taxi for the latest cab rates.

La Guardia Airport *1-718 533 3400, www.panynj.gov/airports/laguardia.*

Seasoned New Yorkers take the **M60 bus** ($2.25), which runs between the airport and 106th Street at Broadway. The ride takes 40-60mins (depending on traffic) and runs from 4.30am to 1.30am daily. The route crosses Manhattan at 125th Street in Harlem. Get off at Lexington Avenue for the 4, 5 and 6 trains; at Malcolm X Boulevard (Lenox Avenue) for the 2 and 3; or at St Nicholas Avenue for the A, B, C and D trains. You can also disembark on Broadway at 116th or 110th Street for the 1 train. Less time-consuming options include New York Airport Service **private buses** (1-212 875 8200, www.nyairportservice.com), which runs frequently between Manhattan and La Guardia (one way $12, round trip $21). **Taxis and car services** charge about $30, plus toll and tip.

MacArthur Airport *1-631 467 3210, www.macarthurairport.com.*

Getting to Manhattan from this airport in Islip, Long Island, 50 miles away, will be more expensive, unless you take the **Long Island Rail Road**. Fares are generally $13; a shuttle from the airport to the station is $5. For **cars**, Colonial Transportation (1-631 589 3500, colonialtransportation.com) will take up to four to Manhattan for $174, including tolls and tip.

Newark Liberty International Airport *1-973 961 6000, www.panynj/airports/newark-liberty.*

Newark has good mass transit access to NYC. The best bet is the 40min, $15 trip by **New Jersey Transit** to or from Penn Station. The airport's monorail, **AirTrain Newark** (www.airtrainnewark.com), is linked to the NJ Transit and Amtrak train systems. **Bus services** operated by Coach USA (1-877 894 9155, www.coachusa.com) run between Newark and Manhattan, stopping outside Grand Central Station (41st Street, between Park & Lexington Avenues), and inside the Port Authority Bus Terminal (one way $15, round trip $25); buses leave every 15-30mins. A **car or taxi** will run at about $60, plus toll and tip.

By bus

Buses aren't very quick and can be uncomfortable, but you probably won't need to book. **Greyhound** (1-800 231 2222, www.greyhound.com) offers long-distance bus travel to destinations across North America. The company has recently responded to the growth of cheaper independent bus companies with its **BoltBus** (1-877 265 8287, www.boltbus.com), serving several East Coast cities and departing from central locations. As well as a fleet of new coaches and free Wi-Fi, it offers low fares. **New Jersey Transit** (1-973 275 5555, www.njtransit.com) runs a bus service to nearly everywhere in the Garden State and parts of New York State. Finally, **Peter Pan** (1-800 343 9999, www.peterpanbus.com) runs extensive services to cities across the North-east; its tickets are also valid on Greyhound buses. Most out-of-town buses come and go from the Port Authority Bus Terminal (*see below*).

George Washington Bridge Bus Station *4211 Broadway, between 178th & 179th Streets, Washington Heights (1-212 564 8484, www.panynj.gov/bus-terminals/george-washington-bridge-bus-station). Subway A, 1 to 181st Street.* **Map** p409 B6. A few bus lines serving New Jersey and Rockland County are based here.

Port Authority Bus Terminal *625 Eighth Avenue, between 40th & 42nd Streets, Garment District (1-212 564 8484, www.panynj.gov/bus-terminals/port-authority-bus-*

terminal). Subway A, C, E to 42nd Street-Port Authority.
Map p410 S13.
This terminus is the hub for many commuter and long-distance services. Though it's perfectly safe, watch out for the occasional pickpocket, especially at night, and note that the food concessions don't open until around 7am.

By car

If you drive into the city, you may face delays, from 15 minutes to two hours, at bridge and tunnel crossings (check www.nyc.gov and www.panynj.gov). Tune in to **WINS** (1010 AM) for traffic reports. Tolls range from $5 to $11. Try to time your arrival and departure against the commuter flow. If you drive to NYC, consider leaving your car in a garage. Street parking is problematic and car theft not unheard of. Garages are dear but plentiful. If you want to park for less than $15 a day, try a garage outside Manhattan and take public transport into the city.

By rail

America's national rail service is run by **Amtrak** (1-800 872 7245, www.amtrak.com). Nationwide routes are slow and infrequent, but there are some good fast services linking the eastern seaboard cities. (For commuter rail services, *see below* **Public transport: Rail**.)

Grand Central Terminal
42nd to 44th Streets, between Vanderbilt & Lexington Avenues, Midtown East. Subway S, 4, 5, 6, 7 to 42nd Street-Grand Central.
Map p404 E24.
Grand Central is home to Metro-North, which runs trains to more than 100 stations in New York State and Connecticut. Schedules are available at the terminal.

Penn Station *31st to 33rd Streets, between Seventh & Eighth Avenues, Garment District. Subway A, C, E, 1, 2, 3 to 34th Street-Penn Station.*
Map p404 D25.
Amtrak, Long Island Rail Road and New Jersey Transit trains depart from this terminal.

PUBLIC TRANSPORT

Changes to schedules can occur at short notice, especially at weekends – pay attention to the posters on subway station walls and announcements you may hear in trains and on subway platforms.

Metropolitan Transportation Authority (MTA) *1-718 330 1234 travel information, 1-718 243 7777 updates, www.mta.info.*
The MTA runs the subway and bus lines, as well as services to points outside Manhattan. News of service interruptions and MTA maps are on its website. Be warned: since 9/11 backpacks, handbags and large containers may be subject to random searches.

Fares & tickets

Although you can pay in cash or coins on the buses, you'll need to buy a **MetroCard** to enter the subway system. The standard fare across the subway and bus network on a MetroCard is $2.25, though a single-ride ticket purchased at a vending machine costs $2.50. You can buy them from booths or vending machines in the stations; from the Official NYC Information Center; from the New York Transit Museum in Brooklyn or Grand Central Terminal; and from many hotels. Free transfers between the subway and buses, or between buses, are available only with a MetroCard. Up to four people can use a **pay-per-use MetroCard**, sold in denominations from $4.50 to $80.

If you put $8 or more on the card, you'll receive a 15 per cent bonus. However, if you're planning to use the subway or buses often, an **unlimited-ride MetroCard** is great value. These cards are offered in two denominations, available at station vending machines but not at booths: a seven-day pass ($29) and a 30-day pass ($104). All are good for unlimited rides during those times, but you can't share a card with your travel companions.

Subway

Far cleaner and safer than it was 20 years ago, the city's subway system is one of the world's largest and cheapest, with a flat fare of $2.25. Trains run around the clock. If you are travelling late at night, board the train from the designated off-peak waiting area, usually near the middle of the platform; this is more secure than the ends of the platform, which are often less populated in the wee hours.

Use the same common-sense safety precautions on the subway that you would in any urban environment. Hold your bag with the opening facing you, keep your wallet in a front pocket and don't wear flashy jewellery. Petty crime levels increase during the holidays.

Stations are most often named after the street on which they're located. Entrances are marked with a green and white globe (open 24 hours) or a red and white globe (limited hours). Many stations have separate entrances for the uptown and downtown platforms – look before you pay. Trains are identified by letters or numbers, colour-coded according to the line on which they run. Local trains stop at every station on the line; express trains stop at major stations only.

The most current subway map is reprinted at the back of this guide (*see pp414-416*); you can also ask MTA workers in service booths for a free copy, or refer to enlarged subway maps displayed in each subway station.

City buses

White and blue MTA buses are the best way to travel crosstown and a pleasant way to travel up- or downtown, as long as you're not in a hurry. They have a digital destination sign on the front, along with a route number preceded by a letter (M for Manhattan, B for Brooklyn, Bx for the Bronx, Q for Queens and S for Staten Island). **Maps** are posted on most buses and at all subway stations; they're also available from the **Official NYC Information Center** (*see p382*). The Manhattan bus map is also reprinted in this guide; *see p413*. All local buses are equipped with wheelchair lifts.

The $2.25 fare is payable with a MetroCard (*see above*) or exact change (coins only; no pennies). MetroCards allow for an automatic transfer from bus to bus, and between bus and subway. If you pay cash, and you're travelling uptown or downtown and want to go crosstown (or vice versa), ask the driver for a transfer when you get on – you'll be given a ticket for use on the second leg of your journey, valid for two hours. MTA's express buses usually head to the outer boroughs for a $5.50 fare.

Rail

The following commuter trains serve NY's hinterland.

Long Island Rail Road *1-718 217 5477, www.mta.info/lirr.*
Provides rail services from Penn Station, Brooklyn and Queens to towns throughout Long Island.

Metro-North Railroad *1-212 532 4900, www.mta.info/mnr.*
Commuter trains serve towns north of Manhattan and leave from Grand Central Terminal.
New Jersey Transit *1-973 275 5555, www.njtransit.com.*
Service from Penn Station reaches most of New Jersey, some points in New York State and Philadelphia.
PATH Trains *1-800 234 7284, www.panynj.gov/path.*
PATH (Port Authority Trans-Hudson) trains run from six stations in Manhattan to various places across the Hudson in New Jersey, including Hoboken, Jersey City and Newark. The 24-hour service costs $1.75 (change or notes).

TAXIS

Yellow cabs are rarely in short supply in New York, except at rush hour and during unpleasant weather. If the centre light atop the taxi is lit, the cab is available and should stop if you flag it down. Jump in and then tell the driver where you're going. (New Yorkers generally give cross-streets rather than addresses.) By law, taxis cannot refuse to take you anywhere inside the five boroughs or to New York airports. Use only yellow medallion (licensed) cabs; avoid unregulated 'gypsy cabs'.

Taxis will carry up to four passengers for the same price: $2.50 plus 40¢ per fifth of a mile or per minute idling, with an extra 50¢ charge (a new state tax), another 50¢ from 8pm to 6am and a $1 surcharge during rush hour (4-8pm Mon-Fri). The average fare for a three-mile ride is $9-$11, depending on the time and traffic. Cabbies rarely allow more than four passengers in a cab (it's illegal, unless the fifth person is a child under seven).

Not all drivers know their way around the city, so it helps if you know where you're going. If you have a problem, take down the medallion and driver's numbers, posted on the partition. Always ask for a receipt – there's a meter number on it. To complain or to trace lost property, call the **Taxi & Limousine Commission** (1-212 227 0700, 8am-4pm Mon-Fri) or visit www.nyc.gov/taxi. Tip 15-20 per cent, as in a restaurant. Most taxis now accept major credit cards.

Late at night, cabs tend to stick to fast-flowing routes. Try the avenues and key streets (Canal, Houston, 14th, 23rd, 34th, 42nd, 57th, 72nd and 86th). Bridge and tunnel exits are good for a steady flow of taxis returning from airports, and cabbies will usually head for nightclubs and big hotels. Otherwise, try the following:

Chinatown Chatham Square, where Mott Street meets the Bowery, is an unofficial taxi stand. You can also try hailing a cab exiting the Manhattan Bridge at Bowery.
Lincoln Center The crowd heads to Columbus Circle; those in the know go to Amsterdam Avenue.
Lower East Side Katz's Deli (Houston Street, at Ludlow Street) is a cabbies' hangout; also try Delancey Street, where cabs come in over the Williamsburg Bridge.
Midtown Try Penn Station, Grand Central Terminal and the Port Authority Bus Terminal.
Soho On the west side, try Sixth Avenue; on the east, the intersection of Houston Street and Broadway.
Times Square There are 30 taxi stands: look for the yellow globes mounted on poles.
Tribeca Cabs head up Hudson Street. The Tribeca Grand (2 Sixth Avenue, between Walker & White Streets) is another good bet.

Car services

Car services are regulated by the **Taxi & Limousine Commission** (*see above*). Unlike cabs, drivers can make only pre-arranged pickups. Don't try to hail one, and be wary of those that offer you a ride. The following companies will pick you up anywhere in the city, at any time, for a set fare.

Carmel *1-212 666 6666.*
Dial 7 *1-212 777 7777.*
Limores *1-212 777 7171.*

DRIVING

Car hire

Car hire is cheaper in the city's outskirts, and in New Jersey and Connecticut, than in Manhattan; book ahead for weekends.

Companies outside New York State exclude loss/damage waiver insurance from their rates. Rental companies in New York State are required by law to insure their own cars (the renter pays the first $100 in damage to the vehicle). UK residents may find cheaper rental insurance at www.insurance4carhire.com.

You will need a credit card to rent a car in the US, and you usually have to be at least 25 years old. All the car-hire companies listed below will add sales tax (8.875 per cent).

Aamcar *1-800 722 6923, 1-212 222 8500, www.aamcar.com.*
Alamo *US: 1-800 462 5266, www.alamo.com. UK: 0870 400 4562, www.alamo.co.uk.*
Avis *US: 1-800 230 4898, www.avis.com. UK: 0844 544 6666, www.avis.co.uk.*
Budget *US: 1-800 527 0700, www.budget.com. UK: 0844 544 3439, www.budget.co.uk.*
Dollar *US: 1-800 800 3665, www.dollar.com. UK: 0800 252 897, www.dollar.co.uk.*
Enterprise *US: 1-800 261 7331, www.enterprise.com. UK: 0870 350 3000, www.enterprise.co.uk.*
Hertz *US: 1-800 654 3131, www.hertz.com. UK: 0870 844 8844, www.hertz.co.uk.*
National *US: 1-800 227 7368, www.nationalcar.com. UK: 0116 217 3884, www.nationalcar.co.uk.*
Thrifty *US: 1-800 847 4389, www.thrifty.com. UK: 01494 751500, www.thrifty.co.uk.*

Parking

Make sure you read parking signs and never park within 15 feet of a fire hydrant (to avoid a $115 ticket and/or having your car towed). Parking is off-limits on most streets for at least a few hours daily. The **Department of Transportation** provides information on daily changes to regulations (dial 311). If precautions fail, call 1-212 971 0771 or 1-212 971 0772 for Manhattan towing and impoundment information; go to www.nyc.gov for phone numbers in other boroughs.

CYCLING

Aside from pleasurable cycling in Central Park, and along the wide bike paths around the perimeter of Manhattan (now virtually encircled by paths), biking in the city streets is only recommended for experienced urban riders. But zipping through bumper-to-bumper traffic holds allure for those with the requisite skills and gear.

WALKING

One of the best ways to take in NYC is on foot. Most of the streets are laid out in a grid pattern and are relatively easy to navigate.

GUIDED TOURS

See pp56-61 **Tour New York**.

Resources A-Z

TRAVEL ADVICE

For up-to-date information on travel to a specific country – including the latest on safety and security, health issues, local laws and customs – contact your home country government's department of foreign affairs. Most have websites with useful advice for would-be travellers.

AUSTRALIA
www.smartraveller.gov.au

CANADA
www.voyage.gc.ca

NEW ZEALAND
www.safetravel.govt.nz

REPUBLIC OF IRELAND
foreignaffairs.gov.ie

UK
www.fco.gov.uk/travel

USA
www.state.gov/travel

ADDRESSES

Addresses follow the standard US format. The room, apartment or suite number usually appears after the street address, followed on the next line by the name of the city and the zip code.

AGE RESTRICTIONS

Buying/drinking alcohol 21
Driving 16
Sex 17
Smoking 18

ATTITUDE & ETIQUETTE

New Yorkers have a reputation for being rude, but 'outspoken' is more apt: they are unlikely to hold their tongues in the face of injustice or inconvenience but they can also be very welcoming and will often go out of their way to offer advice or help.

Some old-fashioned restaurants and swanky clubs operate dress codes (jacket and tie for men, for example, or no baseball caps or ripped jeans; phone to check). However, on the whole, anything goes sartorially.

BUSINESS

Courier services

DHL *1-800 225 5345, www.dhl.com.*
FedEx *1-800 247 4747, www.fedex.com.*
UPS *1-800 742 5877, www.ups.com.*

Messenger services

A to Z Couriers *1-212 253 6500, www.atozcouriers.com.*
Breakaway *1-212 947 7777, www.breakawaycourier.com.*

Office services

All-Language Translation Services *77 W 55th Street, between Fifth & Sixth Avenues, Midtown (1-212 986 1688, www.all-language.com). Subway F to 57th Street.* **Open** 24hrs daily. **Credit** AmEx, DC, MC, V. **Map** p405 E22.
Copy Specialist *44 E 21st Street, at Park Avenue South, Gramercy Park (1-212 533 756, www.thecopyspecialist.com). Subway N, R, 6 to 23rd Street.* **Open** 8.30am-7pm Mon-Fri; 10am-4pm Sat. **Credit** AmEx, DC, MC, V. **Map** p404 E26.
Other locations 71 W 23rd St between Fifth & Sixth Avenues (1-646 336 6999).
FedEx Office *1-800 463 3339, www.fedex.com.*
There are outposts of this efficient computer and copy centre all over the city; many are open 24 hours.

CONSUMER

Better Business Bureau *1-212 533 6200, www.newyork.bbb.org.*
New York City Department of Consumer Affairs *42 Broadway, between Beaver Street & Exchange Place, Financial District (311 local, 1-212 639 9675 out of state, www.nyc.gov/consumer). Subway 4, 5 to Bowling Green.* **Open** 9am-5pm Mon-Fri. **Map** p402 E33.
File complaints on consumer-related matters here.
New York City 311 Call Center *311.*
This non-emergency three-digit number is a means for residents to get answers and register complaints about city issues, from parking regulations to real-estate auctions and consumer tips.

CUSTOMS

US Customs allows foreigners to bring in $100 worth of gifts (the limit is $800 for returning Americans) without paying duty. One carton of 200 cigarettes (or 50 cigars) and one litre of liquor (spirits) are allowed. Plants, meat and fresh produce of any kind cannot be brought into the country. You will have to fill out a form if you carry more than $10,000 in currency. You will be handed a white form on your inbound flight to fill in, confirming that you haven't exceeded any of these allowances.

If you need to bring prescription drugs with you into the US, make sure the container is clearly marked, and bring your doctor's statement or a prescription. Marijuana, cocaine and most opiate derivatives, along with a number of other drugs and chemicals, are not permitted: the possession of them is punishable by a stiff fine and/or imprisonment. Check in with the US Customs Service (www.customs.gov) before you arrive if you're unsure.

UK Customs allows returning visitors to bring only £145 worth of 'gifts, souvenirs and other goods' into the country duty-free, along with the usual duty-free goods.

DISABLED

Under New York City law, all facilities constructed after 1987 must provide complete access for the disabled – restrooms, entrances and exits included. In 1990, the

Americans with Disabilities Act made the same requirement federal law. In the wake of this legislation, many older buildings have added disabled-access features. There has been widespread (though imperfect) compliance with the law, but call ahead to check facilities.New York City can still be very challenging for disabled visitors. One useful resource is Access for All, a guide to NYC's cultural institutions published by Hospital Audiences Inc (1-212 575 7676, www.hospaud.org). The online guide tells how accessible each location really is and includes information on the height of telephones and water fountains; hearing and visual aids; and passenger-loading zones and alternative entrances. HAI's service for the visually impaired provides recordings of commentaries of theatre performances.

All Broadway theatres are equipped with devices for the hearing-impaired; call Sound Associates (1-888 772 7686, www.soundassociates.com) for more information. There are a number of other stage-related resources for the disabled. Telecharge (1-212 239 6200, www.telecharge.com) reserves tickets for wheelchair seating in Broadway and Off Broadway venues.

Lighthouse International
111 E 59th Street, between Park & Lexington Avenues, Upper East Side (1-212 821 9200, www.lighthouse.org). Subway N, R to Lexington Avenue-59th Street; 4, 5, 6 to 59th Street. **Open** 10am-6pm Mon-Fri; 10am-5pm Sat. **Map** p405 E29.
In addition to running a store that sells handy items for the vision-impaired, Lighthouse also provides helpful information for blind residents of and visitors to New York City.

Mayor's Office for People with Disabilities
2nd Floor, 100 Gold Street, between Frankfort & Spruce Streets, Financial District (1-212 788 2830). Subway J, M, Z to Chambers Street; 4, 5, 6 to Brooklyn Bridge-City Hall. **Open** 9am-5pm Mon-Fri. **Map** p402 F32.
This city office provides a broad range of services for the disabled.

New York Society for the Deaf
315 Hudson Street, between Vandam & Spring Streets, Soho (1-212 366 0066, www.fegs.org). Subway C, E to Spring Street; 1 to Houston Street. **Open** 9am-6pm Mon-Thur; 9am-4.30pm Fri. **Map** p403 D30.
Information and a range of services for the deaf and hearing-impaired.

Society for Accessible Travel & Hospitality
1-212 447 7284, www.sath.org.
This non-profit group educates the public about travel facilities for people with disabilities, and promotes travel for the disabled. Membership ($49/yr; $29 reductions) includes access to an information service and a quarterly magazine.

DRUGS

Possession of marijuana can result in anything from a $100 fine and a warning (for a first offence, 25g or less) to felony charges and prison time (for greater amounts and/or repeat offenders). Penalties, ranging from class B misdemeanors to class C felonies, are greater for the sale and cultivation of marijuana.

Possession of 'controlled substances' (cocaine, ecstasy, heroin, etc) is not taken lightly, and charges come with stiff penalties – especially if you are convicted of possession with intent to sell. Convictions carry anything from a mandatory one- to three-year prison sentence to a maximum of 25 years.

ELECTRICITY

The US uses 110-120V, 60-cycle alternating current rather than the 220-240V, 50-cycle AC used in Europe. The transformers that power or recharge newer electronic devices such as laptops are designed to handle either current and may need nothing more than an adaptor for the wall outlet. Other appliances may also require a power converter. Adaptors and converters can be purchased at airport shops, pharmacies, department stores and at branches of electronics chain Radio Shack (www.radioshack.com).

EMBASSIES & CONSULATES

Check the phone book for a complete list of consulates and embassies. *See also p375* **Travel Advice.**

Australia *1-212 351 6500.*
Canada *1-212 596 1628.*
Great Britain *1-212 745 0200.*
Ireland *1-212 319 2555.*
New Zealand *1-212 832 4038.*

EMERGENCIES

In an emergency only, dial **911** for an ambulance, police or the fire department, or call the operator (dial 0). For hospitals, *see below*; for helplines, *see p377*; for the police, *see p380*.

GAY & LESBIAN

For more gay and lesbian resources, including the Lesbian, Gay, Bisexual & Transgender Community Center, *see pp301-310.*

Gay, Lesbian, Bisexual & Transgender National Hotline
1-888 843 4564, www.glnh.org. **Open** 4pm-midnight Mon-Fri; noon-5pm Sat.
This phone service offers excellent peer counselling, legal referrals, details of gay and lesbian organisations, and information on bars, restaurants and hotels. Younger callers can contact the toll-free GLBT National Youth Talk Line (1-800 246 7743, 8pm-midnight Mon-Fri).

HEALTH

Public health care is virtually nonexistent in the US, and private health care is very expensive. Make sure you have comprehensive medical insurance before you leave. For HIV testing, *see p377* Chelsea Clinic; for HIV/AIDS counselling, *see p377* Helplines. For a list of hospitals, *see below.*

For other hospitals, consult the *Yellow Pages* directory.

Accident & emergency

You will be billed for any emergency treatment. Call your travel insurance company before seeking treatment to find out which hospitals accept your insurance. The following hospitals have emergency rooms:

Mount Sinai Hospital
Madison Avenue, at 100th Street, Upper East Side (1-212 241 6500). Subway 6 to 103rd Street. **Map** p406 E16.

New York – Presbyterian Hospital/Weill Cornell Medical Center
525 E 68th Street, at York Avenue, Upper East Side (1-212 746 5454). Subway 6 to 68th Street. **Map** p405 G21.

St Luke's – Roosevelt Hospital
1000 Tenth Avenue, at 59th Street, Upper West Side (1-212 523 4000).

Subway A, B, C, D, 1 to 59th Street-Columbus Circle. **Map** p405 C22.

Clinics

Walk-in clinics offer treatment for minor ailments. Most clinics will require immediate payment for treatments and consultations, though some will send their bill directly to your insurance company if you're a US resident. You will have to file a claim to recover the cost of any prescription medication that is required.

Beth Israel Medical Group
55 E 34th Street, between Madison & Park Avenues, Murray Hill (1-212 252 6000, www.wehealny.org/services/bimg). Subway 6 to 33rd Street. **Open** Walk-in 8am-8pm Mon-Fri; also by appt. **Base fee** from $125. **Credit** AmEx, DC, Disc, MC, V. **Map** p404 E25.
Primary-care facilities offering by-appointment and walk-in services. If you need X-rays or lab tests, go as early as possible (no later than 6pm) Monday to Friday.
Other locations 202 W 23rd Street, at Seventh Avenue (1-212 352 2600).

NY Urgent Hotel Medical Services
Suite 1D, 952 Fifth Avenue, between 76th & 77th Streets, Upper East Side (1-212 737 1212, www.travelmd.com). Subway 6 to 77th Street. **Open** 24hrs; appointments required. **Fees** (higher for nights & weekends) Weekday hotel visit $400. Weekday office visit $200. **Credit** MC, V. **Map** p405 E19.
Specialist medical attention in your Manhattan hotel room or private residence, from a simple prescription to urgent medical care.

Dentists

New York County Dental Society
1-212 573 8500, www.nycdentalsociety.org. **Open** 9am-5pm Mon-Fri.
Local referrals. An emergency line at the number above runs outside office hours; alternatively, use the search facility on the Association's website.

Opticians

See p253.

Pharmacies

For a list of pharmacies (including 24-hour locations), *see p254*. Note that pharmacies in New York will not refill foreign prescriptions and may not sell the same products you use at home.

STDs, HIV & AIDS

For the National STD & AIDS Hotline, *see right* Helplines.

NYC Department of Health Chelsea Health Center
303 Ninth Avenue, at 28th Street, Chelsea (1-212 720 7128). Subway C, E to 23rd Street. **Open** 8.30am-4pm Mon-Fri; 8.30am-noon Sat. Extended hours for HIV testing and counselling only 5-7pm Tue-Thur. **Map** p404 B26.
Hours of local walk-in clinics may change at short notice, so be sure to call ahead before visiting. Arrive early, because day-to-day testing is offered on a first-come, first-served basis. (Check the phone book or see www.nyc.gov for other free clinics.)

Gay Men's Health Crisis
119 W 24th Street, between Sixth & Seventh Avenues, Chelsea (1-212 367 1000, 1-800 243 7692 HIV/AIDS hotline, www.gmhc.org). Subway F, M, 1 to 23rd Street. **Open** *Centre* 10am-6pm Mon-Fri. *Hotline* 10am-6pm Mon, Wed; 1-6pm Fri; recorded information at other times. **Map** p404 D26.
GMHC was the world's first organisation dedicated to helping people with AIDS, and offers testing, counselling and other services on a walk-in and appointment basis.

Contraception & abortion

Parkmed Physicians Center
7th Floor, 800 Second Avenue, between 42nd & 43rd Streets, Midtown East (1-212 686 6066, www.parkmed.com). Subway S, 4, 5, 6, 7 to 42nd Street-Grand Central. **Open** by appt only. **Credit** AmEx, DC, Disc, MC, V. **Map** p404 F24.
Urine pregnancy tests are free. Counselling, contraception services and non-surgical abortions are also available at the centre.

Planned Parenthood of New York City *Margaret Sanger Center, 26 Bleecker Street, at Mott Street, Greenwich Village (1-212 965 7000, 1-800 230 7526, www.ppnyc.org). Subway B, D, F, M to Broadway-Lafayette Street; N, R to Prince Street; 6 to Bleecker Street.* **Open** 8am-4.30pm Mon, Tue; 8am-6.30pm Wed-Fri; 7.30am-4pm Sat. **Credit** AmEx, DC, MC, V. **Map** p403 F29.
The best-known network of family-planning clinics in the US. Counselling and treatment are available for a full range of needs, including abortion, contraception, HIV testing and treatment of STDs.
Other locations 44 Court Street, between Joralemon & Remsen Streets, Brooklyn Heights, Brooklyn (1-212 965 7000).

HELPLINES

All numbers are open 24 hours unless otherwise stated.

Addictions Hotline
1-800 522 5353.
Alcoholics Anonymous
1-212 647 1680. **Open** 9am-10pm daily.
Childhelp USA's National Child Abuse Hotline
1-800 422 4453.
Cocaine Anonymous
1-212 262 2463 recorded information.
National STD & AIDS Hotline
1-800 232 4636.
Pills Anonymous
1-212 874 0700 recorded information.
Safe Horizon Crisis Hotline
1-212 227 3000, www.safehorizon.org.
Counselling for victims of domestic violence, rape or other crimes.
St Luke's – Roosevelt Hospital
1-212 523 4728. **Open** 9am-5pm Mon-Fri.
Samaritans
1-212 673 3000.
Counselling for suicide prevention.
Special Victims Liaison Unit of the NYPD
1-212 267 7273 rape hotline.

ID

Always carry picture ID: even people well over 18 or 21 may be carded when buying tobacco or alcohol, ordering drinks in bars, or entering clubs.

INSURANCE

Non-nationals and US citizens should have travel and medical insurance before travelling. For a list of New York urgent-care facilities, *see p376.*

INTERNET

Cyber Café *250 W 49th Street, between Broadway & Eighth Avenue, Theater District (1-212 333 4109). Subway C, E, 1 to 50th Street; N, R, Q to 49th Street.*

Open 8am-11pm Mon-Fri; 8.30am-11pm Sat, Sun. **Cost** $6.40/30mins; 50¢/printed page. **Credit** AmEx, DC, MC, V. **Map** p404 D23.
This is a standard internet access café that also happens to serve great coffee and snacks.

FedEx Office *1-800 463 3339, www.fedex.com.*
Outposts of this ubiquitous and very efficient computer and copy centre are peppered throughout the city; many are open 24 hours a day.

New York Public Library *www.nypl.org.*
Branches of the NYPL are great places to get online for free, offering both Wi-Fi and computers for public use. (Ask for an out-of-state card, for which you need proof of residence, or a guest pass.)

The three libraries with the most computers available for public internet access are the Science, Industry & Business Library, 188 Madison Avenue, at 34th Street (about 50 computers); the Mid-Manhattan Library, 455 Fifth Avenue, at 40th Street (about 50 computers); the Stephen A Schwartzman Building (Fifth Avenue, at 42nd Street, Midtown), which loans out laptops in addition to its desktop models in the South Hall. All libraries have a computer limit of 45 minutes per day.

NYCWireless *1-212 592 7000, www.nycwireless.net.*
This group has established dozens of hotspots in the city for free wireless access. (For example, most parks below 59th Street are covered.) Visit the website for information and a map.

Starbucks *www.starbucks.com.*
Many branches offer up to two hours of free wireless access per day through AT&T, with activation of a Starbucks card (which you purchase in various amounts and use in the store).

LEFT LUGGAGE

There are luggage-storage facilities at arrivals halls in JFK Airport (Terminal 1: 7am-11pm, $4-$16 per bag per day; call 1-718 751 2947); (Terminal 4: 24hrs, $4-$16 per bag per day; call 1-718 751 4001). At Penn Station, Amtrak offers checked baggage services ($4.50 per bag per day) for some of its ticketed passengers. Due to heightened security, luggage storage is not available at the Port Authority Bus Terminal, Grand Central, or LaGuardia or Newark airports.

One Midtown alternative is to leave bags with the private firm, located between Penn Station and Port Authority, listed below. Some hotels may allow you to leave suitcases with the front desk before check-in or after check-out; if so, be sure to tip the concierge.

Schwartz Travel Services
355 W 36th Street, between Eighth & Ninth Avenues (1-212 290 2626, www.schwartztravel.com). **Open** 8am-11pm daily. **Rates** $7-$10 per bag per day. **No credit cards.** **Other locations** 34 W 46th Street, between Fifth & Sixth Avenues (same phone).

LEGAL HELP

If you're arrested for a minor violation (disorderly conduct, loitering, etc) and you're very polite to the officer during the arrest (and carry proper ID), then you'll probably be fingerprinted, photographed at the station and given a ticket with a date to show up at criminal court. After that, you'll most likely get to go home.

Arguing with a police officer or engaging in more serious criminal activity (such as possession of a weapon, drunk driving, illegal gambling or prostitution, for example) will get you 'processed', which means a 24- to 30-hour journey through the system.

If the courts are backed up (and they usually are), you'll be held temporarily at a precinct pen. You can make a phone call after you've been fingerprinted. When you get through central booking, you'll arrive at 100 Centre Street for arraignment. A judge will decide whether you should be released on bail and will set a court date.

If you can't post bail, then you'll be held at Rikers Island jail.

Legal Aid Society *1-212 577 3300, www.legal-aid.org.* **Open** 9am-5pm Mon-Fri.

Sandback & Michelen Criminal Law *1-800 640 2000.* **Open** 9am-5pm Mon-Fri.
If no one at this firm can help you, then you'll be directed to lawyers who can.

LIBRARIES

See p99 New York Public Library.

LOST PROPERTY

For property lost in the street, contact the police. For lost credit cards or travellers' cheques, *see p380.*

Grand Central Terminal *lower level, near Track 110. 1-212 532 4900.* **Open** 7am-6pm Mon-Fri.
You can call 24 hrs a day to file a claim if you've left something on a Metro-North train.

JFK Airport *1-718 244 4225*, or contact your airline.

La Guardia Airport *1-718 533 3988*, or contact your airline.

Newark Liberty International Airport *1-973 961 6243*, or contact your airline.

Penn Station: Amtrak *1-212 630 7389.* **Open** 7.30am-4pm Mon-Fri.

Penn Station: Long Island Rail Road *1-212 643 5228.* **Open** 7.30am-7pm Mon-Fri.

Penn Station: New Jersey Transit *1-973 275 5555.* **Open** 7am-7pm daily.

Subway & Buses *New York City Metropolitan Transit Authority, 34th Street-Penn Station, near the A-train platform, Garment District (1-212 712 4500).* **Open** 8am-3.30pm Mon, Tue, Fri; 11am-6.30pm Wed, Thur. **Map** p404 D25.
Call if you've left something on a subway train or a bus.

Taxis *1-212 826 3211, 3212, 3213 or 1-212 570 4821, www.nyc.gov/taxi.*
Call for items left in a cab.

MEDIA

Daily newspapers

The **Daily News** (50c; $1 on Sunday) has drifted politically from the Neanderthal right to a more moderate but always tough-minded stance under the ownership of noted real-estate mogul Mort Zuckerman.

Founded in 1801 by Alexander Hamilton, the **New York Post** (25c) is the nation's oldest continuously published daily newspaper. It has swerved sharply to the right under current owner Rupert Murdoch, includes more gossip than any other local paper, and its headlines are often sassy and sensational.

Despite recent financial woes, the **New York Times** ($2) remains the city's, and the nation's, paper of record. Founded as the *New-York Daily Times* in 1851, it has the broadest and deepest coverage of world and national events and, as the masthead proclaims, it delivers 'All the News That's Fit to Print'. The hefty Sunday edition ($5) includes a very well-regarded magazine, as well as book review, travel, real-estate and various other sections.

The **New York Amsterdam News** ($1), one of the nation's longest-running black newspapers, offers a trenchant African-American viewpoint. New York also supports two Spanish-language dailies: **El Diario La Prensa** and **NY Al Día**. **Newsday** (25c) is a Long Island-based daily with a tabloid format but a sober tone. Free tabloids **AM New York** and **New York Metro** offer locally slanted news, arts and entertainment listings.

Weekly newspapers

Downtown journalism is a battlefield, with the **New York Press** pitted against the **Village Voice**. The *Press* is full of irreverence, as well as cynicism and self-absorption. The *Voice* is at turns passionate and ironic but just as often strident and predictable. Both are free.

Most neighbourhoods boast free publications featuring local news, reviews and gossip, such as **Our Town East Side**, **West Side Spirit**, the **West Sider** and **Chelsea Clinton News**.

Magazines

New York magazine is part news weekly, part lifestyle reporting and part listings. Since the 1920s, the **New Yorker** has been known for its fine wit, elegant prose and sophisticated cartoons. It has also evolved into a respected forum for serious long-form journalism.

Based on the tried and trusted format of its London parent magazine, **Time Out New York** is an intelligent, irreverent, indispensable weekly guide to what's going on in the city: arts, restaurants, bars, shops and more.

Since its launch in 1996, the bimonthly **BlackBook Magazine** has covered New York's high fashion and culture with intelligent bravado. **Gotham**, a monthly from the publisher of glossy gab-rags **Hamptons** and **Aspen Peak**, unveiled its larger-than-life celeb-filled pages in 2001. And for two decades now, **Paper** has offered buzz on bars, clubs, downtown boutiques and more.

Radio

Nearly 100 stations serve the New York area. On the AM dial, you can find talk radio and phone-in shows that attract everyone from priests to sports nuts. Flip to FM for music.

College radio is innovative and commercial-free but reception is often compromised by Manhattan's high-rise topography. **WNYU-FM 89.1** and **WKCR-FM 89.9** are, respectively, the stations of New York University and Columbia. **WFUV-FM 90.7**, Fordham University's station, airs a variety of shows, including Beale Street Caravan, the world's most widely distributed blues programme.

American commercial radio is rigidly formatted, which makes most pop stations extremely tedious and repetitive during the day. Tune in on evenings and weekends for more interesting programming. Always popular, **WQHT-FM 97.1**, 'Hot 97,' is a commercial hip hop station with all-day rap and R&B. **WKTU-FM 103.5** is the premier dance music station. **WWPR-FM 105.1**, 'Power 105,' plays top hip hop, and a few old-school hits. **WBLS-FM 107.5** showcases classic and new funk, soul and R&B. **WBGO-FM 88.3** is strictly jazz. **WAXQ-FM 104.3** offers classic rock. **WXRK-FM 92.3**'s alternative music attracts and appals listeners with its 6-10am weekday sleaze fest.

WQEW-AM 1560, 'Radio Disney', has kids' programming. **WNYC-FM 93.9** and **WQXR-FM 105.9** serve up a range of classical music. **WXNY-FM 96.3** and **WQBU-FM 92.7** spin Spanish and Latin.

WABC-AM 770, **WCBS-AM 880**, **WINS-AM 1010** and **WBBR-AM 1130** offer news throughout the day, plus traffic and weather reports. **WNYC-AM 820/FM 93.9**, a commercial-free, public radio station, provides news and current-affairs commentary and broadcasts the BBC World Service. **WBAI-FM 99.5** is a left-leaning community radio station. **WWRL-AM 1600**, the former flagship of defunct Air America, is a more liberal answer to right-wing talk radio.

WFAN-AM 660 airs Giants, Nets, Mets and Devils games. **WCBS-AM 880** covers the Yankees. **WEPN-AM** 1050 is devoted to news and sports talk and is the home of the Jets, Knicks and Rangers. **WBBR-AM 1130** broadcasts Islanders games.

Television

Six major networks broadcast nationwide. All offer ratings-driven variations on a theme.

CBS (Channel 2 in NYC) has the top-rated investigative show, 60 Minutes, on Sundays at 7pm; overall, programming is geared to a middle-aged demographic, but CBS also screens shows such as *CSI* and the reality series *Survivor*. **NBC** (4) is the home of *Law & Order*, the long-running sketch-comedy series *Saturday Night Live* (11.30pm Sat), and popular prime-time shows that include *The Office* and *30 Rock*. **Fox-WNYW** (5) is popular with younger audiences for shows such as *Glee*, *Family Guy*, *24* and *American Idol*. **ABC** (7) is the king of daytime soaps, family-friendly sitcoms and hits like *Desperate Housewives* and *Grey's Anatomy*.

Public TV is on channels 13, 21 and 25. Documentaries, arts shows and science series alternate with Masterpiece (Anglo costume and contemporary dramas packaged for a US audience) and reruns of British sitcoms.

For channel numbers for cable TV channels, such as **Time Warner Cable**, **Cablevision** and **RCN**, check a local newspaper or the Web. **FSN (Fox Sports Network)**, **MSG (Madison Square Garden)**, **ESPN** and **ESPN2** are all-sports stations. **Comedy Central** is all comedy, airing *South Park*, *The Daily Show with Jon Stewart* and its hugely popular spin-off *The Colbert Report*. **Cinemax**, the **Disney Channel**, **HBO**, the **Movie Channel** and **Showtime** are often available in hotels. They show uninterrupted feature films, exclusive specials and series such as *True Blood* and *Curb Your Enthusiasm*.

MONEY

Over the past few years, much of American currency has undergone a subtle facelift, partly to deter increasingly adept counterfeiters; all denominations except the $1 bill have recently been updated by the US Treasury. (However, 'old' money still remains in circulation.) Coins include copper pennies (1¢) and silver-coloured nickels (5¢), dimes (10¢) and quarters (25¢). Half-dollar coins (50¢) and the gold-coloured dollar coins are less common.

All paper money is the same size, so make sure you fork over the right bill. It comes in denominations of $1, $2, $5, $10, $20, $50 and $100 (and higher, but you'll never see those bills). The $2 bills are quite rare. Try to keep some low notes on you because getting change may be a problem with anything bigger than a $20 bill.

ATMs

The city is full of ATMs, located in bank branches, delis and many small shops. Most accept MasterCard, Visa and major bank cards. Some UK banks charge up to £4 per transaction plus a variable payment to cover themselves against any exchange rate fluctuations. Most ATM cards now double as debit cards, if they bear Maestro or Cirrus logos.

Banks & bureaux de change

Banks are generally open from 9am to 6pm Monday to Friday, though some stay open longer and/or on Saturdays. You need photo ID, such as a passport, to cash travellers' cheques. Many banks will not exchange foreign currency; bureaux de change, limited to tourist-trap areas, close at around 6pm or 7pm. In emergencies, most large hotels offer 24-hour exchange facilities, but the rates won't be great.

Chase Bank
1-800 935 9935, www.chase.com.
Chase's website gives information on foreign currency exchange, branch locations and credit cards. For foreign currency delivered in a hurry, call the number listed above.
TD Bank
1-888 751 9000, www.tdbank.com.
All 19 Manhattan branches of the Canadian-owned bank are open seven days a week.
People's Foreign Exchange
60 E 42nd Street, between Madison & Park Avenues, Midtown East (1-212 883 0550). Subway S, 4, 5, 6, 7 to Grand Central. **Open** 9am-5.30pm Mon-Fri; 10.30am-3pm Sat, Sun. **Map** p404 E23.
People's Foreign Exchange offers foreign currency exchange on bank notes and travellers' cheques of any denomination for a $2 fee.
Travelex
29 Broadway, at Morris Street, Financial District (1-212 363 6206, www.travelex.com). Subway 4, 5 to Bowling Green. **Open** 9am-5pm Mon-Sat; 10am-4pm Sun. **Map** p402 E33.
A complete range of foreign-exchange services is offered by Travlex.
Other locations 1590 Broadway, at 48th Street (1-212 265 6063), 9am-9pm daily; 1271 Broadway, at 32nd Street (1-212 679 4365), 9am-9pm daily; 30 Vesey Street, between Broadway & Church Street (1-212 227 8156), 9am-7pm daily.

Credit cards & travellers' cheques

Credit cards are essential for renting cars and booking hotels, and handy for buying tickets over the phone and the internet.

The five major cards accepted in the US are **American Express** (abbreviated as AmEx throughout this book), **Diners Club** (DC), **Discover** (Disc), **MasterCard** (MC) and **Visa** (V). MasterCard and Visa are the most popular; American Express is also widely accepted. Thanks to a 2004 deal between MasterCard and Diners Club, all businesses that accept the former can now accept the latter.

If your cards or travellers' cheques are lost or stolen, call the following numbers:

American Express *1-800 528 2122, 1-800 221 7282 travellers' cheques.*
Diners Club *1-800 234 6377.*
Discover *1-800 347 2683.*
Mastercard/Maestro *1-800 826 2181, 1-800 223 9920 travellers' cheques.*
Visa/Cirrus *1-800 336 8472, 1-800 336 8472 travellers' cheques.*

Tax

Sales tax is 8.875 per cent in New York City, and is applicable to restaurant bills, services and the purchase of just about anything, except most store-bought foods, clothing and shoes (the latter two are exempt when an item costs $110 or less). In the US, sales tax is almost never included in the price of the item, but added on to the final bill at the till. There is no tax refund option for foreign visitors.

Wire services

If you run out of cash, you can have funds wired to you from home through the following companies:
Moneygram *1-800 666 3947, www.moneygram.com.*
Western Union *1-800 325 6000, www.westernunion.com.*

OPENING HOURS

Banks and government offices, including post offices, close on federal holidays. Retail in the city shuts down on Christmas Day and New Year's Day, although movie theatres and some restaurants remain open. Most museums are closed on Mondays, but may open when a public holiday falls on a Monday. New York's subway runs 24 hours a day, 365 days a year, but always check station signs for track or schedule changes, especially during weekends and holidays.

Banks 9am-6pm Mon-Fri; generally also Sat mornings.
Businesses 9am or 10am to 5pm or 6pm Mon-Fri.
Post Offices 9am-5pm Mon-Fri (a few open as early as 7.30am and close as late as 8.30pm); some are open Sat until 3pm or 4pm. The James A Farley Post Office (see below) is open 24 hours daily.
Pubs & Bars 4pm-2am Sun-Thur, noon-4am Fri, Sat (hours vary widely).
Shops 9am, 10am or 11am to 7pm or 8pm Mon-Sat (some open at noon and/or close at 9pm). Many are also open on Sun, usually 11am or noon to 6pm.

POLICE

In an emergency only, dial **911**. The NYPD stations below are in central, tourist-heavy areas of Manhattan. For the location of your nearest police precinct or information about police services, call 1-646 610 5000.

Midtown North Precinct
306 W 54th Street, between Eighth & Ninth Avenues, Hell's Kitchen (1-212 760 8300).
17th Precinct
167 E 51st Street, between Third & Lexington Avenues, Midtown East (1-212 826 3211).
Midtown South Precinct
357 W 35th Street, between Eighth & Ninth Avenues, Garment District (1-212 239 9811).
Central Park Precinct
86th Street & Transverse Road, Central Park (1-212 570 4820).

POSTAL SERVICES

Stamps are available at all US post offices, from drugstore vending machines and at most newsstands. It costs 44¢ to send a 1oz letter within the US. Each additional ounce costs 17¢. Postcards mailed within the US cost 28¢. Airmailed letters or postcards to Canada and Mexico cost 75¢ for the first ounce; to all other countries it's 98¢ for the first ounce. The cost of additional ounces varies by country.

For faster **Express Mail**, you must fill out a form, either at a post office or by arranging a pickup; 24-hour delivery to major US cities is guaranteed. International delivery takes two to three days, with no guarantee. Call 1-800 275 8777 for more information. For couriers and messengers, *see p375*.

James A Farley Post Office
421 Eighth Avenue, between 31st & 33rd Streets, Garment District (1-800 275 8777 24hr information, www.usps.com). Subway A, C, E to 34th Street-Penn Station. **Open** 24hrs daily. *Counter service* 7am-10pm Mon-Fri; 9am-9pm Sat; 11am-7pm Sun. **Credit** DC, MC, V. **Map** p404 D25.
Outside of counter-service hours, you can buy stamps and post packages using automated self-service machines.

General Delivery
390 Ninth Avenue, between 31st & 33rd Streets, Garment District (1-212 330 3099). Subway A, C, E to 34th Street-Penn Station. **Open** 10am-1pm Mon-Fri; 10am-noon Sat. **Map** p404 C25.
US residents without local addresses can receive their post here; it should be addressed to the recipient, General Delivery, 390 Ninth Avenue, New York, NY 10001. You will need to show a passport or ID card when picking up letters.

Poste Restante
Window 73, James A Farley Post Office, 421 Eighth Avenue, between 31st & 33rd Streets, Garment District (1-212 330 2883). Subway A, C, E to 34th Street-Penn Station. **Open** 10am-1pm Mon-Sat. **Map** p404 D25.
Foreign visitors can receive post here; post should be addressed to the recipient, General Post Office, Poste Restante, 421 Eighth Avenue, attn: Window 73, New York, NY 10001. Be sure to bring ID to collect anything.

RELIGION

Here are just a few of New York's many places of worship. Check the phone book for more listings.

Abyssinian Baptist Church
For listings, *see p121*.

Cathedral Church of St John the Divine For listings, *see p119*.

Church of St Paul & St Andrew, United Methodist *263 W 86th Street, between Broadway & West End Avenue, Upper West Side (1-212 362 3179, www.spsanyc.org). Subway 1 to 86th Street.* **Map** p406 C18.

Islamic Cultural Center of New York *1711 Third Avenue, between 96th & 97th Streets, Upper East Side (1-212 722 5234). Subway 6 to 96th Street.* **Map** p406 F17.

Madison Avenue Presbyterian Church *921 Madison Avenue, between 73rd & 74th Streets, Upper East Side (1-212 288 8920, www.mapc.com). Subway 6 to 72nd Street.* **Map** p405 E20.

New York Buddhist Church
331-332 Riverside Drive, between 105th & 106th Streets, Upper West Side (1-212 678 0305, www.newyorkbuddhistchurch.org). Subway 1 to 103rd Street. **Map** p406 B16.

St Patrick's Cathedral
For listings, *see p100*.

UJA – Federation of New York Resource Line *1-877 852 6951, www.ujafedny.org.* **Open** 9am-4pm Mon-Fri.
This hotline provides referrals to other Jewish organisations, groups, temples, philanthropic activities and synagogues.

SAFETY & SECURITY

New York's crime rate, particularly for violent crime, has waned during the past two decades. Most crime occurs late at night, mostly in low-income neighbourhoods. Don't arrive in NYC thinking your safety is at risk wherever you go; it is unlikely that you will ever be bothered.

Still, a bit of common sense won't hurt. Don't flaunt your money and valuables, and try not to look obviously lost. Avoid deserted and poorly lit streets; walk facing oncoming traffic so no one can drive up alongside you undetected, and close to or on the street; muggers prefer to hang back in doorways and shadows. If you are threatened, hand over your valuables at once, then dial 911.

Be extra alert to pickpockets and street hustlers – especially in crowded areas like Times Square.

SMOKING

The 1995 NYC Smoke-Free Air Act makes it illegal to smoke in virtually all indoor public places, including the subway and cinemas; for a list of exceptions, *see p223* Inside Track.

STUDY

Those who study in NYC have access to an endless extracurricular education, as well as a non-stop playground. Foreign students should get hold of an International Student Identity Card (ISIC) in order to secure discounts. These cards can be purchased from your local student-travel agent (go to www.isic.org or ask at your student union or an STA Travel office).

For student-oriented features, listings and guidance, check the free *Time Out New York Student Guide*, distributed on campuses at the start of the academic year.

Manhattan's main universities include: the **City University of New York**'s 23 colleges (1-212 794 5555, www.cuny.edu); **Columbia University** (2960 Broadway, at 116th Street, Morningside Heights, 1-212 854 1754, www.columbia.edu); the **Cooper Union** (30 Cooper Square, between 5th & 6th Streets, East Village, 1-212 353 4100, www.cooper.edu); **Fordham University** (113 W 60th Street, at Columbus Avenue, Upper West Side, 1-212 636 6000, www.fordham.edu); the **New School** (55 W 13th Street, between Fifth & Sixth Avenues, Greenwich Village, 1-212 229 5620, www.newschool.edu); **New York University** (70 Washington Square South, Greenwich Village, 1-212 998 1212, www.nyu.edu); and performing arts school **Juilliard** (60 Lincoln Center Plaza, at Broadway, Upper West Side, 1-212 799 5000, www.juilliard.edu).

TELEPHONES

Dialling & codes

As a rule, you must dial 1 + the area code before a number, even if the place you are calling is in the same area code. The area codes for Manhattan are **212** and **646**; Brooklyn, Queens, Staten Island and the Bronx are **718** and **347**; **917** is now reserved mostly for mobile phones and pagers. Long Island area codes are 516 and 631; codes for New Jersey are 201, 551, 609, 732, 848, 856, 862, 908 and 973. Numbers preceded by **800**, **877** and **888** are free of charge when dialled from within the US.

In an **emergency** dial 911. All calls are free (including those from pay and mobile phones).

For the **operator** dial 0. If you're not used to US phones, then note that the ringing tone is long; the engaged tone, or 'busy signal', is much shorter and higher pitched.

Collect calls are also known as reverse-charge calls. To make one, dial 0 followed by the number, or dial AT&T's 1-800 225 5288, MCI's 1-800 265 5328 or Sprint's 1-800 663 3463.

For **directory assistance**, dial 411 or 1 + area code + 555 1212. Doing so may cost nothing, depending on the pay phone you are using; carrier fees may apply. Long-distance directory assistance may also incur long-distance charges. For a directory of toll-free numbers, dial 1-800 555 1212.

For **international calls** dial 011 + country code (Australia 61; New Zealand 64; UK 44), then the number (omitting any initial zero).

Mobile phones

Most US mobile phones will work in NYC but since the US doesn't have a standard national network, visitors should check with their provider that their phone will work here, and whether they need to unlock a roaming option. Visitors from other countries will need a tri-band handset and a roaming agreement, and may find charges so high that rental (*see p236*), or, depending on the length of their stay, purchase of a US phone (or SIM card) will make better economic sense.

If you carry a mobile phone, make sure you turn it off at restaurants, plays, movies, concerts and museums. New Yorkers are quick to show their annoyance at an ill-timed ring. Some establishments now even post signs designating a cellular-free zone.

Public phones

Functioning public pay phones are becoming increasingly hard to find. Phones take any combination of silver coins: local calls usually cost 50¢ for three minutes. To call long-distance or to make an international call from a pay phone, you need to go through a long-distance company. Most of the pay phones in New York automatically use AT&T, but phones in and around transportation hubs usually contract other long-distance carriers, and charges can be outrageous. MCI and Sprint are respected brand names (see above).

Make the call by either dialling 0 for an operator or dialling direct, which is cheaper. To find out how much it will cost, dial the number, and a computerised voice will tell you how much money to deposit. You can pay for calls with your credit card. The best way to make long-distance calls is with a phone card, available from any post-office branch, many newsagents and delis, or from chain stores such as Duane Reade and Rite Aid (*see p254* Pharmacies).

TIME & DATES

New York is on Eastern Standard Time, which extends from the Atlantic coast to the eastern shore of Lake Michigan and south to the Gulf of Mexico. This is five hours behind Greenwich Mean Time. Clocks are set forward one hour in early March for Daylight Saving Time (Eastern Daylight Time) and back one hour at the beginning of November. Going from east to west, Eastern Time is one hour ahead of Central Time, two hours ahead of Mountain Time and three hours ahead of Pacific Time.

In the United States, the date is written as month, day and year; so 2/8/08 is 8 February 2008.

Forms that foreigners may need to fill in, however, are often the other way round.

TIPPING

In restaurants, it's customary to tip at least 15 per cent, and since NYC tax is 8.875 percent, a quick way to calculate the tip is to double the tax. In many restaurants, when you are with a group of six or more, the tip will be included in the bill. For tipping on taxi fares, *see p374.*

TOILETS

The media had a field day when the first pay toilet to open in the city since 1975 received its 'first flush' by officials in a special ceremony in 2008. 'Public Toilet No.1', as the *New York Post* christened it, is in Madison Square Park (Madison Avenue, between 23rd & 24th Streets, Subway N, R, 6 to 23rd Street) and was due to be followed by around 20 across the city within the following couple of years; progress, however, has been stalled). It costs 25¢ to enter the large stainless steel and tempered glass box (dawdlers and OCD sufferers beware: the door opens after 15 minutes). Below is a list of other convenient rest stops.

Downtown

Battery Park Castle Clinton *Subway 1 to South Ferry; 4, 5 to Bowling Green.*
Tompkins Square Park *Avenue A, at 9th Street. Subway L to First Avenue; 6 to Astor Place.*
Washington Square Park *Thompson Street, at Washington Square South. Subway A, B, C, D, E, F, M to W 4th Street.*

Midtown

Bryant Park *42nd Street, between Fifth & Sixth Avenues. Subway B, D, F, M to 42nd Street-Bryant Park; 7 to Fifth Avenue.*
Grand Central Terminal *42nd Street, at Park Avenue, Lower Concourse. Subway S, 4, 5, 6, 7 to 42nd Street-Grand Central.*
Penn Station *Seventh Avenue, between 31st & 33rd Streets, Subway A, C, E, 1, 2, 3 to 34th Street-Penn Station.*

Uptown

Avery Fisher Hall *Broadway, at 65th Street. Subway 1 to 66th Street-Lincoln Center.*
Charles A Dana Discovery Center *Central Park, north side of Harlem Meer, 110th Street at Malcolm X Boulevard (Lenox Avenue). Subway 2, 3 to 110th Street-Central Park North.*
Delacorte Theater *Central Park, midpark, at 81st Street. Subway B, C to 81st Street-Museum of Natural History.*

TOURIST INFORMATION

Official NYC Information Center *810 Seventh Avenue, between 52nd & 53rd Streets, Midtown (1-212 484 1222, www.nycgo.com). Subway B, D, E to Seventh Avenue.* **Open** 8.30am-6pm Mon-Fri; 9am-5pm Sat, Sun. **Map** p404 D23.
The city's official (private, non-profit) visitors' information centre recently got a high-tech renovation, complete with interactive map tables that allow you to navigate the city's attractions, hotels and restaurants, and send your itineraries to your email address or mobile device. The centre also doles out maps, leaflets, coupons and advice; and sells MetroCards and tickets to attractions such as Top of the Rock, the Statue of Liberty and the Empire State Building, potentially saving you time waiting in line.
Other locations Times Square (*see p383*); Federal Hall, 26 Wall Street, between William & Nassau Streets; Chinatown, triangle of Canal, Walker & Baxter Streets; City Hall, southern tip of City Hall Park, Broadway at Park Row; and Harlem, 144 W 125th Street, between Adam Clayton Powell & Malcolm X Boulevards (inside Studio Museum in Harlem; *see*

THE LOCAL CLIMATE

Average temperatures and monthly rainfall in New York.

	High (°C/°F)	Low (°C/°F)	Rainfall (mm/in)
Jan	2 / 36	-5 / 23	94 / 3.7
Feb	4 / 40	-4 / 24	75 / 3.0
Mar	9 / 48	0 / 32	104 / 4.1
Apr	14 / 58	6 / 42	103 / 4.1
May	20 / 68	12 / 53	114 / 4.5
June	25 / 77	17 / 63	88 / 3.5
July	28 / 83	20 / 68	106 / 4.2
Aug	27 / 81	19 / 66	103 / 4.1
Sep	23 / 74	14 / 58	103 / 4.1
Oct	17 / 63	8 / 47	89 / 3.5
Nov	11 / 52	3 / 38	102 / 4.0
Dec	6 / 42	-2 / 28	98 / 3.9

p121). In the UK: NYC & Company, Colechurch House, 1 London Bridge Walk, London SE1 2SX (020 7367 0900).

Times Square Information Center *1560 Broadway, between 46th & 47th Streets, Theater District (1-212 869 1890, www.timessquarenyc.org). Subway N, Q, R, S, 1, 2, 3, 7 to 42nd Street-Times Square.* **Open** 9am-7pm Mon-Fri; 8am-8pm Sat, Sun. **Map** p404 D24.
This centre offers discount coupons for Broadway tickets, MetroCards, free maps and other useful goods and services, predominantly for the Theater District. There are also ATMs, photo booths and free internet stations on site.

Brooklyn Tourism & Visitors Center *Brooklyn Borough Hall, 209 Joralemon Street, between Court & Adams Streets (1-718 802 3846, www.visitbrooklyn.org).* **Open** 10am-6pm Mon-Fri. Summer also 10am-4pm Sat.
The centre has a wealth of information on attractions, sites and events in the city's largest borough, plus local-interest books and gifts.

VISAS & IMMIGRATION

Visas

Some 35 countries currently participate in the **Visa Waiver Program** (VWP; www.cbp.gov/esta). Citizens of Andorra, Australia, Austria, Belgium, Brunei, Czech Republic, Denmark, Estonia, Finland, France, Germany, Hungary, Iceland, Ireland, Italy, Japan, Latvia, Liechtenstein, Lithuania, Luxembourg, Malta, Monaco, the Netherlands, New Zealand, Norway, Portugal, San Marino, Singapore, Slovakia, Slovenia, South Korea, Spain, Sweden, Switzerland and the UK do not need a visa for stays in the US shorter than 90 days (business or pleasure) as long as they have a machine-readable passport (e-passport) valid for the full 90-day period and a return ticket.

Canadians travelling to the United States will need visas only in special circumstances.

If you do not qualify for entry under the VWP – that is, if you are not from one of the eligible countries or are visiting for any purpose other than pleasure or business – you will need a visa.

If you're in the slightest doubt, check ahead. You can obtain the application forms from your nearest US embassy or consulate or from its website. Find out several months in advance how long the application process is currently taking.

Whether or not you require a visa, you should not travel with a passport that will expire in six months or less.

If you lose your passport when you are inside the US, contact your consulate (*see p376*).

Immigration

Your airline will give all visitors an immigration form to be presented to an official when you land. Fill it in clearly and be prepared to give an address at which you are staying (a hotel is fine).

Upon arrival in the US, you may have to wait an hour or, if you're unlucky, considerably longer, in Immigration, where, owing to tightened security, you can expect slow-moving queues. You may be expected to explain your visit; be polite and prepared. Note that all visitors to the US are now photographed and fingerprinted on arrival on every trip. You will usually be granted an entry permit.

US State Department Visa Information
US: 1-202 663 1225 (8.30am-5pm Mon-Fri, except 11am-noon Wed), http://travel.state.gov. UK: 09055 444546 (60p/min).

WEIGHTS & MEASURES

Despite attempts to bring in metric measurements, you'll find imperial used in almost all contexts in New York and throughout America. People think in ounces, inches, gallons and miles.

WHEN TO GO

There is no bad time to visit New York, and visitor numbers are fairly steady year-round. However, the weather can be unpleasantly hot and humid in summer (especially August) and, although winter snow (usually heaviest in January and February) is picturesque before it gets dirty and slushy, these months are often brutally cold. Late spring and early autumn bring pleasantly moderate temperatures that are perfect for walking and exploring.

Public holidays

New Year's Day 1 Jan
Martin Luther King, Jr Day 3rd Mon in Jan
Presidents Day 3rd Mon in Feb
Memorial Day last Mon in May
Independence Day 4 July
Labor Day 1st Mon in Sept
Columbus Day 2nd Mon in Oct
Veterans Day 11 Nov
Thanksgiving Day 4th Thur in Nov
Christmas Day 25 Dec.

WORK

Non-nationals cannot work in the United States without the appropriate visa; these are hard to get and generally require you to prove that your job could not be done by a US citizen. Contact your local embassy for further details. Some student visas allow part-time work after the first academic year.

UK students who want to spend a summer vacation working in the US should contact the **British Universities North America Club** (BUNAC) for help in securing a temporary job and also the requisite visa (UK: 16 Bowling Green Lane, London EC1R 0QH, 020 7251 3472, www.bunac.org/uk).

Further Reference

BOOKS

Architecture

Richard Berenholtz
New York, New York
Miniature panoramic images of the city through the seasons.
Stanley Greenberg
Invisible New York
A photographic account of hidden architectural triumphs.
New York City Landmarks Preservation Commission
Guide to New York City Landmarks
Karl Sabbagh *Skyscraper*
How the tall ones are built.
Kevin Walsh *Forgotten New York*
Discover overlooked architectural gems and anachronistic remnants.
Norval White & Elliot Willensky
The AIA Guide to New York City
A comprehensive directory of important buildings.

Culture & recollections

Irving Lewis Allen
The City in Slang
NYC-bred words and phrases.
Joseph Berger
The World in a City
The *New York Times* columnist explores the communities located within the five boroughs.
Anatole Broyard
Kafka Was the Rage: A Greenwich Village Memoir
Vivid account of 1940s Village bohemia and its characters.
George Chauncey *Gay New York*
The evolution of gay culture from 1890 to 1940.
Martha Cooper & Henry Chalfant *Subway Art*
A definitive survey of city graffiti.
Naomi Fertitta & Paul Aresu
New York: The Big City and its Little Neighborhoods
This photojournalism/guidebook hybrid illuminates New York's immigrant populations.
Josh Alan Friedman
Tales of Times Square
Sleaze and decay in the old days.
Nelson George *Hip Hop America*
The real history of hip hop, from Grandmaster Flash to Puff Daddy.
Jane Jacobs *The Death and Life of Great American Cities*
A hugely influential critique of modern urban planning.
Chuck Katz
Manhattan on Film 1 & 2
On-location walking tours.
Gillian McCain & Legs McNeil
Please Kill Me
An oral history of the punk scene.
Joseph Mitchell
Up in the Old Hotel
Quirky recollections of New York and New Yorkers from the 1930s to the 1960s.
Thurston Moore & Byron Coley *No Wave*
Musicians reminisce about the downtown post-punk underground scene in this nostalgia trip co-edited by the Sonic Youth frontman.
Frank O'Hara *The Collected Poems of Frank O'Hara*
The great NYC poet found inspiration in his hometown.
Adrienne Onofri
Walking Brooklyn
Thirty tours illuminate the culture and history of the borough.
Sam Stephenson *The Jazz Loft Project: Photographs and Tapes of W Eugene Smith from 821 Sixth Avenue, 1957-1965*
Images and transcripts of conversations from the jazz-obsessed photographer's loft, which became a rehearsal space for some of the era's greatest musicians.
Judith Stonehill *New York's Unique & Unexpected Places*
Fifty special yet less-visited spots.
Time Out
1000 Things To Do in New York
Original and inspirational ideas to appeal to jaded residents and newly arrived visitors.
EB White *Here is New York*
A clear-eyed love letter to Gotham.

History

Herbert Asbury *The Gangs of New York: An Informal History of the Underworld*
A racy journalistic portrait of the city at the turn of the 19th century.
Robert A Caro *The Power Broker*
A biography of Robert Moses, New York's mid-20th-century master builder, and his chequered legacy.
Federal Writers' Project
The WPA Guide to New York City
A wonderful evocation of the 1930s by writers who were employed under FDR's New Deal.
Sanna Feirstein
Naming New York
How Manhattan places got named.
Tom Folsom
The Mad Ones: Crazy Joe Gallo and the Revolution at the Edge of the Underworld
Engaging ride though the world of the Mafia during the 1960s.
Eric Homberger *The Historical Atlas of New York City*
Through maps, photographs, illustrations and essays, this hefty volume charts the metropolis's 400-year heritage.
Clifton Hood *722 Miles: The Building of the Subways and How They Transformed New York*
The birth of the world's longest rapid transit system.
Kenneth T Jackson (ed)
The Encyclopedia of New York City
An ambitious and useful reference guide.
David Levering Lewis
When Harlem Was in Vogue
A study of the Harlem Renaissance.
Jonathan Mahler *Ladies and Gentlemen, the Bronx is Burning*
A gritty snapshot of NYC in 1977.
Mitchell Pacelle *Empire*
The story of the fight to build the Empire State Building.
Clayton Patterson (ed)
Resistance
This collection of essays reflects on the Lower East Side's history as a radical hotbed.
Luc Sante *Low Life*
Opium dens and brothels in New York from the 1840s to the 1920s.
Russell Shorto *The Island at the Center of the World*
How the Dutch colony shaped Manhattan – and America.
Mike Wallace & Edwin G Burrows *Gotham: A History of New York City to 1898*
The first volume in a planned mammoth history of NYC.

Fiction & poetry

Kurt Andersen
Turn of the Century
Millennial Manhattan as seen through the eyes of media players.
Paul Auster
The New York Trilogy: City of Glass, Ghosts and *The Locked Room*
A search for the madness behind the method of Manhattan's grid.
Kevin Baker *Dreamland*
A poetic novel about Coney Island's glory days.

James A Baldwin
Another Country
Racism under the bohemian veneer of the 1960s.
Michael Chabon *The Amazing Adventures of Kavalier and Clay*
Jewish comic-book artists battling with crises of identity in the 1940s.
Ralph Ellison
Invisible Man
Epic examination of race and racism in 1950s Harlem.
Jack Finney *Time and Again*
An illustrator travels back to 19th-century New York City.
Larry Kramer *Faggots*
A devastating satire of gay NYC.
Jonathan Lethem *Chronic City*
The author of *The Fortress of Solitude* packs his latest novel with pop-culture references.
Phillip Lopate (ed)
Writing New York
An excellent anthology of short stories, essays and poems.
Colum McCann
Let the Great World Spin
Interconnected stories set in 1970s New York.
Patrick McGrath *Trauma*
A first-person account of psychic decay that floats a critique of post-9/11 social and political amnesia.
Tim McLoughlin (ed)
Brooklyn Noir 1, 2 & 3
Second-borough crime tales.
Richard Price *Lush Life*
A contemporary murder story set on the Lower East Side.
David Schickler
Kissing in Manhattan
The lives of quirky tenants in a teeming Manhattan block.
Hubert Selby Jr
Last Exit to Brooklyn
Dockland degradation, circa 1950s.
Edith Wharton *Old New York*
Four novellas of 19th-century NYC.
Colson Whitehead *The Colossus of New York: A City in 13 Parts*
A lyrical tribute to city life.
Tom Wolfe
The Bonfire of the Vanities
Rich/poor, black/white – an unmatched slice of 1980s NYC.

FILM

Annie Hall (1977)
Woody Allen and Diane Keaton in this valentine to Manhattan.
Breakfast at Tiffany's (1961)
Audrey Hepburn as the cash-poor, time-rich socialite Holly Golightly.
Dog Day Afternoon (1975)
Al Pacino as a Brooklyn bank robber in Sidney Lumet's classic.
Do the Right Thing (1989)
Racial strife in Brooklyn's Bedford-Stuyvesant in Spike Lee's drama.
The French Connection (1971)
As detective Jimmy 'Popeye' Doyle, Gene Hackman chases down drug traffickers in William Friedkin's much-imitated thriller.
The Godfather (1972) & **The Godfather: Part II** (1974)
Francis Ford Coppola's brilliant commentary on capitalism in America is told through the violent saga of Italian gangsters.
Mean Streets (1973)
Robert De Niro and Harvey Keitel shine as small-time Little Italy hoods in Martin Scorsese's breakthrough film.
Midnight Cowboy (1969)
Street creatures 'Ratso' Rizzo and Joe Buck face an unforgiving Times Square in John Schlesinger's darkly amusing classic.
Spider-Man (2002)
The comic book web-slinger from Forest Hills comes to life in Sam Raimi's pitch-perfect crowd pleaser.
Superfly (1972)
Blaxploitation classic, propelled by legendary Curtis Mayfield soundtrack.
The Taking of Pelham 1 2 3 (2009)
The plot premise may be flawed – in this Denzel Washington/John Travolta remake, as well as in the 1974 original – but it stirs up strap-hangers' darkest fears.
Taxi Driver (1976)
Robert De Niro is a crazed cabbie who sees all of New York as a den of iniquity in Scorsese's drama.

MUSIC

Beastie Boys
'No Sleep Till Brooklyn'
These now middle-aged hip hoppers began showing their love for their fave borough decades ago.
Leonard Cohen
'Chelsea Hotel #2'
Of all the songs inspired by the Chelsea, this bleak vision of doomed love is on a level of its own.
Billy Joel
'New York State of Mind'
This heartfelt ballad exemplifies the city's effect on the souls of its visitors and residents.
Charles Mingus *Mingus Ah Um*
Mingus brought the gospel to jazz and created an NYC masterpiece.
Public Enemy *It Takes a Nation of Millions to Hold Us Back*
A ferociously political tour de force from the Long Island hip hop group whose own Chuck D once called rap 'the CNN for black America'.
The Ramones *Ramones*
Four Queens roughnecks, a few buzzsaw chords, and clipped musings on turning tricks and sniffing glue – it transformed rock 'n' roll.
Frank Sinatra 'Theme from "New York, New York"'
Trite and true, Ol' Blue Eyes' bombastic love letter melts those little-town blues.
Bruce Springsteen
'My City of Ruins'
The Boss praises the city's resilience post-September 11 with this track from *The Rising*.
The Strokes *Is This It*
The effortlessly hip debut of this hometown band garnered praise and worldwide attention.
The Velvet Underground
The Velvet Underground & Nico
Lou Reed and company's first album is still the gold standard of downtown cool.
Wu Tang Clan
Few artists embodied '90s hip hop like the Wu, its members – RZA, GZA and the late ODB among them – coining a cinematic rap aesthetic that influences artists to this day.

WEBSITES

www.timeoutnewyork.com
The recently relaunched *Time Out New York* website covers all the city has to offer. When planning your trip, check the Things to Do, Shopping and individual arts and entertainment sections for up-to-the-minute listings. Search Restaurants & Bars for thousands of reviews written by our critics.
www.clubplanet.com
Follow the city's nocturnal scene and buy tickets to big events.
www.forgotten-ny.com
Discover old New York here.
www.hipguide.com
A very short 'n' sweet site for those looking for what's considered hip.
www.hopstop.com
Works out door-to-door directions on public transportation.
www.manhattanusersguide.com
An insiders' guide to what's going on around town.
www.mta.info
Subway and bus service news is always posted here.
www.nyc.gov
City Hall's official New York City website has lots of useful links.
www.nycgo.com
The website of the official New York City tourism organisation provides information on sights, attractions, hotels, restaurants, shops and more.
www.nytimes.com
'All the News That's Fit to Print' from the *New York Times*.

Content Index

G

H

I

J

K

L

M

N

O

P

Q

R

Venue Index

Billopp House (Conference House) 150

C

D

E

INDEX

INDEX

INDEX

T

U

V

W

Y

Z

Advertisers' Index

Please refer to the relevant pages for contact details

Offset your flight with **Trees for Cities** and make your trip mean something for years to come
www.treesforcities.org/offset
Trees for Cities
Charity registration number 1032154

Maps

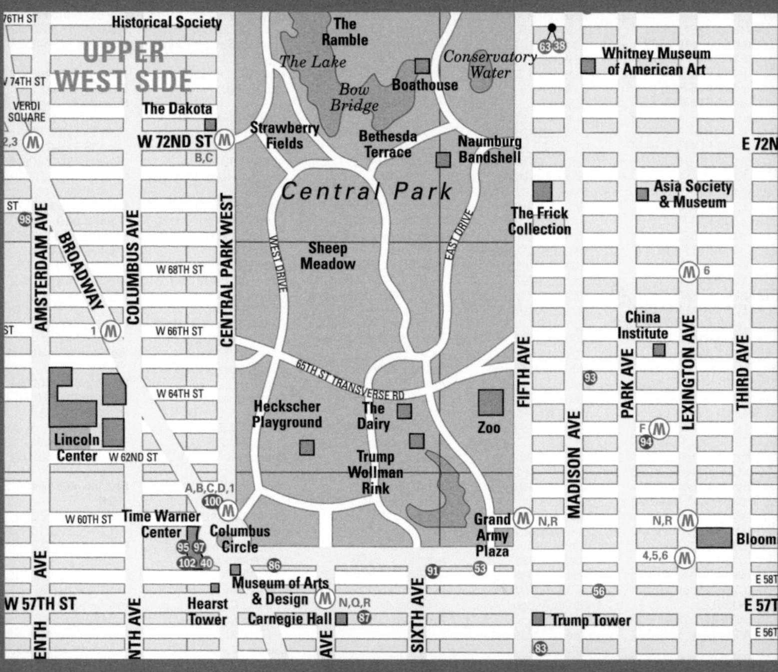

Major sight or landmark	
Hospital or college	
Railway station	
Parks	
River	
Freeway	478
Main road	
Main road tunnel	
Pedestrian road	
Airport	
Church	
Subway station	M
Area name	SOHO

Street Index

STREET INDEX

STREET INDEX

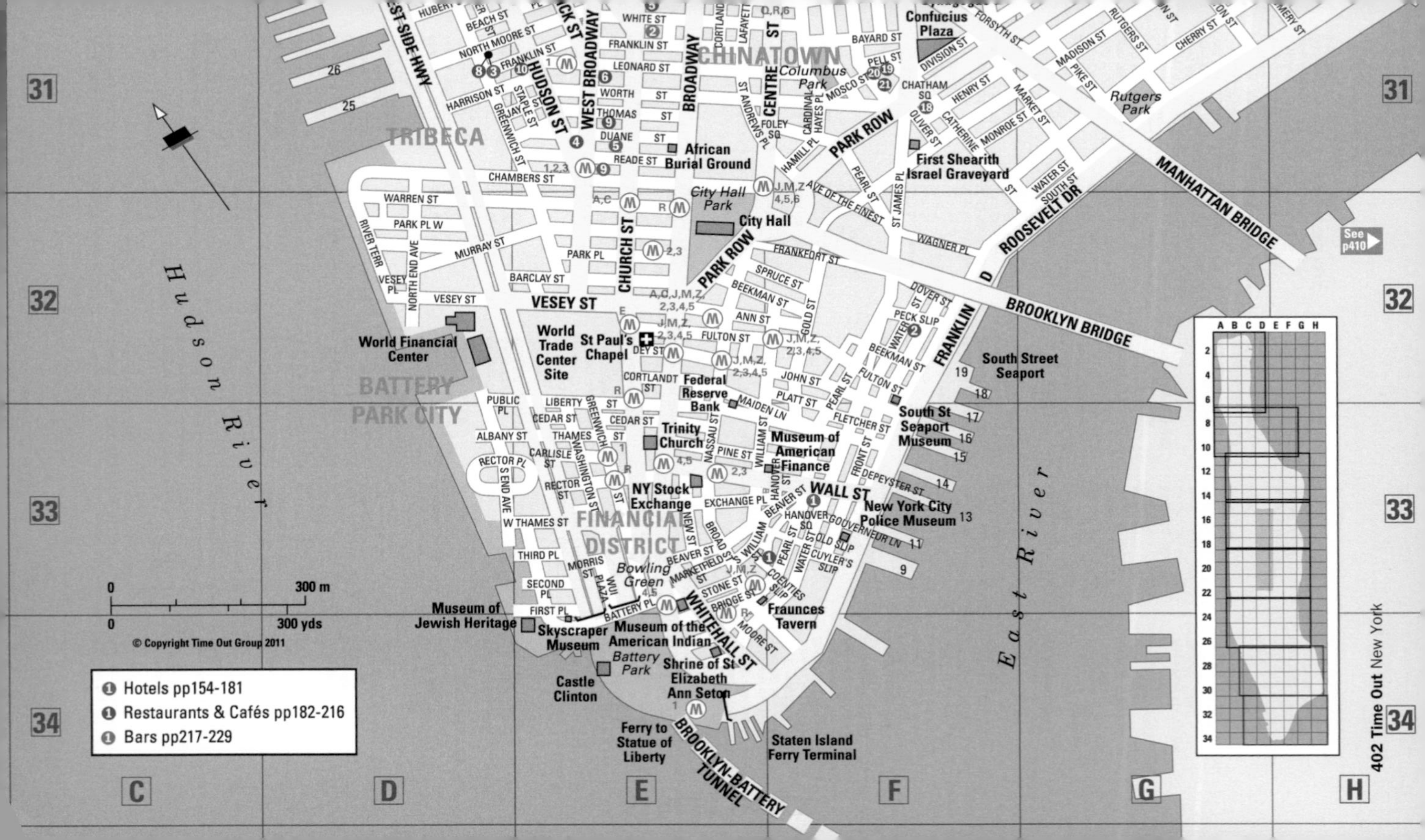

Hotels pp154-181
Restaurants & Cafés pp182-216
Bars pp217-229
© Copyright Time Out Group 2011
0
300 m
300 yds
Hudson River
East River
TRIBECA
BATTERY PARK CITY
FINANCIAL DISTRICT
CHINATOWN
World Financial Center
World Trade Center Site
St Paul's Chapel
Federal Reserve Bank
Trinity Church
NY Stock Exchange
Museum of American Finance
New York City Police Museum
South St Seaport Museum
South Street Seaport
Fraunces Tavern
Staten Island Ferry Terminal
Ferry to Statue of Liberty
Castle Clinton
Battery Park
Bowling Green
Museum of the American Indian
Shrine of St Elizabeth Ann Seton
Skyscraper Museum
Museum of Jewish Heritage
City Hall
City Hall Park
African Burial Ground
First Shearith Israel Graveyard
Columbus Park
Confucius Plaza
Rutgers Park
BROOKLYN BRIDGE
MANHATTAN BRIDGE
BROOKLYN-BATTERY TUNNEL
WEST SIDE HWY
VESEY ST
CHURCH ST
BROADWAY
WEST BROADWAY
HUDSON ST
PARK ROW
CENTRE ST
WALL ST
WHITEHALL ST
FRANKLIN D ROOSEVELT DR
See p410

Hudson River
HOLLAND TUNNEL
WEST SIDE HWY
CANAL ST
MEATPACKING DISTRICT
GANSEVOORT ST
TENTH AVE
High Line
General Theological Seminary of the Episcopal Church
CHELSEA
W 14TH ST
Joyce Theater
EIGHTH AVE
SEVENTH AVE
Rubin Museum of Art
SIXTH AVE
FLATIRON DISTRICT
FIFTH AVE
Theodore Roosevelt Birthplace
BROADWAY
Union Square
PARK AVE SOUTH
Gramercy Park
IRVING PL
National Arts Club
THIRD AVE
RUTHERFORD PL
SECOND AVE
Stuyvesant Square
NATHAN D PERLMAN PL
FIRST AVE
See p404
Stuyvesant Town
E 14TH ST
E 20TH ST
FRANKLIN D ROOSEVELT DR
WEST VILLAGE
HUDSON ST
W HOUSTON ST
VARICK ST
SEVENTH AVE SOUTH
New York City Fire Museum
SOHO
GREENWICH VILLAGE
Washington Square
WASH SQ WEST
WASH SQ EAST
AIA Center for Architecture
LA GUARDIA PL
WEST BROADWAY
Museum of Comic & Cartoon Art
Haughwout Building
Museum of Chinese in America
LAFAYETTE
New York University
Grace Church
FOURTH AVE
ASTOR PL
UNIVERSITY PL
St Mark's Church in-the-Bowery
STUYVESANT ST
Eastern States Buddhist Temple of America
LITTLE ITALY
THE BOWERY
New Museum of Contemporary Art
Lower East Side Tenement Museum
LOWER EAST SIDE
E HOUSTON ST
EAST VILLAGE
AVENUE A
Tompkins Square
AVENUE B
AVENUE C
AVENUE D
Seward Park
EAST BROADWAY
WILLIAMSBURG BRIDGE
East River Park

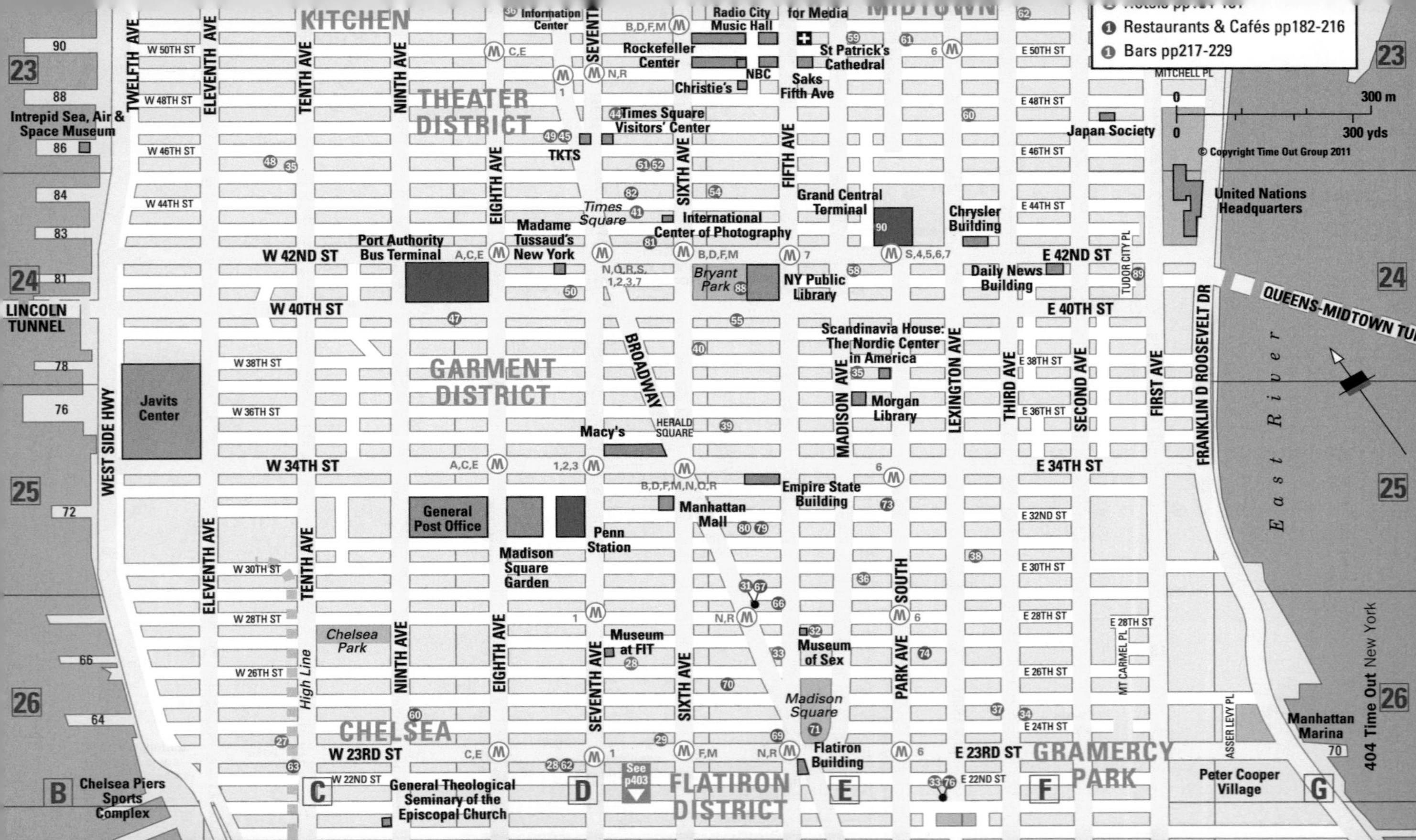

KITCHEN
MIDTOWN
THEATER DISTRICT
GARMENT DISTRICT
CHELSEA
FLATIRON DISTRICT
GRAMERCY PARK
WEST SIDE HWY
TWELFTH AVE
ELEVENTH AVE
TENTH AVE
NINTH AVE
EIGHTH AVE
SEVENTH AVE
SIXTH AVE
FIFTH AVE
MADISON AVE
PARK AVE SOUTH
LEXINGTON AVE
THIRD AVE
SECOND AVE
FIRST AVE
FRANKLIN D ROOSEVELT DR
BROADWAY
W 42ND ST
W 40TH ST
W 34TH ST
W 23RD ST
E 42ND ST
E 40TH ST
E 34TH ST
E 23RD ST
LINCOLN TUNNEL
QUEENS-MIDTOWN TUN
High Line
Intrepid Sea, Air & Space Museum
Information Center
Radio City Music Hall
for Media
Rockefeller Center
St Patrick's Cathedral
NBC
Saks Fifth Ave
Christie's
Times Square Visitors' Center
TKTS
Times Square
International Center of Photography
Grand Central Terminal
Chrysler Building
Madame Tussaud's New York
Port Authority Bus Terminal
Bryant Park
NY Public Library
Daily News Building
Japan Society
United Nations Headquarters
Javits Center
Scandinavia House: The Nordic Center in America
Morgan Library
Macy's
HERALD SQUARE
Empire State Building
Manhattan Mall
General Post Office
Penn Station
Madison Square Garden
Chelsea Park
Museum at FIT
Museum of Sex
Madison Square
Flatiron Building
Chelsea Piers Sports Complex
General Theological Seminary of the Episcopal Church
See p403
Peter Cooper Village
Manhattan Marina
East River
TUDOR CITY PL
MITCHELL PL
MT CARMEL PL
ASSER LEVY PL
Restaurants & Cafés pp182-216
Bars pp217-229
300 m
300 yds
© Copyright Time Out Group 2011

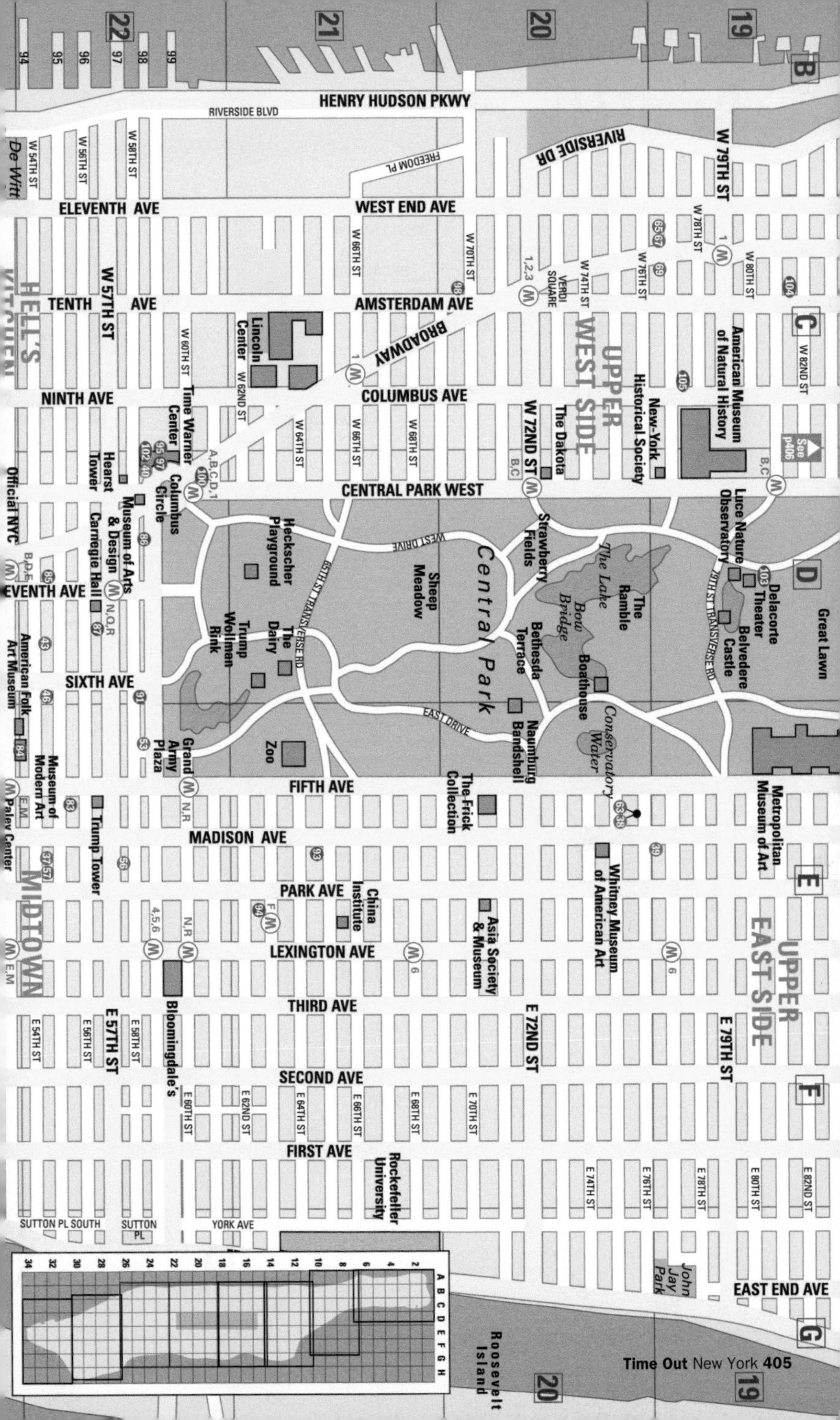

HENRY HUDSON PKWY
RIVERSIDE BLVD
RIVERSIDE DR
FREEDOM PL
ELEVENTH AVE
WEST END AVE
TENTH AVE
AMSTERDAM AVE
BROADWAY
NINTH AVE
COLUMBUS AVE
CENTRAL PARK WEST
SEVENTH AVE
SIXTH AVE
FIFTH AVE
MADISON AVE
PARK AVE
LEXINGTON AVE
THIRD AVE
SECOND AVE
FIRST AVE
YORK AVE
EAST END AVE
SUTTON PL SOUTH
SUTTON PL
W 57TH ST
W 72ND ST
W 79TH ST
E 57TH ST
E 72ND ST
E 79TH ST
HELL'S KITCHEN
UPPER WEST SIDE
UPPER EAST SIDE
MIDTOWN
Central Park
Lincoln Center
Time Warner Center
Columbus Circle
Hearst Tower
Museum of Arts & Design
Carnegie Hall
Official NYC
American Folk Art Museum
Museum of Modern Art
Paley Center
Trump Tower
Grand Army Plaza
Zoo
Trump Wollman Rink
Heckscher Playground
The Dairy
Sheep Meadow
Strawberry Fields
Bethesda Terrace
Naumburg Bandshell
Bow Bridge
The Lake
The Ramble
Boathouse
Conservatory Water
Verdi Square
The Dakota
New-York Historical Society
American Museum of Natural History
Luce Nature Observatory
Delacorte Theater
Belvedere Castle
Great Lawn
Metropolitan Museum of Art
The Frick Collection
Whitney Museum of American Art
Asia Society & Museum
China Institute
Bloomingdale's
Rockefeller University
John Jay Park
Roosevelt Island
De Witt
West Drive
East Drive
65th St Transverse Rd
79th St Transverse Rd
See p406

Hotels pp154-181
Restaurants & Cafés pp182-216
Bars pp217-229
HENRY HUDSON PKWY
RIVERSIDE DRIVE
Riverside Park
Cathedral of St John the Divine
Cathedral Close
MORNINGSIDE DR
CATHEDRAL PARKWAY
W 113TH ST
W 111TH ST
W 109TH ST
W 107TH ST
W 106TH ST
DUKE ELLINGTON BLVD
W 105TH ST
W 103RD ST
W 102ND ST
W 100TH ST
W 98TH ST
W 96TH ST
W 94TH ST
W 92ND ST
BROWNE BLVD
W 90TH ST
W 88TH ST
W 86TH ST
W 84TH ST
WEST END AVE
BROADWAY
AMSTERDAM AVE
COLUMBUS AVE
MANHATTAN AVE
CENTRAL PARK WEST
Symphony Space
Soldiers' & Sailors' Monument
UPPER WEST SIDE
See p405
ADAM CLAYTON POWELL JR BLVD
ST NICHOLAS AVE
MALCOLM X BLVD
CENTRAL PARK NORTH
Harlem Meer
Charles A Dana Discovery Center
WEST DRIVE
EAST DRIVE
The Pool
Conservatory Garden
97TH ST TRANSVERSE RD
Central Park
The Reservoir
86TH ST TRANSVERSE RD
Great Lawn
Metropolitan Museum of Art
FIFTH AVE
MADISON AVE
PARK AVE
LEXINGTON AVE
THIRD AVE
SECOND AVE
FIRST AVE
EAST END AVE
Museum for African Art
EAST HARLEM (EL BARRIO)
El Museo del Barrio
Museum of the City of New York
Jewish Museum
Cooper-Hewitt National Design Museum
Guggenheim Museum
Neue Galerie
E 113TH ST
E 111TH ST
E 109TH ST
E 107TH ST
E 105TH ST
E 103RD ST
E 102ND ST
E 100TH ST
E 98TH ST
E 96TH ST
E 94TH ST
E 92ND ST
E 90TH ST
E 88TH ST
E 86TH ST
E 84TH ST
YORKVILLE
UPPER EAST SIDE
FRANKLIN D ROOSEVELT DR
Jefferson Park
Gracie Mansion
Carl Schurz Park

HENRY HUDSON PKWY
Riverbank State Park
General Grant National Memorial
Riverside Church
Barnard College
Columbia University
MORNINGSIDE HEIGHTS
HAMILTON HEIGHTS
HARLEM
City College of New York
St Nicholas Park
Morningside Park
Marcus Garvey Park
Apollo Theater
Studio Museum in Harlem
Schomburg Center
Abyssinian Baptist Church
TWELFTH AVE
WEST END AVE
AMSTERDAM AVE
MORNINGSIDE
DRIVE
CONVENT AVE
ST NICHOLAS TER
EDGECOMBE AVE
MANHATTAN AVE
FREDERICK DOUGLASS BLVD
ADAM CLAYTON POWELL JR BLVD
MALCOLM X BLVD
MALCOLM X BLVD (LENOX AVE)
MT MORRIS PARK WEST
FIFTH AVE
MADISON AVE
PARK AVE
LEXINGTON AVE
THIRD AVE
SECOND AVE
FIRST AVE
MARTIN LUTHER KING JR BLVD
OLD BROADWAY
HAMILTON PLACE
CLAREMONT AVE
REINHOLD NIEBUHR PL
RIVERSIDE DR WEST
RIVERSIDE DR EAST
ST CLAIR PL
TIEMANN PL
LA SALLE ST
PED BR
CHISUM PL
W 115TH ST
W 116TH ST
W 119TH ST
W 121ST ST
W 123RD ST
W 125TH ST
W 126TH ST
W 127TH ST
W 129TH ST
W 131ST ST
W 133RD ST
W 135TH ST
W 137TH ST
W 139TH ST
W 141ST ST
W 143RD ST
E 115TH ST
E 117TH ST
E 119TH ST
E 121ST ST
E 123RD ST
E 127TH ST
E 129TH ST
E 131ST ST
E 135TH ST
THIRD AVE BRIDGE
ROBERT F KENNEDY BRIDGE (TRIBOROUGH BRIDGE)
See p408
© Copyright Time Out Group 2011
0
300 m
300 yds
B
C
D
E
F
G
11
12
13
14
15

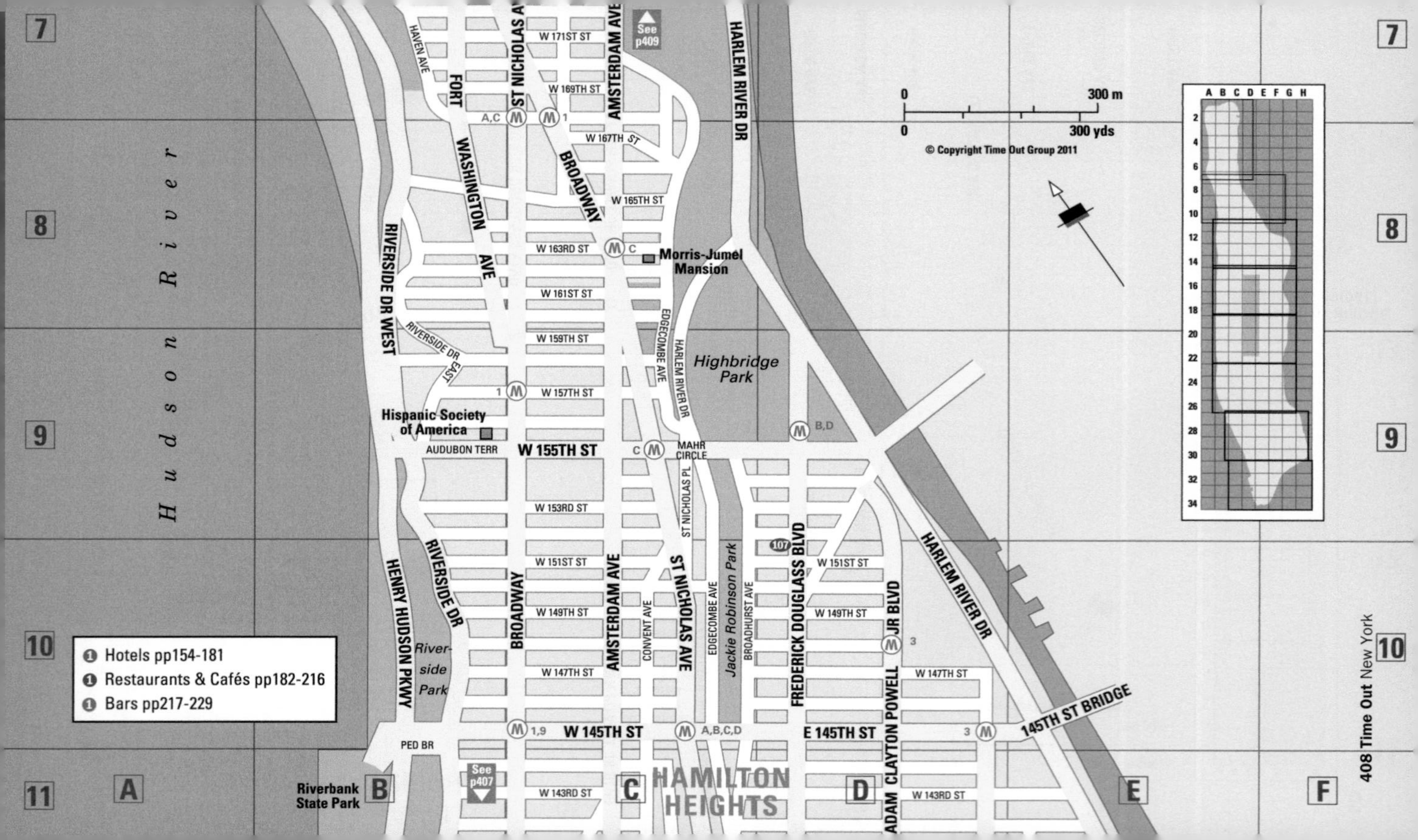

Hudson River
HAVEN AVE
FORT WASHINGTON AVE
ST NICHOLAS AVE
AMSTERDAM AVE
See p409
HARLEM RIVER DR
W 171ST ST
W 169TH ST
W 167TH ST
BROADWAY
W 165TH ST
RIVERSIDE DR WEST
W 163RD ST
Morris-Jumel Mansion
W 161ST ST
EDGECOMBE AVE
RIVERSIDE DR EAST
W 159TH ST
HARLEM RIVER DR
Highbridge Park
W 157TH ST
Hispanic Society of America
AUDUBON TERR
W 155TH ST
MAHR CIRCLE
ST NICHOLAS PL
W 153RD ST
RIVERSIDE DR
HENRY HUDSON PKWY
W 151ST ST
FREDERICK DOUGLASS BLVD
Jackie Robinson Park
BROADHURST AVE
CONVENT AVE
W 149TH ST
ADAM CLAYTON POWELL JR BLVD
Riverside Park
W 147TH ST
W 145TH ST
E 145TH ST
145TH ST BRIDGE
PED BR
See p407
Riverbank State Park
W 143RD ST
HAMILTON HEIGHTS
0 300 m
0 300 yds
© Copyright Time Out Group 2011
Hotels pp154-181
Restaurants & Cafés pp182-216
Bars pp217-229

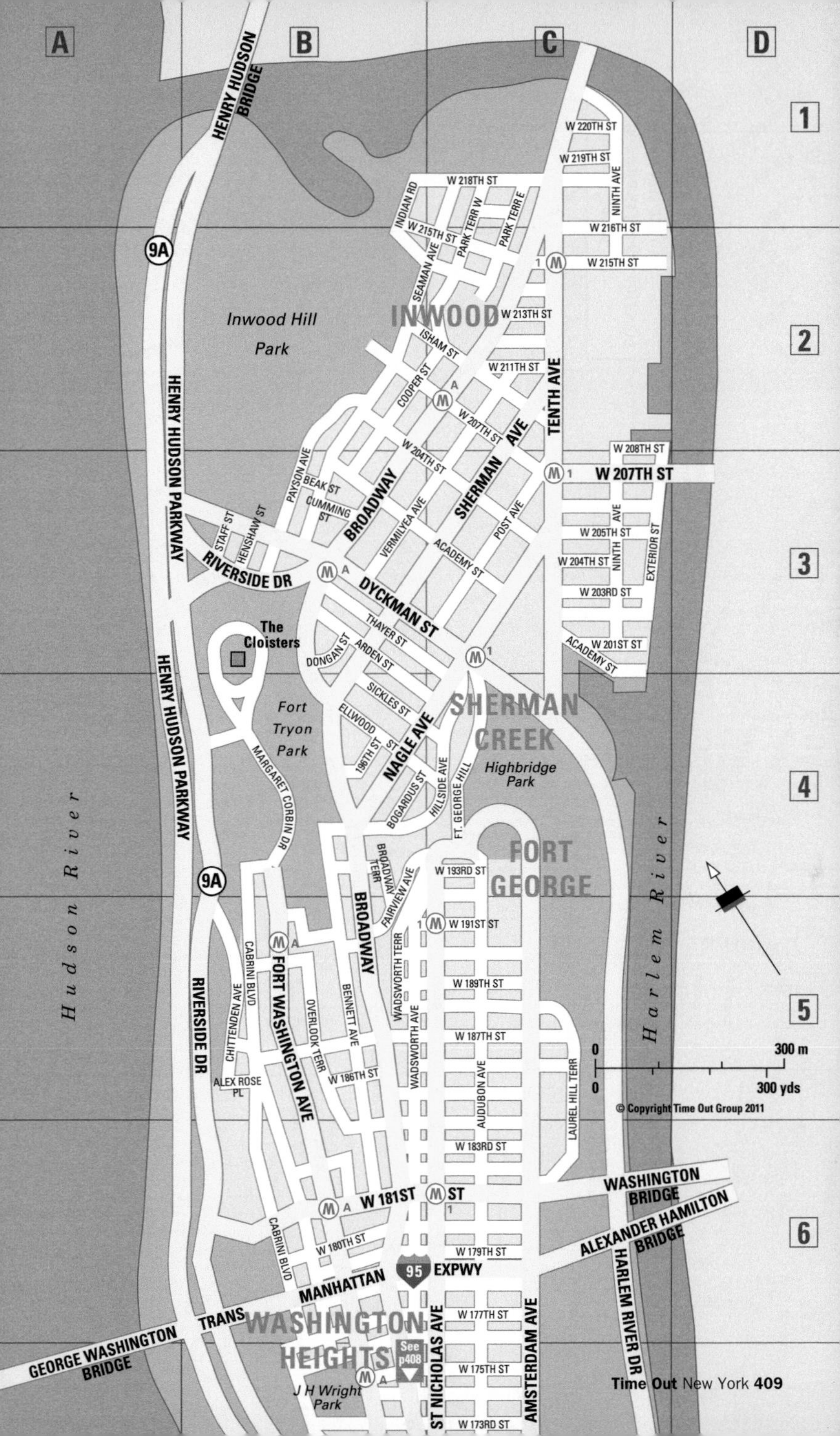
A
B
C
D
1
2
3
4
5
6
HENRY HUDSON BRIDGE
9A
Inwood Hill Park
INWOOD
W 220TH ST
W 219TH ST
W 218TH ST
INDIAN RD
PARK TERR W
PARK TERR E
NINTH AVE
W 216TH ST
W 215TH ST
SEAMAN AVE
W 213TH ST
ISHAM ST
W 211TH ST
TENTH AVE
COOPER ST
W 207TH ST
SHERMAN AVE
W 208TH ST
W 207TH ST
W 204TH ST
PAYSON AVE
BEAK ST
CUMMING ST
BROADWAY
VERMILYEA AVE
POST AVE
HENRY HUDSON PARKWAY
STAFF ST
HENSHAW ST
W 205TH ST
NINTH AVE
EXTERIOR ST
ACADEMY ST
W 204TH ST
W 203RD ST
RIVERSIDE DR
DYCKMAN ST
The Cloisters
THAYER ST
DONGAN ST
ARDEN ST
W 201ST ST
ACADEMY ST
Fort Tryon Park
SICKLES ST
ELLWOOD ST
SHERMAN CREEK
196TH ST
NAGLE AVE
MARGARET CORBIN DR
BOGARDUS ST
HILLSIDE AVE
FT. GEORGE HILL
Highbridge Park
Hudson River
Harlem River
FORT GEORGE
BROADWAY TERR
W 193RD ST
FAIRVIEW AVE
W 191ST ST
CABRINI BLVD
FORT WASHINGTON AVE
OVERLOOK TERR
BENNETT AVE
WADSWORTH TERR
WADSWORTH AVE
W 189TH ST
RIVERSIDE DR
CHITTENDEN AVE
W 187TH ST
AUDUBON AVE
LAUREL HILL TERR
0
300 m
0
300 yds
© Copyright Time Out Group 2011
ALEX ROSE PL
W 186TH ST
W 183RD ST
W 181ST
ST
WASHINGTON BRIDGE
ALEXANDER HAMILTON BRIDGE
CABRINI BLVD
W 180TH ST
W 179TH ST
95 EXPWY
MANHATTAN
TRANS
HARLEM RIVER DR
GEORGE WASHINGTON BRIDGE
WASHINGTON HEIGHTS
W 177TH ST
See p408
ST NICHOLAS AVE
AMSTERDAM AVE
W 175TH ST
J H Wright Park
W 173RD ST

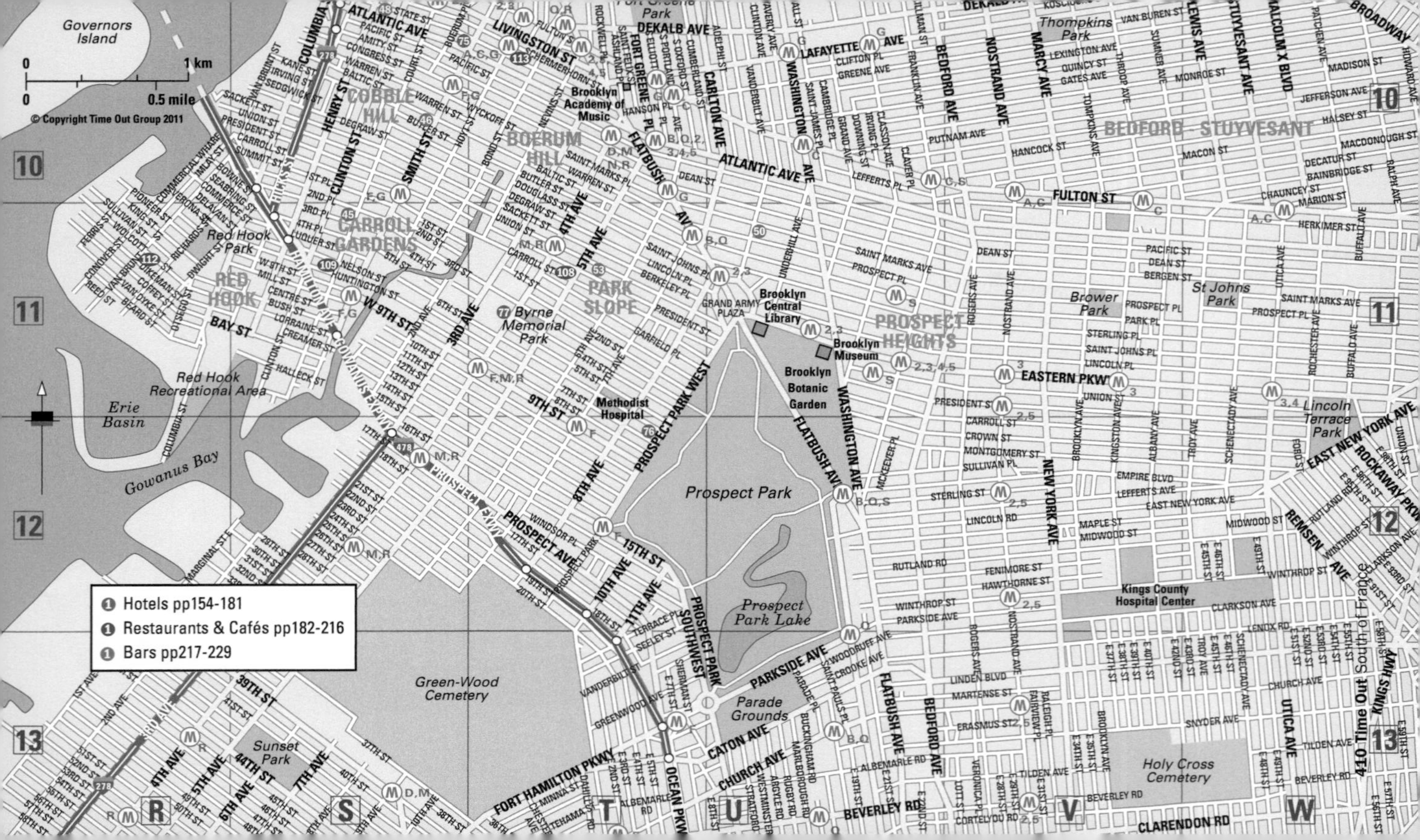

Hotels pp154-181
Restaurants & Cafés pp182-216
Bars pp217-229
© Copyright Time Out Group 2011
0.5 mile
1 km
Governors Island
Erie Basin
Gowanus Bay
Red Hook Recreational Area
RED HOOK
Red Hook Park
CARROLL GARDENS
COBBLE HILL
BOERUM HILL
PARK SLOPE
PROSPECT HEIGHTS
BEDFORD - STUYVESANT
Green-Wood Cemetery
Sunset Park
Prospect Park
Prospect Park Lake
Parade Grounds
Holy Cross Cemetery
Kings County Hospital Center
Brower Park
St Johns Park
Lincoln Terrace Park
Thompkins Park
Byrne Memorial Park
Methodist Hospital
Brooklyn Academy of Music
Brooklyn Central Library
Brooklyn Botanic Garden
Brooklyn Museum
GRAND ARMY PLAZA

Brooklyn
Hudson River
East River
Upper Bay
Wallabout Bay
See pp402-403
See p412
BATTERY PARK CITY
TRIBECA
FINANCIAL DISTRICT
SOHO
GREENWICH VILLAGE
FLATIRON
GRAMERCY PARK
EAST VILLAGE
LITTLE ITALY
CHINATOWN
LOWER EAST SIDE
DUMBO
WILLIAMSBURG
GREENPOINT
BUSHWICK
BROOKLYN HEIGHTS
FORT
Industrial Park
Brooklyn Navy Yard
McCarren Park
McGolrick Park
Cooper Park
English Kills
Empire-Fulton Ferry State Park
BROOKLYN BRIDGE
MANHATTAN BRIDGE
WILLIAMSBURG BRIDGE
KOSCIUSZKO BRIDGE
BROOKLYN-BATTERY TUNNEL
WEST SIDE HWY
FRANKLIN D ROOSEVELT DR
WHITEHALL
CHURCH ST
WEST BROADWAY
BROADWAY
HUDSON ST
VARICK ST
CENTRE ST
PARK ROW
EAST BROADWAY
WILLIAMSBURG BRIDG
E HOUSTON ST
W HOUSTON ST
LAFAYETTE
THE BOWERY
E 14TH ST
AVENUE OF THE AMERICA
FIFTH AVE
PARK AVE SOUTH
THIRD AVE
SECOND AVE
E 23RD ST
W 14TH ST
NASSAU ST
PARK AVE
FLUSHING AVE
MYRTLE AVE
LEE AVE
MARCY AVE
RODNEY ST
BEDFORD AVE
DRIGGS AVE
BERRY ST
NASSAU AVE
UNION AVE
GRAND STREET EXT
BUSHWICK AVE
METROPOLITAN AVE
GRAND ST
VANDERVOORT AVE
HUMBOLDT ST
NORMAN AVE
KINGSLAND AVE
BRIDGEWATER ST
GREENPOINT AVE
MCGUINNESS BLVD
NOSTRAND AVE
BROADWAY
Time Out

Queens
0
1 km
0
0.5 mile
© Copyright Time Out Group 2011
Hotels pp154-181
Restaurants & Cafés pp182-216
Bars pp217-229
U
V
W
X
Y
1
2
3
4
5
Central Park
EAST HARLEM
Jefferson Park
East River
Hell Gate
YORKVILLE
UPPER EAST SIDE
Carl Schurz Park
John Jay Park
Roosevelt Island
ROBERT F KENNEDY BRIDGE (TRIBOROUGH BRIDGE)
Astoria Park
Socrates Sculpture Park
Noguchi Museum
QUEENSBORO BRIDGE
Queens Bridge Park
See pp402-409
LONG ISLAND CITY
Museum of the Moving Image
Sunnyside Yard
MoMA PS1
Dutch Kills
SUNNYSIDE
See pp410-11
Greenland Park
ASTORIA
St Michael's Cemetery
Bowery Bay
LaGuardia Airport
RIKERS ISLAND BRIDGE
JACKSON HEIGHTS
WOODSIDE
New Calvary Cemetery
Calvary Cemetery
Mount Zion Cemetery
MIDDLE VILLAGE
MASPETH
Newtown Creek
PULASKI BRIDGE
Mt Olivet Cemetery
Juniper Valley Park
English Kills
Linden Hill Cemetery
Lutheran Cemetery
Glen Ridge Park
FIFTH AVE
PARK AVE
LEXINGTON AVE
THIRD AVE
SECOND AVE
FIRST AVE
FDR ROOSEVELT DR
E 86TH ST
EAST END AVE
E 79TH ST
VERNON BLVD
21ST ST
34TH AVE
MAIN AVE
ASTORIA BLVD
31ST ST
DITMARS BLVD
STEINWAY ST
31ST AVE
NORTHERN BLVD
QUEENS BLVD
THOMSON AVE
SKILLMAN AVE
43RD AVE
VAN DAM ST
49TH AVE
JACKSON AVE
ROOSEVELT AVE
BROADWAY
WOODSIDE AVE
45TH AVE
BORDEN AVE
GREENPOINT AVE
MCGUINNESS BLVD
NORMAN AVE
MAURICE AVE
GRAND AVE
MASPETH AVE
61ST ST
FRESH POND RD
ELIOT AVE
LOMBARDY ST
VANDERVOORT AVE
GRAND ST
FLUSHING AVE
METROPOLITAN AVE
CENTRAL AVE
82ND ST
81ST ST
69TH ST
58TH ST
48TH ST
39TH ST
11TH ST
49TH AVE
39TH ST
GREENPOINT AVE
New York 411

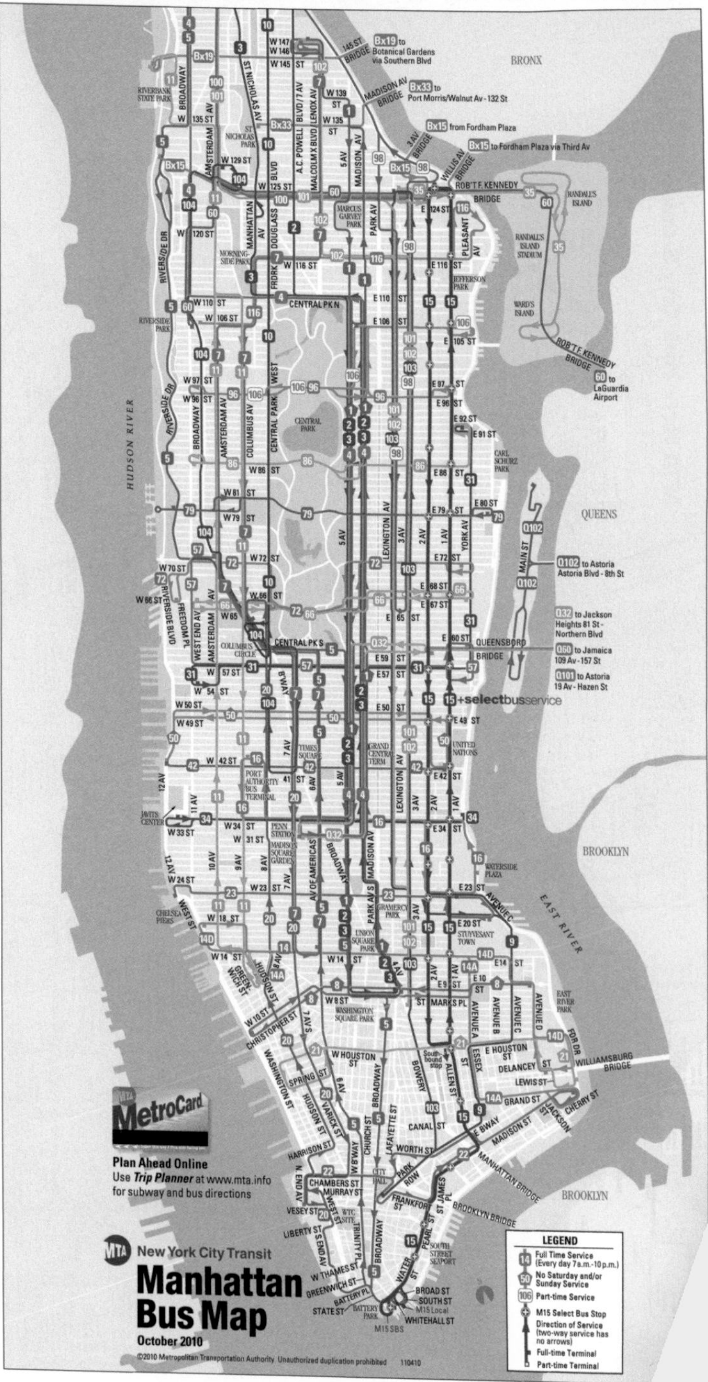

MetroCard
Plan Ahead Online
Use Trip Planner at www.mta.info for subway and bus directions
New York City Transit
Manhattan Bus Map
October 2010
©2010 Metropolitan Transportation Authority. Unauthorized duplication prohibited 110410
LEGEND
Full Time Service (Every day 7 a.m.-10 p.m.)
No Saturday and/or Sunday Service
Part-time Service
M15 Select Bus Stop
Direction of Service (two-way service has no arrows)
Full-time Terminal
Part-time Terminal
Bx19 to Botanical Gardens via Southern Blvd
Bx33 to Port Morris/Walnut Av - 132 St
Bx15 from Fordham Plaza
Bx15 to Fordham Plaza via Third Av
60 to LaGuardia Airport
Q102 to Astoria Astoria Blvd - 8th St
Q32 to Jackson Heights 81 St - Northern Blvd
Q60 to Jamaica 109 Av - 157 St
Q101 to Astoria 19 Av - Hazen St
15 +selectbusservice
BRONX
QUEENS
BROOKLYN
HUDSON RIVER
EAST RIVER
CENTRAL PARK
RANDALL'S ISLAND
WARD'S ISLAND
ROB'T F. KENNEDY BRIDGE
QUEENSBORO BRIDGE
WILLIAMSBURG BRIDGE
MANHATTAN BRIDGE
BROOKLYN BRIDGE
145 ST BRIDGE
MADISON AV BRIDGE
WILLIS AV BRIDGE
3 AV BRIDGE

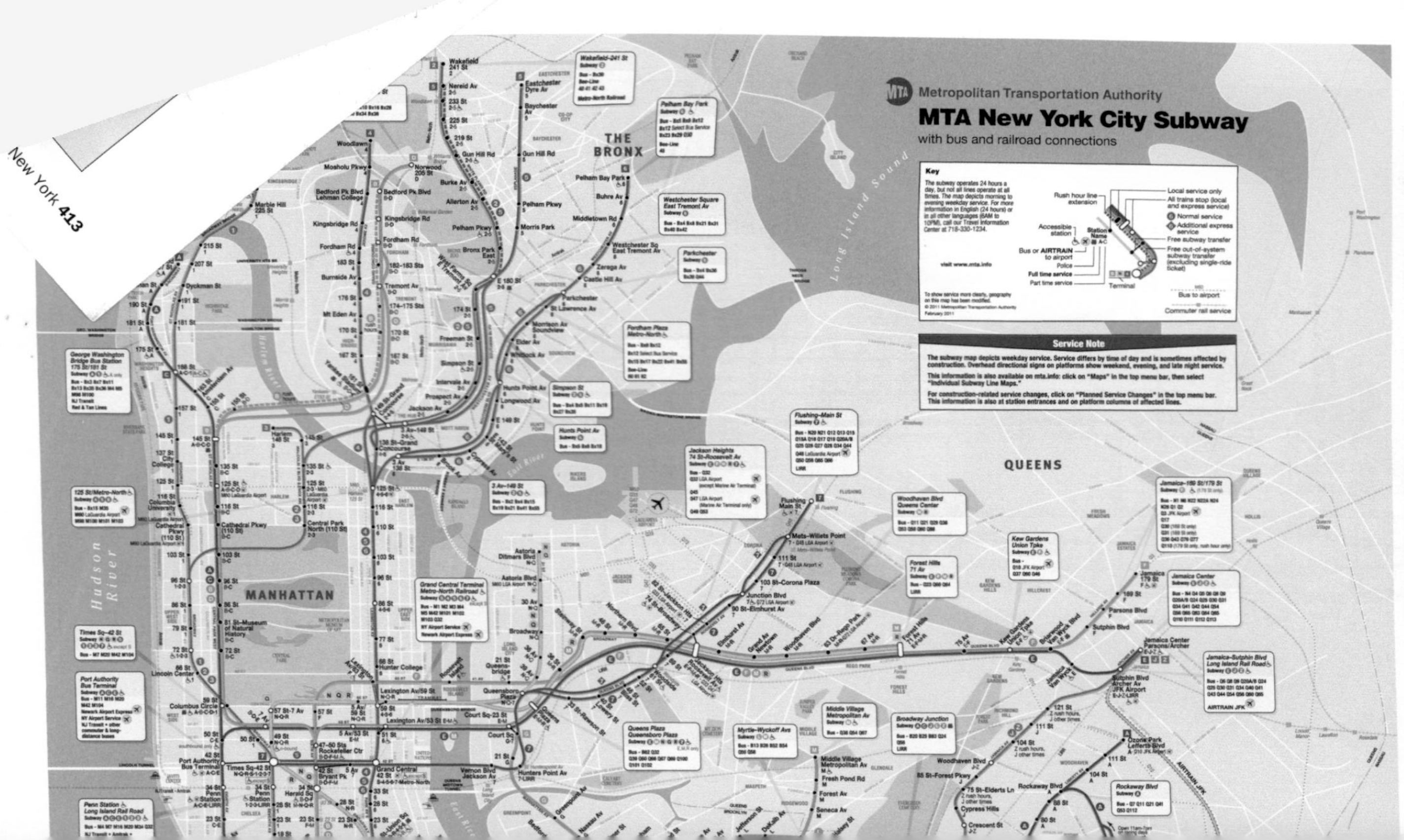
Metropolitan Transportation Authority
MTA New York City Subway
with bus and railroad connections
Key
The subway operates 24 hours a day, but not all lines operate at all times. The map depicts morning to evening weekday service. For more information in English (24 hours) or in all other languages (6AM to 10PM), call our Travel Information Center at 718-330-1234.
visit www.mta.info
Rush hour line extension
Accessible station
Station Name
Bus or AIRTRAIN to airport
Police
Full time service
Part time service
Terminal
Local service only
All trains stop (local and express service)
Normal service
Additional express service
Free subway transfer
Free out-of-system subway transfer (excluding single-ride ticket)
Bus to airport
Commuter rail service
Service Note
The subway map depicts weekday service. Service differs by time of day and is sometimes affected by construction. Overhead directional signs on platforms show weekend, evening, and late night service.
This information is also available on mta.info: click on "Maps" in the top menu bar, then select "Individual Subway Line Maps."
For construction-related service changes, click on "Planned Service Changes" in the top menu bar. This information is also at station entrances and on platform columns of affected lines.
THE BRONX
QUEENS
MANHATTAN
Long Island Sound
Hudson River
Harlem River
East River

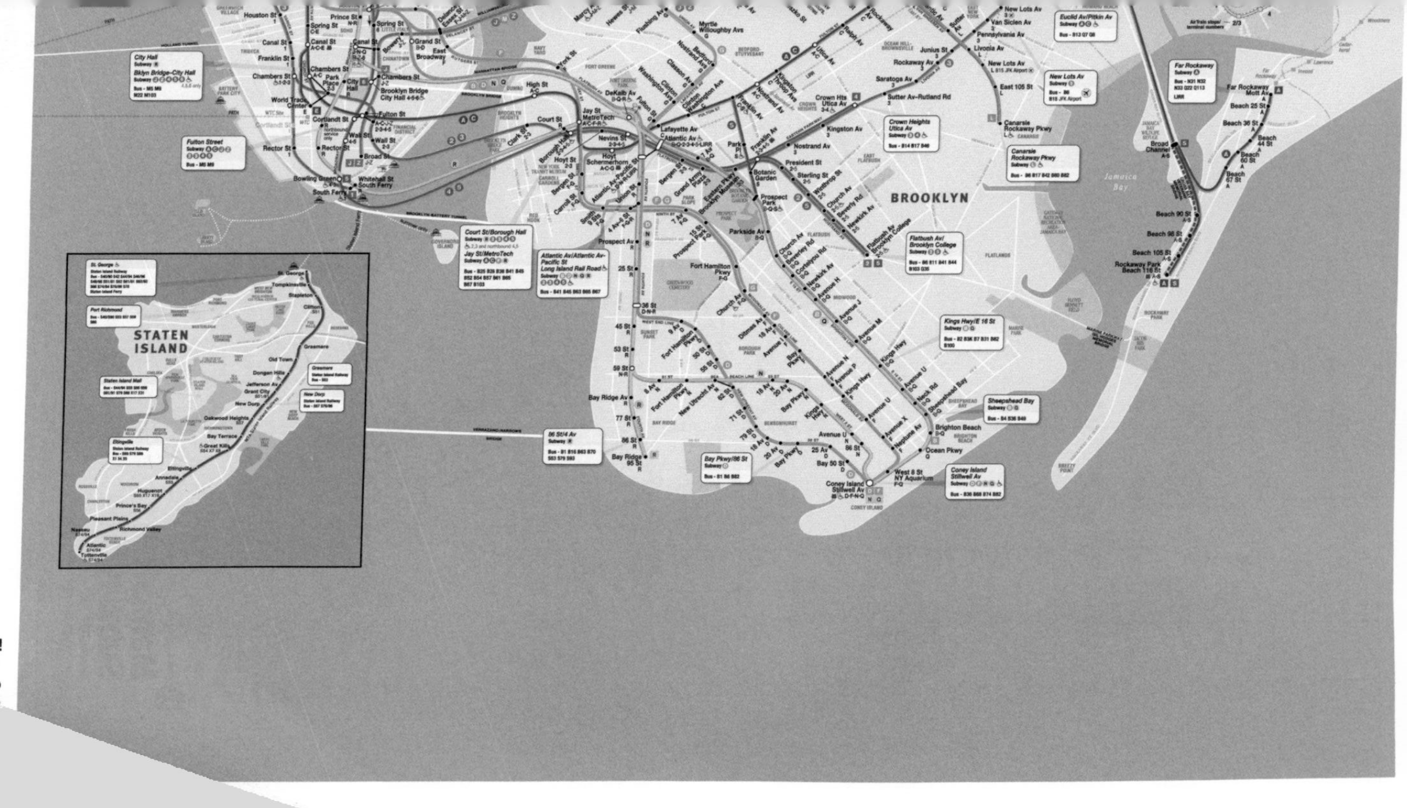
BROOKLYN
STATEN ISLAND
Jamaica Bay
Coney Island Stillwell Av
Brighton Beach
Sheepshead Bay
Bay Ridge 95 St
Far Rockaway Mott Av

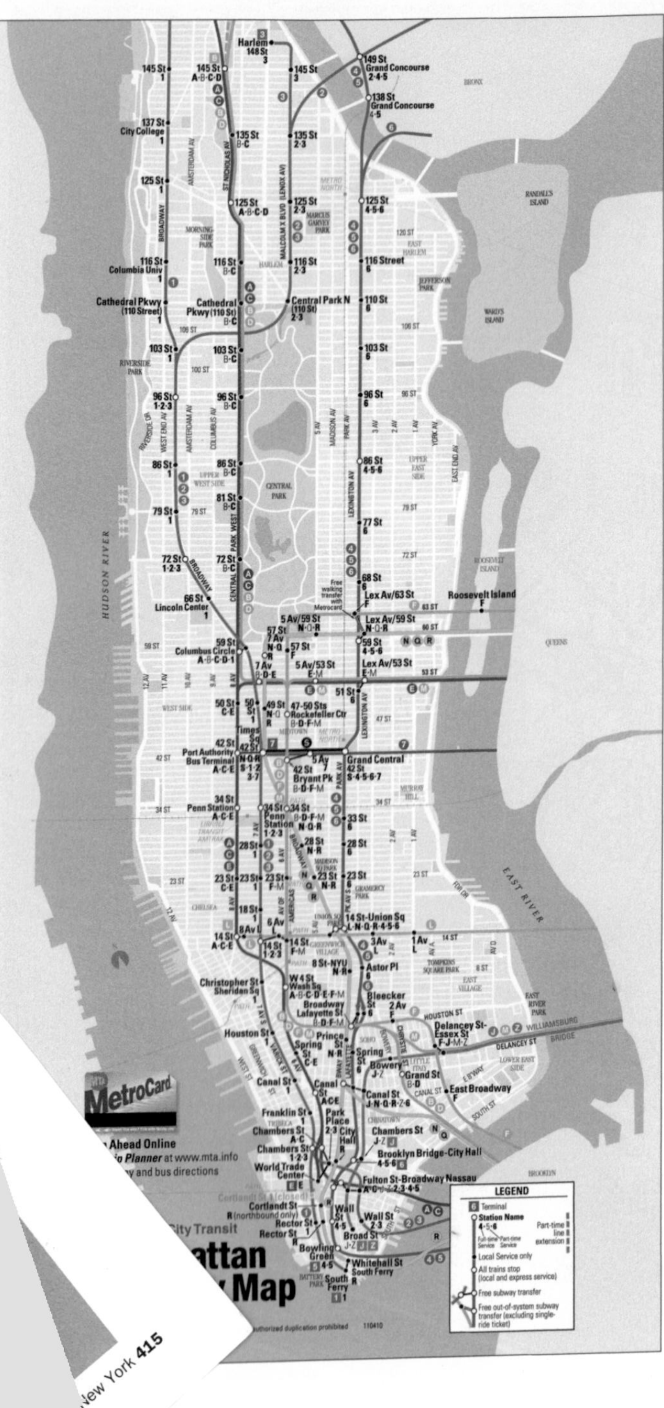

Harlem 148 St 3
145 St 1
145 St A·B·C·D
145 St 3
149 St Grand Concourse 2·4·5
138 St Grand Concourse 4·5
BRONX
137 St City College 1
135 St B·C
135 St 2·3
125 St 1
125 St A·B·C·D
125 St 2·3
125 St 4·5·6
RANDALL'S ISLAND
116 St Columbia Univ 1
116 St B·C
116 St 2·3
116 Street 6
Cathedral Pkwy (110 Street) 1
Cathedral Pkwy (110 St) B·C
Central Park N (110 St) 2·3
110 St 6
WARD'S ISLAND
103 St 1
103 St B·C
103 St 6
96 St 1·2·3
96 St B·C
96 St 6
86 St 1
86 St B·C
86 St 4·5·6
81 St B·C
79 St 1
77 St 6
CENTRAL PARK
HUDSON RIVER
72 St 1·2·3
72 St B·C
68 St 6
66 St Lincoln Center 1
Lex Av/63 St F
Roosevelt Island F
5 Av/59 St N·Q·R
Lex Av/59 St N·Q·R
59 St 4·5·6
59 St Columbus Circle A·B·C·D·1
57 St 7 Av N·Q·R
57 St F
7 Av B·D·E
5 Av/53 St E·M
Lex Av/53 St E·M
51 St 6
QUEENS
50 St C·E
50 St 1
49 St N·Q·R
47-50 Sts Rockefeller Ctr B·D·F·M
Times Sq 42 St N·Q·R S·1·2 3·7
42 St Port Authority Bus Terminal A·C·E
5 Av 7
42 St Bryant Pk B·D·F·M
Grand Central 42 St S·4·5·6·7
34 St Penn Station A·C·E
34 St Penn Station 1·2·3
34 St B·D·F·M N·Q·R
33 St 6
28 St 1
28 St N·R
28 St 6
23 St C·E
23 St 1
23 St F·M
23 St N·R
23 St 6
18 St 1
14 St-Union Sq L·N·Q·R·4·5·6
14 St A·C·E
8 Av L
6 Av L
14 St 1·2·3
14 St F·M
3 Av L
1 Av L
8 St-NYU N·R
Astor Pl 6
EAST RIVER
Christopher St Sheridan Sq 1
W 4 St Wash Sq A·B·C·D·E·F·M
Bleecker St 6
Broadway Lafayette St B·D·F·M
2 Av F
Delancey St-Essex St F·J·M·Z
WILLIAMSBURG BRIDGE
Houston St 1
Prince St N·R
Spring St C·E
Spring St 6
Bowery J·Z
Grand St B·D
Canal St 1
Canal St A·C·E
Canal St J·N·Q·R·Z·6
East Broadway F
Franklin St 1
Park Place 2·3
City Hall R
Chambers St 1·2·3
Chambers St A·C
Chambers St J·Z
Brooklyn Bridge-City Hall 4·5·6
World Trade Center E
Fulton St-Broadway Nassau A·C·J·Z·2·3·4·5
Cortlandt St 1 (closed)
Cortlandt St R (northbound only)
Rector St 1
Rector St R
Wall St 4·5
Wall St 2·3
Broad St J·Z
Bowling Green 4·5
Whitehall St South Ferry R
South Ferry 1
BROOKLYN
MetroCard
Ahead Online
Planner at www.mta.info
and bus directions
City Transit
attan
Map
uthorized duplication prohibited
110410
LEGEND
Terminal
Station Name
4·5·6
Full-time Service
Part-time Service
Part-time line extension
Local Service only
All trains stop (local and express service)
Free subway transfer
Free out-of-system subway transfer (excluding single-ride ticket)